ARTIFICIAL INTELLIGENCE FOR MEDICINE

ARTIFICIAL INTELLIGENCE FOR MEDICINE

An Applied Reference for Methods and Applications

Edited by

SHAI BEN-DAVID

GIUSEPPE CURIGLIANO

DAVID KOFF

BARBARA ALICJA JERECZEK-FOSSA

DAVIDE LA TORRE

GABRIELLA PRAVETTONI

ELSEVIER

ACADEMIC PRESS
An imprint of Elsevier

ISBN 978-0-443-13671-9

For information on all Academic Press publications
visit our website at https://www.elsevier.com/books-and-journals

Publisher: Mara Conner
Acquisitions Editor: Chris Katsaropoulos
Editorial Project Manager: Toni Louise Jackson
Production Project Manager: Anitha Sivaraj
Cover Designer: Miles Hitchen

Typeset by STRAIVE, India

Working together
to grow libraries in
developing countries

www.elsevier.com • www.bookaid.org

Contents

Contributors

Nour Aburaed University of Dubai, Dubai, United Arab Emirates

Mohammed Q. Alkhatib University of Dubai, Dubai, United Arab Emirates

Mina Al-Saad University of Dubai, Dubai, United Arab Emirates

Roberta Amadori Department of Gynaecology and Obstetrics, Ospedale Maggiore della Carità, Novara, Italy

Salvatore Alessio Angileri Diagnostic and Interventional Radiology Department, Fundation IRCCS Cà Granda-Ospedale Maggiore Policlinico, Milan, Italy

Carmen Imma Aquino Department of Gynaecology and Obstetrics, Ospedale Maggiore della Carità; Department of Translational Medicine, University of Piemonte Orientale, Novara, Italy

Pierpaolo Biondetti Diagnostic and Interventional Radiology Department, Fundation IRCCS Cà Granda-Ospedale Maggiore Policlinico, Milan, Italy

Sandra E. Black Sunnybrook Research Institute and the University of Toronto, Toronto, ON, Canada

Silvia Bottini Université Côte d'Azur, Center of Modeling, Simulation and Interactions, Nice; INRAE, Université Cote d'Azur, Institut Sophia Agrobiotech, Sophia-Antipolis, France

Omar Boursalie Department of Electrical, Computer, and Biomedical Engineering, Toronto Metropolitan University, Toronto, ON, Canada

Gianpaolo Carrafiello Diagnostic and Interventional Radiology Department, Fundation IRCCS Cà Granda-Ospedale Maggiore Policlinico; Department of Health Science, Università degli Studi di Milano, Milan, Italy

Serena Carriero Postgraduate School in Radiodiagnostics, Università degli Studi di Milano, Milan, Italy

Nadia Casatta Innovation Department, Diapath S.p.A., Martinengo, Italy

Leo Anthony Celi Department of Medicine, Beth Israel Deaconess Medical Center; Laboratory for Computational Physiology, Massachusetts Institute of Technology, Cambridge; Department of Biostatistics, Harvard T.H. Chan School of Public Health, Boston, MA, United States

Gaia Cervi SORINT.tek, Grassobbio, Italy

Marisa Cobanaj OncoRay, National Center for Radiation Research in Oncology (HZDR), Dresden, Germany

Chiara Corti Division of New Drugs and Early Drug Development for Innovative Therapies, European Institute of Oncology (IEO), IRCCS; Department of Oncology and Hematology-Oncology (DIPO), University of Milan, Milan, Italy

Carmen Criscitiello Division of New Drugs and Early Drug Development for Innovative Therapies, European Institute of Oncology (IEO), IRCCS; Department of Oncology and Hematology-Oncology (DIPO), University of Milan, Milan, Italy

Giuseppe Curigliano Division of Early Drug Development for Innovative Therapies, European Institute of Oncology (IEO), IRCCS; Department of Oncology and Hematology-Oncology (DIPO), University of Milan, Milan, Italy

Hirad Daneshvar Department of Electrical, Computer, and Biomedical Engineering, Toronto Metropolitan University, Toronto, ON, Canada

Valentina De Nicolò Department of Public Health and Infectious Disease, Sapienza University of Rome, Rome, Italy

Edward Christopher Dee Department of Radiation Oncology, Memorial Sloan Kettering Cancer Center, New York, NY, United States

Shuang Di Centre for Data Science and Digital Health, Hamilton Health Sciences, Hamilton; Dalla Lana School of Public Health, University of Toronto, Toronto, ON, Canada

Thomas E. Doyle Department of Electrical and Computer Engineering; School of Biomedical Engineering, McMaster University, Hamilton; Vector Institute, Toronto, ON, Canada

Laura Duncan Hamilton Health Sciences, Hamilton, ON, Canada

Ilaria Durosini Department of Oncology and Hematology-Oncology (DIPO), University of Milan, Milan, Italy

Chiara Frascarelli Division of Pathology, European Institute of Oncology (IEO), IRCCS; Department of Oncology and Hematology-Oncology (DIPO), University of Milan, Milan, Italy

Nicola Fusco Division of Pathology, European Institute of Oncology (IEO), IRCCS; Department of Oncology and Hematology-Oncology (DIPO), University of Milan, Milan, Italy

Vincent Gaudet Department of Electrical and Computer Engineering, University of Waterloo, Waterloo, ON, Canada

Gianluca Gerard SORINT.tek, Grassobbio, Italy

Yasmin Halawani University of Dubai, Dubai, United Arab Emirates

Andrea Icks Institute for Health Services Research and Health Economics, Centre for Health and Society, Medical Faculty and University Hospital Düsseldorf, Heinrich-Heine-University Düsseldorf; Institute for Health Services Research and Health Economics, German Diabetes Center, Leibniz Center for Diabetes Research at Heinrich-Heine-University Düsseldorf, Düsseldorf, Germany

Anna Maria Ierardi Diagnostic and Interventional Radiology Department, Fundation IRCCS Cà Granda-Ospedale Maggiore Policlinico, Milan, Italy

Lars Johannes Isaksson Department of Radiation Oncology, European Institute of Oncology (IEO), IRCCS; Department of Oncology and Hematology-Oncology (DIPO), University of Milan, Milan, Italy

Barbara Alicja Jereczek-Fossa Department of Radiation Oncology, European Institute of Oncology (IEO), IRCCS; Department of Oncology and Hematology-Oncology (DIPO), University of Milan, Milan, Italy

Nadja Kairies-Schwarz Institute for Health Services Research and Health Economics, Centre for Health and Society, Medical Faculty and University Hospital Düsseldorf, Heinrich-Heine-University Düsseldorf, Düsseldorf, Germany

David Koff Department of Radiology, McMaster University, Hamilton, ON, Canada

Davide La Torre SKEMA Business School, Université Côte d'Azur, Nice, France; Department of Oncology and Hematology-Oncology (DIPO), University of Milan, Milan, Italy

Justine Labory Universite Cote d'Azur, Center of Modeling, Simulation and Interaction; Universite Cote d'Azur, Inserm U1081, CNRS UMR 7284, Institute for Research on Cancer and Aging, Nice (IRCAN), Centre hospitalier universitaire (CHU) de Nice, Nice; INRAE, Université Cote d'Azur, Institut Sophia Agrobiotech, Sophia-Antipolis, France

Carolina Lanza Postgraduate School in Radiodiagnostics, Università degli Studi di Milano, Milan, Italy

Carmelo Lupo Innovation Department, Diapath S.p.A., Martinengo; Engineering and Applied Science Department, University of Bergamo, Dalmine, Italy

Muhammad Hasnain Mamdani Department of Medicine, Faculty of Medicine, University of Toronto, Toronto, ON, Canada

Cesare Martinelli Healthcare Practice, Boston Consulting Group, Milan, Italy

Davide Mazzoni Department of Oncology and Hematology-Oncology (DIPO), University of Milan, Milan, Italy

Lucas McCullum Department of Radiation Oncology, MD Anderson Cancer Center, Houston, TX, United States

David McEvoy Michael G. DeGroote School of Medicine, McMaster University, Hamilton, ON, Canada

Walter Nelson CREATE, Hamilton Health Sciences, Hamilton; Department of Statistical Sciences, University of Toronto, Toronto, ON, Canada

Martina Maria Pagin Department of Gynaecology and Obstetrics, Ospedale Maggiore della Carità, Novara, Italy

Alavikunhu Panthakkan University of Dubai, Dubai, United Arab Emirates

Filippo Pesapane Breast Imaging Division, Radiology Department, European Institute of Oncology (IEO), IRCCS, Milan, Italy

Jeremy Petch Centre for Data Science and Digital Health, Hamilton Health Sciences, Hamilton, ON, Canada

Paulo Pires Department of Psychiatry and Behavioural Neurosciences, McMaster University; Hamilton Health Sciences, Hamilton, ON, Canada

Silvia Francesca Maria Pizzoli Department of Oncology and Hematology-Oncology (DIPO), University of Milan, Milan, Italy

Gabriella Pravettoni Department of Oncology and Hematology-Oncology (DIPO), University of Milan; Applied Research Division for Cognitive and Psychological Science, European Institute of Oncology (IEO), IRCCS, Milan, Italy

Marco Repetto CertX SA, Freiburg, Switzerland

Matteo Repetto European Institute of Oncology, IRCCS; Department of Oncology and Hematology (DIPO), University of Milan, Milan, Italy

Gabriele Sala University of Milan, Milan, Italy

Reza Samavi Department of Electrical, Computer, and Biomedical Engineering, Toronto Metropolitan University; Vector Institute, Toronto, ON, Canada

Roberto Sassi Department of Psychiatry, University of British Columbia; British Columbia Children's Hospital, Vancouver, BC, Canada

Milija Strika Department of Oncology and Hematology-Oncology (DIPO), University of Milan; Applied Research Division for Cognitive and Psychological Science, European Institute of Oncology (IEO), IRCCS, Milan, Italy

Paul Summers Radiology Division, Radiology Department, European Institute of Oncology (IEO), IRCCS, Milan, Italy

Daniela Surico Department of Gynaecology and Obstetrics, Ospedale Maggiore della Carità; Department of Translational Medicine, University of Piemonte Orientale, Novara, Italy

Juan Pablo Tabja Bortesi CREATE, Hamilton Health Sciences, Hamilton, ON, Canada

Stefano Triberti Faculty of Human Sciences, Università Telematica Pegaso, Naples, Italy

Gianluca Vago Department of Oncology and Hematology-Oncology (DIPO), University of Milan, Milan, Italy

Stefania Volpe Department of Radiation Oncology, European Institute of Oncology (IEO), IRCCS; Department of Oncology and Hematology-Oncology (DIPO), University of Milan, Milan, Italy

Maisam Wahbah University of Dubai, Dubai, United Arab Emirates

M. Sami Zitouni University of Dubai, Dubai, United Arab Emirates

Katherine Zukotynski Department of Radiology, McMaster University, Hamilton, ON, Canada

About the editors

Shai Ben-David, PhD
University of Waterloo, Waterloo, ON, Canada
Vector Institute, Toronto, ON, Canada

Dr. Shai Ben-David earned his PhD in mathematics from the Hebrew University. Over the years, he has been a professor at the Technion, Haifa, Israel, and held visiting faculty positions at the Australian National University, Cornell University, ETH Zurich, and TTI Chicago. His research interests span a range of topics including logic, theory of distributed computation, machine learning, and complexity theory. He routinely serves as a senior area chair in the major machine learning conferences (NeurIPS, ICML, AISTATS, COLT, and ALT) and won best paper awards in COLT 2006, NeurIPS 2018, and ALT 2023. He is a coauthor of a popular textbook, *Understanding Machine Learning: From Theory to Practice*.

Giuseppe Curigliano, MD, PhD
University of Milan, Milan, Italy
European Institute of Oncology, Milan, Italy

Dr. Giuseppe Curigliano, MD, PhD, is a full professor of medical oncology at the University of Milan and the chief of the Clinical Division of Early Drug Development at the European Institute of Oncology, Milan, Italy. Dr. Curigliano is an expert in advanced drug development in solid tumors, with a specific interest in breast cancer. He contributed to the development of many anticancer treatments currently available as standard of care in the treatment of multiple solid tumors. Dr. Curigliano in 2022 was identified as Clarivate world's most influential researcher. Dr. Curigliano has contributed to over 670 peer-reviewed publications.

David Koff, MD
McMaster University, Hamilton, ON, Canada

Dr. David Koff, professor emeritus and past chair of the Department of Radiology, is the founder and director of MIIRCAM, the Medical Imaging Informatics Research Centre at McMaster University, where he oversees research initiatives on electronic transmission and workflow integration of medical images and AI applications in medical imaging. He codeveloped the Canadian standards for lossy compression. He is a member of the IHE section of the RSNA's Medical Informatics Committee and a cofounder of IHE Canada (Integrating the Healthcare Enterprise).

Barbara Alicja Jereczek, MD, PhD
University of Milan, Milan, Italy
European Institute of Oncology, Milan, Italy

Dr. Barbara Alicja Jereczek-Fossa is a full professor in radiation oncology at the University of Milan, Italy, and the chair of the Division of Radiotherapy at the European Institute of Oncology, Milan. Her research expertise focuses on urological and breast malignancies, oligometastatic cancer, drug-radiation combinations, and innovation in radiotherapy including proton therapy, stereotactic radiotherapy, AI, and radiomics.

Davide La Torre, PhD, HDR
SKEMA Business School, Sophia Antipolis, France
University of Milan, Milan, Italy

Dr. Davide La Torre is a full professor in applied mathematics and computer science at SKEMA Business School in France. His areas of interest in research and instruction are applied mathematics, artificial intelligence, mathematical modeling, and operations research. He has previously held posts as a visiting and permanent university professor in Europe, Canada, the Middle East, Central Asia, and Australia. He has held the positions of department chair and program director at various universities. He has contributed to more than 200 publications listed in Scopus.

Gabriella Pravettoni, PhD
University of Milan, Milan, Italy
European Institute of Oncology, Milan, Italy

Dr. Gabriella Pravettoni is a full professor of cognitive and decision-making psychology at the University of Milan, where, for several years, she has been working on a new dimension of the doctor-patient relationship. She also serves as the director of the Psycho-Oncology Division at the European Institute of Oncology, where she supervises clinical cases and develops and evaluates psychological treatments for cancer patients, putting the findings of several international research projects in which she is involved into clinical practice.

CHAPTER

1

Artificial intelligence in cancer research and precision medicine

Chiara Corti[a,b], Marisa Cobanaj[c], Carmen Criscitiello[a,b], and Giuseppe Curigliano[b,d]

[a]Division of New Drugs and Early Drug Development for Innovative Therapies, European Institute of Oncology (IEO), IRCCS, Milan, Italy [b]Department of Oncology and Hematology-Oncology (DIPO), University of Milan, Milan, Italy [c]OncoRay, National Center for Radiation Research in Oncology (HZDR), Dresden, Germany [d]Division of Early Drug Development for Innovative Therapies, European Institute of Oncology (IEO), IRCCS, Milan, Italy

1. Introduction

Recent unprecedented results in computer vision, automated means of transport, and personalized e-commerce conferred artificial intelligence (AI) great popularity. AI may be defined as the ability of a machine to learn and recognize relationships and patterns from a relevant number of representative examples and to process this information for decision-making purposes on unseen data.[1] AI typically includes machine learning (ML) and deep learning (DL). DL is a subset of ML that focuses on artificial neural networks (ANNs) with multiple fully connected hidden layers (i.e., "deep").

Historically, a critical boost in the application of AI in healthcare has been enabled by the digitalization of patient data, including the adoption of electronic health records (EHRs), imaging, and digital pathology. This transition provides an unprecedented opportunity to derive clinical insights from large-scale analysis of patient data.[2] Indeed, the improved expertise in data capture, the increased ability in aggregation and analytic effort, along with decreasing costs of genome sequencing and related biologic omics, set the foundation and need for novel tools that can meaningfully process these data from multiple sources and types and provide value across biomedical discovery, diagnosis, prognosis, treatment, and prevention, in a multidimensional fashion.[1,3] Such improvements could help overcome the pitfalls associated with applying population-based data to individual patients, including challenges in predicting treatment response and prognosis at the individual level when drawing upon clinical trial data.[4] Furthermore, AI might even help increase healthcare accessibility; for example, automatized point-of-care diagnostics can be established in underserved areas and reduce the required personnel for local supervision.[5]

However, while big data and AI tools have already revolutionized many fields, medicine has partially lagged due to its complexity and multidimensionality, leading to technical challenges in developing and validating solutions that generalize to diverse populations.[4,6,7] On the one hand, AI holds promises for personalized, equitable cancer care and improved health outcomes.[4] For example, digital pathology and radiology are the fields that benefited the most from the implementation of AI in cancer medicine, by contributing to screening, cancer diagnostics, and feature discovery.[8] Such progress could translate not only into a potential reduction of repetitive tasks for pathologists and radiologists, but also into the chance of improving research by discovering hidden patterns.[1] On the other hand, experts of AI in healthcare are becoming increasingly concerned about inner biases and miseducation of algorithms in view of their implementation in daily clinical practice.[9] In fact, it has been already documented that AI could mirror the unconscious thoughts, racism, and biases of the humans who generated these algorithms.[10] So, a potential worsening of existing health disparities is possible, especially without a thoughtful, transparent, and inclusive approach that involves addressing bias in algorithm design and implementation along the cancer care continuum.[3,9,11,12]

Artificial Intelligence for Medicine
https://doi.org/10.1016/B978-0-443-13671-9.00005-3

Additionally, the current AI landscape is increasingly fragmented in healthcare, with concerns regarding AI reproducibility and generalizability, and methodological limitations during algorithm design.[7,13] Also, poor validation can limit clinical translation.[11]

In this chapter, a broad landscape of major applications of AI in cancer care is provided, with a focus on cancer research and precision medicine. Major challenges posed by the implementation of AI in the clinical setting will be discussed. Potentially feasible solutions for mitigating bias are provided, in the light of promoting cancer health equity.

2. Common learning approaches for cancer medicine

AI encompasses a broad range of learning approaches and methods.[2] Supervised learning proved the ability to predict different oncological outcomes, such as tumor detection, survival, or treatment response.[2] Differently, unsupervised learning identifies patterns and subgroups within data where, typically, there is no outcome to predict. Therefore, unsupervised learning usually applies to exploratory analyses.[2]

2.1 Supervised learning

These algorithms include a set of features and predict a chosen outcome, which could be either continuous (regression) or discrete (classification).[2]

2.1.1 Linear models

Linear models relate the independent variables to the outcome of interest through linear equations. Typically, a linear regression model finds a coefficient for each feature, and observation's predictions consist of a weighted combination of these features.[2] The initial assumption is that the outcome linearly relates to the feature values and that there is an additive relationship between features. Other regression models, such as Cox regression (for survival analysis) and logistic regression (for binary classification), likewise presume an additive relationship between features, but require a transformation of the linear function based on the prediction task.[2]

Linear models are often used due to their interpretability and clear-cut methodology. Indeed, such models represent the key elements of many existing risk scores and predictive models, already used in healthcare.[2] Additionally, nonlinearities can be dissected by building interaction variables. As a matter of fact, a linear model does not automatically describe certain interactions between variables such as the effect of tumor size on cancer recurrence risk according to age groups.[2]

2.1.2 Decision tree models

As an alternative to linear models, classification and regression trees have been proposed (Fig. 1).[2] A decision tree typically implies feature splits, which divide observations into subgroups, and leaves, which contain the final subgroups and observations. First, data are separated into two subsets, based on the split that minimizes the error; then, these subsets are in turn split, thus continuing to further levels without modifications in previous splits.[2] The final tree separates the population of interest, and every observation is assigned to a single leaf, based on the feature splits. The splitting can be controlled by a complexity parameter, which allows only splits that meet a certain error improvement threshold. Eventually, the decision tree is pruned to remove splits that do not sufficiently improve the model error.[2]

A single prediction is produced for each leaf. In the case of classification, predictions are generally probabilities, calculated as the frequency of the most common outcome in the leaf; for continuous outcomes, instead, the average numerical value of the outcomes in the leaf is computed.[2]

Nonlinear relationships between features are better captured by a tree-based structure. As a matter of fact, it can set cutoff thresholds, like separating risk levels between patients above or below a certain biometric parameter. Additionally, such models could also describe dependencies between variables.[2]

A recent alternative decision tree algorithm has been introduced, in the form of optimal classification trees. These models use an optimization framework that takes into account the entire structure of the tree when evaluating potential splits and generally demonstrate very good performance while conserving high interpretability.[2]

2.1.3 Ensemble models

Ensemble methods, like random forests, construct multiple decision trees and generate predictions, based on the resultant set of models. Specifically, in random forests, each tree is trained using a random subset of features and data. The final prediction merges the predictions of the single trees. Other ensemble models are gradient boosted machines,

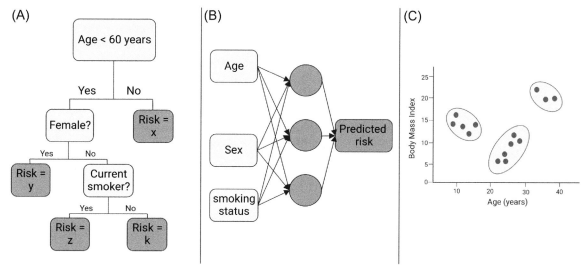

FIG. 1   Example of machine learning models utilized in cancer medicine.[2] An example of a binary classification decision tree (Panel A); an example of a feedforward neural network (Panel B); an example of clusters in two dimensions (Panel C). *Created with biorender.com.*

which iteratively train individual trees. Hence, subsequent trees are constructed to put higher weight on observations that had a high error in previous trees.[2] Coherently, in ensemble methods, there is no single model that explicitly links the input features to the final prediction, since they combine many individual trees. Such reduced interpretability as compared to other models poses challenges in application fields where interpretability is critical to adoption.[2]

2.1.4 Neural networks

Neural network-based models provide a layered network of mathematical transformation that maps features to predicted outcomes (Fig. 1).[2] Specifically, these models map the input features to nodes in a hidden layer through linear functions. Then, these nodes map to an outcome exploiting a nonlinear activation function.[2] Neural network-based dynamics allow for capturing complex interactions between features and the outcome. More recent developments in neural network design include the development of recurrent neural networks, convolutional neural networks (CNNs), and generative adversarial networks.[2] These architectures provide the foundation of DL and, as later discussed, they have become popular due to their ability to process raw images, like those used in radiology and digital pathology. Moreover, they can manage unstructured data formats as well as cases in which the number of input features greatly exceeds the number of observations.

The flip side of power and complexity is related to poor interpretability, which may limit certain clinical applications. Indeed, neural networks are often referred to as "black boxes."[2]

2.2 Unsupervised learning

Unsupervised learning does not predict a specific outcome, but rather it seeks to identify underlying structures within data.[2] Clustering is the model that most commonly finds use in a healthcare setting. For example, clustering EMR data for patients with a certain disease type could offer insight into different patient profiles within the disease. In general, clustering models split the data into a certain number of clusters with the goal of maximizing similarities within clusters and separation between clusters. The two most popular clustering methods are K-means and hierarchical clustering. Cluster interpretation poses a central challenge in unsupervised learning, especially considering the relevance of clustering in exploratory data analysis.[2] Indeed, researchers want to understand the distinguishing features of chosen clusters.[2]

3. Artificial intelligence in cancer screening, detection, and diagnosis

In cancer care, diagnostic accuracy, staging correctness, and time to diagnosis are key determinants of clinical decision-making and treatment outcomes. In this regard, AI's contribution to the digital pathology and imaging fields has been remarkable in recent years, with performance comparable to that of board-certified experts, and an additional advantage of automation and scalability.[1]

To date, the most commonly used DL architecture for image classification in cancer is represented by CNNs, which typically apply a series of nonlinear transformations to structured data to automatically learn relevant features.[1] Because it could be difficult to dissect what features are learned (i.e., "black box"), images should be carefully preprocessed to reduce the risk that the CNN model learns from artifacts.[1] In general, two strategies can be adopted in CNN models: transfer learning and autoencoder. The former relies on training a model on a large dataset, then transferring its knowledge to a smaller dataset. By doing so, the initial convolutional layers extrapolate general, low-level features, such as gradients, edges, and patterns, and the later layers detect specific features within an image, possibly by applying disease-specific data. Conversely, the latter relies on the ability to learn background features from a subset of representative images by the model, which then encodes a compressed representation of the basic features later utilized to initialize the CNN.[1,14,15]

3.1 Digital pathology

The use of digital image analysis in pathology can quickly and accurately identify and quantify specific cell types and can quantitatively assess histological features, morphological patterns, and biologically relevant regions of interest (e.g., tumoral or peritumoral areas, relationships between different immune cell populations).[16] Specifically, quantitative image analysis (QIA) tools also allow to capture data from tissue slides that may not be accessible during manual assessment via routine microscopy.[16] Finally, QIA can also be used to generate high-content data through multiplexing, which allows co-expression and co-localization analysis of multiple markers in situ with respect to the complex spatial context of tissue regions, including the stroma, tumor parenchyma, and invasive margin.[16,17] Thus, the wealth of new information provided by these techniques has created a need for a more consistent and reproducible interpretation of large and complex datasets, along with defining the interaction patterns between cell types and spatial context found in pathological images that define biological underpinnings.[16] So, the need for data reproducibility and the increasing complexity of the analyses described has led to the application of AI in pathology (Fig. 2).[1,16]

To date, several DL-based models that can diagnose and classify cancer from hematoxylin-eosin (H&E)-stained whole slide images (WSIs) of tissues derived from biopsies or surgical resection have been reported.[14] Initially, these model architectures demonstrated great ability in distinguishing cancer cells from healthy tissue within digitized stained slides, with accuracy up to an area under the curve (AUC) > 0.99.[15,18–23] A step forward occurred when deep neural networks (DNNs) were able to distinguish benign versus malignant lesions and to dissect cancer subtypes.[1] For example, deepPath is a scalable, DNN-based image analysis platform for digital pathology, which has recently been shown to classify WSI for The Cancer Genome Atlas (TCGA) lung cancer cohort into normal tissue, lung adenocarcinoma, and lung squamous cell, with a reported AUC of 0.97.[21]

Because optimization and performance improvement of AI-based tools in cancer care rely upon data from individual studies, thus lacking validation in multinational settings, competitions have been proposed to accelerate progress in this field. In the CAMELYON16 challenge, DL-based algorithms to detect breast cancer metastases in H&E-stained WSIs of lymph node sections performed similarly to the best performing pathologists under time constraints in detecting macrometastases and were better in detecting micrometastases.[15,16,24]

Another relevant example is represented by the Prostate cANcer graDe Assessment (PANDA) Challenge, powered by the Karolinska Institute and Google Health.[25] This challenge represents the largest histopathology competition to date, joined by 1290 developers, to catalyze the development of reproducible AI algorithms for Gleason grading, an essential component of clinical decision-making in prostate cancer, using 10,616 digitized prostate biopsies.[25] A diverse set of submitted algorithms reached pathologist-level performance on independent cross-continental cohorts, fully blinded to the algorithm developers.[25] On the United States and European external validation sets, the algorithms achieved agreements of 0.862 (quadratically weighted κ, 95% confidence interval (CI), 0.840–0.884) and 0.868 (95% CI, 0.835–0.900) with expert uropathologists.[25] Successful generalization across different patient populations, laboratories, and reference standards, achieved by a variety of algorithmic approaches, warrants evaluating AI-based Gleason grading in prospective clinical trials.[25]

Given the amount of additional detail and insights that can be gained from combining WSI with ML-based algorithms, this technology can be readily applied to translational research. In this regard, tumor evolution and progression involve many complex cellular and molecular interactions that are spatially and temporally regulated within the tumor microenvironment (TME).[16,26] So, digital pathology approaches, such as quantitative analysis of tumor-infiltrating lymphocytes (TILs), represent an opportunity to gain greater insight into intratumor heterogeneity, spatial patterns of cell phenotypes, and the complex interactions between cancer and the immune system within the TME.[16,26,27] For example, AI-based tools could be used to determine immune cell responses to immunotherapy, such

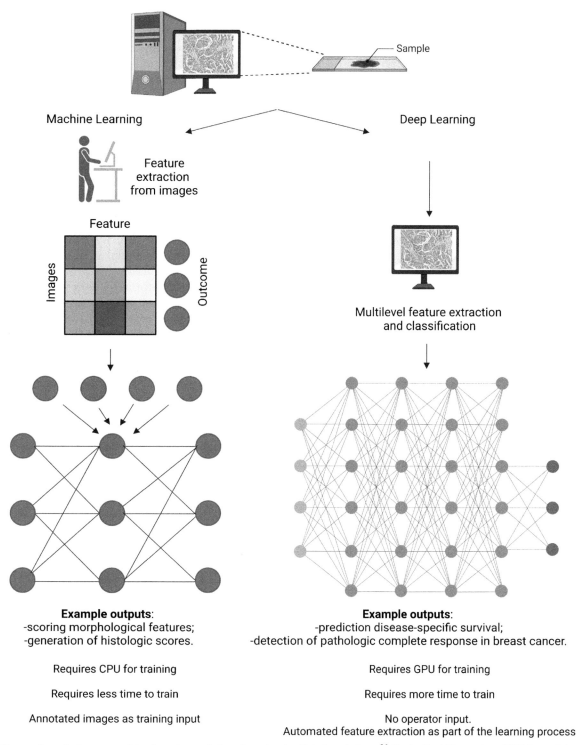

FIG. 2 Comparisons between machine learning and deep learning in digital pathology.[16] Typically, ML requires CPU for training, while DL requires GPU; as for training time, DL usually requires longer time to train; finally, while ML needs annotated images as training output, DL does not imply an operator input. Indeed, automated feature extraction is part of the learning process. Abbreviations: ML, machine learning; DL, deep learning; CPU, central processing units; GPU graphics processing units. *Created with biorender.com.*

as macrophage activation, and lymphocyte infiltration into core tumor regions, to investigate either a possible prognostic role or a predictive role for response to immune checkpoint blockade.[16,28,29] Certainly, the development of novel approaches to concurrently assess multiple biomarkers requires multiple large cohorts to add the scale and robustness necessary to elucidate relationships that may not be apparent to the human eye, and to help overcome observer bias that may mask potential biomarker signals.[4,6,16]

Another relevant application of AI-based tools in digital pathology is related to dissecting determinants of treatment response. In this light, studies on receptor-ligand binding have been performed, as proximity may be indicative of receptor engagement and pathway activation.[16] For instance, lymphocyte-activation gene 3 (LAG-3), expressed on exhausted T cells, principally interacts with major histocompatibility-II (MHC-II) molecules, expressed on the surface of antigen-presenting and tumor cells.[16] Spatial analysis in bladder and gastric cancer tumor cells demonstrated that the density and proximity of LAG-3-positive cells were significantly greater when associated with MHC-II-positive vs. MHC-II-negative tumor cells, suggesting that LAG-3-expressing TILs may be preferentially located in proximity to MHC-II-positive tumor cells, allowing for LAG-3 activation and inhibition of antitumor immunity.[16]

Finally, AI-based approaches may help predict gene mutations from routine histopathology slides.[16] For example, a CNN-based model trained with WSIs of H&E stained hepatocellular carcinoma (HCC) tissue was used to predict the 10 most common prognostic and mutated genes in HCC, with 4 of these (*CTNNB1*, *FMN2*, *TP53*, and *ZFX4*) correctly identified by the model.[30] Similar results were obtained when a DNN was trained to predict the most frequently mutated genes in lung adenocarcinoma, with six (*STK11*, *EGFR*, *FAT1*, *SETBP1*, *KRAS*, and *TP53*) being predicted from WSIs.[21] A CNN-based model has also been used to predict microsatellite instability (MSI) status from tumor tissue.[31] However, current imaging techniques can only identify genetic variants when they directly impact tissue morphology.[16,32] At the same time, AI-based algorithms cannot be applied in cases where actual variant allele frequencies of selected mutations can impact the classification and prognosis of individual diseases.[16,33]

Although guidelines, position papers, directives, AI concepts, best practices and tutorials have been made available to guarantee consistency of AI-based tools applied to digital pathology, several limitations and challenges must be addressed to allow implementation in clinical practice.[34–38] Because the performance of AI applications in digital pathology is largely dependent on the size and quality of the dataset used to train an algorithm, such datasets should be curated by pathologists, ensuring that representative images have been obtained at an appropriate magnification and that all the regions of interest are comprehensively annotated.[16,39] Pathologists should be involved also in the validation process to ensure representativeness of the sample, as well as to evaluate the accuracy and performance of the algorithm.[40,41] Additionally, translation into clinical practice will depend on algorithms being validated across many patient cohorts utilizing data not included in the training set. This will require large amounts of data to be acquired from multiple laboratories to assure the broad applicability required in a clinical setting.[6,16,42] Additional statistical studies will be required for application to properly determine the optimal processes and workflows to ensure full implementation of this technology in clinical practice.[43] Finally, technical concerns related to reproducibility, interpretability, the accuracy of competing devices, financial costs of processing hardware, and regulatory approvals that must accompany studies of clinical utility all represent barriers to implementation of AI-driven tools in digital pathology.[42,44]

3.2 Imaging

When a neoplasm is initially detected, it needs to be distinguished from nonneoplastic mimickers and classified based on its predicted natural history to optimize the type and intensity of treatment.[45] With treatment, which includes cytoreduction through surgery, radiotherapy, and pharmacotherapies, cancer may adapt to the stressors imposed, evolve, and recur.[45] The radiographic appearance of a lesion that increases in size after treatment should prompt a distinction between progressive disease and tissue response to previous loco-regional treatments (e.g., radionecrosis, after radiation therapy); moreover, neoplastic lesions could harbor new molecular aberrations, distinct from the primary tumor, which may confer resistance to further treatments. Such phenomenon may be due to the innate intratumoral heterogeneity of cancers, as well as to the selective pressure of therapy which can sculpt cancer genome evolution.[46]

Imaging evaluation of cancer is typically provided in terms of phenotypic descriptions, by radiologists. Indeed, to complete a radiology report, tumor density, pattern of enhancement, intratumoral cellular and acellular composition, regularity of tumor margins, anatomic relationship to the surrounding tissues, and impact on these structures must be considered.[45] By contrast, radiomics is enabling the digital deciphering of radiographic images into quantitative features, including descriptors of shape, size, and textural patterns.[45] In this regard, AI has already demonstrated its ability to automatically quantify radiographic patterns in medical imaging data.[45]

Within cancer imaging, AI finds three main applications: detection, characterization, and monitoring of tumors.[45] Computer-aided detection has been used to help identify missed cancers in low-dose computer tomography (CT) screening[47]; to detect brain metastases in magnetic resonance imaging (MRI) to improve radiology interpretation time while maintaining high detection sensitivity[48]; to locate microcalcification clusters in screening mammography as an indicator of early breast carcinoma.[49]

In fact, among a variety of imaging modalities developed for breast cancer screening, mammography is the best-studied and the only imaging technique that has been shown to decrease breast cancer mortality in multiple randomized trials.[50] However, it is important to know that mammography may miss up to 20% of underlying breast cancers.[51,52] A recent work conducted involving 128,793 mammograms from 62,185 patients—and of which 3,815 were followed by a cancer diagnosis within 5 years—has demonstrated that the AI-based model Mirai predicts five-year cancer risk from screening mammograms, obtaining AUCs of 0.76, 0.81, and 0.79 on independent test sets from Mass General Hospital, Karolinska, and Chang Gung Memorial Hospital, respectively.[8] This performance constitutes significant advancement over the traditional risk models used in clinical practice today.[8,53–55] Similarly, CT scans were used to develop DNNs that predict occult peritoneal metastasis in gastric cancers with an improved AUC (0.92–0.94), compared with that achieved from clinical and pathologic features (AUC, 0.51–0.63).[56]

Characterization broadly captures diagnosis, staging of tumors, and possibly prognostication and treatment outcome prediction.[45] As for staging, tumors are classified into predefined groups based on differences in their cancer's appearance and spread. These are informative for the expected clinical course and treatment strategies, with TNM classification being the most used worldwide.[45] In this regard, AI has the potential to increase the efficiency, reproducibility, and quality of tumor measurements.[45] An additional level of characterization investigates the biological features of tumors, by correlating radiographic imaging data with biological underpinnings.[45] For example, DNNs have been applied to imaging, as well, for carcinoma and melanoma classification of photographic and dermoscopic images of skin lesions, outperforming the average accuracy shown by 21 board-certified dermatologists (AUC, 0.91–0.94).[57] Another work showed that computer tomography (CT) scans of patients with lung disease can be used to build DNNs that classify textural patterns in the lung (i.e., ground glass opacity and micronodules) with an average accuracy of 0.85.[58] Lastly, a DNN has been trained and tested to distinguish prostate cancer from benign prostate conditions, using magnetic resonance imaging (MRI) from 172 patients with prostate cancer. The reported AUC was 0.84.[59]

AI can contribute to monitoring changes in a tumor over time, either in natural history or in response to treatments.[4,45] In most cases, temporal assessment of metastatic lesions is conventionally limited to predefined metrics, such as the sum of the longest diameter of prespecified target lesions (Response Evaluation Criteria in Solid Tumors, RECIST1.1).[60] Unlike such systems, which tend to simplify a complex tumor geometry and lack generalizability in the case of certain lesion types (e.g., bone), AI-based monitoring tools may be able to capture a huge amount of features across images, thus overcoming those seen and measured by humans.[45]

In conclusion, these promising findings obtained by a variety of algorithms across different patient populations warrant further evaluation and validation in prospective clinical trials. Moreover, with the recent progress made regarding optimization and implementation of liquid biopsies in oncology (i.e., the sampling and analysis of biomarkers from easily accessible biological fluids such as blood and urine), it is likely that treatment response evaluations, as well as the emergence of resistance-associated cancer genetic alterations, will be investigated by combining these approaches with radiomics profiling, in the near future. At the bedside, AI-based tools are expected to integrate all this information in a multidimensional fashion, thus providing a patient-tailored support in clinical decision-making.[45,61]

4. AI and molecular data

Relevant progress in sequencing has been made over the past few decades. Novel technologies have allowed to obtain a huge amount of fine-grained biological data, typically referred to as "-omes," including genome, transcriptome, proteome, metabolome, epigenome, and microbiome.[62] In oncology, genetic and molecular biomarkers are routinely utilized in clinical practice for diagnosis, staging, and treatment allocation.[1,63] As a matter of fact, the Food and Drug Administration (FDA) approved several companion diagnostic prognostic and predictive molecular tests.[64–66] For example, several gene expression profiles have reached clinical practice in breast cancer. Among these, Oncotype DX 21-gene Recurrence Score (RS) is the most well validated. It provides a prognostic signature for outcome with adjuvant endocrine therapy alone and a predictive signature for whether chemotherapy reduces recurrence.[65] The RS was developed by taking into account the 250 most promising candidate genes described in the literature.[67] Then, a reverse transcription polymerase chain reaction-based method was used to generate quantitative expression levels of these candidate genes from samples of 447 patients collected from three datasets.[67] A mathematic formula that includes 16 genes (plus 5 reference genes) was then generated to fine-tune prediction of distant relapse despite endocrine therapy. The outcome of this calculation is known as the RS.[67]

Moreover, cancer treatment can be guided by the presence of specific genetic alterations that are predictive of response to matched targeted therapies. For these reasons, the FDA approved two gene panels (MSK-IMPACT and Foundation One CDx) for analyzing pathogenic variants in solid tumors, in 2017.[68] Such tests detect variations in the coding regions of over 400 genes (MSK-IMPACT) and over 300 genes (Foundation One CDx).[69]

To date, highly multidimensional information provided by combining all the data coming from whole-exome, whole-genome, and targeted panels, transcription profiles from microarray, RNA-seq, and miRNAs, as well as methylation profiles are mainly used for research purposes.[1,4,14] Additionally, the progressively increasing availability of liquid biopsies is providing an abundance of data and is prompting the optimization and automatization of tools able to interpret sequencing results. To better interlock all the pieces of complex cancer data puzzles, in light of imminent clinical application, both powerful statistical methods and ML are needed.[70–72]

Indeed, the combination of multidimensional data is very complex and, to deal with these large datasets, data are often simplified. This may result in partial loss of information.[73] Reduction of data complexity can be achieved through feature selection and feature extraction, and it enables reduction of the amount of storage space needed, lowering of training times, increasing of analysis speed, and removing redundant data.[73] In this regard, the integration of histopathological morphology data with transcriptomics data, which is spatially resolved transcriptomics, constitutes another promising advancement that will allow the integration of gene expression data within a spatial context through DL-based tools.[74]

The use of ML for dissecting molecular data has been around since the early 2000s, when novel approaches such as clustering, support vector machine (SVM), and ANNs were applied to microarray-based expression profiles for cancer classification and subtype detection.[1,2] For example, DNNs have been applied to point mutations to classify tissues into 1 of the 12 TCGA cancer types or healthy tissues obtained from the 1000 Genomes Project.[75] The classifier, trained on the most frequent cancer-specific point mutations obtained from whole-exome sequencing, was able to distinguish between healthy and tumor tissue with high accuracy (AUC, 0.94) but did not perform as well in a multiclass classification task to distinguish all of the 12 cancer types at the same time (AUC, 0.70).[1,75] This work highlighted that accurate cancer classification using mutation data is challenging, possibly because of intratumor heterogeneity and low tumor purity, together with the presence of shared mutations across different cancer types.[1] Another tool, namely, MEDomics, can continuously learn based on multimodal health data inputs. It organizes data and assesses their quality, with the final aim of providing a more accurate prognosis for an individual patient.[76]

In conclusion, the ability to achieve multimodal AI that includes many layers of omics data may enable deep phenotyping of an individual, which means a comprehensive understanding of an individual's biologic uniqueness, with possible impacts on their health.

4.1 Variant calling and gene variant discovery

The process of identifying differences in sequencing data obtained from next-generation sequencing (NGS) is known as variant calling. Since genomic variations that impact the phenotype may result from single base changes, insertions, or deletions, raw sequencing data must be aligned to a reference genome. Data quality is then improved by removing duplicates, filtering single-nucleotide polymorphisms (SNPs), as well as insertions and deletions (indels), realignment, and base recalibration.[76] These processing steps are time-consuming and prone to bias and errors. AI-based tools can be implemented to increase the speed and accuracy of these tasks.[77] For example, CNNs have been successfully applied to preprocessing and variant calling in lung cancer.[45] Another example is Cerebro, a tool that relies on random forest-based ML to incorporate data preprocessing and variation calling into an analysis pipeline that results in the improved identification of tumor-associated mutations.[78] Successful preanalysis has also be achieved through Google's Deep Variant tool, which involves a processing pipeline that relies on DNN to call genetic variants from NGS data.[78] Among standardized workflow software, the open-source OVarFlow aims at automating the process, while optimizing reproducibility and reducing the need for massive computing power.[79] To link a genetic variant to a biological role in disease development and progression, functional validation studies are needed.[80,81] Although in vivo or in vitro studies are the most appropriate in these cases, AI is being investigated as a partial replacement. Some of these in silico tools include PolyPhen and SIFT and try to determine if a mutation can cause cancer by determining the distribution of mutations of interest within the coding region of a protein.[82,83] Indeed, nonrandom distributions are more likely to be associated with the development and progression of cancer.[84]

Despite these tools assisting the selection and classification of variants, validation of these computational models is fundamental. The Critical Assessment of Genome Interpretation (CAGI) is a community experiment to objectively assess computational methods for predicting the phenotypic impacts of genomic variation.[85] CAGI participants are provided genetic variants and make blind predictions of the resulting phenotype.[85] Independent assessors evaluate the predictions by comparing them with experimental and clinical data.[85]

4.2 Targeted therapy directed by genetic testing

The detection of clinically actionable mutations directly from histopathology images is another major interest of AI experts. Indeed, such approaches would be more cost-effective and faster than NGS. In this context, besides classifying subtypes of TCGA lung cancer, deepPath was able to detect six key mutations in lung cancer (i.e., STK11, EGFR, FAT1, SETBP1, KRAS, and TP53), directly from the WSI of 59 patients at AUCs that ranged between 0.73 and 0.85.[1,21] Although these results are promising, understanding which features the DNN model relied on to identify mutation status for each slide is warranted. Another DNN-based approach was able to determine the EGFR mutation status directly from the preoperative CT scans of 844 patients with lung adenocarcinoma with AUC > 0.81.[1,86] Similar results were obtained in nonsmall cell lung cancer, using data from 18F-fluorodeoxyglucose positron emission tomography (18F-FDG-PET) and SResCNN model with AUC > 0.81.[1,87] Of note, MRI images used for feature extraction followed by XGBoost model allowed for the detection of driver mutations (e.g., isocitrate dehydrogenase 1, IDH1) and O-6-methylguanine-DNA methyltransferase (MGMT) methylation status in diffuse low-grade gliomas, with AUC > 0.70.[88] As well, frequent mutations in HCC (i.e., CTNNB1, FMN2, TP53, and ZFX4) have been identified from WSI by the DNN-based Inception-V3 model with AUC > 0.71.[1,30]

Besides mutations in individual genes, AI-based tools have also been applied to mutational footprints, such as microsatellite instability (MSI) status, that is predictive of response to immune checkpoint inhibitors.[89] In this context, the CNN-based model ResNet18 was investigated for classification as either MSI or microsatellite-stable status of predetected tumor regions within H&E slides, with AUC ranging from 0.75 to 0.84, in a cancer-specific fashion. Indeed, the main histologies included were gastric, colorectal, and endometrial cancer, as obtained from 1600 TCGA samples.[1,31] External validation was performed in an external colorectal cancer cohort.[31] Another model, namely, MSI-Net and based on a CNN architecture, was used to classify tissue and MSI status in H&E slides from a colorectal cancer cohort of 100 primary tumors, with AUC of 0.93.[31,90] MSINet was also compared to ResNet18, by retraining this model on the internal cohort adopted (n = 100) for MSINet and by applying it to the TCGA-CRC cohort (n = 479). MSINet and ResNet18 reached AUC of 0.77 and 0.71, respectively. Vice versa, MSINet was retrained on the same training set adopted for ResNet18, and then tested on MSINet internal dataset (n = 100). MSINet and ResNet18 reached AUC of 0.88 and 0.77, respectively.[1,90] Overall, a generally lower performance emerged for the TCGA cohort, which may be related to high heterogeneity in the TCGA datasets.[1]

Another important tissue-agnostic biomarker that is predictive of response to immunotherapy is tumor mutational burden (TMB).[91] Typically, it is assessed through NGS, with consequent high cost and variability across platforms and gene panels. So, AI-based tools have been investigated for TMB estimation directly from histopathology slides.[92] In this context, Image2TMB, a CNN-based image recognition model, was adopted to determine TMB status (high versus low) from frozen H&E slides in the lung adenocarcinoma TCGA cohort (n = 499).[93] Then, a random forest model was used to combine the TMB status probabilities according to three different magnifications (5×, 10×, and 20×), to define whether the TMB is above or below a predefined threshold (AUC, 0.92).[1] Research efforts have also been made to predict TMB from CT scans, with promising results as depicted by a recent study conducted in nonsmall cell lung cancer (AUC, 0.81).[1,94]

Although these methods may not be accurate enough for replacing pathology assessments, the growing potential of AI to detect cancer molecular features is undeniable. Indeed, AI could help screen a large number of tumor samples for specific mutational profiles, ultimately contributing to the design of clinical trials in which subgroups likely to benefit from specific targeted therapies are identified.[1,14,95] Additionally, possible prediction of tumor evolution and resistance to therapy from pattern changes in pathology images collected from longitudinal tumor specimens is expected in next future.[96] Finally, AI may help dissect the functional role of noncoding mutations on gene expression and epigenetic processes.[1,97]

4.3 Early cancer detection and minimal residual disease with liquid biopsy

Liquid biopsies, which consist of the sampling and analysis of biomarkers from easily accessible biological fluids such as blood and urine, can be analyzed to detect circulating tumor cells and plasma cell-free circulating tumor DNA (ctDNA).[98] However, whether these assays aid in prognostication or response classification is still under investigation.[99] For example, a systematic review of 112 studies on HCC concluded that changes in levels of circulating tumor cells could accurately identify patients with recurrence after resection of locoregional therapy.[100–102] Interestingly, a recent work examined the prevalence and dynamics of ctDNA and its association with metastatic recurrence in patients with stages II–III (early, high-risk) hormone receptor-positive breast cancer, more than five years from diagnosis and without clinical evidence of recurrence.[99] One hundred and three patients were enrolled. Whole-exome sequencing was performed on primary tumor tissue to identify somatic mutations tracked via a personalized, tumor-informed ctDNA test to detect minimal residual disease. Plasma was collected at the time of consent and at routine visits every 6–12 months. Patients were followed for clinical recurrence. Overall, 83 of 103 patients had successful sequencing. CtDNA was identified with a median of one year before all cases of distant metastasis.[99] Finally, while the current standard of care for stage II colorectal cancer does not involve a ctDNA-directed approach to postsurgical chemotherapy, the randomized phase II DYNAMIC trial results, presented at the American Society of Clinical Oncology (ASCO) annual meeting 2022, demonstrated similar recurrence-free survival between a ctDNA-guided arm and a standard management arm, thus sparing some patients from receiving adjuvant chemotherapy.

Even though lack of assay standardization and risk of bias often complicate the interpretation of liquid biopsies reports, conspicuous research effort promises to establish such molecular essays in clinical practice in the coming years. This is particularly relevant in the early disease, in which liquid biopsies could contribute to quantifying a possible residual number of circulating cancer cells in the postoperative setting (i.e., minimal residual disease), thus guiding treatment escalation and de-escalation strategies. In the metastatic setting, although liquid biopsies could help in early identification of disease progression and resistance to anticancer systemic treatments, routine use in clinical practice will be established only if an anticipated diagnosis of progressive disease will be translated into improved OS, yet this is not the case in many types of neoplasms.[103]

Finally, several actionable genetic alterations can now be identified by liquid biopsy, with performance similar to that of solid tissue sequencing.[104]

Taking this scenario into account, several AI-driven methodologies have been developed and investigated. For example, Lung-CLiP (Cancer Likelihood in Plasma) is an ML-based approach that estimates the probability that a ctDNA mutation is associated with the tumor.[105] Then, outputs are integrated with copy-number scores in an ensemble classifier with five different algorithms to predict the presence of ctDNA in a blood sample (AUC, 0.69–0.98).[105] Another work focused on predicting the presence of ctDNA in blood across multiple cancer types, by adopting a random forest-based (AUC, 0.91–0.99).[106] CancerSEEK is an AI-based multianalyte blood test that simultaneously evaluates the presence of mutations and eight cancer-associated protein biomarkers.[107] First, samples are classified as cancer-positive by a logistic regression model applied to mutations in 16 genes and expression levels in 8 plasma proteins.[108] Then, the cancer type is predicted using a random forest classifier, with specificity >99% and sensitivity ranging from 33% to 98%, according to the cancer type.[1,108]

In conclusion, as data acquisition from liquid biopsies expands, more advanced DL architectures will possibly reduce the need for manual selection and curation of discriminatory features. Furthermore, multimodal approaches that combine different data types, for example, liquid biopsies and imaging, to enhance early detection and monitor disease risk over time, are awaited in the coming years.[1]

4.4 Translational research

Translational research uses observations from basic science or patient settings to learn more about a disease and to develop powerful new treatment options. In this context, recent efforts in cancer research have focused on dissecting modern hallmarks of cancer, such as the TME. While traditional cancer treatments have been based on neoplastic cells, the totality of noncancerous cells in the tumor, namely, the TME, progressively demonstrated to have an active role in determining tumor behavior and response to therapy.[109] The TME typically includes fibroblasts, immune cells, and cells that comprise the blood vessels; thus, its characterization is crucial for understanding tumor-immune cross-talk in the context of highlighting cancer vulnerabilities.[109]

A recent study highlighted the feasibility of detecting and quantifying TILs, directly from histopathology slides of 13 TCGA cancer types by means of a DNN-based approach.[110] Specifically, two DNNs were trained, to classify TILs and to identify regions of necrosis on the slide to reduce false positives, with final inspection by pathologists to refine the model outputs and a reported AUC of 0.95.[1] Another DNN-based model was trained and tested on histopathology images from breast biopsies of 882 patients to distinguish benign tissue from malignant disease and classify normal versus tumor-associated stroma with an accuracy of 92%.[1,24] Finally, histopathology images from multiplex immunohistochemistry of pancreatic cancer tissue were processed with an autoencoder-based DNN (ColorAE) and a U-Net CNN for biomedical image segmentation, with classification performance ranging from 0.40 to 0.84 (F1 score).[111]

Importantly, as the TME plays a major role in mounting an antitumor immune response, its role became particularly relevant after immune checkpoint inhibitors entered the clinic. In particular, neoantigens, which are mutated peptides arising from tumor-specific mutational events, can be recognized as nonself by the patient's immune system.[112] Usually, after detecting mutations from exome or genome sequencing, an in silico platform simulates the corresponding mutated peptides.[112] After prediction of binding affinity between these mutated peptides and the patient's MHC class I alleles, candidate neoantigens are extrapolated.[112] In this regard, NetMHC, MHCflurry, and EDGE are among the earliest ANN-based neoantigen prediction tools ever designed.[1] More recent approaches involve other models as well, such as random forest (ForestMHC), CNN (ConvMHC and DeepSeqPan), and natural language processing (NLP, HLA-CNN).[98] Additionally, because therapeutic cancer vaccines, instead of being off-the-shelf products, now tend to be designed based upon the unique patient's neoantigen repertoire, a new NLP-based method has been trained on a patient's wild-type immunopeptidome and then tested on patient's mutated to predict de novo peptide sequences of neoantigens.[113] However, this model needs further validation as it was investigated only on mass spectrometry data of a few patients with melanoma, and whether these predicted neoantigens are truly immunogenic still needs to be experimentally investigated.[1]

In the future, systems capable of imaging multiple aspects of the TME, namely, multiplexed imaging platforms, will be increasingly used and integrated with DNN architectures and powerful graphics processing units (GPUs).[1] These technologies will allow not only a detailed study of complex cellular interactions within the TME, but they will be possibly integrated with spatially resolved "-omics." Besides, to deconvolute bulk RNA-seq or microarray profiles into repertoires of resident or infiltrating cell types, DNN have also been investigated, by exploiting existing data from single-cell sequencing.[1] The most well-known methods comprise Scaden and DigitalDLSorter. Of note, since single-cell profiles from only a small subset of tissue types are publicly available to date, this approach has limitations.[1] However, global initiatives, such as The Human Cell Atlas, aiming at comprehensively profiling every cell type of the human body, as well as higher-throughput solutions for scRNA-seq promise to address these unmet needs.[114]

Another relevant application of AI-based tools in translational research is the optimization of tumor cellularity estimation, the fraction of tumor cells in a specimen.[1] Indeed, tumor cellularity could be an important indicator of residual disease after therapy (i.e., pathologic response). To date, pathologists inspect stained tissue slides to estimate tumor cellularity. This approach is laborious and prone to intra- and interobserver variability.[1] Interestingly, although tumor cellularity could be computationally derived also from NGS datasets, concordance is still limited among the different inference methods available; moreover, accuracy could be undermined by heavy dependence on the presence of high numbers of genomic alterations.[1,115] A DNN-based approach has been proposed to overcome these limitations, including H&E-stained WSI from 53 patients with breast cancer, eliminating the need for nuclei segmentation and classification, and feature extraction.[116] In particular, one model was trained to distinguish tumor from healthy tissue, while a second model was trained to output regression scores (0%–100%), referring to tumor cellularity. Concordance was good considering the predicted scores and tumor cellularity as reported by two independent pathologists (correlation 0.82).[116] In conclusion, although applications of AI for translational research are very promising and go far beyond the abovementioned examples, the present results are still initial findings that require further validation on larger datasets and prospective evaluation in independent patient cohorts.

5. Drug development

5.1 Drug discovery and design

Drug discovery and development are typically associated with high costs and time burden, as a single drug could cost billion dollars and can take 10 years of development and testing before potentially being approved by FDA.[117] Additionally, in case of unforeseen side effects or experimental disproof of expected therapeutic activity, this process can fail at any point.[117]

Computational methods can considerably reduce the molecular search space and the time needed to scan the vast biological and chemical domains for both desired and unexpected effects.[117] For example, a new molecule that inactivates a protein driving carcinogenesis might negatively impact vital pathways, potentially resulting in life-threatening complications.[117] So, computational models should be able to scan all the possible interactions among the almost 100,000 proteins that compose the human proteome, in order to find possible safety concerns before bringing a few promising candidates to in vitro and in vivo testing.[117] A fundamental prerequisite for virtual molecule screening is the possibility to predict how drug-like molecules (i.e., ligands) may interact with target proteins (i.e., receptors). Such drug binding predictions need to consider binding kinetics, conformational changes, and chemical and geometrical atomic interactions.[118] This is a very difficult task, considering that >11,000 unique structures of small-molecule ligands have been described, 6444 of which have an experimental binding affinity, thus representing 750,873 protein-ligand atomic interactions, with a specific frequency, geometry, and impact in each interaction type.[119]

Current in silico approaches for tridimensional structural drug binding achieve high quality at a significant computational cost. Indeed, they generate a large set of candidate complexes by means of thorough sampling of possible binding locations; then, scoring and ranking steps are used to retain the most promising instances; finally, an energy-based fine-tuning method is employed to best fit the ligand in the respective pocket locations.[117,120–122]

Since only 19,000 experimental tridimensional complexes are publicly available in the PDBbind database, it is fundamental to integrate DL models with physical, chemical, or biological information, to create trustable models.[117] In this light, novel and faster AI-based approaches have been proposed. EquiBind is a DL model that relies on SE(3)-equivariant graph neural networks and that takes as input a ligand molecular graph with a random associated unbound 3D conformer, as well as a receptor-bound structure.[117] With such built-in geometric reasoning, EquiBind directly predicts bound protein-ligand conformations, with a precise key location, in a single step, without prior knowledge of the protein's target pocket, which is referred to as "blind docking," and incorporates both pose prediction and binding site identification.[117] Moreover, when the model is coupled with existing fine-tuning techniques, the resulting hybrid workflow showed an even better performance.[117]

Other notable examples include a one-class support vector machine model that predicts candidate drug targets in HCC, by integrating gene expression profiles and protein-protein interaction networks (AUC, 0.88).[123] A breast cancer-specific DL-based classification approach was able to predict proteins associated with breast cancer pathogenesis, by integrating numerous cancer databases such as PharmGKB, Cancer Genome Interpreter, and TCGA, thus reporting several potential biomarkers or drug targets.[1,124] Similarly, ECLIPSE is an ML approach that predicts cancer-specific drug targets based on the DepMap data by leveraging both gene-specific and cell line–specific data.[1] Indeed, the DepMap Consortium has made hundreds of loss-of-function screen datasets available to researchers that enable the implementation of diverse AI strategies.[125]

AI has also been applied to design drug structures in silico with desired physiochemical properties and target specificities.[1] For such purpose, reinforcement learning, a growing subset of AI, has been used for in silico molecule generation since it is ideal for complex objectives and allows for interactive feedback.[1] For instance, a recurrent neural network approach, optimized using policy-based reinforcement learning, was able to generate analogues to celecoxib and compound lacking the element sulfur.[126] Another approach exploited a graph CNN model that used reinforcement learning to generate novel molecules, with high accuracy when creating analogues with certain properties.[1] Additionally, a combination of two networks, the generator and the discriminator, has been investigated to build a stronger generator model, which is referred to as generative adversarial networks (GAN).[127] In this context, MolGAN represents a model for generating molecules with prespecified properties. By adopting both GAN and reinforcement learning architecture, it achieved high performance for various properties, including drug likeliness, synthesizability, and solubility (62%, 95%, and 89%, respectively).[127]

Drug property prediction has been investigated also with models different from neural network-based architectures.[128] For example, a random forest model utilized distinct preclinical data types to predict drug toxicity and adverse events.[129] Lastly, a support vector machine model has been developed to predict the absorption, distribution, metabolism, and excretion (ADME) properties of a drug. The model was validated by accurately predicting both the blood-brain barrier permeability and the human intestinal absorption.[128]

Finally, because deep examination of a wide range of molecular features from publicly available datasets (e.g., Dep-Map) documented that reverse-phase protein array data are predictive of cancer cell line dependencies, AI emerges as a versatile tool, not only able to predict therapeutic targets but also to assess the type of experimental data most relevant to a predictive model.[130]

5.2 Drug repurposing

Drug repurposing refers to the possibility of finding a new therapeutic use for a drug, beyond its existing medical indication, and it could represent an economic alternative to conventional drug discovery.[1] Publicly available datasets such as the Library of Integrated Network-Based Cellular Signatures (LINCS) can be used to identify repurposing candidates from drugs that can reverse the expression profiles of cancer-specific gene signatures, obtained by comparing the expression of cancer cells with normal cells.[1,131] DNN-based models have been trained on drug-perturbed transcriptional profiles from LINCS to predict the therapeutic use of some drug categories and to prioritize repurposing candidates according to chemical structural similarities with approved cancer drugs.[132]

Moreover, CDRScan, an ensemble of five CNN-based models trained on cell viability datasets from the Genomics of Drug Sensitivity in Cancer (GDSC) and the COSMIC cell line project (CCLP), predicts which drugs from the GDSC would be most effective, according to the patient's specific somatic mutation profile.[133] PREDICT is a computational pipeline, able to predict novel indications for existing drugs, based on the integration of both drug and disease similarities.[134] This approach has already identified novel indication for known therapies, with associations that find support in the literature.[1]

5.3 Drug activity and efficacy

Due to the increasing availability of large cancer drug efficacy datasets based on cell lines, AI algorithms have been utilized to predict drug activity and efficacy, according to cancer molecular features.[135] In this field, preprocessing often needs to be performed to minimize potential bias and noise, such as cell line authentication or validation of in vivo data.[1,136] In one study, the response of 1001 cancer cell lines to 265 different anticancer compounds was investigated.[137] On this basis, a series of Elastic Net models were built to translate genomic features into drug efficacy (IC50 values).[137] Another work trained a set of three DNNs to predict drug response using data from TCGA and the Cancer Cell Line Encyclopedia. Specifically, one DNN was built to encode mutation information, one was built to encode expression information, and the third one was a drug response predictor network, integrating the first two DNNs.[80] This approach was able to identify both known and novel drug–cancer combinations, with expression data contributing more to accurate predictions than mutation information.[1] Similarly, a DNN-based model was trained on GDSC cell lines and then applied to different genomic datasets with clinical response information.[138] Patients were divided into high-sensitivity and low-sensitivity cohorts according to predicted IC50 values. The DNN-based tool was able to split patients based on survival under certain treatment regimens.[1] To overcome the possible lack of interpretability related to the biological underpinnings that drive a prediction (i.e., "black box"), an interpretable DL model using a visible neural network, namely, DrugCell, has been developed.[139] After integrating this model with another ANN built to modulate a drug's chemical structure, drug response was correctly predicted, also providing additional information about the biological mechanism eliciting a response. So, DrugCell could help forecast synergistic drug combinations, as results were also validated in patient-derived xenograft (PDX), with AUC of 0.75.[139] Interestingly, a multidimensional strategy that combined chemical information with genomics, transcriptomics, and proteomics accurately predicted efficacy for >17,000 compounds across 59 prespecified cell lines in the NCI-60 Human Tumor Cell Lines Screen.[140] Multidimensional strategies, like the integration of genomic features with chemical structures and biological interactions, also allowed to predict cancer drug synergy (DREAM challenge).[141]

6. Predicting treatment outcomes in patients with cancer

Cancer represents a relevant source of morbidity and mortality, worldwide.[51] Consequently, many governments and pharmaceutical companies have implemented large-scale interventional clinical trials to investigate both new therapeutic strategies and experimental compounds.[4] As a result, current clinical practice guidelines generally rely on evidence from large, randomized phase III clinical trials.[4] However, oncologists are well aware of the pitfalls associated with applying population-based data to individual patients, including challenges in predicting treatment response and prognosis at the individual level when drawing upon trial data. Moreover, it is increasingly clear that response to treatment depends not only on tumor characteristics but also on factors such as the TME and, more broadly, on the patient's sociodemographic characteristics.[4] These features are complex and deeply intertwined, posing a challenge to clinicians' ability to predict outcomes.

Although the use of AI in this field has been limited due to insufficient data availability in the past few years, now it is gradually expanding. Indeed, AI could offer a solution in the pursuit of personalized treatment approaches in oncology, capitalizing on the widespread use of clinical (e.g., EHRs), molecular (e.g., sequencing data), radiologic, and digital pathology data. Indeed, ML could ideally automate and merge all these big data to predict response to cancer treatment, thus helping in identifying the best possible anticancer approach for each patient.[4]

In this context, a logistic regression-based classifier was able to predict resistance to immunotherapy in patients with advanced melanoma, after training on treatment-naïve genomic and transcriptomic profiles and clinical features (AUC, 0.73–0.83).[142] Similarly, a XGBoost-based cancer-specific classifier was able to predict response to immune checkpoint blockade after training on one of the largest existing cohorts of matched genomic and transcriptomic profiles from published checkpoint inhibitor studies (AUC, 0.66–0.86).[142] A more sophisticated AI approach involved

CNNs trained and tested on both histopathology slides and clinical characteristics of treatment-naïve patients. Overall, the method was able to predict response to immune checkpoint blockade in patients with advanced melanoma (AUC, 0.80).[143]

Analogous approaches have been investigated in several groups of cancer treatments, besides immunotherapy. For example, a DNN-based tool was developed on data from gene expression, copy-number alteration, and clinical profiles of patients with breast cancer (METABRIC and TCGA), to predict patient outcome after different treatments (AUC > 0.80).[143] In brain cancer and HCC, similar omics-based approaches involving DNN proved the ability to predict patient survival, relying on gene expression, pathway profiles, miRNA expression, and methylation profiles.[144]

As for image-based models, a recent systematic review focusing on 1124 works on treatment outcome prediction in patients with breast cancer documented that the four most published prediction outcome categories were pathologic complete response (pCR) after neoadjuvant chemotherapy (NACT) (25/64, 39%), disease recurrence (16/64, 25%), toxicity (8/64, 12.5%), and response to systemic treatment (8/64, 12.5%). The most common models used were ANN (18/64, 28%), random forest (12/64, 19%), SVM (7/64, 11%), and logistic regression (6/64, 9%).[4] As an example, a CNN-based model was applied to predict response to neoadjuvant chemotherapy in patients with advanced breast cancer from PET/MRI scans of both treatment-naïve and pretreated tumors, with AUC 0.60–0.98.[145] A similar work has been conducted considering pretreatment CT scans in lung cancer to predict disease-free survival.[146] In brain cancer, a CNN-based model with a final layer of Cox regression model was applied to predict patient prognosis from histopathology slides. The performance improved after the inclusion of further genomic markers (IDH1 status and 1p/19q codeletion).[147] In colorectal cancer, CNNs were applied to predict survival from histopathology slides of primary tumors. Interestingly, the model performed better than the consensus assessment provided by three board certified pathologists.[1,148] Another analogue work predicted patient outcome after treatment for early-stage colorectal cancer (chemotherapy, radiation therapy, both or none) from H&E-stained WSI (AUC, 0.71); multivariate survival analysis between patient groups stratified based on the model's predictions showed that the patients predicted to have a poor prognosis indeed had poor cancer-specific survival (adjusted HR, 3.04) compared with those with predicted good prognosis.[1,149] Remarkably, to predict patient sensitivity to different anticancer compounds, an ensemble of six ML algorithms has been trained, using CT scans of patients with nonsmall cell lung cancer (AUC, 0.67–0.82).[150] In a more focused time series model, CNNs with recurrent neural networks applied to longitudinal CT scans of lung tumors were adopted to predict OS in patients after chemoradiation (AUC, 0.74).[1,151]

ML models have also been exploited to fine-tune the individual patient drug dosage for either monotherapies or combination treatments, in a dynamic manner, by means of specific data points collected over time.[152]

7. Methodological challenges

7.1 Validation is crucial to trust AI algorithms

Although AI has indisputable potential to enhance the care of patients with cancer and, more broadly, affect the oncology field, the current AI landscape is remarkably fragmented, with concerns regarding AI reproducibility and generalizability, and methodological limitations during algorithm design.[4,11] Also, poor validation can limit clinical translation.[13] To date, most studies of AI in cancer care are retrospective in nature, and randomized controlled trials specifically designed to compare treatment outcomes with and without an AI-based clinical decision support system are extremely rare in oncology.[4]

Despite considerably improved internal validation techniques, external validation on a structural different population is still limited, and few multicenter studies exist, reducing both confidence in the studies' validity and applicability.[4,153] Moreover, a commonly skewed geographical distribution of AI-based models limits the algorithms' applicability to demographically diverse populations, and to different healthcare systems, such as criteria for reimbursement.[6] Indeed, these factors directly impact the distribution of features in the training and validation cohorts, introducing "collider" bias and leading to deceptive associations in the algorithms.[4,9] This has important implications for sampling methods and database formation. One possible step would be to promote the use of benchmark datasets that represent diverse patient cohorts; the potential benefit would be improved generalizability and recalibration of algorithms, as it has already been seen in some international collaborative efforts.[4] Moreover, comparison of algorithm performance when applied to different ethnicities is often unfeasible due to a relevant underrepresentation of ethnic distributions, potentially further contributing to existing health inequities.[4,6]

7.2 From model discrimination to patient-level outcomes

Model discrimination is frequently reported with the area under the receiver operating characteristic curve (AUROC). However, model calibration, a comparison of the actual output and the expected output given by a system, is often under-reported. Calibration has important implications for patient-level, rather than population-level, performance and is essential for monitoring drifts after model implementation. In fact, a model may have near-perfect discrimination, but if it is poorly calibrated, it would not be reliable from a clinical standpoint.

Coherently, despite a remarkable increase in model development in the recent years, the lack of device creation highlights a relevant gap between AI model development and subsequent device implementation. In fact, broad AI literature shows a discrepancy between the great number of AI publications in 2019 ($n = 12{,}422$) and the limited number of new algorithms being granted FDA approval for clinical use in 2020 ($n = 130$).[4,154]

7.3 Well-curated data are fundamental for algorithm development

A recent systematic review focusing on 1124 works on treatment outcome prediction in patients with breast cancer documented a shortage of publicly available data and code.[4] Specifically, few authors (2/64) were able to share data and code upon direct request, with the rest of the responders unable to share data and code because of institutional ethics, risk of patient privacy violations, or confidentiality over the code, even if many articles contained data sharing statements that suggested that data would be made available upon request.[4] These findings highlight the need for internationally achievable anonymization and curation of data, with subsequent dissemination to the research community, such as through publicly available and secure sites.[9]

Code availability should become the rule rather than the exception. The importance of access to well-curated data is fundamental for algorithm development, as is the access process transparency. Moreover, how missing data and outliers are managed should always be reported. Considering that missing data are quite inevitable in EHRs, modeling might rely on skewed data in case of a disproportionate loss between different subgroups of patients, which is parallel to attrition bias in randomized clinical trials.[155]

To accelerate generalizability, there is a clear need for standardized structuring, formatting, and curating of collected data. For this purpose, close collaboration between clinicians, data scientists, and AI engineers will be required.[156] Moreover, reciprocal familiarization of clinicians with AI, as well as data scientists and AI engineers with clinical medicine, would facilitate progress in the field.[155] Finally, the risk of bias in the reporting methodology has been highlighted by various works focused on critical appraisal of AI-based research.[4,155] This bias does not appear to be specific to certain medical specialties, rather it appears to be a consistent problem throughout the field of AI in healthcare.[157]

Overall, addressing these critical issues will be fundamental to ensure reproducibility of algorithmic performance. Surely, overcoming these barriers requires coordination at the level of the institutions as well as professional societies.[158]

7.4 How to mitigate dataset shift and calibration drift

Progression toward AI maturity in healthcare is still limited.[4,155] Such limited adoption of AI into the clinic despite an accelerated development of algorithms should take into account that ML algorithms are highly data-dependent and affected by both the context and the specific timepoints in which a dataset is generated. The clinical environment is typically highly dynamic and patient populations are heterogeneous, to the point that a model that works well in one time period or in one hospital may fail in another. Some variation refers to predictable and unavoidable variability in the system (common-cause variation) and can be mitigated by improving its characterization using independent data and by calibrating the model. Special-cause variations are unexpected decreases in model performance due to shifts in the joint distribution between the model inputs and the target variables, which are typically referred to as dataset shifts. The goal of AI monitoring should be to raise an alarm when calibration drift and special-cause variation are present and help teams identify necessary corrections to the model or the data generation/collection process.[159,160] In contrast to AI monitoring, the aim of model updating should be to correct for observed decreases in model performance, to prevent such decreases from occurring, and even improve model performance over time.[4]

7.5 Regulating a data flow

The goal of optimizing personalized treatment strategies, and more generally, cancer care, to individual patients will require integration of a bidirectional data flow: from patients to algorithms for training, and from trained algorithms to patients, further highlighting the importance of integrating data science with clinical medicine.[155] The main challenge in this flow of data is the availability of large, interoperable cancer datasets that contain the abundant, longitudinal data required for producing generalizable models. In this regard, making anonymized patient data publicly available could contribute to larger datasets resulting from diverse patient cohorts, thus facilitating international collaborative research efforts.[4,155] Another benefit deriving from a continuous flow of new data could reside in a constant verification and reevaluation of patient care, and its related outcomes, a process that is critical for AI algorithm implementation. Doing so would require new approaches to data governance, including solutions that both easily adapt to a rapid turnover of data and comply with General Data Protection Regulation (GDPR) standards.[4,160,161]

Moreover, while the use of pharmaceuticals and medical devices is generally well coded in EHRs, the use of emergent digital technologies and AI-based interventions is less well identified. So, a clear record of which patients have been exposed to specific AI technologies would be necessary to enable monitoring of outcomes and tracking of safety issues.[158] In the near future, we hope that the proliferation of standardized interoperable electronic health systems will result in higher-quality data and in broader adoption of syndicated approaches for ML.[162] In this perspective, we believe that patients with cancer will benefit from evidence coming from larger and more comprehensive datasets, which may complement local conditions and expertise, hopefully reducing the bias associated with anecdotal experience.[4,163,164]

8. Future perspectives

AI is undoubtedly experiencing explosive growth in the past years in oncology and related specialties. Notably, the branches where AI is currently gaining more impact are represented by radiology, pathology, and radiation oncology. In this scenario, one of the most promising expectancies for AI is the possibility to integrate different and composite data derived from multidimensional approaches for oncological patients. The powerful tools of AI are the only ones that can manage the enormous amounts of data from different analyses, including information derived from EHRs, imaging, and NGS, which can now be interpreted, thanks to dynamic and high-quality reference databases (e.g., ClinVar, COSMIC), with increasingly more standardized guidelines for reporting and interpretation (e.g., American College of Medical Genetics (ACMG)—standards and guidelines for the interpretation of the sequence variants).[164–167]

However, current methodological weaknesses should be urgently addressed as they could limit the clinical impact of AI and, potentially, worsen existing health disparities (Fig. 3). It is becoming increasingly clear that socioeconomic disparities, differences in race and gender could affect disease risk and recurrence. Indeed, race-specific variations in the occurrence and frequency of genomic aberrations have been reported for various cancer types.[169] So, AI could ideally bring together not only clinical information but also build a broader characterization of each patient's uniqueness, in their socioeconomic context.

For example, AI applied to breast cancer treatment outcomes documented a substantial risk of bias.[4] Rigorous adherence to standards, and broad changes in our approach to data and reproducibility, would facilitate the translation of algorithmic data science into feasible tools and, hopefully, improved patient care. Furthermore, existing datasets that are commonly used to train and test AI models in cancer are still inherently biased toward certain racial and ethnic groups. Specifically, TCGA, the largest repository of varied cancer datasets, is predominantly composed of white individuals with European ancestry.[169] Other biases exist within the commonly used large datasets. Again, the TCGA cohorts are mainly comprised of primary tumors with very limited availability of metastatic tumors.[1] Another intrinsic potential cause of bias is related to how data are used, especially when they come from the most underutilized, yet rich, data source, which is EHRs. The main reasons involve EHRs being unstructured, with high levels of noise, sparseness, and inconsistencies, requiring dedicated curation and data cleaning. These challenges are being actively addressed by standards such as the Observational Medical Outcomes Partnership Common Data Model, which is focused on restructuring patient data into easy-to-use databases with standardized disease codes and harmonized vocabulary.[1]

Finally, interrogation of algorithms for bias, postdeployment monitoring and algorithm update for data and calibration drift are important and resource-intensive tasks that are better performed by high-skilled groups, with

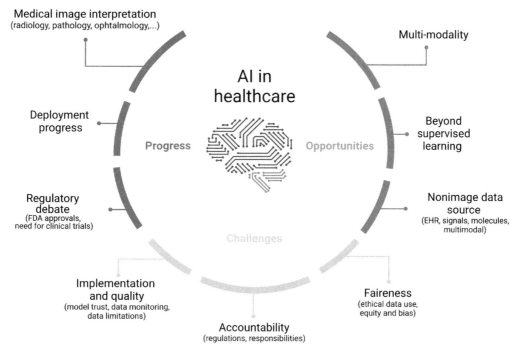

FIG. 3 Overview of the progress, challenges, and opportunity of AI in cancer medicine.[168] *Created with biorender.com.*

appropriate diversity based on the context of the local health systems where such algorithms will be applied.[158] As a matter of fact, such highly complex systems are sensitive to changes in the environment and liable to performance decay.[9] Even after their successful integration into clinical practice, AI algorithms should be continuously monitored and updated to ensure their long-term safety and effectiveness; the latest performance metrics should be promptly communicated to end-users and the model should be revised or even suspended when substantial decay in performance is observed. So, to bring AI into maturity in clinical care, the creation of hospital units responsible for quality assurance and improvement of these algorithms is desirable.[9]

From a regulatory standpoint, the need to ensure the safety, efficacy, and fairness of clinical AI is indisputable. Hence, as the number of applications of clinical AI is increasing, a fundamental challenge for regulators is arising, also taking into account the need for adaptations, considering the heterogeneity of local health systems and inevitable data drift.[158] In fact, clinical AI, like any technology in healthcare, is associated with risks including missed diagnosis, incorrect treatment, and exacerbation of inequity. In particular, the regressive impact of clinical AI on inequity was recently studied when a large insurer's algorithm that generated clinical risk scores for patients based on their healthcare costs was analyzed.[170] Specifically, because black patients with similar disease severity to white patients tend to access less care, and thus cost a payer less, the prediction model underestimated black patients' illness severity, resulting in fewer resources dedicated to black patients compared with white patients for the same true illness severity.[158,170]

Nevertheless, current regulatory approaches have been adapted from approaches designed to assess the safety and efficacy of drugs and conventional medical devices. Indeed, the FDA considers clinical AI as a software-based medical device.[158] Typically, this involves the approval of a "static" model after which reapplication must be carried out for any change in data, algorithm or intended use.[158] More recently, the FDA has proposed a regulatory framework for modifications to AI. This expands on the existing approach with new postauthorization considerations that are of greater importance for clinical AI.[171] In particular, predetermined change control plans are recommended, which place the onus on the manufacturers of algorithms to specify which parameters they intend to modify in the future as well as the intended methodology to operationalize changes.[158,172]

It is worth noticing that the comparative ease of developing a new AI algorithm, compared to a new drug or conventional physical medical device, is expected to create a volume problem for existing regulators[173]; moreover, AI technologies should necessarily change in response to changes in the underlying data, thus further increasing the aforementioned volume problem.[173]

9. Conclusion

In conclusion, ML offers great promise in oncology. It can be used to derive risk cohorts, predict prognosis, inform treatment plans, and aid with diagnosis and early interventions. Given the proliferation of patient data that are available, data-driven approaches can enhance our understanding of cancer and its effect on individuals. Although ML presents numerous technical and organizational challenges, it is a worthwhile endeavor that will likely transform cancer care.

References

1. Bhinder B, Gilvary C, Madhukar NS, Elemento O. Artificial intelligence in cancer research and precision medicine. *Cancer Discov.* 2021;11 (4):900–915. https://doi.org/10.1158/2159-8290.CD-21-0090.
2. Bertsimas D, Wiberg H. Machine learning in oncology: methods, applications, and challenges. *JCO Clin Cancer Inform.* 2020;4:885–894. https://doi.org/10.1200/CCI.20.00072.
3. Dankwa-Mullan I, Weeraratne D. Artificial intelligence and machine learning technologies in cancer care: addressing disparities, bias, and data diversity. *Cancer Discov.* 2022;12(6):1423–1427. https://doi.org/10.1158/2159-8290.CD-22-0373.
4. Corti C, Cobanaj M, Marian F, et al. Artificial intelligence for prediction of treatment outcomes in breast cancer: systematic review of design, reporting standards, and bias. *Cancer Treat Rev.* 2022;108, 102410. https://doi.org/10.1016/j.ctrv.2022.102410.
5. Trapani D, Ginsburg O, Fadelu T, et al. Global challenges and policy solutions in breast cancer control. *Cancer Treat Rev.* 2022;104, 102339. https://doi.org/10.1016/j.ctrv.2022.102339.
6. Swami N, Corti C, Curigliano G, et al. Exploring biases in predictive modelling across diverse populations. *The Lancet Healthy Longevity.* 2022;3 (2):E88. https://doi.org/10.1016/S2666-7568(21)00307-X.
7. Badawi O, Brennan T, Celi LA, et al. Making big data useful for health care: a summary of the inaugural mit critical data conference. *JMIR Med Inform.* 2014;2(2), e22. https://doi.org/10.2196/medinform.3447.
8. Yala A, Mikhael PG, Strand F, et al. Multi-institutional validation of a mammography-based breast cancer risk model. *J Clin Oncol.* 2022;40 (16):1732–1740. https://doi.org/10.1200/JCO.21.01337.
9. Feng J, Phillips RV, Malenica I, et al. Clinical artificial intelligence quality improvement: towards continual monitoring and updating of AI algorithms in healthcare. *NPJ Digit Med.* 2022;5(1):66. https://doi.org/10.1038/s41746-022-00611-y.
10. Gichoya JW, Banerjee I, Bhimireddy AR, et al. AI recognition of patient race in medical imaging: a modelling study. *Lancet Digit Health.* 2022;4 (6):e406–e414. https://doi.org/10.1016/S2589-7500(22)00063-2.
11. Futoma J, Simons M, Panch T, et al. The myth of generalisability in clinical research and machine learning in health care. *Lancet Digit Health.* 2020;2(9):e489–e492. https://doi.org/10.1016/S2589-7500(20)30186-2.
12. Braveman P, Gottlieb L. The social determinants of health: it's time to consider the causes of the causes. *Public Health Rep.* 2014;129(Suppl. 2):19–31. https://doi.org/10.1177/00333549141291S206.
13. Celi LA, Mark RG, Stone DJ, Montgomery RA. "Big data" in the intensive care unit. Closing the data loop. *Am J Respir Crit Care Med.* 2013;187 (11):1157–1160. https://doi.org/10.1164/rccm.201212-2311ED.
14. Khosravi P, Kazemi E, Imielinski M, et al. Deep convolutional neural networks enable discrimination of heterogeneous digital pathology images. *EBioMedicine.* 2018;27:317–328. https://doi.org/10.1016/j.ebiom.2017.12.026.
15. Ehteshami Bejnordi B, Veta M, Johannes van Diest P, et al. Diagnostic assessment of deep learning algorithms for detection of lymph node metastases in women with breast cancer. *JAMA.* 2017;318(22):2199–2210. https://doi.org/10.1001/jama.2017.14585.
16. Baxi V, Edwards R, Montalto M, Saha S. Digital pathology and artificial intelligence in translational medicine and clinical practice. *Mod Pathol.* 2022;35(1):23–32. https://doi.org/10.1038/s41379-021-00919-2.
17. Dixon AR, Bathany C, Tsuei M, et al. Recent developments in multiplexing techniques for immunohistochemistry. *Expert Rev Mol Diagn.* 2015;15 (9):1171–1186. https://doi.org/10.1586/14737159.2015.1069182.
18. Liu Y, Kohlberger T, Norouzi M, et al. Artificial intelligence-based breast cancer nodal metastasis detection: insights into the black box for pathologists. *Arch Pathol Lab Med.* 2019;143(7):859–868. https://doi.org/10.5858/arpa.2018-0147-OA.
19. Li S, Jiang H, Pang W. Joint multiple fully connected convolutional neural network with extreme learning machine for hepatocellular carcinoma nuclei grading. *Comput Biol Med.* 2017;84:156–167. https://doi.org/10.1016/j.compbiomed.2017.03.017.
20. Korbar B, Olofson AM, Miraflor AP, et al. Deep learning for classification of colorectal polyps on whole-slide images. *J Pathol Inform.* 2017;8:30. https://doi.org/10.4103/jpi.jpi_34_17.
21. Coudray N, Ocampo PS, Sakellaropoulos T, et al. Classification and mutation prediction from non-small cell lung cancer histopathology images using deep learning. *Nat Med.* 2018;24(10):1559–1567. https://doi.org/10.1038/s41591-018-0177-5.
22. Iizuka O, Kanavati F, Kato K, et al. Deep learning models for histopathological classification of gastric and colonic epithelial tumours. *Sci Rep.* 2020;10(1):1504. https://doi.org/10.1038/s41598-020-58467-9.
23. Campanella G, Hanna MG, Geneslaw L, et al. Clinical-grade computational pathology using weakly supervised deep learning on whole slide images. *Nat Med.* 2019;25(8):1301–1309. https://doi.org/10.1038/s41591-019-0508-1.
24. Ehteshami Bejnordi B, Mullooly M, Pfeiffer RM, et al. Using deep convolutional neural networks to identify and classify tumor-associated stroma in diagnostic breast biopsies. *Mod Pathol.* 2018;31(10):1502–1512. https://doi.org/10.1038/s41379-018-0073-z.
25. Bulten W, Kartasalo K, Chen PC, et al. Artificial intelligence for diagnosis and Gleason grading of prostate cancer: the PANDA challenge. *Nat Med.* 2022;28(1):154–163. https://doi.org/10.1038/s41591-021-01620-2.
26. Heindl A, Nawaz S, Yuan Y. Mapping spatial heterogeneity in the tumor microenvironment: a new era for digital pathology. *Lab Invest.* 2015;95 (4):377–384. https://doi.org/10.1038/labinvest.2014.155.

27. Ercoli G, Lopez G, Ciapponi C, et al. Building up a high-throughput screening platform to assess the heterogeneity of HER2 gene amplification in breast cancers. *J Vis Exp.* 2017;(130). https://doi.org/10.3791/56686.

28. Pavillon N, Hobro AJ, Akira S, Smith NI. Noninvasive detection of macrophage activation with single-cell resolution through machine learning. *Proc Natl Acad Sci U S A.* 2018;115(12):E2676–E2685. https://doi.org/10.1073/pnas.1711872115.

29. Sun R, Limkin EJ, Vakalopoulou M, et al. A radiomics approach to assess tumour-infiltrating CD8 cells and response to anti-PD-1 or anti-PD-L1 immunotherapy: an imaging biomarker, retrospective multicohort study. *Lancet Oncol.* 2018;19(9):1180–1191. https://doi.org/10.1016/S1470-2045(18)30413-3.

30. Chen M, Zhang B, Topatana W, et al. Classification and mutation prediction based on histopathology H&E images in liver cancer using deep learning. *NPJ Precis Oncol.* 2020;4:14. https://doi.org/10.1038/s41698-020-0120-3.

31. Kather JN, Pearson AT, Halama N, et al. Deep learning can predict microsatellite instability directly from histology in gastrointestinal cancer. *Nat Med.* 2019;25(7):1054–1056. https://doi.org/10.1038/s41591-019-0462-y.

32. Shamai G, Binenbaum Y, Slossberg R, et al. Artificial intelligence algorithms to assess hormonal status from tissue microarrays in patients with breast cancer. *JAMA Netw Open.* 2019;2(7), e197700. https://doi.org/10.1001/jamanetworkopen.2019.7700.

33. Sallman DA, Padron E. Integrating mutation variant allele frequency into clinical practice in myeloid malignancies. *Hematol Oncol Stem Cell Ther.* 2016;9(3):89–95. https://doi.org/10.1016/j.hemonc.2016.04.003.

34. Pantanowitz L, Dickinson K, Evans AJ, et al. American Telemedicine Association clinical guidelines for telepathology. *J Pathol Inform.* 2014;5 (1):39. https://doi.org/10.4103/2153-3539.143329.

35. Garcia-Alvarez A, Papakonstantinou A, Oliveira M. Brain metastases in HER2-positive breast cancer: current and novel treatment strategies. *Cancers (Basel).* 2021;13(12). https://doi.org/10.3390/cancers13122927.

36. Long RE, Smith A, Machotka SV, et al. Scientific and Regulatory Policy Committee (SRPC) paper: validation of digital pathology systems in the regulated nonclinical environment. *Toxicol Pathol.* 2013;41(1):115–124. https://doi.org/10.1177/0192623312451162.

37. Abels E, Pantanowitz L, Aeffner F, et al. Computational pathology definitions, best practices, and recommendations for regulatory guidance: a white paper from the Digital Pathology Association. *J Pathol.* 2019;249(3):286–294. https://doi.org/10.1002/path.5331.

38. Janowczyk A, Madabhushi A. Deep learning for digital pathology image analysis: a comprehensive tutorial with selected use cases. *J Pathol Inform.* 2016;7:29. https://doi.org/10.4103/2153-3539.186902.

39. Bera K, Schalper KA, Rimm DL, et al. Artificial intelligence in digital pathology—new tools for diagnosis and precision oncology. *Nat Rev Clin Oncol.* 2019;16(11):703–715. https://doi.org/10.1038/s41571-019-0252-y.

40. Bui MM, Riben MW, Allison KH, et al. Quantitative image analysis of human epidermal growth factor receptor 2 immunohistochemistry for breast cancer: guideline from the College of American Pathologists. *Arch Pathol Lab Med.* 2019;143(10):1180–1195. https://doi.org/10.5858/arpa.2018-0378-CP.

41. Pantanowitz L, Sinard JH, Henricks WH, et al. Validating whole slide imaging for diagnostic purposes in pathology: guideline from the College of American Pathologists Pathology and Laboratory Quality Center. *Arch Pathol Lab Med.* 2013;137(12):1710–1722. https://doi.org/10.5858/arpa.2013-0093-CP.

42. Collins GS, Reitsma JB, Altman DG, Moons KG. Transparent reporting of a multivariable prediction model for individual prognosis or diagnosis (TRIPOD): the TRIPOD statement. *BMJ.* 2015;350, g7594. https://doi.org/10.1136/bmj.g7594.

43. Serag A, Ion-Margineanu A, Qureshi H, et al. Translational AI and deep learning in diagnostic pathology. *Front Med (Lausanne).* 2019;6:185. https://doi.org/10.3389/fmed.2019.00185.

44. Bodén ACS, Molin J, Garvin S, et al. The human-in-the-loop: an evaluation of pathologists' interaction with artificial intelligence in clinical practice. *Histopathology.* 2021;79(2):210–218. https://doi.org/10.1111/his.14356.

45. Bi WL, Hosny A, Schabath MB, et al. Artificial intelligence in cancer imaging: clinical challenges and applications. *CA Cancer J Clin.* 2019;69 (2):127–157. https://doi.org/10.3322/caac.21552.

46. Venkatesan S, Swanton C, Taylor BS, Costello JF. Treatment-induced mutagenesis and selective pressures sculpt cancer evolution. *Cold Spring Harb Perspect Med.* 2017;7(8). https://doi.org/10.1101/cshperspect.a026617.

47. Liang M, Tang W, Xu DM, et al. Low-dose CT screening for lung cancer: computer-aided detection of missed lung cancers. *Radiology.* 2016;281 (1):279–288. https://doi.org/10.1148/radiol.2016150063.

48. Ambrosini RD, Wang P, O'Dell WG. Computer-aided detection of metastatic brain tumors using automated three-dimensional template matching. *J Magn Reson Imaging.* 2010;31(1):85–93. https://doi.org/10.1002/jmri.22009.

49. Kumar MNA, Sheshadri HS. Computer aided detection of clustered microcalcification: a survey. *Curr Med Imaging Rev.* 2019;15(2):132–149. https://doi.org/10.2174/1573405614666181012103750.

50. Screening IUPoBC. The benefits and harms of breast cancer screening: an independent review. *Lancet.* 2012;380(9855):1778–1786. https://doi.org/10.1016/S0140-6736(12)61611-0.

51. Siegel RL, Miller KD, Jemal A. Cancer statistics, 2020. *CA Cancer J Clin.* 2020;70(1):7–30. https://doi.org/10.3322/caac.21590.

52. Sprague BL, Coley RY, Kerlikowske K, et al. Assessment of radiologist performance in breast cancer screening using digital breast tomosynthesis vs digital mammography. *JAMA Netw Open.* 2020;3(3), e201759. https://doi.org/10.1001/jamanetworkopen.2020.1759.

53. Gail MH, Costantino JP, Pee D, et al. Projecting individualized absolute invasive breast cancer risk in African American women. *J Natl Cancer Inst.* 2007;99(23):1782–1792. https://doi.org/10.1093/jnci/djm223.

54. Matsuno RK, Costantino JP, Ziegler RG, et al. Projecting individualized absolute invasive breast cancer risk in Asian and Pacific Islander American women. *J Natl Cancer Inst.* 2011;103(12):951–961. https://doi.org/10.1093/jnci/djr154.

55. Boggs DA, Rosenberg L, Adams-Campbell LL, Palmer JR. Prospective approach to breast cancer risk prediction in African American women: the black women's health study model. *J Clin Oncol.* 2015;33(9):1038–1044. https://doi.org/10.1200/JCO.2014.57.2750.

56. Jiang Y, Liang X, Wang W, et al. Noninvasive prediction of occult peritoneal metastasis in gastric cancer using deep learning. *JAMA Netw Open.* 2021;4(1), e2032269. https://doi.org/10.1001/jamanetworkopen.2020.32269.

57. Esteva A, Kuprel B, Novoa RA, et al. Dermatologist-level classification of skin cancer with deep neural networks. *Nature.* 2017;542 (7639):115–118. https://doi.org/10.1038/nature21056.

58. Anthimopoulos M, Christodoulidis S, Ebner L, et al. Lung pattern classification for interstitial lung diseases using a deep convolutional neural network. *IEEE Trans Med Imaging.* 2016;35(5):1207–1216. https://doi.org/10.1109/TMI.2016.2535865.

59. Wang X, Yang W, Weinreb J, et al. Searching for prostate cancer by fully automated magnetic resonance imaging classification: deep learning versus non-deep learning. *Sci Rep.* 2017;7(1):15415. https://doi.org/10.1038/s41598-017-15720-y.

60. Eisenhauer EA, Therasse P, Bogaerts J, et al. New response evaluation criteria in solid tumours: revised RECIST guideline (version 1.1). *Eur J Cancer.* 2009;45(2):228–247. https://doi.org/10.1016/j.ejca.2008.10.026.

61. Bennett CC, Hauser K. Artificial intelligence framework for simulating clinical decision-making: a Markov decision process approach. *Artif Intell Med.* 2013;57(1):9–19. https://doi.org/10.1016/j.artmed.2012.12.003.

62. Karczewski KJ, Snyder MP. Integrative omics for health and disease. *Nat Rev Genet.* 2018;19(5):299–310. https://doi.org/10.1038/nrg.2018.4.

63. Corti C, Antonarelli G, Criscitiello C, et al. Targeting brain metastases in breast cancer. *Cancer Treat Rev.* 2022;103, 102324. https://doi.org/10.1016/j.ctrv.2021.102324.

64. Sidransky D. Emerging molecular markers of cancer. *Nat Rev Cancer.* 2002;2(3):210–219. https://doi.org/10.1038/nrc755.

65. Sparano JA, Gray RJ, Makower DF, et al. Adjuvant chemotherapy guided by a 21-gene expression assay in breast cancer. *N Engl J Med.* 2018;379 (2):111–121. https://doi.org/10.1056/NEJMoa1804710.

66. Hequet D, Harrissart G, Krief D, et al. Prosigna test in breast cancer: real-life experience. *Breast Cancer Res Treat.* 2021;188(1):141–147. https://doi.org/10.1007/s10549-021-06191-x.

67. Paik S, Shak S, Tang G, et al. A multigene assay to predict recurrence of tamoxifen-treated, node-negative breast cancer. *N Engl J Med.* 2004;351 (27):2817–2826. https://doi.org/10.1056/NEJMoa041588.

68. Consortium APG. AACR project GENIE: powering precision medicine through an International Consortium. *Cancer Discov.* 2017;7(8):818–831. https://doi.org/10.1158/2159-8290.CD-17-0151.

69. Ashley EA, Butte AJ, Wheeler MT, et al. Clinical assessment incorporating a personal genome. *Lancet.* 2010;375(9725):1525–1535. https://doi.org/10.1016/S0140-6736(10)60452-7.

70. Zhou Q, Zhou Z, Chen C, et al. Grading of hepatocellular carcinoma using 3D SE-DenseNet in dynamic enhanced MR images. *Comput Biol Med.* 2019;107:47–57. https://doi.org/10.1016/j.compbiomed.2019.01.026.

71. Grewal JK, Tessier-Cloutier B, Jones M, et al. Application of a neural network whole transcriptome-based pan-cancer method for diagnosis of primary and metastatic cancers. *JAMA Netw Open.* 2019;2(4), e192597. https://doi.org/10.1001/jamanetworkopen.2019.2597.

72. Mostavi M, Chiu YC, Huang Y, Chen Y. Convolutional neural network models for cancer type prediction based on gene expression. *BMC Med Genomics.* 2020;13(Suppl. 5):44. https://doi.org/10.1186/s12920-020-0677-2.

73. Ballester PJ, Carmona J. Artificial intelligence for the next generation of precision oncology. *NPJ Precis Oncol.* 2021;5(1):79. https://doi.org/10.1038/s41698-021-00216-w.

74. Marx V. Method of the Year: spatially resolved transcriptomics. *Nat Methods.* 2021;18(1):9–14. https://doi.org/10.1038/s41592-020-01033-y.

75. Sun Y, Zhu S, Ma K, et al. Identification of 12 cancer types through genome deep learning. *Sci Rep.* 2019;9(1):17256. https://doi.org/10.1038/s41598-019-53989-3.

76. Morin O, Vallières M, Braunstein S, et al. An artificial intelligence framework integrating longitudinal electronic health records with real-world data enables continuous pan-cancer prognostication. *Nat Cancer.* 2021;2(7):709–722. https://doi.org/10.1038/s43018-021-00236-2.

77. Bewicke-Copley F, Arjun Kumar E, Palladino G, et al. Applications and analysis of targeted genomic sequencing in cancer studies. *Comput Struct Biotechnol J.* 2019;17:1348–1359. https://doi.org/10.1016/j.csbj.2019.10.004.

78. Wood DE, White JR, Georgiadis A, et al. A machine learning approach for somatic mutation discovery. *Sci Transl Med.* 2018;10(457). https://doi.org/10.1126/scitranslmed.aar7939.

79. Bathke J, Lühken G. OVarFlow: a resource optimized GATK 4 based Open source Variant calling workFlow. *BMC Bioinformatics.* 2021;22(1):402. https://doi.org/10.1186/s12859-021-04317-y.

80. Chiu YC, Chen HH, Zhang T, et al. Predicting drug response of tumors from integrated genomic profiles by deep neural networks. *BMC Med Genomics.* 2019;12(Suppl. 1):18. https://doi.org/10.1186/s12920-018-0460-9.

81. Alexandrov LB, Nik-Zainal S, Wedge DC, et al. Signatures of mutational processes in human cancer. *Nature.* 2013;500(7463):415–421. https://doi.org/10.1038/nature12477.

82. Vaser R, Adusumalli S, Leng SN, et al. SIFT missense predictions for genomes. *Nat Protoc.* 2016;11(1):1–9. https://doi.org/10.1038/nprot.2015.123.

83. Adzhubei IA, Schmidt S, Peshkin L, et al. A method and server for predicting damaging missense mutations. *Nat Methods.* 2010;7(4):248–249. https://doi.org/10.1038/nmeth0410-248.

84. Porta-Pardo E, Kamburov A, Tamborero D, et al. Comparison of algorithms for the detection of cancer drivers at subgene resolution. *Nat Methods.* 2017;14(8):782–788. https://doi.org/10.1038/nmeth.4364.

85. Andreoletti G, Pal LR, Moult J, Brenner SE. Reports from the fifth edition of CAGI: the Critical Assessment of Genome Interpretation. *Hum Mutat.* 2019;40(9):1197–1201. https://doi.org/10.1002/humu.23876.

86. Wang S, Shi J, Ye Z, et al. Predicting EGFR mutation status in lung adenocarcinoma on computed tomography image using deep learning. *Eur Respir J.* 2019;53(3). https://doi.org/10.1183/13993003.00986-2018.

87. Mu W, Jiang L, Zhang J, et al. Non-invasive decision support for NSCLC treatment using PET/CT radiomics. *Nat Commun.* 2020;11(1):5228. https://doi.org/10.1038/s41467-020-19116-x.

88. Shboul ZA, Chen JM, Iftekharuddin K. Prediction of molecular mutations in diffuse low-grade gliomas using MR imaging features. *Sci Rep.* 2020;10(1):3711. https://doi.org/10.1038/s41598-020-60550-0.

89. Sidaway P. MSI-H: a truly agnostic biomarker? *Nat Rev Clin Oncol.* 2020;17(2):68. https://doi.org/10.1038/s41571-019-0310-5.

90. Yamashita R, Long J, Longacre T, et al. Deep learning model for the prediction of microsatellite instability in colorectal cancer: a diagnostic study. *Lancet Oncol.* 2021;22(1):132–141. https://doi.org/10.1016/S1470-2045(20)30535-0.

91. Chan TA, Yarchoan M, Jaffee E, et al. Development of tumor mutation burden as an immunotherapy biomarker: utility for the oncology clinic. *Ann Oncol.* 2019;30(1):44–56. https://doi.org/10.1093/annonc/mdy495.

92. Krøigård AB, Thomassen M, Lænkholm AV, et al. Evaluation of nine somatic variant callers for detection of somatic mutations in exome and targeted deep sequencing data. *PloS One.* 2016;11(3), e0151664. https://doi.org/10.1371/journal.pone.0151664.

93. Jain MS, Massoud TF. Predicting tumour mutational burden from histopathological images using multiscale deep learning. *Nat Mach Intell.* 2020;2:356–362.

94. He B, Dong D, She Y, et al. Predicting response to immunotherapy in advanced non-small-cell lung cancer using tumor mutational burden radiomic biomarker. *J Immunother Cancer.* 2020;8(2). https://doi.org/10.1136/jitc-2020-000550.

95. Xu Z, Verma A, Naveed U, et al. Deep learning predicts chromosomal instability from histopathology images. *iScience.* 2021;24(5), 102394. https://doi.org/10.1016/j.isci.2021.102394.

96. Bai H, Wang Z, Chen K, et al. Influence of chemotherapy on EGFR mutation status among patients with non-small-cell lung cancer. *J Clin Oncol.* 2012;30(25):3077–3083. https://doi.org/10.1200/JCO.2011.39.3744.

97. Zhou J, Theesfeld CL, Yao K, et al. Deep learning sequence-based ab initio prediction of variant effects on expression and disease risk. *Nat Genet.* 2018;50(8):1171–1179. https://doi.org/10.1038/s41588-018-0160-6.

98. Bhinder B, Elemento O. Computational methods in tumor immunology. *Methods Enzymol.* 2020;636:209–259. https://doi.org/10.1016/bs.mie.2020.01.001.

99. Lipsyc-Sharf M, de Bruin EC, Santos K, et al. Circulating tumor DNA and late recurrence in high-risk hormone receptor-positive, human epidermal growth factor receptor 2-negative breast cancer. *J Clin Oncol.* 2022; JCO2200908. https://doi.org/10.1200/JCO.22.00908.

100. Park S, Lee EJ, Rim CH, Seong J. Plasma cell-free DNA as a predictive marker after radiotherapy for hepatocellular carcinoma. *Yonsei Med J.* 2018;59(4):470–479. https://doi.org/10.3349/ymj.2018.59.4.470.

101. Alunni-Fabbroni M, Rönsch K, Huber T, et al. Circulating DNA as prognostic biomarker in patients with advanced hepatocellular carcinoma: a translational exploratory study from the SORAMIC trial. *J Transl Med.* 2019;17(1):328. https://doi.org/10.1186/s12967-019-2079-9.

102. Chen VL, Xu D, Wicha MS, et al. Utility of liquid biopsy analysis in detection of hepatocellular carcinoma, determination of prognosis, and disease monitoring: a systematic review. *Clin Gastroenterol Hepatol.* 2020;18(13):2879–2902.e9. https://doi.org/10.1016/j.cgh.2020.04.019.

103. Ignatiadis M, Sledge GW, Jeffrey SS. Liquid biopsy enters the clinic—implementation issues and future challenges. *Nat Rev Clin Oncol.* 2021;18 (5):297–312. https://doi.org/10.1038/s41571-020-00457-x.

104. André F, Ciruelos E, Rubovszky G, et al. Alpelisib for PIK3CA-mutated, hormone receptor–positive advanced breast cancer. *N Engl J Med.* 2019;380(20):1929–1940. https://doi.org/10.1056/NEJMoa1813904.

105. Chabon JJ, Hamilton EG, Kurtz DM, et al. Integrating genomic features for non-invasive early lung cancer detection. *Nature.* 2020;580 (7802):245–251. https://doi.org/10.1038/s41586-020-2140-0.

106. Mouliere F, Chandrananda D, Piskorz AM, et al. Enhanced detection of circulating tumor DNA by fragment size analysis. *Sci Transl Med.* 2018;10(466). https://doi.org/10.1126/scitranslmed.aat4921.

107. Killock D. Diagnosis: CancerSEEK and destroy—a blood test for early cancer detection. *Nat Rev Clin Oncol.* 2018;15(3):133. https://doi.org/10.1038/nrclinonc.2018.21.

108. Cohen JD, Li L, Wang Y, et al. Detection and localization of surgically resectable cancers with a multi-analyte blood test. *Science.* 2018;359 (6378):926–930. https://doi.org/10.1126/science.aar3247.

109. Wang JJ, Lei KF, Han F. Tumor microenvironment: recent advances in various cancer treatments. *Eur Rev Med Pharmacol Sci.* 2018;22 (12):3855–3864. https://doi.org/10.26355/eurrev_201806_15270.

110. Saltz J, Gupta R, Hou L, et al. Spatial organization and molecular correlation of tumor-infiltrating lymphocytes using deep learning on pathology images. *Cell Rep.* 2018;23(1):181–193.e7. https://doi.org/10.1016/j.celrep.2018.03.086.

111. Fassler DJ, Abousamra S, Gupta R, et al. Deep learning-based image analysis methods for brightfield-acquired multiplex immunohistochemistry images. *Diagn Pathol.* 2020;15(1):100. https://doi.org/10.1186/s13000-020-01003-0.

112. Antonarelli G, Corti C, Tarantino P, et al. Therapeutic cancer vaccines revamping: technology advancements and pitfalls. *Ann Oncol.* 2021;32 (12):1537–1551. https://doi.org/10.1016/j.annonc.2021.08.2153.

113. Finotello F, Rieder D, Hackl H, Trajanoski Z. Next-generation computational tools for interrogating cancer immunity. *Nat Rev Genet.* 2019;20 (12):724–746. https://doi.org/10.1038/s41576-019-0166-7.

114. Regev A, Teichmann SA, Lander ES, et al. The human cell atlas. *Elife.* 2017;6. https://doi.org/10.7554/eLife.27041.

115. Haider S, Tyekucheva S, Prandi D, et al. Systematic assessment of tumor purity and its clinical implications. *JCO Precis Oncol.* 2020;4. https://doi.org/10.1200/PO.20.00016.

116. Akbar S, Peikari M, Salama S, et al. Automated and manual quantification of tumour cellularity in digital slides for tumour burden assessment. *Sci Rep.* 2019;9(1):14099. https://doi.org/10.1038/s41598-019-50568-4.

117. Stark H, Ganea OE, Pattanaik L, et al. EQUIBIND: geometric deep learning for drug binding structure prediction. The ICLR 2022 Workshop on Geometrical and Topological Representation Learning, 2022. https://gt-rl.github.io/.

118. Du X, Li Y, Xia YL, et al. Insights into protein-ligand interactions: mechanisms, models, and methods. *Int J Mol Sci.* 2016;17(2). https://doi.org/10.3390/ijms17020144.

119. Ferreira de Freitas R, Schapira M. A systematic analysis of atomic protein-ligand interactions in the PDB. *Medchemcomm.* 2017;8(10):1970–1981. https://doi.org/10.1039/c7md00381a.

120. McNutt AT, Francoeur P, Aggarwal R, et al. GNINA 1.0: molecular docking with deep learning. *J Chem.* 2021;13(1):43. https://doi.org/10.1186/s13321-021-00522-2.

121. Friesner RA, Banks JL, Murphy RB, et al. Glide: a new approach for rapid, accurate docking and scoring. 1. Method and assessment of docking accuracy. *J Med Chem.* 2004;47(7):1739–1749. https://doi.org/10.1021/jm0306430.

122. Hassan NM, Alhossary AA, Mu Y, Kwoh CK. Protein-ligand blind docking using QuickVina-W with inter-process spatio-temporal integration. *Sci Rep.* 2017;7(1):15451. https://doi.org/10.1038/s41598-017-15571-7.

123. Tong Z, Zhou Y, Wang J. Identifying potential drug targets in hepatocellular carcinoma based on network analysis and one-class support vector machine. *Sci Rep.* 2019;9(1):10442. https://doi.org/10.1038/s41598-019-46540-x.

124. Tamborero D, Rubio-Perez C, Deu-Pons J, et al. Cancer genome interpreter annotates the biological and clinical relevance of tumor alterations. *Genome Med.* 2018;10(1):25. https://doi.org/10.1186/s13073-018-0531-8.

125. Tsherniak A, Vazquez F, Montgomery PG, et al. Defining a cancer dependency map. *Cell.* 2017;170(3):564–576.e16. https://doi.org/10.1016/j.cell.2017.06.010.

126. Olivecrona M, Blaschke T, Engkvist O, Chen H. Molecular de-novo design through deep reinforcement learning. *J Chem.* 2017;9(1):48. https://doi.org/10.1186/s13321-017-0235-x.

127. Maziarka Ł, Pocha A, Kaczmarczyk J, et al. Mol-CycleGAN: a generative model for molecular optimization. *J Chem*. 2020;12(1):2. https://doi.org/10.1186/s13321-019-0404-1.

128. Shen J, Cheng F, Xu Y, et al. Estimation of ADME properties with substructure pattern recognition. *J Chem Inf Model*. 2010;50(6):1034–1041. https://doi.org/10.1021/ci100104j.

129. Gayvert KM, Madhukar NS, Elemento O. A data-driven approach to predicting successes and failures of clinical trials. *Cell Chem Biol*. 2016;23 (10):1294–1301. https://doi.org/10.1016/j.chembiol.2016.07.023.

130. Chen MM, Li J, Mills GB, Liang H. Predicting cancer cell line dependencies from the protein expression data of reverse-phase protein arrays. *JCO Clin Cancer Inform*. 2020;4:357–366. https://doi.org/10.1200/CCI.19.00144.

131. Chen B, Ma L, Paik H, et al. Reversal of cancer gene expression correlates with drug efficacy and reveals therapeutic targets. *Nat Commun*. 2017;8:16022. https://doi.org/10.1038/ncomms16022.

132. Li B, Dai C, Wang L, et al. A novel drug repurposing approach for non-small cell lung cancer using deep learning. *PloS One*. 2020;15(6), e0233112. https://doi.org/10.1371/journal.pone.0233112.

133. Chang Y, Park H, Yang HJ, et al. Cancer drug response profile scan (CDRscan): a deep learning model that predicts drug effectiveness from cancer genomic signature. *Sci Rep*. 2018;8(1):8857. https://doi.org/10.1038/s41598-018-27214-6.

134. Gottlieb A, Stein GY, Ruppin E, Sharan R. PREDICT: a method for inferring novel drug indications with application to personalized medicine. *Mol Syst Biol*. 2011;7:496. https://doi.org/10.1038/msb.2011.26.

135. Smirnov P, Kofia V, Maru A, et al. PharmacoDB: an integrative database for mining in vitro anticancer drug screening studies. *Nucleic Acids Res*. 2018;46(D1):D994–D1002. https://doi.org/10.1093/nar/gkx911.

136. Cheung ST, Chan SL, Lo KW. Contaminated and misidentified cell lines commonly use in cancer research. *Mol Carcinog*. 2020;59(6):573–574. https://doi.org/10.1002/mc.23189.

137. Iorio F, Knijnenburg TA, Vis DJ, et al. A landscape of pharmacogenomic interactions in cancer. *Cell*. 2016;166(3):740–754. https://doi.org/10.1016/j.cell.2016.06.017.

138. Sakellaropoulos T, Vougas K, Narang S, et al. A deep learning framework for predicting response to therapy in cancer. *Cell Rep*. 2019;29 (11):3367–3373.e4. https://doi.org/10.1016/j.celrep.2019.11.017.

139. Kuenzi BM, Park J, Fong SH, et al. Predicting drug response and synergy using a deep learning model of human cancer cells. *Cancer Cell*. 2020;38 (5):672–684.e6. https://doi.org/10.1016/j.ccell.2020.09.014.

140. Cortés-Ciriano I, van Westen GJ, Bouvier G, et al. Improved large-scale prediction of growth inhibition patterns using the NCI60 cancer cell line panel. *Bioinformatics*. 2016;32(1):85–95. https://doi.org/10.1093/bioinformatics/btv529.

141. Menden MP, Wang D, Mason MJ, et al. Community assessment to advance computational prediction of cancer drug combinations in a pharmacogenomic screen. *Nat Commun*. 2019;10(1):2674. https://doi.org/10.1038/s41467-019-09799-2.

142. Liu D, Schilling B, Sucker A, et al. Integrative molecular and clinical modeling of clinical outcomes to PD1 blockade in patients with metastatic melanoma. *Nat Med*. 2019;25(12):1916–1927. https://doi.org/10.1038/s41591-019-0654-5.

143. Johannet P, Coudray N, Donnelly DM, et al. Using machine learning algorithms to predict immunotherapy response in patients with advanced melanoma. *Clin Cancer Res*. 2021;27(1):131–140. https://doi.org/10.1158/1078-0432.CCR-20-2415.

144. Chaudhary K, Poirion OB, Lu L, Garmire LX. Deep learning-based multi-omics integration robustly predicts survival in liver cancer. *Clin Cancer Res*. 2018;24(6):1248–1259. https://doi.org/10.1158/1078-0432.CCR-17-0853.

145. Choi JH, Kim HA, Kim W, et al. Early prediction of neoadjuvant chemotherapy response for advanced breast cancer using PET/MRI image deep learning. *Sci Rep*. 2020;10(1):21149. https://doi.org/10.1038/s41598-020-77875-5.

146. Lou B, Doken S, Zhuang T, et al. An image-based deep learning framework for individualizing radiotherapy dose. *Lancet Digit Health*. 2019;1(3): e136–e147. https://doi.org/10.1016/S2589-7500(19)30058-5.

147. Mobadersany P, Yousefi S, Amgad M, et al. Predicting cancer outcomes from histology and genomics using convolutional networks. *Proc Natl Acad Sci U S A*. 2018;115(13):E2970–E2979. https://doi.org/10.1073/pnas.1717139115.

148. Bychkov D, Linder N, Turkki R, et al. Deep learning based tissue analysis predicts outcome in colorectal cancer. *Sci Rep*. 2018;8(1):3395. https://doi.org/10.1038/s41598-018-21758-3.

149. Skrede OJ, De Raedt S, Kleppe A, et al. Deep learning for prediction of colorectal cancer outcome: a discovery and validation study. *Lancet*. 2020;395(10221):350–360. https://doi.org/10.1016/S0140-6736(19)32998-8.

150. Dercle L, Fronheiser M, Lu L, et al. Identification of non-small cell lung cancer sensitive to systemic cancer therapies using radiomics. *Clin Cancer Res*. 2020;26(9):2151–2162. https://doi.org/10.1158/1078-0432.CCR-19-2942.

151. Xu Y, Hosny A, Zeleznik R, et al. Deep learning predicts lung cancer treatment response from serial medical imaging. *Clin Cancer Res*. 2019;25 (11):3266–3275. https://doi.org/10.1158/1078-0432.CCR-18-2495.

152. Blasiak A, Khong J, Kee T. CURATE.AI: optimizing personalized medicine with artificial intelligence. *SLAS Technol*. 2020;25(2):95–105. https://doi.org/10.1177/2472630319890316.

153. Ramspek CL, Jager KJ, Dekker FW, et al. External validation of prognostic models: what, why, how, when and where? *Clin Kidney J*. 2021;14 (1):49–58. https://doi.org/10.1093/ckj/sfaa188.

154. Benjamens S, Dhunnoo P, Meskó B. The state of artificial intelligence-based FDA-approved medical devices and algorithms: an online database. *NPJ Digit Med*. 2020;3:118. https://doi.org/10.1038/s41746-020-00324-0.

155. Gallifant J, Zhang J, Del Pilar Arias Lopez M, et al. Artificial intelligence for mechanical ventilation: systematic review of design, reporting standards, and bias. *Br J Anaesth*. 2022;128(2):343–351. https://doi.org/10.1016/j.bja.2021.09.025.

156. Lehne M, Sass J, Essenwanger A, et al. Why digital medicine depends on interoperability. *NPJ Digit Med*. 2019;2:79. https://doi.org/10.1038/s41746-019-0158-1.

157. Cirillo D, Catuara-Solarz S, Morey C, et al. Sex and gender differences and biases in artificial intelligence for biomedicine and healthcare. *NPJ Digit Med*. 2020;3:81. https://doi.org/10.1038/s41746-020-0288-5.

158. Panch T, Duralde E, Mattie H, et al. A distributed approach to the regulation of clinical AI. *PLOS Digit Health*. 2022;1(5), e0000040. https://doi.org/10.1371/journal.pdig.0000040.

159. Yoshida E, Fei S, Bavuso K, et al. The value of monitoring clinical decision support interventions. *Appl Clin Inform*. 2018;9(1):163–173. https://doi.org/10.1055/s-0038-1632397.

160. Lee CS, Lee AY. Clinical applications of continual learning machine learning. *Lancet Digit Health*. 2020;2(6):e279–e281. https://doi.org/10.1016/S2589-7500(20)30102-3.

161. OPTIMA. IMI Innovative Medicines Initiative. 2022. https://www.imi.europa.eu/.

162. Rieke N, Hancox J, Li W, et al. The future of digital health with federated learning. *NPJ Digit Med*. 2020;3:119. https://doi.org/10.1038/s41746-020-00323-1.

163. Warren LR, Clarke J, Arora S, Darzi A. Improving data sharing between acute hospitals in England: an overview of health record system distribution and retrospective observational analysis of inter-hospital transitions of care. *BMJ Open*. 2019;9(12), e031637. https://doi.org/10.1136/bmjopen-2019-031637.

164. Lubin IM, Aziz N, Babb LJ, et al. Principles and recommendations for standardizing the use of the next-generation sequencing variant file in clinical settings. *J Mol Diagn*. 2017;19(3):417–426. https://doi.org/10.1016/j.jmoldx.2016.12.001.

165. Yao K, Singh A, Sridhar K, et al. Artificial intelligence in pathology: a simple and practical guide. *Adv Anat Pathol*. 2020;27(6):385–393. https://doi.org/10.1097/PAP.0000000000000277.

166. Richards S, Aziz N, Bale S, et al. Standards and guidelines for the interpretation of sequence variants: a joint consensus recommendation of the American College of Medical Genetics and Genomics and the Association for Molecular Pathology. *Genet Med*. 2015;17(5):405–424. https://doi.org/10.1038/gim.2015.30.

167. Fraikin G. Fabric genomics announces AI-based ACMG Classification solution for genetic testing with hereditary panels. *Businesswire*. 2019.

168. Rajpurkar P, Chen E, Banerjee O, Topol EJ. AI in health and medicine. *Nat Med*. 2022;28(1):31–38. https://doi.org/10.1038/s41591-021-01614-0.

169. Yuan J, Hu Z, Mahal BA, et al. Integrated analysis of genetic ancestry and genomic alterations across cancers. *Cancer Cell*. 2018;34(4):549–560.e9. https://doi.org/10.1016/j.ccell.2018.08.019.

170. Obermeyer Z, Powers B, Vogeli C, Mullainathan S. Dissecting racial bias in an algorithm used to manage the health of populations. *Science*. 2019;366(6464):447–453. https://doi.org/10.1126/science.aax2342.

171. US Food & Drug Administration. Proposed regulatory framework for modifications to artificial intelligence/machine learning (AI/ML)-based software as a medical device (SaMD). In: *Discussion paper and request for feedback 2019*; 2021. Available from: https://www-fda-gov.pros2.lib.unimi.it/files/medical%20devices/published/US-FDA-Artificial-Intelligence-and-achine-Learning-Discussion-Paper.pdf. Accessed 10 July 2021.

172. U.S. Food and Drug Administration. Artificial Intelligence/Machine Learning (AI/ML)-Based Software as a Medical Device (SaMD) Action Plan; 2021.

173. Meskó B, Görög M. A short guide for medical professionals in the era of artificial intelligence. *NPJ Digit Med*. 2020;3:126. https://doi.org/10.1038/s41746-020-00333-z.

2

Machine learning in computational pathology through self-supervised learning and vision transformers

Carmelo Lupo[a,b], *Nadia Casatta*[a], *Gianluca Gerard*[c], *Gaia Cervi*[c], *Nicola Fusco*[d,e], *and Giuseppe Curigliano*[d,f]

[a]Innovation Department, Diapath S.p.A., Martinengo, Italy [b]Engineering and Applied Science Department, University of Bergamo, Dalmine, Italy [c]SORINT.tek, Grassobbio, Italy [d]Department of Oncology and Hematology-Oncology (DIPO), University of Milan, Milan, Italy [e]Division of Pathology, European Institute of Oncology (IEO), IRCCS, Milan, Italy [f]Division of Early Drug Development for Innovative Therapies, European Institute of Oncology (IEO), IRCCS, Milan, Italy

1. Introduction

AI-based histopathologic evaluation requires good-quality samples, achieved through a virtuous workflow that begins in surgery and ends through multistep process in pathology using quality technology and reagents to standardize preanalytical and analytical conditions.[1] Good FFPE requires good tissue handling, properly fixation, and validated tissue processing protocols and of course, also good staining (hematoxylin and eosin, H&E) is needed. In computational pathology, the H&E quality is mandatory; the histological images will not only be a group of cells with morphological details but will also be groups of pixels that need to be identified and classified by AI models. Indeed, AI has the potential to aid cancer diagnosis by assisting pathologists' accuracy in diagnosis, going beyond the limitations of the human eye. The present changes in the evaluation of breast cancer features for the definition of the best therapy for patients is a clear example of the urgent need of reliable, objective, and specific tools in the field. The updates of current guidelines focus more on the identification of HER2-overexpressing tumors rather than accurately differentiating HER2 scores in the low range. It is reported that best practices would now be to distinguish IHC score 0 from 1+ for clinical relevance, going beyond the very poor concordance among pathologists in classifying tumors as either IHC score 1+ or 0.[2] While in the past such a threshold has never had any true impact on clinical decision-making, now the clinical implications of such distinction are clear.[3–7]

AI offers the possibility of discriminating on H&E images characteristics of the tissue that are not distinguishable to the human eye. Recent works show the possibility to define the state of some markers starting from the H&E image alone.[8–10]

However, although considerable progress has already been made in anatomic pathology both in terms of algorithm performance and the development of new strategies, many challenges need to be addressed to incorporate AI into clinical practice.[11,12] Recently developed projects mainly focus on fully supervised learning approaches and heavily rely on expert-based manual annotation, in consideration of the fact that labeling is an expensive and complex task. More recently, over the past years, deep learning has witnessed a surge in self-supervised learning as a paradigm for learning feature representations without the need for labeled data. In 2022, the Vision Transformer (ViT) emerged as a strong competitor to convolutional neural networks (CNNs) in computer vision tasks. While transformer models have become the de facto status quo in natural language processing (NLP), their recent application in computer vision has gained attention since its first publication at ICLR 2021 conference.[13] The self-attention mechanism represents a key component of the transformer architecture, which is used to capture long-range dependencies and contextual information in the input data, making this system freer to inductive biases compared to CNNs. This way the model attends to different regions of the input data, based on their relevance to the task at hand. In March 2022, Chen and Krishnan published their work on the use of DINO (self-Distillation with NO labels), a recently released supervised self-learning technique based on Vision Transformers, applied to WSI.[14] At present, the factor mostly limiting the use of deep learning models in the medico-diagnostic field is the lack of generalizability: it often happens that algorithms in line with the state of the art show a decisive drop in performance during external validation. The ability to handle, without costly retraining, diverse datasets is, in fact, critical to design clinically viable solutions.[11] Therefore, we approached the potential of this system by validating Chen et al.'s experiment on newly unseen datasets. Because of the attention mechanism underlying ViTs, the model is expected to be able to derive the parts of the histopathological image that have the most information content and belong to diagnosis-related tissue phenotypes. Here, we present the method we developed to support the pathologist's work, especially for personnel with less work experience. Based on the needs of the pathology laboratories, the following areas of interest were pinpointed: identification of the presence of areas of tumor in colon and lung biopsy and distinction of HER2 gene status in breast cancer samples, a molecular biomarker that recently acquired a new significance following the recent need to characterize HER-2 low sensitive tumors, as anticipated earlier.

2. Methods

2.1 Preliminary work

Given the optimal performances achieved by the feature extractor ViT_{256}–16 on the publicly available dataset of colon-rectal cancer (CRC-100 K),[15] in the first phase, we tested the generalization capabilities of the model on a dataset of lung and colorectal cancer. The dataset comprises 25,000 H&E patches belonging to different five classes: colon adenocarcinoma, benign colonic tissue, lung adenocarcinoma, lung squamous cell carcinoma (SCC), and benign lung tissue.[16] The samples of SCC, lung adenocarcinoma, and colon adenocarcinoma were retrieved from different 50 subjects each. From each image, we generated nine nonoverlapping tiles of 256×256 pixels, and the dataset was randomly split into training (80%) and validation set (20%). As no other information was given (e.g., patient number), apart from the patch classification, no other criterion was considered in the partitioning. Once extracted the embeddings, we trained a KNN algorithm to test the classification performances for each class by measuring AUC, precision, and recall.

2.2 Dataset

To test the performances of the model in a scenario closer to the clinical practice, where entire tissue biopsy images are being analyzed by clinicians, we selected a publicly available dataset of WSIs of invasive breast cancer carcinoma positive/negative for the molecular biomarker HER2 published by Farahmand et al.[17] The dataset comprises 186 cases of HER2-positive (90 HER2+) and -negative (96 HER2-) WSIs retrieved from the Yale Pathology electronic database. The HER2-positive cases were labeled as those with 3+ score by immunohistochemistry (IHC) as defined by ASCO/CAP clinical practice guidelines.[18] For each WSI, digitalized at $20\times$ magnification (0.5 µm/pixel), the regions of interest (ROIs) associated to HER2 ± areas of invasive carcinoma were annotated. Given the nontrivial resources in terms of computing power and storage necessary to handle over 60 GB of data, we initially considered a subset of 58 samples.

2.3 Data preprocessing

The dataset was randomly partitioned at patient-level into training (70%), validation (20%), and test set (10%) in a stratified fashion to ensure equal class representativeness across all sets. No other feature was considered. As WSIs are very large in size, tissue identification from background, shadows, water, pen marks, etc. rapidly reduce the quantity and increase the quality of the image data being analyzed. Each image was scaled down by a factor of 32, and a series of filters were applied for tissue segmentation.[19] The code provides a series of filters that can be combined in a customized way: here, we masked out background regions by setting nontissue pixels to 0 for their gray, red, green, and blue channels.

Following the flow reported in Fig. 1, this way it was possible to filter out signs of red, blue, or green pen frequently found in WSIs from clinical practice. Then, each slide was broken into nonoverlapping tiles of dimensions 4096×4096 pixels retrieved from slide's highest resolution (level 0). To selectively choose how "good" a tile is compared to other tiles, we assigned scores to tiles based on tissue percentage and color characteristics: only tiles with tissue percentage higher than 0 were retained, and the remaining were labeled as "Low Tissue" or "Tissue" if the tissue percentage was lower than 10% or higher. Finally, each tile was labeled with its correspondent class (HER2+ or HER2-) if at least 50% of pixels were within the ROI (Fig. 2).

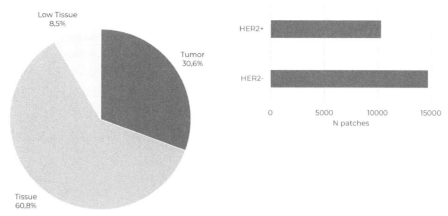

FIG. 1   Data preprocessing workflow.

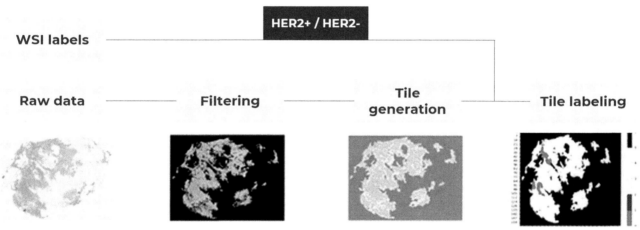

FIG. 2   Pie chart representing the percentage of patches 256×256 in the training set by class (left). Bar chart with the percentage of samples in the training set colored by biomarker type (right).

2.4 Model description—Hierarchical image pyramid transformer (HIPT) architecture

WSIs at $20\times$ magnification exhibit a hierarchical structure of visual tokens (Fig. 3): 16×16 images cover individual cells, 256×256 images capture cell-to-cell interactions (e.g., tumor cellularity), and 4096×4096 images encompass interactions and organization of group of cells within the tissue microenvironment. Motivated by the natural hierarchical structure inherent in WSIs and the recent progress in the integration of multiscale information in ViT-based models, a new transformer-based architecture called the Hierarchical Image Pyramid Transformer (HIPT) was proposed by the authors that aggregates in a bottom-up fashion visual tokens to finally form a slide-level representation.[14] For ease of notation, we refer to x_{16} images as being at the cell-level, x_{256} images as being at the patch-level, x_{4096} images as being at the region-level, with the overall WSI being the slide-level. Finally, we denoted the ViT working on x_L with $[l \times l]$ tokens as $ViT_L - l$ and CLS_L its correspondent output. Therefore, the problem is formulated as follows:

$$HIPT(x_{WSI}) = ViT_{WSI} - 4096\left(\left\{CLS_{4096}^{(k)}\right\}_{k=1}^{M}\right)$$

$$CLS_{4096}^{(k)} = ViT_{4096} - 256\left(\left\{CLS_{256}^{(j)}\right\}_{i=1}^{256}\right) \tag{1}$$

$$CLS_{256}^{(j)} = ViT_{256} - 16\left(\left\{x_{16}^{(i)}\right\}_{i=1}^{256}\right)$$

where 256 is the sequence length of $[16 \times 16]$- and $[256 \times 256]$-patching in x_{256} and x_{4096} images, respectively, and M is the total number of x_{4096} images in x_{WSI}. Given a x_{256} patch, the ViT unrolls the image as a sequence of nonoverlapping

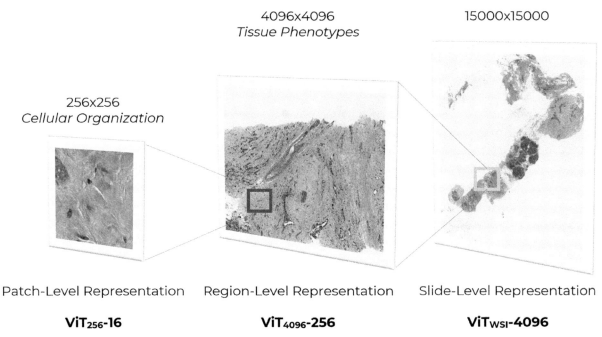

FIG. 3 Hierarchical Image Pyramid Transformer (HIPT) architecture.

$[16 \times 16]$ tokens followed by a linear embedding layer with added position embeddings to produce a set of 384-dim embeddings $\{x_{16}^{(i)}\}_{i=1}^{256} \in \mathbb{R}^{256 \times 384}$ with a learnable [CLS] token. The output of the ViT_{256}–16, the [CLS] tokens, is used as input sequence for the ViT_{4096}–256 which output a CLS token of dimension $d = 192$.

Both ViT_{256}–16 and ViT_{256}–4096 were pretrained in self-supervised manner by leveraging self-DIstillation with NO labels (DINO) architecture[10] in two subsequent steps on a large set of WSIs covering 33 cancer types retrieved from The Genome Cancer Atlas (TCGA) database.[20]

2.5 Feature extraction

In the code released by the authors,[21] both ViT_{256}–16 and ViT_{256}–4096 models are made available. To capture cell-to-cell dependencies, for each patch, x_{256} we extracted its corresponding embeddings ([CLS]$_{256}$) by employing the ViT_{256}–16. Likewise, as both models capture different tissue topological information, we concatenate to each token [CLS]$_{256}$ its corresponding embedding at region-level ([CLS]$_{4096}$) using the ViT_{256}–4096. Thus, for each region x_{4096}, a vector of dimension 256×576 was extracted, being 256 the number of patches x_{256} and 576 the result of the concatenation between the tokens [CLS]$_{256}$ and [CLS]$_{4096}$. This was done to understand if the integration of the region-level information to the local context may help in the distinction between tissue/carcinoma and HER2+/HER2- invasive carcinoma (Fig. 4).

2.6 Feature selection: Principal component analysis (PCA)

For testing whether the selection of the topmost informative inputs increases the performance of the KNN classifier, we applied a principal component analysis (PCA) on the 1×576 feature vector. As the features have a strongly variable range, they were standardized to a unique range to contribute equally to the analysis.[22] Next, the PCA was fit onto the training data to retain only 68 features, accounting for 90% of the variance. The same procedure was applied to both validation and test set.

2.7 Feature classification: K Nearest Neighbor algorithm

K-Nearest Neighbor algorithm (KNN) is a nonparametric, supervised learning classifier, which uses proximity to make predictions about the grouping of an individual data point.[23] As this algorithm is often used in combination to self-supervised ViTs,[24] the quality of the feature extractors was evaluated by using the KNN as classifier on the extracted embeddings according to the scheme described earlier. Different values of k (20, 40, 60, 80, 100, 120) were assessed on the validation set with same distance metrics (Minkowski distance) and distance-based weight function to

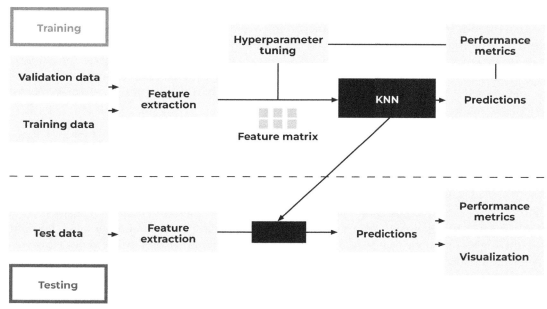

FIG. 4 Diagram of the pipeline after the data preparation.

TABLE 1 Summary of composition of training, validation, and test set per WSI number, number of regions, and number of patches divided by class.

	Training set	Validation set	Test set
Number of WSI	40	12	6
Number of regions (x_{4096})	1014	409	165
Number of patches (x_{256})	81,469 HER2+: 10,364 HER2-: 14,585 Tissue: 49,566 Low-tissue: 6954	36,135 HER2+: 3039 HER2-: 3793 Tissue: 27,124 Low-tissue: 2179	10,745

reduce the influence of outliers and noise. As visible from Table 1, the class percentage of the training data appears to be strongly skewed toward the "Tissue" class, with fewer samples of class "HER2+" or "HER2-." To lower the bias toward the majority class, we randomly downsampled the patches of the "Tissue" class, retaining 15,000 samples for the training set and 5000 samples for the validation set. The best performing set of hyperparameters was determined considering the area under curve (AUC)–receiver characteristic operator (ROC) curve along with precision and recall metrics given the great class imbalance of the dataset. In fact, when dealing with datasets in which the number of samples of negative class is much higher than one of the positive classes, the AUC can be a misleading metrics to approximate the real performance of the model.[25] The patch-level performance on the test set was evaluated both numerically by the metrics mentioned earlier and visually by comparing the prediction heatmaps with ground truth. Automated Slide Analysis Platform (ASAP) is an easy-to-use interface for visualizing, annotating, and automatically analyzing multiresolution histopathology images.[26] The available code[27] was adapted to derive for each WSI a mask file to be visualized in ASAP. In our opinion, this last step is crucial to better understand what types of misclassifications are most frequent and if the model can identify characteristics associated to explainable knowledge by the team of clinicians.

3. Results

3.1 Results of preliminary work on LC25000 dataset

The results obtained in this preliminary study were optimal: in fact, the model achieved an average AUC of 0.99 across the three classes of lung tissue and the two classes of colon tissue samples. This result is in line with what was presented in the publication paper: the authors tested the potential of the ViT_{256}–16 on patch-level tissue phenotyping task on a dataset of colon-rectal cancer (CRC-100 K) achieving overall AUC of 0.987. Despite the optimal results, important factors need to be considered. Primarily, *LC25000* is a manually curated dataset in which the entire area belongs to the same class, no experimental biases are present (e.g., no background noise as bubbles, no regions at the edge between background-tissue or tissue-tumor), and each class is equally present. Secondarily, as the number of samples per patient is unknown, it was not possible to perform a patient-wise partitioning, leading to probably inflated results and data leakage problems.[28]

3.2 Evaluation of performances of KNN

As visible from Tables 2, 3 and 4, the KNN classifier trained on only x_{256} vision and aggregated with x_{4096} can discriminate with good performances regions of invasive carcinoma and normal tissue. In fact, when aggregating the HER2+ and HER2- labels into a single-class "Tumor" class, recall and precision increase considerably. On the other hand, both types of embeddings do not extract features imputable to a specific biomarker label: for both HER2+ and HER2- classes, the highest number of misclassifications is against the other biomarker type. However, adding the region-level information to x_{256} vision seems to have a beneficial impact on the distinction of the two classes, making the precision and recall rise by 0.03/0.05 points. To be noticed, the KNN classifier seems to better distinguish the

TABLE 2   Confusion matrix and performance measure of KNN classifier trained on patch-level embeddings and tested on validation set with $k=60$.

		Predicted			
		HER2+	HER2-	Low Tissue	Tissue
Real	HER2+	989	1534	48	468
	HER2-	1716	1562	31	484
	Low tissue	8	1	2001	169
	Tissue	540	1005	344	3111
		HER2+	HER2-	Low Tissue	Tissue
AUC		0.6834	0.6634	0.9866	0.8404
Precision		0.3040	0.3807	0.8254	0.7351
Recall		0.3254	0.4118	0.9183	0.6222

TABLE 3   Confusion matrix and performance measure of KNN classifier trained on patch-level and region-level embeddings and tested on validation set with $k=120$.

		Predicted			
		HER2+	HER2-	Low Tissue	Tissue
Real	HER2+	1123	1486	63	367
	HER2-	1755	1659	51	338
	Low tissue	9	0	2003	167
	Tissue	520	857	562	3061
		HER2+	HER2-	Low Tissue	Tissue
AUC		0.6379	0.6334	0.9840	0.8597
Precision		0.3333	0.4137	0.7627	0.7917
Recall		0.3751	0.4421	0.9219	0.6182

TABLE 4 Confusion matrix and performance measure of KNN classifier trained on patch-level and region-level embeddings after PCA and tested on validation set with $k=20$.

		Predicted			
		HER2+	HER2-	Low Tissue	Tissue
Real	HER2+	1225	1300	39	475
	HER2-	1483	1732	19	559
	Low tissue	4	5	1918	252
	Tissue	569	622	232	3577
		HER2+	HER2-	Low Tissue	Tissue
AUC		0.6374	0.6418	0.9843	0.8689
Precision		0.3733	0.4733	0.8686	0.7355
Recall		0.4030	0.4566	0.8802	0.7154

HER2- condition compared to HER2+ condition. This phenomenon appears to be in clear contrast to what reported by Farahmand et al.,[17] whose model performed equally on both HER2 conditions with AUC reaching 0.88. Therefore, in this respect, further investigation needs to be conducted starting from the inclusion of all training samples in the analysis. On the other hand, the model well discriminates patches in which the tissue presence is low, most frequently occurring at the edge between tissue regions and background or where the tissue has a frayed profile. Noteworthy, over 1/5 of the total amount of "Tissue" samples in the validation set are wrongly predicted as carcinoma regions and 1/5 of the total amount of "Tissue" predictions are in fact tumor regions. This is probably since an image is labeled as cancerous if at least 50% of the pixels are within the ROI. Therefore, the features extracted by the ViT may be closer to the tumor classes. This phenomenon is less observable when aggregating the x_{256} and x_{4096} visions because the addition of the region-level information probably facilitates the distinction between the two "Tissue" and "Tumor" classes. By comparing the results obtained by the KNN with and without prior PCA (Tables 3 and 4), we can see that precision and recall are a few points apart. Therefore, the PCA does not seem to reveal any additional information that may help the classifier to better distinguish the HER2+/− condition.

In the test set, we observe the same phenomenon as for the validation set with the good performances achieved by the tissue-related classes and when considering the two biomarker types as a unique class (Table 5). The recall value for "Tumor" class in both validation and test set is over 0.90, whereas the precision value is far lower (0.86 for validation and 0.47 for test set). Thus, the model can correctly discriminate most carcinoma regions, but at the same time, it often spots tumor areas within the tissue environment and vice versa. Even though in cancer diagnosis it is preferable to

TABLE 5 Confusion matrix and performance measure of KNN classifier trained on patch-level and region-level embeddings and tested on test set with $k=120$.

		Predicted			
		HER2+	HER2-	Low Tissue	Tissue
Real	HER2+	631	415	36	66
	HER2-	408	708	8	707
	Low tissue	2	2	1068	4
	Tissue	1380	985	896	3388
		HER2+	HER2-	Low Tissue	Tissue
AUC		0.7886	0.7366	0.9780	0.7373
Precision		0.2606	0.3355	0.5318	0.8055
Recall		0.5496	0.3866	0.9561	0.5095

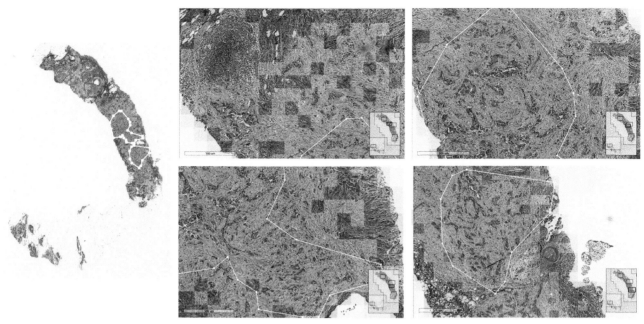

FIG. 5 Visualization of KNN predictions on HER2+ WSI within ASAP: on the left, the entire WSI, on the right, some significant close-ups at 500 µm. The contour line in green marks the region annotated by the pathologist. The regions predicted as HER2 negative and positive are colored in light blue and green (gray and light gray in print version), respectively. The areas predicted as "Tissue" and "Low Tissue" are highlighted in red and yellow (gray and light gray in print version).

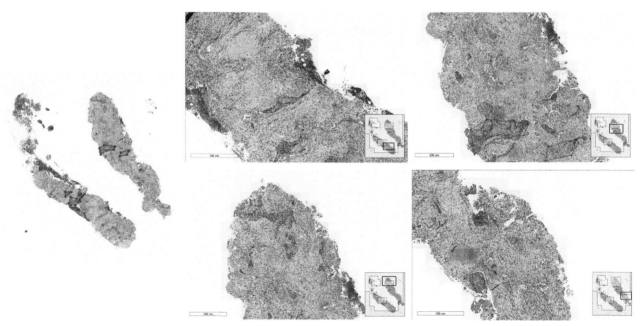

FIG. 6 Visualization of KNN predictions on HER2+ WSI. The contour line in green (light gray in print version) marks the region annotated by the pathologist.

have an extremely sensitive system, to better investigate the nature of this phenomenon, the mask files were analyzed with the ASAP tool. As visible in the Figs. 5–8, the system can correctly spot the tumor regions annotated by the pathologist. Likewise, it highlights regions within each WSI that may potentially guide the analysis of the technician. In fact, the model correctly identifies as either HER2+ or HER2- areas in which are present cell atypia, infiltrating and intraductal carcinoma, lymphocytic infiltrate, etc.

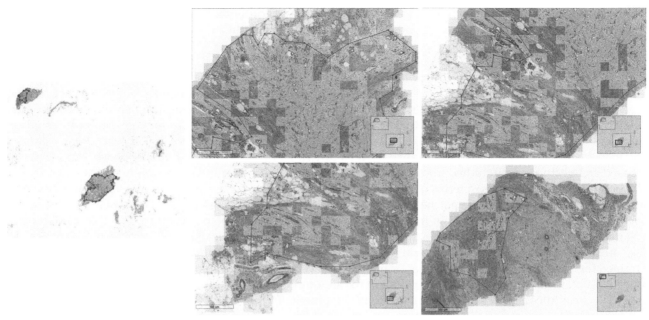

FIG. 7 Visualization of KNN predictions on HER2-WSI. The contour line in purple (gray in print version) marks the region annotated by the pathologist.

FIG. 8 Visualization of KNN predictions on HER2-WSI. The contour line in blue (gray in print version) marks the region annotated by the pathologist.

4. Discussion and future perspectives

The assignment of a personalized therapy that is most appropriate for each patient requires an increasing expertise of the pathologist. The possibility to delegate to a virtual pathologist the management and diagnosis of the simplest cases, as well as an initial evaluative screening of a significant number of biopsy specimens would greatly simplifies the routine management of a pathology anatomy laboratory, along with the speed up of reporting and diagnosis formulation timelines. As an example, the preventing screening campaigns for various diseases generate huge number of samples to be screened, and an AI system that can perform initial screening on a high number of specimens would allow the pathologist to focus on complex cases, where nowadays AI cannot intervene. The following areas of interest were identified based on the real need of pathology laboratories to simplify and optimize the current workflow:

- Colon and lung biopsy: identification of the presence of neoplastic areas;
- Breast cancer: ability to distinguish HER2 score in H&E WSI.

Although the model proposed by Chen et al. has been trained on a large amount of data, our experience has shown limited generalization capabilities for predicting HER2 levels of expression in breast cancer specimens. Accordingly, we aimed at developing an algorithm that takes advantage of the promising ViT technology but ensures adequate performance in terms of generalizability when tested on external public and/or private datasets. First, a focus was made on the increase of the specificity of the extracted features after undergoing a fine-tuning phase. In addition, other ViT-based architectures were studied from reviewing the state of the art on traditional computer vision tasks, in order to test potential and limitations in terms of performance and computational resource usage. Even though the distinction between positive and negative patches for HER2 still represents a challenging task at current stage, the model we propose here can discriminate cancerous from normal tissue regions with good precision and recall on a hold-out dataset. Moreover, as reported in the Figs. 5–8, the KNN classifier trained on the features extracted by both ViT_{256}–16 and ViT_{256}–4096 can correctly spot morphological features of specific tumors. Considering that the feature extractors were not trained for this specific task, the good performances achieved on lung and colon cancer dataset as well as the promising results obtained on HER2 dataset regardless of the annotation policy, we suggest that this hierarchical infrastructure of ViTs constitutes a good starting point for the development of future models trained for ad-hoc tasks. Testing the algorithm on WSI, whose corresponding immunohistochemical image is available, would allow a better understanding of the potential and limitations of this approach. Ultimately, based on the multiple instance learning framework, a slide-level classification could also be reached by training a neural network by using the features extracted by the ViTs. This type of approach to WSI analysis, together with the design of a functional interface for the end user, will be the basis for a tool that can directly be tested, validated, and implemented in a real-world environment within a clinical setting of a reference institution of excellence. Following this path, AI will soon be able to avoid the execution of IHC tests that recognize the presence or overexpression of specific markers, leading to significant savings in terms of time and costs. It will no longer be necessary to carry out time-consuming analyses; therefore, the turnaround time (TAT, or time to diagnosis) will be reduced, offering the patient the possibility of receiving the most appropriate therapy in less time. Laboratories may avoid to be equipped with instrumentations and platforms for perform validated IHC testing nor with specialized personnel to read the appropriate immunoreactivity of the patients' samples. It is easy to imagine how, in the short future, these AI potentials could be applied not only to breast cancer, but also, for example, to the status of estrogen and progesterone receptors, to the identification of melanoma, or to the detection and diagnosis of microsatellite instability state in colon cancer. AI models could be available to all pathological services worldwide as a CADx (computer-aided diagnosis) tool to support the pathologist's daily diagnostic activity. This type of tool would allow the improvement of TAT performance, as well as guaranteeing greater diagnostic accuracy in peripheral centers (developing areas of the planet) where the expertise of professionals is not always comparable to that of professionals operating in reference centers also according to the specific training courses and the available cases. Thanks to the optimization of timing in terms of efficiency and diagnostic accuracy, this technological progress sees a great positive social impact in the path of "democratization" of the usability of a timely and correct diagnosis in a capillary manner for individual patients. The developed AI model would also provide a great benefit to clinicians such as oncologists in managing the patient's therapeutic process.

References

1. Caramelo A, Polónia A, Vale J, et al. Demonstrating the interference of tissue processing in the evaluation of tissue biomarkers: the case of PD-L1. *Pathol Res Pract.* 2023; 154605. https://doi.org/10.1016/j.prp.2023.154605.
2. Wolff AC, Somerfield MR, Dowsett M, et al. Human epidermal growth factor receptor 2 testing in breast cancer: American Society of Clinical Oncology–College of American Pathologists Guideline Update. *Arch Pathol Lab Med.* 2023. https://doi.org/10.5858/arpa.2023-0950-SA.
3. Corti C, Giugliano F, Nicolò E, Tarantino P, Criscitiello C, Curigliano G. HER2-low breast Cancer: a new subtype? *Curr Treatment Opt Oncol Springer.* 2023. https://doi.org/10.1007/s11864-023-01068-1.
4. Idossa D, Borrero M, Blaes A. ERBB2-low (also known as HER2-low) breast Cancer. *JAMA Oncol.* 2023. https://doi.org/10.1001/jamaoncol.2022.6889.
5. Swain SM, Shastry M, Hamilton E. Targeting HER2-positive breast cancer: advances and future directions. *Nat Rev Drug Discov.* 2022;2022:1–26. https://doi.org/10.1038/s41573-022-00579-0.
6. Schlam I, Tolaney SM, Tarantino P. How I treat HER2-low advanced breast cancer. *Breast.* 2023;67:116–123. https://doi.org/10.1016/j.breast.2023.01.005.
7. Venetis K, Crimini E, Sajjadi E, et al. HER2 low, ultra-low, and novel complementary biomarkers: expanding the Spectrum of HER2 positivity in breast Cancer. *Front Mol Biosc Front Media SA.* 2022. https://doi.org/10.3389/fmolb.2022.834651.

8. Mayer C, Ofek E, Fridrich DE, et al. Direct identification of ALK and ROS1 fusions in non-small cell lung cancer from hematoxylin and eosin-stained slides using deep learning algorithms. *Mod Pathol.* 2022;35(12):1882–1887. https://doi.org/10.1038/s41379-022-01141-4.

9. Conde-Sousa E, Vale J, Feng M, et al. HEROHE challenge: predicting HER2 status in breast cancer from hematoxylin–eosin whole-slide imaging. *J Imaging.* 2022;8(8). https://doi.org/10.3390/jimaging8080213.

10. Lu W, Toss M, Rakha E, Rajpoot N, Minhas F. SlideGraph+: Whole Slide Image Level Graphs to Predict HER2Status in Breast Cancer; 2021.

11. van der Laak J, Litjens G, Ciompi F. Deep learning in histopathology: the path to the clinic. *Nat Med.* 2021;27(5):775–784. https://doi.org/10.1038/s41591-021-01343-4.

12. Cazzato G, Massaro A, Colagrande A, et al. Artificial intelligence applied to a first screening of Naevoid melanoma: a new use of fast random Forest algorithm in Dermatopathology. *Curr Oncol.* 2023;30:6066–6078. https://doi.org/10.3390/curroncol30070452.

13. Dosovitskiy A, Beyer L, Kolesnikov A, et al. An Image Is Worth 16x16 Words: Transformers for Image Recognition at Scale; 2020. http://arxiv.org/abs/2010.11929.

14. Chen RJ, Krishnan RG. Self-supervised vision transformers learn visual concepts in histopathology; 2022. https://doi.org/10.48550/arxiv.2203.00585.

15. Kather JN, Halama N, Marx A. 100,000 Histological images of human colorectal cancer and healthy tissue; 2018. https://doi.org/10.5281/ZENODO.1214456.

16. Borkowski AA, Bui MM, Brannon Thomas L, Wilson CP, Deland LA, Mastorides SM. Lung and colon cancer histopathological image dataset (LC25000). *ArXiv.* 2019. https://doi.org/10.48550/arXiv.1912.12142.

17. Farahmand S, Fernandez AI, Ahmed FS, et al. Deep learning trained on hematoxylin and eosin tumor region of Interest predicts HER2 status and trastuzumab treatment response in HER2+ breast cancer. *Mod Pathol.* 2021;35(1):44–51. https://doi.org/10.1038/s41379-021-00911-w.

18. Wolff AC, Elizabeth Hale Hammond M, Allison KH, et al. Human epidermal growth factor receptor 2 testing in breast cancer: American society of clinical oncology/college of American pathologists clinical practice guideline focused update. *J Clin Oncol.* 2018;36(20):2105–2122. https://doi.org/10.1200/JCO.2018.77.8738.

19. Mike D, Fei H, Nakul J, Deron E. Predicting breast Cancer proliferation scores with TensorFlow. *Keras, Apache Spark.* 2019. https://github.com/CODAIT/deep-histopath>. Accessed 23 June 2021.

20. National Cancer Institute. The Cancer Genome Atlas Program. https://www.cancer.gov/about-nci/organization/ccg/research/structural-genomics/tcga. Accessed 14 September 2022.

21. Chen RJ, Chen C, Li Y, et al. Scaling vision transformers to gigapixel images via hierarchical self-supervised learning; 2022. https://doi.org/10.48550/arxiv.2206.02647.

22. Jollife IT, Cadima J. Principal component analysis: A review and recent developments. *Philos Trans Roy Soc A: Math Phys Eng Sci Roy Soc Lond.* 2016. https://doi.org/10.1098/rsta.2015.0202.

23. Zhang, Z. Introduction to machine learning: k-nearest neighbors. Hemodialysis Int, J Transl Med. doi:10.21037/atm.2016.03.37.

24. Caron M, Touvron H, Misra I, et al. Emerging properties in self-supervised vision transformers. *Proc IEEE Int Conf Comput Vision.* 2021;9630–9640. https://doi.org/10.48550/arxiv.2104.14294.

25. Johnson JM, Khoshgoftaar TM. Survey on deep learning with class imbalance. *J Big Data.* 2019;6(1):1–54. https://doi.org/10.1186/S40537-019-0192-5/TABLES/18.

26. Geert L, Hans P, Hans M, Peter B, Yuichiro H, Nick O. ASAP—Automated Slide Analysis Platform; 2023. https://github.com/computationalpathologygroup/ASAP>. Accessed 23 June 2021.

27. Litjens G, Bandi P, Bejnordi BE, et al. 1399 H&E-stained sentinel lymph node sections of breast cancer patients: the CAMELYON dataset. *GigaScience.* 2018;7(6):1–8. https://doi.org/10.1093/GIGASCIENCE/GIY065.

28. Bussola N, Marcolini A, Maggio V, Jurman G, Furlanello C. AI slipping on tiles: Data leakage in digital pathology. In: *Pattern Recognition. ICPR International Workshops and Challenges.* Springer International Publishing; 2021:167–182.

3

Artificial intelligence in small-molecule drug discovery

Cesare Martinelli[a], Matteo Repetto[b,c], and Giuseppe Curigliano[d,e]

[a]Healthcare Practice, Boston Consulting Group, Milan, Italy [b]European Institute of Oncology, IRCCS, Milan, Italy [c]Department of Oncology and Hematology (DIPO), University of Milan, Milan, Italy [d]Division of Early Drug Development for Innovative Therapies, European Institute of Oncology (IEO), IRCCS, Milan, Italy [e]Department of Oncology and Hematology-Oncology (DIPO), University of Milan, Milan, Italy

1. AI in small-molecule discovery

The process of drug design and discovery involves multiple steps, including target recognition, hit discovery, lead creation, optimization of the lead, recognition of preclinical drug candidates, preclinical studies, and clinical research.[1] Thanks to technological advances, the process has increased in complexity over the years, requiring high investments and time: reports indicate that standard research and development cycle of authorization new drug is around 14 years, with an overall investment of around 2 billion dollars.[2] However, despite the large efforts deployed in the preclinical phase to scan and test thousands of potential drug candidates, the success rate of drugs entering in clinical trial phase remains below 15%,[2] with estimated losses per clinical trial fail between 800M$ and 1.4B$.[3]

In this context, AI technology has attracted the interest of researchers and pharmaceutical companies, thanks to its capability to rapidly and effectively analyze large volumes of data, with potent generalization capabilities that can enhance efficacy and decrease costs and time of the overall R&D process[4]: multiple Big Pharma companies (e.g., Pfizer, Novartis, Bayer, Roche, and Eli Lilly) are exploring this space, also leveraging partnerships with AI companies (Table 1).[1]

For decades, multiple machine learning algorithms have been employed in drug discovering, including linear regression, nearest neighbors, Bayesian classification, support vector machines, decision trees, and neural network,[5] though with limited impact, also because these approaches require manual generation of features from data, limiting their applications when the data sets involve millions of compounds as in drug discovery.[4]

However, the rapid increase in computational power, the improved accessibility of data, and the development of new, more automated, deep learning algorithms, such as deep neural networks, have improved molecular modeling predictions and are expected to dramatically enhance analytical capabilities, thus increasing the adoption of AI in drug discovery along the R&D process.[1]

1.1 Review of the different applications of AI in drug discovery

The applications of AI in drug discovery can be clustered in the following macro-areas

1. New drug target screening
2. Drug design
3. Drug screening and characterization
4. Pharmacokinetic and toxicity predictions
5. Drug repurposing
6. De novo chemical design and synthesis planning
7. Pharmaceutical product development
8. Clinical trial design and monitoring

TABLE 1   Partnerships between Pharma and AI companies.

Pharma company	AI company	Purpose
Pfizer	IBM Watson	Identification of new drug targets
Pfizer	XtalPi	Leverage Quantum Mechanics and ML to predict 3D structure of molecules and binding characteristics
Bayer	Exscientia	New lead structure optimization
Bayer	Sensyne Health	Finding of advanced treatments
Novartis	Microsoft	Generative chemistry, cell and gene treatments, smart delivery of therapies
Novartis	IBM Watson	Improvement of health outcomes for breast cancer patients
Sanofi	BenevolentAI	Leverage neural networks to address idiopathic pulmonary fibrosis and chronic kidney disease
Janssen	BenevolentAI	Develop and commercialize innovative drug candidates
Takeda	Numerate	Locate drug molecules to treat multiple disorders
Eli Lilly	Atomwise	Develop drugs on futuristic protein targets
Roche	OWKIN	Machine learning-based clinical trials and drug discovery

1.1.1 New drug target screening

The first application on AI in drug discovery is related to the opportunity to find new protein-phenotype or protein-function associations by mapping new network pathways connecting genes, proteins, and biological functions.[3] In fact, the function of one in three proteins of the human genome still remains largely unknown or poorly understood, and in-depth biological insights are limited to a limited number of proteins.[3] In this direction, ML algorithms can be developed to prioritize novel, potential drug targets in poorly understood diseases, as Papadimitriou et al. showed through a ML predictor called "Variant Combinations Pathogenicity Predictor," consisting of an ensemble of 500 individual random forest predictors.[6]

This and other ML methods can identify combinations of genetic variants or disease-causing abnormalities, including cases where causal genes are still unknown. It is expected that the advances in data integration and the development of novel AI algorithms and disease causality models will establish new unbiased ways for target selection and prioritization.[3]

1.1.2 Drug design

The potential applications of AI in drug design span from predictions of molecular interactions (e.g., drug-protein, protein-protein) and 3D structure to de novo drug design.

The prediction of 3D structure of protein out of its amino acid sequence is vital to successfully scan potential lead molecules that can fit with the active sites of the target proteins, also because the experimental evaluation of the 3D structures is too costly and time-consuming to be performed on standard basis.

Due to the high number of interactions and potential conformation spaces, traditional approaches for the prediction of the full tertiary structure of human proteins require enormous computational power. For this reason, non-AI-based algorithms, such as simulated annealing, usually split protein folding into multiple subproblems, including secondary structure, solvent-accessible surface area, torsion angles, etc., that subsequently are joined together.[1]

AI algorithms can leverage large datasets of protein arrays to efficaciously predict tertiary structure. Though the exact envisage of 3D structures starting from amino acidic sequence has not been yet reached, the rapid improvement of Deep Learning (DL) has enabled unprecedented precision, nearly accomplishing the goal: during the 14th critical assessment of protein structure prediction (CASP14), AlphaFold, the deep learning algorithm developed by DeepMind, outperformed non-AI algorithms by being able to regularly predict undisclosed structures of 87 proteins with atomic accuracy, even in cases when homologous structure was not available (i.e., the cases when previous methods encountered most problems), opening promising opportunities for drug discovery.[7]

Molecular interaction predictions could have multiple applications in medicine, from better clarification of multiple biochemical and pathological processes (e.g., kinase interactions, receptor signal transduction, etc.), to the development of highly specific small molecules targeting selected binding sites to increase or decrease the biological activity in specific pathological processes. Therefore, a detailed understanding of the interface region of active sites is crucial for designing novel targeted therapies[1] and tests them through docking simulations to evaluate drug target binding affinity (DBTA).

Currently, molecular interactions are mainly predicted from amino acid and protein structures: in fact, as soon as the 3D protein structure has been experimentally characterized, the knowledge of the protein template structure is simple and reliable owing to the conservative nature of most active sites' interfaces, enabling large precision in both the in silico produced and the experimental protein structure.[1]

In this direction, multiple docking tools have been developed to simulate the interaction of small molecules with target proteins, mainly leveraging the complementarity ("key-lock interaction") principle.

However, the availability of protein structures is limited: for instance, there are limited structural details for 80% of protein-protein interactions known in yeast, bacteria, and/or humans.[1] Therefore, AI applications can

- expand docking analysis also to proteins with amino acid sequence only, lacking 3D characterization that can be predicted through AI
- enhance docking precision, also in case of docking with in silico-mutated structures to predict mutation resistance to novel drug candidates
- predict the chances of off-target effects and adverse event issues due to structural similarity between different molecules, thus helping to optimize the drug to increase its selectivity[4]
- directly perform target binding affinity evaluation overlooking full 3D structure knowledge

Regarding the last point, AI methods can evaluate the drug binding affinity by considering either the features or similarities between the drug and its target (some methods consider both)[4]:

- Feature-based analysis recognizes the chemical moieties of the drug and the target to determine the feature vectors
- Similarity-based analysis scores the similarity between drug and target and assumes that similar drugs will interact with the same targets

Leveraging amino acid sequence data alone, Zeng et al. set up a web server known as complex contact to autonomously predict acknowledged protein complexes. The server first explores the sequence homologs among the tested proteins and then builds two paired multiple sequence alignments (MSA). Then, it utilizes the deep residual neural network (ResNet) and coevolutionary analysis approaches for predicting interprotein contact,[8] greatly outperforming previous prediction-based methods.

Another example is DeepAffinity, an interpretable deep learning algorithm that uses both convolutional and recurrent neural networks and both labeled and unlabeled data to predict drug-target affinity.[4]

1.1.3 Drug screening and characterization

AI tools can strongly enhance virtual screening (VS) processes. VS is a computational drug discovery approach typically leveraged for searching within large libraries of small-molecule potential active candidates that can bind with a defined target (e.g., receptors, enzymes, etc.).

VS is performed using computer programs, and AI is the perfect complement to perform this process at a highly reduced time and increased efficiency, further enabling high-throughput screening approaches.

VS is performed following to different strategies:

- Ligand-based virtual screening (LBVS)
- Structure-based virtual screening (SBVS).

LBVS relies on the observed data of inactive and active ligands, using the conformational, chemical, and physicochemical similarities between the already known active ligands to predict and recognize new highly bioactive ligands.[1]

LBVS can be performed leveraging multiple machine learning methods, including random forest, support vector machine, decision tree, K-nearest neighbor, and Naïve Bayes classifiers, with a substantial improvement in success rate of hit predictions.

As an example, Xiao et al. leveraged the open-source chassis TensorFlow to develop a deep neural network for LBVS with 0.01%–0.09% false-positive rate.[9]

On the other side, the SBVS is typically employed using the preacquired three-dimensional structure of the target through the abovementioned computational or experimental methods. This method is typically employed to investigate the interactions and docking possibilities between the conceivable binding site residues on the 3D structure and the library of active ligands.[1] Even though SBVS generally exhibits superior predictive performance compared to LBVS, the need for 3D structures limits its application.

This need is best fulfilled by AI algorithms: these algorithms, including Boosting, Random Forest, and support vector machine, can better explore the nonlinear reliance of molecular interactions among the candidate ligands and the target. Deep learning can enable a further step forward, since the conventional ML algorithms require manual identification and extraction of features to be performed, a step that can be automated with DL techniques. An example of the advances in this space is the work performed by Mendolia et al., who presented a novel convolutional neural network trained on molecular fingerprints[a] to predict the biological activity of candidate compounds vs the cyclin-dependent kinase 1 (CDK1) target, with extremely good prediction results (98.55% accuracy in active-only selection and 98.88% in high precision discrimination).[10]

Following the high-throughput screening, the drug discovery process requires quantitative structure-activity relationship (QSAR) assessment. This procedure employs mathematical methods to build a quantitative correlation map between the physicochemical properties (e.g., solubility, degree of ionization, partition coefficient, intrinsic permeability), the chemical structure, and the biological activity of the drug candidates,[1,4] for example, including immunotoxicity predictions. The correlation is then leveraged to assess the candidates and select only the molecules with a favorable profile to progress to synthesis and laboratory testing stages. The purpose of this step is to fine-tune the screening of molecules with the required properties and allow better visibility over the virtually screened compounds, without losing too much experimental time.

The steps required in the QSAR method include data collection and pretreatment, selection or generation of molecular descriptors, development of an analytical model, assessment and interpretation of the model, and its applications on the candidate compounds.

AI is a crucial enabler of QSAR, thanks to the opportunity to build effective model to correlate biological activity and chemical structure, and deep learning approaches are the best alternative as QSAR models become increasingly complex: for example, the first success case in the application of deep learning to solve a QSAR issue was achieved by Dahl et al. that developed an integrated DL model to win the 2012 Merck Kaggle Molecular Activity Challenge.[11] In the same manner, other groups developed neural networks to predict physicochemical properties of molecules, such as the solubility, the lipophilicity, and the intestinal absorptivity.[4]

1.1.4 Pharmacokinetic and toxicity predictions

After the drug screening process, the candidate leads of hits must be assessed to evaluate their pharmacokinetic (i.e., absorption, distribution, metabolism, and excretion (ADME)) and toxicity properties, as a first step to ensure drug candidates' safety for humans.

The ADME-T properties are among the most relevant issues causing failure in drug development,[1] and therefore, their early assessment and optimization are crucial to enhance the success rates of drug development.

Since in vivo toxicological experiments are time-consuming and expensive, computer-assisted ADME-T prediction has become the preferred method in drug discovery: it has been suggested that large-scale utilization of computer-based algorithms could reduce by 50% the cost of drug development.[1]

Several ML models, including support vector machine, Gaussian process, random forest, and deep learning, have been used for ADME-T predictions, showing robustness and tolerance of noisy data.

Most relevant applications of DL in this space include the Tox21 Data challenge, instigated by US federal agencies, that assessed the performance of several computational approaches to predict drugs toxicity, eventually reducing the number of in vivo and in vitro experiments. Among the winners of the challenge, Mayr and colleagues developed a DL-enabled prediction pipelined named DeepTox that leverages well-known toxicophore characteristics to predict

---

[a] Molecular fingerprints are computational methods to represent the chemical space, used as molecular descriptors in AI to represent the chemical structure of a compound in a way that is easy to be handled by AI algorithms. Other molecular representations include quantitative molecular descriptors that use quantitative properties directly derived from molecular structure (e.g., potential energy measurements, electron density around the molecule, coordinates of atoms, etc.), graph-based representations (that recently gained traction and model molecules as graphs where the nodes are represented by atoms and edges are represented by bonds), and SMILES strings.[4] SMILES stands for "Simplified Molecular Input Line Entry System" and is a natural language notation system used for describing the structure of chemical species using short ASCII strings that could be leveraged to perform AI analysis based on natural language processing algorithms and rules.[30]

toxicity properties of new compounds using a multitask learning approach.[12] Furthermore, development in ADME-T predictors includes the following:

- "one-shot learning" methods by Altae-Tran et al.,[13] enabling ADME-T analysis on sparse datasets
- XenoSite, FAME, and SMARTCyp, working on predicting the sites of drug metabolism
- CypRules, MetaSite, MetaPred, SMARTCyp, and WhichCyp, aiming to identify the specific isoforms of CYP450 that are in involved in each drug metabolism[4]
- PrOCTOR, random forest model considering drug-likeliness properties, molecular features, target-based features, and target protein to generate a score to forecast whether a drug would fail in clinical trials due to toxicity issues. It also recognized FDA-approved drugs that later reported adverse drug events[14]
- The web platform ADMETlab 2.0, leveraging a multitask graph neural network[15]

Nevertheless, more research is needed to develop a globally applicable ADTME-T predictor.

1.1.5 Drug repurposing

Drug repurposing is the evaluation of the therapeutic efficacy of already approved drugs for new indications. This approach significantly reduces the risks of failure, leveraging well-known safety data in the already approved indications, thus following a both time-saving and economic approach. In fact, repurposing of existing drug qualifies it directly for Phase II clinical trials.[4]

Drug repurposing can leverage AI algorithms in drug-target interactions (DTI) analysis with a similar approach to the one described in the previous paragraphs, particularly regarding molecular docking.

The rationale of this methodology relies on structurally complementarity between the ligand and the candidate molecules, assuming that structurally similar molecules have similar biological activities (structure-based approaches). The small molecules evaluated for repurposing are therefore analyzed through docking operations on the crystal structure of the target in scope.

Is therefore apparent how AI can ease this process, leveraging 3D structure prediction of targets and high computational power to screen more candidates, with reliable, multilevel results rendition.

Frequently employed ML methods are binary classifiers, including support vector machines, artificial neural networks, random forest, and deep learning.[1] An example of DL application is DTINet, a computational operation developed by Luo et al. to envisage new DTIs from already approved drugs.[16]

Other ML approaches in drug repurposing consider drug–drug, disease–disease similarity, the similarity between targets, chemical structure, and gene expression profiles.[4]

1.1.6 De novo chemical design and synthesis planning

AI in the de novo design of molecules has the potential to positively impact the pharmaceutical sector thanks of its various advantages, such as the opportunity of online learning and simultaneous optimization of the already-learned data, as well as the suggestion of possible synthesis routes for newly designed compounds with swifter lead design and development.[4]

De novo drug design leverages the 3D structure of the target molecule to generate new molecules active on the target. This computer-based strategy employs specific algorithms to design new molecules and screen novel chemical structures with a predetermined activity on the target. These novel structures have to fulfill specific requisites in terms of biological activity, pharmacokinetic, ADME, and synthesis scalability.[1]

These constraints can be implemented in a structure-based approach to optimize the newly generated drug candidates that are able to bind in target's binding pocket.

In fact, compounds found through this approach are typically difficult to synthetize and can benefit from a more comprehensive, AI-enabled evaluation.

In this case, a development pipeline that incorporates AI could start with ligand-based techniques to produce large libraries of promising chemical compounds that will be then screened with AI techniques to select only the compounds with better ADME characteristics and synthesis feasibility.

In addition, AI approaches can find drug-protein interactions that cover regions of the chemical space that have not been analyzed yet but might have the potential for lead-like characteristics.[1]

Another approach in this field is to generate alternative representations of already known ligand compounds, leveraging conversion rules based on chemists' knowledge[1]: with this approach, new compounds with desired properties can be generated, leveraging a continuous representation of the starting compound that is obtained with a deep neural network.[17]

Some other examples include the following:

- Putin et al., who developed a deep neural network named "reinforced adversarial neural computer (RANC)" based on reinforcement learning for de novo design of small organic molecules.[18] This platform was trained with molecules represented as SMILES strings. It then generated molecules with predefined chemical descriptors in terms of MW, partition coefficient, and topological polar surface area (TPSA)
- Merk et al., using a generative AI model (i.e., a model based on two competing DNN: a generator, trained to generate new molecules and a discriminator, trained to screen generated molecules and discriminate those with high probability to come from real world: in this setting, the generator learns to generate molecules progressively more similar to real molecules) to design retinoid X and PPAR agonist molecules, with a desired therapeutic effect without requiring complex rules. The authors successfully designed five molecules, four out of which have shown good modulatory activity in cell assays[19]
- Zhavoronkov et al.,[20] who developed another generative model, the Generative Tensorial Reinforcement Learning (GENTRL), that produced in vivo active DDR1 and DDR2 inhibitors in only 21 days. This was an important milestone for the use of generative chemistry in drug discovery since the generated molecules have been proven to be synthesizable, are active in vitro, metabolically stable, and show in vivo activity in disease-relevant models.

The last step in this field is the prediction of the synthetic feasibility of the identified compound. At present, many efforts have been made to predict the synthetic reactions needed to get the compound, but limited industrially actionable results have been reached due to the complexity of the task and the high number of synthesis rules to be implemented in the algorithms. Nevertheless, data-driven synthetic planning approaches are expected to impact this space in the near future.[1] A significant example of the potential progress in this space is Chematica program[21] (renamed Synthia, property of Merck group[22]), which can encode a set of rules into the machine and propose possible synthesizing routes for eight medicinally essential targets. This program has proven to be efficient both in terms better productivity and reduced costs, can provide alternate synthesizing strategies for patented products, and is said to be helpful in the synthesis of compounds that have not yet been synthesized.[21]

In conclusion, given the promising in vitro and in vivo results of molecules designed with generative reinforcement learning technologies, AI is poised to become an integral part of the drug design cycle,[3] even though synthesis and experimental validation still remain the bottleneck for the preclinical testing of these discoveries.

1.1.7 Pharmaceutical product development

After the discovery of a novel molecule, the subsequent incorporation in a suitable dosage form with predetermined delivery characteristics is required. In this field, AI can replace older trial-and-error approaches.[4] Various computational algorithms can address issues typically encountered in formulation design, such as stability, dissolution, and porosity.

AI tools leverage rule-based systems to prioritize the best type, quantity, and nature of the excipients based on physicochemical characteristics of the drug, monitoring the entire process through a feedback mechanism that can enable further adjustments.[4]

Guo et al.[23] integrated expert systems (ES) and an artificial neural network to create a hybrid system for the development of direct-filling hard gelatin capsules of piroxicam according to its dissolution profile characteristics:

- The Model Expert System (MES) makes decisions and recommendations for formulation development based on the input parameters.
- The artificial neural network uses backpropagation findings to link formulation parameters to the desired response, jointly controlled by the control module, to ensure smoother formulation development

1.1.8 Clinical trial design and monitoring

The limited success rate of clinical trials entering phase I is one of the major issues in drug development. Apart from poor performance of the drug candidate themselves (due to inefficacy or toxicity) that can be addressed by AI in the preclinical steps, other causes of clinical trial failures include inappropriate patient selection, shortage of technical requirements, and poor trial organization. AI models can address these issues as well, leveraging the current large availability of clinical data.

For example, a better and faster patient enrollment could dramatically improve clinical trials' effectiveness: it has been reported that patients' enrollment takes one-third of clinical trial timeline. AI can help in better patients' profiling and selection for Phase II and Phase III trials, leveraging patient-specific genome profile analysis, enabling earlier prediction of drug efficacy on recruited patients.

Another issue in clinical trial is related to the high drop-out rates: it has been reported that patients' drop-outs account for 30% of clinical trial failures. Moreover, drop-outs' replacements have a negative impact on clinical trial timeline and costs. AI support in this space could involve either closer monitoring of patients with mobile software or early prediction of drop-out probability based on patient's personal data.[4]

As an example, IBM Watson developed a system for clinical trial matching that utilized large volume of structured and unstructured electronic medical records data to elaborate detailed profile of clinical findings used to better compare patients to clinical trial eligibility criteria[3]: in this way, clinicians do not need to manually sort patients' medical record and can optimize the patients' enrollment.

In addition, AI can enable earlier prediction of clinical trials' likelihood of success, leveraging clinical data acquired in early phases or interim data collections to avoid the start of large, expensive phase III clinical trials for less promising molecules.[3]

Lastly, AI has the potential to enable in silico clinical trials, through the computer-based synthesis of patient's physiological and pathological information, aiming to produce patient-specific and subpopulation-specific predictions for diagnosis, prognosis, posology, and treatment planning.[3]

1.2 AI potential in drug discovery

As explained above, AI is expected to revolutionize the entire pharmaceutical and medical sectors. Overall interest on AI is supported by strong investments of Pharma companies, boosting impressive market figures: the global pharmaceutical market of AI is showing very high growth rates, from 200M$ in 2015 to 700M$ in 2018, with projected growth rates around 40% until 2024 and an expected size of 5B$ in 2024.[4]

Consequently, it is expected that around 2B$ revenues will be generated in the pharmaceutical sector by 2022 through AI-based solutions, supported by an investment of more than 7B$ distributed across 300+ deals between 2013 and 2018 further accelerated in latest years: according to a recent BCG report, investments in AI-enabled drug discovery topped 2.4B$ in 2020 and reached more than 5.2B$ in 2021.[24]

1.3 State of development pipeline of AI-discovered small molecules

Although AI algorithms have generated many novel targets and novel compounds addressing different diseases and therapeutic areas, still no compound generated through AI has reached commercialization for public use yet.[25]

Nevertheless, the advances in this space are apparent. In a recently published article,[26] a BCG team selected 24 AI-native drug companies and mapped the development pipeline of 20 of them between 2010 and 2021 leveraging publicly available data. During the time considered, these companies experienced rapid pipeline growth (36% average annual growth), mainly driven by assets in preclinical stage. The total number of disclosed programs and preclinical assets from these companies reached c. 160 units. The same set of companies has about 15 assets in clinical development.

Impressively, when compared to top 20 Pharma companies (c. 330 disclosed discovery programs and preclinical assets and c. 430 assets in phase I clinical trials), these numbers appear sizable, especially in the preclinical stages (AI companies, most of which started less than 10 years ago, show discovery production volume of around 50% of the in-house discovery of "big-pharmas"). Nevertheless, it remains to be seen how many of these AI-enabled preclinical programs will reach clinical trial stage and how successful will they be.

Considering therapeutic area and target classes, the same article showed that for the section of assets for which detailed target information was available (about a quarter of the abovementioned 330 assets), AI companies still focus on well-established target classes, in fact:

- 34% are kinases
- 30% are nonkinase enzymes
- 13% are G-protein-coupled receptors
- 4% are catalytic receptors
- 5% are transcription factors
- 13% other protein targets

The authors explain the selective focus on well-established targets (which is not the case for top-20 Pharma companies that have a more balanced mix) with a set of multiple factors, such as aim to de-risk pipelines by focusing on target with well-explained biochemistry function, wish to prove the effectiveness of AI technology addressing well-known challenges, and most importantly, larger availability of data that are leveraged to train the AI algorithms.

Despite the overall trend, there are some selected examples of AI-derived compounds for novel targets, with the potential to become first-in-class in their space. These targets include tyrosine phosphatase SHP2, DNA helicase WRN, and paracaspase MATL1.

Regarding therapeutic area, AI programs focus on areas with high unmet medical need and wide availability of well-established targets:

- 36% oncology
- 15% central nervous system
- 6% immunology
- 12% systemic antiinfectives
- 31% others

In terms of chemical structure and properties, there are few publicly available data, hindering the opportunity of comprehensive analysis.

Nevertheless, it is worth mentioning some interesting assets:

1. A novel, allosteric TYK2 inhibitor exhibiting at least 20-fold more selectivity over other members of the Janus Kinase (JAK) family, thus expected to have a more favorable profile compared to products currently marketed, whose application in clinical practice is limited by their poor selectivity. The molecular structure of this new asset is quite similar to approved ones; the only difference seems to be related to wider interaction with TYK2, with an expansion into underrepresented areas of chemical space
2. Two small molecules targeting serotonin receptors (a 5-HT1A agonist and a bispecific 5-HT1A agonist and 5-HT2A antagonist) that recently entered the clinic trial phase. Chemical space analysis suggests that these molecules occupy similar space to previously approved drugs and show similar structures. The similarity might derive from the similar training set that has been used to generate and test these molecules.

In the same article, authors reconstructed the approximate timeline for selected Pharma-AI partnership and discovery programs. The authors reported multiple AI-enabled programs completing the entire discovery and preclinical journey in less than 4 years, compared to historic timelines in the industry of 5–6 years, which is particularly encouraging given the nascent stage of AI technology in drug discovery.

The authors conclude that AI programs are showing promising sings in terms of early discovery efficiency, speed, and productivity, as well as some glimpses of increase molecular diversity in terms of targets and mechanism of action. For other dimensions, such as impact on costs and clinical development success rates, it is too early to draw conclusions.

1.4 Future outlook and challenges

Compared with medical image recognition, AI drug discovery has experienced more limited advances. One of the reasons for this difference may be related to the high quality needed in Pharma R&D that sets the standard for AI at a higher level. Therefore, it has been suggested that the safety and efficacy endpoints should hat to be better leveraged in AI development to evaluate AI methods' performance in order to enhance AI adoption in drug discovery.[27] In addition, more complex biologic data should be used to develop an AI model, in order to better resemble biologic phenomena.

One of the other issues that ML experts are finding in the adoption of ML in drug discovery is related to the splitting of training and testing data that could potentially hinder generality and transferability of the AI findings.[1] The common strategy of random splitting is often not the best for chemical data.[1] To address this issue, multiple open-source algorithms have been published, such as MoleculeNet[28] and ATOM Modeling PipeLine,[29] to benchmark different machine learning and splitting methods and develop new, optimized, AI-enabled drug discovery pipelines.

Related to this, one of the most important requirements to develop high-performing DL methods is the availability of a high quality and volume data sets to perform DL algorithms training.[1] Increasing data availability is therefore crucial to improve DL efficacy and avoid overfitting issues that hinder the validity of this models.

In this field, it is noteworthy to mention that only a small fraction of drug discovery data overall is available for ML training, especially because pharmaceutical companies typically do no share data on preclinical candidate drugs, particularly limiting the number of in vitro findings and negative data (i.e., molecules already characterized and discarded/withdrawn) that are crucial to train ML algorithms.[3]

Another issue of current AI algorithms is the limited interpretability of most of these methods, typically called "black boxes." It is expected that emerging explainable AI models could increase models' transparency, thus enabling easier communication with data scientists, chemists, and biologists and improve algorithm pertinency to the biological space.

The selection of the best model to use is another complex problem to be solved, since it is not always easy to choose the most suitable AI model to the needs of research tasks among the several ones proposed in the literature. In this regard, hyperparameter optimization might be one of the solutions, even though parameter adjustment is still a computationally burdensome operation.

Other challenges include lack of skilled personnel in AI among Pharma companies that limit the adoption of these technologies.[4] To fully benefit from AI revolution, multiple professional figures are needed, such as skilled data scientists, software engineers with a sound knowledge of AI technology, and scientists capable of sharing domain knowledge to AI developers, along with a clear definition of company's business targets and R&D goals.

As suggested in a recent BCG report,[24] to achieve the full potential of AI a full end-to-end transformation of the discovery process and pipeline is required: companies must therefore make investments in data, technologies, new skills, and behaviors throughout the whole R&D organization. An example of this new approach is shown by the recent initiatives of AI-native biotech companies that implemented end-to-end development pipelines and processes along with a large ecosystem of partnerships among academic institutions, contract research organization, and other industry partners with a comprehensive redefinition of their value chain.[24]

References

1. Tripathi N, Goshisht MK, Sahu SK, Arora C. Applications of artificial intelligence to drug design and discovery. *Mol Divers.* 2021;25:1634–1664.
2. Lim S. The Process and Costs of Drug Development (2022). FTLO Science; 3 November 2022 [Online] [Riportato: 7 November 2022.] https://ftloscience.com/.
3. Zhavoronkov A, et al. Will artificial intelligence for drug discovery impact clinical pharmacology? *Clin Pharmacol Ther.* 2020;107(4):780–785.
4. Debleena P, et al. Artificial intelligence in drug discovery and development. *Drug Discov Today.* 2021;26(1):80–93.
5. Melville JL, Burke EK, Hirst JD. Machine learning in virtual screening. *Comb Chem High Throughput Screen.* 2009;12:332–343.
6. Papadimitriou S, et al. Predicting disease-causing variant combinations. *PNAS.* 2019;116(24):11878–11887.
7. Jumper J, et al. Highly accurate protein structure prediction. *Nature.* 2021;596:583–589.
8. Zenge H, et al. ComplexContact: a web server for inter-protein contact. *Nucleic Acids Res.* 2018;46:W432–W437.
9. Xiao T, et al. Development of ligand-based big data deep neural network models for virtual screening of large compound libraries. *Mol Inform.* 2018;37(11):1800031.
10. Mendolia I, et al. Convolutional architectures for virtual screening. *BMC Bioinform.* 2020;21(suppl 8):310.
11. Ma J, et al. Deep neural nets as a method for quantitative structure-activity relationships. *J Chem Inf Model.* 2015;55(2):263–274.
12. Mayr A, et al. DeepTox: toxicity prediction using deep learning. *Front Environ Sci.* 2016;3:80.
13. Altae-Tran H, et al. Low data drug discovery with one-shot learning. *ACS Cent Sci.* 2017;3:283–293.
14. Gayvert KM, et al. A data-driven approach to predicting successes and failures of clinical trials. *Cell Chem Biol.* 2016;23(10):1294–1301.
15. ADMETlab 2.0. ADMETlab 2.0 [Online] [Riportato: 8 November 2022] https://admetmesh.scbdd.com/.
16. Luo YL, et al. A network integration approach for drug-target interaction prediction and computational drug repositioning from heterogeneous information. *Nat Commun.* 2017;8:573.
17. Gòmez-Bombarelli R, et al. Automatic chemical design using a data-driven continuous representation of molecules. *ACS Cent Sci.* 2018;4(2):268–276.
18. Putin E, et al. Reinforced adversarial neural computer for de novo molecular design. *J Chem Inf Model.* 2018;58(6):1194–1204.
19. Merk D, et al. Tuning artificial intelligence on the de novo design of natural-product-inspired retinoid X receptor modulators. *Commun Chem.* 2018;1:68.
20. Zhavoronkov A, et al. Deep learning enables rapid identification of potent DDR1 kinase inhibitors. *Nat Biotechnol.* 2019;37:1038–1040.
21. Grzybowski BA, et al. Chematica: a story of computer code that started to think like a chemist. *Chem.* 2018;4(3):390–398.
22. *Software di analisi retrosintetica SYNTHIA™.* sigmaaldrich.com. [Online] Merck. [Riportato: 2022 November 2022]. https://www.sigmaaldrich.com/IT/it/services/software-and-digital-platforms/synthia-retrosynthesis-software.
23. Guo M, et al. Development, a prototype intelligent hybrid system for hard gelatin capsule formulation. *Pharm Technol.* 2002;26(9):44–52.
24. Ayers M, Jayatunga M, Goldader J, Meier C. Adopting AI in Drug Discovery. Boston Consulting Group; 2022.
25. Gupta R, et al. Artificial intelligence to deep learning: machine intelligence approach for drug discovery. *Mol Divers.* 2021;25(3):1315–1360.
26. Jayatunga MKP, Xie W, Ruder L, Schulze U, Meier C. AI in small-molecule drug discovery: a coming wave? *Nat Rev Drug Discov.* 2022;21:175–176.
27. Bender A, Cortés-Ciriano I. Artificial intelligence in drug discovery: what is realistic, what are illusions? Part 1: ways to make an impact, and why we are not there yet. *Drug Discov Today.* 2021;26(2):511–524.
28. Wu Z, et al. MoleculeNet: a benchmark for molecular machine learning. *Chem Sci.* 2017;9(2):513–530.
29. ATOM Consortium. ATOM Modeling PipeLine (AMPL) for Drug Discovery [Online] [Riportato: 7 November 2022] https://github.com/ATOMScience-org/AMPL.
30. Pillai N, et al. Machine Learning guided early drug discovery of small molecules. *Drugdiscov Today.* 2022;27(8):2209–2215.

4

AI/ML and drug repurposing in lung cancer: State of the art and potential roles for retinoids

Gabriele Sala[a], Davide La Torre[b,c], Marco Repetto[d], and Giuseppe Curigliano[c,e]

[a]University of Milan, Milan, Italy [b]SKEMA Business School, Université Côte d'Azur, Nice, France [c]Department of Oncology and Hematology-Oncology (DIPO), University of Milan, Milan, Italy [d]CertX SA, Freiburg, Switzerland [e]Division of Early Drug Development for Innovative Therapies, European Institute of Oncology (IEO), IRCCS, Milan, Italy

1. Introduction

Recent advances in AI and ML have revolutionized medical research. Improved hardware and cost reductions have led to the development of sophisticated tools that accelerate preclinical and clinical investigations. Researchers now leverage artificial intelligence/machine learning (AI/ML) techniques to quickly analyze vast amounts of data, including genetic, proteomic, and transcriptomic profiles, as well as unstructured clinical charts. This enables them to gain insights that were previously impossible. Moreover, collaboration between research and clinical teams has become easier, thanks to reduced barriers and the availability of public clinical data. This fosters the exchange of ideas across scientific domains.

For example, deep learning (DL) tools showed great promise in the clinical setting for the diagnosis of diseases starting from radiological and pathological images. In many cases, the performance of ML-based tools exceeded that of clinical experts.[1] This is particularly promising in the case of rare or difficult to diagnose conditions, or when specialists are not available.

The application of AI-based tools has been introduced in the field of cancer genetics to analyze mutations and other genetic aberrations that are correlated with the onset and progression of various types of cancer. These tools have the capability to assist physicians not only with diagnosis but also with a precise characterization of various forms of tumors. For example, a study found that a convoluted neural network (CNN) model has been found to be able, up to a certain point, to predict which genes in tumor tissue samples are mutated based upon the analysis of histological samples without the need for an annotation performed by a pathologist.[2] In addition, in recent years, the scientific community has commenced to examine the potential applications of AI and ML technologies in the realm of drug repurposing for the treatment of various forms of tumors. Researchers are exploring innovative methods that integrate clinical and transcriptomic data with information on the chemical structures of established compounds to uncover new clinical uses for drugs that are already approved for use.[3]

In this chapter, we explore the state of the art of the use of AI/ML tools for drug repurposing in the field of cancer research, with a focus on lung adenocarcinomas. Also, a brief description of the most popular AI/ML tools and frameworks that are used for this scope will be presented. Finally, an illustrative approach to analyzing big data will be suggested to examine the potential impact of less commonly studied genes on predicting the occurrence of metastasis in cancer patients. This approach focuses on investigating genetic abnormalities within these genes to determine their correlation with the presence of metastasis at the time of diagnosis.

2. Drug repurposing

The journey of transitioning a new molecular entity from a laboratory setting to the bedside of a cancer patient is a complex and extensive process. For example, the discovery of protein tyrosine phosphorylation by the laboratory of Tony Hunter in 1979 serves as a testament to this, as it took more than two decades for the approval of the first drug inhibiting this process, imatinib, for use in clinical settings.[4] There have been significant advancements from that initial milestone, with more than 30 tyrosine kinase inhibitors and therapeutic monoclonal antibodies now approved for the treatment of various types of cancer.

Currently, the substantial amount of financial investments that is necessary to identify, study, produce, and commercialize new chemotherapeutic drugs, calculated in billions of dollars in investment for each molecule,[5] poses significant burdens to these efforts. This phenomenon is commonly referred to as *high attrition rate*. On the side, another approach that is gaining momentum during recent years is the concept of *drug repurposing*. Drug repurposing, also known as drug repositioning,[6] can be defined to as a strategy for identifying new uses for approved drugs outside the scope of the original indication.[7] Repurposing existing drugs has the potential to reduce the cost and time associated with the development of new drugs because most of the preclinical testing and safety assessment has already been completed.[7] This is especially true in the context of rare diseases.[8,9]

In addition, serendipitous discoveries have also historically played a significant role in drug development, with unexpected positive effects observed in clinical trials or real-world use.[10] For instance, sildenafil, originally developed to treat cardiovascular conditions, was later found to have a remarkable impact on erectile dysfunction. Similarly, thalidomide, initially marketed as a sedative, was later discovered to possess potent antiinflammatory properties, leading to its application in treating certain types of cancers and autoimmune disorders.

Systematic drug repurposing might start from the following approaches, each one of which offers unique perspectives on identifying new therapeutic indications for existing drugs[10,11]:

1. *Drug-centric approach*: This approach focuses on the drug itself and looks for new targets or indications that it could be used for.
2. *Target-centric approach*: This approach involves pairing a proven drug and its known target with a novel indication, where the old and new indications usually exhibit considerable differences. This method entails studying the distinct molecular targets involved in a disease's pathology and employing an existing drug that has been shown to regulate those specific targets.
3. *Disease-centric approach*: This approach involves pairing diseases lacking effective treatments, or having partially effective treatments, with approved or unsuccessful compounds that have therapeutic potential. It entails identifying diseases that share similar underlying biological mechanisms with the target disease of the original drug.

Moreover, strategies aimed at drug repurposing can be categorized into two main approaches: experimental and computational.[12] The experimental methods encompass various techniques such as in vitro high-throughput screening as well as in vivo models for phenotypic screening. On the other hand, computational approaches involve the examination of preexisting data sources, which include chemical structures, gene expression data, proteomic data, and electronic health records (EHRs). The success of both these approaches heavily relies on the accessibility and quality of the data used for the analyses. The progress made in genome-wide association studies (GWAS), in this context, has significantly contributed to the availability of reliable data for drug repurposing.[13] Through GWAS, it is possible to obtain information about and to test hundreds of thousands of genetic variants across many genomes to find those statistically associated with a specific trait or disease. This methodology has generated a myriad of robust associations for a range of traits and diseases, and the number of associated variants is expected to grow steadily.[14] By providing vast amounts of genetic reliable data, GWAS studies offer crucial data suitable for drug repurposing research.

2.1 Drug repurposing in cancer

Considerable strides have been taken thus far to explore novel prospects for utilizing existing medications in the treatment of cancer. Extensive investigations, both in preclinical and clinical settings, have encompassed various domains, spanning from molecular-level genetic studies to the analysis of real-world patient information. A number of molecules have been, and still are, under experimentation for their repurposing as chemotherapeutic drugs.

For example, a recent review by Turabi et al.[15] cited molecules such as niclosamide (an antiparasitic drug) as a potential candidate for colorectal cancer, minocycline (an antibiotic) against prostate cancer, bisphosphonates (antiosteoporosis agents) against ovarian cancer, and other classes of molecules such as steroidal and nonsteroidal antiinflammatory, statins and many more as potential repurposeable candidates in various types of tumors.

The interest toward drug repurposing for lung cancer patients is exemplified also in a work by Jain et al.[16] who enlisted 18 different repurposed drugs or combinations of drugs in NSCLC patients, ranging from antibiotics to treatment for psychiatric conditions. A further example of drug that has been identified as a potential repurposable molecule for the treatment of NSCLC is Nebivolol.[17] From a biological perspective, Peyvandipour et al.[18] proposed a system biology approach to drug repurposing that integrates drug target and disease-related genes information retrieved from publicly available datasets into a network and integrate it with known molecular pathways to test which genes are most perturbed by certain drugs. Other authors[19] tested approaches that leverage on the knowledge about long noncoding RNA (lncRNA) genetic regions that are known to be related to survival in cancer patients and to be affected by certain existing drugs to build an index that is informative of the repurposing potential of such drugs.

2.2 AI/ML approaches in drug repurposing in cancer research

Historically, cancer treatment has centered around the "magic bullet" strategy, targeting individual oncogenes and tumor suppressor genes.[20] This approach has long been regarded as a fundamental pillar in cancer therapy. However, recent discoveries illuminating the heterogeneous nature of tumors have cast doubt on the efficacy of the traditional approach. In fact, some authors[21] call for a new approach, a so-called "shrapnel" approach, which focuses on pathway perturbations and global molecular and physiological patterns to tackle the growth of cancer cells.

At present, the primary challenge lies in extracting profound biological insights from the vast amount of complex information rather than merely obtaining the data itself.[22] Artificial intelligence and machine learning-based tools are leveraged more and more in cancer reseach,[23,24] including within the field of lung adenocarcinoma,[25] thanks to the ability that they offer to find meaningful patterns in the complexity of the available data.

Whereas the scope of this chapter is not to delve too much into the details of such approaches, it is worth mentioning a few examples of possible applications of AI/ML tools[26]:

- *Tools to improve literature searches*: By coupling automatic text retrieval from the web (e.g., from PubMed) and natural language processing-based analysis systems with manual interpretation of the resulting information, it could be possible to find potentially novel and meaningful connections between molecules and different types of cancer.
- *EHR-based methods*: EHRs are an immense source of clinical information. With tools such as the abovementioned natural language processing algorithms, it is possible to extract data from EHR notes of cancer patients treated with various molecules and to structure it into databases amenable to further analyses.
- *Computational methods for drug-target interactions*: These include, for example, tools that allow researchers to predict the binding affinity, or other quantitative measures, of molecules to their ligands in novel contexts.

However, it is crucial to acknowledge that not all ML techniques are suitable for all types of data or hypotheses. It is imperative to consider the specific characteristics of the data and hypothesis in question when selecting an appropriate ML approach. Before reviewing the current literature about AI/ML tools in drug repurposing, let us clarify some technical terms.

2.2.1 AI: A few definitions

Some of the terms used in the field of AI are the following[27]:

- The term "artificial intelligence" refers to the development of computer systems that can perform tasks that typically require human intelligence, such as visual perception, speech recognition, decision making, and language translation.
- Machine learning is a subfield of artificial intelligence that focuses on the development of algorithms and statistical models that allow computers to "learn" from data, without being explicitly programmed.
- An algorithm is a step-by-step procedure for solving a problem. In the context of AI and ML, algorithms are used to analyze and process data to make predictions or decisions.
- The term "data" refers to information that can be processed by computers. In the context of AI and ML, data are used to train and evaluate algorithms, with the goal of improving their accuracy and performance.
- Deep learning is a subfield of machine learning that focuses on the use of neural networks with multiple layers to analyze and process complex data.
- A neural network is a type of machine learning model that is designed to recognize patterns in data by simulating the structure and function of the human brain.

2.2.2 How ML algorithms work

A machine learning algorithm learns through a process called training. During training, the algorithm is fed a large set of data, and it learns to recognize patterns and relationships in that data. The algorithm then uses these learned patterns to make predictions or classifications on new data. The accuracy of the algorithm's predictions is then measured, and, if necessary, the algorithm is fine-tuned to improve its performance. This process is repeated until the algorithm reaches an acceptable level of accuracy.

From a general point of view, ML training methods can be broadly divided into supervised and unsupervised categories.[22] In supervised methods, the dataset used to train the algorithm has been previously labeled with the correct answers. Then, the algorithm learns from it and builds a model that can be used to predict the correct outcome for new data. On the other hand, in unsupervised methods, the dataset used to train the algorithm is not labeled; hence, the algorithm must find a way to cluster the data into groups to build a model.

There are several advantages to using supervised methods. One is that it is easier to train the algorithm since the correct answers are already known. Another advantage is that the resulting model is more accurate since the algorithm has been able to learn from the dataset. Finally, supervised methods of machine learning are more effective when there is a large amount of training data available. Unsupervised machine learning methods, on the other hand, are better than supervised methods when the problem involves discovering hidden patterns or relationships in data, rather than predicting a specific outcome. They can be used when labeled data are not available. This can be the case when the cost of collecting labeled data is high, there is no labeled data, or labels are difficult to obtain. For example, in medical research, unsupervised ML methods could be used to identify subtypes of a disease based on gene expression data, allowing for a more personalized approach to treatment. Unsupervised methods can also provide a better understanding of the data, since they do not rely on humans for information. Finally, unsupervised methods are often easier to implement since they do not require the same amount of training data as supervised methods.

2.2.2.1 Classifiers

A classifier is a machine learning algorithm that is used to categorize input data into one of several predefined categories or classes.[28] It is a type of supervised learning algorithm that learns from a training dataset, which includes labeled examples of the input data and their associated classes, and then uses this information to predict the class of new, unseen data. Classifiers can be used for a wide range of applications, including sentiment analysis, spam filtering, image classification, and medical diagnosis.

The process of classification involves understanding and grouping together similar ideas or objects. By using already sorted training datasets, machine learning programs can put future datasets into categories by utilizing various algorithms.[29] The goal of any classification algorithm is to find the right mapping function that will take an input (x) and categorize it correctly into an output (y).

A few types of classification algorithms, or classifiers, are as follows:

- Logistic Regression
- K-Nearest Neighbors
- Support Vector Machines
- Kernel SVM
- Naïve Bayes
- Decision Tree Classification
- Random Forest Classification

In this chapter, we will see a practical application of a few of these classifiers:

- Decision Tree: it is a machine learning algorithm that uses a series of if-then questions to categorize input data into one of several predefined classes.[30] The algorithm works by asking a series of questions that consider all possible outcomes, and each question is designed to further refine the classification of the input data. This process is repeated until some termination condition is reached, such as a minimum number of samples in a node, a maximum depth of the tree, or a minimum improvement in the accuracy of the classifier. The goal is to arrive at the most accurate classification by the end of the series of questions.
- Random Forest: it is a popular type of ensemble learning algorithm that is used for classification tasks. As the name suggests, this algorithm is based on the concept of a forest, where multiple trees (decision trees, to be specific) are grown on various subsets of the input data.[31] The key idea behind using multiple trees is that each tree makes its own prediction for the class of a given input, and the final output is determined by taking the majority vote from all the predictions made by the individual trees.

– Gradient Boosting: it is a powerful machine learning technique that aims to produce accurate prediction models by combining multiple weak prediction models. The process of gradient boosting starts with a set of weak learners, which are simple models that make predictions about the response variable.[32] Through iterative refinement, these weak learners are gradually combined and improved to form a stronger, more accurate prediction model.

3. Lung adenocarcinoma

Lung cancer adenocarcinoma (LCA) is a highly aggressive form of cancer, representing the predominant type of lung cancer in the United States and ranking as the second most commonly diagnosed tumor globally among both men and women.[33] LCA presents itself with a broad spectrum of genetic and environmental risk factors. These factors include mutations, copy number variations, and epigenetic modifications. Furthermore, environmental hazards like smoking and air pollution are known to elevate the likelihood of LCA development. In addition, the concept of hereditary predisposition to cancer is gaining significant attention among clinicians and researchers.[34]

Lung carcinoma is divided into two main categories: small cell lung cancer (SCLC) and non–small cell lung cancer (NSCLC). SCLC accounts for 15% of cases and is fast-growing and often metastatic at diagnosis, mainly affecting smokers. NSCLC accounts for 85% of cases, and its progression varies depending on its histologic type, with 40% of patients having metastases outside of the chest at diagnosis.

The diagnosis of lung adenocarcinoma is confirmed using various methods, including chest x-ray, CT or combined PET-CT scans, cytopathology examination of pleural fluid or sputum, bronchoscopy-guided biopsy, and core biopsy, and in some cases, an open lung biopsy.

The staging of non–small cell lung cancer (NSCLC) is classified into four categories, namely, stage I to stage IV, using the TNM system. This system evaluates the cancer's extent by considering the tumor size, its proximity to the lung and neighbor structures, the presence of cancer cells in lymph nodes that drain the lung, and the occurrence of distant metastases.

Lung carcinomas tend to metastasize preferentially in the brain, liver, bones, and adrenal glands.[35] Other organs are usually not involved until the disease is in its later stages, though this could be not always the case. Though discussing this process extensively falls outside the scope of this project, it is worth mentioning that several genetic alterations have been found to play a role in the development of lung cancer metastases.

For SCLC, the five-year survival rate is 20% for limited stage and less than 1% for extensive stage. For NSCLC, the five-year survival rate varies from 60% to 70% for stage I to less than 1% for stage IV. Recent advancements in targeted therapies and chemotherapy have improved the survival rate for NSCLC to 18%, with longer survival for early-stage disease and stage IV patients with specific mutations.

The complexity of LCA and its diverse risk factors make it a challenging form of cancer to treat, especially when diagnosed at a later stage. Much interest is focused on identifying pharmacological agents that can hinder the ability of cancer cells to penetrate the extracellular matrix (ECM) and to create secondary metastatic tumors.[36]

3.1 AI/ML tools and drug repurposing for lung cancer

In recent times, there has been a remarkable increase in attention within the AI/ML field concerning the practice of repurposing drugs to uncover innovative treatments for lung cancer. A few examples of these progresses are reported here.

Chen et al.[37] proposed a computational method to identify novel genes that contribute to the development of lung adenocarcinoma. It involves constructing a large network of protein–protein interactions, searching for connections between dysfunctional genes that might have the potential to contribute to the tumorigenesis process on multiple levels.

Ramesh et al.[25] used a machine learning model to identify 497 active compounds from a list of 2509 molecules. After further validation, the authors found that Montelukast (DB00471) showed significant anticancer activity and could be a promising candidate for the management of RET-specific NSCLC.

Li et al.[3] analyzed transcriptomic data of 12,797 genes from three cell lines and information about the chemical structures of 75 molecules to build an in vitro classification model based on ML classifiers. The authors found one candidate molecule, pimozide, that might be suitable for further in vivo or in vitro experiments in NSCLC patients.

In another drug repurposing study,[38] the transcriptomics profile of NSCLC and healthy patients' samples was analyzed and resulted in the extraction of two significant gene modules. Transcription factor genes regulating these gene modules were extracted, and a list of drugs targeting these genes was obtained. This study suggested that at least 16 drugs have potential for becoming repurposed drugs for treating NSCLC.

Another study[39] combined two methods: machine learning algorithms and topological parameter-based classification. In this study, seven potential drugs were discovered for early-stage NSCLC and 11 for late-stage NSCLC. With this study, the authors also wish to inspire future studies and to extend their proposed method to treat other diseases.

In this chapter, a new proposed strategy is presented for analyzing big data to facilitate drug repurposing in lung cancer treatment. The strategy utilizes publicly accessible datasets of -omics data from lung cancer patients, which are available on the cBioPortal platform. Alongside, simple machine learning methods are employed. This disease-focused drug repurposing approach aims to provide the reader with an intuitive introduction to the application of AI/ML in medicine.

3.2 Retinoids and lung cancer?

Retinoids are a diverse group of compounds that have their origins in vitamin A. They are known to play a crucial role in the treatment of various skin conditions. There are over 4000 types of retinoids, each of which has a unique mechanism of action. They exert their effects by binding to different binding proteins and nuclear receptors, such as retinol-binding protein (RBP), cellular retinoic acid-binding protein (CRABP), retinoid X receptor (RXR), and retinoic acid receptor (RAR). These receptors then regulate the gene expression by binding to target genes and activating their transcription. The exact way in which they influence cell survival, differentiation, and transformation into cancer cells is still not completely understood.[40]

Retinoic acid receptor alpha (RARA) has been at the center of hematologists' attention due to its role in acute promyelocytic leukemia (APL).[41] In recent years, however, research suggested that retinoids and their cellular receptors[42] may have potential therapeutic benefits not only in patients with APL, but also against other types of cancer, including lung adenocarcinoma.[43] A few authors also suggest a potential role for retinoids against cancer while used in combination with standard chemotherapies.[44,45] However, other sources report a lack of retinoic acid activity in cancer patients[46] and in the treatment of lung cancer,[47] or even detrimental effects of topic retinoids in lung carcinogenesis.[48] Some authors suspect that this contradictory evidence and an apparent lack of effects of retinoids in tumorigenesis may be explained by other factors such as altered metabolism of retinoids due to genetic mutations ATRA's catabolic enzymes.[49]

Therefore, it seems that despite unclear and sometimes conflicting results, retinoids continue to spark interest in clinical research for their role as mediators of cellular differentiation.[50] In the following section, we aim to demonstrate the application of machine learning (ML) in lung cancer research, with a focus on genetic data related to retinoid receptors-associated genes.

4. AI/ML, lung cancer and drug repurposing: A practical example

The following section presents an illustrative example of utilizing a rather simple AI algorithm to analyze a dataset containing genetic information from actual lung cancer patients. The objective is to identify potential correlations between a clinical variable and abnormalities in both related and seemingly unrelated genes. In this example, we will demonstrate the process of training classifiers that aim at predicting the presence/absence of metastases in different types of lung cancer adenocarcinoma based on genetic alterations in a set of genes traditionally associated with lung cancer development. Although our primary focus is not to establish a clinical-genetic relationship, we aim at showing the capabilities of AI/ML tools in the context of clinical research.

In addition, our primary focus will be on accessibility. We believe that democratizing AI/ML tools is crucial to enable widespread adoption and innovation. By emphasizing that the tools and methods showcased are freely available, we aim to empower individuals from diverse backgrounds to explore the potential of AI/ML in their respective fields.

4.1 Clinical database and software

The clinical database that was analyzed in this chapter is composed of 29 studies on lung cancer patients encompassing a total of 12,434 samples (as of June 2023). These studies were chosen and queried through cBioPortal. The *cBioPortal for Cancer Genomics* is a platform that provides researchers with convenient and streamlined access to multidimensional genomic data sets.[51]

The genes used for training the model were selected based on the most relevant literature, highlighting those with evidence of a genetic contribution to the growth of lung cancer cells and those that are most commonly altered in samples from lung cancer patients: EGFR, KRAS, ALK, RET, ERBB2, BRAF, MET, ROS1, and BRCA2.[52] (To provide a comprehensive review of each of the gene's contribution to the pathogenesis of lung cancer is out of scope for this chapter.) Only cases that had both mutations and copy number alterations data were chosen (patients $n = 8724$, samples $n = 10{,}763$). Queried genes were altered in 7999 (74%) of queried samples.

The hypothesis is that the inclusion of alterations in certain genes improves the performance of a classification model so that a discussion might be started about how these genes may play a role in the development of lung cancer metastases. Three additional gene classes were added to the model for analysis:

1. *ATP-Binding Cassette (ABC)* subtypes A10 (ABCA10) and A12 (ABCA12), due to growing interest in their involvement in tumor and metastasis initiation.[53]
2. *Connexins (Cx)* GJA1, GJB1, GJC1, GJA3: the connection between their mutations and cancer pathogenesis is not yet solid, and studying these proteins in cancer is challenging due to the multitude of possible combinations within a single connexon.[54]
3. The families of *Retinoic Acid Receptors* A (subtypes RARA and RARB) and X (subtypes RXRA and RXRB): there is a growing body of evidence regarding the role of retinoic acid in cell differentiation and tumorigenesis in solid tumors.[49]

Within the provided example, it will be shown that not only retinoic acid receptor genes contribute to the model predictive power, but also the ABCA and Cxs play a role.

Data from the cBioPortal included demographic information, as well as clinical information such as the Tumor Mutational Burden (TMB) score. In particular, TMB score, which is considered a predictive biomarker for immunotherapy response in cancer,[55] was chosen to be included instead of other demographic information as it shows significant correlations with certain demographic factors such as age, gender, height, weight, smoking, and race in specific patient cohorts.

The target variable that the models will aim to predict is the M stage.

The code of the algorithm was written in Python. The following were the software used:

– DeepNote platform freeware, kernel version 3.9, and
– Microsoft Visual Studio Code version 1.73.0, kernel version 3.9.7.

4.2 Methods

After software fine-tuning and data import, data were "wrangled," or managed, in such a way that it was amenable for further analysis. The final *genetic dataset* is composed by 2589 unique entries and has 96 variables (Fig. 1).

	Sample ID	EGFR	KRAS	ALK	RET	ERBB2	BRAF	MET	ROS1	BRCA2	...	RARB: HOMDEL	RARB: FUSION	RXRA: MUT	RXRA: AMP	RXRA: HOMDEL	RXRA: FUSION	RXRB: MUT	RXRB: AMP	RXRB: HOMDEL	RXRB: FUSION
0	LUAD-D02326	no alteration	no alteration	no alteration	no alteration	Y772_A775dup (driver)	no alteration	no alteration	no alteration	no alteration	...	no alteration	no alteration	no alteration	no alteration	no alteration	no alteration	no alteration	no alteration	no alteration	no alteration
1	LUAD-S01341	no alteration	no alteration	no alteration	no alteration	Y772_A775dup (driver)	no alteration	no alteration	no alteration	no alteration	...	no alteration	no alteration	no alteration	no alteration	no alteration	no alteration	no alteration	no alteration	no alteration	no alteration
2	LUAD-U6SJ7	no alteration	G12C (driver)	no alteration	no alteration	no alteration	no alteration	no alteration	no alteration	no alteration	...	no alteration	no alteration	no alteration	no alteration	no alteration	no alteration	no alteration	no alteration	no alteration	no alteration
3	LUAD-E01014	G719A (driver)	no alteration	no alteration	no alteration	no alteration	no alteration	no alteration	no alteration	no alteration	...	no alteration	no alteration	no alteration	no alteration	no alteration	no alteration	no alteration	no alteration	no alteration	no alteration
4	LUAD-S01404	no alteration	G12C (driver)	no alteration	no alteration	no alteration	no alteration	no alteration	no alteration	no alteration	...	no alteration	no alteration	no alteration	no alteration	no alteration	no alteration	no alteration	no alteration	no alteration	no alteration
...	...	...	...	...	...	...	...	...	...	...	...	...	...	...	...	...	...	...	...	...	...
2584	TCGA-NK-A5CT-01	no alteration	no alteration	no alteration	no alteration	no alteration	no alteration	no alteration	no alteration	no alteration	...	no alteration	no alteration	no alteration	no alteration	no alteration	no alteration	no alteration	no alteration	no alteration	no alteration
2585	TCGA-NK-A5D1-01	no alteration	no alteration	no alteration	no alteration	no alteration	no alteration	no alteration	no alteration	no alteration	...	no alteration	no alteration	no alteration	no alteration	no alteration	no alteration	no alteration	no alteration	no alteration	no alteration
2586	TCGA-NK-A7XE-01	no alteration	no alteration	no alteration	no alteration	no alteration	no alteration	no alteration	no alteration	no alteration	...	no alteration	no alteration	no alteration	no alteration	no alteration	no alteration	no alteration	no alteration	no alteration	no alteration
2587	TCGA-O2-A52V-01	no alteration	no alteration	no alteration	no alteration	no alteration	no alteration	no alteration	no alteration	no alteration	...	no alteration	no alteration	no alteration	no alteration	no alteration	no alteration	no alteration	no alteration	no alteration	no alteration
2588	TCGA-XC-AA0X-01	no alteration	no alteration	no alteration	no alteration	no alteration	no alteration	no alteration	no alteration	no alteration	...	no alteration	no alteration	no alteration	no alteration	no alteration	no alteration	no alteration	no alteration	no alteration	no alteration

2589 rows × 96 columns

FIG. 1 Final genetic dataset.

In addition to columns containing identification data about the samples, the remain columns contain, for every given gene, the following information:

- MUT: presence or absence of genetic mutations down to the specific alteration sequenced.
- AMP: presence or absence of amplification of the gene.
- HOMDEL: presence or absence of homologous deletion of the gene.

Then, the dataset containing *clinical data* was analyzed. After this, we removed the duplicate entries and the entries that contained NaN (missing) values. Then, we merged the two databases and eliminated duplicate entries, obtaining the following (Fig. 2):

The dataset comprises a total of 972 samples and 101 variables. Further simplifying included the reduction of the feature "Cancer Type" values only to lung adenocarcinoma and lung squamous cell carcinoma, the pruning of the entries that had the "Mx" value within the target feature and the simplification of all the M1 subtypes (M1a, M1b) into the M1 information.

For a classifier to be trained on categorical features, an array of dummy variables was created starting from the original dataset (Fig. 3).

The resulting database that was used for training the model is a 762×648 array. It is reasonable to anticipate that we will not obtain high prediction scores because the number of features is almost equal to the number of rows; hence, it is hardly possible that a proper classification model might be found.

The main score that was used to evaluate these results, by the authors' choice given the nature of the categorization task, was the F1 score. This score keeps the balance between precision and recall scores (which, for completeness, are also presented within the results). The F1 score often used when class distribution is uneven, but it can also be defined as a statistical measure of the accuracy of an individual test.

4.3 Data resampling and features selection

Given the current clinical hypothesis, it is reasonable to say that there could be an imbalance between the cases with metastases and without metastases (Fig. 4):

In this experiment, 731 samples came from patients who had metastases, whereas 31 come from patients who presented with metastases; hence, we can say that the dataset it is heavily imbalanced. When a dataset is imbalanced

1908	TCGA-77-A5GA-01	no alteration	no alteration	no alteration	no alteration	no alteration	no alteration	no alteration	no alteration	no alteration	...	no alteration	no alteration	no alteration	no alteration	no alteration	4.56666666667	Male	99	Lung Squamous Cell Carcinoma
1909	TCGA-90-6837-01	no alteration	no alteration	no alteration	no alteration	no alteration	no alteration	no alteration	no alteration	no alteration	...	no alteration	no alteration	no alteration	no alteration	no alteration	0.0666666666667	Male	40	Lung Squamous Cell Carcinoma
1910	TCGA-51-6867-01	no alteration	no alteration	no alteration	no alteration	no alteration	no alteration	no alteration	no alteration	no alteration	...	no alteration	no alteration	no alteration	no alteration	no alteration	18.1	Female	40	Lung Squamous Cell Carcinoma
1911	TCGA-NK-A5D1-01	no alteration	no alteration	no alteration	no alteration	no alteration	no alteration	no alteration	no alteration	no alteration	...	no alteration	no alteration	no alteration	no alteration	no alteration	3.13333333333	Male	90	Lung Squamous Cell Carcinoma

972 rows × 101 columns

FIG. 2 Merged databases, without duplicate entries.

	TMB (nonsynonymous)CLINICAL	Cancer Type DetailedCLINICAL_Lung Adenocarcinoma	Cancer Type DetailedCLINICAL_Lung Squamous Cell Carcinoma	M StageCLINICAL_M0	M StageCLINICAL_M1	M StageCLINICAL_Mx	EGFR: AMP_AMP (driver)	EGFR: AMP_HOMDEL	EGFR: AMP_no alteration	EGFR: HOMDEL_AMP (driver)	...	RARB: AMP_no alteration	RARB: HOMDEL_HOMDEL	RARB: HOMDEL_no alteration	MUT_E
0	6.300000	1	0	0	1	0	0	0	1	0	...	1	0	1	
2	9.633333	1	0	1	0	0	0	0	1	0	...	1	0	1	
4	9.833333	1	0	1	0	0	0	0	1	0	...	1	0	1	
6	54.233333	1	0	1	0	0	0	0	1	0	...	1	0	1	
8	4.066667	1	0	1	0	0	0	0	1	0	...	1	0	1	
...	...	...	...	...	...	...	...	...	...	...	...	...	...	...	
1907	4.700000	0	1	1	0	0	0	0	1	0	...	1	0	1	
1908	4.566667	0	1	1	0	0	0	0	1	0	...	1	0	1	
1909	0.066667	0	1	0	0	1	0	0	1	0	...	1	0	1	
1910	18.100000	0	1	1	0	0	0	0	1	0	...	1	0	1	
1911	3.133333	0	1	1	0	0	0	0	1	0	...	1	0	1	

972 rows × 648 columns

FIG. 3 Array of dummy features used for working on categorical variables.

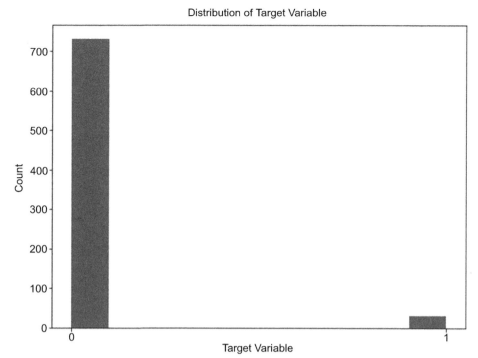

FIG. 4 *N* of cases showing imbalance between classes.

toward one class of the target variable over the other, there are different methods for creating an artificial dataset which is more balanced. Among the methods that we tested for this project, there are the following[56,57]:

- *Oversampling* of the least common class: it involves randomly duplicating examples from the minority class and adding them to the training dataset.
- *Undersampling* of the commonest class: it involves randomly selecting examples from the majority class to delete from the training dataset.
- *SMOTE-NC*: the Synthetic Minority Over-sampling Technique for Nominal and Continuous (SMOTE-NC) addresses the challenge of imbalanced datasets containing both numerical and categorical variables by generating synthetic samples of the minority class that are not identical replicas of existing samples to balance it with the majority class.

Before delving into the data, it is worth mentioning the risk of overfitting. In machine learning, overfitting refers to a model that models the training data too well. It happens when a model learns the detail and noise in the training data to the extent that it negatively impacts the performance of the model when it is applied on new data. In other words, an overfit model is one that is very close to the training data but not generalizable to other cases.[58] Given the results of this experiment, we must consider the risk that the model will be over-fitted to the rather small training dataset.

First, we trained the model on the whole dataset that comprised all the features, after resampling its data through these three methods. We used the Decision Tree, Random Forest, and Gradient Boosting classifiers. In order to do this, we split the dataset into a training and a test dataset and then we trained each classifier on each resampled data (Fig. 5).

Apart from the accuracy, ROC AUC, and balanced accuracy scores, the other scores are all near the 0.5 value. Such scores could indicate that the model is not more reliable in classifying the samples than tossing a coin. There is little doubt that the number of samples are way too few with respect to the features that the model was trained on for it to be able to perform well for classification purposes. Hence, a further analysis step was added to the model to select the n number of features that contribute the most to maximizing the selected score. This method is called *cross-validation*, and it is commonly used to assess how well a model will perform on unseen data.

Cross-validation involves dividing the available dataset into multiple subsets or "folds." The model is then trained on a portion of the data (known as the training set) and evaluated on the remaining data (known as the validation set). This process is repeated several times, with different subsets of the data used for training and validation in each iteration. The performance metrics obtained from each iteration are averaged to provide an overall assessment of the

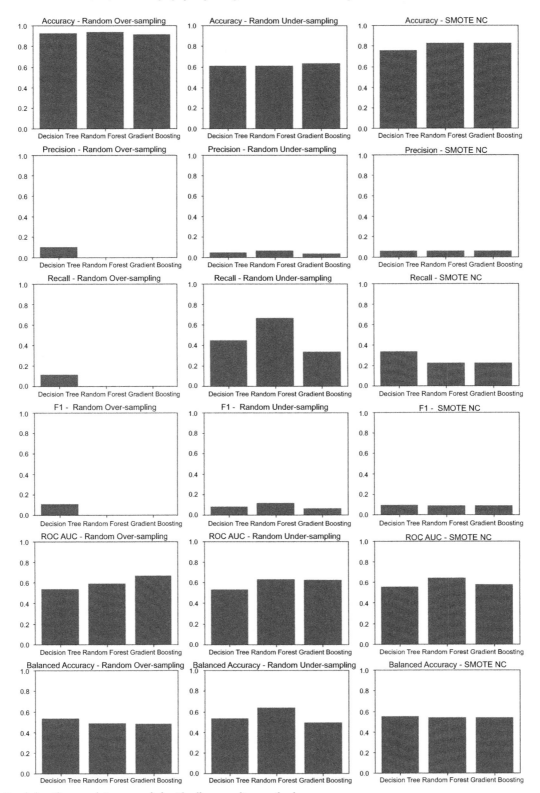

FIG. 5 Results of classifiers on data resampled with all resampling method.

Resampling Method	Classifier	Num Features	Feature	Max F1
Random Over-sampling	Decision Tree	36	Cancer Type DetailedCLINICAL_Lung Adenocarcinoma	0.847334
Random Over-sampling	Random Forest	35	Cancer Type DetailedCLINICAL_Lung Adenocarcinoma	0.849989
Random Over-sampling	Gradient Boosting	37	Cancer Type DetailedCLINICAL_Lung Adenocarcinoma	0.838134
Random Under-sampling	Decision Tree	12	Cancer Type DetailedCLINICAL_Lung Adenocarcinoma	0.629744
Random Under-sampling	Random Forest	16	Cancer Type DetailedCLINICAL_Lung Adenocarcinoma	0.704029
Random Under-sampling	Gradient Boosting	12	Cancer Type DetailedCLINICAL_Lung Adenocarcinoma	0.649744
SMOTE NC	Decision Tree	38	Cancer Type DetailedCLINICAL_Lung Adenocarcinoma	0.804972
SMOTE NC	Random Forest	39	Cancer Type DetailedCLINICAL_Lung Adenocarcinoma	0.803332
SMOTE NC	Gradient Boosting	33	Cancer Type DetailedCLINICAL_Lung Adenocarcinoma	0.793641

FIG. 6   Resulting F1 scores and number of features selected for every combination of classifier and resampling method.

model's performance. Cross-validation helps in assessing how well the model generalizes to unseen data and provides a more reliable estimate of its performance compared to using a single train-test split. In order to have a more specific model, we decided to limit the analysis to the data on adenocarcinoma samples only.

The following table lists the highest values of F1 score for each combination of classifier and resampling method (Fig. 6). For each case, the number of features selected during the cross-validation step is also shown:

4.4 Results

The following histograms indicate the number of selected features that maximizes the F1 score for each combination of classifier and resampling method, and the maximum F1 score (indicated on the x axis in the histogram):

The y-axis with the label "Frequency" in the histogram indicates the number of occurrences or frequency of F1 scores falling within each bin (Fig. 7). Each bin represents a range of F1 scores, and the height of each bar in the histogram represents the count or frequency of F1 scores that fall within that range.

From the graphs, it seems that, given a certain number of selected features, it is possible to obtain values of the F1 score that, in certain cases, can go higher than 0.849. Although this value does not indicate a clinical correlation between the values of the selected features and the presence or absence of metastases, also considering the risk of over-fitting, it is interesting to note that within the list of selected features we might find some pattern that could be of interest for further research. For example, the highest values of F1 scores were obtained when the random over-sampling method was applied to all the three classifiers analyzed, with F1 scores ranging from 0.838 to 0.849. The second-highest results were obtained through the SMOTE-NC oversampling method. The features included in the first three cases included the following:

- TMB (nonsynonymous)CLINICAL
- *EGFR*: MUT_E746_A750del (driver), EGFR: MUT_E866K, EGFR: MUT_L833V (driver), EGFR: K754_I759del (driver), EGFR: MUT_L858R (driver), EGFR: MUT_L861Q (driver)

Also, the following features were selected by the model for the case with the highest F1 score:

- *KRAS*: AMP_AMP (driver), KRAS: HOMDEL_AMP (driver), KRAS: MUT_G12A (driver), KRAS: MUT_G12C (driver), KRAS: MUT_G12D (driver), KRAS: MUT_G12D (driver), G12C (driver), KRAS: MUT_G12V (driver), KRAS: G12C (driver), KRAS: MUT_G13C (driver), KRAS: MUT_G13D (driver)
- *BRAF*: MUT_N581S (driver), BRAF: MUT_V600E (driver)
- ALK: MUT_no alteration, ERBB2: MUT_no alteration, BRAF: MUT_no alteration, MET: MUT_no alteration, ROS1: MUT_no alteration, BRCA2: MUT_no alteration → interestingly enough, no precise mutations within these genes were selected.

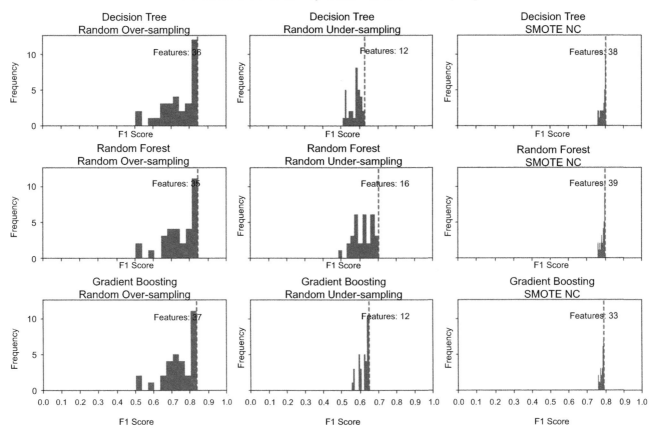

FIG. 7   N of selected features that maximizes the F1 score for each combination of classifier and resampling method.

Interestingly, in addition to the abovementioned, well-characterized putative genes, the model also selected the following features:

- *ABCA10*: MUT_C945*
- *ABCA12*: MUT_E564*, ABCA12: MUT_F2467I, ABCA12: MUT_H1097Q, ABCA12: MUT_L1924I, ABCA12: MUT_L901S,
- *GJA1*: MUT_R101Q,
- *RARA*: MUT_K164N.

While it is not surprising that the RARA mutation was selected during the model optimization (it was the a priori hypothesis of this experiment), what is more intriguing is the consistent selection of multiple mutations within the ABCA10, ABCA12, and Cx genes across various combinations of classifier-resampling methods that yielded the highest F1 scores. This pattern remained consistent even when the random oversampling, undersampling, and SMOTE methods were employed in all three instances.

Considering the intricate nature of the task at hand, it comes as no surprise that drawing precise conclusions regarding the role of these "newly identified mutations" from the obtained results is challenging, at least. The complexity of the problem necessitates caution in interpreting the findings. However, intriguingly, these results could potentially serve as a steppingstone for further exploration and investigation. The fact that the constructed model demonstrates improved performance when incorporating this information sparks speculation and encourages further research endeavors.

4.5 Discussion

This project had the scope of testing a method to build models that would classify lung cancer patient populations into "metastatic" vs "nonmetastatic" categories based upon a mix of genetic and clinical data. This rationale was based upon the idea of training machine learning algorithms (classifiers) on real patients' data and to see how these algorithms improve by selecting only certain genetic mutations.

During this experiment, a certain number of assumptions were made during the design of the model to reach a compromise between the usability of the model and its performance. These assumptions were related to how the dataset was constructed, on the quality of the data inputted, and on how to handle ambiguous results.

In this study, we outlined several AI/ML tools accessible to the general public, along with their purpose in identifying patterns and ultimately generating clinical hypotheses. These hypotheses can be valuable for conducting drug repurposing experiments. However, as it was noted earlier, this project was inherently affected by limitations due to the assumptions that had been made. For example:

- The information regarding smoking status was not included to limit the potential risk for introducing noise into the model.
- Demographic information such as age, gender, race was not included into the model.
- The focus was on lung cancer adenocarcinoma. This was an arbitrary decision to reduce the number of variables but it also limited the informative power of the model.
- Not all possible classifiers and sampling methods were analyzed.
- The decision to focus on the F1 score for the interpretation of the results was made due to the imbalanced nature of the dataset and on the nature of the classification task. However, consideration of changes in precision or other scores could has proven useful.

Lastly, it is crucial to emphasize that the process of matching genetic profiles with a specific disease state is not a straightforward correlation that directly leads to the identification of a viable drug candidates. While genetic profiling provides valuable insights into the underlying mechanisms and genetic variants associated with cancer, it is only one piece of a complex puzzle in the realm of its pathogenesis.

5. Conclusions

In conclusion, AI/ML-based tools have the potential to revolutionize the way we diagnose and treat cancer, including lung cancer adenocarcinoma (LCA). AI/ML-based tools can be used to identify novel molecular patterns and new potential targets for existing drugs.

AI/ML-based tools hold promise in enhancing the prognosis and treatment of patients with LCA by effectively reducing the time and financial burdens associated with the traditional drug development process. These tools have the capability to revolutionize our comprehension of the intricate molecular mechanisms that underlie LCA, unveiling novel therapeutic targets that may exist within the realm of currently available drugs. While a priori hypotheses have traditionally served as the cornerstone of scientific experimentation, it is crucial to acknowledge the significance of remaining open to alternative possibilities. This principle is particularly pertinent in the realm of oncology, where a wealth of well-established and robust information already exists, but the landscape of knowledge is poised to expand exponentially in the forthcoming years. The advent of AI/ML technologies has the potential to propel us into a future where our understanding of LCA and its treatment options surpasses current boundaries, enabling us to make significant strides in improving patient outcomes and ultimately conquering this disease.

Declaration of interests/disclaimer

G.S. was an employee of Lusofarmaco SpA and GlaxoSmithKline SpA and is now an employee of Novartis Pharma SpA. No potential conflict of interest is expected from the contribution to this book.

For information regarding the code used within this chapter please write to gabrielesala88@gmail.com.

References

1. Shimizu H, Nakayama KI. Artificial intelligence in oncology. *Cancer Sci.* 2020;111(5):1452–1460. https://doi.org/10.1111/CAS.14377.
2. Coudray N, Ocampo PS, Sakellaropoulos T, et al. Classification and mutation prediction from non-small cell lung cancer histopathology images using deep learning. *Nat Med.* 2018;24(10):1559–1567. https://doi.org/10.1038/S41591-018-0177-5.
3. Li B, Dai C, Wang L, et al. A novel drug repurposing approach for non-small cell lung cancer using deep learning. *PloS One.* 2020;15(6), e0233112. https://doi.org/10.1371/JOURNAL.PONE.0233112.
4. Yu JS. From discovery of tyrosine phosphorylation to targeted cancer therapies: the 2018 tang prize in biopharmaceutical science. *Biom J.* 2019;42 (2):80–83. https://doi.org/10.1016/J.BJ.2019.03.004.

5. Pammolli F, Magazzini L, Riccaboni M. The productivity crisis in pharmaceutical R&D. *Nat Rev Drug Discov.* 2011;10(6):428–438. https://doi.org/10.1038/NRD3405.

6. Corsello SM, Bittker JA, Liu Z, et al. The Drug Repurposing Hub: a next-generation drug library and information resource. *Nat Med.* 2017;23(4):405–408. https://doi.org/10.1038/nm.4306.

7. Pushpakom S, Iorio F, Eyers PA, et al. Drug repurposing: progress, challenges and recommendations. *Nat Rev Drug Discov.* 2019;18(1):41–58. https://doi.org/10.1038/NRD.2018.168.

8. Pantziarka P, Verbaanderd C, Huys I, Bouche G, Meheus L. Repurposing drugs in oncology: from candidate selection to clinical adoption. *Semin Cancer Biol.* 2021;68:186–191. https://doi.org/10.1016/J.SEMCANCER.2020.01.008.

9. Sleire L, Førde-Tislevoll HE, Netland IA, Leiss L, Skeie BS, Enger PØ. Drug repurposing in cancer. *Pharmacol Res.* 2017;124:74–91. https://doi.org/10.1016/J.PHRS.2017.07.013.

10. Parisi D, Adasme MF, Sveshnikova A, Bolz SN, Moreau Y, Schroeder M. Drug repositioning or target repositioning: a structural perspective of drug-target-indication relationship for available repurposed drugs. *Comput Struct Biotechnol J.* 2020;18:1043. https://doi.org/10.1016/J.CSBJ.2020.04.004.

11. Jarada TN, Rokne JG, Alhajj R. A review of computational drug repositioning: strategies, approaches, opportunities, challenges, and directions. *J Chem.* 2020;12(1):1–23. https://doi.org/10.1186/S13321-020-00450-7/TABLES/3.

12. Tan GSQ, Sloan EK, Lambert P, Kirkpatrick CMJ, Ilomäki J. Drug repurposing using real-world data. *Drug Discov Today.* 2023;28(1), 103422. https://doi.org/10.1016/j.drudis.2022.103422.

13. Reay WR, Cairns MJ. Advancing the use of genome-wide association studies for drug repurposing. *Nat Rev Genet.* 2021;22(10):658–671. https://doi.org/10.1038/s41576-021-00387-z.

14. Uffelmann E, Huang QQ, Munung NS, et al. Genome-wide association studies. *Nature Reviews Methods Primers.* 2021;1(1):59. https://doi.org/10.1038/s43586-021-00056-9.

15. Turabi KS, Deshmukh A, Paul S, et al. Drug repurposing—an emerging strategy in cancer therapeutics. *Naunyn Schmiedebergs Arch Pharmacol.* 2022;395(10):1139–1158. https://doi.org/10.1007/S00210-022-02263-X.

16. Jain AS, Prasad A, Pradeep S, et al. Everything old is new again: drug repurposing approach for non-small cell lung Cancer targeting MAPK signaling pathway. *Front Oncol.* 2021;11:4011. https://doi.org/10.3389/FONC.2021.741326/BIBTEX.

17. Thirunavukkarasu M.K., Karuppasamy R. Drug repurposing combined with MM/PBSA based validation strategies towards MEK inhibitors screening. Published online 2021. https://doi.org/10.1080/07391102.2021.1970629.

18. Peyvandipour A, Saberian N, Shafi A, Donato M, Draghici S. A novel computational approach for drug repurposing using systems biology. *Bioinformatics.* 2018;34(16):2817–2825. https://doi.org/10.1093/BIOINFORMATICS/BTY133.

19. Li A, Huang HT, Huang HC, Juan HF. LncTx: a network-based method to repurpose drugs acting on the survival-related lncRNAs in lung cancer. *Comput Struct Biotechnol J.* 2021;19:3990–4002. https://doi.org/10.1016/J.CSBJ.2021.07.007.

20. Strebhardt K, Ullrich A. Paul Ehrlich's magic bullet concept: 100 years of progress. *Nat Rev Cancer.* 2008;8(6):473–480. https://doi.org/10.1038/nrc2394.

21. Hernández-Lemus E, Martínez-García M. Pathway-based drug-repurposing schemes in Cancer: the role of translational bioinformatics. *Front Oncol.* 2021;10:2996. https://doi.org/10.3389/FONC.2020.605680/BIBTEX.

22. Xu C, Jackson SA. Machine learning and complex biological data. *Genome Biol.* 2019;20(1):1–4. https://doi.org/10.1186/S13059-019-1689-0/FIGURES/2.

23. Issa NT, Stathias V, Schürer S, Dakshanamurthy S. Machine and deep learning approaches for cancer drug repurposing. *Semin Cancer Biol.* 2021;68:132–142. https://doi.org/10.1016/J.SEMCANCER.2019.12.011.

24. Tanoli Z, Vähä-Koskela M, Aittokallio T. Artificial intelligence, machine learning, and drug repurposing in cancer. *Expert Opin Drug Discovery.* 2021;16(9):977–989. https://doi.org/10.1080/17460441.2021.1883585.

25. Ramesh P, Karuppasamy R, Veerappapillai S. Machine learning driven drug repurposing strategy for identification of potential RET inhibitors against non-small cell lung cancer. *Med Oncol.* 2023;40(56). https://doi.org/10.1007/S12032-022-01924-4.

26. Wieder R, Adam N. Drug repositioning for cancer in the era of AI, big omics, and real-world data. *Crit Rev Oncol Hematol.* 2022;175, 103730. https://doi.org/10.1016/J.CRITREVONC.2022.103730.

27. Helm JM, Swiergosz AM, Haeberle HS, et al. Machine learning and artificial intelligence: definitions, applications, and future directions. *Curr Rev Musculoskelet Med.* 2020;13(1):69–76. https://doi.org/10.1007/s12178-020-09600-8.

28. Classifier Definition. DeepAI. https://deepai.org/machine-learning-glossary-and-terms/classifier. Accessed 11 February 2023.

29. 5 Types of Classification Algorithms in Machine Learning. n.d. Accessed 20 November 2022. https://monkeylearn.com/blog/classification-algorithms/.

30. Machine Learning Classifiers. n.d. What is classification? | by Sidath Asiri | Towards Data Science. Accessed 20 November 2022. https://towardsdatascience.com/machine-learning-classifiers-a5cc4e1b0623.

31. Javatpoint, n.d. Machine Learning Random Forest Algorithm—Javatpoint. Accessed 20 November 2022. https://www.javatpoint.com/machine-learning-random-forest-algorithm.

32. DeepAI, n.d., Gradient Boosting Definition | DeepAI. Accessed 20 November 2022. https://deepai.org/machine-learning-glossary-and-terms/gradient-boosting.

33. Chalela R, Curull V, Enríquez C, Pijuan L, Bellosillo B, Gea J. Lung adenocarcinoma: from molecular basis to genome-guided therapy and immunotherapy. *J Thorac Dis.* 2017;9(7):2142–2158. https://doi.org/10.21037/JTD.2017.06.20.

34. Benusiglio PR, Fallet V, Sanchis-Borja M, Coulet F, Cadranel J. Lung cancer is also a hereditary disease. *Eur Respir Rev.* 2021;30(162). https://doi.org/10.1183/16000617.0045-2021.

35. Popper HH. Progression and metastasis of lung cancer. *Cancer Metastasis Rev.* 2016;35(1):75. https://doi.org/10.1007/S10555-016-9618-0.

36. Balkwill F, Mantovani A. Inflammation and cancer: Back to Virchow? *Lancet.* 2001;357(9255):539–545. https://doi.org/10.1016/S0140-6736(00)04046-0.

37. Chen L., Huang T., Zhang Y.H., Jiang Y., Zheng M., Cai Y.D. Identification of novel candidate drivers connecting different dysfunctional levels for lung adenocarcinoma using protein-protein interactions and a shortest path approach. Sci Rep 2016;6(1):1–10. https://doi.org/10.1038/srep29849.

38. MotieGhader H, Tabrizi-Nezhadi P, Deldar Abad Paskeh M, et al. Drug repositioning in non-small cell lung cancer (NSCLC) using gene co-expression and drug–gene interaction networks analysis. *Sci Rep.* 2022;12(1):1–15. https://doi.org/10.1038/s41598-022-13719-8.

39. Huang CH, Chang PMH, Hsu CW, Huang CYF, Ng KL. Drug repositioning for non-small cell lung cancer by using machine learning algorithms and topological graph theory. *BMC Bioinformatics.* 2016;17(1):13–26. https://doi.org/10.1186/S12859-015-0845-0/FIGURES/2.

40. Bushue N, Wan YJY. Retinoid pathway and Cancer therapeutics. *Adv Drug Deliv Rev.* 2010;62(13):1285. https://doi.org/10.1016/J.ADDR.2010.07.003.

41. Yilmaz M, Kantarjian H, Ravandi F. Acute promyelocytic leukemia current treatment algorithms. *Blood. Cancer J.* 2021;11(6). https://doi.org/10.1038/S41408-021-00514-3.

42. Bogos K, Renyi-Vamos F, Kovacs G, Tovari J, Dome B. Role of retinoic receptors in lung carcinogenesis. *J Exp Clin Cancer Res.* 2008;27(1):1–7. https://doi.org/10.1186/1756-9966-27-18/TABLES/1.

43. Toma S., Raffo P., Isnardi L., Palumbo R. Retinoids in lung cancer chemoprevention and treatment. Third International Congress on Cancer - Chemotherapy of Non-Small-Cell Lung Cancer: New Achievements, 29-31 May 1998 - Venice, Italy 1998;10:S95–S102. https://doi.org/10.1093/annonc/10.suppl_5.S95.

44. Tripathi SK, Pandey K, Panda M, Spinella MJ, Rengasamy KR, Biswal BK. The potential of retinoids for combination therapy of lung cancer: updates and future directions. *Pharmacol Res.* 2019;147, 104331. https://doi.org/10.1016/J.PHRS.2019.104331.

45. Averbuch SD. Lung Cancer Prevention: Retinoids and the Epidermal Growth Factor Receptor-A Phoenix Rising?. http://aacrjournals.org/clincancerres/article-pdf/8/1/1/2301569/df0102000001.pdf. Accessed 21 January 2023.

46. Freemantle SJ, Dragnev KH, Dmitrovsky E. The retinoic acid paradox in Cancer chemoprevention. *JNCI: J Natl Cancer Inst.* 2006;98(7):426–427. https://doi.org/10.1093/JNCI/DJJ116.

47. Fritz H, Kennedy D, Fergusson D, et al. Vitamin a and retinoid derivatives for lung Cancer: a systematic review and Meta analysis. *PloS One.* 2011;6(6). https://doi.org/10.1371/JOURNAL.PONE.0021107.

48. Rosenberg EW, Skinner RB. Topical retinoids: another piece for the retinoid-cigarette-lung cancer puzzle? *J Thorac Oncol.* 2006;1(7):732. https://doi.org/10.1097/01243894-200609000-00023.

49. Hunsu VO, Facey COB, Fields JZ, Boman BM. Retinoids as chemo-preventive and molecular-targeted anti-cancer therapies. *Int J Mol Sci.* 2021;22 (14):7731. https://doi.org/10.3390/IJMS22147731.

50. Hada M, Mondul AM, Weinstein SJ, Albanes D. Serum retinol and risk of overall and site-specific cancer in the ATBC study. *Am J Epidemiol.* 2020;189(6):532–542. https://doi.org/10.1093/AJE/KWZ226.

51. cBioPortal FAQs. https://docs.cbioportal.org/user-guide/faq/#what-is-the-cbioportal-for-cancer-genomics. Accessed 20 November 2022.

52. Villalobos P, Wistuba II. Lung cancer biomarkers. *Hematol Oncol Clin North Am.* 2017;31(1):13. https://doi.org/10.1016/J.HOC.2016.08.006.

53. Nobili S, Lapucci A, Landini I, Coronnello M, Roviello G, Mini E. Role of ATP-binding cassette transporters in cancer initiation and progression. *Semin Cancer Biol.* 2020;60:72–95. https://doi.org/10.1016/J.SEMCANCER.2019.08.006.

54. Nalewajska M., Marchelek-My M., Opara-Bajerowicz M., Dziedziejko V., Pawlik A. Molecular Sciences Connexins-Therapeutic Targets in Cancers, https://doi.org/10.3390/ijms21239119.

55. Li M, Gao X, Wang X. Identification of tumor mutation burden-associated molecular and clinical features in cancer by analyzing multi-omics data. *Front Immunol.* 2023;14. https://doi.org/10.3389/fimmu.2023.1090838.

56. MachineLearningMastery.com. Random Oversampling and Undersampling for Imbalanced Classification—MachineLearningMastery.com. https://machinelearningmastery.com/random-oversampling-and-undersampling-for-imbalanced-classification/. Accessed 20 November 2022.

57. Wongvorachan T, He S, Bulut O. A comparison of undersampling, oversampling, and SMOTE methods for dealing with imbalanced classification in educational data mining. *Inform.* 2023;14(1):54. https://doi.org/10.3390/info14010054.

58. Ying X. An overview of overfitting and its solutions. *J Phys Conf Ser.* 2019;1168, 022022. https://doi.org/10.1088/1742-6596/1168/2/022022.

CHAPTER

5

Artificial intelligence and digital worlds: New frontiers of integration between AI and other technological tools

Silvia Francesca Maria Pizzoli[a], Ilaria Durosini[a], Milija Strika[a,b], and Gabriella Pravettoni[a,b]

[a]Department of Oncology and Hematology-Oncology (DIPO), University of Milan, Milan, Italy [b]Applied Research Division for Cognitive and Psychological Science, European Institute of Oncology (IEO), IRCCS, Milan, Italy

1. Introduction

Artificial intelligence (AI) is revolutionizing the field of medicine, potentially transforming the healthcare system in numerous ways. AI-powered medical tools can help in the diagnosis of different diseases, the identification of treatment plans, the general improvement of patients' health management, and the support of healthcare system organizations.[1–4] Overall, AI is an extremely valuable asset for professionals who are required to comprehend data and make informed decisions.[5,6] For example, in the field of oncology, AI can be used to support physicians and decision-making processes. Currently, there is an available AI system for supporting oncologists in decision-making in the field of cancer care (IBM Watson for Oncology). Such a system is capable of analyzing patients' data and comparing it with data stored as historical cases of hospitals, providing a list of treatment choices and options to support the oncologists in making informed decisions, and finally identifying possible clinical trials (from https://clinicaltrials.gov/) tailored on the features of the specific patients. The decisions and treatment schemas supported by this AI seem to be concordant with those taken by multidisciplinary teams, even if further evidence is needed.[7] Another example is the application of AI in the field of radiology,[8] where artificial entities can be used to support radiologists in overcoming their cognitive burden by assisting them with the interpretation of mammograms and identifying suspicious lesions. Other benefits are the reduction of the economic burden of mammography screening by reducing the number of unnecessary diagnostic tests and the improvement of the efficiency of radiologists.

In recent years, apart from the uses of AI outputs in medical diagnosis and disease screening, other technological and digital tools advancements began to be integrated into medical education and training programs, allowing, for instance, healthcare professionals to practice and refine their skills in a simulated environment. This provides a more efficient and cost-effective means of learning that can better prepare healthcare professionals for real-world scenarios.

Integrating AI with other technological tools such as Virtual Reality, the Metaverse, and wearables for recording psychophysiological data presents a wealth of new possibilities. For example, AI can enhance Virtual Reality experiences by creating more realistic and personalized environments; wearables can provide valuable data for personalized healthcare and wellness, including monitoring of vital signs, sleep patterns, and emotional states, while the Metaverse can be made more immersive and interactive through the use of AI-powered chatbots and intelligent agents.

The combination of these technologies has the potential to revolutionize a variety of fields, from entertainment and education to healthcare and wellness, and create entirely new opportunities for human-machine interaction.

Overall, AI and related technologies have tremendous potential to transform the healthcare landscape but must be carefully integrated and managed to ensure their maximum benefit and mitigate potential risks.

In this chapter, we try to shed light on the new possibilities of integrations between AI and other technologies usually used in clinical practice to better understand their possible applications in the context of care, supporting patients' participation to care, personal emotions, and personal motivations.[9–11] We focused on AI and Virtual Reality, AI and Metaverse, AI and smartphones/wearables devices, and AI as a language for standalone support in the medical field. These paragraphs do not aim to be exhaustive of all the possible integrations of AI with new technologies, but they represent an area of potential interest for understanding AI's role in healthcare. Physicians' and patients' psychological points of view, as well as obstacles, facilitators, and future directions of AI, will also be discussed.

2. AI and Virtual Reality

Nowadays, scientific evidence highlights the importance of the use of new technologies in healthcare for the promotion of patient's well-being. A technology frequently used for the treatment and management of medical patients is Virtual Reality (VR). Through VR, people can immerse themselves in a virtual environment, interacting and exploring this world similar to the real ones. VR allowed users to be immersed in a scenario with sensorial stimulation and promoted the development of a *sense of presence*. From a psychological point of view, the *sense of presence* refers to the subjective feeling of "being there" and behaving in the VR as if it were the actual reality.[12] The immersion into virtual scenarios allowed the creation of a vivid, realistic, and emotionally salient illusion to be in a new reality.[13]

Over the years, some researchers explored the benefits of applying VR in the treatment of complex psychiatric conditions and medical care. For example, an innovative application of VR in healthcare is related to the treatment of eating disorders,[14] which are conditions difficult to treat and that affect young people's mental and physical health worldwide.[15] According to the *Diagnostic and Statistical Manual of Mental Disorders-5*,[16] patients suffering from eating disorders may have dysfunctional eating habits and distorted cognition about their bodies and tend to obsessively pursue the idea of a "perfect body," overestimating their body weight.[17] VR can help patients to normalize their eating patterns, modify the distorted perception of their body, as well as achieve a more realistic perception of dissatisfaction with some physical parts of themselves.[14,18]

Additionally, VR is currently used in the oncological context for the promotion of physical and psychological benefits in mood states.[19] Indeed, receiving a life-threatening diagnosis exposes people to negative emotions (e.g., depression, anxiety, fear) and PTSD symptoms,[20] for which VR can provide valuable benefits.

Other examples of VR application are related to the treatment of a variety of psychological diseases, such as post-traumatic stress disorder,[21] Parkinson's disease, Alzheimer's, and other psychological (e.g., anxiety, depression) and neurophysiological (e.g., pain) disorders.[22–28]

A great advantage of VR hardware and software lies in the possibility of integrating this tool with other technologies, such as AI. Specifically, AI could improve the use of VR through deep learning tools. Deep learning is a class of machine learning algorithms that imitates the way humans obtain certain types of knowledge, and it can improve computer vision by instilling intelligence into VR technologies. The term "deep" refers to the multitude of levels through which data are transformed. Deep learning enables learning representations of data with multiple levels of abstraction,[29] thus being able to learn to represent the real world as a result of other more abstract concepts and representations.

Thus, the first advantage of integrating AI and deep learning in VR is related to content creation: creating VR content in 3D takes a lot of time and effort. Through AI and deep learning, the time for content creation could be drastically reduced and the integration of these technologies could lead to the creation of environments that are rich in detail and, more important, personalized for users.

Second, the integration between AI and VR allowed the reproduction of complex interactions tailored to human behaviors. In VR, users can interact with the virtual world in the same way they interact with the real one: for example, they can walk, grab objects, or open doors. Coding complex body movements is incredibly difficult and time-consuming. Thanks to deep and machine learning, it is possible to reproduce complex movements in the virtual environment.[30] Avatars, similar to real humans, can move, interact, and act in space. This might be tremendously useful for the creation of intervention programs tailored to patients' needs and cognitive and bodily features, for example, for patients with eating disorders or breast cancer survivors struggling with their body image. Bodily illusions are indeed already been proposed in the field of anorexia nervosa and VR.[14]

Third, VR and AI can be integrated to facilitate clinicians' training. Clinicians can use VR to simulate surgery in advance and use machine learning techniques to present high-definition medical images to patients, allowing a virtual medical simulation.[31] For example, the virtual operative assistant (VOA) is a platform that allows the virtual training of neurosurgeons using virtual reality surgical simulators. VOA permits the identification of specific components of the psychomotor skills of the hands and compares students' performances with other performance metrics, reducing the need for constant supervision through personalized feedback.

Fourth, VR and AI can be used to further promote patients' well-being and medical symptom reduction with a personalized approach. Virtual environments are used to support patients' emotions and mental health using specific psychological techniques adapted for new technologies. An example is Bubble, a novel intervention that integrates AI and VR for the treatment of the sensation of heat associated with signs of cutaneous vasodilatation and subsequent drop in core temperature associated with palpitations, panic, anxiety, and irritability in cancer patients (i.e., hot flashes[32,33]). The intervention with Bubble took place in a winter environment called Frosty, which allows calm and relaxation, and helps patients to reduce hot flashes.[32] Traditional and evidence-based cognitive behavioral techniques and mindfulness techniques were reproduced in the virtual context and allowed the effective reduction of mental distress and targeted symptoms. AI algorithms guarantee a personalized experience for the user's experience on the bases of their choices, their answers to some questions, and their movements within the virtual environment.

These examples allow us to understand possible areas of integration of AI into VR, highlighting the utility of new technologies for the tailored promotion of well-being and a better understanding of complex clinical information.

3. AI and the metaverse

More recently, a 3-D virtual world where users can interact with each other through personal avatars and within a computer-generated environment is rapidly spreading through the entire population, the Metaverse. Adolescents, young adults, adults, and older may use the Metaverse to promote education, health, and social connections. Indeed, the virtual bridge between the physical and virtual worlds allows social interactions, trade, travel, going to concerts, attending conferences, etc.[34]

Concerning the healthcare area, a 2022 perspective paper describes four main possible future applications for Metaverse and AI in medicine (MeTAI[35]). Virtual comparative scanning is one of the proposed applications[35] and deals with the possibility of integrating data from physical and virtual worlds to create "computational avatars," which are individualized avatars tailored to the patient's profile and with anatomical properties that can be visualized and modified by scanners and AI-driven graphical tools to insert, remove, and modify diseases in these avatars. According to this possibility, potential pathologies might be simulated and scanned within the patient's avatar. The use of detailed patient avatars can help physicians explain and show medical problems and treatment options to patients, thus helping to reduce patient anxiety and improve patient's outcomes.[35]

Bringing the Metaverse into medicine and healthcare could also lead benefits in doctor-patient relationship. For example, the UAE chain Aster DM Healthcare has created the first virtual medical facility, Medcare Women & Children Hospital, to enable an immersive remote doctor-patient experience equal to the physical one (www.asterdmhealthcare.com). To do this, Medcare Women & Children Hospital has partnered with Biometaverse becoming the first hospital in the Metaverse. The objective of this initiative is to provide healthcare services, including real-time consultations through the hospital's team of doctors. The expectation is to replace traditional telemedicine services with interactions in the Metaverse, to have a more collaborative and better doctor-patient experience. Despite the enormous potential of this invention, there are still many details that need to be improved: thinking about how patients will be able to be connected to the virtual environment, how to interact with physical needs, and reinventing the healthcare business model.

Another example of the application of the Metaverse in medicine can be found in the project of Skalidis and colleagues, who created "CardioVerse"—an eventual cardiology-targeted Metaverse for the digital treatment of cardiological problems.[34] CardioVerse allows cardiologists and cardiac surgeons to conduct virtual consultations with their patients and follow them through the course of care. CardioVerse does not aim to substitute digital examinations for physical ones but only to improve the quality of the examinations themselves and the quality of care and life of the patients. Overall, the possibilities offered by CardioVerse are manifold: virtual consultations, medical education, health app monitoring, and VR interventions.[34] The future use of "medical" avatars scanned with AI technologies[35] might be implemented in Metaverse spaces for medical consultations too. Currently, some challenges need to be addressed to implement the use of CardioVerse. The main obstacles will be the security of patient data processing and technical, legislative, and regulatory issues.[34] Once researchers find a way to deal with these issues, the CardioVerse platform will bring benefits to the medical world.

Metaverse might also be used as a virtual shared space for physician training. As a training tool for physicians, it allows for hands-on training in a simulated and safe virtual environment, which can be especially useful for the practice of high-risk or expensive procedures or for managing rare medical conditions. In 2021, an application of the

Metaverse as a training aid for lung cancer surgery has already been proposed.[36] The idea of employing remote training came from the social isolation pandemic issues and ended up in a training course for surgeons. Virtual training in VR, compared to traditional training, also showed comparable effects on orthopedic surgical trainees.[37] The virtual nature of the Metaverse allows for greater flexibility in scheduling and access to training materials, as physicians can access the platform from anywhere with an internet connection. Using a Metaverse application for medical training can also help lower the costs associated with traditional in-person training and courses, such as travel expenses and facility rental fees.

The Metaverse might also provide a collaborative learning environment, where physicians can work remotely but together with colleagues to develop treatment plans or share knowledge and experience. The use of Metaverse as a collaborative learning environment has already been proposed in the educational field,[38] and it is reasonable to think that educational and collaborative learning sessions might be carried out also within professionals working in the same or different hospitals. The same might be applied to patients' communities or patients' education. Similar applications, meant to inform patients about treatments' features and anxiety management[39] or on mental illnesses,[40] have already been applied in VR.

In future applications, patients could use the Metaverse to participate in virtual support groups and therapy sessions, providing a more accessible and inclusive form of healthcare. Evidence on virtual and remote support groups for patients already suggests promising results,[41] and it is reasonable to guess that future support groups in the Metaverse might enhance engagement and a sense of involvement.

Furthermore, researchers could use the Metaverse to conduct clinical trials and experiments, allowing them to study the effects of treatments and therapies in a virtual environment before moving to real-world testing. The Metaverse has thus the potential to transform the context of care and improve access to healthcare for individuals all over the world.

In conclusion, the Metaverse offers new opportunities for medicine, helping to improve medical training, simulation, and research. However, it is important to stress that this technology is still under development, and further research is needed to fully assess its impact and implications on medical practice.

4. AI, smartphones, and wearables devices

Combining AI with smartphones and wearable devices has the potential to revolutionize human life by providing personalized insights and promoting—for example—an individual's physical and mental health.

An approach called *digital phenotyping* allows the assemblage of real-time biometric and personal data with digital tools (smartphones and wearables) to assess and measure behaviors and psychophysiological variables that can be used to describe and predict complex medical or psychophysiological conditions. The expression *digital phenotyping* was initially used in psychiatry to identify a method to collect data on social and behavioral symptoms of psychosis (schizophrenia).[42] *Digital phenotyping* might be used for diagnosis and clinical assessment, predict changes and trajectories in clinical conditions, and deliver tailored remote or traditional interventions according to specific individual real-time data. It can also be used in psychiatric and psychological fields for the assessment of personality[43] and mood disorders[44] and for identifying unhealthy lifestyles and preventing chronic diseases.[45]

Smartphone applications and wearables such as fitness trackers and smartwatches can collect vast amounts of data on various biometric and behavioral measures, and AI-machine learning algorithms are useful to generate insights and identify patterns that could indicate the onset of certain health conditions. A vast amount of digital data can be used to define and track phenotypes of interest, such as cognitive functioning, behavioral and sleep patterns, physical activity, speech, social behaviors, and interactions.[46] Digital data on these phenotypes can be gathered through different modalities: from implicit monitoring with sensors to the explicit collection of data via patient-reported outcomes (e.g., questionnaires[47]). A more recent conceptualization of digital phenotyping suggests a slightly more complex classification of digital data: (1) sensor data recorded by smartphones sensors such as Bluetooth or GPS (temperature, speed, location, and distance); (2) activity data that are generated when persons interact and use their digital devices (text messages, screen activity logs, calls), including also self-report questionnaires or diaries, and social media data generated by users' posts on Facebook, Twitter, and Instagram (language used, timing and content of posts on[48]). These sources of information can provide a large amount of valuable data to characterize phenotypes, such as social behavior, and develop the individual's digital phenotype.[49]

Nowadays, much more complex passive data can be integrated into these types of studies. Actigraphy, for instance, is a device placed on the wrist that can precisely and reliably estimate physical activity behaviors or sleep–wake activity.[50] The analysis of the sleep–wake activity and sleep circles provided valuable insights into assessing rapid changes in risk factors for suicide among high-risk suicidal samples.[51,52]

The approach of digital phenotyping turned out to be beneficial also during the COVID-19 pandemic. COVID-19 appeared worldwide with serious physical and psychological consequences for the entire population.[9,10] A 2022 study on postacute COVID-19 syndrome observed and analyzed psychological data (which includes symptoms affecting mood, anxiety levels, sleep quality, and pain) for four weeks with digital phenotyping in 695 college students with high levels of stress.[53] Active data were constituted by clinical assessment surveys to be completed by students every two weeks, while passive data were taken from phone sensor data such as GPS, accelerometer, and screen states. The results showed that patterns of changes in sleep–wake activity could be used to track and capture the evolving phenomenon of postacute COVID-19 syndrome. Another study on students during the pandemic revealed that the approach of digital phenotyping could be useful in tracking mental health issues in times of social isolation.[54] Specifically, in 2021, 100 students were enrolled in an observational study to assess if and how digital biomarkers of complex behavior can correlate with mental health states. For 28 days, participants were asked to provide data in the form of completion of self-report questionnaires on mood assessment and allow for the passive collection of GPS, accelerometer, phone call, and screen time data. A final traditional visit to assess depression and mental health was carried out. The results showed that digital self-report assessment of depression correlated with the gold standard procedure of traditional visits, while sleep patterns recorded through sensors correlated with depression and stress.

Overall, *digital phenotyping* might be a method to integrate digital data, machine learning, and AI to detect fast-changing behaviors or indexes with the measurements of more stable or self-reported traits. The integration of different sources of data might indeed provide a tailored prediction of health and well-being risks, also providing cost-savings and ecological data. Despite the promising results, there are also limitations to this approach, such as the need for large and diverse datasets to develop accurate AI models and concerns around data privacy and security. Moreover, wearables may only be suitable for some individuals, especially those with limited access to technology or those uncomfortable with constant monitoring. Despite the advantages, the psychological and ethical implications of applying digital phenotyping in clinical practice should be carefully addressed. *Digital phenotyping* might also give rise to the so-called "Observer effect" or "Hawthorne effect".[55] According to this psychological effect, people might behave differently or modify their choice in response to the awareness of being observed and studied.

5. AI language in healthcare

Besides the applications of AI with other technological tools and specific hardware (VR, AR, Metaverse), there are also implementations of AI on its own in the healthcare setting. Up to this point, we have talked about the application of new technologies in conjunction with artificial intelligence, now it is useful to focus on some application examples of AI in the healthcare context.

A recent example of AI services is Babylon Health, a digital health service provider that enables, through an AI platform, virtual clinical services for patients.[56] Machine learning systems are integrated into Babylon Health to learn as much available real-world data from laboratories and medical records as possible and use it to, for example, predict disease risk, recommend optimal interventions, or even identify diagnostic codes from medical records. To be able to do this, AI must be able to understand patients and what they are communicating, so Babylon's developers used natural language processing (NPL[57]). NPL refers to AI algorithms that can process and understand natural language, and it has enormous application benefits in medicine. When used to read notes written by physicians, it can be able to predict patient outcomes and generate patterns of diagnosis that can detect certain chronic diseases in their early stages.[58] In addition to this functionality, NPL is also capable of reproducing natural language that can be used in the interface with patients to ask questions and obtain information about their health status, in the form of chatbots.[58] Finally, Babylon also allows patients to talk to a network of professionals who can give advice about disease management, answer questions, and reassure patients in need.

Another example of AI application as a standalone in medicine is deep learning-based automatic detection (DLAD), an algorithm for radiological diagnostics.[59] The algorithm can recognize four major groups of respiratory diseases by analyzing chest X-rays: malignant neoplasms, pneumonia, active tuberculosis, and pneumothorax. The algorithm was created based on hundreds of thousands of patient data and demonstrated better diagnostic accuracy than a comparison group of radiologists.[59] Therefore, DLAD makes it possible to improve the detection performance of malignant pulmonary nodules in chest radiographs and also improve the performance of physicians when used as a coadjuvant reader. This might be especially true in the context of the high cognitive burden of the physicians or the case of incidental findings when lesions and incidental signs are captured by imaging data when the person is receiving unrelated exams.[60] Anyway, we must keep in mind that this technology, like all others, can never replace the figure of the physician, but only represents an aid and facilitator.

A similar scope can be found in SkinVision, an application based on a machine learning algorithm that can quickly assess suspicious skin changes just by taking a picture with your mobile phone.[61] The application can give users a binary assessment of the risk, which can be low or high, but in no way provides a diagnosis. The AI algorithm on which SkinVision is based is only able to provide a risk assessment. Still, when there is a case of high risk of melanoma, the user receives advice from the customer care team based on an image assessment made by a dermatologist. So this is another example of how AI can assist the work of the doctor but never replace it.[62]

A recent advantage of fast-spreading AI technology is OpenAI Chat Generative Pretrained Transformer (ChatGPT; www.openai.com), a prototype machine learning-based chatbot designed to give textual responses similar to what a human being would give. Launched in November 2022, ChatGPT is rapidly spreading within the population, covering a wide range of topics. It can write paragraphs and letters, answer questions, and create stories and poems. ChatGPT could also be used in the healthcare area to create unique memory devices ("create a mnemonic for the names of leg muscles") and explain complex concepts in more or less complex language ("explain to me what gastric hypomotility is as if I were a 10-year-old, a first-year medical student, or a gastroenterology colleague").

To provide a practical example of using ChatGPT, we asked the following question: "What are the latest findings in the field of breast cancer? Can you also provide me with examples of papers on the topic?" The AI answered with a bullet list of the possible approaches to treat breast cancer and test the specific cancer type. However, one of the main problems with ChatGPT is its potential to generate inaccurate or incomplete information. The suggested literature in the answer was indeed quite inconsistent with actual scientific relevant literature. This bias might affect professionals trying to re-perceive information on ChatGPT quickly and promote misleading information. Another concern regarding ChatGPT is related to the possible bias that might arise from the small sample sizes of machine learning training data or reflecting universal internet biases.

In the scientific field, some authors began to disclose the use of ChatGPT as an author of a scientific publication. The choice was discussed since AI cannot be considered responsible for its "choices" of content[63] and, even more interestingly, Gaggioli[64] argued that the use of AI should be disclosed even if it has been used during any stage of the study, including data analysis and data visualization. This would prevent potential misconduct and highlight benefits in increasing the efficiency of chatbots, allowing for a transparent and ethical review process.[64] The disclosure of the specific use of AI during research, data analysis, and paper writing might be a first step in the direction of transparency and in the assessment of the potential benefits and limits of using AI in the field.

Despite the possible benefits of this AI technology, from a psychological point of view, the area is under continuous exploration. Nowadays, people are showing deep interest in ChatGPT and trying to discover and use them in their lives. It is important to recognize that people have started to communicate with AI technology and, as in other learning processes, some missteps and mistakes may occur. Therefore, it is important to use technology to support, but not substitute, the human figure, reflecting on the user's communicative intention behind using AI and their general attitudes toward technologies.

6. Limits, barriers, and future directions of the use of AI and its integrations with other technologies in medicine

AI has shown great promise in the field of medicine, with potential applications ranging from diagnosis and treatment and personalized medicine. However, there are several limits and future directions that must be considered.

First, it is essential to integrate AI with new technologies in an easy and user-friendly way to ensure widespread adoption. If users do not know how AI works, the stronger the concerns, the higher the perceptions of risk, and the lower the benefits associated with using AI will also be.[65] It is fundamental to better integrate individuals' knowledge about AI and its uses in clinical practice to improve the doctor-patient relationship so that perceptions of risk associated with the use of this technology can be diminished and they can enjoy its benefits.[65]

A key aspect of the use of AI in medicine is the importance of the doctor-patient relationship.[6] While AI tools can provide valuable insights and support clinical decision-making, the human touch and communication between doctors and patients remain critical for effective care. Patients must feel involved and trusty in the AI-powered tool to accept their diagnosis, express their preferences, and be engaged in decision-making about their health,[66,67] and this is where the relationship between doctors and patients comes into play. Patients need to be able to trust their doctors, and part of that trust comes from being able to understand the rationale behind diagnoses and treatment plans.[68] Clinical decision-making may become hindered or postponed if the recommendations provided by artificial entities are challenging to clarify or comprehend to patients.[69] Interestingly, a recent scoping review described possible applications of AI in terms of an instrument to support and enhance compassion in the medical practice by supporting communication and awareness of suffering.[70]

To engage patients in the informed use of AI, it might be considered to disseminate explanatory videos on the use of AI in medicine, illustrating how it works and what the possible advantages and limitations of this technology are. The use of information videos on medical procedures already proved to enhance patients' satisfaction and information gain.[71] Another solution might be the creation of interactive websites dedicated to the AI topic, where patients can find information about AI applications in the healthcare setting and at need ask questions and receive answers from physicians involved in the use of this technology. In addition, to achieve widespread adoption of artificial intelligence, AI systems must be regulated by the relevant authorities and used in synergy with traditional techniques.[1]

Reducing disparities in accessing internet information on AI and explanations of AI and technological devices might be a further step to ensure that everyone can benefit from AI advancements, regardless of sociodemographic or economic status. It has been shown, for instance, that older adults usually face barriers in online searching information behavior and that current intervention still has opportunities to improve.[72] Significant steps would be, for example, the development of tailored platforms and information aids for the elderly.[72]

The explainability of the outputs is another crucial aspect for building trust and ensuring that physicians can confidently rely on AI recommendations. AI models can be difficult to explain, and this can lead to a lack of transparency and trust in AI. The concept of explainable artificial intelligence (XAI) is thus essential, and a recent work described how AI should address the following aims to be understandable for clinical users: (1) Understandability, (2) Clinical relevance, (3) Truthfulness, (4) Informative plausibility, and (5) Computational efficiency.[73]

Barriers and facilitators of both patients and doctors who are going to interact with AI must be explicitly considered when integrating AI with other technologies.

Specifically, it should be taken into consideration the presence of psycho-social variables that might shape the interaction between the person and the AI and related technologies. The presence of online communities on the topic and the possibility of real-time interaction are, for example, factors that facilitate the exploration of technologies and information-seeking behaviors.[74] Age, gender, socioeconomic status as well as health literacy[74] might be other factors to be considered when developing health interventions integrating AI with other technologies.

Overall, while there are certainly limits to what AI can currently do, there are also many exciting future directions for AI research. As AI continues to evolve, it has the potential to transform many aspects of our lives, from the way we work to the way we interact with technology.

Acknowledgments

S.F.M.P. and I.D. were supported by Fondazione Umberto Veronesi. M.S. is a PhD student within the European School of Molecular Medicine (SEMM).

References

1. Davenport T, Kalakota R. The potential for artificial intelligence in healthcare. *Future Healthcare J.* 2019;6(2):94–98. https://doi.org/10.7861/futurehosp.6-2-94.
2. Hamet P, Tremblay J. Artificial intelligence in medicine. *Metabolism: Clin Exp.* 2017;69S:S36–S40. https://doi.org/10.1016/j.metabol.2017.01.011.
3. Jiang F, Jiang Y, Zhi H, et al. Artificial intelligence in healthcare: past, present and future. *Stroke Vascular Neurol.* 2017;2(4):230–243. https://doi.org/10.1136/svn-2017-000101.
4. Somashekhar SP, Sepúlveda MJ, Puglielli S, et al. Watson for oncology and breast cancer treatment recommendations: agreement with an expert multidisciplinary tumor board. *Ann Oncol.* 2018;29(2):418–423. https://doi.org/10.1093/annonc/mdx781.
5. Triberti S, Durosini I, La Torre D, Sebri V, Savioni L, Pravettoni G. Artificial intelligence in healthcare practice: how to tackle the "human" challenge. In: *Handbook of artificial intelligence in healthcare: Vol 2: Practicalities and Prospects*; 2022:43–60.
6. Triberti S, Durosini I, Lin J, La Torre D, Ruiz Galán M. Editorial: on the "human" in human-artificial intelligence interaction. *Front Psychol.* 2021;12, 808995. https://doi.org/10.3389/fpsyg.2021.808995.
7. Jie Z, Zhiying Z, Li L. A meta-analysis of Watson for oncology in clinical application. *Sci Rep.* 2021;11:5792. https://doi.org/10.1038/s41598-021-84973-5.
8. Pesapane F, Codari M, Sardanelli F. Artificial intelligence in medical imaging: threat or opportunity? Radiologists again at the forefront of innovation in medicine. *Eur Radiol Exp.* 2018;2(1):35. https://doi.org/10.1186/s41747-018-0061-6.
9. Durosini I, Savioni L, Triberti S, Guiddi P, Pravettoni G. The motivation journey: A grounded theory study on female Cancer Survivors' experience of a psychological intervention for quality of life. *Int J Environ Res Public Health.* 2021;18(3):950. https://doi.org/10.3390/ijerph18030950.
10. Durosini I, Triberti S, Savioni L, Pravettoni G. In the eye of a quiet storm: A critical incident study on the quarantine experience during the coronavirus pandemic. *PloS One.* 2021;16(2), e0247121.

11. Durosini I, Triberti S, Savioni L, Sebri V, Pravettoni G. The role of emotion- related abilities in the quality of life of breast cancer survivors: a systematic review. *Int J Environ Res Public Health.* 2022;19(19):12704.

12. Sanchez-Vives MV, Slater M. From presence to consciousness through virtual reality. *Nat Rev Neurosci.* 2005;6(4):332–339. https://doi.org/10.1038/nrn1651.

13. Riva G. Virtual reality in clinical psychology. *Comprehen Clin Psychol.* 2022;91.

14. Riva G, Malighetti C, Serino S. Virtual reality in the treatment of eating disorders. *Clin Psychol Psychother.* 2021;28(3):477–488. https://doi.org/10.1002/cpp.2622.

15. Silén Y, Keski-Rahkonen A. Worldwide prevalence of DSM-5 eating disorders among young people. *Curr Opin Psychiatry.* 2022;35(6):362–371. https://doi.org/10.1097/YCO.0000000000000818.

16. American Psychiatric Association. Diagnostic and Statistical Manual of Mental Disorders. 5th ed. Washington, DC: American Psychiatric Publishing; 2013.

17. Clus D, Larsen ME, Lemey C, Berrouiguet S. The use of virtual reality in patients with eating disorders: systematic review. *J Med Internet Res.* 2018;20(4), e157. https://doi.org/10.2196/jmir.7898.

18. Brizzi G, Sansoni M, Riva G. The BODY-FRIEND project: using new technology to learn about how people with anorexia feel about their bodies. *Cyberpsychol Behav Soc Netw.* 2023;26(2):141–143. https://doi.org/10.1089/cyber.2023.29267.

19. Baños RM, Espinoza M, García-Palacios A, et al. A positive psychological intervention using virtual reality for patients with advanced cancer in a hospital setting: a pilot study to assess feasibility. *Support Care Cancer.* 2013;21:263–270.

20. Cordova MJ, Riba MB, Spiegel D. Post-traumatic stress disorder and cancer. *Lancet Psychiatry.* 2017;4(4):330–338. https://doi.org/10.1016/S2215-0366(17)30014-7.

21. Kothgassner OD, Goreis A, Kafka JX, Van Eickels RL, Plener PL, Felnhofer A. Virtual reality exposure therapy for posttraumatic stress disorder (PTSD): a meta-analysis. *Eur J Psychotraumatol.* 2019;10(1):1654782. https://doi.org/10.1080/20008198.2019.1654782.

22. Freeman D, Reeve S, Robinson A, et al. Virtual reality in the assessment, understanding, and treatment of mental health disorders. *Psychol Med.* 2017;47(14):2393–2400. https://doi.org/10.1017/S003329171700040.

23. Oliveira J, Gamito P, Souto T, et al. Virtual reality-based cognitive stimulation on people with mild to moderate dementia due to Alzheimer's disease: A pilot randomized controlled trial. *Int J Environ Res Public Health.* 2021;18(10):5290. https://doi.org/10.3390/ijerph1810529.

24. Pizzoli SFM, Marzorati C, Mazzoni D, Pravettoni G. Web-based relaxation intervention for stress during social isolation: randomized controlled trial. *JMIR Ment Health.* 2020;7(12), e22757. https://doi.org/10.2196/22757.

25. Pizzoli SFM, Marzorati C, Mazzoni D, Pravettoni G. An Internet-based intervention to alleviate stress during social isolation with guided relaxation and meditation: protocol for a randomized controlled trial. *JMIR Res Protoc.* 2020;9(6), e19236. https://doi.org/10.2196/19236. 32530814. PMCID: PMC7301689.

26. Pizzoli SFM, Triberti S, Monzani D, et al. Comparison of relaxation techniques in virtual reality for breast cancer patients. In: Cardoso A, Restivo MT, eds. *Proceedings of the 2019 5th Experiment at International Conference, exp.at 2019.* Institute of Electrical and Electronics Engineers Inc.; 2019:348–351. https://doi.org/10.1109/EXPAT.2019.8876542.

27. Rousseaux F, Faymonville ME, Nyssen AS, et al. Can hypnosis and virtual reality reduce anxiety, pain and fatigue among patients who undergo cardiac surgery: a randomised controlled trial. *Trials.* 2020;21(1):330. https://doi.org/10.1186/s13063-020-4222-6.

28. van Gelderen MJ, Nijdam MJ, Haagen JFG, Vermetten E. Interactive motion-assisted exposure therapy for veterans with treatment-resistant posttraumatic stress disorder: a randomized controlled trial. *Psychother Psychosom.* 2020;89(4):215–227. https://doi.org/10.1159/000505977.

29. LeCun Y, Bengio Y, Hinton G. Deep learning. *Nature.* 2015;521(7553):436–444. https://doi.org/10.1038/nature14539.

30. Wang M, Lyu XQ, Li YJ, et al. VR content creation and exploration with deep learning: A survey. *Comp Visual Media.* 2020;6:3–28. https://doi.org/10.1007/s41095-020-0162-z.

31. Lin Q. Application and development of virtual reality technology in artificial intelligence deep learning. *IOP Conf Ser: Mater Sci Eng.* 2020. https://doi.org/10.1088/1757-899X/740/1/012151.

32. Horesh D, Kohavi S, Shilony-Nalaboff L, et al. Virtual reality combined with artificial intelligence (VR- AI) reduces hot flashes and improves psychological well-being in women with breast and ovarian Cancer: A pilot study. *Healthcare (Basel, Switzerland).* 2022;10(11):2261. https://doi.org/10.3390/healthcare10112261.

33. Hunter MS, Coventry S, Hamed H, Fentiman I, Grunfeld EA. Evaluation of a group cognitive behavioural intervention for women suffering from menopausal symptoms following breast cancer treatment. *Psychooncology.* 2009;18(5):560–563. https://doi.org/10.1002/pon.1414.

34. Skalidis, I., Muller, O., & Fournier, S. (2022). CardioVerse: the cardiovascular medicine in the era of Metaverse. Trends Cardiovasc Med, S1050-1738(22)00071–8. Advance online publication. doi:https://doi.org/10.1016/j.tcm.2022.05.004.

35. Wang G, Badal A, Jia X, et al. Development of metaverse for intelligent healthcare. *Nature Mach Intelligence.* 2022;4:922–929. https://doi.org/10.1038/s42256-022-00549-6.

36. Koo H. Training in lung cancer surgery through the metaverse, including extended reality, in the smart operating room of Seoul National University Bundang hospital, Korea. *J Educ Eval Health Prof.* 2021;18:33. https://doi.org/10.3352/jeehp.2021.18.33.

37. Zaid MB, Dilallo M, Shau D, Ward DT. Virtual reality as a learning tool for trainees in unicompartmental knee arthroplasty: a randomized controlled trial. *J Am Acad Orthop Surg.* 2022;30(2):84–90. https://doi.org/10.5435/JAAOS-D-20-01357.

38. Jovanović A, Milosavljević A. Vortex Metaverse platform for gamified collaborative learning. *Electronics.* 2022;11(3):317. https://doi.org/10.3390/electronics11030317.

39. Jimenez YA, Cumming S, Wang W, Stuart K, Thwaites DI, Lewis SJ. Patient education using virtual reality increases knowledge and positive experience for breast cancer patients undergoing radiation therapy. *Support Care Cancer.* 2018;26(8):2879–2888. https://doi.org/10.1007/s00520-018-4114-4.

40. Tay JL, Xie H, Sim K. Effectiveness of augmented and virtual reality-based interventions in improving knowledge, attitudes, empathy and stigma regarding people with mental illnesses—A scoping review. *J Person Med.* 2023;13(1):112. https://doi.org/10.3390/jpm13010112.

41. Vosburg RW, Seitz C. Increasing support group attendance for metabolic and bariatric surgery patients with online groups. *Clin Obesity.* 2022;12 (3), e12517. https://doi.org/10.1111/cob.12517.

42. Torous J, Kiang MV, Lorme J, Onnela JP. New tools for new research in psychiatry: A scalable and customizable platform to empower data driven smartphone research. *JMIR Mental Health.* 2016;3(2), e5165. https://doi.org/10.2196/mental.5165.

43. Montag C, Elhai JD. A new agenda for personality psychology in the digital age? *Personal Individ Differ.* 2019;147:128–134. https://doi.org/10.1016/j.paid.2019.03.045.

44. Maatoug R, Oudin A, Adrien V, et al. Digital phenotype of mood disorders: a conceptual and critical review. *Front Psych.* 2022;13, 895860. https://doi.org/10.3389/fpsyt.2022.895860.

45. Skinner AL, Attwood AS, Baddeley R, Evans-Reeves K, Bauld L, Munafò MR. Digital phenotyping and the development and delivery of health guidelines and behaviour change interventions. *Addiction.* 2017;112(7):1281–1285. https://doi.org/10.1111/ADD.13746.

46. Onnela JP. Opportunities and challenges in the collection and analysis of digital phenotyping data. *Neuropsychopharmacology.* 2021;46(1):45–54. https://doi.org/10.1038/S41386-020-0771-3.

47. Sequeira L, Battaglia M, Perrotta S, Merikangas K, Strauss J. Digital phenotyping with Mobile and wearable devices: advanced symptom measurement in child and adolescent depression. *J Am Acad Child Adolesc Psychiatry.* 2019;58(9):841–845. https://doi.org/10.1016/J.JAAC.2019.04.011.

48. Birk RH, Samuel G. Digital phenotyping for mental health: reviewing the challenges of using data to monitor and predict mental health problems. *Curr Psychiatry Rep.* 2022;24(10):523–528. https://doi.org/10.1007/S11920-022-01358-9.

49. Barrigon ML, Courtet P, Oquendo M, Baca-García E. Precision medicine and suicide: an opportunity for digital health. *Curr Psychiatry Rep.* 2019;21(12). https://doi.org/10.1007/S11920-019-1119-8.

50. Smith MT, McCrae CS, Cheung J, et al. Use of Actigraphy for the evaluation of sleep disorders and circadian rhythm sleep-wake disorders: an American Academy of sleep medicine systematic review, Meta-Analysis, and GRADE assessment. *J Clin Sleep Med.* 2018;14(7):1209. https://doi.org/10.5664/JCSM.7228.

51. Ballard ED, Gilbert JR, Wusinich C, Zarate Jr CA. New methods for assessing rapid changes in suicide risk. *Front Psych.* 2021;12, 598434. https://doi.org/10.3389/fpsyt.2021.598434.

52. Littlewood DL, Kyle SD, Carter LA, Peters S, Pratt D, Gooding P. Short sleep duration and poor sleep quality predict next-day suicidal ideation: an ecological momentary assessment study. *Psychol Med.* 2019;49(3):403–411. https://doi.org/10.1017/S0033291718001009.

53. Patel SK, Torous J. Exploring the neuropsychiatric sequelae of perceived COVID-19 exposure in college students: A pilot digital phenotyping study. *Front Psych.* 2022;12, 788926. https://doi.org/10.3389/fpsyt.2021.788926.

54. Melcher J, Lavoie J, Hays R, et al. Digital phenotyping of student mental health during COVID-19: an observational study of 100 college students. *J Am Coll Health.* 2021;1–13. https://doi.org/10.1080/07448481.2021.1905650.

55. Franke RH, Kaul JD. The Hawthorne experiments: first statistical interpretation. *Am Sociol Rev.* 1978;43(5):623. https://doi.org/10.2307/2094540.

56. Marr B. The amazing ways Babylon health is using artificial intelligence to make healthcare universally accessible. In: *Forbes;* 2021. Retrieved from https://www.forbes.com/sites/bernardmarr/2021/06/28/the-amazing-ways-babylon-health-is-using-artificial-intelligence-to-make-healthcare-universally-accessible.

57. Nguyen TL, Do TTH. Artificial intelligence in healthcare: A new technology benefit for both patients and doctors. In: *2019 Portland International Conference on Management of Engineering and Technology (PICMET), Portland, OR, USA;* 2019:1–15. https://doi.org/10.23919/PICMET.2019.8893884.

58. Locke S, Bashall A, Al-Adely S, Moore J, Wilson A, Kitchen GB. Natural language processing in medicine: a review. *Trends in Anaesthesia Crit Care.* 2021. https://doi.org/10.1016/j.tacc.2021.02.007.

59. Nam JG, Park S, Hwang EJ, et al. Development and validation of deep learning-based automatic detection algorithm for malignant pulmonary nodules on chest radiographs. *Radiology.* 2019;290(1):218–228. https://doi.org/10.1148/radiol.2018180237.

60. O'Sullivan J, Muntinga T, Grigg S, Ioannidis J. Prevalence and outcomes of incidental imaging findings: umbrella review. *BMJ.* 2018;361. https://doi.org/10.1136/bmj.k2387.

61. SkinVision (2023). https://www.skinvision.com/.

62. de Carvalho TM, Noels E, Wakkee M, Udrea A, Nijsten T. Development of smartphone apps for skin Cancer risk assessment: Progress and promise. *JMIR Dermatol.* 2019;2(1), e13376. https://doi.org/10.2196/13376.

63. Stokel-Walker C. ChatGPT listed as author on research papers: many scientists disapprove. *Nature.* 2023;613(7945):620–621. https://doi.org/10.1038/d41586-023-00107-z.

64. Gaggioli A. Ethics: disclose use of AI in scientific manuscripts. *Nature.* 2023;614(7948):413.

65. Esmaeilzadeh P. Use of AI-based tools for healthcare purposes: a survey study from consumers' perspectives. *BMC Med Inform Decis Mak.* 2020;20 (1):170. https://doi.org/10.1186/s12911-020-01191-1.

66. Monzani D, Vergani L, Pizzoli SFM, et al. Sexism interacts with patient-physician gender concordance in influencing patient control preferences: findings from a vignette experimental design (2020). *Appl Psychol Health Well Being.* 2020;12(2):471–492. https://doi.org/10.1111/aphw.12193.

67. Monzani D, Vergani L, Marton G, Pizzoli SF, Pravettoni G. When in doubt, Google it: distress-related information seeking in Italy during the COVID-19 pandemic. *BMC Public Health.* 2021;21:1–10.

68. Alexandra D, et al. The use of artificial intelligence (AI) in the radiology field: what is the state of doctor-patient communication in cancer diagnosis? *Cancers.* 2023;15(2). https://doi.org/10.3390/cancers15020470.

69. La Torre D, Colapinto C, Durosini I, Triberti S. Team formation for human-artificial intelligence collaboration in the workplace: A goal programming model to Foster organizational change. *IEEE Trans Eng Manage.* 2021. https://doi.org/10.1109/TEM.2021.3077195. Advance online publication.

70. Morrow E, Zidaru T, Ross F, et al. Artificial intelligence technologies and compassion in healthcare: A systematic scoping review. *Front Psychol.* 2023;13, 971044. https://doi.org/10.3389/fpsyg.2022.971044.

71. Snyder-Ramos SA, Seintsch H, Böttiger BW, Motsch J, Martin E, Bauer M. Patient satisfaction and information gain after the preanesthetic visit: a comparison of face-to-face interview, brochure, and video. *Anesth Analg.* 2005;100(6):1753–1758. https://doi.org/10.1213/01. ANE.0000153010.49776.E5.

72. Zhao YC, Zhao M, Song S. Online health information seeking behaviors among older adults: systematic scoping review. *J Med Internet Res.* 2022;24(2). https://doi.org/10.2196/34790.

73. Jin W, Li X, Fatehi M, Hamarneh G. Guidelines and evaluation of clinical explainable AI in medical image analysis. *Med Image Anal.* 2023;84, 102684. https://doi.org/10.1016/j.media.2022.102684.

74. Jia X, Pang Y, Liu LS. Online health information seeking behavior: A systematic review. *Healthcare (Basel, Switzerland).* 2021;9(12):1740. https://doi.org/10.3390/healthcare9121740.

6

The dual path of the technology acceptance model: An application of machine learning cardiotocography in delivery rooms

Davide Mazzoni[a], Martina Maria Pagin[b], Roberta Amadori[b], Daniela Surico[b,c], Stefano Triberti[d], Carmen Imma Aquino[b,c], and Gabriella Pravettoni[a,e]

[a]Department of Oncology and Hematology-Oncology (DIPO), University of Milan, Milan, Italy [b]Department of Gynaecology and Obstetrics, Ospedale Maggiore della Carità, Novara, Italy [c]Department of Translational Medicine, University of Piemonte Orientale, Novara, Italy [d]Faculty of Human Sciences, Università Telematica Pegaso, Naples, Italy [e]Applied Research Division for Cognitive and Psychological Science, European Institute of Oncology (IEO), IRCCS, Milan, Italy

1. Introduction

The evaluation of fetal well-being during labor is one of the crucial points for the care of women and infants' health. In this regard, cardiotocography (CTG) is a technique for monitoring fetal heartbeat and uterine contractions during pregnancy and labor. CTG is nowadays widely used for assessing fetal well-being, with the aim to reduce the risk of unnecessary and invasive obstetric interventions and to improve maternal-fetal outcomes.[1,2] Despite the international guidelines for its use and interpretation, some issues are still debated, and a uniform approach for defining terminology, classifying characters, and similar interpretation of results is still needed.[3]

One of the main issues due to the use of this technology is related to the interobserver and intraobserver variability in its interpretation.[4,5] More specifically, the differences in the identification and classification of decelerations, that is, the evaluation of variability and the classification of CTG as suspect/pathological, are a long-known issue.[6,7] In this regard, the American College of Obstetricians and Gynecologists (ACOG)[8] guidelines show the highest interobserver agreement for category II tracings and the lowest interobserver agreement for category I and III tracings.

Another issue is represented by the many types of classifications available in the literature. The aim of a recent study[9] was to compare interobserver agreement, reliability, and accuracy of CTG analysis when performed according to the International Federation of Gynecology and Obstetrics (FIGO) (2015), ACOG (2009), and United Kingdom National Institute for Health and Care Excellence – NICE (2014) guidelines.[10,11] The results showed that the interobserver agreement was not strongly affected by clinicians' years of practice, and the quality (e.g., degree of reliability, sensitivity, and specificity) in the prediction of acidemia also depended on the adopted guideline. In the study by Bhatia et al.,[12] the percentage of agreement was identical across the three systems for both normal cardiotocography results and for intermediate or ambiguous data. However, the interobserver agreement of cardiotocography classification appeared to be suboptimal.[12] These results suggest that, if CTG is an integral part of intrapartum care, some limitations due to the modest interobserver agreement partially reduce its usefulness and efficacy in clinical practice. Such variability in the interpretations could be an important source of mistakes or misunderstandings in the consequent decision-making process.

Artificial Intelligence for Medicine
https://doi.org/10.1016/B978-0-443-13671-9.00002-8

In the last two decades, several authors have suggested that the use of additional high-tech advances, such as remote computer-analyzed technologies and Artificial Intelligence, may partially overcome these limits, thus minimizing the most severe outcomes. For example, some research groups developed computerized systems to support the CTG interpretation and the subsequent decision-making in labor.[13] At the beginning of this millennium, a working group from Plymouth University developed a computerized decision support system for the management of childbirth.[13] This software extracted data from CTG and clinical history, analyzed these data to interpret the CTG in the unique single context of that woman in labor, and offered recommendations for the management of labor. K2 Medical Systems, a spin-off company from the working group of the Plymouth University, has developed a data system collection (called 'Guardian') to manage the information from the monitored labors. This system does not interpret the collected data but acts as an interface to collect, organize, and display data from multiple sources. A specific system has also been developed to extract data such as baseline rate, variability, accelerations, decelerations, quality signal, and contractions. From the analysis of these characteristics, the software could show advice using a color-based system. This software could be used as clinical decision support and as a tool for the clinical Audit. The validation studies[14–16] demonstrated that the software's performance was similar to an expert obstetrician and sometimes better than the usual practical clinic.

Another study by Brocklehurst and colleagues[17] was based on the application of a decision-support system in labor. They found no difference in the incidence of poor neonatal outcomes, such as neonatal encephalopathy and admission to the neonatal unit, comparing the decision-support group with the no-decision-support group. Finally, a recent systematic review[18] had the objective to evaluate whether intrapartum cardiotocography with computer analysis decreased the incidence of newborn metabolic acidosis or obstetric intervention when compared with visual analysis. The use of computer analysis of fetal monitoring signals during labor did not significantly reduce the rate of metabolic acidosis or obstetric intervention.

2. The development of artificial intelligence tools for interpreting CTG

Artificial Intelligence (AI) is spreading in clinical practice. It can be viewed both as a discipline and a technology. As a new discipline, in the last few years it has supplied a large contribution to the progress in many disciplines, such as philosophy, mathematics, psychology, cybernetic, and cognitive science. As a technology, one of its distinctive features is the ability to analyze large quantities of data and find recurring models that the human mind cannot evaluate.[19] AI could be a good tool to support doctors in daily practice, i.e., the Watson for Oncology by IBM used for the oncologic diagnosis and therapy. The possible applications of AI in medicine are potentially unlimited. It is possible to resume many of them within a general categorization including AI to support medical diagnosis or identification of personalized treatment; AI to improve patient engagement; and AI to empower health organizations' structure and management.[20] Among those, there is also the area of Obstetricians and Gynaecology, as evidenced by Desai's study.[21] AI could be used for the diagnosis of preterm labor, ovarian cancer, medically assisted procreation, and to interpret CTGs.[22]

The past "experience" is crucial in guiding the CTG interpretation and deep learning systems enable computers to observe and learn from patterns. In this sense, it is hoped that deep learning approaches could lead to an improvement of CTG interpretation, thus lowering the rate of unnecessary medical interventions.[23]

To support these ideas, some works focused on the development of an appropriate technology to interpret CTG in labor. In a 2019 study by Iraji,[24] different approaches based on AI have been compared to predict fetal well-being. In the same year, Zhao[25] presented an 8-layer convolutional neural network to predict fetal acidemia through the analysis of fetal heart rate (FHR), and results were promising. Finally, none of the techniques now available were demonstrated to be absolutely better than the others in evaluating FHR: a combined approach appeared to be more promising.[26]

A recent literature review by Aeberhard et al.[27] summarized 40 different studies investigating at least one algorithm or system to classify CTG tracings. The authors conclude that several promising approaches exist in this area, but none of them has gained significant acceptance in clinical practice. Further investigation and refinement of the algorithms and features are needed to achieve a validated decision-support system.

3. The professionals' acceptance of AI technologies

Although many researchers have been creating the best technique to interpret CTG, very few things are known about the opinion of the clinicians. However, a very common obstacle is represented by the acceptance of technologies in the practical clinic.[19] Acceptance is considered one of the essential conditions for the introduction and the success of a technology, as in the healthcare system. Furthermore, the study of acceptance of AI has been identified as one of the main areas for the research and policy-making about AI implementation, especially in health care.[28] Indeed, human attitudes and behavior could generate organizational and practical issues independently of the actual effectiveness of a given technology and ultimately could affect the usage of the technology in the long run or eventually its abandonment.

Even if there doesn't exist a unanimous agreement about the definition of acceptance, some authors define it as a phenomenon that reflects the point until which the potential users are ready to use a particular system.[29] The Technology Acceptance Model (TAM) represents one of the most validated principal theoretical models and has been introduced in the 80s by Fred Davis[30] to predict the acceptance or the refusal of a new technology. It is an adaptation of the "Theory of reasoned action," developed by Fishbein and Ajzen in 1975[31,32] and the "Theory of planned behaviour" (TPB)[33,52] that explains and predicts the behavior of people in a specific situation. The TAM[30] presumes that the most important predictors of the behavioral intention to use a technology (Intention-to-use; INT) are as follows:

- Perceived Utility (PU) defined as the degree to which a person believes that using a particular system would enhance his or her job performance;
- Perceived Ease of Use (PEU) defined as the degree to which a person believes that using a particular system would be free of effort.

TAM is one of the most powerful and solid models to predict the acceptance of technology using the perceived utility and the ease-of-use predictors. TAM has been efficaciously applied to a number of technologies in a wide range of sectors,[34–36] including various technologies to be employed in the health sector.[37–39] However, to our knowledge, it has never been applied to the intention to use an AI tool in delivery rooms. Moreover, we must consider that different extended versions of the TAM exist, and different factors have been proposed to integrate the core model in different contexts. Indeed, there could be some variables (not included in the original model) related to the human and social changing process that could influence the acceptance of technology.[38,40] In this regard, we suggest that at least two factors could play an important role in the acceptance and usage of an AI tool for CTG.

The first one has to do with the *responsibility* that the professionals perceive about the possibility of errors during childbirth. Responsibility involves both worries about caused damages and possible omissions.[41] In this sense, professionals could be more willing to use the tool because they will see the usefulness of reducing their sense of responsibility for possible negative outcomes. In other words, perceived responsibility could have a positive effect on the intention to use the tool, increasing the perceived meaning and usefulness that is attributed to the tool itself.

The second one has to do with the sense of self-efficacy, which could have an impact on the perceived easiness of the tool. Indeed, according to the TPB,[33] a person would be as likely to perform a given behavior as much that behavior is controllable. Such controllability does not depend only on the features of the tool but also on what the professional thinks about his/her own capacity to face problems in general. It is thus possible that a general sense of efficacy would predict the intention to use the tool through the perceived easiness.

In summary, at the root of the TAM in the context of delivery rooms, we hypothesize the existence of two paths: an instrumental one based on self-efficacy and ease of use; a second one, based on the sense of responsibility and utility.

4. Aims and hypotheses

The aim of this study was to investigate the factors associated with the acceptance of an AI-based tool aimed at interpreting the CTG by a group of midwives.

More specifically, according to the TAM model, we hypothesized that the perceived usefulness (H1) and the easiness of use (H2) would predict the intention to use the tool.

Moreover, in line with the above-mentioned literature, we hypothesized that personal responsibility (H3) and self-efficacy at work (H4) would be associated with the intention to use the tool.

Finally, we wanted to move a step further, testing a model in which the effect of personal responsibility on behavioral intention was mediated by the perceived usefulness (H5), and the effect of self-efficacy was be mediated by the easiness of use (H6) (see Fig. 1).

5. Methods

The study questionnaire was administered through the Qualtrics platform for data collection. The invitation to take part in the study with the link to the informed consent was delivered through professional associations and their social

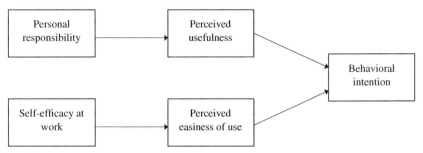

FIG. 1   The hypothesized model.

network pages. After completing the informed consent, the participants filled in the questionnaire. All the answers were registered anonymously. The questionnaire completion lasted around 15 min. The study protocol was approved by the Ethical Committee of the University of Milan. The questionnaire covered the following variables:

- Age, years of professional activity, and sex were assessed through single items;
- *Personal responsibility* was assessed through the 17 items of the Responsibility scales of the Obsessive Beliefs Questionnaire[42]) in the Italian translation by Dorz et al.[41] These items focused on the perceived responsibility that the professional usually attributes to himself/herself both for caused damages and for possible omissions. Examples of items were "I should make sure others are protected from any negative consequences of my decisions or actions" and "For me, not preventing harm is as bad as causing harm". The internal consistency of the scale was acceptable ($\alpha = .87$), and a mean index was used in the analyses.
- *Self-efficacy at work* was assessed with an adaptation of the 10-item General Self-Efficacy Scale[43] to the working contexts, in the Italian translation by Sibilia et al.[44] An example of the item was "At work, I can always manage to solve difficult problems if I try hard enough". The internal consistency of the scale was acceptable ($\alpha = .93$), and a mean index was used in the analyses.

5.1 The TAM variables

The items of the TAM variables (perceived usefulness, easiness of use, behavioral intention to use) were adapted from the original model by Davis.[45,46]

Participants were asked to read a brief text, presenting the essential characteristics of the AI tool and then to answers to the items assessing the TAM variables. The AI tool was described as a system that, after being adequately trained through many traces associated with neonatal outcomes, would be able to evaluate the prelabor risk factors and the CTG trace in progress, providing indications to the professional on the most appropriate to undertake: "Waiting behavior," in the case of a normal CTG; "Reevaluation" in the case of suspicious CTG; "Immediate intervention" in the case of pathological CTG.

Perceived usefulness was assessed through four items. An example of item was "I would find the AI system supporting CTG reading helpful in my work." The internal consistency of the scale was acceptable ($\alpha = .88$), and a mean index was used in the analyses.

Perceived easiness of use was assessed through four items. An example of item was "I would find it easy to use the AI system supporting CTG reading." The internal consistency of the scale was acceptable ($\alpha = .92$), and a mean index was used in the analyses.

Finally, the behavioral intention to use the tool was assessed through a single item, referring to the above-described AI tool: "I would use it regularly in my job." For all the psychological variables (responsibility, self-efficacy, perceived usefulness, easiness of use, behavioral intention to use) the possible answers ranged from 1 (strongly disagree) to 7 (strongly agree).

5.2 Analyses

In order to test our hypotheses, the analyses followed different steps. First, descriptive statistics and correlations between the key variables were calculated. Second, to test our main predictions (H1–H2 and H3–H4), two linear regressions were performed. After checking for acceptable values of the multicollinearity (tolerance, VIF), in the first model, the behavioral intention to use the AI tool was inserted as the dependent variable, while perceived usefulness and perceived ease of use were inserted as predictors (consistently with the core of the TAM model). In the second model, also personal responsibility and self-efficacy at work were inserted as predictors.

Third, in order to test the last group of hypotheses (H5 and H6), a mediation model was tested through the macro PROCESS,[47] and 10,000 bootstrap resamples were used to generate bias-corrected bootstrap 95% confidence intervals for indirect effects. In our model, personal responsibility and self-efficacy were inserted as independent (exogenous) variables. PROCESS allows testing one independent variable at a time. In the first model, personal responsibility was inserted as an independent variable and self-efficacy as a covariate. In the second one, self-efficacy was inserted as an independent variable and personal responsibility as a covariate. The behavioral intention to use the tool was the dependent variable. Perceived usefulness and perceived ease of use were inserted as parallel mediators of the relationships between personal responsibility/self-efficacy and the intention to use the tool.

6. Results

The final sample consisted of 302 midwives. Almost all of them were females (301, 99.3%), while two participants preferred not to declare. The mean age of the respondents was 34.21 years (SD = 9.71), and they reported an average practice of 10.08 years (DS = 9.86). Descriptive statistics and correlations of the key variables are presented in Table 1. The results show that the behavioral intention to use the tool correlated with all the psychological variables. The normality of the distributions of all the variables was acceptable (skewness ranging from −0.34 to 0.08; kurtosis ranging from −0.76 to −0.19).

Table 2 presents the results of the linear regression analyses. Standardized coefficients (β) are reported and accompanied by the p values. The results showed acceptable levels of the variance inflation factor (VIF) that was equal to 1.29 for both variables in Model I and ranged from 1.05 to 1.40 in Model II. These results, together with the correlation coefficients (Table 1), suggest that multicollinearity was not a problem.

As shown in Table 2, our first group of hypotheses (H1, H2) was confirmed, with perceived usefulness and perceived easiness of use showing positive and significant effects on the behavioral intention to use the technology. The TAM main hypotheses were thus confirmed. However, when self-efficacy and responsibility were introduced in Model II, they did not show a significant effect on the intention to use the tool.

In order to test our final group of hypotheses, personal responsibility and self-efficacy were inserted as independent variables, while the behavioral intention to use the tool was the dependent variable. Perceived usefulness and perceived ease of use were inserted as mediators. The results showed that responsibility had a positive significant effect on perceived usefulness (β = .22; CI: .144, .446), and in less extent on perceived easiness (β = .14; CI: .043, .321). Self-efficacy showed a significant effect on perceived easiness (β = .28; CI: .226, .502) but not on usefulness (β = .09; CI: −.030, .269).

As hypothesized, the indirect effect of responsibility through usefulness was significant (β = .12; CI: .051, 190), and the indirect effect of self-efficacy through perceived easiness was significant (β = .05; CI: .055, 159). The indirect effect of self-efficacy through perceived usefulness was not significant (β = .05; CI: −.018, .114), while the indirect effect of responsibility through easiness of use was slightly significant (β = .05; CI: .008, .096).

TABLE 1 Descriptives and correlations of the key variables.

	Mean (standard deviation)	2.	3.	4.	5.
1. Personal responsibility	4.55 (.96)	.054 (p = .349)	.221 (p < −.001)	.156 (p = .007)	.237 (p < .001)
2. Self-efficacy at work	4.55 (.97)	–	.100 (p = .082)	.292 (p < .001)	.126 (p = .029)
3. Perceived usefulness	4.22 (1.31)		–	.473 (p < .001)	.737 (p < .001)
4. Perceived easiness of use	4.91 (1.24)			–	.625 (p < .001)
5. Behavioral intention to use the tool	4.17 (1.68)				–

Notes. All the variables were measured on a scale ranging from 1 to 7.

TABLE 2 Results of the linear regression.

	Model I	Model II
Personal responsibility		.059[a] $p = .094$
Self-efficacy at work		−.040 $p = .273$
Perceived usefulness	.569 $p < .001$	.556 $p < .001$
Perceived easiness of use	.356 $p < .001$	.365 $p < .001$
R^2	.642	.647
Adjusted R^2	.640	.642
F	(2, 300) 269.045; $p < .001$	(4, 298) 136.396; $p < .001$

[a] *Standardized coefficients are reported.*

7. Discussion

In this chapter, we presented the results of a study in which we investigated the psychological factors associated with the acceptance of an AI-based tool aimed at interpreting the CTG by a group of midwives. Some important results are worth to be discussed. First, we could notice that, on average, our respondents showed a positive attitude toward a similar tool. Indeed, the scores on all the TAM dimensions (usefulness, easiness of use, intention to use it) were slightly higher than the scale midpoint. Despite this tool is not currently available for the respondents, there is a strong rationale for its potential in reducing the issues connected with the interobserver and intraobserver variability in the interpretation of CTG and in the consequent decisions[27].

Second, our results confirmed the core of the TAM model.[30,4648] Perceived usefulness and easiness of use showed a significant and strong effect on behavioral intention. The two main predictors are able to explain a good proportion of variance. These results add to the previous literature on the TAM, extending the contexts in which the TAM can be fruitfully applied.

Typically, easiness of use, in particular, can be regarded as the more controversial of the two predictors[45,49]: it could lead to negative or ambiguous results, for example, when the technology is expected to play an important role in making decisions that rely on professionals' knowledge (i.e., professionals may feel that a user-friendly version of the technology is not "serious" enough). However, in this area, users seem to appreciate easiness of use, because it allows them to concentrate on the delicate clinical decisions they have to make.

Third, this study extended the TAM model, considering two variables, self-efficacy and responsibility, that appear particularly relevant in the context of delivery rooms. Self-efficacy at work showed a positive effect on the easiness of use, thus suggesting the existence of an *agency path*, in which the focus is on the perceived ability to face the work challenges in general, and the use of a new AI tool in particular. This resonates with the environmental control, which reflects perceptions of internal and external constraints on behavior.[33,50]

The perceived responsibility (for caused damages and for possible omissions) showed a significant effect on the perceived usefulness. This suggests the existence of a *meaning path*, according to which the importance of the tool has to do with its possibility to reduce the perceived responsibility of the midwives.

Some limitations must be recognized. First, due to the cross-sectional design, some cautions should be taken in the interpretation of any causal direction, and this is particularly true for mediation models. Future studies with longitudinal data will be able to solve this issue, at least partially. Second, our dependent variable is measured through a single item assessing the behavioral intention (i.e., the intention to use the tool) rather than the real behavior. Even if several other studies adopted this measure from the TAM, we believe that future studies assessing the current behavior will lead to conclusions that are more robust. Third, due to the sampling method, our result cannot be considered as representative of the midwives' population, because of selection biases. For example, it is possible that the respondents who voluntarily took part in the study were already interested in the topic.

Despite these limitations, our results have also some implications for clinical practice, providing some useful insights that could be part of midwives' education about CTG and their responsibilities during childbirth. A 2001 study[51] showed that, from the analysis of deliveries with babies born with low Apgar Score, in 74%, there was evidence of "substandard care" in labor. Implementing cyclical audit, monthly feedback meetings, and training sessions in cardiotocography, the percentage decreases to 23%. Implementing the ability to interpret CTGs could have a strong effect on neonatal conditions.

According to our results, in the midwives' education, it would be important to reflect on the potential impact of their perceived responsibility. Indeed, our results showed that also the midwives' perceived responsibility (besides the gynecologists' one) could have an impact on their attitudes toward a new AI technology to support the CTG interpretation.

This research constitutes an example of a preliminary analysis of acceptance of an AI-driven resource in a specific healthcare context by professionals, which is a fundamental step to take toward the fruitful implementation of such resources in medicine.[28] Future studies may employ methods focused on the actual implementation of similar technologies within the hospital, in order to capture important information about their actual effects on care management and effectiveness.

Acknowledgments

This work was partially supported by the Italian Ministry of Health with Ricerca Corrente and 5x1000 funds.

Conflict of interest disclosure

The authors have no conflict of interest to declare.

References

1. Al Wattar BH, Honess E, Bunnewell S, et al. Effectiveness of intrapartum fetal surveillance to improve maternal and neonatal outcomes: a systematic review and network meta-analysis. *CMAJ.* 2021;193(14):E468–E477. https://doi.org/10.1503/cmaj.202538.
2. Robertson L, Knight H, Prosser Snelling E, et al. Each baby counts: National quality improvement programme to reduce intrapartum-related deaths and brain injuries in term babies. *Semin Fetal Neonatal Med.* 2017;22(3):193–198. https://doi.org/10.1016/j.siny.2017.02.001.
3. Mohan M, Ramawat J, La Monica G, et al. Electronic intrapartum fetal monitoring: a systematic review of international clinical practice guidelines. *AJOG Global Reports.* 2021;1(2), 100008. https://doi.org/10.1016/j.xagr.2021.100008.
4. Amadori R, Aquino CI, Osella E, et al. The application of intrauterine resuscitation maneuvers in delivery room: actual and expected Use. *Midwifery.* 2022;107, 103279. https://doi.org/10.1016/j.midw.2022.103279.
5. Blackwell SC, Grobman WA, Antoniewicz L, Hutchinson M, Bannerman CG. Interobserver and intraobserver reliability of the NICHD 3-tier fetal heart rate interpretation system. *Am J Obstet Gynecol.* 2011;205(4):378–e1. https://doi.org/10.1016/j.ajog.2011.06.086.
6. Aquino CI, Vaianella E, Amadori R, et al. Ethnicity impact on fetal monitoring during labour. *Italian J Gynæcol Obstetr.* 2022;34(3):167–171. https://doi.org/10.36129/jog.2021.05.
7. Ayres-de-Campos D, Bernardes J, Costa-Pereira A, Pereira-Leite L. Inconsistencies in classification by experts of cardiotocograms and subsequent clinical decision. *Br J Obstet Gynaecol.* 1999;106(12):1307–1310. https://doi.org/10.1111/j.1471-0528.1999.tb08187.x.
8. American College of Obstetricians and Gynecologist. Practice Bulletin n. 106: Intrapartum fetal heart rate monitoring: nomenclature, interpretation, and general management principles. *Obstet Gynecol.* 2009;114(1):192–202. https://doi.org/10.1097/AOG.0b013e3181aef106.
9. Santo S, Ayres-de-Campos D, Costa-Santos C, et al. Agreement and accuracy using the FIGO, ACOG and NICE cardiotocography interpretation guidelines. *Acta Obstet Gynecol Scand.* 2017;96(2):166–175. https://doi.org/10.1111/aogs.13064.
10. National Collaborating Centre for Women's and Children's Health (UK). Intrapartum care: care of healthy women and their babies during childbirth; 2014.
11. Visser GH, Ayres-de-Campos D, FIGO Intrapartum Fetal Monitoring Expert Consensus Panel. FIGO consensus guidelines on intrapartum fetal monitoring: Adjunctive technologies. *Int J Gynaecol Obstet.* 2015;131(1):25–29. https://doi.org/10.1016/j.ijgo.2015.06.021.
12. Bhatia M, Mahtani KR, Nunan D, Reddy A. A cross-sectional comparison of three guidelines for intrapartum cardiotocography. *Int J Gynaecol Obstet.* 2017;138(1):89–93. https://doi.org/10.1002/ijgo.12161.
13. Harris M. An investigation of labour ward care to inform the design of a computerised decision support system for the management of childbirth; 2002. Doctoral dissertation, University of Plymouth.
14. Keith RD, Greene KR. 4 Development, evaluation and validation of an intelligent system for the management of labour. *Bailliere's Clin.* 1994.
15. Keith RD, Beckley S, Garibaldi JM, Westgate JA, Ifeachor EC, Greene KR. A ulticenter comparative study of 17 experts and an intelligent computer system for managing labour using the cardiotocogram. *BJOG.* 1995;102(9):688–700.
16. Skinner JF, Harris M, Greene KR. Computerised decision support for managing labour using the cardiotocogram: 500 cases with the range of abnormality. In: *Harrogate: 28th British Congress of Obstetrics and Gynaecology*; 1998, June.
17. Brocklehurst P, Field D, Greene K, et al. Computerised interpretation of fetal heart rate during labour (INFANT): a randomised controlled trial. *The Lancet.* 2017;389(10080):1719–1729. https://doi.org/10.1016/S0140-6736(17)30568-8.
18. Campanile M, D'Alessandro P, Della Corte L, et al. Intrapartum cardiotocography with and without computer analysis: a systematic review and meta-analysis of randomized controlled trials. *J Matern Fetal Neonatal Med.* 2020;33(13):2284–2290. https://doi.org/10.1080/14767058.2018.1542676.
19. Pravettoni G, Triberti S. Il medico 4.0: Come cambia la relazione medico-paziente nell'era delle nuove tecnologie. Edra; 2019.

20. Triberti S, Durosini I, Pravettoni G. A "third wheel" effect in health decision making involving artificial entities: a psychological perspective. *Front Public Health*. 2020;8:117. https://doi.org/10.3389/fpubh.2020.00117.

21. Desai GS. Artificial intelligence: the future of obstetrics and gynecology. *J Obstetr Gynecol India*. 2018;68(4):326–327. https://doi.org/10.1007/s13224-018-1118-4.

22. Emin EI, Emin E, Papalois A, Willmott F, Clarke S, Sideris M. Artificial intelligence in obstetrics and gynaecology: is this the way forward? *In Vivo*. 2019;33(5):1547–1551. https://doi.org/10.21873/invivo.11635.

23. Balayla J, Shrem G. Use of artificial intelligence (AI) in the interpretation of intrapartum fetal heart rate (FHR) tracings: a systematic review and meta-analysis. *Arch Gynecol Obstet*. 2019;300:7–14. https://doi.org/10.1007/s00404-019-05151-7.

24. Iraji MS. Prediction of fetal state from the cardiotocogram recordings using neural network models. *Artif Intell Med*. 2019;96:33–44. https://doi.org/10.1016/j.artmed.2019.03.005.

25. Zhao Z, Deng Y, Zhang Y, Zhang Y, Zhang X, Shao L. DeepFHR: intelligent prediction of fetal Acidemia using fetal heart rate signals based on convolutional neural network. *BMC Med Inform Decis Mak*. 2019;19(1):1–15. https://doi.org/10.1186/s12911-019-1007-5.

26. Ponsiglione AM, Cosentino C, Cesarelli G, Amato F, Romano M. A comprehensive review of techniques for processing and analyzing fetal heart rate signals. *Sensors*. 2021;21(18):6136. https://doi.org/10.3390/s21186136.

27. Aeberhard JL, Radan A-P, Delgado-Gonzalo R, et al. Artificial intelligence and machine learning in cardiotocography: a scoping review. *Eur J Obstet Gynecol Reprod Biol*. 2023;281:54–62. https://doi.org/10.1016/j.ejogrb.2022.12.008. PMID: 36535071.

28. Triberti S, Durosini I, Lin J, La Torre D, Ruiz Galán M. On the "Human" in human-artificial intelligence interaction. *Front Psychol*. 2021;12, 808995. https://doi.org/10.3389/fpsyg.2021.808995.

29. Ausserer K, Risser R. Intelligent transport systems and services-chances and risks. In: *ICTCT-Workshop*; 2005.

30. Davis FD. Perceived usefulness, perceived ease of use, and user acceptance of information technology. *MIS Q*. 1989;13:319–340. https://doi.org/10.2307/249008.

31. Ajzen I, Fishbein M. Attitude-behavior relations: a theoretical analysis and review of empirical research. *Psychol Bull*. 1977;84(5):888–918. https://doi.org/10.1037/0033-2909.84.5.888.

32. Fishbein M, Ajzen I. Belief, Attitude, Intention, and Behavior: An Introduction to Theory and Research. Reading, MA: Addison-Wesley; 1975.

33. Ajzen I. The theory of planned behavior. *Organ Behav Hum Decis Process*. 1991;50(2):179–211. https://doi.org/10.1016/0749-5978(91)90020-T.

34. Carissoli C, Di Natale AF, Caputo M, et al. Parental attitudes toward videogames at school. *Comput Schools*. 2019;36(3):188–204. https://doi.org/10.1080/07380569.2019.1643277.

35. Fussell SG, Truong D. Using virtual reality for dynamic learning: an extended technology acceptance model. *Virtual Reality*. 2022;26(1):249–267. https://doi.org/10.1080/10494820.2021.2009880.

36. Levy Y, Green BD. An empirical study of computer self-efficacy and the technology acceptance model in the military: A case of a US Navy combat information system. *J Organ End User Comput (JOEUC)*. 2009;21(3):1–23.

37. Gorini A, Mazzocco K, Triberti S, Sebri V, Savioni L, Pravettoni G. A P5 Approach to m-Health: design suggestions for advanced mobile health technology. *Front Psychol*. 2018;9:2066. https://doi.org/10.3389/fpsyg.2018.02066.

38. Holden RJ, Karsh BT. The technology acceptance model: its past and its future in health care. *J Biomed Inform*. 2010;43(1):159–172.

39. Strudwick G. Predicting nurses' use of healthcare technology using the technology acceptance model: an integrative review. CIN. *Comput Inform Nurs*. 2015;33(5):189–198. https://doi.org/10.1097/CIN.0000000000000142.

40. Legris P, Ingham J, Collerette P. Why do people use information technology? A critical review of the technology acceptance model. *Inf Manag*. 2003;40(3):191–204. https://doi.org/10.1016/S0378-7206(01)00143-4.

41. Dorz S, Novara C, Pastore M, Sica C, Sanavio E. Presentazione della versione italiana dell'Obsessive Beliefs Questionnaire (OBQ): struttura fattoriale e analisi di attendibilità (parte I). *Psicoter Cognit Comport*. 2009;15(2):139–170.

42. Obsessive Compulsive Cognitions Working Group. Development and initial validation of the obsessive belief questionnaire and the interpretation of intrusion inventory. *Behav Res Ther*. 2001;39:987–1006. https://doi.org/10.1016/s0005-7967(00)00085-1.

43. Schwarzer R, Jerusalem M. Generalized self-efficacy scale. In: Weinman IJ, Wright S, Johnston M, eds. *Measures in Health Psychology: A User's Portfolio. Causal and Control beliefs*. Windsor, UK: NFER-NELSON; 1995:35–37.

44. Sibilia L, Schwarzer R, Jerusalem M. Italian Adaptation of the General Self-Efficacy Scale, 1995; 2019. Available from: http://userpage.fu-berlin.de/~health/italian.htm.

45. Venkatesh V, Morris MG, Davis GB, Davis FD. User acceptance of information technology: toward a unified view. *MIS Q*. 2003;27(3):425–478. https://doi.org/10.2307/30036540.

46. Davis FD. A technology acceptance model for empirically testing new end-user information systems: theory and results; 1986. [doctoral dissertation] Cambridge (MA): MIT Sloan School of Management.

47. Hayes AF. Introduction to mediation, moderation, and conditional process analysis: a regression-based approach. 2nd ed. Guilford Press; 2018.

48. King WR, He J. A meta-analysis of the technology acceptance model. *Inf Manag*. 2006;43(6):740–755. https://doi.org/10.1016/j.im.2006.05.003.

49. Hubert M, Blut M, Brock C, Zhang RW, Koch V, Riedl R. The influence of acceptance and adoption drivers on smart home usage. *Eur J Market*. 2019;53(6):1073–1098. https://doi.org/10.1108/EJM-12-2016-0794.

50. Taylor S, Todd PA. Understanding information technology usage: a test of competing models. *Inform Syst Res*. 1995;6(2):144–176.

51. Young P, Hamilton R, Hodgett S, et al. Reducing risk by improving standards of intrapartum fetal care. *J R Soc Med*. 2001;94(5):226–231. https://doi.org/10.1177/014107680109400507.

52. Prati G, Mazzoni D, Zani B. Perceived behavioural control, subjective norms, attitudes and intention to use condom: a longitudinal cross-lagged design. *Psychol Health*. 2014;29(10):1119–1136. https://doi.org/10.1080/08870446.2014.913043. PMID: 24724800.

7

Artificial intelligence in diagnostic and predictive pathology

Chiara Frascarelli[a,b], Nicola Fusco[a,b], and Gianluca Vago[b]

[a]Division of Pathology, European Institute of Oncology (IEO), IRCCS, Milan, Italy
[b]Department of Oncology and Hematology-Oncology (DIPO), University of Milan, Milan, Italy

1. Introduction: Artificial intelligence in healthcare systems

Modern healthcare systems employ electronic health records (EHR) to systematically collect patient health information in a digital format.[1] The databases created by EHR contain large, but regrettably, heterogeneous datasets that combine structured data elements, such as diagnoses (International Classification of Diseases-10), procedures (Current Procedural Terminology code), and medications (RxNorm), but also rich unstructured data, including pathology reports and clinical narratives.[2] To date, unstructured textual elements represent more than 80% of the data stored in EHR, thus limiting the systematization of dedicated wide and comprehensive databases.

Large healthcare systems realized the importance of the analysis of EHR-based data early on and created data warehouses, which are used both for research and clinical purposes.[3] Such data warehouses not only contain EHR data but they are often enriched with claims data, imaging data, digital pathology, "omics" data, and "wearable-generated" data (e.g., nutrition, at-home vitals monitoring, physical activity status) from digital devices (e.g., smartphones and smartwatches).[4]

Artificial intelligence (AI) methods, in particular machine learning (ML) and deep learning, are well suited to deal with both the data type and looming questions in health care. In particular, AI can aid physicians in the complex task of risk-stratifying patients for interventions, identifying those most at risk of imminent decompensating, and evaluating multiple small outcomes to optimize overall patient outcomes. Integrating physicians into model development and educating them in this field will be the next paradigm shift in medical education.[5]

The subfields of ML and deep learning networks have shown success in providing solutions to the healthcare questions of risk stratification and optimizing patient outcomes. The use of this technology will exponentially expand as it becomes increasingly integrated into large healthcare systems.

2. State of the art for digital pathology

Traditional pathology approaches have played an integral role in the delivery of diagnosis, biomarkers testing, and classification of disease.[6] Technological advances and the increased focus on precision medicine have recently paved the way for the development of digital pathology-based approaches for quantitative pathologic assessments, namely whole-slide imaging (WSI) and AI-based solutions, allowing us to explore and extract information beyond human visual perception.[7]

The development of AI tools for the analysis of histological images based on neural networks is necessary to enhance the potential of precision medicine.[4] Novel machine learning algorithms can lead to a quantum leap in biomarkers' validation and application in the clinical practice for patients with cancer.

Artificial Intelligence for Medicine
https://doi.org/10.1016/B978-0-443-13671-9.00018-1

81

2.1 From modern cyto- and histopathology to the digitalization era

Pathology has historically played a crucial role in the drug development process, including preclinical research to facilitate target identification, define drug mechanism of action and pharmacodynamics, and enable toxicology assessments.[8,9] More recently, pathology has formed a bridge between drug discovery, translational, and clinical research programs that are striving to decipher disease pathophysiology in the context of the mechanism of action, patient selection, or patient stratification.[10,11] In this era of ultra-personalized medicine and unprecedented technological advances, pathology is bound to change dramatically.[12] The reason is that the last decades have seen a remarkable increase in the development of different ancillary techniques able to provide actionable information in addition to that provided by histopathological analyses.[13] This (r)evolution has entailed a progressive adaptation to new clinical challenges, placing pathologists at the forefront of the era of precision medicine.[14] Indeed, with the introduction of different molecular tools (e.g., next-generation sequencing, NGS) to investigate the underlying biological mechanisms of cancer development, molecular pathologists have now gained a pivotal role in the therapeutic decision-making process by facilitating the translation of biomarker discoveries to the clinical application.[3,15]

Cytopathology is a well-established diagnostic approach owing to its low cost, reliability, and minimal invasiveness compared with other methodologies. In recent years, several efforts have been made to standardize and optimize the classification systems in cytopathology to facilitate communication between cytopathologists and other physicians.[16] The revival of molecular cytopathology in today's clinical practice stems from the need to address some of the many challenges posed by precision medicine. Indeed, we have highlighted many reasons why molecular cytopathologists play a critical role in modern multidisciplinary team (MDT) meetings by providing timely and accurate diagnoses, as well as support for the overall clinical decision-making process.

Remarkably, since its inception in the 1600s up to our days, the optical microscope has remained the gold standard diagnostic tool for histological examination worldwide. Tissues are generally visualized with hematoxylin and eosin (H&E) staining agents. Thus, for decades, pathologists have visualized cellular morphological structures of tissues in "pink and purple." Ample descriptions of anatomical-pathological pictures have been characterized and defined based on this technique and its artifacts. However, in today's era of technological revolution, the field of anatomic pathology is bound to change once again, progressing from morphology-based diagnosis to molecular-based diagnosis.[6]

Histopathology involves the examination of tissue sections to identify microscopic manifestations of diseases.[17] Tissue samples are collected via biopsies or surgical resections and are then prepared to undergo further analyses.[18,19] The manual analysis is a time-consuming task lasting up to one hour per image.[20] However, heterogeneous tissue morphologies, arbitrary selection of the tissue regions to be analyzed in detail, and subjective evaluation of findings generally lead to a low interpathologist agreement on the diagnosis.[21–24]

2.2 Pathology as the core of translational clinical research

The need for high-throughput approaches integrating different layers of information and enabling complex analyses clashes with the intrinsic qualitative nature of morphological evaluation and reporting.[25] Digitalization of pathology data has infringed these limitations, opening a full spectrum of opportunities for tissue-based investigations.

The integrated adoption of pathologist-guided and/or AI-assisted segmentation of tissue structures and cell components conjugates the suitability of analytical methods typical of single-cell resolved science (e.g., clustering analyses, dimensionality reduction methods) with spatial information, offering an unprecedented level of insight into the biology of normal and diseased tissues.[26]

High-resolution tissue imaging based on new-generation slide scanners further extends the inference of pieces of information beyond the quantitative analysis of cell morphotype/phenotype and cell-cell or cell-contexture interactions, opening a window over the topographic organization of nuclear content and related mechanobiology.[27]

The possibility to exploit in situ transcriptional analyses to discover and validate the correspondence between emerging digital patterns and the underlying molecular networks represents the current edge of tissue-driven research, with genome-level assays making their way into the field.[28] In the scenario of such a multi-omics harmonization—now including what we can identify as patronymics—the preanalytical phases and quality controls of surgical pathology lab best practices represent the cornerstones. The confluence of mergeable digital pathology data into repositories for proper comparison and data analysis routines will likely represent the bottleneck of patronymics in the forthcoming years when tissue-driven research will face the rapid refinement of tissue-based molecular/genetics methods and the exponential increase in the availability of digital pathology platforms.[29]

3. Integrating computational pathology and bioinformatics

The incorporation of scientific research through clinical informatics, including genomics, proteomics, bioinformatics, and biostatistics, into clinical practice, unlocks innovative approaches to patient care. Computational pathology is a burgeoning subspecialty in pathology that promises a better-integrated solution to WSIs, multi-omics data, and clinical informatics. However, computational pathology faces several challenges, including the ability to integrate raw data from different sources, limitation of hardware processing capacity, and a lack of specific training programs, as well as issues on ethics and larger societal acceptable practices that are still solidifying. The establishment of the entire industry of computational pathology requires far-reaching changes in the three essential elements connecting patients and doctors: the local laboratory, the scan center, and the central cloud hub/portal for data processing and retrieval. Computational pathology, unlocked through information integration and advanced digital communication networks, has the potential to improve clinical workflow efficiency and diagnostic quality, and ultimately create personalized diagnosis and treatment plans for patients.[30]

3.1 Role of bioinformatics in the clinical management of patients with cancer

Cancer is one of the commonest causes of patient death in the clinic and a complex disease occurring in multiple organs per system, multiple systems per organ, or both, in the body. The poor diagnoses, therapies, and prognoses of the disease could be mainly due to the variation of severities, durations, locations, sensitivity, and resistance against drugs, cell differentiation, and origin, and understanding of pathogenesis. With increasing evidence that the interaction and network between genes and proteins play an important role in the investigation of cancer molecular mechanisms, it is necessary and important to introduce a new concept of Systems Clinical Medicine into cancer research, to integrate systems biology, clinical science, omics-based technology, bioinformatics, and computational science to improve diagnosis, therapies, and prognosis of diseases. Cancer bioinformatics is a critical and important part of the systems of clinical medicine in cancer and the core tool and approach to carry out the investigations of cancer in systems of clinical medicine.[31]

The applicability, specificity, and integration of methodologies, software, computational tools, and databases that can be used to explore the molecular mechanisms of cancer and identify and validate novel biomarkers, network biomarkers, and individualized medicine in cancer should be seriously considered.[32]

Cancer bioinformatics is expected to play a more important role in the identification and validation of biomarkers, specific to clinical phenotypes related to early diagnoses, measurements to monitor the progress of the disease and the response to therapy, and predictors for the improvement of patient's life quality. Of gene-, protein-, peptide-, chemical- or physic-based variables in cancer, biomarkers were investigated from a single one to multiple markers, from the expression to functional indication, and from the network to dynamic network. Network biomarkers as a new type of biomarkers with protein-protein interactions were investigated with the integration of knowledge on protein annotations, interaction, and signaling pathways. Alterations of network biomarkers can be monitored and evaluated at different stages and time points during the development of diseases, named dynamic network biomarkers, as one of the new strategies. Dynamic network biomarkers were expected to be correlated with clinical informatics, including patient complaints, history, therapies, clinical symptoms and signs, physician's examinations, biochemical analyses, imaging profiles, pathologies, and other measurements.[33]

3.2 The introduction of artificial intelligence in anatomic pathology laboratories

The introduction of digital pathology and AI in clinical laboratories represents another major paradigm shift in anatomic pathology. Briefly, the term digital pathology is often inappropriately restricted to the employment of glass slide scanners used to obtain WSIs for sharing purposes. However, the whole gamut of this broad field runs from the complete automation of the entire anatomic pathology workflow to the application of digitized slides for primary diagnosis and consultation purposes. Moreover, digital pathology has recently been integrated with image analysis and AI tools, which further streamline the overall laboratory work of clinical pathologists.[34] All these modifications would require the optimization of the precious yet scarce biological material for cancer characterization. In this setting, one of the most immediate applications of WSI might be the digitization of cytological smears destined for molecular analysis. Creating databases of scanned cyto/histological samples could serve multiple purposes.

3.3 Basics of machine learning

When working with images, common tasks include classification, detection, segmentation, and instance segmentation. Supervised learning and unsupervised learning are the two classifications in which machine learning can be divided. Unsupervised learning analyses and clusters unlabeled datasets, while supervised learning trains the model using human-provided labels. Some degree of supervision is almost always necessary for medical AI systems. The annotations/labels, usually known as ground truth that are being introduced during the algorithm training phase impact on the accuracy and quality of the generated data. To ensure the accuracy of data, annotations must be handled by preferably more than one experienced pathologist. The model is usually evaluated using testing data, a small subset of data never fed into training.[35]

3.4 Whole-slide imaging, machine learning, and the impact on patient outcome

Digital pathology refers to the environment that includes tools and systems for digitizing pathology slides and associated metadata, in addition to their storage, evaluation, and analysis, as well as supporting infrastructure. WSI has been proven in multiple studies to have an excellent correlation with traditional light microscopy diagnosis[36] and to be a reliable tool for routine surgical pathology diagnosis.[37,38] Indeed, WSI technology provides some advantages over traditional microscopy, including portability, ease of sharing and retrieving images, and task balance.[39] The establishment of the digital pathology environment contributed to the development of a new branch of pathology known as computational pathology (CPATH).[40]

The term computational pathology has become a buzzword among the digital pathology community, yet it often leads to confusion due to its use in different contexts.[41–43] The expert authors of the Digital Pathology Association (DPA) define CPATH as the "omics" or "big-data" approach to pathology, where multiple sources of patient information including pathology image data and meta-data are combined to extract patterns and analyze features.[44]

Traditional digital image analysis focuses on three broad categories of measurements: localization, classification, and quantification of image objects. This method is an iterative process where typically a few parameters are manually tuned, built into an algorithm, and often tested only on a region of the slide image.[45] Aspects that fail a quality control review are tweaked until the algorithm performance meets pre-determined analysis criteria.

ML has facilitated significant advancements within the field of image analysis, as it often allows the generation of more robust algorithms that need fewer iterative optimizations for each dataset, compared with methods where parameters are manually tuned. Supervised ML techniques, in which an algorithm is trained using ground truth labels, are particularly effective in image segmentation (detection of specific objects) and classification (such as tumor diagnosis) tasks.[46] The ground truth may be a category or label assigned to a dataset that guides an algorithm.

These early studies applied ML to histopathology using small, manually selected regions of interest, but later research showed that these techniques could work equally well on WSIs.[47] In DP, ML-enhanced image analysis is now widely employed by researchers and implemented in several commercially available image analysis software products.

Researchers quickly found that ML algorithms could be used in novel ways that were not limited to information contained only in the slide image. ML algorithms could be used to extract an enormous number of features in an image. For example, ML-powered image analysis can be used to identify objects in a histology image which may be used to generate "histologic primitives" such as nuclei, tumor cells, etc. that a human would consider an 'object'.[48] When these features are correlated with non-image patient features from the medical record, such as response to a specific treatment, algorithms can be developed that may predict these responses from images alone. The image features need not necessarily be "objects" that may be recognized by a human. For example, Beck et al. examined "a rich quantitative feature set" consisting of 6642 engineered features expressing characteristics of both breast cancer epithelium and stroma[46] and correlated these to patient outcomes. They identified a small number of stromal morphological features that yielded mutually independent prognostic information about breast cancer. It is possible to go a step further and train a deep learning algorithm in such a way that an enormous number of image features are automatically extracted and used to obtain patient outcome-related predictions from images.[49] There is a trade-off: the larger the number and level of abstraction of image feature used for the predictions, the greater the difficulty in understanding those predictions (see our section on understanding algorithms).

Nevertheless, these types of analyses are what many consider to be the biggest promise of CPATH, particularly in the field of oncology, where it may increase the speed and accuracy of diagnosis.

3.5 Beyond human visual perception: The role of computational pathology

Integrating AI into the workflow of the pathology department can perform quality control of the preanalytic, analytic, and postanalytic phases of the pathology department's work process, allowing quality control of scan images and formalin-fixed paraffin-embedded tissue blocks, integrated diagnosis with joining clinical information, ordering necessary pathology studies including immunohistochemistry and molecular studies, automating repetitive tasks, on-demand consultation, and cloud server management, which, finally allow precision medicine by enabling us to use a wide range of patient data, including pathological images, to develop disease-preventive and treatment methods tailored to individual patient features. To achieve the above-mentioned goals, there are crucial elements required for CPATH.[50] One of the promises of CPATH is that it can be used to build a clinical decision support tool for the precision diagnosis of the patient. For example, algorithms have been described that identify images likely to contain tumor cells,[51] compute mitotic counts,[52] improve the accuracy and precision of immunohistochemistry scoring,[20,53] or apply standardized histological scoring criteria such as the Gleason score,[54] which can be critically important in the management of cancer and guiding treatment strategy.[55] Spatial relationships among immune cells within the stromal or tumor compartments of the tumor microenvironment can also be evaluated using deep learning tools and correlated to response with immunotherapy.[56]

The capacity of ML to identify new image features may lead to the discovery of previously unrecognized morphological characteristics with a clinical relevance that have not been used in visual assessment by pathologists, either because these features had not previously been discovered or because they are beyond human visual perception. For example, deep learning is capable of assessing morphological information from the stroma neighboring ductal carcinoma in situ (DCIS) breast lesions which correlate with DCIS grade.[57] It should be noted that even though pathologists recognize morphological changes as a consequence of the presence of a tumor, they may not currently directly use this information in diagnostics or to offer prognostic insight. The fact that deep learning is able to exploit such "hidden" features is promising as it may yield prognostic information not currently utilized. Once identified, it may be possible to re-engineer a simpler image analysis algorithm to identify the specific feature, which clinicians can accept more easily accept.

4. Model for next-generation computational pathology

Despite considerable technical advancements in CPATH in recent years, the deployment of deep learning algorithms in real clinical settings is still far from adequate. This is because most algorithms used in current clinical practice are limited to traditional image analysis of immunohistochemical stains, which do not employ advanced ML techniques such as deep learning.[44] Moreover, to be implemented into existing or future workflows, the CPATH algorithm must be scientifically validated, have considerable clinical benefit, and not cause harm or confuse people at the same time.[58] Implementation of CPATH may require a significant investment in IT infrastructure. In general, data to be analyzed are captured as images of tissue sections, often scanned at $20\times$ or $40\times$ objective magnification. In clinical practice, pathology images are commonly larger than 50,000 by 50,000 pixels [60]. As a benchmark, this can translate into estimated image file sizes ranging from 0.5 to 4 GB for $40\times$, depending on the size of the scan area and the type of image compression.

The large size of these images may present a problem for evaluation, storage, and inventory management. The primary computing obstacles that users face are processor speed and memory requirements of local workstations, data storage requirements, and limitations of the network. For CPATH to perform effectively, there must be safeguards to ensure that images are fully loaded and that the analysis algorithm is not interrupted due to insufficient bandwidth, processing power, or memory. Additional considerations when running deep learning algorithms include, but are not limited to, the number of intended users, flexibility of the server or cloud configuration to accommodate new algorithms or case-loads, cyber security, and associated costs.

The performance of any image processing is highly dependent on processor speed.[59] Deep learning is best performed using graphics processing units (GPUs), which can provide significant performance enhancement over central processing units (CPUs).[60] Most computers are designed to perform computations on their local CPU and use the GPU simply to render graphics. In order to implement deep learning algorithm, it may be necessary to purchase a more powerful GPU; these are generally more expensive and tend to generate more heat. Some laboratories may, therefore, choose to dedicate high-performance workstations strictly for deep learning. However, some vendors offer the ability to perform image analysis at the server or cloud level, which may provide significantly more resources and can potentially distribute deep learning capabilities to a much larger user base.

The large size of WSIs presents a potential hurdle for efficient processing in environments that lack sufficient bandwidth. Several data transfer considerations have to be done depending on the network implementation. First, digital slide data from the whole-slide scanner must be transferred to its network storage location, which requires the file in its entirety. Second, the digital slide must be transferred from its network storage location to the image analysis environment (which may reside locally, elsewhere on the network, or in the cloud), which can often be accomplished more efficiently, since the entire image is unlikely to be analyzed at once. Training a deep learning network on an entire slide image at full resolution is currently very challenging, so it usually operates on a smaller tiled image or patch.[61] Downscaling (reducing resolution) of these images is one possible approach, but this may lead to loss of discriminative details as using small, high-resolution tiles may lose tissue context. The optimal resolution and tile size for analysis are highly case-dependent.[62] If only small regions of interest are to be processed, or if the processing can occur at a reduced magnification, smaller portions of the virtual slide file need to be transferred due to the pyramid structure of most WSI file formats.[63]

CPATH algorithms must be trained with high-quality data so that they can deal with the diverse datasets encountered in real-world clinical practice. Even in deep learning, the ground truth should be manually incorporated into the dataset to train appropriate diagnostic contexts in supervised learning to classify, segment, and predict images based on it.[64] The ground truth can be derived from pathology reports grading patient outcomes or tumors, as well as scores assessed by molecular experiments, depending on the study's goals, which are still determined by human experts and need a significant amount of manual labor to obtain a "correct" dataset.[44] Although datasets created by professional pathologists are of excellent quality, vast quantities are difficult to obtain due to the time, cost, and repetitive and arduous tasks required. As a result, publicly available datasets have been continuously created, such as the ones from TCGA or grand challenges, with the help of weakly supervised learning. Alternative efforts have recently been made to gather massive scales of annotated images by crowdsourcing online. Hughes et al. used a crowdsourced image presentation platform to demonstrate deep learning performance comparable to that of a single professional pathologist,[65] while López-Pérez et al. used a crowdsourced deep learning algorithm to help a group of doctors or medical students who were not pathologists make annotations comparable to an expert in breast cancer images.[63] Crowdsourcing may generate some noise, but it shows that inexperienced users could assist with pathological annotation and dataset generation. Obtaining quality data entails more than just obtaining a sufficient raw pathological image slide of a single disease from a patient or hospital; it also includes preparing materials to analyze and process the image to extract useful data for deep learning model training.

Another issue relies on the fact that supervised algorithms should be developed using a wide variety of data sources, to more robustly handle variations when exposed to other datasets.

Training the deep learning model on large and diverse datasets may lower the generalization error to some extent.[32]

The amount and quality of input data determine the performance of the deep learning algorithm.[66,67] Although the size of datasets has been growing over the years with the development of CPATH, even if algorithms trained using learning datasets perform well on test sets, it is difficult to be certain that algorithms perform well on actual clinical encounters because clinical data come from significantly more diverse sources than studies. Similarly, when evaluating the performance of deep learning algorithms with a specific validation set for each grand challenge, it is also difficult to predict whether they will perform well in actual clinical practice. Color variation is a representative example of the variation of data. Color variation is caused by differences in raw materials, staining techniques used across different pathology labs, patient inter-variability, and different slide scanners, which affect not just color but also overall data variation.[68]

A principal concern with the use of deep learning is that it is very difficult to understand some of the features and neural pathways used to make decisions. In particular, when deep learning is used to automatically extract features from an image that are directly correlated to clinical endpoints, without including a segmentation step where image objects are first extracted (see the section on correlating images to patient response), it is particularly challenging to understand why the algorithm reached its conclusions. Artificial neural networks have accordingly been described as a "black box." This has led to several concerns: difficulty in correcting an underperforming algorithm; lack of transparency, clarity, and provability for humans who may not trust how an algorithm generates reliable results; and regulatory concerns because, unlike traditional image analysis, in deep learning, the image features are abstracted in a way that is very difficult for a human to understand. In response, there have been efforts to convert deep learning algorithms into a "glass box" by clarifying the inputs and their relation to measured outputs, making it more interpretable by a human using a variety of techniques.[69–72] By providing information to the reviewing pathologist about the histopathologic features used by the algorithm in a particular instance, trust in the algorithm can be fostered, and synergy between pathologist and machine can be achieved that may exceed the performance of either AI or pathologist alone.[73]

Other than the importance of understanding the algorithms, several steps of validation are conducted during the lengthy process of developing a CPATH algorithm to test its performance and safety. To train models and evaluate performance, CPATH studies on typical supervised algorithms separate annotated data into individual learning datasets and test datasets, the majority of which employ datasets with features fairly similar to those of learning datasets in the so-called "internal verification" stage. Afterward, through so-called "external validation," which uses data for tests that have not been used for training, it is feasible to roughly evaluate if the algorithm performs well with the data it would encounter in real clinical practice.[74] However, simply because the CPATH algorithm performed well at this phase, it is hard to ascertain whether it will function equally well in practical practice.[75] While many studies on the CPATH algorithm are being conducted, most studies use autonomous standards due to a lack of established clinical verification standards and institutional validation. Even if deep learning algorithms perform well and are employed with provisional permission, it is difficult to confirm that their performance exhibits the same confirmed effect when the algorithm is upgraded in the subsequent operation process.

A general principle in training any machine learning algorithm is to split the annotated data into "training" and "test" datasets and ensure that these sets are independent when assessing performance. Histopathological assessments by the pathologist are considered the gold standard, but the algorithm data may be more reproducible than human assessment. This may be partially overcome by comparing the algorithm data to patient outcomes, to see whether it is better able to predict outcomes compared with manual pathology assessment/scoring. However, the best methods to determine the reliability of an algorithm applied to novel datasets are an area of active debate.[46]

AI tool creation must take into account the requirement for research and ethics approval, which is typically necessary during the research and clinical trial stages. Providing transparency of the data used in developing an algorithm fosters interpretability and openness of scientific discovery, and increases acceptance and trust of the results. However, not exposing the data used by a deep learning model allows companies to create proprietary models that may not be validated or challenged in the public space. On the other hand, exposing the private data of a patient (e.g., digital image with associated identifiable unique mutations) can present ethical concerns that violate privacy and, as a result, may prompt restrictive governance policies and security models. Developers must follow the ethics of using patient data for research and commercial advantages. Recognizing the usefulness of patient data for research and the difficulties in obtaining agreement for its use, the corresponding institution should establish a proper scheme to provide individual patients some influence over how their data are used.[76] Individual institutional review boards may have additional local protocols for permitting one to opt out of data use for research, and all of these elements must be understood and followed throughout the design stage of AI tool creation.[77] There are many parallels to be found with the AI development pipeline; while successful items will most likely transit through the full pathway, supported by various resources, many products will, however, fail at some point. Each stage of the pipeline, including the justification of the tool for review and, is recommended for usage in clinical guidelines, can benefit from measurable outcomes of success to make informed judgments about which products should be promoted.[78] This usually calls for proof of cost or resource savings, quality improvements, and patient impact and is thus frequently challenging to demonstrate, especially when the solution entails major transformation and process redesign.

Whether one uses a cloud-based AI solution for pathology diagnostics depends on several things, such as the preferred workflow, frequency of instrument use, software and hardware costs, and whether or not the IT security risk group is willing to allow the use of cloud-based solutions. Cloud-based systems must include a business associate's agreement, end-to-end encryption, and unambiguous data-use agreements to prevent data breaches and inappropriate use of patient data.[77]

Given the volume of data, their highly confidential nature, and the need to respect the rights of individuals—both for ethical reasons and to comply with the law—organizations should develop formal mechanisms to comprehensively address these issues, rather than address them ad hoc.[44]

5. Final remarks

AI currently has enormous potential to improve pathology practice by reducing errors, improving reproducibility, and facilitating expert communication, all of which were previously difficult with microscopic glass slides. Recent trends in AI applications should be affordable, practical, interoperable, explainable, generalizable, manageable, and reimbursable.[77]

Within the field of CPATH, the techniques for ML-enhanced image analysis and its combination with other data sources have evolved to the point where they may soon be ready to be translated from the research environment into practicing clinical laboratories. Although the promises of CPATH are great, manifold hurdles need to be overcome.[78]

Regulators, vendors, and healthcare providers can all help to drive the field forward to benefit patients. Many researchers are convinced that AI, in general, and deep learning, in particular, could help with many repetitive tasks using digital pathology because of recent successes in image recognition. However, there are currently only a few AI-driven software tools in this field. As a result, we believe pathologists should be involved from the start, even when developing algorithms, to ensure that these eagerly anticipated software packages are improved or even replaced by AI algorithms. Despite popular belief, AI will be difficult to implement in pathology. AI tools are likely to be approved by regulators such as the Food and Drug Administration.

The quantitative nature of CPATH has the potential to transform pathology laboratory and clinical practices. Case stratification, expedited review and annotation, and the output of meaningful models to guide treatment decisions and predict patterns in medical fields are all possibilities. The pathology community needs more research to develop safe and reliable AI. As clinical AI's requirements become clearer, this gap will close.

Finally, healthcare institutions could be encouraged to pool anonymized patient data and make them publicly accessible, so that researchers around the world may cooperate to develop more accurate diagnostic algorithms. Deep learning is a numbers game, and obtaining sufficient training data is often the primary hurdle, which can be addressed by collaborative data-sharing initiatives, similar to what exists in biomedical imaging 61 but where digital pathology lags.

AI in pathology is young and will continue to mature as researchers, doctors, industry, regulatory agencies, and patient advocacy groups innovate and bring new technology to healthcare practitioners. To accomplish its successful application, robust and standardized computational, clinical, and laboratory practices must be established concurrently and validated across multiple partnering sites.

References

1. Meystre SM, et al. Extracting information from textual documents in the electronic health record: a review of recent research. *Yearb Med Inform.* 2008;128–144.
2. Giordano C, et al. Accessing artificial intelligence for clinical decision-making. *Front Digit Health.* 2021;3, 645232.
3. Pisapia P, et al. The evolving landscape of anatomic pathology. *Crit Rev Oncol Hematol.* 2022;178, 103776.
4. Baxi V, et al. Digital pathology and artificial intelligence in translational medicine and clinical practice. *Mod Pathol.* 2022;35(1):23–32.
5. Jubb AM, Koeppen H, Reis-Filho JS. Pathology in drug discovery and development. *J Pathol.* 2014;232(2):99–102.
6. Krupinski EA, Graham AR, Weinstein RS. Characterizing the development of visual search expertise in pathology residents viewing whole slide images. *Hum Pathol.* 2013;44(3):357–364.
7. Kramer JA, Sagartz JE, Morris DL. The application of discovery toxicology and pathology towards the design of safer pharmaceutical lead candidates. *Nat Rev Drug Discov.* 2007;6(8):636–649.
8. Carbone DP, et al. First-line Nivolumab in stage IV or recurrent non-small-cell lung Cancer. *N Engl J Med.* 2017;376(25):2415–2426.
9. Nagtegaal ID, et al. Pathology is a necessary and informative tool in oncology clinical trials. *J Pathol.* 2014;232(2):185–189.
10. Angerilli V, et al. The role of the pathologist in the next-generation era of tumor molecular characterization. *Diagnostics (Basel).* 2021;11(2):339–354.
11. Pitman MB, Black-Schaffer WS. Post-fine-needle aspiration biopsy communication and the integrated and standardized cytopathology report. *Cancer Cytopathol.* 2017;125(S6):486–493.
12. Fusco N, Malapelle U, Criscitiello C. Editorial: diagnosis and treatment of breast Cancer in 2022: the rise of novel molecular biomarkers. *Front Mol Biosci.* 2022;9:1117323.
13. Venetis K, et al. HER2 low, ultra-low, and novel complementary biomarkers: expanding the spectrum of HER2 positivity in breast cancer. *Front Mol Biosci.* 2022. https://doi.org/10.3389/fmolb.2022.834651.
14. Invernizzi M, et al. Integrating molecular biomarkers in breast cancer rehabilitation. What is the current evidence? A systematic review of randomized controlled trials. *Front Mol Biosci.* 2022;9, 930361.
15. Cappello F, et al. FFPE-based NGS approaches into clinical practice: the limits of glory from a pathologist viewpoint. *J Pers Med.* 2022;12(5):750–768.
16. Gurcan MN, et al. Histopathological image analysis: a review. *IEEE Rev Biomed Eng.* 2009;2:147–171.
17. Wei JW, et al. Pathologist level classification of histologic patterns on resected lung adenocarcinoma slides with deep neural networks. *Sci Rep.* 2019;9(1):3358.
18. Bonizzi G, et al. Biobank for translational medicine: standard operating procedures for optimal sample management. *J Vis Exp.* 2022;189.
19. Bonizzi G, et al. Standard operating procedures for biobank in oncology. *Front Mol Biosci.* 2022;9, 967310.
20. Arvaniti E, et al. Automated Gleason grading of prostate cancer tissue microarrays via deep learning. *Sci Rep.* 2018;8(1):12054.
21. Vennalaganti P, et al. Discordance among pathologists in the United States and Europe in diagnosis of low-grade dysplasia for patients with Barrett's esophagus. *Gastroenterology.* 2017;152(3):564–570.e4.
22. Costantini M, et al. Interobserver agreement in the histologic diagnosis of colorectal polyps. The experience of the multicenter adenoma colorectal study (SMAC). *J Clin Epidemiol.* 2003;56(3):209–214.
23. Tripodo C, et al. A spatially resolved dark- versus light-zone microenvironment signature subdivides germinal center-related aggressive B cell lymphomas. *iScience.* 2020;23(10), 101562.
24. Morello G, et al. T cells expressing receptor recombination/revision machinery are detected in the tumor microenvironment and expanded in Genomically over-unstable models. *Cancer Immunol Res.* 2021;9(7):825–837.

25. Marletta S, et al. Artificial intelligence-based tools applied to pathological diagnosis of microbiological diseases. *Pathol Res Pract.* 2023;243, 154362.

26. L'Imperio V, et al. Spatial transcriptome of a germinal center plasmablastic burst hints at MYD88/CD79B mutants-enriched diffuse large B-cell lymphomas. *Eur J Immunol.* 2022;52(8):1350–1361. https://doi.org/10.1002/eji.202149746.

27. Caputo A, et al. Real-world digital pathology: considerations and ruminations of four young pathologists. *J Clin Pathol.* 2023;68–70.

28. Cui M, Zhang DY. Artificial intelligence and computational pathology. *Lab Invest.* 2021;101(4):412–422.

29. Wu D, Rice CM, Wang X. Cancer bioinformatics: a new approach to systems clinical medicine. *BMC Bioinform.* 2012;13(1):71.

30. Laczny C, et al. miRTrail - a comprehensive webserver for analyzing gene and miRNA patterns to enhance the understanding of regulatory mechanisms in diseases. *BMC Bioinform.* 2012;13(1):36.

31. Wang X. Role of clinical bioinformatics in the development of network-based biomarkers. *J Clin Bioinforma.* 2011;1(1):28.

32. Niazi MKK, Parwani AV, Gurcan MN. Digital pathology and artificial intelligence. *Lancet Oncol.* 2019;20(5):e253–e261.

33. Chan RCK, et al. Artificial intelligence in breast cancer histopathology. *Histopathology.* 2023;82(1):198–210.

34. Saco A, et al. Validation of whole-slide imaging for Histolopathogical diagnosis: current state. *Pathobiology.* 2016;83(2–3):89–98.

35. Al-Janabi S, et al. Whole slide images for primary diagnostics of gastrointestinal tract pathology: a feasibility study. *Hum Pathol.* 2012;43 (5):702–707.

36. Snead DR, et al. Validation of digital pathology imaging for primary histopathological diagnosis. *Histopathology.* 2016;68(7):1063–1072.

37. Williams BJ, Bottoms D, Treanor D. Future-proofing pathology: the case for clinical adoption of digital pathology. *J Clin Pathol.* 2017;70 (12):1010–1018.

38. Astrachan O, et al. The present and future of computational thinking. *ACM SIGCSE Bulletin.* 2009;41:549–550.

39. Louis DN, et al. Computational pathology: a path ahead. *Arch Pathol Lab Med.* 2016;140(1):41–50.

40. Louis DN, et al. Computational pathology: an emerging definition. *Arch Pathol Lab Med.* 2014;138(9):1133–1138.

41. Fuchs TJ, Buhmann JM. Computational pathology: challenges and promises for tissue analysis. *Comput Med Imaging Graph.* 2011;35(7–8):515–530.

42. Abels E, et al. Computational pathology definitions, best practices, and recommendations for regulatory guidance: a white paper from the digital pathology association. *J Pathol.* 2019;249(3):286–294.

43. Aeffner F, et al. Introduction to digital image analysis in whole-slide imaging: a white paper from the digital pathology association. *J Pathol Inform.* 2019;10:9.

44. Madabhushi A, Lee G. Image analysis and machine learning in digital pathology: challenges and opportunities. *Med Image Anal.* 2016;33:170–175.

45. Litjens G, et al. A survey on deep learning in medical image analysis. *Med Image Anal.* 2017;42:60–88.

46. Beck AH, et al. Systematic analysis of breast cancer morphology uncovers stromal features associated with survival. *Sci Transl Med.* 2011;3(108). 108ra113.

47. Mobadersany P, et al. Predicting cancer outcomes from histology and genomics using convolutional networks. *Proc Natl Acad Sci U S A.* 2018;115 (13):E2970–e2979.

48. Kim I, et al. Application of artificial intelligence in pathology: trends and challenges. *Diagnostics.* 2022;12:2794.

49. Cruz-Roa A, et al. Accurate and reproducible invasive breast cancer detection in whole-slide images: a deep learning approach for quantifying tumor extent. *Sci Rep.* 2017;7:46450.

50. Tellez D, et al. Whole-slide mitosis detection in H&E Breast Histology Using PHH3 as a reference to train distilled stain-invariant convolutional networks. *IEEE Trans Med Imaging.* 2018;37(9):2126–2136.

51. Jakobsen MR, et al. Comparison between digital image analysis and visual assessment of immunohistochemical HER2 expression in breast cancer. *Pathol Res Pract.* 2018;214(12):2087–2092.

52. Stålhammar G, et al. Digital image analysis of Ki67 in hot spots is superior to both manual Ki67 and mitotic counts in breast cancer. *Histopathology.* 2018;72(6):974–989.

53. Qaiser T, et al. HER2 challenge contest: a detailed assessment of automated HER2 scoring algorithms in whole slide images of breast cancer tissues. *Histopathology.* 2018;72(2):227–238.

54. Saltz J, et al. Spatial organization and molecular correlation of tumor-infiltrating lymphocytes using deep learning on pathology images. *Cell Rep.* 2018;23(1):181–193.e7.

55. Dong F, et al. Computational pathology to discriminate benign from malignant intraductal proliferations of the breast. *PloS One.* 2014;9(12), e114885.

56. Huss R, Coupland SE. Software-assisted decision support in digital histopathology. *J Pathol.* 2020;250(5):685–692.

57. Tizhoosh HR, Pantanowitz L. Artificial intelligence and digital pathology: challenges and opportunities. *J Pathol Inform.* 2018;9:38.

58. Zarella MD, Feldscher A. Laboratory computer performance in a digital pathology environment: outcomes from a single institution. *J Pathol Inform.* 2018;9:44.

59. Hou L, et al. Patch-based convolutional neural network for whole slide tissue image classification. *Proc IEEE Comput Soc Conf Comput Vis Pattern Recognit.* 2016;2016:2424–2433.

60. Zarella MD, et al. Estimation of fine-scale histologic features at low magnification. *Arch Pathol Lab Med.* 2018;142(11):1394–1402.

61. Shen D, Wu G, Suk HI. Deep learning in medical image analysis. *Annu Rev Biomed Eng.* 2017;19:221–248.

62. Hughes AJ, et al. Quanti.Us: a tool for rapid, flexible, crowd-based annotation of images. *Nat Methods.* 2018;15(8):587–590.

63. López-Pérez M, et al. Learning from crowds in digital pathology using scalable variational Gaussian processes. *Sci Rep.* 2021;11(1):11612.

64. Narla A, et al. Automated classification of skin lesions: from pixels to practice. *J Invest Dermatol.* 2018;138(10):2108–2110.

65. Bera K, et al. Artificial intelligence in digital pathology - new tools for diagnosis and precision oncology. *Nat Rev Clin Oncol.* 2019;16(11):703–715.

66. Wu Y, et al. Recent advances of deep learning for computational histopathology: principles and applications. *Cancers (Basel).* 2022;14 (5):1199–1219.

67. Wen S, et al. Comparison of different classifiers with active learning to support quality control in nucleus segmentation in pathology images. *AMIA Jt Summits Transl Sci Proc.* 2018;2017:227–236.

68. Guidotti R, Monreale A, Ruggieri S, Turini F, Giannotti F, Pedreschi D. A survey of methods for explaining Black box models. *ACM Comput Surv.* 2018;51(5).

69. Selvaraju RR, et al. Grad-CAM: visual explanations from deep networks via gradient-based localization. *Int J Comput Vision*. 2020;128(2):336–359.
70. Ribeiro MT, Singh S, Guestrin C. Why should I trust you?: Explaining the predictions of any classifier. In: *Proceedings of the 22nd ACM SIGKDD International Conference on Knowledge Discovery and Data Mining*. Association for Computing Machinery; 2016:1135–1144.
71. Steiner DF, et al. Impact of deep learning assistance on the histopathologic review of lymph nodes for metastatic breast Cancer. *Am J Surg Pathol*. 2018;42(12):1636–1646.
72. van der Laak J, Litjens G, Ciompi F. Deep learning in histopathology: the path to the clinic. *Nat Med*. 2021;27(5):775–784.
73. Kleppe A, et al. Designing deep learning studies in cancer diagnostics. *Nat Rev Cancer*. 2021;21(3):199–211.
74. Colling R, et al. Artificial intelligence in digital pathology: a roadmap to routine use in clinical practice. *J Pathol*. 2019;249(2):143–150.
75. Acs B, Rantalainen M, Hartman J. Artificial intelligence as the next step towards precision pathology. *J Intern Med*. 2020;288(1):62–81.
76. Koromina M, Pandi MT, Patrinos GP. Rethinking drug repositioning and development with artificial intelligence, machine learning, and omics. *Omics*. 2019;23(11):539–548.
77. Cheng JY, et al. Challenges in the development, deployment, and regulation of artificial intelligence in anatomic pathology. *Am J Pathol*. 2021;191 (10):1684–1692.
78. Ching T, et al. Opportunities and obstacles for deep learning in biology and medicine. *J R Soc Interface*. 2018;15(141):387–434.

8

Artificial intelligence in the oncology workflow: Applications, limitations, and future perspectives

Marisa Cobanaj[a], Chiara Corti[b,c], Edward Christopher Dee[d], Lucas McCullum[e], Leo Anthony Celi[f,g,h], Giuseppe Curigliano[c,i], and Carmen Criscitiello[b,c]

[a]OncoRay, National Center for Radiation Research in Oncology (HZDR), Dresden, Germany [b]Division of New Drugs and Early Drug Development for Innovative Therapies, European Institute of Oncology (IEO), IRCCS, Milan, Italy [c]Department of Oncology and Hematology-Oncology (DIPO), University of Milan, Milan, Italy [d]Department of Radiation Oncology, Memorial Sloan Kettering Cancer Center, New York, NY, United States [e]Department of Radiation Oncology, MD Anderson Cancer Center, Houston, TX, United States [f]Department of Medicine, Beth Israel Deaconess Medical Center, Boston, MA, United States [g]Laboratory for Computational Physiology, Massachusetts Institute of Technology, Cambridge, MA, United States [h]Department of Biostatistics, Harvard T.H. Chan School of Public Health, Boston, MA, United States [i]Division of Early Drug Development for Innovative Therapies, European Institute of Oncology (IEO), IRCCS, Milan, Italy

1. Introduction

Cancer is among the most common causes of morbidity and mortality worldwide. According to the World Health Organization (WHO), almost 19.3 million new cancer cases occurred in 2020, with this number expected to increase. In 2040, 30.2 million new cancer cases are estimated to be diagnosed.[1] Although advances in cancer prevention, screening, and treatment increased cancer survival rates—especially for high-income countries[2]—nearly 10 million cancer-related deaths occurred in 2020, almost one in six deaths.[3] Therefore, promoting and supporting innovation in cancer care is of primary importance.

Artificial intelligence (AI) has contributed to addressing challenges in many medical specialties, including the oncology field. On the grounds of the digitalization of medical data and novel computational technologies, AI has the potential to improve the availability and quality of cancer care worldwide. Applications range from cancer prevention, diagnosis, and prognosis to treatment development, delivery, and evaluation.[4]

In the last two decades, patient-centered approaches have been developed and implemented, with increasing effort focusing on multidisciplinary tumor boards and integrated multimodal treatment strategies, including surgery, systemic treatments, and radiation therapy (RT). Specifically, RT is recommended for more than 50% of cancer patients in both curative and palliative settings.[5–7] However, owing to technological advances, the RT workflow has become increasingly complex and reliant on human–machine interactions. Related time-consuming tasks require important manual input and result in increased variability in care quality. In this scenario, AI gained growing attention as a powerful tool to provide faster, higher quality, and safer radiation treatment delivery by optimization and automation in the clinical workflow.

In this review, we discuss the progress of AI in oncology, with a focus on radiation treatment from a workflow perspective. For insight, an overview of innovative employed AI methods will be provided. Opportunities, applicability, and efficiency of AI solutions will be systematically addressed with examples for each stage of the RT workflow

Artificial Intelligence for Medicine
https://doi.org/10.1016/B978-0-443-13671-9.00013-2

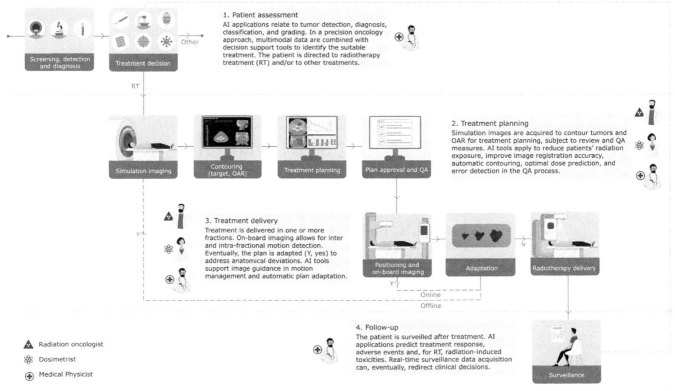

FIG. 1   AI applications in the radiotherapy workflow. Schematic overview of AI applications in the radiotherapy (RT) workflow, conceptually divided into three domains: (1) assessment, (2) treatment planning and delivery, and (3) surveillance. The workflow begins with the patient consult. During this time, useful information derived from screening and diagnostic tools are evaluated. To assess the potential benefit of treatment, tumor stage, gene signatures, and overall patient status (e.g., age, comorbidities, functional status, tumor, and critical healthy tissues proximity) are considered to build predictive models of treatment outcome and define a treatment strategy. If the patient is directed to RT, a simulation appointment during which medical images are acquired for treatment planning follows. Subsequently, the treatment plan is created and subjected to approval, review, and quality assurance (QA) measures prior to delivery of radiation to the patient. Finally, the patient then receives follow-up care. Many clinical figures are involved, such as radiation oncologists, medical physicists, and dosimetrists. AI tools have the potential to shift their focus from repetitive and laborious tasks, such as tumor and organ segmentation, plan design, and QA, respectively, toward the management of nonroutine, high-risk issues, and the development and implementation of solutions that require human acumen.[8–10]

(Fig. 1). In the first section, algorithms' adoption in the patient assessment stage, encompassing screening, diagnosis, and treatment decisions as part of the broad oncology workflow, will be presented. In the second section, the major applications in the treatment planning and delivery stages of the RT workflow will be highlighted. In the last section, implementations in patient follow-up care will be described. Finally, challenges, recommendations, and future implications of AI-powered cancer care will be debated.

2. AI methods in oncology

In 1955, emeritus Stanford Professor John McCarthy introduced AI as "the science and engineering of making intelligent machines."[11] AI refers to computers' capability to perform tasks mimicking human intelligence, such as visual perception and pattern recognition for decision-making and problem-solving purposes.[12] Machine learning (ML) and deep learning (DL) are subfields of AI. DL is, in turn, a subfield of ML (Fig. 2).

ML is an actionable discipline extended from the computational learning theory in AI. ML algorithms are operated by computer programs to learn from data; especially for unstructured data, machines often proved better and more unbiased decision-making skills than the human learner. Learning from given data objects, the class of future data to be tested can be revealed, so data-driven predictions or decisions be performed without human assistance.[13,14]

In this scenario, the advent of artificial neural network (ANN) models introduced great innovation. ANN consists of a group of related input/output units, whose connection is expressed by a weighted edge. In the learning stage, weights are optimized based on the agreement between predicted output and labeled test data.[13,14] ANN models with multiple self-learning hidden layers that include several neurons herald a new era for DL. Hidden

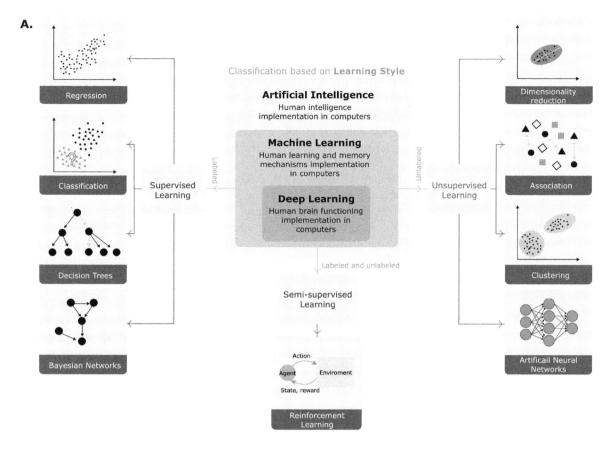

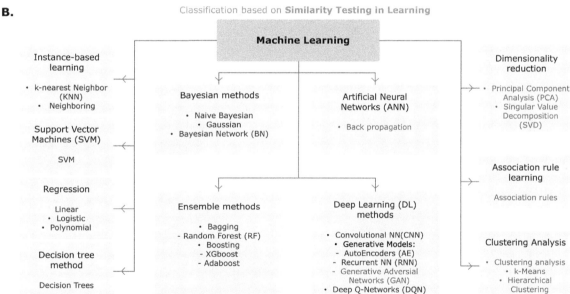

FIG. 2   Classification of machine learning models. (A) According to input data employment in the learning process, ML algorithms can be classified into (1) *Supervised Learning*: Input data/features are labeled (training set). The model is constructed through training of the training dataset, improved by receiving feedback predictions (validation set, part of the training set), and tested through incoming data (without known labels, test set).[13,14] (2) *Unsupervised Learning*: Input data are not labeled. The model is constructed by exploring the structures in the input data to extract general rules, going through a mathematical process to reduce redundancy, or organizing data by similarity testing.[13,14] (3) *Semi-supervised Learning*: Input data are both labeled and unlabeled. The model learns the structures to organize the data to make predictions and different assumptions are made to model the unlabeled data.[13] (B) According to the similarity testing functions employed in the learning process, ML algorithms can be classified into twelve categories. For example, (1) *regression* relies on statistical learning, (2) *instance-based learning (or memory-based learning)* methods apply similarity measures, stored in the database, (3) *tree-based methods* are based on tree-structured decision models, (4) *Bayesian methods* are based on statistical decision theory, (5) *clustering analysis* relies on similarity tests to group data, (6) *neural networks* are based on cognitive models, inspired by the structure and function of biological neurons to model the complex relationships between, (7) *deep learning* methods are based on much deeper and complex neural networks, and (8) *ensemble methods* are composed of multiple weaker independently trained models, whose prediction results are combined.[13,14] Algorithm examples are listed for each category, highlighted in color according to their learning style class (ref. panel A).

layers simulate biological neurons making the output of the previous layer as input of the next layer. The layer-wise learning structure of the deep network simulates the hierarchical structure of information processing by the human brain.[13,14]

DL's inventive learning approach differs from the one of "nondeep" ML, which is more dependent on human intervention. As a general rule, a feature hierarchy process is necessary to differentiate categories of data and create structured inputs, required by the learning process. In conventional ML, human intervention is required to determine the hierarchy of features (so-called handcrafted features[15]). DL, instead, can automate much of the feature extraction process itself and accept also raw unstructured data. Hence, part of the human intervention is not necessary, and usage of larger data sets is possible.[16,17]

With conventional ML methods, the limited generalizability related to the variation of the input data and task scope achieved varying degrees of clinical utility and the adoption of AI in medicine declined.[18] The multimodal nature of DL and the ability to discern complex and nonlinear relationships in data[19] offers algorithm generalizability which might ultimately result in better clinical decision-making and thus improved quality of care.

Besides, natural language processing (NLP) is an adjacent field within AI, involved in converting unstructured data (i.e., electronic health records (EHRs) clinical notes, and diagnostic/procedural reports) into discrete data elements to enrich complex databases, hence the power of derived models.[20]

Together with the digitalization of healthcare data (e.g., EHRs and medical imaging) and the enhanced parallel computing capability (e.g., architectures such as graphics processing units, GPUs) and cloud storage, the advent of DL announced practice-changing and boosted unprecedented development of AI-based applications for medicine.[21] In the context of cancer care, noteworthy aspects include diagnostic accuracy, tumor classification and grading, novel anti-cancer drug discovery, treatment decision optimization for personalized therapy (patient outcome and treatment response prediction), and automated RT workflow (Fig. 3).

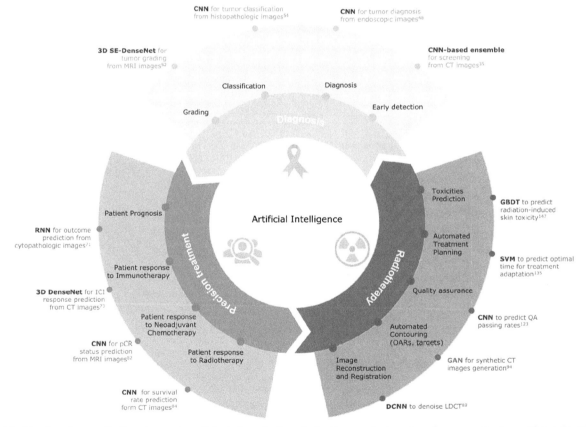

FIG. 3   Machine learning applications in oncology. Selected applications in the three main domains of cancer patient care (*diagnosis, radiotherapy, precision treatment*) are reported for each stage of the oncologic workflow. Application examples are listed for each field, highlighted in color according to their learning style class (ref. panel A, Fig. 2). CT=Computed tomography. LDCT=Low dose computed tomography. MRI=Magnetic resonance imaging. pCR=Pathologic complete response. CNN=Convolutional neural networks. DCNN=Deep CNN. RNN=Recurrent neural network. 3D SE-DenseNet=Three-dimensional squeeze-and-excitation densely connected convolutional network. AE=Autoencoders. GAN=Generative adversial networks. SVM=Support vector machines. GBDT=Gradient Boost Decision Tree. OAR=Organ at risk.

3. AI in diagnosis and treatment decision

The clinical cancer therapy workflow starts with the oncologic consultation. An inspection of the patient's symptoms, medical history, physical evaluation, genomic data, diagnostic examinations, prognosis, and treatment response prediction allows the oncologist to define a tailored treatment decision strategy. Early cancer detection and accuracy in diagnosis, classification, and grading are the main fields of interest of AI applications, especially DL-based, addressed by means of image and multiomics data analysis tools.

In cancer-related image analysis, DL methods outperformed conventional computer-aided detection (CAD) systems in many cases,[20] simplifying the pipelines of conventional CAD diagnosis and reducing false-positive rates.[22] As for multiomics-based data analysis, DL approaches proved higher accuracies in specific tasks than the state-of-the-art genomic-informed clinical models.[23] Indeed, the introduction of more advanced testing (e.g., gene expression assays and next-generation sequencing, NGS, of somatic and germline genomes) provided an ever-expanding list of disease-related features. On the other side, while increasing the potential resolving power, they create a net of interactions among emerging and established disease factors, elevating complexity level beyond comprehension supported by traditional approaches. Still, DL techniques proved to be the only feasible means of synthesizing the magnitude and interdependence of such multimodal data, indispensable to approach the intricacy of the biological system and provide an accurate interpretation of an individual's cancer status.[20]

We anticipate that convolutional neural networks (CNNs) will be largely mentioned in this first stage of the clinical workflow, being very efficient at capturing the spatial and temporal dependencies of the input in settings such as images or sequential data.[23,24] They are currently adopted in the detection, segmentation, and classification of cancer lesions in medical images and deep sequencing.[15,23–27] CNNs consist of three stacking main layers: convolutional, pooling, and fully connected layers. Layer by layer, the pixels' values of the original images are converted to the final prediction scores. The convolutional layers combine input data (feature map) with convolutional kernels (filters) to create a transformed feature map. Based on learned parameters, filters are automatically adjusted to extract the most useful features of interest.

3.1 Screening and early detection

Cancer screening programs proved to reduce the requirement of invasive treatments and/or mortality for many common cancers, like breast,[28] cervical,[29] colorectal,[30,31] and lung tumors.[32,33]

As for cancer-related image analysis, efficient AI applications rely on radiologic,[33–38] endoscopic,[39] and cytopathologic images[40] for precancerous lesion detection.[22]

In radiological imaging, several DL models achieved excellent accuracies for breast cancer screening.[34–38] A CNN-based ensemble classifier for computed tomography (CT) imaging identified breast cancer lesions in two large datasets, representative of different screening cohorts and practices. Compared to the original decisions in the clinical practice and to an independent study evaluating six radiologists' performance, AI support proved a reduction in the number of false positives and false negatives. The area under the curve (AUC) for the AI system was 11.5% higher than the average AUC achieved by the six radiologists (0.62 vs 0.74).[38] Similarly, in lung cancer screening, a three-dimensional (3D) CNN model for low-dose CT (LDCT) imaging identified cancer lesions in two cohorts of patients, with no prior computed tomography (CT) imaging performed and with prior CT available.[33] Compared to six independent radiologists' evaluations, the model proved absolute reductions of 11% in false positives and 5% in false negatives in the first case and similar performance in the latter case. The model achieved a state-of-the-art performance (AUC, 0.94). Notably, Sybil, another model based on 3D CNN, further allowed to accurately predict an individual's future lung cancer risk within one year from a single LDCT on three different data sets (National Lung Screening Trial, NLST, Massachusetts General Hospital, MGH, and Chang Gung Memorial Hospital, CGMH, with an AUC of 0.92, 0.86, and 0.80, respectively),[41] correctly lateralizing future cancers' location and LDCT's likelihood of high-risk score. In endoscopic imaging, a CCN-based model for diagnostic colorectal colonoscopy predicted polyp rate and adenoma detection rate (ADR).[39] Compared to conventional colonoscopy, the AI-based colonoscopy significantly increased adenoma detection rates and the mean number of diminutive adenomas found per patient (29.1% vs. 20.3%). Finally, in cytopathologic imaging, a DL classifier detected cervical epithelial cells stained both with brown cytoplasmic stain (p16) and red nuclear (Ki-67) with abnormal morphology (p16/Ki-67 dual-stained, DS).[40] Learning approaches included CCN with 4 layers (CNN4) and Inception-v3 with 48 layers (IncV3). Compared to conventional Pap and manual DS in three independent epidemiological studies of cervical precancers, the AI-based DS proved equal sensitivity and substantially higher specificity. With respect to Pap, an objective and automated DS evaluation reduced avoidable colposcopies by one-third (41.9% vs 60.1%, $P < 0.001$). Both the above-mentioned automatic optical biopsy models were trained on tissue biopsy-based gold standards.

Regarding multiomics (exome, transcriptome, and epigenome) data analysis, successful AI-based screening systems relate to liquid biopsies, allowing for whole-blood pan-cancer detection from deep sequencing.[22,42,43] Whole blood is the common medium shared by tumor markers and represents an attractive option for rapid, noninvasive, and simple processing testing. Multi-cancer early detection (MCED) tests have been developed to differentiate circulating tumor DNAs (ctDNAs) or other analytes, such as protein biomarkers, from those of noncancer cells.[42] Promising results have been obtained with CancerSEEK,[44,45] with proved specificities >99%. Sensitivity, instead, depends on cancer type and stage, ranging from 39% in stage I disease to approximately 84% in stage III disease. A logistic regression model is used to classify samples as cancer-positive to 16 gene mutations and expression levels of eight plasma proteins, then a random forest model identifies cancer type. CancerSEEK received Breakthrough Device designation from the U.S. Food and Drug Administration (FDA) for patho-genomics and transcriptomics in pancreatic and ovarian cancers. Additional validation of the test is ongoing in a prospective, observational study. Further interest in AI applications for pan-cancer tests is enhanced by the potential to enable cost-effective screening methods over single-organ approaches for less common cancers and cancer types that currently have no effective screening method.[42]

3.2 Diagnosis, classification, and grading

In cancer-related image analysis, AI applications are built on radiologic,[46–50] endoscopic,[51–55] and histopathologic images[56–61] for accurate diagnosis, cancer subtype classification, and tumor grading.[22] As for multiomics-data analysis, AI is employed in mentioned tasks by learning the transcriptome patterns.[20]

In radiological imaging for diagnostic purposes, successful DL methods have been implemented for colorectal,[46] liver,[47] and nasopharyngeal (NPC)[48] cancer.[20,22] For example, a 3D residual neural network (ResNet)-based SVM classifier for CT imaging identified peritoneal metastasis of synchronous peritoneal carcinomatosis in colorectal cancer. The performance of the algorithm, compared to contrast-enhanced CT evaluated by radiologists, resulted in higher accuracy (AUC of 0.99 vs 0.79).[46] As for endoscopic imaging in diagnosis, applications interest gastrointestinal lesions,[51] polyps,[52] and esophageal[54] cancer detection.[20,22] A CNN-based gastrointestinal AI diagnostic system (GRAIDS) for gastroscopy recognized upper gastrointestinal cancers in a multicenter study. Accuracy levels (from 91.5% to 97.7%) reached expert endoscopists' ones and surpassed those of competent and trainee endoscopists.[51] Regarding histopathologic diagnostic slides, DL has numerous applications in breast cancer.[27,56,62] In CAMELYON16, a researcher challenge competition for diagnosing breast cancer, a GoogLeNet-based classifier for whole-slide imaging (WSI) identified metastasis in lymph nodes stained with hematoxylin–eosin (H&E). The model outperformed pathologist's interpretation, limited to routine workflow time constraints (AUC of 0.99 vs 0.88).[56]

In radiological imaging for classification and grading objectives, DL models were applied to liver[49] and prostate[50] tumors.[20,22] A 3D densely connected CCN (3D SE-DenseNet) combined with squeeze-and-excitation networks (SENets) for MR imaging classified hepatocellular carcinoma (HCC) grading with an accuracy of 83%.[49] Concerning endoscopic imaging in tumor classification, AI application examples apply to colorectal polyps.[55] A DNN-based model assisted a CAD system in identifying diminutive (less than 5 mm) neoplastic or hyperplastic colorectal polyps with an accuracy of 90.1%, in a shorter time with respect to endoscopists. Perfect intra-observer agreement was reported, while a low level of intra-observer and inter-observer agreement occurred among endoscopists. Another successful classification tool AI-based in image analysis applies to skin lesions.[63,64] A single CCN algorithm for dermoscopic imaging distinguished keratinocyte carcinomas (most common cancer) vs benign seborrheic keratoses; and malignant melanomas (deadliest cancer) vs benign nevi. Performance was comparable to the evaluation of 21 certified dermatologists.[63] Finally, DL-based tumor classification and grading with histopathologic images were implemented for lung lesions,[57] prostate,[58,59] brain,[60] and breast[61] cancer.[20,22] DeepPATH, an Inception-v3 architecture-based model for WSI analysis (training dataset from The Cancer Genome Atlas, TCGA), classified tissues into three classes (normal, lung adenocarcinoma, LUAD, and lung squamous cell carcinoma, LUSC) with an AUC of 0.97.[57] Moreover, a DL system for WSI of prostatectomies automated Gleason grading of prostate adenocarcinoma. The model achieved a significantly higher accuracy with respect to experts' evaluation (accuracy 70% vs 61%).[59]

Regarding multiomics-data analysis in cancer classification and grading, AI relies on whole transcriptome[65,66] RNA sequencing.[20] SCOPE, a Supervised Cancer Origin Prediction Using Expression algorithm trained on TCGA, incorporated multiple tumor profiles to identify cancer status for 40 classes of untreated primary cancers (mesothelioma and treatment-resistant metastatic cancers) and discriminate it against adjacent normal tissues. Moreover, SCOPE identified the origin site in 15 cases of cancers with unknown primary origin.[65] Besides, AI-based analysis of multiomics data combined with clinically annotated data is successfully employed in drug-susceptibility genes identification, variant detection, and cancer research.[4,67,68]

Overall, these applications encourage the adoption of AI in cancer diagnosis, classification, and grading, whose performances are comparable or even superior to trained experts' evaluation.[22] Taking on time-consuming tasks, AI enables clinical figures to better allocate their efforts to high-level decision-making tasks, whose complexity is related to the presence of confounding factors for the diagnosis.[27] Moreover, when training on large-scale archives, AI provides advantages in scalability and builds computational unanimity that compensates for interobserver variability in clinical practice.[69] Therefore, to improve workflow efficiency, the translation of AI-based models from research to clinical practice is promoted.

3.3 Treatment decision and precision therapy

The goal of precision medicine in oncology is to identify suitable treatments for individual patients, according to their disease prognosis and their expected response to different therapeutic interventions (immunotherapy, chemotherapy, targeted therapy, surgery, and radiotherapy).[22] This way, specific treatments can be delivered to subpopulations of patients who will benefit from them, while side effects (e.g., unnecessary toxicity, delays in surgery, avoidable costs) will spare groups who will not. In this light, the term 'precision medicine' is preferred to 'personalized medicine.'[70–72,]

Patients' clinical outcome and treatment response are correlated with individual tumor characteristics, genetic content, and, generally, sociodemographic characteristics. Radiation oncologists often rely on various diagnostic tools (i.e., medical imaging, bloodwork, and genomics) to define the appropriate combination of treatments. However, the large volume of data that needs to be explored and these data's complex interconnection is orders of magnitude beyond the cognitive capacity of a single human.[20,72] To guide oncologists in treatment selection, supports of AI for medical imaging assessments and NLP for EHR are fundamental. Based on large databases, they can better predict individual patient outcomes[73–75] and response to therapies.[76–81]

The Response Evaluation Criteria in Solid Tumors (RECIST), most popular metric adopted for treatment response evaluation, is based on the tumors' changes in size. AI algorithms can potentially better assess tumor response and predict outcomes by considering more informative changes in tumor phenotype than changes in size alone.[82] In this scenario, radiomic analysis, a branch of medical imaging analytics, plays a major role. Radiomic methods allow for automated extraction of quantitative features (i.e., size, shape, image intensity, texture, relationships between voxels, and fractal characteristics) to characterize radiologic images, providing computer vision–based insights not appreciable otherwise.[20,71,83] Moreover, they can correlate genetic, histologic, and other related data with radiomic signatures to create *radiomic biomarkers*.[71]

In immunotherapy, several drugs have been recognized for the treatment of a wide range of tumors, including melanoma, nonsmall cell lung cancer (NSCLC), bladder, and gastrointestinal cancer. However, 50%–80% of patients are unresponsive to immunotherapy drugs such as immune checkpoint inhibitors (ICI).[22] Immunotherapy treatment response is currently based on biomarkers of the immunogenic tumor microenvironment (e.g., programmed death-ligand 1 (PD-L1) expression, tumor mutational burden (TMB), microsatellite instability (MSI), and somatic copy number alterations), called *predictive* or *treatment selection biomarkers*.[84] AI applications have been developed to relate promising predictive biomarkers of immunotherapy response with radiomic and pathomics data (i.e., radiomic biomarkers identification). For instance, a 3D-DenseNet model combined tumor mutational burden (TMB) data—a significant predictor of ICIs efficacy—with CT images to investigate the correlation between the radiomic signature and TMB and include its predictive value for ICI response in advanced NSCLC. The individual noninvasive radiomic biomarker, TMBRB, could distinguish High-TMB from Low-TMB with an AUC of 0.81 on the test cohort, superior to that of a histological subtype and radiomic model.[76] On the other side, since several potential predictive biomarkers of ICI response lack scalability, require extensive resources, or still need to be validated for clinical implementation,[84] different pipelines have been developed. A multivariable classifier integrated histology specimens with clinical data, readily available through the standard of care, to predict response in advanced melanoma. The classifier proved to accurately stratify patients into responders and nonresponders with an AUC of 0.80.[77] Still, invasive and difficult procedures (i.e., biopsies) are required to acquire biomarker data, which remain limited to the specific tumor region. Innovatively, another DL tool (fully connected deep NLP model) was proposed to directly predict the response (in terms of gold-standard RECIST) and progression-free survival using radiology text reports for NSCLC patients treated with a programmed cell death protein 1 (PD-1) blockade protein. This model promises to facilitate the analysis of large real-world oncology estimating objective response metrics (RECIST) at a greater scale and without the negatives of biopsies.[78]

As for neoadjuvant chemotherapy (NAC), DL algorithms have been adopted to estimate treatment responses to NAC for breast[8,79,80] and rectal[81] cancer.[22] Several models apply radiomics on pre-NAC magnetic resonance imaging (MRI) data to predict the pathological complete response (pCR) before the NAC, with AUC ranging from 0.78 to 0.86.[8] Again, since no radiomic or DL model has been validated yet to change the clinical decision-making of NAC, other solutions have been considered. As the structural and functional change in tumor microenvironment after NAC can reflect the therapeutic response effect, a CNN model was proposed to predict the pCR status after NAC by combining pre-NAC and post-NAC MRI. An exceptional performance, with an AUC of 0.97, was achieved considering both data sets, while it was lower using only pre-NAC or post-NAC data.[79]

Finally, regarding radiotherapy treatment, AI applications have been implemented to estimate treatment responses to RT for the lung[9,85] and the brain[86] cancer.[24] Even for RT, although radiomics-based tools are still largely confined to research, many undergoing studies focus on radiomics-analysis for treatment response prediction.[9,85–87] For example, a CNN model based on pretreatment CT planning data predicted clinical outcomes of early NSCLC patients treated with stereotactic body RT (SBRT).[9] Radiomic features proved to be prognostic for some outcomes that conventional imaging metrics (volume and diameter) could not predict. Besides, another CCN model based on pretreatment and posttreatment CT images of patients with locally advanced NSCLC significantly predicted survival and cancer-specific outcomes (progression, migration, invasion, distant metastases, and local-regional recurrence).[85] Lastly, also in the context of RT, AI applications have been developed to identify predictive biomarkers. A logistic regression model was adopted to predict response to RT by means of genomic signatures (e.g., involved in DNA damage repair and radiosensitivity), identified considering the transcriptome differences (from TCGA database across 15 cancer types) between RT responder and nonresponder groups. The model performed with an AUC up to 0.97 and has potential application as a biomarker.

Although standardization of imaging systems within/across institutions (which remains a major challenge for radiomics[84]) is not accomplished yet and more work is required for reproducible AI models, these AI applications can impact cancer care quality through analysis of better practices and trends.

4. AI in radiotherapy treatment

If the patient is directed to RT, the subsequent RT workflow stage involves radiation dose prescription to the tumor and normal structures avoidance in accordance with established dose constraints, for treatment plan design. However, due to changes in tumor radiosensitivity and deviations in the anatomical arrangement of the tumor and surrounding tissues, this is not a straightforward task. AI applications support radiotherapy personalization,[87] providing genomic-adjusted radiation dose for radiosensitivity and optimization of dose prescription,[88] based on tumor and nearby organ contours.[82] To define constraints for treatment plan preparation, simulation imaging is performed according to the oncologist's instructions (e.g., patient immobilization, scan range, treatment site, patient preparation in terms of organ's filling or contrast injection).[82,83,89]

4.1 Simulation imaging

Simulation involves multiple types of medical images: CT images, which provide electron density information for radiation dose calculation,[88] MRI scans, capable of soft tissue contrast for tumor and organ segmentation,[90] or both image modalities, allowing for image fusion with registration techniques to combine them.[82,89]

CT is a widespread imaging technique due to its low cost, acquisition speed, and high spatial resolution. However, it provides an additional dose to the patient, introducing further risks when increasing the number of images (i.e., four-dimensional CT, 4DCT) for treatment planning and monitoring,[89] especially if a high number of fractions (e.g., 30 or more) is required. Therefore, AI applications aimed to reduce imparted dose, while guaranteeing image quality (degraded by increased noise due to reduced exposure) suitable for RT planning, by timely acting on the reconstruction pipeline. AI approaches either perform denoising after image reconstruction (image-to-image approaches) or during the reconstruction process (iterative-learning approaches).[89] Among image-to-image approaches, deep CNN (DCNN) methods have been used to map LDCT images toward their corresponding normal-dose counterparts.[89] In iterative-learning approaches, prior functions (for image smoothness and edge maintenance) are learned for iterative reconstruction from sinograms. Currently, prior functions are manually designed or learned with conventional ML algorithms (e.g., PCA), assuming that reconstructed images lie within a linear manifold model trained from normal-dose images. However, the manifold is usually highly nonlinear. Recently, DL methods have been adopted for appropriate modeling, improving the image reconstruction quality.[91] Still, CT imaging is related to uncertainty in tumor location due to poor soft-tissue contrast. To provide additional information for target delineation and contouring, a supporting image, such as MRI, is aligned with the planning CT image.

MRI, unlike CT, does not impart additional dose to the patient and provides superior soft-tissue contrast, offering both anatomical and functional imaging for a more accurate delineation of tumor and organs while also providing simultaneous information for the assessment of treatment response.[10] However, a better soft-tissue capacity is paid at the expense of a lack of electron density information for dose calculation and treatment plan preparation. Conventional ML models (e.g., atlas-based) have already been implemented to create synthetic CT (sCT) images from MRI, thus providing MRI with the capability to calculate radiation dose.[92] Newly, DL models addressed this issue with direct encoder–decoder networks and generative adversarial networks (GANs). Direct encoder–decoder networks map end-to-end MRIs to corresponding CTs, while GANs pit image "generators" against "discriminators" to ensure that synthesized images are as realistic as possible.[89] It has been reported that DCNN outperforms sCT generation by conventional atlas-based method, both in terms of accuracy (mean absolute error, MAE, 84.8 vs 94.5 Hounsfield units, HU) and computation speed of the sCT.[93] GANs are based on two adversarial CNNs: a generator, trained to synthesize images that resemble real CT (sCT), and a discriminator, trained to differentiate sCT from real CT (binary classification problem). Regarding GANs' performance, recent studies reported an MAE of around 76 HU for the brain sCTs and 40 HU for the pelvis sCTs. The mean dose difference between the sCT and the reference CT was <2% and <1%, respectively.[94]

Hence, AI methods have begun to open the way for MR-only RT workflow. Novel technology development turned this possibility into reality integrating MR scanners with linear accelerators, the so-called MR-Linac systems.[95] Due to the magnetic field (MF) interference between the radiation beam (i.e., beam deflection by the MF of the MRI scanner) and the MRI system (i.e., artifacts on MRI images by the MF of the beam accelerator), low-field (LF) MR systems are integrated (0.35–1.5 T).[96] In recent years, the built-in MRI and linear accelerator systems have evolved to become nearly independent of each other, allowing for near-zero MF distortion during gantry rotation and negligible electron return effect (which is accounted for in the treatment planning system (TPS)).[97] Further AI applications are taking over the challenge of providing good image quality for LF MRI.[98] Moreover, high-resolution and low-noise MRI acquisition time is long and needs to be adapted to RT workflow time constraints. Therefore, AI methods also aim to reduce MRI scan times—while guaranteeing adequate resolution and signal-to-noise ratio (SNR) for tumor and organ delineation—by enabling detailed reconstructed images from undersampled MRI data (i.e., sparse k-space acquisitions and compressed sensing techniques).[95] Most recent enhancements to the MRI fast acquisition methods have begun to use MRI fingerprinting, where tissue properties are quickly acquired and postprocessed using dictionaries and ML to generate any scan (e.g., T2-weighted, FLAIR, DWI, etc.).[99] An MR-only RT workflow is appealing in terms of reduced uncertainty (related to the unnecessary alignment procedure to CT scans) and clinical efficiency and costs (number of imaging appointments).[82]

4.1.1 Image registration

Image registration is an optimization process, performed by medical physicists and dosimetrists to align multimodal data in the treatment planning stage and before treatment fractions delivery (CT and supporting image, predominantly MRI), and longitudinal data (at subsequent time samples) in the delivered-dose monitoring stage.[82,89]

The clinical desire to exactly quantify the registration spatial error for treatment margins definition faces two main challenges: the different nature of images, which does not allow conventional measures of similarity to be generalizable, and the variability of image content (e.g., tumor change in size throughout the treatment), which does not allow for a simple voxel-wise correspondence.[89] Therefore, DL models are applied to *area-based methods* (based on similarity measurements),[100] focusing on learning more efficient similarity metrics from training data. For instance, a deep similarity learning method trained a binary classifier to learn the patch-wise correspondence of images. The output was then used as the similarity score, outperforming conventional similarity metrics.[101] Besides, novel DL models consider *feature-based methods* (based on salient feature detection),[100] to face the issue of image content variability by allowing deformable registrations. In this case, an AE network was trained to hierarchically learn features as a preprocessing step.[89] Additionally, to deal with the multi-modality issue, some DL methods employed learning algorithms either to construct a shared latent representation of anatomical structures across different modalities or for cross-modal image synthesis, reducing the task to a monomodal registration.[102] However, these applications still need to be properly validated in a clinical setting.[89]

4.1.2 Segmentation

Segmentation is a crucial stage: tumor and OAR delineation guide dose prescription constraints. Therefore, inappropriate contouring might lead to underdosing of the tumor or overdosing of healthy tissues, ultimately affecting the success of the treatment.[82] Manually performed on a slice-by-slice basis, it turns out to be a complicated process subject to interobserver variability.[20,22,82,89] Therefore, substantial efforts of AI applications in the RT workflow have focused on automatic segmentation. Current segmentation procedure assistance integrates prior knowledge in the segmentation process (e.g., organs' relative position or expected size changes). Semi-automatic methods in clinical practice, such as atlases, consider segmented reference images. Hence, the registration procedure, selection strategy, and required subsequent manual iterations introduce uncertainty components.[82,89] AI has the potential to enable almost completely or possibly even fully automated segmentation approaches. Recent AI methods more efficiently incorporate prior knowledge in the form of parameterized models by labeling each voxel in the learning process.[89] In OAR segmentation, DL models proved outstanding results for head-and-neck (H&N),[103–105] lung,[106] and NPC[107] cancer.[82] A DL auto-contouring approach for OARs in H&N tumor demonstrated improved performance with respect to atlas-based approaches, both in terms of time reduction (about 40%) and accuracy (higher dice similarity coefficient, DSC, and lower Hausdorff distance, HD).[105] Tumor volume segmentation, on the other hand, is an even more challenging application, due to variability in tumors' shapes, sizes, locations, and internal architecture. Various AI approaches led to significant improvement in gross tumor volume (GTV) and clinical tumor volume (CTV) delineation in brain,[108] breast,[109] lung,[110,111] rectal,[112] and NPC[113] cancer.[22] Most significantly, recent efforts in clinical validation for radiotherapy targeting involved model validation in external datasets (including clinical trials and diagnostic radiology data) and end-user testing. A U-Nets full CNN (FCNN) segmenting primary NSCLC tumors and involved lymph nodes in CT images yielded target volumes with equivalent radiation dose coverage to those of experts and a 65% reduction in segmentation time.[111] Another FCNN (3D CNN of *VoxResNet*, FCNN) architecture extracting representative MRI-based features for NPC GTV segmentation proved a high level of accuracy compared with ground truth (DSC 0.79, HU 2.0 mm) and assisting oncologists in a multicenter evaluation (median DSC, 0.74 vs 0.78, reduced intra-/interobserver variation and time by 36.4%, 54.5%, and 39.4%, respectively).[113]

However, AI models for registration and segmentation purposes are trained on historical registration clinical data sets, considered as ground truth. Although improved simulation of the task as performed by clinicians, they are limited to the clinical correctness and protocols adopted.[89] Nonetheless, AI-based performances, largely beneficial in automatizing and speeding up time-consuming processes, might encourage institutions to pursue standardization.[89]

Lastly, the introduction of AI-based segmentation tools in the market calls in turn for AI-based quality assurance (QA) tools to identify eventual errors. QA of auto-segmentations is a workforce-demanding and time-consuming task, therefore another potential field of application for AI.[82]

4.2 Treatment planning

Treatment planning is an optimization process meant to maximize dose delivered to the tumor and competitively minimize the dose delivered to surrounding healthy tissues[22,82,89] establishing specific dosimetry objectives.[22,82] First, an appropriate treatment technique is selected (e.g., fixed beam intensity-modulated RT, IMRT, volumetric modulated arc therapy, VMAT, and protons).[83] Then, iteratively, positioning, fractionation, distribution, and other machine parameters (e.g., radiation beam angles and weights[83]) are set in a trial-and-error-based approach.[22,82,89] Finally, the plan is evaluated and approved. As the above-mentioned RT workflow steps, it is a labor-intensive and time-consuming task, whose performance quality depends on clinical physicists' experience. As a result, it involves a high degree of intra-[22,82,89] and inter institutional[82] variability.

Therefore, many algorithms have been developed to support medical physicists, dosimetrists, and radiation oncologists in the treatment planning and evaluation tasks, either automating the planning process and/or optimizing dosimetric trade-offs. In clinical practice, automated rule implementation and reasoning (ARIR) approaches are employed to automatize repetitive tasks by means of hard-coded rules[89,114] with timesaving benefits.[115] The TPS receives as input the patient's anatomy and the dosimetric requirements and, following a binary logic from simple clinical guidelines, simulates manual treatment planning, allowing for iterative adjustments after performance evaluation.[114] Knowledge-based planning (KBP) is adopted to assist radiation oncologists in initial decision-making, considering associations between geometric and dosimetric parameters (e.g., beam arrangements and DVH constraints in inverse planning) from a selection of previous plans defined with best clinical knowledge.[96,116] Besides advantages in time-sparing and reduced variability, KBP-based plans are generally superior to manual planning in OAR sparing.[89] The drawback is the need for re-optimization, which is a time-consuming process, in case the planner changes the dosimetric trade-off during the evaluation.[114] To address this limitation, multicriteria optimization (MCO) approaches, instead of a single plan, generate multiple optimal plans (so-called Pareto surface) simultaneously, allowing real-time evaluation of results for different trade-offs.[89,114]

Although these approaches have improved planning quality reliability, still remain suboptimal since they cannot provide estimations of patient-specific achievable dose distributions. DL-based methods, by means of a comprehensive analysis of patient-individual anatomy, aim to incorporate parameters of treatment prescription and delivery technique into AI decision-making.[22,82,114] For instance, novel KB modeling approaches, based on NNs, are trained on prior plans to predict voxel-by-voxel dose optimization dose values considering patient's contours and anatomy.[117,118] Specifically, CNNs' architectures allow for automatic feature extraction (instead of handcrafted features) and direct contour-to-dose mapping learning. Furthermore, GANs' models have been proposed in a reinforcement learning approach, where the two networks are represented by a dose-distribution predictor (discriminator), that learns from produced plans (simulations), and a planning producer (generator), that optimizes parameters (actions) using the predicted plan distribution.[83,89,114] The predicted 3D dose distribution outperforms other AI algorithms in terms of OAR dose sparing, tumor coverage, and similarity to clinical plan in terms of gamma pass-rate.[116] Although, once more, restricted to the quality of the data they are trained with, fast, automatic, and reliable planning processes can support useful insights for radiation oncologists.[89,119]

4.3 Patient-specific and machine QA

Once the radiation oncologist approves the treatment plan, QA checks are performed by medical physicists to guarantee appropriate setting and performance of elements involved in the treatment delivery stage.

In patient-specific QA, treatment plans are evaluated to detect eventual human or treatment machine system (software and hardware altogether) errors that can affect the treatment delivery performance to the specific patient.[82] For this purpose, treatment plan parameters (e.g., delineated targets and OARs, beam configurations, monitor units (MU), energies, and fractions[89]) are checked and delivered doses compared to planned ones (e.g., in terms of target coverage, normal tissue sparing, and dose homogeneity[89]) employing phantoms designed with dosimeters.[82] Yet again, AI applications address repetitive manual tasks to expedite QA procedures, detecting rare errors and potential contributing factors, which would otherwise require further investigation.[82] Regarding target and OAR contour quality, a CNN method together with a QA network based on ResNet have been introduced to automatically predict the segmentation quality level—in terms of DSC—on CT images. The tool can differentiate between high-quality and low-quality contours (AUC of 0.96, 0.93, and 0.88 for good, medium, and bad quality level prediction, respectively), thus directing medical physics to review the low-quality ones.[120] As for the physical parameters of the patient-specific treatment plan, clustering algorithms have been employed in identifying potential outliers.[89] Finally, in relation to dose distribution, AI-based applications are potentially able to enhance the quality of delivered treatments by predicting differences between planned and delivered treatment variables and incorporating them into dose calculations to increase QA passing rates.[89] Notably, a CCN has been implemented to predict a priori individualized IMRT QA passing rates automatically extracting features from fluence maps of beam intensity, with results comparable to a system designed by physicist experts (MAE of 0.70 vs 0.74).[121] Moreover, the model proved to successfully detect small setup errors in the measurement process as well as a mismatch of the linear accelerator (Linac).[122]

Besides, in machine QA, single parts of the treatment machine are periodically checked in terms of accuracy and precision. The large amount of data acquired provide AI algorithms with the capability to predict errors and trends (e.g., positional multileaf collimator errors and beam symmetry trends).[82,83] For instance, ANN time-series predictive models have been used to monitor Linac's performance over time.[123]

4.4 Treatment set-up and delivery

Advances in TPS and computer-run radiation delivery are beneficial in terms of precise dose allocation to the target volume and improved OAR sparing.[124] On the other hand, this requires accurately reproducing patient's position during the simulation imaging stage on which the treatment plan is based. Therefore, image guidance during the course of the RT treatment (i.e., image-guided radiotherapy, IGRT), is a fundamental requirement to ensure a correct treatment plan delivery.[124]

4.4.1 Image guidance

Cone-beam CT (CBCT) is the usual on-board image modality involved in patient setup and treatment monitoring, although megavoltage (MV) images may also be acquired for assistance. For the purpose of adaptive RT (ART), it is more beneficial to improve CBCT image quality to CT level and perform dose evaluation on registered planning CTs rather than employing CBCT for direct dose calculation, due to the inherent reduced image quality and inaccurate HU mapping.[125] Hence, AI has been applied to improve the image quality of CBCT.[125–127] Remarkably, a GAN model trained to perform a direct scatter correction of CBCT in the image space (i.e., after reconstruction) and a DNN (U-Net) for a correction in the projection space (i.e., before reconstruction) improved MAE from 158 HU to 57 HU and 39 HU, respectively. The dose calculation accuracy was suitable for VMAT, while needed improvement for IMRT.[126] Other multimodality imaging techniques are being used for on board imaging (e.g., MRI, PET, ultrasounds),[128] leading to further opportunities for AI applications.

4.4.2 Motion management

To realize the pretreatment positioning of the patient, a rigid registration (RR) is performed to align the on-board imaging (acquired in the treatment location) to the planning CT, shifting the patient's couch. Patient or organ motion during the treatment delivery (i.e., *intra-fractional motion*[129]) needs to be addressed to preserve the treatment delivery precision. Current motion management methods limit or monitor the respiratory and abdominal motion range (i.e., gating techniques).[130] Inter- and intraindividual variability concerning the extent, frequency, and other organs' mobility complicates tumor motion modeling. AI methods have been employed in dynamic motion-management models capable of adapting to patient motion variability combining individual predictors.[82,89] By means of external markers, NNs successfully predicted tumor position in advance in case of variable breathing patterns and uncorrelated anatomical movements, enabling more accurate tumor tracking.[82,89,131]

4.4.3 Adaptive treatment

Importantly, anatomical changes between simulation imaging and delivery of treatment fraction (i.e., *inter-fractional motion*[129]) need to be considered, evaluating the need for an *offline* re-planning process, involving additional simulation imaging, contouring, and treatment planning.[89] Defining whether a re-planning stage is beneficial in the treatment is a key point in the RT workflow. Such a decision should consider not only the anatomical deviation range but also patient-specific characteristics and, on the other side, the impact of a treatment delivery delay. Recently, AI addressed this topic and investigated methods to automatically adapt the previous treatment plan according to individual's responses, defined as KB response-ART (KBR-ART). With an RL approach, a set of algorithms are trained to learn the radiotherapy environment and search for the optimal dose based on their knowledge of clinical, dosimetric, radiomics, and biomarkers data.[132] Moreover, AI applications have been implemented to predict the optimal time for adaptation. A representative case is an SVM used for time-series evaluation of volume and dose variations in H&N cancer, which identified an average 58% of patients potentially benefitting from re-planning in the fourth week, in agreement with the radiation oncologist's evaluation.[133]

Still, even with AI support, re-planning is a time-consuming process. The adoption of MRI as on-board image modality (MRgRT) and its novel capability of performing real-time imaging,[134] promoted *online* adaptive treatment modality (oART).[135] The treatment plan is adapted daily with real-time tumor and OAR images while the patient remains in the treatment position.[136,137] To limit patients' staying on the treatment couch and open the Linac for more treatment sessions, the treatment adaptation task needs to be investigated using AI approaches. A recent conditional GAN (cGAN) model has been implemented to rapidly predict deliverable adaptive plans for on-board MR imaging (MRgOART).[138] For plans predicted in less than 20s, the passing rate of the dose was 88%, ensuring 95% of the prescription dose to the planning target volume (PTV) and an average increase of 7.6% to OARs. Finally, CBCT on-board imaging commercial solutions[139] and clinical implementations[137] are already available.

5. AI in cancer surveillance

At the end of the treatment, a follow-up data collection of the patient is fundamental in predicting treatments outcome for the above-mentioned purpose of precision medicine. The evolution of imaging changes (e.g., stability/change in tumor size, loss of enhancement, PET avidity),[83] response of tumor markers[83,140] and phenotypic diversity[80,141] can be considered to monitor tumor evolution hence efficacy and/or adverse effects of therapies. Relying on cancer surveillance data, AI applications have been implemented to enable timely, personalized treatment adjustments to improve outcome from the personalized medicine perspective. For instance, an AI-driven platform has been clinically tested in immunotherapy to advise drug dosage in relation to individual patients' phenotypic output (phenotypic personalized medicine, PPM) and in relation to the evolution of their response to treatment.[22,142] PPM-based approaches demonstrated encouraging results in limiting side effects by appropriate drug adjustment.[22,142]

As for RT, the presence of radiation-induced toxicity reduces the consistency of RECIST definitions of response and counsels' reliability on multi-modal patient-specific data. AI is supposed to incorporate pre- and posttreatment images, clinical and molecular data, and radiation dose distributions, to more robustly predict tissue complications and severe toxicities and enable a proactive, rather than reactive, fine-tuning of radiation dose.[82,88,143,144] For this purpose, a radiobiological model has been already discussed,[144] and successful approaches have already focused on subsets of these data for radiation toxicity prediction. For example, a gradient boosting decision tree (GBDT) model, combined with a multiple-variable logistic regression, was developed to predict radiation-induced acute skin toxicity based on images and clinical and dosimetric information of breast cancer patients. PTV dose-related regions of interest (ROIs) and skin dose-related ROIs were contoured to extract radiomic features. A combination of 20 radiomics features and 8 clinical and dosimetric variables achieved an AUC of 0.91. Notably, multiple cancer centers data and internal cross-fold validation increase reliability of the predictive model.[145] Overall, research in the radiomic field, as in other areas, provides promising results to predict outcome in time for RT treatment escalation and/or application of a different treatment modalities. Still, it is essential to remember that these techniques require extremely large datasets, which sets a challenge for the RT community where limited datasets are the norm due to the complex barriers surrounding data sharing in the field.[83]

6. Challenges and adoption barriers of AI models in oncology

While a wide range of AI applications is proposed in oncology, several challenges need to be faced to translate them into clinical practice. Large, high-quality, and representative datasets in model training and suitable validation are prerequisites to improve performance in clinically applied AI.[82,89,143] On the other side, efforts of resources and time are necessary to familiarize with the technology—both in terms of utility and limitations—and ensure safe and appropriate clinical use.[146]

6.1 Database construction

The trustworthiness of AI relies on training on a massive amount of data, which prevents overfitting, thus decrease in performance in external validation dataset.[20,72] The modernization of the healthcare setting is already promoting a full digital representation of the patient's medical data. This holds especially in oncology, where diagnostic, treatment, and surveillance data details (e.g., diagnostic, and monitoring/on-board images, prescribed pharmaceuticals, and radiation doses, delivered dose distributions, genomic and transcriptomic sequences) are in digital form and, by definition, provided with temporal and/or spatial allocation. Hence, the volume of data that needs to be collected and managed is rapidly growing (about 7 GB per single patient, with raw genomic data entailing around 70% of it).[147] To store these huge datasets in a noncare zone, anonymize them and regulate access for study purposes,[21] translational research platforms need to be established.[147]

Besides availability and accessibility, standardization is a must to create quality data and address the diversity of features for automatic multicentric data extraction and integration. To regulate fields and terms in EHR, treatment procedures, and genomic annotations, around 440 biomedical ontologies have been already defined (e.g., SNOMED, NCI Thesaurus, CTCAE, and the UMLS meta-thesaurus).[147] Furthermore, the Radiation Oncology Ontology (ROO) has been introduced to include terms such as region of interest (ROI), target volumes (GTV, CTV, PTV), and dose-volume histograms (DVH).[148] If criteria of data anonymization, accessibility to a noncare platform regulation, and standardization are met, the only requirement left to create and validate truly integrative and scalable models is a multicentric sharing of data for a representative and balanced training cohort.[20,143,147]

However, reality still does not reflect this scenario. Firstly, efforts in standardization need to be reinforced. Often, the plethora of generated data still requires laborious curation and cleaning to be employed in AI model development.[82] This applies especially to unstructured EHR data, with a significant degree of noise, sparseness, and inconsistency. The Observational Medical Outcomes Partnership (OMOP), Common Data Model (CDM), is currently making headway in providing standardized disease codes and vocabulary to structure observational health records into easy-to-use databases.[4] Secondly, and more importantly, given the concerns of real data protection and patient control over their sensible medical records, data[4] are usually confined as property of individual institutions and data-sharing platforms are little put into practice. The applicability of AI models is directly affected in multiple aspects. The significant heterogeneity in medical data across institutions decreases model's performance when applied at different centers. Moreover, the consequently limited data availability reduces the training dataset size, thus increasing chances of model overfitting on it (especially for DL architectures based on a huge number of features) and decreasing generalizability across other populations.[4,20,22,143,147]

To avoid biases related to data collection, data-sharing solutions that enable contributions and learning across institutional and international borders should be promoted and adopted in view of a rewardable medical and scientific interest. Some progress is on course with the establishment of privacy-preserving distributed DL (DDL)[148,149] and multicenter data-sharing agreements.[150,151] Without actually sharing local datasets, DDL provides privacy-preserving solutions to enable multiple research groups to cooperatively implement a common DL model. Data security concerns related to sensitive medical information can be addressed by current digital forensics improvements in personal health signatures for a variety of data modalities (e.g., DNA sequencing, CT or MRI imaging, and diagnosis reports, especially in case of rare diseases).[152] Some steps toward the development of open-source and open-access archives for cancer-related data collections have been moved. The Cancer Imaging Archive (TCIA) and The Cancer Genome Atlas (TCGA) provide examples of multicenter cancer-related images and genomic data collection, respectively. However, inherent biases toward certain minoritized racial and ethnic groups persist. The TCGA, especially, is predominantly composed of white individuals with European ancestry and mainly comprises primary tumors, with restricted cases of metastatic tumors.[4]

6.2 Model commissioning

Given the above-mentioned dataset-related limitations, a rigorous experimental design is mandatory in building models. Model's commissioning is twofold: to an initial algorithm training and (*internal*) validation phase intended to tune the model to the clinical necessity, a subsequent test phase (*external* validation) follows to ensure model's reproducibility prior to clinical use.[146] The training/validation phase implies a partition of the available dataset in a training and validation set (typically 80%–20%, respectively). The test phase involves instead an independent evaluation of the final performance to investigate model's robustness.

To prevent model development from introducing algorithmic biases, the datasets should reflect clinical diversities, inequities, and disparities (in terms of socio-economic factors and health systems practices[153]) of the population the model will be ultimately applied to.[143] Developing efficient algorithms on populations not demographically, socio-economically, and genotypically representative of the addressed cohort might have hazardous consequences.[154,155] This was the case of a hypertrophic cardiomyopathy genetic test built on a dataset characterized by mostly White Americans. Being mutations significantly more common among Black Americans than White American, the test misclassified benign variants as pathogenic for African ancestry patients.[154] It turns out that instead of disease features, the model might learn the dataset distribution (i.e., shortcut learning), influenced by clinical, demographic, or technology-related confounders.[156] Detecting these shortcuts and removing disparities in race and subsequent patterns of health service utilization to ensure not codified or exacerbated algorithms is not an easy task. Even balancing dataset classes (e.g., majority class down-sample or minority class up-sample) might not be sufficient and lead to poor performance, since included cohorts might not reflect populations that did not access the healthcare system at all. The problem is not only AI-related but also local practices need to be considered.

Additionally, in the current status quo, despite great improvements in internal validation practices, external validation is still infrequent and limited by huge costs and a lack of proper protocols. Usually, single-institution clinical data (un-representative of other institutions' realities and minoritarian groups), limited in confounders information, are employed. Biases cannot be detected in such a test set—if any—and the model fails when applied to different clinical settings (i.e., "out of distribution" data) during the test phase.[153]

Not to forget, the reproducibility of the model output is challenging even within the same clinical environment it was developed for: AI models are subject to data drift over time, caused by changes in data formatting, clinical practice (equipment and protocols)[146] or natural drift not present during model commissioning, and change in features' relationship (covariate shift).[4,20,147,153] A feedback system is required to monitor models' validity and advise for the necessity of model re-training.[20,146,153]

Finally, concerning dataset employment, it is important to remark that for precision medicine, a variety of data (e.g., clinical, laboratory, imaging, and epidemiological data)[4,22] should be integrated into the model. Precise medicine should also be encouraged by follow-up data collection to guide treatment decisions and early predict and manage adverse events and relapses according to the patient's current state of knowledge.[147] On the other side, increased development of fusion models and larger feature space for training can aggravate the shortcut learning issue.

Beside dataset-related aspects, the patient-per-feature ratio is another factor to be considered for model commissioning, especially when integrating thousands of information (e.g., genomics) in DL models. A small ratio will result in overfitting (i.e., overtraining) and random errors or training dataset noise description, limiting reliability on another population as mentioned above.[147] In addition, the algorithm selection is a crucial aspect. The outcome of different ML techniques should be compared in model commissioning, opting for the best-performing one. Only about 17% of the published AI studies in oncology were estimated to test more than one ML method.[147]

As a last note, a collaborative ecosystem to leverage the data set is necessary. To support transparency, reproducibility, and quality check in similar healthcare systems and populations, ultimately novel algorithm development and best practices refinement, improvements should be directed in systematic algorithm source code and training condition report.[4,20,72,147,153] Therefore, the data-sharing agreements for publicly available datasets should also require users to share their queries, git hubs, collabs, and Jupiter notebooks upon publication of their work.

6.3 Clinical implementation

Despite improvements in model development, many AI tools remain at the proof-of-concept stage, widening the gap between model development and device implementation.[153] Improved resolving power comes at the expense of our understanding capacity and ability to predict failures. The "black-box" nature of many AI algorithms—especially DL, relying on convoluted hidden layers of data interaction—is emphasized by a large number of parameters involved.[20,22,82,83,143,153] The consequent limited clinical adoption urges the need to establish trust in AI systems providing *interpretability* (understanding what an algorithm is doing) and *explainability* (elucidating the underlying mechanics) of models.[82] Explanatory AI (XAI) is a branch of AI aiming at providing some level of transparency to the decision process beneath complex algorithms. Research is still ongoing, but progress made so far in explanation of deep network processing, representation, and producing systems is promising.[157] Despite the lack of interpretability, a rigorous model implementation based on active monitoring of model's performance and constant assessment of suitable training data can prevent errors and systematic biases.

A correct implementation into clinical reality would require a dedicated multidisciplinary team of relevant experts (e.g., physicians, physicists, biologists, technicians, and IT specialists) with basic knowledge of AI and insight into the specific model, including the target patient cohorts, to support risk analysis and identify eventual systematic errors. Early detection of possible risks or malfunctions can improve the model's robustness against failure. Furthermore, they are required to train and instruct the final users on the proper use and interpretation of the model output.[146]

Besides, implementation in healthcare systems arises many relevant regulatory, ethical, and legal issues. From a regulatory standpoint, the U.S. Food and Drug Administration and the European Union currently classify AI technologies as "software as a medical device," providing regulations and draft guidance for AI algorithms application in medical practice and clinical workflows.[158,159] In terms of ethics, AI applications are already subject to inherent racial bias issues. Moreover, an ever-increasing reliance on AI will likely turn the patient–doctor relationship into a patient–healthcare system relationship. From a legal point of view, this might affect the concept of personal responsibility of the doctor for the patient and redefine the liable party in case of incorrect AI-based decisions.[22,82] Also, patients' right to an explanation of algorithms' output[160] and data protection laws are all points to be addressed.[82] Opportunely, some framework is recently being set by the Medical Device Regulation (MDR) regarding clinical applications and liabilities related to in-house created models, and the General Data Protection Regulation (GDPR) on the subject of privacy compliance. Also, the 2013/59/EURATOM directive introduced the obligation to perform risk analysis for AI-based software.[146]

7. Conclusions and future perspectives

AI gains in accuracy, reproducibility, and consistency are poised to redefine the roles of clinical figures involved in the cancer treatment workflow, from patient consult to follow-up (Fig. 1). The automatization of repetitive tasks requiring labor-intensive input is expected to unhamper the clinical workforce and transfer their responsibilities to quality control of AI output and high-value activities, such as complex decision-making tasks and clinical management.[82] To assist the implementation of AI solutions, the training of medical figures will need to shift from lengthy apprenticeships, meant to gain expertise in performing manual activities, to education in integrating and interpreting information from large datasets in order to support clinical evaluation.[20,82,143,147] An excellent model to consider for such initiatives is represented by the Information Exchange and Data Transformation (INFORMED) fellowship in Oncology Data Science.[161,162] Furthermore, extracurricular enrichment in datathon competitions, that team up clinicians, data scientists, and social scientists to analyze real-world health-related data, should be incentivized to provide clinicians with invaluable insights into data curation and model development and data scientists into the clinical context, thus facilitating the integration of AI technology into routine practice.

Under these circumstances, AI tools are expected to improve performance standardization and reduce interobserver variation in a time-sparing methodology, ultimately translating into an enhanced quality of treatments. These benefits are of primary importance in the current global health scenery, especially for resource-constrained (in workforce and equipment) clinical settings.[20,82,83] Indeed, while more than half of all cancer patients live in low-income or middle-income countries, according to the WHO comprehensive treatment is available in less than 15% of low-income countries but in more than 90% of high-income ones.[163] AI applications have the potential to alleviate expert personnel deficiencies by providing specialized knowledge across disease sites and equipment shortages by maximizing the usage of available devices.

The enthusiasm around AI and big data is obviously well justified. Still, many challenges, a number of which have been mentioned, need to be stressed to encourage proactive solutions. Crucially, the little inclination for multi-institutional data sharing must be surmounted to benefit from the use of distributed learning. Since real-world data disproportions cannot be grasped by a single institution alone, it is crucial to include data exchange in the AI pipeline to build robust models and prevent health biases. Well-intentioned privacy-preserving policies turn into detrimental procedures for marginalized and under-represented populations when neglecting the risk of data privatization.[4,20,153,164] Efforts in the current legal framework need to be reinforced for the purpose of privacy, equity, and safety coexistence. Currently, the FDA's approval process for medical devices and software considers primarily white men and lacks concrete measures for various races, ethnicities, and social environments inclusion. To achieve health equity, the FDA should ask developers of AI solutions for transparency on patient composition in employed datasets and mandate, not just recommend, validation on diverse patient populations.[164]

Besides, model performance needs to be continuously monitored and recalibrated to address dataset shifts related to changes in clinical practice, patient demographic variation, and hardware and software revolution for data capture. In this regard, FDA announced the need for a regulatory approach that spans the lifecycle of AI-based software.[165] To guarantee a safe operation of the model while improving treatment, re-evaluation plans of new medical devices have been discussed but still not clearly addressed. While postapproval changes of traditional devices may require additional FDA review, this approach might not be suitable for AI-based software, whose inherent continuous learning necessity might lead to outputs that differ from those reviewed prior to approval. Prospective clinical trials are necessary for a priori AI-based software evaluation to address algorithmic biases. Meanwhile, it is fundamental to ensure the safety and effectiveness of AI-based software in its postapproval period by a list of safe allowable changes for models' adjustment to new data without further FDA review. Even so, anticipated changes may accumulate over time and generate an unexpected difference in the software's performance. Postmarket device monitoring programs can be based on appropriate guardrails or, alternatively, on periodical reviews to guarantee the risk–benefit profile for the software. FDA should keep the entitlement to remove the software from the market in case of potential serious harm.[165]

Equally important, algorithm retraining on patient status changes, either continuous in real-time or semicontinuous in scheduled slots (e.g., nightly runs), should be envisioned in the future pipeline to fully exploit the potential of a patient-centered health model.[20,147] Hyperindividualized approaches in cancer detection, treatment interventions, systemic cancer therapeutics and radiation dosages, and surveillance examinations might substantially improve patients' quality care and outcome.[20]

Finally, the FDA should promote a high level of transparency to allow patients and clinicians to make cognizant decisions. Clinical evidence used to support the initial approval should be publicly shared in a straightforward language and distributed through peer-reviewed literature.[165]

In conclusion, the oncology field is highly algorithmic and data centric. AI-based models can fail during the whole AI lifecycle: biases might be introduced during data collection (i.e., limited diversity), model development (i.e., algorithmic biases), evaluation and test (i.e., external validation), and implementation (i.e., model monitoring). Model's fairness requires clinicians, AI engineers, data scientists, social scientists, and industry partnership in a common goal-oriented cooperation to sustain the equity value to the greatest extent possible.[153,166] In the current time of socio-economic disparities and cost reductions, greater efficiency achieved by AI solutions can translate the fee-for-service to an even quality-based care. To realize the full potential of AI and not constrain it to scope and values, a synergy of the international oncology community is necessary for coordination of talent, training, investment, and resources.[143] The road ahead is challenging, but the cancer care transformation holds huge promises.

Funding

This research did not receive any specific grant from funding agencies in the public, commercial, or not-for-profit sectors.

Acknowledgments

MC contributed to the literature search, conception, design of the article, and drafted the first version of the manuscript. CCo, LM, and EDC contributed to the literature search and provided critical revisions to the manuscript. LAC and GC provided critical revisions to the manuscript. CCr provided critical revisions of the manuscript and supervision. All the authors provided final approval to the submitted work.

Competing interests

MC and LM have no potential conflicts of interest to disclose. CCo is funded in part through the IEO-Monzino "Career Development" grant. ECD is funded in part through the NIH/NCI Support Grant P30 CA008748. CCr reports personal fees for consulting, advisory roles, and speakers' bureau from Lilly, Roche, Novartis, MSD, Seagen, Gilead, and Pfizer. LAC is funded by the National Institute of Health through NIBIB R01 EB017205. GC reports honoraria for speaker's engagement: Roche, Seattle Genetics, Novartis, Lilly, Pfizer, Foundation Medicine, NanoString, Samsung, Celltrion, BMS, MSD; honoraria for providing consultancy: Roche, Seattle Genetics, NanoString; honoraria for participating in Advisory Board: Roche, Lilly, Pfizer, Foundation Medicine, Samsung, Celltrion, Mylan; honoraria for writing engagement: Novartis, BMS; honoraria for participation in Ellipsis Scientific Affairs Group; Institutional research funding for conducting phase I and II clinical trials: Pfizer, Roche, Novartis, Sanofi, Celgene, Servier, Orion, AstraZeneca, Seattle Genetics, AbbVie, Tesaro, BMS, Merck Serono, Merck Sharp Dome, Janssen-Cilag, Philogen, Bayer, Medivation, Medimmune. All the competing interests were outside the submitted work.

References

1. Ferlay J. et al. Global Cancer Observatory: Cancer Tomorrow. Lyon, France: International Agency for Research on Cancer; 2020. https://gco.iarc.fr/tomorrow.
2. Allemani C, et al. Global surveillance of trends in cancer survival 2000–14 (CONCORD-3): analysis of individual records for 37513025 patients diagnosed with one of 18 cancers from 322 population-based registries in 71 countries. *The Lancet*. 2018;391:1023–1075.
3. Sung H, et al. Global Cancer Statistics 2020: GLOBOCAN estimates of incidence and mortality worldwide for 36 cancers in 185 countries. *CA Cancer J Clin*. 2021;71:209–249.
4. Corti C, et al. Artificial intelligence in cancer research and precision medicine: applications, limitations and priorities to drive transformation in the delivery of equitable and unbiased care. *Cancer Treat Rev*. 2023;112.
5. Delaney G, Jacob S, Featherstone C, Barton M. The role of radiotherapy in cancer treatment. *Cancer*. 2005;104:1129–1137.
6. Borras JM, et al. The impact of cancer incidence and stage on optimal utilization of radiotherapy: methodology of a population based analysis by the ESTRO-HERO project. *Radiother Oncol*. 2015;116:45–50.
7. Borras JM, et al. The optimal utilization proportion of external beam radiotherapy in European countries: An ESTRO-HERO analysis. *Radiother Oncol*. 2015;116:38–44.
8. Liu Z, et al. Radiomics of multiparametric MRI for pretreatment prediction of pathologic complete response to neoadjuvant chemotherapy in breast cancer: a multicenter study. *Clin Cancer Res*. 2019;25:3538–3547.
9. Huynh E, et al. CT-based radiomic analysis of stereotactic body radiation therapy patients with lung cancer. *Radiother Oncol*. 2016;120:258–266.
10. Li M, Zhang Q, Yang K. Role of MRI-based functional imaging in improving the therapeutic index of radiotherapy in cancer treatment. Preprint at *Front Oncol*. 2021;11. https://doi.org/10.3389/fonc.2021.645177.
11. McCarthy J, Minsky M, Rochester N, Shannon CE. A proposal for the Dartmouth summer research project on artificial intelligence, August 31, 1955. *AI Mag*. 2006;27:12–14.
12. Bellman R. An Introduction to Artificial Intelligence: Can Computers Think? In; 1978.
13. Hwang K, Chen M. Big-data analytics for Cloud, Iot and cognitive computing. Wiley; 2017.
14. Rajkomar A, Dean J, Kohane I. Machine learning in medicine. *N Engl J Med*. 2019;380:1347–1358.
15. Litjens G, et al. A survey on deep learning in medical image analysis. *Med Image Anal*. 2017;42:60–88.
16. Wainberg M, Merico D, Delong A, Frey BJ. Deep learning in biomedicine. *Nat Biotechnol*. 2018;36(9):829–838.
17. Meyer P, Noblet V, Mazzara C, Lallement A. Survey on deep learning for radiotherapy. *Comput Biol Med*. 2018;98:126–146.
18. Kaul V, Enslin S, Gross SA. History of artificial intelligence in medicine. *Gastrointest Endosc*. 2020;92:807–812.
19. Ngiam J, et al. Multimodal deep learning. In: *International Conference on Machine Learning*; 2011.
20. Shreve JT, Khanani SA, Haddad TC. Artificial intelligence in oncology: current capabilities, future opportunities, and ethical considerations. *Am Soc Clin Oncol Educ Book*. 2022;842–851. https://doi.org/10.1200/edbk_350652.
21. Topol, E.J. High-performance medicine: the convergence of human and artificial intelligence. *Nat Med 2019*. 2019;25;44–56.
22. Chen ZH, et al. Artificial intelligence for assisting cancer diagnosis and treatment in the era of precision medicine. *Cancer Commun*. 2021;41:1100–1115.
23. Montesinos-López OA, et al. A review of deep learning applications for genomic selection. *BMC Genomics*. 2021;22:19.

24. Yadav, S.S. & Jadhav, S.M. Deep convolutional neural network based medical image classification for disease diagnosis. https://doi.org/10.1186/s40537-019-0276-2.

25. Koumakis L. Deep learning models in genomics; are we there yet? *Comput Struct Biotechnol J.* 2020;18:1466.

26. Krizhevsky A, Sutskever I, Hinton GE. ImageNet classification with deep convolutional neural networks. *Commun ACM.* 2017;60.

27. Bi WL, et al. Artificial intelligence in cancer imaging: clinical challenges and applications. *CA Cancer J Clin.* 2019;69:127–157.

28. Maroni, R. et al. A case-control study to evaluate the impact of the breast screening programme on mortality in England. Br J Cancer. https://doi.org/10.1038/s41416-020-01163-2.

29. Jansen EEL, et al. Effect of organised cervical cancer screening on cervical cancer mortality in Europe: a systematic review. *Eur J Cancer.* 2020;127:207–223.

30. Zhang J, et al. Colonoscopic screening is associated with reduced colorectal Cancer incidence and mortality: a systematic review and meta-analysis. *J Cancer.* 2020;11:5953–5970.

31. Mori Y, Kudo SE, Berzin TM, Misawa M, Takeda K. Computer-aided diagnosis for colonoscopy. *Endoscopy.* 2017;49:813–819.

32. Duffy SW, Field JK. Mortality reduction with low-dose CT screening for lung cancer. *N Engl J Med.* 2020;382:572–573.

33. Jacobs C, et al. Deep learning for lung Cancer detection on screening CT scans: results of a large-scale public competition and an observer study with 11 radiologists. *Radiol Artif Intell.* 2021;3.

34. Huynh BQ, Li H, Giger ML. Digital mammographic tumor classification using transfer learning from deep convolutional neural networks; 2016. https://doi.org/10.1117/1.JMI.3.3.034501.

35. Kooi T, et al. Large scale deep learning for computer aided detection of mammographic lesions. *Med Image Anal.* 2017;35:303–312.

36. Carneiro G, Nascimento J, Bradley AP. Automated analysis of unregistered multi-view mammograms with deep learning. *IEEE Trans Med Imaging.* 2017;36:2355–2365.

37. Dhungel N, Carneiro G, Bradley AP. A deep learning approach for the analysis of masses in mammograms with minimal user intervention. *Med Image Anal.* 2017;37:114–128.

38. Mckinney SM, et al. International evaluation of an AI system for breast cancer screening. *Nature.* 2020;577:89.

39. Wang P, et al. Real-time automatic detection system increases colonoscopic polyp and adenoma detection rates: a prospective randomised controlled study. *Gut.* 2019;68:1813–1819.

40. Wentzensen, N. et al. Accuracy and efficiency of deep-learning-based automation of dual stain cytology in cervical cancer screening. https://doi.org/10.1093/jnci/djaa066.

41. Mikhael PG, et al. Sybil: a validated deep learning model to predict future lung cancer risk from a single low-dose chest computed tomography. *J Clin Oncol.* 2023. https://doi.org/10.1200/jco.22.01345.

42. Ahlquist DA. Universal cancer screening: revolutionary, rational, and realizable. *NPJ Precis Oncol.* 2018;2:23.

43. Hackshaw A, Clarke CA, Hartman AR. New genomic technologies for multi-cancer early detection: rethinking the scope of cancer screening. *Cancer Cell.* 2022;40:109–113.

44. Cohen JD, et al. Detection and localization of surgically resectable cancers with a multi-analyte blood test. *Science.* 2018;359:926.

45. Duffy MJ, DIamandis EP, Crown J. Circulating tumor DNA (ctDNA) as a pan-cancer screening test: is it finally on the horizon? *Clin Chem Lab Med.* 2021;59:1353–1361.

46. Yuan Z, et al. Development and validation of an image-based deep learning algorithm for detection of synchronous peritoneal Carcinomatosis in colorectal Cancer. *Ann Surg.* 2022;275:E645–E651.

47. Rundo F, et al. Deep learning for accurate diagnosis of liver tumor based on magnetic resonance imaging and clinical data. *Front Oncol.* 2020;10:680.

48. Wang Y-W, et al. Can parameters other than minimal axial diameter in MRI and PET/CT further improve diagnostic accuracy for equivocal retropharyngeal lymph nodes in nasopharyngeal carcinoma?; 2016. https://doi.org/10.1371/journal.pone.0163741.

49. Zhou Q, et al. Grading of hepatocellular carcinoma using 3D SE-DenseNet in dynamic enhanced MR images. *Comput Biol Med.* 2019;107:47–57.

50. Abraham B, Nair MS. Automated grading of prostate cancer using convolutional neural network and ordinal class classifier. *Inform Med Unlocked.* 2019;17.

51. Luo H, et al. Real-time artificial intelligence for detection of upper gastrointestinal cancer by endoscopy: a multicentre, case-control, diagnostic study. *Lancet Oncol.* 2019;20:1645–1654.

52. Komeda Y, et al. Artificial intelligence-based endoscopic diagnosis of colorectal polyps using residual networks. *PloS One.* 2021;16.

53. Wang P, et al. Development and validation of a deep-learning algorithm for the detection of polyps during colonoscopy. *Nature Biomed Eng.* 2018;10(2):741–748.

54. Zhang SM, Wang YJ, Zhang ST. Accuracy of artificial intelligence-assisted detection eof esophageal cancer and neoplasms on endoscopic images: A systematic review and meta-analysis; 2021. https://doi.org/10.1111/1751-2980.12992.

55. Chen PJ, et al. Accurate classification of diminutive colorectal polyps using computer-aided analysis. *Gastroenterology.* 2018;154:568–575.

56. Bejnordi BE, et al. Diagnostic assessment of deep learning algorithms for detection of lymph node metastases in women with breast Cancer. *JAMA.* 2017;318.2199–2210.

57. Coudray N, et al. Classification and mutation prediction from non–small cell lung cancer histopathology images using deep learning. *Nat Med.* 2018;24(10):1559–1567.

58. Nagpal, K. et al. Development and validation of a deep learning algorithm for improving Gleason scoring of prostate cancer. https://doi.org/10.1038/s41746-019-0112-2.

59. Arvaniti E, et al. Automated Gleason grading of prostate cancer tissue microarrays via deep learning. *Sci Rep.* 2018;8:12054.

60. Mohsen H, El-Dahshan E-SA, El-Horbaty E-SM, Salem A-BM. Classification using deep learning neural networks for brain tumors. *Future Comput Inform J.* 2018;3:68–71.

61. Motlagh, M.H. et al. Breast cancer histopathological image classification: a deep learning approach. https://doi.org/10.1101/242818.

62. Dabeer S, Khan MM, Islam S. Cancer diagnosis in histopathological image: CNN based approach. *Inform Med Unlocked.* 2019;16.

63. Esteva A, et al. Dermatologist-level classification of skin cancer with deep neural networks; 2017. https://doi.org/10.1038/nature21056.

64. Yu L, Chen H, Dou Q, Qin J, Heng PA. Automated melanoma recognition in Dermoscopy images via very deep residual networks. *IEEE Trans Med Imaging.* 2017;36:994–1004.

65. Grewal JK, et al. Application of a neural network whole transcriptome-based pan-cancer method for diagnosis of primary and metastatic cancers. *JAMA Netw Open.* 2019;2:e192597.

66. Wang K, et al. Dissecting cancer heterogeneity based on dimension reduction of transcriptomic profiles using extreme learning machines; 2018. https://doi.org/10.1371/journal.pone.0203824.

67. Zhou J, et al. Deep learning sequence-based ab initio prediction of variant effects on expression and disease risk. *Nat Genet.* 2018;50.

68. Davis, R.J. et al. Pan-cancer transcriptional signatures predictive of oncogenic mutations reveal that Fbw7 regulates cancer cell oxidative metabolism. https://doi.org/10.1073/pnas.1718338115.

69. Tizhoosh HR, et al. Searching images for consensus: can AI remove observer variability in pathology? *Am J Pathol.* 2021;191:1702–1708.

70. National Research Council. Toward Precision Medicine: Building a Knowledge Network for Biomedical Research and a New Taxonomy of Disease; 2011:1–128. https://doi.org/10.17226/13284.

71. Shaw A, et al. Editorial: breakthrough in imaging-guided precision medicine in oncology. *Front Oncol.* 2022;vol. 12. Preprint at. https://doi.org/10.3389/fonc.2022.908561.

72. Corti C, et al. Artificial intelligence for prediction of treatment outcomes in breast cancer: systematic review of design, reporting standards, and bias. *Cancer Treat Rev.* 2022;108.

73. Chen D, et al. Developing prognostic systems of cancer patients by ensemble clustering. *J Biomed Biotechnol.* 2009. https://doi.org/10.1155/2009/632786.

74. Bychkov D, et al. Deep learning based tissue analysis predicts outcome in colorectal cancer. *Sci Rep.* 2018;8:3395.

75. Janssen BV, et al. Imaging-based machine-learning models to predict clinical outcomes and identify biomarkers in pancreatic cancer: a scoping review. *Ann Surg.* 2022;275:560–567.

76. He B, et al. Predicting response to immunotherapy in advanced non-small-cell lung cancer using tumor mutational burden radiomic biomarker. *J Immunother Cancer.* 2020;8:e000550.

77. Johannet P, et al. Using machine learning algorithms to predict immunotherapy response in patients with advanced melanoma. *Clin Cancer Res.* 2021;27:131–140.

78. Arbour KC, et al. Deep learning to estimate RECIST in patients with nSCLC treated with PD-1 blockade K. *Cancer Discov.* 2021;11:59–67.

79. Qu YH, et al. Prediction of pathological complete response to neoadjuvant chemotherapy in breast cancer using a deep learning (DL) method. *Thorac Cancer.* 2020;11:651.

80. Li F, et al. Deep learning-based predictive biomarker of pathological complete response to neoadjuvant chemotherapy from histological images in breast cancer. *J Transl Med.* 2021;19:1–13.

81. Feng L, et al. Development and validation of a radiopathomics model to predict pathological complete response to neoadjuvant chemoradiotherapy in locally advanced rectal cancer: a multicentre observational study. *Lancet Digit Health.* 2022;4:e8–e17.

82. Huynh E, et al. Artificial intelligence in radiation oncology. *Nat Rev Clin Oncol.* 2020;17:771–781. Preprint at. https://doi.org/10.1038/s41571-020-0417-8.

83. Feng M, Valdes G, Dixit N, Solberg TD. Machine learning in radiation oncology: opportunities, requirements, and needs. *Front Oncol.* 2018;8.

84. Janes H, Pepe MS, Mcshane LM, Sargent DJ, Heagerty PJ. The fundamental difficulty with evaluating the accuracy of biomarkers for guiding treatment. *J Natl Cancer Inst.* 2015;107:157.

85. Xu, Y. et al., Precision medicine and imaging deep learning predicts lung cancer treatment response from serial medical imaging. https://doi.org/10.1158/1078-0432.CCR-18-2495.

86. Jalalifar SA, Soliman H, Sahgal A, Sadeghi-Naini A. Predicting the outcome of radiotherapy in brain metastasis by integrating the clinical and MRI-based deep learning features. *Med Phys.* 2022;49:7167–7178.

87. Scott JG, et al. Personalizing radiotherapy prescription dose using genomic markers of radiosensitivity and normal tissue toxicity in NSCLC. *J Thorac Oncol.* 2021;16:428–438.

88. Nguyen, D. et al., A feasibility study for predicting optimal radiation therapy dose distributions of prostate cancer patients from patient anatomy using deep learning. https://doi.org/10.1038/s41598-018-37741-x.

89. Jarrett D, Stride E, Vallis K, Gooding MJ. Applications and limitations of machine learning in radiation oncology. *Br J Radiol.* 2019;92.

90. Devic S. MRI simulation for radiotherapy treatment planning. *Med Phys.* 2012;39:6701–6711.

91. Wu D, Kim K, el Fakhri G, Li Q. Iterative low-dose CT reconstruction with priors trained by artificial neural network. *IEEE Trans Med Imaging.* 2017;36:2479–2486.

92. Lee, J., Carass, A., Jog, A. & Prince, J.L. Multi-atlas-based CT synthesis from conventional MRI with patch-based refinement for MRI-based radiotherapy planning. https://doi.org/10.1117/12.2254571.

93. Han X. MR-based synthetic CT generation using a deep convolutional neural network method. *Med Phys.* 2017;44:1408–1419.

94. Boulanger M, et al. Deep learning methods to generate synthetic CT from MRI in radiotherapy: a literature review. *Phys Med.* 2021;89:265–281.

95. Jonsson J, Nyholm T, Söderkvist K. The rationale for MR-only treatment planning for external radiotherapy; 2019. https://doi.org/10.1016/j.ctro.2019.03.005.

96. Kurz C, et al. Medical physics challenges in clinical MR-guided radiotherapy. *Radiat Oncol.* 2020;15. Preprint at. https://doi.org/10.1186/s13014-020-01524-4.

97. Jackson S, Glitzner M, Tijssen RHN, Raaymakers BW. MRI B0 homogeneity and geometric distortion with continuous linac gantry rotation on an Elekta Unity MR-linac. *Phys Med Biol.* 2019;64:12NT01.

98. Bahrami K, Shi F, Rekik I, Shen D. Convolutional neural network for reconstruction of 7T-like images from 3T MRI using appearance and anatomical features. In: *Lecture Notes in Computer Science (including subseries Lecture Notes in Artificial Intelligence and Lecture Notes in Bioinformatics).* 10008 LNCS; 2016:39–47.

99. Bruijnen T, et al. Technical feasibility of magnetic resonance fingerprinting on a 1.5T MRI-linac. *Phys Med Biol.* 2020;65. 22NT01.

100. Ma J, et al. Image matching from handcrafted to deep features: a survey. *Int J Comput Vis.* 2021;129:23–79.

101. Cheng X, Zhang L, Zheng Y. Deep similarity learning for multimodal medical images. *Comput Methods Biomech Biomed Eng Imaging Vis.* 2018;6:248–252.

102. Chen X, Diaz-Pinto A, Ravikumar N, Frangi AF. Progress in biomedical engineering. In: *Deep Learning in Medical Image Registration*; 2020. https://doi.org/10.1088/2516-1091/abd37c.

103. Ibragimov B, Xing L. Segmentation of organs-at-risks in head and neck CT images using convolutional neural networks; 2017. https://doi.org/10.1002/mp.12045.

104. Guo D, et al. Organ at risk segmentation for head and neck cancer using stratified learning and neural architecture search. In: *Proceedings of the IEEE/CVF Conference on Computer Vision and Pattern Recognition*; 2020:4223–4232.

105. Ng CKC, Leung VWS, Hung RHM. Clinical evaluation of deep learning and atlas-based auto-contouring for head and neck radiation therapy. *Appl Sci (Switzerland)*. 2022;12. https://doi.org/10.3390/app122211681. 11681–11681.

106. Lustberg T, et al. Clinical evaluation of atlas and deep learning based automatic contouring for lung cancer. *Radiother Oncol*. 2018;126:312–317.

107. Liang S, et al. Deep-learning-based detection and segmentation of organs at risk in nasopharyngeal carcinoma computed tomographic images for radiotherapy planning. *Eur Radiol*. 2019;29:1961–1967.

108. Ranjbarzadeh, R. et al. Brain tumor segmentation based on deep learning and an attention mechanism using MRI multi-modalities brain images. Sci Rep 11, 10930 (123AD).

109. Men K, et al. Fully automatic and robust segmentation of the clinical target volume for radiotherapy of breast cancer using big data and deep learning. *Phys Med*. 2018;50:13–19.

110. Hepel JT, et al. Deep learning improved clinical target volume contouring quality and efficiency for postoperative radiation therapy in non-small cell lung Cancer. *Cell Lung Cancer Front Oncol*. 2019;9:1192.

111. Hosny A, et al. Clinical validation of deep learning algorithms for radiotherapy targeting of non-small-cell lung cancer: an observational study. *Lancet Digit Health*. 2022;4:e657–e666.

112. Men K, Dai J, Li Y. Automatic segmentation of the clinical target volume and organs at risk in the planning CT for rectal cancer using deep dilated convolutional neural networks. *Med Phys*. 2017;44:6377–6389.

113. Lin L, et al. Deep learning for automated contouring of primary tumor volumes by MRI for nasopharyngeal carcinoma. *Radiology*. 2019;291:677–686.

114. Wang C, Zhu X, Hong JC, Zheng D. Artificial intelligence in radiotherapy treatment planning: present and future. *Technol Cancer Res Treat*. 2019;18. Preprint at. https://doi.org/10.1177/1533033819873922.

115. Gallio E, et al. Evaluation of a commercial automatic treatment planning system for liver stereotactic body radiation therapy treatments. *Phys Med*. 2018;46:153–159.

116. Ge Y, Wu QJ. Knowledge-based planning for intensity-modulated radiation therapy: a review of data-driven approaches. *Med Phys*. 2019;46:2760–2775.

117. Shiraishi S, Moore KL. Knowledge-based prediction of three-dimensional dose distributions for external beam radiotherapy. *Med Phys*. 2016;43:378–387.

118. Fan J, et al. Automatic treatment planning based on three-dimensional dose distribution predicted from deep learning technique. *Med Phys*. 2019;46:370–381.

119. Mahmood R, Babier A, Mcniven A, Chan TCY. Automated treatment planning in radiation therapy using generative adversarial networks. *Proc Mach Learn Res*. 2018;85:1–15.

120. Allen Li X, et al. CNN-based quality assurance for automatic segmentation of breast Cancer in radiotherapy. *Breast Cancer Radiotherapy Front Oncol*. 2020;1:524.

121. Interian Y, et al. Deep nets vs expert designed features in medical physics: an IMRT QA case study. *Med Phys*. 2018;45:2672–2680.

122. Valdes G, et al. A mathematical framework for virtual IMRT QA using machine learning. *Med Phys*. 2016;43:4323–4334.

123. Li Q, Chan MF. Predictive time-series modeling using artificial neural networks for Linac beam symmetry: an empirical study. *Ann N Y Acad Sci*. 2017;1387:84.

124. Dawson LA, Sharpe MB. Image-guided radiotherapy: rationale, benefits, and limitations. *Lancet Oncol*. 2006;7:848–858.

125. Zhang Y, et al. Improving CBCT quality to CT level using deep-learning with generative adversarial network HHS public access. *Med Phys*. 2021;48:2816–2826.

126. Kurz C, et al. Cone-beam CT intensity correction for adaptive radiotherapy of the prostate using deep learning. *Phys Med*. 2018;52:48.

127. Kida, S. et al. Cone beam computed tomography image quality improvement using a deep convolutional neural network. https://doi.org/10.7759/cureus.2548.

128. Lim-Reinders S, Keller BM, Al-Ward S, Sahgal A, Kim A. Online adaptive radiation therapy. *Int J Radiat Oncol Biol Phys*. 2017;99:994–1003.

129. Langen KM, Jones DTL. Organ motion and its management. *Int J Radiat Oncol Biol Phys*. 2001;50:265–278.

130. Brandner ED, Chetty IJ, Giaddui TG, Xiao Y, Huq MS. Motion management strategies and technical issues associated with stereotactic body radiotherapy of thoracic and upper abdominal tumors: a review from NRG oncology; 2017. https://doi.org/10.1002/mp.12227.

131. Isaksson M, Jalden J, Murphy MJ. On using an adaptive neural network to predict lung tumor motion during respiration for radiotherapy applications. *Med Phys*. 2005;32:3801–3809.

132. Tseng HH, Luo Y, ten Haken RK, el Naqa I. The role of machine learning in knowledge-based response-adapted radiotherapy. *Front Oncol*. 2018;8. Preprint at. https://doi.org/10.3389/fonc.2018.00266.

133. Guidi G, et al. A machine learning tool for re-planning and adaptive RT: a multicenter cohort investigation. *Phys Med*. 2016;32:1659–1666.

134. Nayak KS, Lim Y, Campbell-Washburn AE, Steeden J. Real-time magnetic resonance imaging. *J Magn Reson Imaging*. 2022;55:81–99.

135. Buchanan L, et al. Deep learning-based prediction of deliverable adaptive plans for MR-guided adaptive radiotherapy: a feasibility study. *Front Oncol*. 2023. https://doi.org/10.3389/fonc.2023.939951.

136. Lamb J, et al. Online adaptive radiation therapy: implementation of a new process of care. *Cureus*. 2017;9.

137. Sibolt P, et al. Clinical implementation of artificial intelligence-driven cone-beam computed tomography-guided online adaptive radiotherapy in the pelvic region. *Phys Imaging Radiat Oncol*. 2021;17:1–7.

138. Cusumano D, et al. Artificial intelligence in magnetic resonance guided radiotherapy: medical and physical considerations on state of art and future perspectives. *Phys Med: Eur J Med Phys*. 2021;85:175–191.

139. Archambault Y, et al. Making on-line adaptive radiotherapy possible using artificial intelligence and machine learning for efficient daily re-planning. *Med Phys Int J*. 2020;8.

140. Yang, Y. et al. Elevated tumor markers for monitoring tumor response to immunotherapy, https://doi.org/10.1016/j.eclinm.2022.101381.

141. Navin NE. Tumor evolution in response to chemotherapy: Phenotype versus genotype. *Cell Rep.* 2014;6:417–419. Preprint at https://doi.org/10.1016/j.celrep.2014.01.035.

142. Blasiak A, Khong J, Kee T. CURATE.AI: optimizing personalized medicine with artificial intelligence. *SLAS Technol.* 2020;25:95–105. Preprint at https://doi.org/10.1177/2472630319890316.

143. Thompson RF, et al. Artificial intelligence in radiation oncology: a specialty-wide disruptive transformation? *Radiother Oncol.* 2018;129:421–426. Preprint at https://doi.org/10.1016/j.radonc.2018.05.030.

144. Lambin P, et al. Predicting outcomes in radiation oncology-multifactorial decision support systems. *Nat Rev Clin Oncol.* 2013;10:27–40. Preprint at https://doi.org/10.1038/nrclinonc.2012.196.

145. Feng H, et al. Prediction of radiation-induced acute skin toxicity in breast cancer patients using data encapsulation screening and dose-gradient-based multi-region radiomics technique: a multicenter study. *Front Oncol.* 2022;12:5648.

146. Vandewinckele L, et al. Overview of artificial intelligence-based applications in radiotherapy: Recommendations for implementation and quality assurance. *Radiother Oncol.* 2020;153:55–66. Preprint at https://doi.org/10.1016/j.radonc.2020.09.008.

147. Bibault JE, Giraud P, Burgun A. Big data and machine learning in radiation oncology: State of the art and future prospects. *Cancer Lett.* 2016;382:110–117. Preprint at https://doi.org/10.1016/j.canlet.2016.05.033.

148. Traverso A, van Soest J, Wee L, Dekker A. The radiation oncology ontology (ROO): publishing linked data in radiation oncology using semantic web and ontology techniques. *Med Phys.* 2018;45:e854–e862.

149. Froelicher, D. et al., Scalable Privacy-Preserving Distributed Learning.

150. Beier M, et al. Multicenter data sharing for collaboration in sleep medicine. In: *2015 15th IEEE/ACM International Symposium on Cluster, Cloud and Grid Computing*; 2015:880–889. https://doi.org/10.1109/CCGrid.2015.148.

151. Batlle JC, et al. Data sharing of imaging in an evolving health care world: report of the ACR data sharing workgroup, part 1: data ethics of privacy, consent, and anonymization. *J Am Coll Radiol.* 2021;18:1646–1654.

152. Rocher L, Hendrickx JM, de Montjoye YA. Estimating the success of re-identifications in incomplete datasets using generative models. *Nat Commun.* 2019;10.

153. Marshall DC, Komorowski M. Is artificial intelligence ready to solve mechanical ventilation? Computer says blow. *Br J Anaesth.* 2022;128:231–233. Preprint at https://doi.org/10.1016/j.bja.2021.10.050.

154. Manrai AK, et al. Genetic misdiagnoses and the potential for health disparities. *N Engl J Med.* 2016;375:655–665.

155. Obermeyer Z, Powers B, Vogeli C, Mullainathan S. Dissecting racial bias in an algorithm used to manage the health of populations. *Science.* 2019;366:447–453.

156. Zemel R, Brendel W, Bethge M, Wichmann FA. Shortcut learning in deep neural networks. *Nat Mach Intell.* 2020. https://doi.org/10.1038/s42256-020-00257-z.

157. Gilpin LH, et al. Explaining explanations: an overview of interpretability of machine learning; 2019.

158. Lekadir K, Quaglio G, Garmendia AT, Gallin C. Artificial intelligence in healthcare: applications, risks, and ethical and societal impacts; 2022. https://doi.org/10.2861/568473.

159. The Food and Drug Administration. Software as a Medical Device (SaMD) Action Plan, 09/22/2021. Available at: https://shorturl.at/foM04. Accessed on July 1, 2022.

160. Goodman B, Flaxman S. European Union Regulations on Algorithmic Decision-Making and a 'Right to Explanation'; 2016. https://doi.org/10.1609/aimag.v38i3.2741.

161. Khozin S, Kim G, Pazdur R. Regulatory watch: From big data to smart data: FDA's INFORMED initiative. *Nat Rev Drug Discov.* 2017. https://doi.org/10.1038/nrd.2017.26.

162. NCI Fellowship. Growing the Field—NCI Fellowship Opportunities in Data Science. https://datascience.cancer.gov/news-events/blog/growing-field-nci-fellowship-opportunities-data-science.

163. World Health Organization. Assessing national capacity for the prevention and control of noncommunicable diseases: report of the 2019 global survey, Geneva: World Health Organization; 2020. https://apps.who.int/iris/handle/10665/331452.

164. Hammond, A., Jain, B., Anthony Celi, L. & Cody Stanford, F., An extension to the FDA approval process is needed to achieve AI equity. https://doi.org/10.1038/s42256-023-00614-8.

165. Hwang TJ, Kesselheim AS, Vokinger KN. Lifecycle regulation of artificial intelligence- and machine learning-based software devices in medicine. *JAMA.* 2019;322:2285–2286.

166. MIT. An MIT Technology Review Series: AI Colonialism. MIT Technology Review; 2022. https://www.technologyreview.com/supertopic/ai-colonialism-supertopic/.

SOK: Application of machine learning models in child and youth mental health decision-making

Hirad Daneshvar[a], Omar Boursalie[a], Reza Samavi[a,b], Thomas E. Doyle[b,c,d], Laura Duncan[e], Paulo Pires[e,f], and Roberto Sassi[g,h]

[a]Department of Electrical, Computer, and Biomedical Engineering, Toronto Metropolitan University, Toronto, ON, Canada [b]Vector Institute, Toronto, ON, Canada [c]Department of Electrical and Computer Engineering, McMaster University, Hamilton, ON, Canada [d]School of Biomedical Engineering, McMaster University, Hamilton, ON, Canada [e]Hamilton Health Sciences, Hamilton, ON, Canada [f]Department of Psychiatry and Behavioural Neurosciences, McMaster University, Hamilton, ON, Canada [g]Department of Psychiatry, University of British Columbia, Vancouver, BC, Canada [h]British Columbia Children's Hospital, Vancouver, BC, Canada

1. Introduction

Healthcare professionals have to weigh knowledge, experience, evidence, cost, time, etc., to make decisions that will have optimal outcomes for patients' health. Historically, the healthcare system has relied on human intelligence-based decision-making, where health professionals make decisions based on their experience, patient interviews, analysis of clinical tests, and other wide-ranging factors. There is growing interest in using artificial intelligence (AI) to augment human intelligence in decision-making to improve efficiency, performance, and, hopefully, patient outcomes. The core of AI is machine learning algorithms (MLA),[1] which are trained to make predictions (e.g., suicide risk[2]) and classifications (e.g., Alzheimer's disease detection[3]) by learning trends and relationships from a dataset without human guidance. However, predictions and classifications are not decisions (e.g., admit the patient if their heart disease risk is above 50%). An important challenge in integrating AI into the decision-making process is bridging the gap between researchers developing AI models and health professionals and patients using the deployed models. Researchers make simplifications and abstractions when developing their models. On the other hand, health professionals are specialists with unique terminologies and concepts for their field and expectations that AI cannot achieve. The following real-world scenario demonstrates the importance of deliberate collaboration between researchers and health professionals in integrating AI into clinical decision-making.

The authors of this paper are currently developing emergency department (ED) readmission prediction models to assist health professionals to identify patients who may need a different type or amount of intervention. This research is a collaboration between AI researchers at Toronto Metropolitan and McMaster University and mental health professionals at McMaster and British Columbia's Children's Hospitals. Our aim is to explore the potential utility of readmission prediction models at McMaster Children's Hospital's Child and Youth Outpatient Services Program (CYMHP). Artificial intelligence researchers must understand the clinical data and preexisting workflows from which data are generated. In contrast, health professionals need to understand the strengths and limitations of AI models.

Previous studies[4-6] have reviewed the application of AI in general healthcare. However, mental healthcare has unique requirements, terminologies, and concepts. For example, mental disorder diagnoses are based on health professionals' experiences, patient interviews, and clinical judgment. This is sometimes augmented with analysis of patients' responses to standardized assessments and questionnaires about their mental health. Current literature reviews on AI in mental healthcare, group publications by application,[7] data types,[8] and patient populations.[9] Shatte et al.[7] found that AI applications in mental health can be grouped into diagnosis, prognosis, treatment, public health, research, and clinical administration domains. Researchers mainly target the detection and diagnosis of depression, schizophrenia, and Alzheimer's disease. Su et al.[8] reviewed AI applications, challenges, and opportunities in mental health based on the type of data analyzed: clinical, genomics, audio and visual expression, and social media data. The review by Le Glaz et al.[9] focused on AI applications based on populations: patients whose records are available in research databases and patients seen in ED and psychiatry departments with additional mental health information in their medical records and from their social media. Le Glaz et al. found that AI applications in mental health focus on extracting symptoms, predicting disorder severity, and comparing therapy effectiveness to confirm clinical hypotheses. However, existing reviews did not investigate how AI can be integrated into a mental healthcare decision-making workflow in a clinical setting. Existing reviews also did not describe the data preprocessing, evaluation, ethical considerations, and operationalization (deployment) stages essential to integrating AI into clinical workflows.

The paper's contributions and structure are as follows: Section 2 reviews terminology and concepts and defines our study methodology and scope. Section 3 presents our case study for human intelligence-based decision-making at CYMHP. Section 4 presents our literature review on the applications of AI in mental health. Section 5 presents open research challenges. Finally, we conclude in Section 6.

2. Methodology

Due to the inconsistent definitions in Ref. 10, we define the terminology used in clinical and AI communities in this section. We then define the methodology and scope of our study.

2.1 Decision-making terminology

A decision is a choice between two or more actions, recommendations, or judgments.[11] Agents, entities with specialized knowledge interacting in a shared environment (e.g., health professionals, patients, and AI), make decisions individually or as a group.[12] A primary decision-maker is responsible for making the final decision because agents can disagree with each other. Subsequently, we define decision-making as the process by which a primary decision-maker identifies, evaluates, and makes decisions. For example, a health professional (primary decision-maker) decides to admit a patient (agent) to the hospital (decision) after evaluating their symptoms against clinical guidelines (decision-making process).

Computational (analytical) thinking can be executed by humans (human intelligence) or machines (AI) and involves problem decomposition, pattern recognition, abstraction, and algorithms.[13] We identified three decision-making systems in the literature: human intelligence-based, AI-based, and AI-assisted (Table 1). In human intelligence-based decision-making, a health professional makes the final decision based on their experiences and analysis of clinical data, literature, and guidelines. Simon[19] describes human decision-making as a sequential process consisting of gathering information, investigating and evaluating options, and making a decision with feedback loops between steps. In AI-based decision-making, the AI makes the final decision by analyzing clinical datasets. The core of AI is MLA, where models are trained to make predictions and classifications by learning trends and relationships from a dataset without human guidance. Note that predictions and classifications are not decisions. Additional logic is required to derive decisions from AI outputs (e.g., admit the patient if disease risk is above 50%). Human and AI-based systems may reach similar decisions using different approaches. For example, a health professional's decision to admit a patient could be based on their interview, while the AI agent's decision is based on vital sign analysis. In AI-assisted decision-making, the predictions and classifications are additional inputs used to augment, not replace, the decision-making process of the health professional who makes the final decision. The health professional can also provide feedback to the AI to improve performance. In all decision-making systems, humans ultimately choose whether to implement (or veto) the decision from the health professional or AI.

TABLE 1 Properties of human and AI-based and AI-assisted decision-making.

		Human intelligence-based	AI-based	AI-assisted
Agents	Health Professional(s)	Yes[14]	No	Yes[14,15]
	Patient and Caregiver(s)	Yes[14]	Yes	Yes[14,15]
	AI	No[14]	Yes[16]	Yes[14,15]
Computers and Data are Involved		Yes[16]	Yes[16]	Yes[16]
Human–AI Collaboration		No	No[17]	Yes[14,15,17]
Primary Decision-Maker		Health professionals	AI	Health professional[15]
Responsible for Decision		Health professionals	Unclear[16]	Health professional[15]
Decision Implementation		Health professionals and patients	Patients	Health professionals and patients
AI to Human Communication		–	Yes	Yes[15]
Human to AI Communication		–	No	Yes (Human-in-the-loop)[14]
AI Agent Provides		–	Actions and recommendations[16,18]	Predictions and classifications[18]
Decision based on	Health Professionals' Judgments	Yes[14]	No[16]	Yes[14,15]
	Literature, Recommendations, and Guidelines	Yes	Yes[15,16]	Yes[15]
	Clinical Data (e.g., medical histories, imaging, and blood tests)	Yes (Analyzed by human agent[15])	Yes (Analyzed by AI agent[15])	Yes (Analyzed by a human or AI agent[15])
	AI Model Outputs	No	Yes[15,16]	Yes[14,15]
Same decision made with different health professional(s)?		No	–	No

2.2 Mental healthcare data terminology

Human, AI-based, and AI-assisted decision-making requires collecting and analyzing healthcare data. We describe the properties of the data available in mental healthcare in Table 2 based on the following dimensions:

- *Source*: The USA Agency for Healthcare Research and Quality defines patient-generated health data (PGHD) as data recorded by patients or their caregivers.[58] Subsequently, we define clinically generated health data (CGHD) as data recorded by health professionals and administrators.
- *Sample Intervals*: Medical data represent observations of a patient's health over time. The intervals between sequential observations can be approximately uniform (regularly sampled) or nonuniform (irregularly sampled) over a specified period.[59] We define the observation period from a patient's first entry in a hospital database until the present or the patient's death. As a result, CGHD recorded during infrequent hospital visits, including medical device recordings, are irregularly sampled data. In contrast, PGHD is regularly sampled data because there can be uniform intervals between observations.
- *Modality*: Tabular data are stored in a table with rows and columns.[60] Text, audio, image, and video data represent words,[51] analog audio (discrete samples of sound wave's amplitude),[33] images (pixels),[54] and video (audio and images) in a digital format, respectively.
- *Quantitative*: Data can be measured, expressed as continuous or discrete values, and analyzed using numerical methods.[61]
- *Qualitative*: Data are descriptive, expressed using numeric codes, and cannot be analyzed using numerical methods.[62] Qualitative data with and without a natural order or hierarchy are called ordinal and nominal, respectively.
- *Format*: Structured data are stored in formats searchable in relational databases, while unstructured data are not.[61] Semistructured data are unstructured but include metadata searchable in databases.
- *Electronic Health Record (EHR)*: Data can be accessed from hospital databases.

TABLE 2 Mental healthcare data properties.

	Source		Sample intervals		Modality				Quant.			Qual.	Format			Electronic health record	Machine learning publications
	Clinically Generated Health Data (CGHD)	Patient-Generated Health Data (PGHD)	Regular	Irregular	Tabular	Text	Image	Video	Continuous	Discrete	Ordinal	Nominal	Unstructured	Semistructured	Structured		
(a) Clinical Notes	X			X		X					X	X	X			X	20
(b) Demographic Records	X	X	X	X	X				X	X	X	X			X	X	2,21
(c) Diagnostic Codes	X			X	X						X				X	X	2,22
(d) Intervention Codes	X			X	X						X				X	X	2,22
(e) Prescription Records	X			X	X						X				X	X	2,22
(f) Medical Device Recordings	X			X	X				X				X			X	23
(g) Medical Images	X			X			X	X	X					X		X	3,24,25
(h) Laboratory Reports	X			X	X	X			X	X			X			X	2
(i) Genomics Reports	X			X	X	X			X	X			X			X	26–30
(j) Insurance and Healthcare Provider Claims	X			X	X	X					X		X				21
(k) Questionnaire Responses		X		X	X	X					X	X	X				31–37
(l) Nonmedical Sensor Recordings		X	X	X	X	X			X				X				34,38–42
(m) Smartphone App Outputs (Embedded Sensors Only)		X	X	X	X	X			X	X	X	X	X		X		33,34, 43,44
(n) Social Media Posts		X	X	X		X	X					X		X			45–51, 52–57

2.2.1 Clinically generated health data

The main CGHD used by mental healthcare professionals are clinical notes (Table 2a), which contain subjective patient assessments, psychotherapy and progress notes, treatment plans, and discharge summaries.[63] Assessments include patients and their families' medical and mental health history, demographic, socio-economic, and biological background. Psychotherapy and progress notes are the health professional's observations that patients, billing, and insurance providers cannot view. Treatment plans summarize the patients' mental health history, diagnoses, and progress and describe future goals and proposed services for billing and auditing. Discharge summaries communicate follow-up plans to caregivers and other healthcare professionals once patients complete a treatment program or are discharged from the hospital.

In addition to clinical notes, patients' demographic, diagnostic, intervention, and medication information (Table 2b–e) are recorded by health professionals[64] into the hospital databases. International Classification of Disease (ICD)[65] codes are used for reporting morbidity and mortality data for epidemiology, billing, and research.[61] Mental disorders can also be recorded using the Diagnostic and Statistical Manual of Mental Disorders (DSM) codes.[66] However, overlapping mental health diagnoses and treatments are challenging to standardize using quantitative codes[64] compared to medical fields based on physical health. In addition, the ICD and DSM standards disagree on mental health definitions.[67] Health professionals' uncertainties, observations, and judgments are not captured by diagnostic codes.

Unlike other medical fields, health professionals use medical devices, imaging, laboratory, and genomics testing (Table 2f–i) to exclude physical diseases with symptoms similar to mental illness (e.g., brain tumors). Subsequently, researchers investigate using medical test data to understand brain function, establish baselines, and identify functional and biological biomarkers to be used as ground truths for mental healthcare.[66,67]

Clinically generated health data are stored in various hospital databases.[68] The administration database may contain demographic, diagnostic, and intervention data. Inpatient (admitted to hospital) databases have demographic, diagnostic, intervention, prescription, and medical device data from the intensive care unit (ICU), general hospital, and discharge summaries. Outpatient (treated without admission to hospital) databases contain demographic, diagnostic, intervention, prescription, and medical device data from ED, day surgeries, and community-based care. A picture archiving and communication system (PACS) and laboratory system store medical images and lab reports.

2.2.2 Patient-generated health data

Patient-generated health data are becoming more common as the use of patient-reported outcome measures and measurement-based care approaches has increased. Self-reported measures and assessments are collected in the form of questionnaires completed by patients and their caregivers (Table 2k), which contain structured (e.g., multiple choice) and unstructured (e.g., text) responses regarding their health. Self-assessment questionnaires can be completed at irregular (e.g., medical appointments) or regular (e.g., daily on a smartphone) intervals. Mental health professionals use patients' self-reported questionnaires, medical histories, and observations from patient interviews to diagnose and treat mental diseases.

Outside of the clinical setting, patients can use PGHD to establish physiological and behavioral baselines to monitor their health during daily life.[67] Many PGHD sources are nonmedical equivalents to CGHD. Nonmedical sensors (Table 2l) are being used to monitor a variety of patients' biological, physical (e.g., speech patterns), behavioral (e.g., activity level), and environmental (e.g., location) conditions outside of the clinical settings. Patient online portals and smartphone apps (Table 2m) can be used by patients to track their appointments, clinical assessments, progress, and treatment plans. Smartphone apps can also be used to track mood, diet, exercise, and medication compliance and to deliver interventions. Social media (Table 2n) content is written by patients and posted online. The large amounts of generated PGHD are challenging to analyze, combine, harmonize, and capture manually.

Some PGHD data may be stored in the medical record, while some may be stored in mental health clinics separately from the hospital systems. Other PGHD (Table 2l–n) may be recorded in private databases not accessible by hospitals.

2.3 Literature review methodology and scope

Section 3 describes our case study in human intelligence-based decision-making in a CYMHP at McMaster Children's Hospital in Hamilton, Canada. Section 4 reports our literature review on AI-based and assisted decision-making systems in mental health. We focused on MLA because it is the core component of AI. Our review is based on the PRISMA (Preferred Reporting Items for Systematic Reviews and Meta-Analyses) methodology.[69] Since our review focus is on AI applications in mental health, we did not follow the complete PRISMA guidelines or conduct a meta-analysis, and one author reviewed the publications. We reviewed journals, conferences, and textbooks published between January 2010 and 2023. We included publications written in English that contained at least one engineering (machine or deep learning, neural networks, AI, or natural language processing (NLP)) and medical (mental health or psychiatry) term in the paper's title, abstract, or keywords. Fifty-nine publications met our inclusion criteria in the Google Scholar and Association for Computing Machinery (ACM) Digital Library databases. Nineteen publications that did not focus on mental health or present results applying MLA to a mental health dataset (e.g., surveys, literature reviews, and taxonomies) were excluded. Overall, forty publications were identified for our review. We review AI in general mental healthcare due to a minimal number of publications (4/40) focusing on child and youth mental health.

3. Human intelligence-based decision-making in mental health

3.1 How data are used in human intelligence-based decision-making in child and youth mental health

3.1.1 Overview

In CYMHP, CGHD and PGHD are used to make clinical and administrative decisions at the patient, service provider, program, and system level. This could include referral, treatment, service delivery, triage/prioritization, case management, program planning, or resource allocation. Decisions are more or less amenable to being supported through clinical decision support systems depending on the medical department and patient population.[70] Clinically generated data are often referred to as health administrative data and are generated in EHR systems by clinicians or staff. Patient-generated data are becoming increasingly common and may exist inside or outside of the EHR.

To date, CYMHP has relied heavily on human intelligence-based approaches because (1) mental health is a complex and multifaceted part of overall health,[71] and (2) measurement, assessment, and diagnostic formulation for child and youth mental health disorders and mental health-related needs are more challenging than for other medical conditions, illness and diseases, such as asthma, diabetes, and arthritis.[72] The measurement and classification of mental illness remain a challenge, with traditional disease categories being primarily constructed from expert opinions and empirically derived behavioral syndromes rather than relying on clear pathophysiological underpinnings.[73] Not surprisingly, disease staging (a method of measuring the severity of clearly defined illnesses), with its associated outcome prediction value, is a much better-established discipline in other branches of medicine. Disease staging often involves the assessment of multiple validated biological markers that carry some predictive value regarding certain treatment modalities or likely clinical outcomes (e.g., the Tumour, Node, Metastasis (TNM) system for cancer staging or the WHO clinical staging of HIV disease). The adequate staging of medical illnesses allows for a more precise allocation of resources, with the goal of providing more intense levels of support for the patients with the highest needs. Unfortunately, no such level of precision in clinical staging is currently available for mental illnesses.

One model of human intelligence-based decision-making using PGHD is measurement-based care (MBC), which is the systematic evaluation of patient signs or symptoms at regular clinical intervals to inform treatment. Although vastly underused in mental health,[74] it is considered a key component of evidence-based mental health treatment.[75] MBC is best provided by using PGHD, such as self-report symptom checklists, since they are brief, simple, inexpensive to implement; pose a little burden to respondents; can be administered in almost any setting to multiple informants (e.g., parents, teachers, and youth) using various modes of administration (e.g., in person, by mail, online); and exhibit relatively little between-subject variation in completion times.[76] Patient-generated health data can be used to inform the level of intensity and modality of mental healthcare for children and youth requesting mental health support. At a group level, MBC can be used to determine the appropriate allocation of services within an agency and delivery of optimal intensity of care for youth on a waiting list. Moreover, when used repeatedly during the episode of care (e.g., before and after a certain intervention, after every therapy session, or at regular intervals during treatment), these PGHD can be used to test the effectiveness of particular treatment modalities and to inform clinicians in "real-time" whether clinical improvement is achieved.

3.1.2 Case study: McMaster Children's hospital child and youth mental health program

McMaster Children's Hospital CYMHP in Hamilton, Ontario, provides a case study in understanding the role of human intelligence-based approaches in clinical decision-making in child and youth mental health outpatient services. In particular, we focus on the identification of clinical needs at intake to services as part of an MBC approach. Fig. 1 illustrates the service pathway for a child/youth seeking mental health outpatient services at McMaster Children's Hospital's Child and Youth Mental Health Outpatient Program.

Patients enter McMaster Children's Hospital through (1) referral by a family physician or local centralized referral organization to CYMHP; or (2) presentation to the ED. Once referred to CYMHP, families are placed on a waiting list

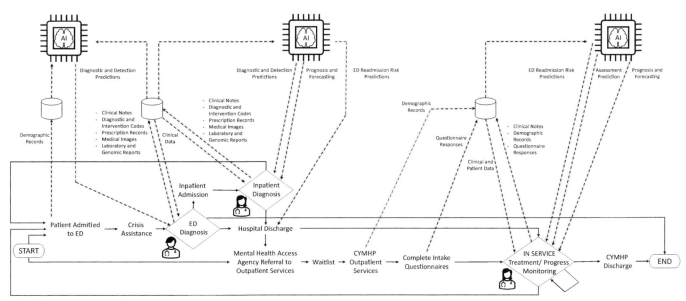

FIG. 1   Patient mental healthcare pathway (solid lines) through the ED (second row from bottom), inpatient (third row from bottom), and outpatient (first row from bottom) services. Human decisions (diamond) are made using CGHD and PGHD at each step in the pathway (dashed lines). In the future, AI predictions (dashed lines going out from the AI boxes) can assist human decision-making.

until an appointment can be made. In advance of their first appointment and entry to services, youth (age 12–17) and parents/caregivers of children and youth (age 4–17) complete a standardized intake questionnaire that assesses the mental health-related needs of the child youth and the main concerns they are seeking services to address. This questionnaire includes validated health measures that validly and reliably assess mental health disorder symptoms. Following questionnaire completion at intake, the youth and/or caregivers enter the service. The information collected is summarized in a clinician report and reviewed by clinicians. Clinicians also complete a clinical interview with children, youth, and families, which is documented in the EHR in the form of notes. This information may be gathered over several sessions depending on the complexity of the case and the need for any further assessments. Once the clinician is satisfied, they have the necessary information, and they generate a treatment plan for the patient based on their clinical judgment.

Additional assessments may be completed during service until discharge. At discharge, youth and caregivers complete discharge questionnaires. At any point during outpatient service, if the child/youth experiences a significant crisis, they may also access services via the ED. For children/youth entering service through the ED, crisis assistance is offered, and they are either discharged or referred to inpatient admission for further service. At discharge from the ED or inpatient services, a child/youth may be referred to CYMHP for additional support and treatment. At each point in the service pathway, CGHD or PGHD may be generated.

3.2 Challenges to data use in human intelligence-based decision-making in child and youth mental health

There are a number of challenges to the use of data in this type of scenario that generalize to other decision-making in child and youth mental health.[77] First, CGHD and PGHD are high in volume, dimensionality, and heterogeneity, which are hard for human intelligence to process in an efficient, timely, and optimized way.[78] Second, the use of clinical judgment is impossible to fully explicate in a way that can be easily reproduced by other untrained humans or clinical decision support systems.[79] Third, the format, access point, temporality, and availability of data are variable, which can change their role in the decision-making process. Finally, human intelligence-based approaches are subject to several biases, conscious and unconscious.[80]

Regarding the use of PGHD in MBC specifically, the level of complexity in collecting self-report information is amplified by the frequent presence of multiple informants (e.g., parents and teachers). Other demographic and clinical factors may exert a larger prognostic or treatment-moderating influence in youth compared with adults, such as parental mental health, parental divorce, abuse, trauma, school environment, and other socio-economic factors. Over the last decade, the amount of data that healthcare practitioners need to consider when assessing patients has dramatically expanded. Genomic, metabolic, epigenetic, imaging, personal, and family clinical history, for instance, may all impact treatment response and clinical outcomes on an individual level.[81] Furthermore, the increased availability of digital technologies in healthcare (e.g., electronic medical records, biometric data from wearable devices or smartphones) has produced massive amounts of data with potential relevance for treatment decisions.[82–84] Deriving clinical meaning from such a vast number of variables is an overwhelming task for any single practitioner. Integrating "big data" from such heterogenous sources holds great promise in mental health, given the complex net of relationships between brain functioning, environmental, and experiential characteristics associated with psychiatric symptoms. By addressing some of these challenges, AI-based decision-making holds promise for future directions in child and youth mental healthcare,[85] which include precision medicine[86] and deep learning health system approaches.[82,87,88]

4. Sok AI-assisted and AI-based decision-making in mental health

In this section, we review the AI-assisted and AI-based mental health systems based on their development stages: data preparation (Section 4.1), modeling (Section 4.2), evaluation (Section 4.3), and operationalization (Section 4.4).

4.1 Data preparation

The raw CGHD (Section 2.2.1) and PGHD (Section 2.2.2) cannot be directly analyzed using MLA due to issues, such as missing values in some samples (rows) or having a lot of input data columns for the MLA (also called features).[89] Data preparation (preprocessing) is the cleaning, integration, reduction, and transformation of raw data into a set of features that are suitable as MLA inputs.[90] Data cleaning addresses noisy, inconsistent, and incomplete data common in health datasets.[91] When working with text data, lemmatization should be performed, which is turning the third-person format into the first-person format and all verbs into the present tense, followed by turning words into their root forms.[51,55] Missing values are common when working with tabular data, such as questionnaire responses. Imputation techniques, such as statistical (e.g., mean or median) and deep learning imputation, estimate missing data using the remaining data in the dataset.[31] Tabular data, such as data gathered by sensors, can be noisy and should be preprocessed to clean and better utilize data. Having noisy data is not specific to tabular data. Image and video data are not always ready to be used by MLAs and need to be cleaned. Often a specific part of the image or video needs to be detected, such as a patient's face, for emotion detection, before being able to use MLAs. To do so, transforming the area of interest, such as cropping, resizing, and turning the images to gray scale, should be performed to remove and smooth the noise before using the image for the prediction task.[92]

Data reduction is selecting a subset of features and samples to construct a data subset representative of the original dataset. The number of features available in tabular data, also referred to as the dimensionality of the data, can affect the MLA. Statistical and linear algebra methods can be used to reduce the dimensionality of the input data, such as the work done by Iliou et al. for data used in depression type prediction.[32] Dimensionality reduction techniques can also be applied to video data. Principal component analysis (PCA) can be used to reduce the number of features of input video that can be used for mental health prediction tasks, such as mental disorder recognition.[93] The PCA method is a statistical method used to reduce the dimensionality of the data by analyzing the data and extracting the important features.

Data transformation is constructing features from the subset of all available columns that the MLA will analyze. Data transformation techniques include normalization, discretization, encoding, and data fusion. Data normalization is the process of scaling numerical values to the same scale, preventing the samples with higher values from dominating the others.[94] Data discretization is the transformation of continuous values in our dataset into different buckets, for example, converting the age feature into different categories for mental health analysis using MLA.[95] Some of the features in our dataset can contain categorical features. Categorical features are nonnumerical features with discrete values (e.g., hair color). Since MLAs need numerical attributes, we need to turn our categorical features into numeric values, by mapping the categories to numbers, an approach called encoding. An example of encoding is converting the ICD-10 diagnostic codes to numeric values for predicting future ED visits of mental health patients.[96] If multiple records of a single subject (e.g., patient) exist, we would need to fuse them into a single representation, a process called data fusion.[97] One advantage of data fusion can be representing the hierarchy available in the data from multiple sources. Data fusion can also help find causal links in the data.[98] Text preprocessing begins with Tokenization, which splits the document into sentences and sentences into words, lowercasing the words and removing the punctuations, stop words, links, and numbers.[51,55] Often video and audio data need to be transformed before being inputted into a model. One popular video and audio preprocessing step is to transform the input data into multiple instances of the same length, an approach called sliding window.[99]

4.2 Modeling

Machine learning algorithms (Section 4.2.1) have been used in mental health for diagnosis and detection (Section 4.2.2), prognosis and forecasting (Section 4.2.3), and assessment (Section 4.2.4).

4.2.1 Machine learning models

This section discusses different MLAs, for example, decision trees and Support Vector Machine (SVM). One of the widely used MLAs is the decision tree algorithm. The decision tree algorithm creates a hierarchical model based on the input features. Each node in the decision tree represents a feature, and the connections between the nodes represent the values the feature can take. The final leaf nodes of the tree represent the final decision (i.e., label).[1] The SVM algorithm used for classification tasks maps the inputs to a feature space and separates classes by finding margins between them. The margin is found in such a way that the classification error is minimized. Another widely used MLA for prediction tasks like depression detection is the Naïve Bayes algorithm, which is based on the Bayes theorem and conditional probability.

One branch of MLAs is the use of Artificial Neural Network (ANN), known as deep learning. Artificial Neural Networks learn the existing nonlinear relationship in the data to achieve the task (e.g., classification).[1] One of the most popular ANNs is the multilayer perceptron (MLP). An MLP is a network of ANNs with input layer (i.e., input neurons), output layer (i.e., one or multiple output neurons related to the task), and multiple hidden layers (i.e., layers between the input and the output layers). The values are transmitted from the input layer to the output layer. There are different types of ANNs, for example, Convolutional Neural Network (CNN) and Recurrent Neural Network (RNN). A popular MLA used for image classification tasks is called CNN, which has convolution layers, pooling layers, and fully connected layer. The convolution layers are used to process the input, i.e., the image, and learn different patterns in the image. Then, the pooling layer is used to reduce the dimension of the feature map provided by the convolution layer. Finally, the fully connected layer is used for the image classification task[100] (e.g., emotion detection). When the input data consist of sequential or time series, such as a sequence of a patient's visit to the ED, traditional MLAs are not suitable. For example, when a patient has multiple visits to the ED, the previous visits should be used to predict the next visit. The RNN approaches use memory to learn from inputs in the previous timesteps of the time series and predict the future.[1]

Natural language processing methods are MLA used to work with text, such as clinical notes. Since text can be seen as a sequence of words, RNN approaches can be used.[100] Recent advancements in large language models (LLMs), such as Bidirectional Encoder Representations from Transformers (BERT) and Generative Pretrained Transformer (GPT), are being used for NLP. One approach is using a pretrained LLM, i.e., an LLM that has been trained on a generic task, and fine-tuning for the desired task.[101] When fine-tuning the LLM, the pretrained LLM learns to perform better on the specific task, for example, predicting the diagnostic code from clinical notes. In the mental health domain, a pretrained LLM, such as BERT, can be fine-tuned on mental health discussions available on social media and used for mental health-related tasks, such as depression detection from user's text written on social media platforms.[57]

4.2.2 Diagnosis and detection

Machine learning algorithms have been used to diagnose mental health disorders as summarized in Table 3. Current MLAs have used medical images, genomics reports, questionnaire responses, nonmedical sensor recordings, smartphone app outputs, and social media and micro-blog posts (Table 2g, i, k–n) to predict different mental health-related disorders. Neuroimages are capable of providing evidence of neuropsychiatric disorders. Studies have used neuroimages for detecting patients with a specific mental disorder. For example, Schnack et al. used SVM with MRI scans to distinguish schizophrenia from bipolar patients.[25] Some mental health conditions are related to aging, and medical images, such as brain MRI, have been studied to find age-related diseases. For example, Sheela Kumari et al. applied ANN,[24] and Doan et al. applied Linked Independent Component Analysis (LICA)[3] to brain MRI for the diagnosis of Alzheimer's disease.

Some mental health conditions, such as manic-depressive illness, might be linked to a complex genetic disorder. Therefore, analyzing genomics sequences with machine learning approaches can be used for diagnosis. Laksshman et al. investigated bipolar disorder prediction using exome sequencing data, which is a type of genome sequence, using deep CNN.[29] Exome sequence can also be used to predict mental disorders using machine learning. Supervised MLAs, such as Random Forest and XGBoost, are effective in predicting schizophrenia using genomic sequences.[30]

Mental health professionals use patient-reported questionnaires to assess a patient's mental health status. As a result, mental health questionnaire responses can be used as MLA inputs for diagnosis tasks. Iliou et al. used responses to the BDI for detecting depression using the Nearest Neighbor classifier, Random Forest, MLP, and SVM.[32] Similarly, Oak used responses to questionnaires with a Radial Bias Function Network (RBFN) model to detect depression.[33]

TABLE 3 Summary of the discussed work in the diagnosis and detection category.

	Data	Modality	Machine learning algorithms	Predictive task
(g)	Medical Images	Image	LICA,[3] ANN,[24] SVM[25]	Alzheimer's Disease,[3,24] Distinguish Schizophrenia from Bipolar Patients[25]
(i)	Genomics Reports	Tabular	Deep CNN,[29] SVM, XGBoost, Random Forest[30]	Bipolar Disorder,[29] Schizophrenia Disorder[30]
(k)	Questionnaire Responses	Tabular	Nearest Neighbor Classifier,[32] Random Forest,[32,35] MLP,[32] SVM,[32] RBFN,[33] XGBoost,[35] Decision Tree,[35] Gaussian Naïve Bayes[35]	Depression[32,33,35]
(l)	Nonmedical Sensor Recordings	Speech	Multilinear Logistic Regression[40]	Alzheimer's Disease[40]
		Tabular	Naïve Bayes Classifier[44]	Stress,[43] Manic and Stress States of Patients with Bipolar Disorder[44]
(m)	Smartphone App Outputs	Speech	RBFN[33]	Depression[33]
(n)	Social Media Posts	Text	Logistic Regression,[45] SVM,[46] ULM,[47] CLM,[47] LIWC,[47] BiLSTM,[48] GloVe Embedding,[48] Decision Tree,[49] CNN,[50] NER,[50] RNN,[50] DNN,[52] BoW,[54] ELMo,[54] FastText,[54] LLM[57]	Depression,[52,54,57] Bipolar Disorder,[45] PTSD,[47] Substance Use,[49] Suicide Risk[46,48,50]
		Image	ResNet[54]	Depression[54]
(n)	Micro-blog Posts	Text	Word Embedding and CNN[51]	Depression[51]

Nonmedical devices or sensor data that can provide helpful information have also been explored. The data can be in the form of speech and captured through different microphones. For example, Fraser et al. applied multilinear logistic regression[40] to identify Alzheimer's disease from narratives. Alternatively, the data can be tabular, containing values of different sensors, such as the speed at which the person is walking. Carneiro et al. used user interaction with touchscreen devices and device sensors to detect stress.[43] The phone call logs, the sounds captured using the mobile phone's microphone, and other sensor data (such as GPS data) have been utilized with the Naïve Bayes classifier to detect manic and stress states of patients diagnosed with bipolar disorder by Grünerbl et al.[44]

Smartphones and smartphone apps are pervasively used and have become part of people's everyday lives.[102] The output provided by different smartphone apps, such as an app that records the user's voice or sleep patterns, can provide useful information for the diagnosis task. One data type that could be gathered through smartphones is the user's speech, which can contain valuable information for detecting mental health disorders, such as depression. For example, to determine whether the speaker can be diagnosed with depression, Oak[33] used speech data collected from participants of their study who used a smartphone app and applied RBFN. The features extracted from the user's speech, such as length of pause and talking speed, can indicate some mental health-related disorders.

One of the most popular AI approaches in mental health is using NLP techniques with user-generated text data, such as social media or micro-blog posts. User-generated text data can contain indications of different mental health problems, such as depression, that machine learning approaches can utilize. Jia used user's posts on social media posts and applied Deep Neural Network (DNN) to detect depression.[52] Budenz et al. used social media posts with a logistic regression model to detect bipolar disorder.[45]

4.2.3 Prognosis and forecasting

In the prognosis and forecasting task, patient data are given to the MLA to predict the course of a disease or to predict future mental state as summarized in Table 4. It is common to use the patient's medical history to predict the course of a disease or future events. The data types mainly used in prognosis and forecasting tasks are clinical notes, demographic records, diagnostic codes, intervention codes, prescription records, medical device recordings, laboratory reports, genomics reports, insurance and healthcare provider claims, questionnaire responses, nonmedical sensor recordings, and social media and micro-blog posts (Table 2a–f, h–l, n).

A good source of information for prognosis and forecasting is the EHR, which contains data related to the history of patients' clinical encounters. Machine learning algorithms can be used to analyze clinically generated texts and notes written by clinicians to predict the future state of a disease. Since clinical notes contain information regarding the

TABLE 4   Summary of the discussed work in the prognosis and forecasting category.

	Data	Modality	Machine learning algorithms	Predictive task
(a)	Clinical Notes	Text	SVM, Logistic Regression, Random Forest[20]	Psychosis Onset[20]
(b)	Demographic Records	Tabular	Logistic Regression Classifier[2]	Suicide Risk Prediction[2]
(c)	Diagnostic Codes	Tabular	LSTM-Based Model,[22] Logistic Regression Classifier[2]	Current Illness State and Next Disease Occurrence,[22] Suicide Risk Prediction[2]
(d)	Intervention Codes			
(e)	Prescription Records			
(f)	Medical Device Recordings	Tabular	SVM[23]	Stress Monitoring[23]
(h)	Laboratory Reports	Tabular	Logistic Regression Classifier[2]	Suicide Risk Prediction[2]
(i)	Genomics Reports	Tabular	Deep Boltzmann Machine-Based Model[28]	Disease[28]
(j)	Insurance and Healthcare Provider Claims	Tabular	SVM,[21] XGBoost[21]	Opioid Use Post Surgery[21]
(k)	Questionnaire Responses	Tabular	Random Forest,[31] Ensemble Model[37]	Therapy Outcomes,[31] Personalized Treatment Response[37]
(n)	Micro-blog Posts	Text	Regression[56]	User's Stage When Quitting Smoking[56]

course of the disorder up to its current state, they can be a rich source of information for the prognosis task. For example, Viani et al. used SVM, Logistic Regression, and Random Forest algorithms[20] to find psychosis onset information from EHR text.

The EHR can also contain structured data, such as demographic records, medications, diagnoses, intervention codes, and laboratory records. Since a patient might visit a hospital multiple times, the EHR contains the history of a patient's visits. Based on the patient's history of diagnostic codes, intervention codes, or prescription records, MLAs can extract patterns that might help predict the patient's future mental health status. For example, Pham et al. used Long Short-Term Memory (LSTM) to process the structured data available in medical records to infer the current illness state and predict the next disease occurrence.[22]

Medical device recordings have been used in healthcare to predict future events, such as predicting future cardiac disease from electrocardiography (ECG) signals.[103] Most recordings are stored in a structural (i.e., tabular) format. In mental health, some medical sensor readings, such as electroencephalography (EEG) signals, are being gathered and can be analyzed with machine learning approaches for prognosis and forecasting tasks. For example, Ha et al. used different sensor data, such as EEG, with SVM to create a mental health management system.[23]

Since mental health conditions might be linked to genomics, genomics reports could be utilized with machine learning approaches to predict patients' future mental health states. Wang et al. utilized connections from gene regulatory networks with an interpretable deep Boltzmann machine-based model to improve disease prediction.[28]

Besides EHR, insurance and health providers also store lists of diagnostic codes, intervention codes, and prescription records as part of the claims data. Therefore, insurance and healthcare provider claims can also be used for prognosis and forecasting. Similar to EHRs, insurance claims can also contain the history of a patient's claims. As a result, MLAs can extract patterns from patients' insurance claim histories. Hur et al. used patient demographics, type of surgery, and their data 12 months before the surgery and applied SVM and XGBoost to predict postoperative opioid use.[21] The authors used the insurance claims history of patients to obtain the inputs to the MLA they trained.

In mental healthcare, clinicians often use patient-reported outcome measures, which may indicate future mental health problems. This can be predicted using machine learning approaches. Personalized treatment plans can also be predicted by analyzing the course of a disease. For example, Hornstein et al. used self-reported questionnaires to predict therapy outcomes for depression and anxiety by training Random Forest algorithm.[31] Gyorda et al. used questionnaires to predict personalized treatment plans.[37]

Social media or micro-blogs can also be a good source of information for which MLA and NLP approaches can be used. Topics, psycho-linguistic features, and language styles of users are potential sources of information that could be used by machine learning approaches to improve healthcare research. For example, Nguyen et al. used psycho-linguistic features and content topics extracted from user-generated posts regarding user's interest in quitting smoking with a Regression algorithm to differentiate posts of users who were in the first week of quitting from others.[56]

Data from different modalities captured through different means could be utilized by AI approaches for predicting future mental health problems or prognosis. Similar to methods used for diagnosis and detection, methods developed for prognosis can be used for either AI-assisted decision-making or AI-based decision-making. Table 4 summarizes the work discussed in this category.

4.2.4 Assessment

In assessment tasks, the purpose is to assess the mental health of a group or an individual. Data types mainly used in assessment tasks include genomics reports, questionnaire responses, nonmedical sensor recordings, and social media and micro-blog posts (Table 2i,k,l,n).

Genomic data can be utilized by machine learning approaches to investigate mental health states. For example, Khan and Wang investigated prioritizing genetic variants that may contribute to mental disorders using Multilayer Neural Networks.[26] The authors developed a deep learning model that analyzes a person's whole genome sequence data and provides a prioritized list of variants. Khan et al. further expanded their study of using genetic variants by adding general gene scores and disease-specific scores to the score the model in their previous study[26] generated and applied DNN.[27]

Questionnaires and surveys can also have helpful information that could be utilized with AI algorithms for assessment tasks. Responses to questionnaires recorded at certain times, for example, during the COVID-19 lockdown, can contain indicators of mental health-related risks. Machine learning algorithms can identify the indicators and help assess the respondents' mental health. For example, Sano et al.'s[34] approach to finding contributing factors to academic performance and measuring sleep quality, stress levels, and mental health used various data, including surveys by using an SVM model.

Acoustic features of speech data can provide useful information regarding a patient's health status. Nonmedical devices, such as a headset, can be used to capture a patient's speech during an interview and passed to an MLA to assess the patient's mental health state. For example, Kliper et al. used speech data with SVM model to alert possible underlying mental health conditions of individuals.[42] Bedi et al. also used speech data with SVM model to predict the changes to the mental state based on the drugs an individual uses.[39]

Mobile phones and wearable devices are being used pervasively. Sensors available in the mentioned devices can provide useful data for assessing an individual's mental health state, such as the work done by Sano et al.[34] using various data, including mobile phone and wearable sensors, to find factors contributing to academic performance and measure sleep quality, stress level, and mental health by applying SVM model. Guo et al. used sensor data and applied the K-Nearest Neighbors (k−NN) algorithm to sense human emotions.[41] Besides mobile phones and wearable sensors, smart home settings use sensors that can produce useful information.

Different social and micro-blog platforms, such as Reddit, can be a rich source of information for assessment tasks. Posts published by users on micro-blog platforms can help identify different mental health insights during a specific time, such as the pandemic. As an example, Low et al. used Reddit posts with Linear Models, Tree Ensemble Classifiers, and a Clustering approach to find that usage of tokens, such as economic stress, increased during the COVID-19 pandemic.[53] Mittal et al. also used user posts on Reddit and applied SVM, Random Forest, Multinomial Naïve Bayes, and Stochastic Gradient Descent (SGD) classifier to identify those with suicidal thoughts.[55]

Assessing an individual's mental health status or the mental health status of a group can help lower the impact of mental health problems in public. There are different data sources, especially sources being used pervasively by users (e.g., social platforms and mobile devices with different sensors), that can provide rich datasets for machine learning approaches to analyze. The approaches can be used in AI-assisted decision-making to help clinicians make better decisions or in AI-based decision-making. Table 5 summarizes the work discussed in the assessment category.

4.3 Evaluation

Machine learning algorithms are increasingly evaluated using multiple criteria, such as task performance, explainability, fairness, robustness, security, privacy, and trust throughout the MLA development pipeline.[104] In task performance,[27] the trained model's predictive or classification performance (e.g., accuracy, sensitivity, and specificity) is evaluated on held-out test data not used to train the model. By evaluating the MLA's task performance, we assess if the model is memorizing (overfitting) or cannot capture the relationships between the inputs and outputs of the training set (underfitting). The MLA's task performance is compared to alternative models, gold standards, or subject-domain experts to evaluate the model's suitability for deployment. For example, Du et al. compared the results of their proposed approach for suicide tweets classification with other approaches.[50] However, high task performance in a lab setting (e.g., above 90% accuracy) does not guarantee the model will perform well in a clinical environment with new data.[105] In addition, a model can achieve high task performance while performing poorly for the remaining evaluation criteria.

TABLE 5 Summary of the discussed work in the assessment category.

	Data	Modality	Machine learning algorithms	Predictive task
(i)	Genomics Reports	Tabular	Multilayer Neural Network,[26] Deep Neural Network[27]	Prioritizing Contributing Genetic Variants to Mental Disorder[26,27]
(k)	Questionnaire Responses	Tabular	SVM,[34,36] Random Forest, MLP, XGBoost, KNN, Logistic Regression, Decision Trees[36]	Finding Contributing Factors to Mental Health,[34] Finding Impact of COVID-19 Lockdown on the Mental Health of Children and Adolescents[36]
(l)	Nonmedical Sensor Recordings	Speech	SVM[39,42]	Finding Possible Underlying Mental Health Conditions,[42] Finding Changes to Mental Health State based on Drug Usage[39]
		Tabular	SVM,[34] k-NN,[41] HMM[38]	Finding Contributing Factors to Mental Health,[34] Sensing Human Emotions,[41] Predicting Emergency Psychiatric State[38]
(n)	Micro-blog Posts	Text	Linear Models, Tree Ensemble Classifiers, Clustering,[53] SVM, Random Forest, Multinomial Naïve Bayes Algorithm, SGD Classifier[55]	Usage of Tokens During COVID-19,[53] Identify Users with Suicidal Thoughts[55]

Explainability is the model's ability to provide details on its functions in a form meaningful to a stakeholder (e.g., health professionals, patients, caregivers, and regulators).[106] Early MLAs are interpretable (white box). For example, a decision tree's prediction can be communicated to stakeholders by displaying the sequence of decisions made at each branch in the tree. On the other hand, CNN and transformers are not natively interpretable (black boxes). The explainable AI field focuses on developing tools to improve the explainability of black-box models, which often have improved performance compared to white-box models. For example, CNN has achieved start-of-the-art task performance in image processing but does not natively have a mechanism to explain its predictions. One explainability mechanism is saliency maps, which display the inputs given the most attention (weight) by the CNN. In AI-assisted decision-making, explainability is important for the final decision-maker (health professional) to consider the AI predictions with additional information sources (e.g., medical tests). In AI-based decision-making, explainability is important to communicating the decision-making process to the patient, who vetoes or implements the decision. Researchers also use explainability to identify problems and biases in their models. Ahmed et al. proposed an MLA that can detect depression from patient writings using a deep attention model and used weighted terms to explain the model's predictions.[107] To determine the reasons for the prediction, the approach uses rule-based classification. For example, in a text written by a patient, the patient indicated that they want depression to win and be at peace in heaven, which triggered the model to predict depression based on the text.

Fairness evaluates the model's performance on subgroups in a dataset to identify bias and discrimination.[108] Fairness is crucial in healthcare to ensure equitable diagnosis and treatment. A model can achieve high task performance (e.g., accuracy) but not be fair to marginalize vulnerable groups. Disparity causes MLAs with high accuracy to be unfair toward specific groups. Rodolfa et al. used a post hoc method to mitigate disparity in the application of AI in an inmate's mental health setting in which race can be a sensitive attribute leading to having unfair MLAs.[109] There are methodologies for improving AI fairness, such as under and over-sampling.[110]

Robustness[111] evaluates the MLA's generalization ability beyond its training and test data. Ideally, the model's predictions or classifications should not change when applied to new data similar to the training set. However, an overfit model that memorized patterns specific to the train and test sets will not perform well on new data. One technique for assessing robustness is to evaluate the model on external data from a different location (e.g., a hospital). Another technique is to evaluate the model's sensitivity to input data perturbations that change the model's classifications. Researchers can also evaluate how the model performance changes under data drift when the underlying patterns and distributions being modeled change over time. After a certain amount of data drift, the model is no longer valid and needs to be retrained or retired. For example, Harrigian et al. investigated the robustness of MLA for depression detection using social platform posts[112] and explored the generalization ability of the trained models across multiple social media platforms, such as Twitter or Reddit. Harrigian et al. found that the performance of an MLA trained on data from one social media platform, such as Twitter (source dataset) for a specific task, such as depression detection, drops when using the same trained model on data from a different social platform, for example, Reddit (target dataset), for the same predictive task. However, the difference between the MLA's performance on the source data and the target dataset will differ when changing the datasets. A key area of robustness is measuring the model's uncertainty or confidence for its predictions or classifications.[113] Like explainability, some MLAs communicate uncertainty natively (e.g., Bayesian networks), while others do not (e.g., CNN). Note that the model's class probability does not necessarily reflect the model's confidence or uncertainty in its prediction (e.g., a model can be 90% certain in its prediction a patient has a 75% chance of readmission). In AI-assisted decision-making, uncertainty is important for the health professional to weigh different sources of information to make a decision. In AI-based decision-making, uncertainty helps patients accept or veto the model's recommended decision.

Security evaluates an MLA's ability to function as intended when attacked, while privacy refers to a stakeholder's ability to control their information.[114] Security and privacy are critical in mental healthcare. There are specific security and privacy guidelines and regulations, such as Personal Information Protection Act (PIPA), the Personal Health Information Protection Act (PHIPA), General Data Protection Regulation (GDPR), and the Personal Information Protection and Electronic Documents Act (PIPEDA), for MLAs. Model security and privacy can be evaluated by simulating adversarial attacks against the model to produce misclassifications or to reveal information about the model's architecture, configuration, and training data.[115] Studies have also been able to retrieve private information that deep learning models have memorized during training.[116] For example, Rabi et al. used user-generated data, such as speech, which are privacy-sensitive to assess mental health.[117] To not allow reconstruction, the authors did not record the raw audio, but instead, they recorded some features, for example, the total number of auto-correlation peaks, that helped infer when a human was speaking and if there was a conversation happening.

Trust in AI is the positive expectation of an AI agent's future performance when delegated to a position always occupied by a human without supervision.[118] In AI-assisted decision-making, health professionals must trust the AI agent before incorporating the agent's classifications and predictions into the health professional's decision-making process. In AI-based decision-making, the patient's trust in the AI agent is crucial because the agent operates without a health professional's supervision. Unlike quantitative task performance metrics, trust is stochastic and subjective, and depends on multiple criteria. All the evaluation criteria described in this section can contribute to stakeholders' trust in AI. Multiple trust frameworks have been proposed to define the importance of the evaluation criteria for establishing trust in different application areas. For example, Chandler et al. proposed a framework to evaluate the trustworthiness of AI in psychiatry based on explainability and robustness.[119]

4.4 Operationalization

Operationalization is the deployment of the trained model.[120] In AI-assisted decision-making, the model is integrated into a clinical environment and workflow.[104] As a result, operationalization involves addressing technical challenges, such as deploying the model in the clinical environment's preexisting computing infrastructure, accessing clinical data, and communicating the model's classification or predictions to health professionals.[121] Health professionals are also educated about the model, interpreting the model's classifications or predictions, and recommending clinical actions. After installation, the MLA is run in silent mode, where classifications and predictions are made in real-time but not acted upon by health professionals.[122] The silent mode enables researchers to evaluate the model's performance in the clinical environment from a technical perspective, identify and review errors, and build buy-in and trust from health professionals. After silent mode, the model is fully deployed into the clinical workflow, and prospective validation studies and clinical trials on the model's performance are conducted.[123] The model is monitored and maintained after deployment to address user concerns and performance degradation. Hirsch et al. described the challenges of a MLA called CORE-MI, which uses speech and language processing techniques to be used in therapy sessions that transcribe and evaluate the quality of therapy sessions.[124] The purpose of the use of the CORE-MI approach is to provide a visual summary and to be used for provider training and supervision in clinics. Hirsch et al. used phased deployment to improve the accuracy of their approach. In phased deployment, MLAs would first run through multiple sessions in educational settings in training clinics and universities. Therefore, the students using the approach would provide feedback. By the time MLAs would be ready to be deployed in nontraining clinical settings, it is expected that the phased deployment approach improve the accuracy of MLAs.

Developers have more operationalization control in AI-based decision-making systems because the model is not part of a preexisting clinical workflow. For example, data collected by mobile devices are transmitted to a remote server for analysis, and the results are communicated to the user by a smartphone application.[125] Technical challenges (e.g., computational and network requirements) are addressed during operationalization in controlled settings instead of silent deployment.[126] Documentation is essential in AI-based decision-making systems because the model decisions are communicated directly to patients. Clinical trials are conducted to receive regulatory approval. Prospective validation studies, monitoring, and maintenance are conducted after deployment.

5. Discussion and open research challenges

5.1 Discussion

Mental healthcare lacks measurable biological markers (biomarkers) and well-validated clinical tests to predict mental health diagnoses or treatment effectiveness.[127] Subsequently, the CGHD and PGHD used in mental healthcare are primarily text-based, such as clinical notes and questionnaire responses (Table 2a and k), respectively. In human intelligence-based decision-making, health professionals make decisions based on their interactions with patients, interpretation of patients' clinical notes and questionnaire responses, and domain knowledge. However, it is challenging for humans to review the growing volume of data for each patient. Instead, the clinicians focus on the most recent data. This opens up the opportunity for AI approaches to be used in the mental health domain. Current applied AI approaches in mental health using both CGHD and PGHD data. Although most of the work focuses on using PGHD through social media platforms, data from different modalities, such as text and audio, have been utilized. The previously discussed approaches can be used for both AI-assisted decision-making and AI-based decision-making.

Currently, most research in using AI in mental health has been done in the lab environment. However, there is no guarantee that the developed approaches yield close to the same performance in the clinical setting as the developed approach in the lab environment.[105] Most developed AI approaches do not consider the clinical workflow used by clinicians but are working independently. The clinician considers specific data in the clinical workflow and plans future treatment paths. The clinician has been left out of the AI pipeline for most of the discussed work. The machine learning algorithm is trained on a set of data and tested for a specific task without considering the stage in the clinical pipeline, ethical considerations, or input from patients and caregivers.

Instead of developing an AI algorithm independent from clinical workflow, we can train, deploy, and integrate different AI models in different stages of the clinical workflow, as can be seen in Fig. 1. In each stage, relevant data are passed to the model. The model's predictions are then presented to the clinician. The clinician uses the AI prediction, available data, and their expertise to make a decision. As a result, the data the clinicians are used to working with would be augmented with the AI predictions. This approach would allow clinicians to use all available data from different modalities through the AI predictions. To transition from human intelligence-based decision-making in youth mental health to AI-assisted decision-making in youth mental health, we need to address challenges in both developing AI methods to be used in the mental health domain (Section 5.2) and mental health clinicians' concerns regarding AI-assisted decision-making (Section 5.3).

5.2 Open research challenges in AI in mental health

After reviewing the current state of the knowledge about AI algorithms in mental health, we identified a need for more work in three open research areas: data fusion, utilizing data semantics, and model explainability. There are challenges associated with each of the open research areas with respect to the machine learning pipelines. For example, data fusion occurs in the preprocessing stage resulting in a dataset with multiple modalities. However, in the modeling stage, we need to develop models capable of analyzing the fused data. To use the semantics, we need first to identify the semantics from the current raw data. Finally, for the explainability of the model, we should provide proper evaluation techniques that take the audience (i.e., expert clinicians, patients, and caregivers) into account.

5.2.1 Data fusion

In our case study example, self-reported questionnaires, containing both qualitative and quantitative questions, are used by clinicians for decision-making. Additionally, patients' healthcare service utilization history is available through the use of EHRs. The EHRs mostly contain a sequence of a patient's visits to a hospital. The pattern of a patient's access to healthcare can also be a good source of information. Fusing the two datasets, i.e., self-reported questionnaire information and the patient's medical history, results in a rich dataset to work with. However, having a dataset with different types of data causes heterogeneity. Therefore, the AI model should be able to process heterogeneous data. Additionally, effectively fusing data from multiple sources is challenging as there may be multiple ways of data fusion.

5.2.2 Data semantics

Data from different sources, i.e., questionnaires and the EHRs, contain semantics, such as the timeline of different medical events that occurred during a patient's life asked in the questionnaires or the services utilized during each visit to the ED and diagnostic codes provided by each service provider. There are two types of semantics in the data sources:

(1) the semantics between features of a data source, such as the relationship between different questions in a questionnaire, and (2) the semantics between two data sources, such as the link between events recorded in the EHRs and the questions of the questionnaire. Most MLAs cannot utilize the available semantics. Therefore, both the data fusion technique and the MLA should be able to utilize the available semantics. Although some work has been done in utilizing semantics between features of EHR data of mental health youths,[96] more work needs to be done, especially in utilizing semantics of the fused dataset.

5.2.3 Model explainability

To promote the use of AI approaches in mental health, healthcare professionals should trust the approach. One approach in developing trustworthy AI approaches is providing explanations. In youth/child mental health, the AI approach can provide explanations to both the end user (i.e., clinician) and the youth and their families. The explanations should be suitable for the user based on their expertise and understanding of the field.[106] One important challenge, other than the method for creating explanations, is the evaluation of the model's explainability.

5.3 Open research challenges in AI-assisted decision-making in mental health

Integrating AI into clinical workflows opens new research opportunities, such as investigating how health professionals' decision-making processes adapt to AI, how AI models change after deployment, and identifying where AI can most benefit the clinical decision-making pathway. Human decision-making processes change when augmented with AI. Studies show that humans augmented with AI focused on reviewing areas in image segmentation that the model had incorrectly classified.[128] However, our review found that AI's prediction and classification performance were evaluated against humans (human vs AI). In AI-assisted clinical decision-making, there is a need for new frameworks and metrics to document and evaluate how human performance changes when augmented with AI (human vs human + AI). For example, researchers evaluate radiologists' performance reviewing imaging scans with and without AI assistance compared to ground truths (autopsy). However, establishing metrics and frameworks to evaluate human-based decision-making in mental health is challenging because of the lack of quantitative ground truths. A potential evaluation mechanism is to compare the performance of a mental health professional augmented with AI to a group of experts (i.e., human-based decision-making VS. AI-assisted decision-making).

The deployment of AI into clinical workflows results in feedback loops when the model is updated with new data generated from the AI-assisted decision-making process. Feedback loops can have adverse effects on the AI model's performance. For example, correctly identifying high-risk patients allows them to be engaged with earlier by health professionals. In future updates, the model may mistakenly learn that high-risk symptoms are now low-risk because patients with those symptoms avoided future ED visits. Feedback loops may also bias models initially trained to be fair. Feedback loops are especially concerning in mental healthcare due to the subjectivity of diagnoses and lack of ground truths. Investigating feedback loops requires mechanisms to evaluate models after deployment in clinical workflows.

Researchers can investigate how human-based decision-making changes when augmented with AI and feedback loops for each decision-making point in Fig. 1. However, different health professionals make decisions at each point based on various data modalities. Furthermore, AI models have strengths and weaknesses that impact their effectiveness in assisting health professionals at each decision point. Identifying where AI can benefit most in a clinical workflow is essential. Guidelines on AI in mental health decision-making will then assist health professionals and developers in understanding the trade-offs of integrating AI into their clinical workflows at each decision point.

6. Conclusion

Advances in AI provide opportunities to augment human decision-making in mental health. Our review introduces AI researchers to the applications of their models within a clinical workflow and health professionals to the capabilities of AI. Collaborating AI researchers and health professionals will have a shared understanding of the terminologies, concepts, and capabilities of AI and clinical decision-making in mental healthcare. We presented a case study of human decision-making at CYMHP. We categorized the use of AI in the mental health decision-making process into three decision points: diagnosis and detection, prognosis and forecasting, and assessment. We performed a literature review on the applications of AI in mental healthcare. Reviewed studies focus on developing classification and prediction models without considering integration into a clinic workflow. We propose open research questions for applying AI to augment clinical decision-making.

Our study has limitations. First, we did not follow the complete PRISMA methodology as we did not conduct a meta-analysis, and only the lead author reviewed the publications. In addition, our case study is specific to child and youth mental healthcare in a hospital outpatient setting. Our next step is to expand our investigation on human-based decision-making to additional hospitals and clinics. We are also investigating techniques to fuse heterogeneous clinical notes and mental health questionnaires for analysis using AI. Finally, we are developing proof-of-concept readmission prediction models for deployment in CYMHP.

Acknowledgments

This study is supported by the Pediatric Mental Health Learning Health System research project and funded by the Hamilton Health Sciences RFA Research Strategic Initiative Program and Natural Sciences and Engineering Research Council of Canada (NSERC) Discovery grants.

References

1. Mitchell T. Machine Learning. New York: McGraw-Hill; 2007.
2. Su C, Aseltine R, Doshi R, Chen K, Rogers SC, Wang F. ML for suicide risk prediction in children and adolescents with EHRs. *Transl Psychiatry.* 2020;10(1):413–423. https://doi.org/10.1038/s41398-020-01100-0.
3. Trung Doan N, Engvig A, Zaske K, et al. Distinguishing early and late brain aging from the Alzheimer's disease Spectrum: consistent morphological patterns across independent samples. *Neuroimage.* 2017;158:282–295. https://doi.org/10.1016/j.neuroimage.2017.06.070.
4. Shickel B, Tighe P, Bihorac A, Rashidi P. Deep EHR: a survey of recent advances in deep learning techniques for EHR analysis. *IEEE J Biomed Health Inform.* 2018;22(5):1589–1604. https://doi.org/10.1109/JBHI.2017.2767063.
5. Tobore I, Li J, Yuhang L, et al. Deep learning intervention for health care challenges: some biomedical domain considerations. *JMIR Mhealth Uhealth.* 2019;7(8):1–36. https://doi.org/10.2196/11966.
6. Piccialli F, Somma V, Giampaolo F, Cuomo S, Fortino G. A survey on deep learning in medicine: why, how and when? *Inform Fusion.* 2021;66:111–137. https://doi.org/10.1016/j.inffus.2020.09.006.
7. Shatte A, Hutchinson D, Teague S. ML in mental health: a scoping review of methods and applications. *Psychol Med.* 2019;49:1426–1448. https://doi.org/10.1017/S0033291719000151.
8. Su C, Xu Z, Pathak J, Wang F. Deep learning in mental health outcome research: a scoping review. *Transl Psychiatry.* 2020;10(1):1–26. https://doi.org/10.1038/s41398-020-0780-3.
9. Le Glaz A, Haralambous Y, Kim-Dufor P, et al. ML and NLP in mental health: systematic review. *J Med Internet Res.* 2021;23(5):1–20. https://doi.org/10.2196/15708.
10. Shoham Y, Leyton-Brown K. Multiagent Systems: Algorithmic, Game-Theoretic, and Logical Foundations. Cambridge University Press; 2008.
11. Harvey I, Roberts C. Clinical guidelines, medical litigation, and the current medical Defence system. *Lancet.* 1987;329(8525):145–147. https://doi.org/10.1016/S0140-6736(87)91976-3.
12. Poole D, Mackworth A. AI: Foundations of Computational Agents. Cambridge University Press; 2017.
13. Wing J. Computational thinking and thinking about computing. *Philo Trans Roy Soc A: Math Phys Eng Sci.* 2008;366(1881):3717–3725. https://doi.org/10.1098/rsta.2008.0118.
14. Zahedi Z, Sreedharan S, Kambhampati S. A Mental-Model Centric Landscape of Human-AI Symbiosis. In: *AAAI R^2HCAI*; 2023.
15. Gondocs D, Dorfle V. AI in medical diagnosis: AI prediction vs human judgment. In: *AAAI R^2HCAI*; 2023.
16. Bates D, Kuperman G, Wang S, et al. Ten commandments for effective clinical decision support: making the practice of evidence-based medicine a reality. *J American Med Inform Assoc.* 2003;10(6):523–530. https://doi.org/10.1197/jamia.M1370.
17. Lai Y, Kankanhalli A, Ong D. Human-AI collaboration in healthcare: A Review and Research Agenda. In: *ICSS*; 2021.
18. Verghese A, Shah N, Harrington R. What this computer needs is a physician: humanism and AI. *J American Med Assoc.* 2018;319(1):19–20. https://doi.org/10.1001/jama.2017.19198.
19. Simon H. The New Science of Management Decision. Harper & Brothers; 1960.
20. Viani N, Botelle R, Kerwin J, et al. A NLP approach for identifying temporal disease onset information from mental healthcare text. *Sci Rep.* 2021;11:1–12. https://doi.org/10.1038/s41598-020-80457-0.
21. Hur JH, Tang ST, Gunaseelan V. Predicting postoperative opioid use with ML and insurance claims in opioid-naive patients. *Am J Surg.* 2021;222(3):659–665. https://doi.org/10.1016/j.amjsurg.2021.03.058.
22. Pham T, Tran T, Phung D, Venkatesh S. Predicting healthcare trajectories from medical records: a deep learning approach. *J Biomed Inform.* 2017;69:218–229. https://doi.org/10.1016/j.jbi.2017.04.001.
23. Ha U, Lee Y, Kim H, et al. A wearable EEG-HEG-HRV multimodal system with simultaneous monitoring of tES for mental health management. *IEEE Trans Biomed Circuits Syst.* 2015;9(6):758–766. https://doi.org/10.1109/TBCAS.2015.2504959.
24. Sheela Kumari R, Varghese T, Kesavadas C, Albert Singh N, Mathuranath P. Longitudinal evaluation of structural changes in frontotemporal dementia using artificial neural networks. In: *FICTA*; 2014. https://doi.org/10.1007/978-3-319-02931-3_20.
25. Schnack H, Nieuwenhuis M, van Haren N, et al. Can structural MRI aid in clinical classification? A ML study in two independent samples of patients with schizophrenia, bipolar disorder and healthy subjects. *Neuroimage.* 2014;84:299–306. https://doi.org/10.1016/j.neuroimage.2013.08.053.

26. Khan A, Wang K. A deep learning based scoring system for prioritizing susceptibility variants for mental disorders. In: *BIBM*; 2017. https://doi.org/10.1109/BIBM.2017.8217916.

27. Khan A, Liu Q, Wang K. iMEGES: integrated mental-disorder GEnome score by deep neural network for prioritizing the susceptibility genes for mental disorders in personal genomes. *J Bioinform*. 2018;19(17):96–107. https://doi.org/10.1186/s12859-018-2469-7.

28. Wang D, Liu S, Warrell J, et al. Comprehensive functional genomic resource and integrative model for the human brain. *Science*. 2018;362 (6420):1–13. https://doi.org/10.1126/science.aat8464.

29. Sundaram L, Bhat R, Viswanath V, Li X. DeepBipolar: identifying genomic mutations for bipolar disorder via deep learning. *Hum Mutat*. 2017;38(9):1217–1224. https://doi.org/10.1002/humu.23272.

30. Trakadis Y, Sardaar S, Chen A, Fulginiti V, Krishnan A. ML in schizophrenia genomics, a case-control study using 5,090 exomes. *Amer J Med Genetics*. 2019;180(2):103–112. https://doi.org/10.1002/ajmg.b.32638.

31. Hornstein S, Forman-Hoffman V, Nazander A, Ranta K, Hilbert K. Predicting therapy outcome in a digital mental health intervention for depression and anxiety: a ML approach. *Digital Health*. 2021;7:1–11. https://doi.org/10.1177/20552076211060659.

32. Iliou T, Konstantopoulou G, Ntekouli M, et al. ILIOU ML preprocessing method for depression type prediction. *Evol Syst*. 2019;10(1):29–39. https://doi.org/10.1007/s12530-017-9205-9.

33. Oak S. Depression detection and analysis. *AAAI Spring Symp Ser*. 2017.

34. Sano A, Phillips A, Yu A, et al. Recognizing academic performance, sleep quality, stress level, and mental health using personality traits, wearable sensors and Mobile phones. *BSN*. 2015. https://doi.org/10.1109/BSN.2015.7299420.

35. Haque U, Kabir E, Khanam R. Detection of child depression using ML methods. *PloS One*. 2021;16(12):1–13. https://doi.org/10.1371/journal.pone.0261131.

36. Ntakolia C, Priftis D, Charakopoulou-Travlou M, et al. An explainable ML approach for COVID-19's impact on mood states of children and adolescents during the first lockdown in Greece. *Healthcare*. 2022;10(1):1–28. https://doi.org/10.3390/healthcare10010149.

37. Gyorda J, Nemesure M, Price G, Jacobson N. Applying ensemble ML models to predict individual response to a digitally delivered worry postponement intervention. *J Affect Disord*. 2023;320:201–210. https://doi.org/10.1016/j.jad.2022.09.112.

38. Alam M, Abedin S, Al Ameen M, Hong C. Web of objects based ambient assisted living framework for emergency psychiatric state prediction. *Sensors*. 2016;16(9):1–23. https://doi.org/10.3390/s16091431.

39. Bedi G, Cecchi G, Slezak D, Carrillo F, Sigman M, de Wit H. A window into the intoxicated mind? Speech as an index of psychoactive drug effects. *Neuropsychopharmacol*. 2014;39(10):2340–2348. https://doi.org/10.1038/npp.2014.80.

40. Fraser K, Meltzer J, Rudzicz F. Linguistic features identify Alzheimer's disease in narrative speech. *J Alzheimer Disease*. 2016;49:407–422. https://doi.org/10.3233/JAD-150520.

41. Guo R, Li S, He L, Gao W, Qi H, Owens G. Pervasive and unobtrusive emotion sensing for human mental health. In: *IPCTHW*; 2013. https://doi.org/10.4108/icst.pervasivehealth.2013.252133.

42. Kliper R, Portuguese S, Weinshall D. Prosodic analysis of speech and the underlying mental state. In: *PCPMH*; 2016. https://doi.org/10.1007/978-3-319-32270-4_6.

43. Carneiro D, Castillo J, Novais P. Multimodal behavioral analysis for non-invasive stress detection. *Expert Syst Appl*. 2012;39(18):13376–13389. https://doi.org/10.1016/j.eswa.2012.05.065.

44. Grünerbl A, Muaremi A, Osmani V, et al. Smartphone-based recognition of states and state changes in bipolar disorder patients. *IEEE J Biomed Health Inform*. 2015;19(1):140–148. https://doi.org/10.1109/JBHI.2014.2343154.

45. Budenz A, Klassen A, Purtle J, Tov EY, Yudell M, Massey P. Mental illness and bipolar disorder on twitter: implications for stigma and social support. *J Ment Health*. 2019;29(2):191–199. https://doi.org/10.1080/09638237.2019.1677878.

46. Cheng Q, Li TM, Kwok C-L, Zhu T, Yip PS. Assessing suicide risk and emotional distress in Chinese social media: a text mining and ML study. *J Med Internet Res*. 2017;19(7):1–10. https://doi.org/10.2196/jmir.7276.

47. Coppersmith G, Harman C, Dredze M. Measuring post traumatic stress disorder in twitter. In: *ICWSM*; 2014. https://doi.org/10.1609/icwsm.v8i1.14574.

48. Coppersmith G, Leary R, Crutchley P, Fine A. NLP of social media as screening for suicide risk. *Biomed Inform Insights*. 2018;10:1–11. https://doi.org/10.1177/1178222618792860.

49. Dou Z-Y, Barman-Adhikari A, Fang F, Yadav A. Harnessing social media to identify homeless youth at-risk of substance use. In: *CAII*; 2021. https://doi.org/10.1609/aaai.v35i17.17732.

50. Du J, Zhang Y, Luo J, et al. Extracting psychiatric stressors for suicide from social media using deep learning. *BMC Med Inform Decis Mak*. 2018;18 (2):78–87. https://doi.org/10.1186/s12911-018-0632-8.

51. Figueredo J, Calumby R. On text preprocessing for early detection of depression on social media. In: *SBCAS*; 2020. https://doi.org/10.5753/sbcas.2020.11504.

52. Jia J. Mental health computing via harvesting social media data. In: *ECAI*; 2018. https://doi.org/10.24963/ijcai.2018/808.

53. Low D, Rumker L, Talkar T, Torous J, Cecchi G, Ghosh S. NLP reveals vulnerable mental health support groups and heightened health anxiety on Reddit during COVID-19: observational study. *J Med Internet Res*. 2020;22:1–16. https://doi.org/10.2196/22635.

54. Mann P, Paes A, Matsushima E. See and read: detecting depression symptoms in higher education students using multimodal social media data. In: *ICWSM*; 2020. https://doi.org/10.1609/icwsm.v14i1.7313.

55. Mittal A, Goyal A, Mittal M. Data preprocessing based connecting suicidal and help-seeking Behaviours. In: *ICCMC*; 2021. https://doi.org/10.1109/ICCMC51019.2021.9418452.

56. Nguyen T, Borland R, Yearwood J, Yong H-H, Venkatesh S, Phung D. Discriminative cues for different stages of smoking cessation in online community. In: *WISE*; 2016. https://doi.org/10.1007/978-3-319-48743-4_12.

57. Ji S, Zhang T, Ansari L, Fu J, Tiwari P, Cambria E. MentalBERT: Publicly Available Pretrained Language Models for Mental Healthcare. In: *LREC*; 2021 [arXiv:2110.15621].

58. Gliklich R, Leavy M, Dreyer N. Tools and Technologies for Registry Interoperability, Registries for Evaluating Patient Outcomes: A User's Guide. United States of America Agency for Healthcare Research and Quality; 2019.

59. Longford N. Studying Human Populations: An Advanced Course in Statistics. Springer; 2008.

60. Tennison J, Kellogg G, Herman I. Model for Tabular Data and Metadata on the Web, W3C Recommendation; 2015.

61. MIT Critical Data. Secondary analysis of EHR. *Springer Nature*. 2016. https://doi.org/10.1007/978-3-319-43742-2.

62. Dettori J, Norvell D. The anatomy of data. *Global Spine J*. 2018;8(3):311–313. https://doi.org/10.1177/2192568217746998.

63. Bell J, Kilic C, Prabakaran R, et al. Use of EHRs in identifying drug and alcohol misuse among psychiatric in-patients. *Psychiatrist*. 2013;37(1):15–20. https://doi.org/10.1192/pb.bp.111.038240.

64. Cresswell K, Morrison Z, Sheikh A, Kalra D. There are too many, but never enough: qualitative case study investigating routine coding of clinical information in depression. *PloS One*. 2012;7(8):1–10. https://doi.org/10.1371/journal.pone.0043831.

65. CIHI. Canadian Coding Standards for Version 2010 ICD-10-CA and CCI; 2010. Tech rep, 2010.

66. Liang Y, Zheng X, Zeng D. A survey on big data-driven digital phenotyping of mental health. *Inf Fusion*. 2019;52:290–307. https://doi.org/10.1016/j.inffus.2019.04.001.

67. Moukaddam N, Sano A, Salas R, Hamma Z, Sabharwal A. Turning data into better mental health: past, present, and future, front. *Digit Health*. 2022;4:1–13. https://doi.org/10.3389/fdgth.2022.916810.

68. Institute of Medicine. Health Data in the Information Age: Use, Disclosure, and Privacy. The National Academies Press; 1994. https://doi.org/10.17226/2312.

69. Page M, Moher D, Bossuyt P, et al. PRISMA 2020 Explanation and elaboration: updated guidance and exemplars for reporting systematic reviews. *BMJ*. 2021;372:1–36. https://doi.org/10.1136/bmj.n160.

70. Sutton R, Pincock D, Baumgart D, Sadowski D, Fedorak R, Kroeker K. An overview of clinical decision support systems: benefits, risks, and strategies for success. *npj Digit Med*. 2020;3(1):1–10. https://doi.org/10.1038/s41746-020-0221-y.

71. Silk J, Nath S, Siegel L, Kendall P. Conceptualizing mental disorders in children: where have we been and where are we going? *Dev Psychopathol*. 2000;12(4):713–735. https://doi.org/10.1017/S0954579400004090.

72. Editorial. Biologically-inspired biomarkers for mental disorders. *EBioMedicine*. 2017;17:1–2. https://doi.org/10.1016/j.ebiom.2017.03.015.

73. Bzdok D, Meyer-Lindenberg A. ML for precision psychiatry: opportunities and challenges. *Biol Psychiatry Cogn Neurosci Neuroimaging*. 2018;3(3):223–230. https://doi.org/10.1016/j.bpsc.2017.11.007.

74. Lewis C, Boyd M, Puspitasari A, et al. Implementing measurement-based care in behavioral health: a review. *JAMA Psychiatry*. 2019;76(3):324–335. https://doi.org/10.1001/jamapsychiatry.2018.3329.

75. Jensen-Doss A, Haimes E, Smith A, et al. Monitoring treatment Progress and providing feedback is viewed favorably but rarely used in practice. *Adm Policy Ment Health*. 2018;45(1):48–61. https://doi.org/10.1007/s10488-016-0763-0.

76. Boyle M, Duncan L, Georgiades K, et al. Classifying child and adolescent psychiatric disorder by problem checklists and standardized interviews. *Int J Methods Psychiatr Res*. 2017;26(4):1–9. https://doi.org/10.1002/mpr.1544.

77. Aboraya A, Nasrallah H, Elswick D, et al. Measurement-based care in psychiatry: past, present, and future. *Innov Clin Neurosci*. 2018;15(11):13–26.

78. Pastorino R, De Vito C, Migliara G, et al. Benefits and challenges of big data in healthcare: an overview of the European initiatives. *Eur J Public Health*. 2019;29(3):23–27. https://doi.org/10.1093/eurpub/ckz168.

79. Benner P, Hughes R, Sutphen M. Clinical Reasoning, Decision Making, and Action: Thinking Critically and Clinically. Agency for Healthcare Research and Quality; 2008.

80. Timmons A, Duong J, Fiallo N, et al. A call to action on assessing and mitigating Bias in AI applications for mental health. *Perspect Psychol Sci*. 2022;1–35. https://doi.org/10.1177/17456916221134490.

81. Beam A, Kohane I. Big data and ML in health care. *JAMA*. 2018;319(13):1317–1318. https://doi.org/10.1001/jama.2017.18391.

82. Mitchell M, Kan L. Digital technology and the future of health systems. *Health Syst Reform*. 2019;5(2):113–120. https://doi.org/10.1080/23288604.2019.1583040.

83. Weber G, Mandl K, Kohane I. Finding the missing link for big biomedical data. *JAMA*. 2014;311(24):2479–2480. https://doi.org/10.1001/jama.2014.4228.

84. Simon G. Big data from health Records in Mental Health Care: hardly clairvoyant but already useful. *JAMA Psychiatry*. 2019;76(4):349–350. https://doi.org/10.1001/jamapsychiatry.2018.4510.

85. Koutsouleris N, Hauser T, Skvortsova V, De Choudhury M. From promise to practice: towards the realisation of AI-informed mental health care. *Lancet Digital Health*. 2022;4(11):829–840. https://doi.org/10.1016/S2589-7500(22)00153-4.

86. Hulsen T, Jamuar S, Moody A, et al. From big data to precision medicine. *Front Med*. 2019;6:1–34. https://doi.org/10.3389/fmed.2019.00034.

87. Naylor D. On the prospects for a (deep) learning health care system. *JAMA*. 2018;320(11):1099–1100. https://doi.org/10.1001/jama.2018.11103.

88. Norgeot B, Glicksberg B, Butte A. A call for deep-learning healthcare. *Nature Med*. 2019;25(1):14–15. https://doi.org/10.1038/s41591-018-0320-3.

89. Han J, Pei J, Tong H. Data Mining: Concepts and Techniques. Morgan Kaufmann; 2022.

90. García S, Luengo J, Herrera F. Data Preprocessing in Data Mining. Springer; 2015.

91. Wells B, Chagin K, Nowacki A, Kattan M. Strategies for handling missing data in EHR derived data. *EGEMS*. 2013;1(3). https://doi.org/10.13063/2327-9214.1035.

92. Fei Z, Yang E, Li DD-U, et al. Deep convolution network based emotion analysis towards mental health care. *Neurocomputing*. 2020;388:212–227. https://doi.org/10.1016/j.neucom.2020.01.034.

93. Zhang Z, Lin W, Liu M, Mahmoud M. Multimodal deep learning framework for mental disorder recognition. In: *FG*; 2020. https://doi.org/10.1109/FG47880.2020.00033.

94. Singh D, Singh B. Investigating the impact of data normalization on classification performance. *Appl Soft Comput*. 2020;97:1–23. https://doi.org/10.1016/j.asoc.2019.105524.

95. Sankar A, Juliet S. Investigations on ML models for mental health analysis and prediction. In: *ICEEICT*; 2023. https://doi.org/10.1109/ICEEICT56924.2023.10157385.

96. Daneshvar H, Samavi R. Heterogeneous patient graph embedding in readmission prediction. In: *CCAI*; 2022.

97. Bleiholder J, Naumann F. Data fusion. *ACM Comput Surveys*. 2009;41(1):1–41. https://doi.org/10.1145/1456650.1456651.

98. Holzinger A, Malle B, Saranti A, Pfeifer B. Towards multi-modal Causability with graph neural networks enabling information fusion for explainable AI. *Inf Fusion*. 2021;71:28–37. https://doi.org/10.1016/j.inffus.2021.01.008.

99. Shinde S, Tambe A, Vishwakarma A, Mhatre S. Automated depression detection using audio features. *Int Research J Eng Technol*. 2020;7(5):1–5.

100. Zhang Q, Yang LT, Chen Z, Li P. A survey on deep learning for big data. *Inform Fusion*. 2018;42:146–157. https://doi.org/10.1016/j.inffus.2017.10.006.

101. Min B, Ross H, Sulem E, et al. Recent advances in NLP via large pre-trained language models: a survey. *ACM Comput Surv*. 2023. https://doi.org/10.1145/3605943.

102. Li T, Xia T, Wang H, et al. Smartphone app usage analysis: datasets, methods, and applications. *IEEE Comm Surveys Tutorials*. 2022;24(2):937–966. https://doi.org/10.1109/COMST.2022.3163176.

103. Suhail M, Razak T. Cardiac disease detection from ECG signal using discrete wavelet transform with ML method. *Diabetes Res Clin Pract*. 2022;187. https://doi.org/10.1016/j.diabres.2022.109852.

104. Studer S, Bui T, Drescher C, et al. Towards CRISPML(Q): a ML process model with quality assurance methodology. *Mach Learning Know Extraction*. 2021;3(2):392–413. https://doi.org/10.3390/make3020020.

105. Nwanosike E, Conway B, Merchant H, Hasan S. Potential applications and performance of ML techniques and algorithms in clinical practice: a systematic review. *Int J Med Inform*. 2022;159:1–11. https://doi.org/10.1016/j.ijmedinf.2021.104679.

106. Barredo Arrieta A, Díaz-Rodríguez N, Del Ser J, et al. Explainable AI (XAI): concepts, taxonomies, opportunities and challenges toward responsible AI. *Inf Fusion*. 2020;58:82–115. https://doi.org/10.1016/j.inffus.2019.12.012.

107. Ahmed U, Jhaveri R, Srivastava G, Lin JC-W. Explainable deep attention active learning for sentimental analytics of mental disorder. *ACM Trans Asian Low-Resour Lang Inf Process*. 2022;1–20. https://doi.org/10.1145/3551890.

108. Mehrabi N, Morstatter F, Saxena N, Lerman K, Galstyan A. A survey on Bias and fairness in ML. *ACM Comput Surv*. 2021;54(6):1–35. https://doi.org/10.1145/3457607.

109. Rodolfa K, Lamba H, Ghani R. Empirical observation of negligible fairness–accuracy trade-offs in ML for public policy. *Nature Mach Intell*. 2021;3(10):896–904. https://doi.org/10.1038/s42256-021-00396-x.

110. Valentim I, Lourenço N, Antunes N. The impact of data preparation on the fairness of software systems. In: *ISSRE*; 2019. https://doi.org/10.1109/ISSRE.2019.00046.

111. Carlini N, Wagner D. Towards evaluating the robustness of neural networks. In: *SP*; 2017. https://doi.org/10.1109/SP.2017.49.

112. Harrigian K, Aguirre C, Dredze M. Do models of mental health based on social media data generalize? In: *EMNLP*; 2020. https://doi.org/10.18653/v1/2020.findings-emnlp.337.

113. Abdar M, Pourpanah F, Hussain S, et al. A review of uncertainty quantification in deep learning: techniques, applications, and challenges. *Info Fusion*. 2021;76:243–297. https://doi.org/10.1016/j.inffus.2021.05.008.

114. Price W, Cohen I. Privacy in the age of medical big data. *Nat Med*. 2019;25:37–43. https://doi.org/10.1038/s41591-018-0272-7.

115. Liu X, Xie L, Wang Y, et al. Privacy and security issues in deep learning: a survey. *IEEE Access*. 2021;9:4566–4593. https://doi.org/10.1109/ACCESS.2020.3045078.

116. Nasr M, Shokri R, Houmansadr A. Comprehensive privacy analysis of deep learning: passive and active white-box inference attacks against centralized and federated learning. In: *SP*; 2019. https://doi.org/10.1109/SP.2019.00065.

117. Rabbi M, Ali S, Choudhury T, Berke E. Passive and in-situ assessment of mental and physical well-being using Mobile sensors. In: *ICUC*; 2011. https://doi.org/10.1145/2030112.2030164.

118. Hong Y, Lian J, Xu L, et al. Statistical perspectives on reliability of AI systems. *Quality Eng*. 2022;35(1):56–78. https://doi.org/10.1080/08982112.2022.2089854.

119. Chandler C, Foltz P, Elvevåg B. Using ML in psychiatry: the need to establish a framework that nurtures trustworthiness. *Schizophr Bull*. 2019;46(1):11–14. https://doi.org/10.1093/schbul/sbz105.

120. Reddy S, Rogers W, Makinen V-P, et al. Evaluation framework to guide implementation of AI systems into healthcare settings. *BMJ Health Care Inform*. 2021;28(1):1–7. https://doi.org/10.1136/bmjhci-2021-100444.

121. Coiera E. The last mile: where AI meets reality. *J Med Internet Res*. 2019;21(11):1–4. https://doi.org/10.2196/16323.

122. Pou-Prom C, Murray J, Kuzulugil S, Mamdani M, Verma AA. From compute to care: lessons learned from deploying an early warning system into clinical practice. *Frontiers Digital Health*. 2022;4. https://doi.org/10.3389/fdgth.2022.932123.

123. Plana D, Shung D, Grimshaw A, Saraf A, Sung JJ, Kann B. Randomized clinical trials of ML interventions in health care: a systematic review. *JAMA Netw Open*. 2022;5(9):1–14. https://doi.org/10.1001/jamanetworkopen.2022.33946.

124. Hirsch T, Merced K, Narayanan S, Imel Z, Atkins D. Designing contestability: interaction design, ML, and mental health. In: *DIS*; 2017. https://doi.org/10.1145/3064663.3064703.

125. Garcia-Ceja E, Riegler M, Nordgreen T, Jakobsen P, Oedegaard K, Tørresen J. Mental health monitoring with multimodal sensing and ML: a survey. *Pervasive Mobile Comput*. 2018;51:1–26. https://doi.org/10.1016/j.pmcj.2018.09.003.

126. Giurgiu I, Riva O, Alonso G. Dynamic software deployment from clouds to Mobile devices. In: *Middleware*; 2012. https://doi.org/10.1007/978-3-642-35170-9_20.

127. Strimbu K, Tavel J. What are biomarkers? *Curr Opin HIV AIDS*. 2010;5:463–466. https://doi.org/10.1097/COH.0b013e32833ed177.

128. Fails J, Olsen D. Interactive ML. In: *ICIUI*; 2003. https://doi.org/10.1145/604045.604056.

10

Cancer detection in hyperspectral imagery using artificial intelligence: Current trends and future directions

Nour Aburaed*, Mina Al-Saad, M. Sami Zitouni, Mohammed Q. Alkhatib, Maisam Wahbah, Yasmin Halawani, and Alavikunhu Panthakkan

University of Dubai, Dubai, United Arab Emirates

1. Introduction

Cancer is one of the most serious health problems in the world. It is now the leading cause of mortality in nearly every country.[1] According to a World Health Organization (WHO) report published in 2022, cancer is identified as one of the leading causes of death, accounting for about 16% of deaths worldwide.[2] Early detection and diagnosis of cancer increases the probability of better treatment and viability. The standard method of assessing cancer and monitoring its progression in an organ consists of taking a sample or biopsy of the suspect tissue, and then performing microscopic analysis of the cells using white light laboratory microscopes. After that, an experienced pathologist can visually differentiate between a tumor and a healthy tissue based on the structure, appearance, and arrangement of the cells. Identifying cancer from microscopic biopsy images is a labor-intensive and time-consuming procedure, subjective in nature, and may vary from one expert to another.[3] Nowadays, with the increasing awareness of cancer prevention and the vast amount of data generated every day from parallel streams of screening, doctors need to analyze a large number of medical images. Therefore, it is important to develop an automated computer-aided diagnosis (CAD) system to effectively and accurately identify lesions from images with minimal human intervention. Hyperspectral imaging (HSI) is a developing imaging modality technique that has a double function of spectroscopy and imaging to capture both spatial and spectral information, providing hundreds of spectral bands for each pixel in the 2D plane. Hyperspectral technology provides a noninvasive disease diagnosis in the majority of medical applications. This type of image can collect information along the electromagnetic (EM) spectrum, covering a wide range of wavelengths that generally includes the visible, near-infrared, and mid-infrared portions of the spectrum rather than assigning primary colors (red, green, blue) to each pixel. The advantage of HSI over conventional imaging is a three-dimensional dataset of spatial and spectral information that can be provided, called hypercube image data. This imaging technology was originally designed for NASA satellite imaging and remote sensing.[4] In recent years, HSI has become a trending topic in the detection and diagnosis of diseases, in particular cancer.

Nowadays, artificial intelligence (AI) technology is gaining momentum in healthcare and medical field due to the unique advantages that AI and deep learning (DL) algorithms can offer by making the processing of large-scale data possible and easier, which allows autonomous extraction of features from medical images with minimal human intervention. Moreover, advances in AI technology combined with those in medical imaging have led to the gradual conversion of digital medical images into high-dimensional data which is convenient for data mining and data science techniques.[5] With the ability to analyze large amounts of data quickly and accurately, AI can help healthcare professionals make more informed decisions and improve patient outcomes.[6] In the field of oncology, AI can be used to

---

* All the authors contributed equally to this work.

analyze medical images, detect cancer at an early stage, and predict treatment response. With the increasing availability of electronic health records, large-scale genomics datasets, and imaging technologies, AI has the potential to bring about a new era of personalized medicine, where treatment plans are tailored to the unique needs of each patient. The development of AI applications for cancer is a rapidly evolving field and holds immense promise for improving patient care and advancing our understanding of this complex disease. Earlier research conducted by the West Virginia University (WVU) Optical Imaging group at the WVU Cancer Institute has demonstrated that HSI and DL-based classification methods could distinguish efficiently between tumor and normal tissue in animal experiments for different tumor sizes.[7]

This chapter discusses the latest trends in using HSI combined with AI for cancer detection, in addition to the challenges and future direction of this field. This chapter is organized as follows: Section 2 introduces HSI and their vital role in healthcare field, Section 3 presents the fundamentals of AI methods that are currently being used, Section 4 explores the applications of AI combined with HSI in cancer detection and diagnosis, Section 5 illustrates the meta-analysis of a total of 65 relevant papers published between 2017 and 2023, Section 6 explains the current challenges faced in this field, as well as additional algorithms that could be applied in the coming decade, and finally, Section 7 summarizes and concludes this chapter.

2. Hyperspectral imaging

One of the main applications of the principles of optical spectroscopy is HSI, which gathers data from hundreds of continuous, narrow bands of the EM spectrum, including visible light, near-infrared, and shortwave infrared. As opposed to conventional multispectral imaging (MSI), this produces a 3D spatial and spectral depiction of the scene being captured, known as a hypercube. The difference between HSI and MSI is illustrated in Fig. 1. In terms of image

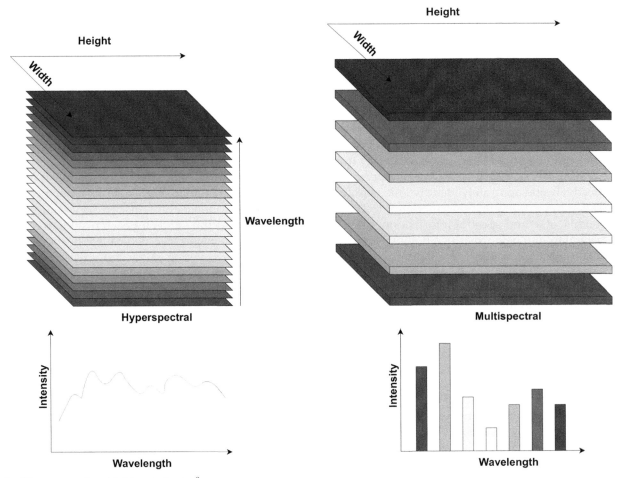

FIG. 1   Hyperspectral vs. Multispectral cube.[8]

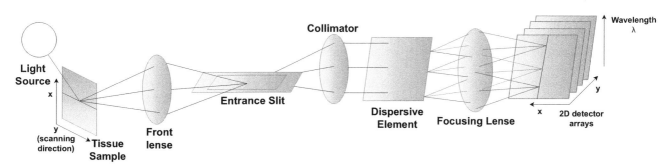

FIG. 2   Illustration of a pushbroom HSI system.[9]

resolution, it is stated that HSI has high spectral resolution. Thus, HSI is capable of assigning a unique spectral signature to each spatial pixel of an object depending on its light reflectance, which eases object detection tasks. Thanks to this unique capability, HSI provides an advantage over MSI, and it is frequently deployed in a wide range of applications, including remote sensing and health care. HSI is utilized in medical imaging to give precise molecular and functional information about tissues. In order to construct a high-dimensional depiction of the tissue being examined, it captures images of said tissue at various wavelengths and merges them. The identification of numerous biomarkers, the detection of disease, and the tracking of the efficacy of treatments can all be done using this information. For instance, HSI has been used to observe brain blood flow, monitor blood oxygenation, and find cancer in tissues. HSI is an active area of research in the realm of medical imaging and has the potential to offer significant diagnostic and therapeutic information in a non-invasive manner.

There are several different acquisition modes of HSI, which are classified into four categories; pushbroom, whiskbroom, snapshot, and staring.[10] An example of a typical pushbroom HSI system is shown in Fig. 2. The TIVITA CMOS pushbroom HS camera is frequently used in medical biological tissue detection to produce HSI of size $640 \times 480 \times 100$ collected at a spectral range of 500–1000 nm. Additionally, it can be utilized for HSI-based RGB image reconstruction.[11] In Section 4, the need for real-time processing and computational complexity reduction will be emphasized. Therefore, handheld HSI systems are popularly used. This device is capable of quick imaging and uses fast spectral capture of a single image, which makes it easier to manage common image processing techniques and facilitates ease of use.[11]

3. AI concepts and background

The concept of AI was first introduced in 1956 with the goal of building machines that can think and perform complicated tasks in a manner similar to human beings and, thereby share the same basic features.[12] In recent years, AI has become a hot research topic and achieved tremendous progress in health care and clinical research industry. AI presents noninvasive and quantitative assessment techniques for early detection and diagnosis of different types of diseases. Furthermore, the advances in computing power offered by graphics processing unit (GPU) and the accessibility of vast data made it possible to train AI systems more effectively.[13] Nowadays, with the availability of HSI that offers high spectral resolution, it is possible to capture more detailed spectral information below and beyond the visual range which can be utilized for cancer detection and classification tasks.[14] HSI can provide enough deep knowledge about various cancerous tissue parts and their spatial distribution from the spectral feature of each pixel in the HSI. The massive amount of hyperspectral data makes the manual interpretation of these images more challenging if not impossible, tedious, and prone to human error as the performance highly depends on expert's experience. Thus, it is very essential to develop a computer-aided solution that can assist in cancer diagnosis and detection procedures.[15]

Traditional machine learning (ML) approaches, which are a subset of AI, were introduced earlier for hyperspectral medical image analysis.[16,17] Most of these methods lean toward classification models for identification and diagnosis of disease. They are essentially based on analyzing the patterns in the data using some mathematical algorithms and then making decisions either with supervised learning, where the algorithm is allowed to learn from examples of input data and their corresponding outcome, or unsupervised learning, where no outcome data are provided.[11] Examples of ML algorithms that are widely used in hyperspectral medical image analysis are support vector machine (SVM),[18] K-nearest neighbors (KNN),[19] linear discriminant analysis (LDA),[20] random forest (RF),[21] and artificial neural network (ANN).[14] Although ML technologies show promising classification results, the performance of these approaches depends on manually extracting discriminant features, which is considered time-consuming and easily influenced by subjective factors. DL, which is considered a subset of ANN, came as an answer to this shortcoming. The hyperspectral classification based on DL techniques has attracted increased attention in the field of medical analysis due to their ability to extract effective feature hierarchies from the existing data more efficiently and automatically. Moreover, DL algorithms have been generally widely used in the HSI classification, especially in the field of remote sensing.[22]

The term DL refers to how these algorithms are constructed and arranged by stacking numerous hidden layers to learn from the data. Several studies showed that DL can be used as a potential approach for the improvement of cancer detection accuracy for a variety of cancer types. Convolutional neural networks (CNNs) are an example of DL methods, which were designed for image analysis tasks such as segmentation[23] and classification.[24] The term is derived from convolution operation, which is a mathematical linear action between matrices. The basic building blocks of CNNs consist of a convolution layer, pooling layer, and fully connected layer.[25] Other types of layers may be included, such as dropout and batch normalization. The convolutional layer is used to extract feature maps from the input image, while the pooling layer is used as a dimensionality reduction layer to reduce the dimension of the extracted feature information and, thus, it can simplify the network calculation complexity and improve the calculation speed. A fully connected layer is used to combine all the features together and send the output value to the classifier for the final prediction result.[26]

4. Cancer applications

4.1 Skin

Skin cancer is a growing concern worldwide,[27] with melanoma being one of the most aggressive and deadliest forms of skin cancer. Early and accurate diagnosis of melanoma is critical to improving patient outcomes, and significant effort has been put into developing methods for skin cancer detection. In recent years, advances in imaging technology and ML have led to the development of new techniques for skin cancer diagnosis. These techniques offer the potential to revolutionize the detection and diagnosis of skin cancer by improving speed, accuracy, and patient outcomes. At the same time, the use of HSI for skin cancer detection has also gained significant attention recently. Researchers have used HSI to develop algorithms that can distinguish between healthy and cancerous skin, and they have shown that HSI can be used to accurately diagnose skin cancer in a noninvasive manner.[28]

Leon et al.[28] proposed a framework based on a supervised classification with an automatic fine-tuning of the model hyperparameters. The goal of the research was to use HSI technology as a non-invasive clinical support system for pigmented skin lesions (PSLs) during dermatological routine practice. Data were collected by a snapshot HS camera that is capable of having images in the visual and near-infrared (VNIR) spectral range from 450 to 950 nm, having a spectral resolution of 8 nm, which results in 125 bands. The research was conducted on 61 patients with a total of 76 samples. The performance was validated by taking 10 samples from 8 patients. The results obtained showed SVM Linear classifier offered better results when compared to SVM sigmoid and SVM radial basis function (SVM-RBF), providing an area under curve (AUC) of 0.89.

An encoder-decoder structure, namely hyper-net, was proposed by Wang et al.[29] In this study, skin tissues were collected from 125 patients, ranging from 7 to 65 years old, diagnosed with melanoma. The 125 patients were divided into three separate datasets for training, validation, and testing, with 85 patients used for training, 20 for validation, and 20 for testing. Images were captured using a microscopic HSI (MHSI) system,[30] which is designed to incorporate with microscopic system for pathology smear analysis. The captured 3D hypercube consists of 60 bands. The ground truth for each image was generated by two professional pathologists, with any disagreements reviewed by one or more expert pathologists. The images were preprocessed by calibrating and selecting a subset of spectra based on their mutual information, with 16 consecutive bands from 670 nm to 783 nm selected. The large hyperspectral pathology images were divided into overlapping image cubes to act as a form of augmentation during training and to address patch edge artifacts during testing. The annotations were first performed on the large images and then divided into smaller patches. A total of 4760 patches were used for training, 1116 for validation, and 1120 for testing. Segmentation was performed using the proposed hyper-net. The proposed model outperforms other state-of-the-art models in terms of dice coefficient (up to 0.91) and achieved up to 92.67% accuracy.

Liu et al.[16] used a pushbroom MHSI system to collect data in 151 bands ranging from 465.5 nm to 905.1 nm with a spectral resolution of approximately 3 nm. In total, there were 34 cases of basal cell carcinoma (BCC), 63 cases of squamous cell carcinoma (SCC), and 39 cases of malignant melanoma (MM). The research focused on the SCC staging study, in which there were 13 cases of stage I, 37 cases of stage II, and 13 cases of stage III. The performance of the classification was evaluated by testing 300 blind samples. Experimental results showed that the random forest model obtained the optimal SCC staging results with the highest staging accuracy and kappa value of 0.952 and 0.928, respectively.

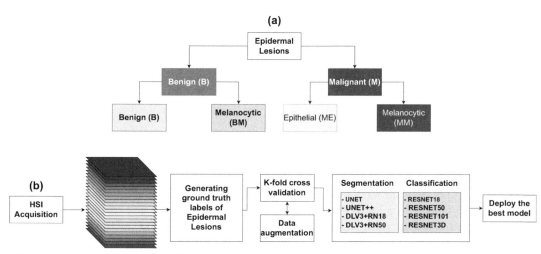

FIG. 3 Proposed experimental framework used in.[31] (A) Taxonomy of the epidermal lesions included in the HS database. (B) Proposed processing framework using low-power Nvidia Jetson GPU for algorithm deployment to reach real-time performance.

In a recent study proposed by La Silva et al.,[31] eight CNN architectures were trained to both classify and perform the semantic segmentation of the HS skin lesion images. First, the data were collected on-site at two hospitals. The campaign was carried out from March 2018 to June 2019. The database was composed of 76 HSI; 40 benign and 36 malignant skin lesions, from 61 subjects. The system used for image acquisition is composed of a snapshot camera capable of capturing VNIR spectrum (450–950 nm). Full description of the proposed framework is seen in Fig. 3. Experimental results show that U-Net++ is the most suitable for segmentation tasks with an average AUC over 0.6. While ResNet3D and ResNet50 have the best performance for classification tasks with AUC over 0.9, U-Net++ is more suitable for real-time semantic segmentation tasks when deployed on a low-power Nvidia Jetson GPU device. The GPU was embedded into a portable and handheld medical instrument containing an HS camera. Experts can then employ the created AI system's application in future clinical settings since it can classify and segment epidermal lesions in almost 1.2 s.

Hirano et al.[32] studied the use of hyperspectral data and GoogLeNet[33] for Melanoma classification. The total number of HSI records was 619, including 283 melanomas and 336 non-melanomas. The spectral range used in this study was 500.1–749.3 nm with 84 bands. First, each HSI went through a "mini network" to perform dimensionality reduction as a preprocessing step before the data are passed to GoogLeNet, which was trained on ImageNet dataset. The system was evaluated by fivefold cross-validation and the reported sensitivity, specificity, and accuracy were 69.1%, 75.7%, and 72.7%, respectively. To enhance the performance, data augmentation (vertical, horizontal, and diagonal flips) was performed to increase the amount of training data. This led to an increase in the reported results to 72.%, 81.2%, and 77.2%. It nearly matched dermatologists' accuracy, however, it fell short of that found in several earlier studies. This result indicates that the number of datasets is insufficient and that sufficient deductions could not be achieved by reducing the number of wavelengths.

To overcome the redundancy within the spectral bands, Vinokuro et al.[34] proposed the use of a selected number of bands instead of the full hypercube. An acousto-optical video spectrometer was used to take images of the area being studied resulting in 151 spectral bands between 440 and 750 nm. The number of images was 2592 obtained from 96 subjects. Seventy-five percent of the images were used for training and the rest for validation. The study was carried out in narrow spectral regions of 530–570 nm and 600–606 nm. For four kinds of neoplasms: melanoma, nevus, BCC, and papilloma, the results were evaluated by following a 10-fold cross-validation approach. Classification accuracy of 92% was achieved.

A Vision Transformers (ViT)[35] approach was utilized by La Silva et al.[36] The hyperspectral collection of in vivo skin cancer samples contains 76 photos taken from 61 different people. A total of 46 photos show malignant lesions, whereas 30 show benign skin cancer. Since the original dataset is small, data augmentation was applied to the real data. Each captured image has 125 spectral bands that extend from 450 to 950 nm in the VNIR spectrum. The four classes used in the labeling process are benign epithelial (BE), benign melanocytic (BM), malignant epithelial (ME), and malignant melanocytic (MM). Results show that the proposed architecture is capable of classifying the benign and malignant melanocytic lesions with high accuracy and specificity while adopting a 10-fold cross-validation.

A pilot study on the use of CNNs to differentiate malignant from benign skin tumors was proposed by Lindholm et al.[37] The study was carried out on 42 samples extracted from 33 patients with an average age of 66 years. A total of 17 patients had a history of one or several skin cancers, while six had a history of one or several other cancers.

Thirty-one percent of the lesions were located on the head or neck, including three lesions on particularly complex sites, namely the ear, eyelid, and corner of the eye. The imager used in this study was preset to capture 33 bands within VNIR range. The proposed approach achieved a sensitivity of 87% and a specificity of 93% for recognizing melanoma from pigmented nevi and healthy skin with a pixel-wise analysis. The sensitivity and specificity were boosted to 95% and 97%, respectively, by using majority voting.

4.2 Brain

Brain cancer refers to a group of diseases in which abnormal cells form in the tissues of the brain. These cells can grow and form tumors, which can disrupt normal brain function and cause serious health problems.[39] One of the most aggressive and prevalent types of brain cancer is glioblastoma (GBM), which is characterized by its rapid growth, high resistance to treatment, and poor prognosis. Early detection and diagnosis of brain cancer are crucial for improving patient outcomes, but traditional imaging techniques such as magnetic resonance imaging (MRI) and computed tomography (CT) scans can be limited in their ability to accurately identify the presence and extent of the disease. This highlights the need for more advanced techniques, such as HSI, that can help improve the accuracy of brain cancer detection and classification, with the aid of AI and ML. Thus, many recent works have been presented to this end.

A research by Fabelo et al.[40] introduced a method for classifying HSI that considers both spatial and spectral characteristics. The work aimed to help neurosurgeons accurately identify tumor boundaries during surgery without significant removal of healthy tissue or leaving behind tumor tissue. The method is a combination of supervised and unsupervised ML. First, a supervised pixel-wise classification is performed using SVM. Then, a spatially homogenized map is generated using a dimensional reduction algorithm and KNN filtering. After that, an unsupervised clustering approach is used to create a segmentation map, which is combined with the supervised classification through a majority voting approach. The method was tested on five HSI of GBM tumors and validated by specialists, showing promising results with accurate tumor delineation.

As an extension to,[40] a DL-based framework for processing HSI of in vivo human brain tissue for GBM tumor identification was proposed by Fabelo et al.[41,42] The effectiveness of the proposed framework was tested using 26 in vivo HSI cubes from 16 patients. These works also aimed to assist operating surgeon to achieve precise tumor resection by providing guidance through generating a thematic map with a delineated parenchymal area of the brain, thus identifying the tumor location. Using a proposed DL method that combines 1D-CNN and 2D-CNN, an overall accuracy of 80% was achieved in leave-one-out cross-validation for multiclass classification. Furthermore, a visualization tool was developed to enable surgeons to adjust the thematic map during the surgical procedure to select the most suitable classification threshold based on the current situation.

A framework for a hyperspectral database of in vivo human brain tissue generation was also presented by Fabelo et al.[38] The data were gathered using a special HSI acquisition system that could collect information in the VNIR range of 400–1000 nm. The conducted in vivo brain HSI acquisition procedure is illustrated in Fig. 4. To evaluate the consistency of the system, two consecutive images of the same scene were captured and compared. The results showed that the system performed best in the range of 450–900 nm. Thirty-six HSI were collected from 22 different patients and resulted in more than 300,000 spectral signatures being labeled using a semi-automated method based on the spectral angle mapper algorithm. Four classes were established: normal tissue, tumor tissue, blood vessels, and background elements.

On the other hand, Ortega et al.[43] investigated automatic identification of GBM and non-tumor tissue on hematoxylin and eosin-stained histological slides of human brain tissue using DL. An HSI microscope, with a spectral range

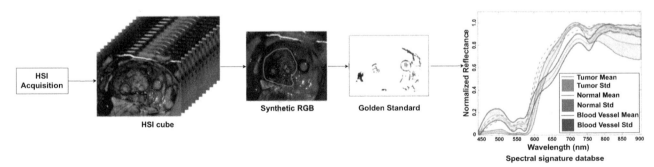

FIG. 4 Acquisition procedure of in vivo brain HSI in.[38] HSI acquisition system used during a neurosurgical operation. The golden standard map contains pixels labeled in four different classes: normal brain tissue (green, light gray in print version), tumor tissue (red, gray in print version), blood vessel (blue, dark gray in print version), and background (black). The spectral signature database is generated from the aforementioned four classes.

from 400 to 1000 nm, was utilized to acquire 517 HSI cubes from 13 GBM patients. To perform the classification between nontumor and tumor tissue, a CNN was trained using the collected data. A fourfold cross-validation was conducted, where each fold was trained with nine patients and only five of them provided both tumor and non-tumor samples. An average accuracy of 85% was achieved, representing a 5% average improvement compared to the results obtained using RGB images.

A study was presented by Martinez et al.[44] to determine the most relevant spectral ranges in the VNIR region for accurately detecting brain cancer in vivo using HSI. An optimization-based methodology has been proposed to identify the most relevant wavelengths that result in high classification accuracy with supervised SVM, while using the smallest number of spectral bands. The results showed that the proposed methodology was able to improve tumor identification accuracy by approximately 5% using only 48 bands compared to the reference results obtained using 128 bands. This offers the possibility of developing customized sensors for real-time HSI. The authors concluded that the most important spectral ranges for this task include wavelengths between 440.5 and 465.96 nm, 498.71–509.62 nm, 556.91–575.1 nm, 593.29–615.12 nm, 636.94–666.05 nm, 698.79–731.53 nm, and 884.32–902.51 nm.

The classification of multiclass brain tumors using in vivo brain HSI and supervised ML was studied and discussed by Ruiz et al.[45] In this work, 4 HSI with spectral information distributed within 25 bands along the spectral range between 655 and 975 nm, from four patients with grade IV GBM brain tumors were involved. Two conventional ML techniques were considered, SVM and RF. The images were used to train and test the models based on five different classes: healthy tissue, tumor, venous blood vessel, arterial blood vessel, and dura mater. The presented results showed that SVM performed better than RF, achieving an average accuracy of up to 97%.

In an extended and more recent research by Urbanos et al.,[21] 13 in vivo HSI from 12 patients with grade III and IV gliomas were studied. In addition to the conventional SVM and RF classifiers used in,[45] a CNN classifier was trained on the collected HSI dataset based on the same five classes in.[45] An overall accuracy between 60% and 95% was achieved using different training conditions.

Leon et al.[46] investigated the benefits of fusing the outputs of two HSI cameras covering the VNIR 400–1700 nm spectral ranges, for an intraoperative system developed to delineate brain tumor tissue during neurosurgical procedures. The HSI was registered using intensity-based and feature-based techniques with various geometric transformations to create a fused HSI cube with a wide spectral range of 435–1638 nm. The fusion process was verified using four HSI datasets. Additionally, segmentation and classification methods, including, SVM, RF, and KNN, were evaluated to compare the performance of using the VNIR and NIR data separately to the fused data. The results indicated that the proposed fusion method can improve the classification accuracy by up to 21% compared to using each data modality independently.

Hao et al.[47] proposed an approach for accurately identifying GBM tumors in in vivo human brain HSI. In order to make full use of the spectral and spatial information in HSI, this work combines the outputs of multiple DL models, including 1D-CNN and 2D-CNN. In this method, spectral phasor analysis and data oversampling were performed, then features were extracted using 1D-CNN and 2D-CNN for classification. After that, fusion and optimization of classification results were done using edge-preserving filtering, and finally, background segmentation was performed using FCN. The proposed method was tested on two real human brain hyperspectral datasets and achieved an overall accuracy of 96.69% for four-class classification and 96.34% for GBM tumor identification.

4.3 Head and neck

Head and neck cancer is one of the most common cancer types worldwide.[48] Such type of cancer can spread in multiple tissue species in the head and neck area such as the gingiva, oral mucosa, mandible, retromolar trigone, maxillary, floor of mouth, mandibular surfaces, tongue, pharynx, larynx, and the thyroid.[49] Due to the various benefits of the HSI technique, it has been employed for the detection of head and neck cancer tissues in human subjects,[50] as well as in animal models (mice).[24,51]

This section is divided into three subsections; the first one discusses the studies that considered cancer tumors in the various types of the oral cavity tissues; the second one is dedicated to the studies concerning the cancer specimen from the tongue structure; the final subsection covers the recent studies associated with the general types of tissues in the head and neck, including thyroid or salivary gland tumors.

4.3.1 Oral cavity

Thiem et al.[52] collected 316 HSI samples of healthy human-oral mucosa, muscle, and fat from 174 patients using an HS camera that covers the wavelength range from 500 to 1000 nm. The classification of healthy oral cavity tissues was performed using a six-layer deep neural network employing the HS-reflectance values. The fivefold cross-validation results in an accuracy>0.8, sensitivity>0.57, specificity>0.79, and error < 0.21. Although the study presented a proof of principle showing the successful classification of the specific HS-reflectance signature into the different oral tissue types, there is a gap in accuracy which requires further analysis of convolutional blocks and images.

The study reported by Bengs et al. in Ref. 53 demonstrated the feasibility of in vivo head and neck tumor type classification for multiple hyperspectral bands (only spectral, mostly spatial, or combined spatial and spectral information) using 3D recurrent-convolutional models. The data were collected from 98 patients in which polychrome V monochromator was the light source for HSI, and a monochromatic CCD-camera was employed to obtain images with a spectral range of 430–680 nm. The performance of the DL model was validated using cross fold which resulted in 0.694 sensitivity, 0.689 specificity, 0.695 F-score, and 0.763 AUC.

Jeyaraj et al.[54] analyzed 100 multidimensional cubic patches of HSI data sets for the classification of cancerous tumor using a structure of regression-based partitioned CNN learning algorithm with two partitioned layers for labeling and classification. The work considered the method of bagging and boosting for feature selection, as well as the image intensity values along with texture's spatial and spectral information. The sevenfold cross-validation showed an increased quality of diagnosis with an accuracy value of 0.914, sensitivity of 0.91, specificity of 0.94, and AUC of 0.965.

4.3.2 Tongue

It has been demonstrated by Trajanovski et al.[55] that some channel selection and filtering in VNIR spectrum are beneficial for achieving better performance. That is because important information about the tumor is encoded in various channels. The work considered a clinical dataset with limited samples of tongue squamous cell carcinoma. HSIs within 400–700 nm spectral range were created using line sensors by moving the specimen on a translation stage under the camera through the scanning line. The DL semantic segmentation method has been validated using leave-patients-out. The cross-validation results were 0.958 accuracy, 0.873 sensitivity, 0.975 specificity, 0.891 ± 0.053 F-score, and 0.924 ± 0.036 AUC.

A dual-stream network that utilizes the combined spectral and structural information in the hypercube has been introduced by Weijtmans et al. in Ref. 56 for tumor detection. The work considered a limited data set of tongue squamous cell carcinoma data from seven patients. HSI scan results in a data cube for each tissue sample in which the imaging system uses a line-by-line scanning method to form small patches spanning all bands, which is then used to select bigger patches. The obtained HSI spanned a spectral range of 480–920 nm. The introduced model outperformed the spectral and structural techniques, despite the limited analysis and the fact that the method's lengthy imaging procedure made it difficult to employ in real-time applications. The leave-one-patient-out cross-validation results of the classification approach should have an accuracy of 0.798 ± 0.083, sensitivity of 0.864 ± 0.125, specificity of 0.731 ± 0.188, and AUC of 0.904 ± 0.053.

4.3.3 General tissues in head and neck

The work reported by Halicek et al. in Ref. 57 collected 293 tissue specimens from 102 patients with head and neck squamous cell carcinoma. The employed DL architecture was a customized CNN to optimize the hypercube data in image patches. It demonstrated that label-free, autofluorescence imaging, and reflectance-based HSI methods can reliably detect the margin of cancer within minutes in images that span a spectral range of 450–900 nm with 91 bands. The introduced cancer margin classification method was validated using fivefold cross-validation, which showed an accuracy of 0.88–0.97, and an AUC of 0.77–0.91 for reflectance-based HSI intra-patients.

Fei et al. presented in Ref. 58 a pilot study on surgical tissue specimens of head and neck cancer patients using a label-free reflectance HSI for tumor margin assessment. The three tissue types were normal tissue, visible tumor, and tumor with adjacent normal tissue. Samples were collected from 16 patients and prepared for HSI, autofluorescence imaging, and fluorescence imaging with vital dyes. The reflectance HSI spanned a spectral range of 450–950 nm. The introduced ML-based quantification pipeline was used to classify normal and cancerous tissue and was validated using cross-validation, which resulted in an accuracy of 0.90 ± 0.08 for oral cavity and 0.94 ± 0.06 for thyroid. The reported sensitivity values for oral cavity and thyroid tissues were 0.89 ± 0.09, and 0.94 ± 0.06, respectively. The specificity values were 0.91 ± 0.06 for oral cavity and 0.95 ± 0.06 for thyroid.

The study conducted by Halicek et al.[60] acquired 216 ex-vivo surgical specimen from 82 patients diagnosed with thyroid and salivary gland cancer. The study confirmed that HSI of 91 bands ranging between 450 and 900 nm in autofluorescence and broadband reflectance modes has a high potential in detecting and classifying cancer tumors. The used CNN method was validated using fivefold cross-validation scheme, which resulted in average accuracy values of 0.89 in the parotid group, and 0.84 for the autofluorescence imaging approach for the other group. The later approach achieved the highest sensitivity values; 0.99 on average for the parotid group, and 0.77 on average for

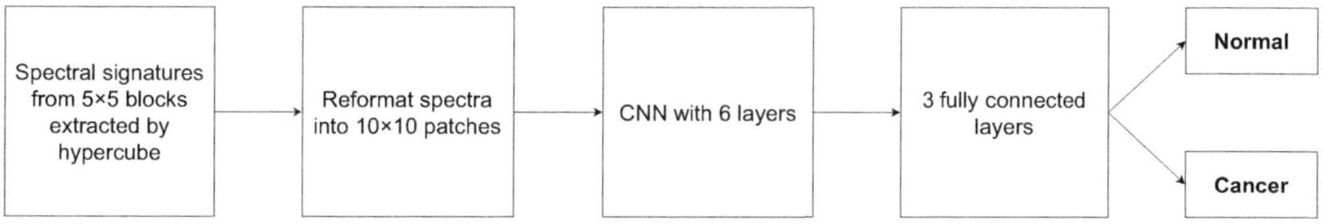

FIG. 5   The DL architecture and data processing block diagram.[59]

the other group. Moreover, HSI resulted in the highest specificity of 0.79 in the parotid group, and 0.87 in the human-eye method for the other group. At last, the AUC values were 0.90 for the classification of thyroid tumors and 0.92 for HSI of salivary glands.

The work introduced in Ref. 59 diagnosed upper aerodigestive tract sites as well as the thyroid for 50 patients with 88 tissue samples using a CRI maestro imaging system to obtain the database of HSI (450–900 nm, 91 bands) from tissue specimens. The classification has been established using CNN. which can produce near real-time tissue labeling for intraoperative detection. The DL architecture as well as the data processing block diagram are depicted in Fig. 5. To separate spectral bands, xenon white-light illumination source was used in addition to a liquid crystal tunable filter and a 16-bit charge-coupled device. Leave-one-out cross-validation resulted in accuracy, sensitivity, and specificity of 0.80 ± 0.14, 0.81 ± 0.19, and 0.78 ± 0.20, respectively.

4.4 Gastric

Gastric cancer is a type of cancer where malignant cells form in the lining of the stomach can invade other organs such as the esophagus, pancreas, colon, small intestine, and peritoneum.[61] Tumors in this type of cancer, grow from mucosa, the innermost tissue layer, and spread to the other layers of the stomach wall. Symptoms can vary from stomach discomfort, food indigestion, mild nausea, to finding trouble swallowing food, vomiting, blood in the stool, yellowing of the eyes and skin, and others. Fast cancer identification is of paramount importance to increase the patients' survival rates. Traditional diagnostic methods include physical examinations of the body and screening of the patient's illness history, blood sample collection, and checking against several bio-markers that might return abnormal values, upper endoscopy examination starting from the esophagus to the first part of the small intestine screening for unusual areas, in addition to x-rays, CT-scans, and biopsy collection.[61]

In Ref. 14, the researchers used principal component analysis (PCA), to extract features from the captured images, which is then followed by either an ANN or SVM classification algorithm. Image data were prepared from six types of cultured cells, and imaging was performed using sisuChema Short Wave Infrared (SWIR) hyper-spectral pushbroom imaging system. The models' ability to identify migrated tumors in the NIR regions of 920–2514 nm have shown an overall accuracy of 87.4% and 88.9% using ANN SVM, respectively, using the one-vs-one (OVO) multiclass technique.

The authors in Ref. 62, focused on the spectral bands between 360 and 550 nm to differentiate between benign and cancerous colon cells. The samples were removed from the patients during surgery, and then QImaging Corporation's Rolera EM-C^2 camera was used to capture the images. HSI and panchromatic images from 13 patients were fed into a CNN to compare their classification performance. The CNN consisted of three convolution layers and one FC layer. The classification accuracy was 74.1% with an F-score of 0.747. The output was superior to the one obtained through logistic regression classifier, which showed an accuracy of 70.6% and an F-score of 0.561. Although promising results were demonstrated in Ref. 14,62, more samples are required to determine the validity of the models.

A continuous HSI classification process during free-hand endoscopic procedure is developed in Ref. 63. Full data flow process begins with free-hand endoscopy procedure, where white light images and hyperspectral line-scan data are obtained. Then the captured data are normalized before feeding it into the five-layered CNN. And finally, the classified output data are overlaid over the white light image. Large volumes of multidimensional real-time data generated from spatial-scanning hyperspectral endoscope (HySE) require real-time analysis. Three hundred HySE images were fed into a five-layered CNN. Intact pig esophagus and human esophagus biopsies were used in testing the trained CNN. Pixel-wise CNN achieved the highest accuracy compared to other ML algorithms such as slice-wise CNN and SVM. Yet, its classification speed is lower than the imaging speed of the HySE system.

The work presented in Ref. 64 utilized real-time NIR HSI in the region from 1000 to 1600 nm. SVM was used on images that deployed the least absolute shrinkage and selection operator (LASSO) to reduce their dimension and, hence, the processing time. The specimens included in the study were taken from six stomachs. Images from these specimens were captured by CVN800HS, Sumitomo Electric Industries, as an HS camera with the innermost layer, mucous, surface on top. With 95 selected wavelengths, the SVM model was able to achieve 82.2% classification accuracy, 93% sensitivity, and 0.8% specificity. They also demonstrated that the model can provide similar results with only four wavelengths, which makes it attractive for real-time processing.

Motivated by the need for an automatic computer-assisted diagnostic tool to rapidly detect cancerous tissues during an intervention, the researchers in Ref. 65 combined colonic and esophagogastric datasets and fed them into ML models to classify normal and cancerous cells regardless of the type of cancer. The researchers have also introduced patient-specific decision threshold tuning in order to incorporate information specific to the patient and increase the detection accuracy. The dataset was collected from 10 patients with esophagogastric cancer and 12 patients with colon cancer. One hypercube was created for each patient, with images being captured from samples 5 min after their resection. HSI images covered spectral range 500–1000 nm. RF, logistic regression, multilayer perceptron (MLP), linear SVM, radial basis functions (RBFs), and 3D-CNN were trained on the collected HSI images. Due to the limited dataset size, all models were trained and tested using the leave-one-patient-put cross-validation (LOPOCV) approach. The combined training set positively affected RBF-SVM and MLP models. Although the shallow 3D-CNN outperformed the other ML models with a higher mean and lower standard deviation on receiver operator curve AUC (ROC-AUC), it did not benefit from the enlarged dataset. Next, the authors explored the impact of cross-dataset training on ML models. Results suggest that the hyperspectral information gained from training the model with data from a different tissue and cancer type improves the performance of the ML model.

In Ref. 66, the authors used color reproduction to convert white-light images (WLIs) to narrowband endoscopic HSI (NBI) with 415 nm and 540 nm wavelengths. Smart spectrum cloud, Hitspectra Intelligent Technology Co., Ltd., Kaohsiung City, Taiwan HSI was used in the process of converting esophageal cancer images into spectral images. Single-shot multibox detector (SSD) based on the VGG-16 network architecture, which consists of 13 convolution layers and three FC layers, was used to classify the images into three categories: normal, dysplasia, and SCC. The dataset was divided into three categories depending on the utilized imaging technique, namely: WLIs, NBI, and HSI. The model with HSI images scored the highest mean for all metrics with accuracy 90.7%, precision 90.1%, sensitivity 83.0%, F-score 86.1%, and AP 83.7%. Kappa, which evaluates the consistency between the classified output result and pathological analysis, was higher than the threshold 0.6 in all categories, indicating that the utilized model is feasible for esophageal cancer detection. Nonetheless, some results were not as expected indicating that the dataset still needs to be improved.

The study presented in Ref. 67, aimed to explore several ML algorithms to distinguish between normal cells and colorectal cancer (CRC) ones. Samples were collected from 54 patients undergoing CRC resections or endoscopically nonresectable adenomas. The extracted specimen was divided ex-situ while exposing the mucosal side. TIVITA® Tissue system was used to capture the HSI images in the range of 500–1000 nm. Hybercubes were generated by combining the 2D spatial data with a third dimension consisting of spectral data. A 50 cm distance was kept between the camera and the specimen. Then, images were categorized by a pathologist and a surgeon into three classes: healthy, adenomatous margin, and cancer. The data were preprocessed using Savitzky–Golay filter, then normalized, and finally down-sampled to achieve a balanced dataset. Three LOPOCV were performed with MLP model. The model was able to reach a 94% accuracy.

The researchers in Ref. 68, focused on esophageal cancer classification. An MLP with two hidden layers was used to classify HSI, which was within the spectral region 500–1000 nm and collected from 95 patients, into three categories: squamous epithelium cells, esophageal adenocarcinoma cells, and tumor stroma cells. SVM, LR, and MLP were tested, where the first two methods showed high variance and, hence, were discarded. LOPOCV was used with MLP in four different cases. Accuracy, sensitivity, and specificity of the background class were the highest with values over 90% for all performance indicators. The accuracy of the esophageal adenocarcinoma cells and tumor stroma class along with the sensitivity and specificity metrics were higher than 77%, and the highest F-score value was 82%. The sensitivity of the squamous epithelium was the lowest at 53%, while its accuracy was 80% approximately.

4.5 Other types

4.5.1 Breast

Breast cancer is a type of cancer that starts in the cells of the breast. It develops when the cells in the breast grow uncontrollably and divide to form a mass called a tumor. It can occur in both women and men, although it is more common in women. Breast cancer is the second most prevalent type of cancer overall, and improving survival depends on early identification and treatment. It develops when abnormal cells in breast tissue grow out of control, and if it is not found and treated quickly, it can spread to other regions of the body. Breast cancer symptoms include a lump in the

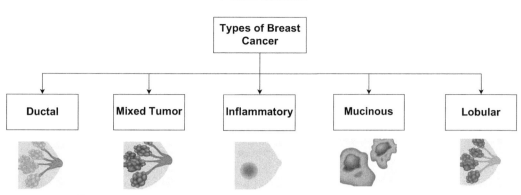

FIG. 6   Types of breast cancer.[69]

breast, changes in the size or shape of the breast, changes in the skin of the breast, and changes in the nipple. Although the actual origin of breast cancer is unknown, a person's risk of developing breast cancer can be increased by a number of variables such as age, genetics, hormone exposure, and lifestyle. Breast cancer can be diagnosed by a number of tests, including a physical examination, a mammogram, an ultrasound scan, a biopsy, and a magnetic resonance imaging. Treatment for breast cancer depends on the type and stage of the cancer and the patient's general health. Treatment options include surgery, radiotherapy, chemotherapy, hormone therapy, or a combination of these. Early detection is the key to successful treatment of breast cancer. As seen in Fig. 6, there are several different types of breast cancer, including ductal breast cancer, lobular breast cancer, inflammatory breast cancer, mucinous breast cancer, and mixed tumor breast cancer.

DL algorithms have the potential to detect breast cancer. Similar to the aforementioned types of cancer, CNNs are one popular approach for this task. Another approach is to use DL algorithms to examine medical records, including the patient's history, symptoms, and test results to identify risk factors and predict the likelihood of breast cancer. DL algorithms have the potential to greatly enhance the accessibility and accuracy of breast cancer detection, resulting in earlier diagnosis and better patient outcomes. In Ref. 70, Zhang et al. discussed HSI as an imaging technique to diagnose and detect breast cancer. In Ref. 43, Ortega et al. proposed a combined DL and HSI technique with AUCs of more than 0.89 using 2D-CNN for the detection of minute variations in the molecular and cellular structure of the tissue that could point to the existence of breast cancer cells. The proposed method has the potential to completely transform how breast cancer is detected and treated.

4.5.2 Blood

Blood cancer is a type of cancer that affects the blood cells, which include red blood cells, white blood cells, and platelets. Blood cancer is a serious and potentially fatal disease that affects the production of blood cells in the body. It can cause abnormal blood cell production and interfere with immune system function, resulting in anemia, infection, and bleeding. Symptoms of blood cancer include fatigue, weakness, fever, weight loss, and easy bruising or bleeding. Blood cancers include leukemia, lymphoma, and multiple myeloma. Early detection and treatment of blood cancer can improve survival and reduce the severity of symptoms. Physical examination, blood tests, and biopsy of the affected tissue are used to diagnose blood cancer. Treatment for blood cancer is determined by the type and stage of the cancer as well as the patient's overall health. Understanding the various types of blood cancer, their causes, symptoms, and treatment options is critical for accurate diagnosis and treatment of the disease.

By analyzing the unique spectral signatures of tissues, HSI can be a powerful tool for detecting blood cancers. To improve the accuracy and speed of cancer detection, DL algorithms are applied to HSI data. A typical HSI and DL blood cancer detection approach involves capturing an HSI of the tissue and then processing it with a DL algorithm to identify the spectral signatures of cancer cells. In Ref. 71, Abunadi et al. proposed various hybrid techniques, such as CNN + SVM, AlexNet+SVM, and ResNet+SVM models to provide powerful analytical and diagnostic tools with high efficiency for blood cancer classification. In Ref. 72, Huang et al. proposed a kernel fusion approach based on the Gabor kernel and CNN kernel to enhance the performance of the conventional CNN for the categorization of medical HSI with an accuracy of 95.69%. The use of HSI and DL algorithms has the potential to revolutionize the detection of blood cancer and have several advantages in the diagnosis and classification tasks, including high accuracy, speed, and improved diagnostic consistency.

4.5.3 Liver

The liver is a vital organ that filters toxins from the blood, produces bile for digestion, and stores glucose for energy. Liver cancer is a type of cancer that begins in the liver. There are two types of liver cancer: hepatocellular carcinoma, which is the most common type of liver cancer, and cholangiocarcinoma. Both types of liver cancer can cause similar symptoms, such as abdominal pain, weight loss, and skin and eye yellowing. Early detection and treatment are critical for improving the prognosis and survival of liver cancer patients. Various medical imaging and biopsy techniques can detect and classify liver cancer. Ultrasound, CT, MRI, positron emission tomography, and biopsy are common techniques. In addition to these techniques, blood tests and liver function tests may be used to determine the presence and extent of liver cancer. The results of these tests can also aid in determining the best treatment option. DL can be a powerful tool for detecting and classifying liver cancer, allowing doctors to diagnose the disease earlier and provide more effective treatment options. HSI can be used to capture detailed images of the liver and surrounding tissue, while DL algorithms can be trained to identify and classify different types of liver tumors based on their spectral characteristics. HSI approach for the diagnosis and detection of liver cancer was discussed by Zhang et al. in Ref. 43. With the use of this method, spectral and spatial information can be extracted from tissue using imaging and spectroscopy capabilities in a noninvasive manner. In Ref. 73, Wang et al. discussed how the combination of HSI and DL techniques can revolutionize the field of liver cancer detection and classification by providing medical professionals with faster, more accurate, and cost-effective diagnostic solutions.

4.5.4 Kidney

The kidneys are two organs in the abdomen that help remove waste and excess fluid from the blood. Kidney cancer can develop in any part of the kidney. Blood in the urine, a mass or lump in the abdomen, side pain, and fatigue are all symptoms of kidney cancer. Kidney cancer is one of the most common cancers, and early detection and diagnosis are critical for successful treatment. There are several subtypes of kidney cancer, including clear cell renal cell carcinoma, papillary renal cell carcinoma, chromophobe renal cell carcinoma, collecting duct carcinoma, and renal medullary carcinoma. Traditional imaging techniques, such as CT and MRI, are frequently used to diagnose kidney cancer, but they do not always provide an accurate diagnosis. HSI is used to detect kidney cancer because abnormal cells in cancerous tissue have a different spectral signature than normal cells. In Ref. 74, Markgraf et al. proposed an organ evaluation strategy based on supervised learning methods trained with blood and urine markers for assessing the functional status of normothermically perfused kidneys. In the validation and test sets, the proposed classifiers achieved 75% and 83% accuracy, respectively. DL techniques can provide more accurate and efficient diagnoses than traditional diagnostic methods, thereby improving patient outcomes. CNNs and RNNs are two popular DL techniques for detecting kidney cancer. In Ref. 75, Sommer et al. implemented an optimized KidneyResNet DL model for classifying kidney cancer using HSI with an accuracy of 96% and 100% validation and test sets, respectively. HSI is a promising tool for the detection and classification of kidney cancer, especially as a noninvasive and efficient method for its early diagnosis and treatment.

5. Meta-analysis

This chapter demonstrated the various 65 studies that were systematically reviewed AI with HSI imaging applications in cancer diagnosis. Fig. 7 shows the overview of databases that were used in this review. The selected studies were published between 2017 and 2023. It must be noted that the analysis was based on data collected up to February 2023; therefore, there is a high possibility that additional publications may occur in the journals being published in the later months of 2023. Overall, it seems that the number of publications is on the rise with the exception of the year 2020. This indicates a continued interest in this area of research considering the challenges and gaps still present in it, as will be discussed in Section 6.

The main types of cancer applications using HSI discussed in this chapter are brain, skin, head and neck, gastric, and other cancer categories such as blood, liver, and kidney. The articles were systematically classified into these specific cancer types. Fig. 8 shows the total publication of each type between 2017 and 2023. Research on gastric cancer has been steadily increasing, but skin cancer particularly witnessed a sharp increase in 2022. Overall, it appears that brain, gastric, and skin cancer are the top three topics in this area of research.

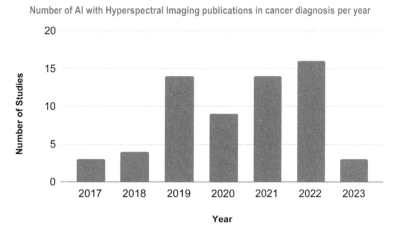

FIG. 7   Publications on AI with HSI in cancer diagnosis between 2017 and 2023 (ongoing).

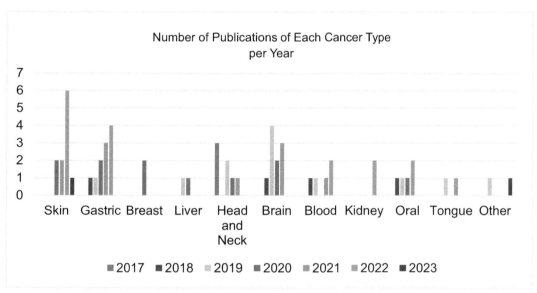

FIG. 8   Publications of each cancer type between 2017 and 2023 (ongoing).

According to Fig. 9, it appears that the most frequently used evaluation metric is accuracy, followed by sensitivity and specificity, and then F-score, followed by AUC. Accuracy by itself is not a reliable metric. For example, in segmentation cases, if an image consists of 90% background, the accuracy will be high even with inaccurate segmentation of the infected tissue. In other words, it does not hold well with imbalanced data. Hence, it needs to be paired with other metrics, such as the other frequently used ones.

Fig. 10 illustrates that the most widely utilized spectral range is approximately 400–1000 nm, which falls within VNIR, and it indicates that it is the most useful range for this task. Considering the high dimensionality of hypercubes and the desire to produce results in real time, the studied research papers indicate that the number of used bands can be as large as 826, or as small as 25. A large number of bands leads to redundant information that can affect training results negatively and cause a high computational complexity. Most studies use 150 bands or less, and some go as low as 25 bands.

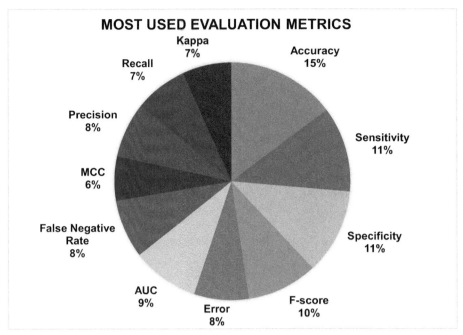

FIG. 9 The most frequently used metrics for evaluating HSI classification and segmentation techniques.

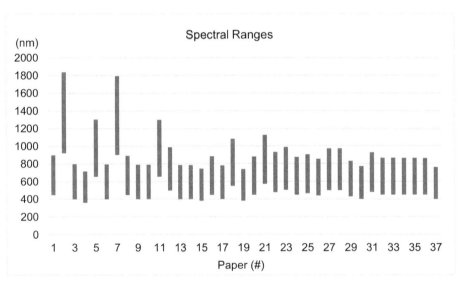

FIG. 10 Commonly utilized spectral ranges in HSI for cancer detection.

6. Recommendations and future directions

The future direction of this area of research lies in tackling the most commonly faced challenges. When it comes to cancer detection generally, it is crucial to avoid false detection results, particularly false-negative (FN) cases. Thus, it is insufficient to rely on accuracy alone as an evaluation metric, and that is why it is essential to include sensitivity and specificity in the reported results. Furthermore, there is still a gap between the predicted results and the expert's opinion, which calls for a further boost in the algorithm's general reliability and resilience in terms of performance. It is of essential importance that the algorithms deliver results in real time. The curse of dimensionality that HSI suffers from leads to an undesirably high computational complexity. Simultaneously, the lack of data quantity presents a clear challenge when training CNNs. Transfer learning (TL) is a powerful approach for training a small dataset without overfitting. In this method, a pretrained model previously trained on a large dataset to perform a specific task is reused as a starting point and fine-tuned to another task using a different dataset with limited samples. Data augmentation is another way to solve this issue. Moreover, semi-supervised learning (SSL) methods have attracted much research attention recently due to their capability of full use of both vast numbers of unlabeled samples and the limited numbers of labeled samples which in turn can improve the detection performance. However, it is believed that generative adversarial networks (GANs)[76]; one example of SSL, can be used to generate more samples, but this approach has not been explored for HSI in cancer detection thus far. So far, several research studies proved that analyzing images in the frequency domain provides better results compared to the spatial domain. This is true for HSI as well, according to this study. However, this has not been attempted for HSI cancer detection thus far. Complex-valued neural networks (CVNNs)[77] present a potential solution that is worth investigating for the purpose of boosting the detection accuracy and other metrics. Finally, the authors recommend investigating operational neural networks[78] for HSI cancer detection, as these networks have proven their ability to generalize better than the standard CNNs even with a limited amount of data.

7. Conclusions

HSI combines the power of imaging and spectroscopy and provides both spectral and spatial information. Spatial information helps to investigate the morphology and changes intuitively, while the spectral information acts as fingerprints that reflects the object-specific information. It can offer information about tissue samples in a noninvasive manner and in real time. Without a doubt, DL is the most discussed topic today in medical imaging research, both diagnostic and therapeutic. By implementing AI in medical HSI, this combination can have great potential for improving the accuracy and reliability in disease detection, diagnosis, monitoring, and image-guided surgeries. In this chapter, the AI and DL techniques for medical HSI have been discussed by studying published research papers relevant to the topic within the years 2017–2023. In general, the majority of these studies are within brain, gastric, and skin cancer topics. The literature indicates that the high dimensionality of HSI and data scarcity present two of the big challenges in this area of research. Tackling these challenges while ensuring low time complexity and boosting the accuracy of the outcome is the ideal way to move forward in this area of research.

References

1. Aldhyani TH, Nair R, Alzain E, Alkahtani H, Koundal D. Deep learning model for the detection of real time breast cancer images using improved dilation-based method. *Diagnostics*. 2022;12:2505.
2. Sebastian AM, Peter D. Artificial intelligence in cancer research: trends, challenges and future directions. *Life*. 2022;12:1991.
3. Schröder A, Maktabi M, Thieme R, Jansen-Winkeln B, Gockel I, Chalopin C. Evaluation of artificial neural networks for the detection of esophagus tumor cells in microscopic hyperspectral images. In: *2022 25th Euromicro Conference on Digital System Design (DSD), IEEE*; 2022:827–834.
4. Fei B, Akbari H, Halig LV. Hyperspectral imaging and spectral-spatial classification for cancer detection. In: *2012 5th International Conference on BioMedical Engineering and Informatics, IEEE*; 2012:62–64.
5. Walter W, Pohlkamp C, Meggendorfer M, et al. Artificial intelligence in hematological diagnostics: game changer or gadget? *Blood Rev*. 2022. 101019.
6. Zitouni MS, Lih Oh S, Vicnesh J, Khandoker A, Acharya UR. Automated recognition of major depressive disorder from cardiovascular and respiratory physiological signals. *Front Psych*. 2022;13:2773.
7. Khouj Y, Dawson J, Coad J, Vona-Davis L. Hyperspectral imaging and k-means classification for histologic evaluation of ductal carcinoma in situ. *Front Oncol*. 2018;8:17.
8. Aburaed N, Alkhatib MQ, Marshall S, Zabalza J, Al Ahmad H. A review of spatial enhancement of hyperspectral remote sensing imaging techniques. *IEEE J Select Top Appl Earth Observ Remote Sens*. 2023;16:2275–2300.
9. Lu G, Fei B. Medical hyperspectral imaging: a review. *J Biomed Opt*. 2014;19, 010901.
10. Li Q, He X, Wang Y, Liu H, Xu D, Guo F. Review of spectral imaging technology in biomedical engineering: achievements and challenges. *J Biomed Opt*. 2013;18, 100901.
11. Cui R, Yu H, Xu T, et al. Deep learning in medical hyperspectral images: a review. *Sensors*. 2022;22:9790.
12. Sadeeq HT, Ameen SY, Abdulazeez AM. Cancer diagnosis based on artificial intelligence, machine learning, and deep learning. In: *2022 International Conference on Innovation and Intelligence for Informatics, Computing, and Technologies (3ICT), IEEE*; 2022:656–661.
13. Bhardwaj P, Kumar Y, Bhandari G. Ai-enabled computational techniques for cancer diagnosis. In: *2021 IEEE 8th Uttar Pradesh Section International Conference on Electrical, Electronics and Computer Engineering (UPCON)*; 2021:1–7.
14. Nathan M, Kabatznik A, Mahmood A. Hyperspectral imaging for cancer detection and classification. In: *2018 3rd Biennial South African Biomedical Engineering Conference (SAIBMEC), IEEE*; 2018:1–4.
15. Pertzborn D, Nguyen H-N, Hüttmann K, et al. Intraoperative assessment of tumor margins in tissue sections with hyperspectral imaging and machine learning. *Cancer*. 2023;15:213.
16. Liu L, Qi M, Li Y, et al. Staging of skin cancer based on hyperspectral microscopic imaging and machine learning. *Biosensors*. 2022;12:790.

17. Quintana L, Ortega S, Leon R, et al. In the use of artificial intelligence and hyperspectral imaging in digital pathology for breast cancer cell identification. In: *Medical Imaging 2022: Digital and Computational Pathology*. vol. 12039. SPIE; 2022:73–82.

18. Gopi A, Reshmi C. A noninvasive cancer detection using hyperspectral images. In: *2017 International Conference on Wireless Communications, Signal Processing and Networking (WiSPNET), IEEE*; 2017:2051–2055.

19. Florimbi G, Fabelo H, Torti E, et al. Accelerating the k-nearest neighbors filtering algorithm to optimize the real-time classification of human brain tumor in hyperspectral images. *Sensors*. 2018;18:2314.

20. Madooei A, Abdlaty RM, Doerwald-Munoz L, et al. Hyperspectral image processing for detection and grading of skin erythema. In: *Medical Imaging 2017: Image Processing*. vol. 10133. SPIE; 2017:577–583.

21. Urbanos G, Martín A, Vázquez G, et al. Supervised machine learning methods and hyperspectral imaging techniques jointly applied for brain cancer classification. *Sensors*. 2021;21:3827.

22. Alkhatib MQ, Al-Saad M, Aburaed N, et al. Tri-cnn: a three branch model for hyperspectral image classification. *Remote Sens (Basel)*. 2023;15:316.

23. Bir P, Balas VE. A review on medical image analysis with convolutional neural networks. In: *2020 IEEE International Conference on Computing, Power and Communication Technologies (GUCON), IEEE*; 2020:870–876.

24. Ma L, Lu G, Wang D, et al. Deep learning based classification for head and neck cancer detection with hyperspectral imaging in an animal model. In: *Medical Imaging 2017: Biomedical Applications in Molecular, Structural, and Functional Imaging*. vol. 10137. SPIE; 2017:632–639.

25. Hu B, Du J, Zhang Z, Wang Q. Tumor tissue classification based on micro-hyperspectral technology and deep learning, biomedical. *Opt Express*. 2019;10:6370–6389.

26. Zhao Y, Hu B, Wang Y, Yin X, Jiang Y, Zhu X. Identification of gastric cancer with convolutional neural networks: a systematic review. *Multimed Tools Appl*. 2022;81:11717–11736.

27. Urban K, Mehrmal S, Uppal P, Giesey RL, Delost GR. The global burden of skin cancer: a longitudinal analysis from the global burden of disease study, 1990–2017. *JAAD Int*. 2021;2:98–108.

28. Leon R, Martinez-Vega B, Fabelo H, et al. Non-invasive skin cancer diagnosis using hyperspectral imaging for in-situ clinical support. *J Clin Med*. 2020;9:1662.

29. Wang Q, Sun L, Wang Y, et al. Identification of melanoma from hyperspectral pathology image using 3d convolutional networks. *IEEE Trans Med Imaging*. 2021;40:218–227.

30. Li Q, Zhou M, Liu H, Wang Y, Guo F. Red blood cell count automation using microscopic hyperspectral imaging technology. *Appl Spectrosc*. 2015;69:1372–1380.

31. La Salvia M, Torti E, Leon R, et al. Neural networks-based on-site dermatologic diagnosis through hyperspectral epidermal images. *Sensors*. 2022;22:7139.

32. Hirano G, Nemoto M, Kimura Y, et al. Automatic diagnosis of melanoma using hyperspectral data and googlenet. *Skin Res Technol*. 2020;26:891–897.

33. Szegedy C, Liu W, Jia Y, et al. Going deeper with convolutions. In: *Proceedings of the IEEE Conference on Computer Vision and Pattern Recognition*; 2015:1–9.

34. Vinokurov V, Khristoforova Y, Myakinin O, et al. Neural network classifier for hyperspectral images of skin pathologies. In: *Journal of Physics: Conference Series*. vol. 2127. IOP Publishing; 2021:012026.

35. Dosovitskiy A, Beyer L, Kolesnikov A, et al. An image is worth 16x16 words: Transformers for image recognition at scale. In: *arXiv preprint arXiv:2010.11929*; 2020.

36. La Salvia M, Torti E, Gazzoni M, et al. Attention-based skin cancer classification through hyperspectral imaging. In: *2022 25th Euromicro Conference on Digital System Design (DSD), IEEE*; 2022:871–876.

37. Lindholm V, Raita-Hakola A-M, Annala L, et al. Differentiating malignant from benign pigmented or non-pigmented skin tumours—a pilot study on 3d hyperspectral imaging of complex skin surfaces and convolutional neural networks. *J Clin Med*. 2022;11:1914.

38. Fabelo H, Ortega S, Szolna A, et al. In-vivo hyperspectral human brain image database for brain cancer detection. *IEEE Access*. 2019;7:39098–39116.

39. Tandel GS, Biswas M, Kakde OG, et al. A review on a deep learning perspective in brain cancer classification. *Cancer*. 2019;11:111.

40. Fabelo H, Ortega S, Ravi D, et al. Spatio-spectral classification of hyperspectral images for brain cancer detection during surgical operations. *PloS One*. 2018;13, e0193721.

41. Fabelo H, Halicek M, Ortega S, et al. Deep learning-based framework for in vivo identification of glioblastoma tumor using hyperspectral images of human brain. *Sensors*. 2019;19:920.

42. Fabelo H, Halicek M, Ortega S, et al. Surgical aid visualization system for glioblastoma tumor identification based on deep learning and in-vivo hyperspectral images of human patients. In: *Medical Imaging 2019: Image-Guided Procedures, Robotic Interventions, and Modeling*. vol. 10951. SPIE; 2019:254–264.

43. Ortega S, Halicek M, Fabelo H, et al. Hyperspectral imaging for the detection of glioblastoma tumor cells in H&E slides using convolutional neural networks. *Sensors*. 2020;20:1911.

44. Martinez B, Leon R, Fabelo H, et al. Most relevant spectral bands identification for brain cancer detection using hyperspectral imaging. *Sensors*. 2019;19:5481.

45. Ruiz L, Martín A, Urbanos G, et al. Multiclass brain tumor classification using hyperspectral imaging and supervised machine learning. In: *Conference on Design of Circuits and Integrated Systems (DCIS)*. IEEE; 2020:1–6.

46. Leon R, Fabelo H, Ortega S, et al. Vnir–nir hyperspectral imaging fusion targeting intraoperative brain cancer detection. *Sci Rep*. 2021;11:19696.

47. Hao Q, Pei Y, Zhou R, et al. Fusing multiple deep models for in vivo human brain hyperspectral image classification to identify glioblastoma tumor. *IEEE Trans Instrum Meas*. 2021;70:1–14.

48. Zhou X, Ma L, Brown W, et al. Automatic detection of head and neck squamous cell carcinoma on pathologic slides using polarized hyperspectral imaging and machine learning. In: Tomaszewski JE, Ward AD, eds. *Medical Imaging 2021: Digital Pathology*. vol. 11603. SPIE: International Society for Optics and Photonics; 2021:116030Q. https://doi.org/10.1117/12.2582330.

49. M. Halicek, J.V. Little, X. Wang, M. Patel, C.C. Griffith, A.Y. Chen, B. Fei, Tumor margin classification of head and neck cancer using hyperspectral imaging and convolutional neural networks, in: B. Fei, R. J. W. III (Eds.), Medical Imaging 2018: Image-Guided Procedures, Robotic Interventions, and Modeling, vol. 10576, International Society for Optics and Photonics, SPIE, 2018, p. 1057605. https://doi.org/10.1117/12.2293167.

50. Khan U, Paheding S, Elkin CP, Devabhaktuni VK. Trends in deep learning for medical hyperspectral image analysis. *IEEE Access.* 2021;9:79534–79548.
51. Ma L, Lu G, Wang D, Qin X, Chen ZG, Fei B. Adaptive deep learning for head and neck cancer detection using hyperspectral imaging. *Visual Comput Ind, Biomed Art.* 2019;2:1–12.
52. Thiem DGE, Römer P, Gielisch M, et al. Hyperspectral imaging and artificial intelligence to detect oral malignancy—part 1—automated tissue classification of oral muscle, fat and mucosa using a light-weight 6-layer deep neural network. *Head Face Med.* 2021;17:38.
53. Bengs M, Gessert N, Laffers W, et al. Spectral-spatial recurrent-convolutional networks for in-vivo hyperspectral tumor type classification. In: Martel AL, Abolmaesumi P, Stoyanov D, Mateus D, Zuluaga MA, Zhou SK, Racoceanu D, Joskowicz L, eds. *Medical Image Computing and Computer Assisted Intervention—MICCAI 2020.* Cham: Springer International Publishing; 2020:690–699.
54. Jeyaraj P, Samuel Nadar E. Computer-assisted medical image classification for early diagnosis of oral cancer employing deep learning algorithm. *J Cancer Res Clin Oncol.* 2019;145.
55. Trajanovski S, Shan C, Weijtmans PJ, de Koning SGB, Ruers TJ. Tongue tumor detection in hyperspectral images using deep learning semantic segmentation. *IEEE Trans Biomed Eng.* 2020;68:1330–1340.
56. Weijtmans P, Shan C, Tan T, Brouwer de Koning S, Ruers T. A dual stream network for tumor detection in hyperspectral images. In: *2019 IEEE 16th International Symposium on Biomedical Imaging (ISBI 2019)*; 2019:1256–1259. https://doi.org/10.1109/ISBI.2019.8759566.
57. Halicek M, Dormer JD, Little JV, et al. Hyperspectral imaging of head and neck squamous cell carcinoma for cancer margin detection in surgical specimens from 102 patients using deep learning. *Cancer.* 2019;11(9), 1367.
58. Fei B, Lu G, Wang X, et al. Label-free reflectance hyperspectral imaging for tumor margin assessment: a pilot study on surgical specimens of cancer patients. *J Biomed Opt.* 2017;22, 086009.
59. Halicek M, Lu G, Little JV, et al. Deep convolutional neural networks for classifying head and neck cancer using hyperspectral imaging. *J Biomed Opt.* 2017;22:060503.
60. Halicek M, Dormer JD, Little JV, Chen AY, Fei B. Tumor detection of the thyroid and salivary glands using hyperspectral imaging and deep learning, biomed. *Opt Express.* 2020;11:1383–1400.
61. PDQ® Adult Treatment Editorial Board. PDQ Gastric Cancer Treatment. Bethesda, MD: National Cancer Institute; 2022. https://www.cancer.gov/types/stomach/patient/stomach-treatment-pdq. [Accessed 2023-02-09].
62. Mobilia S, Sirkeci-Mergen B, Deal J, Rich TC, Leavesley SJ. Classification of hyperspectral colon cancer images using convolutional neural networks. In: *2019 IEEE Data Science Workshop (DSW)*; 2019:232–236. https://doi.org/10.1109/DSW.2019.8755582.
63. Grigoroiu A, Yoon J, Bohndiek SE. Deep learning applied to hyperspectral endoscopy for online spectral classification. *Sci Rep.* 2020;10:1–10.
64. Yahata A, Takemura H, Takamatsu T, et al. Wavelength selection of near-infrared hyperspectral imaging for gastric cancer detection. In: *2021 6th International Conference on Intelligent Informatics and Biomedical Sciences (ICIIBMS)*. vol. 6; 2021:219–223. https://doi.org/10.1109/ICIIBMS52876.2021.9651625.
65. Collins T, Maktabi M, Barberio M, et al. Automatic recognition of colon and esophagogastric cancer with machine learning and hyperspectral imaging. *Diagnostics.* 2021;11:1810.
66. Tsai T-J, Mukundan A, Chi Y-S, et al. Intelligent identification of early esophageal cancer by band-selective hyperspectral imaging. *Cancer.* 2022;14:4292.
67. Jansen-Winkeln B, Barberio M, Chalopin C, et al. Feedforward artificial neural network-based colorectal cancer detection using hyperspectral imaging: a step towards automatic optical biopsy. *Cancer.* 2021;13:967.
68. Maktabi M, Wichmann Y, Köhler H, et al. Tumor cell identification and classification in esophageal adenocarcinoma specimens by hyperspectral imaging. *Sci Rep.* 2022;12:1–14.
69. Cassata C. Types of breast cancer; 2022. URL: https://www.everydayhealth.com/breast-cancer/guide/types/.
70. Zhang Y, Wu X, He L, et al. Applications of hyperspectral imaging in the detection and diagnosis of solid tumors. *Transl Cancer Res.* 2020;9:1265.
71. Abunadi I, Senan EM. Multi-method diagnosis of blood microscopic sample for early detection of acute lymphoblastic leukemia based on deep learning and hybrid techniques. *Sensors.* 2022;22:1629.
72. Huang Q, Li W, Xie X. Convolutional neural network for medical hyperspectral image classification with kernel fusion. In: *BIBE 2018; International Conference on Biological Information and Biomedical Engineering.* VDE; 2018:1–4.
73. Wang R, He Y, Yao C, et al. Classification and segmentation of hyperspectral data of hepatocellular carcinoma samples using 1-d convolutional neural network. *Cytometry A.* 2020;97:31–38.
74. Markgraf W, Malberg H. Preoperative function assessment of ex vivo kidneys with supervised machine learning based on blood and urine markers measured during normothermic machine perfusion. *Biomedicine.* 2022;10:3055.
75. Sommer F, Sun B, Fischer J, et al. Hyperspectral imaging during normothermic machine perfusion—a functional classification of ex vivo kidneys based on convolutional neural networks. *Biomedicine.* 2022;10:397.
76. Goodfellow I, Pouget-Abadie J, Mirza M, et al. Generative adversarial nets. In: Ghahramani Z, Welling M, Cortes C, Lawrence N, Weinberger K, eds. *Advances in Neural Information Processing Systems.* vol. 27. Curran Associates, Inc.; 2014. URL: https://proceedings.neurips.cc/paper/2014/file/5ca3e9b122f61f8f06494c97b1afccf3-Paper.pdf.
77. Aburaed N, Alkhatib MQ, Marshall S, Zabalza J, Ahmad HA. Complex-valued neural network for hyperspectral single image super resolution. In: Barnett NJ, Gowen AA, Liang H, eds. *Hyperspectral Imaging and Applications.* Vol. II, vol. 12338. SPIE: International Society for Optics and Photonics; 2023:123380H. https://doi.org/10.1117/12.2645086.
78. Kiranyaz S, Ince T, Iosifidis A, Gabbouj M. Operational neural networks. *Neural Comput Applic.* 2020;32:6645–6668.

11

Global research trends of Artificial Intelligence and Machine Learning applied in medicine: A bibliometric analysis (2012–2022)

Valentina De Nicolò[a] and Davide La Torre[b,c]

[a]Department of Public Health and Infectious Disease, Sapienza University of Rome, Rome, Italy [b]SKEMA Business School, Université Côte d'Azur, Nice, France [c]Department of Oncology and Hematology-Oncology (DIPO), University of Milan, Milan, Italy

1. Introduction

The earliest work in Medical Artificial Intelligence dates to the early 1970s, about 15 years after the conation of the term "Artificial Intelligence," which occurred in 1956 at the famous Dartmouth College Conference. In the same place, 50 years later (2006), another conference took place to celebrate the Dartmouth Summer Research Project to assess how far AI has progressed and where it has gone or should have been going. However, since the 1950s, AI has been applied in medicine since physicians first attempted to improve their diagnoses using computer-aided programs.[1] Gunn, who first utilized computer analysis for abdominal pain diagnosis in 1976, has remained in history as one of the most memorable examples.[2,3]

By 1978, the leading journal in the field (Artificial Intelligence, Elsevier, Amsterdam) had devoted a special issue[4] solely to AIM research papers. Over the next decade, the community continued to grow, and with the formation of the American Association for Artificial Intelligence in 1980, a unique subgroup on medical applications (AAAI-M) was created.

Since the early 1990s, the wide range of research and development activities of Artificial Intelligence in medicine (AIM) had reached a period of "adolescence" in which interactions with the outside world were not only natural but mandatory.[5] However, the interest and advances in medical AI applications have surged in recent years, thanks to the enhanced computing power of modern computers[6,7] and the vast amount of digital data now available. As a result, AIM has come closer over the years to statistics and operations research, linguistics, communications, engineering, theoretical computer science, computer systems architecture, brain, and cognitive science,[8] until reaching the current situation in which it could be potentially applied to every type of healthcare data. Popular AI techniques include Machine Learning methods for structured data, such as Support Vector Machine and Neural Networks, and modern Deep Learning, as well as Natural Language Processing for unstructured data.[9]

AIM has branched out to various healthcare applications, such as health services management, predictive medicine, clinical decision-making, patient data, and diagnostics.[10] The further development of modern advanced "AI-based platform" (AIP) should include AI-based personalized medicine (AIPM) that allows practitioners to find cures tuned for patients.[11]

That research field can be considered significant enough to warrant bibliometric analysis since there are thousands of papers concerning AI and ML in medicine and large volumes of bibliometric data.[12] Moreover, in recent years, the bibliometric methodology has become increasingly popular due to the usefulness of bibliometric databases and software that simplify the collection and assessment of vast volumes of data, including this vibrant field of Artificial Intelligence.[13]

Bibliometrics is used to do many things: to evaluate the impact of the research output; to identify areas of research strength and weaknesses; to find out potential research collaboration opportunities; to identify research trends and growth of knowledge, forecasting future publishing trends; to determine authorship and its trends in documents on different fields; to predict the productivity of publishers, individual authors, organizations, and countries; and to identify journals with the most significant impact in various research areas.

2. Methods

The data source was The Science Citation Index Expanded (SCI-Expanded) of Clarivate Analytics' Web of Science Core Collection (WoSCC). This platform applies a strict screening process according to Bradford's law, which states that bibliometrics includes only notable academic publications from many areas. The SCI-E (Science Citation Index Expanded), as WoSCC's journal citation subdatabase, is a multidisciplinary comprehensive indexing database covering the field of natural science, with more than 9200 global significant authoritative journals encompassing 178 topic categories.

2.1 Search strategy

To guarantee that no data updates were made, the examination of the information of papers concerning Artificial Intelligence in the field of medicine and healthcare and the research of databases were conducted and finished in one day. Articles' titles, keywords, abstracts, authors, institutions, and reference data were acquired and archived in plain text format.

The research formula was the following:

1#: (((TS = (medicine) OR TS = (healthcare)) AND DT = (Article OR Review) AND LA = (English) AND DOP = (2012/2022))) [486,420 results].
2#: (((TS = (artificial intelligence) OR TS = (machine learning) OR TS = (deep learning)) AND DT = (Article OR Review) AND LA = (English) AND DOP = (2012/2022))) [269,100 results].
3#: 1#: AND 2# [11,357 results].

This research was conducted on October 15, 2022, in the WoS. From a total of 11,357 papers registered between June 2012 and October 2022 in the WoS SCI-Expanded, 2834 have been included in the following bibliometric analysis.

2.2 Screening strategy

In this research, all journal papers about Artificial Intelligence and Machine Learning in medicine applications and healthcare were included for screening. The research analysis papers were limited to those that (1) focused on healthcare or medical applications, excluding everything related to pediatrics; (2) involved Artificial Intelligence, Machine Learning, or Deep Learning technologies; (3) were published in review articles, articles, peer-reviewed journals, conference proceedings, and early access articles. Books and book chapters were not included in the following bibliometric analysis because, for the leading-edge research in the field and the rapid development of these technologies, it should not have been updated.

The preliminary screening procedure categorized papers into includes, excludes, or ensures. Then, articles marked as ensured were screened for a second time according to the practical inclusion and exclusion criteria and discussed until a consensus was reached. After that, the set of papers was screened for title and abstract. Finally, a full-text screening was done only when necessary, according to the bibliometric analysis methodology.

According to the screening criteria, after removing duplicate and inapplicable papers, 8439 were excluded, either because they did not involve Artificial Intelligence technologies or did not focus on medicine or healthcare application. Finally, as the strategy flowchart, 2834 publications were gathered from the Web of Science (SCI-E), panning the previous 10 years. These papers have been included in further bibliometric analysis (Fig. 1).

2.3 Bibliometric analysis

Bibliometric analysis is a rigorous, popular, and measurable method for exploring and analyzing large volumes of scientific data and identifying developmental trends in particular fields. Its ability to handle large databases makes it

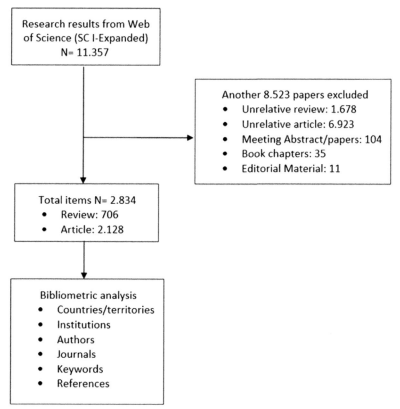

FIG. 1 Flowchart detailing the paper collection and screening process.

possible to get insights from a large corpus. Nowadays, bibliometric analysis is getting very popular and has gained a reputation as a legitimate scientific tool with applications in various areas[14] and has proven to be a beneficial method to provide objective, quantifiable, and reproducible data. Researchers have classified bibliometric tools into two categories: performance analysis and science mapping,[15] as shown in Fig. 2. This study takes advantage of both sets of tools.

We rigorously perform this bibliometric analysis according to the bibliometric methodology published in different guidelines and overviews like "How to conduct a bibliometric analysis: An overview and guidelines,"[16] published on September 2021 in the Journal of Business Research, to compute the growth rate of publications, characteristics of research activities (topics and keywords), publication patterns (countries and journals), and research hotspot tendencies in Artificial Intelligence and Machine Learning applied to medicine and healthcare.

2.4 Software tools for conducting science mapping bibliometric analysis

Different kinds of software were provided to analyze the data and generate visualization knowledge maps. We used the tools and the most employed bibliometric analysis utilized in other important publications.[17–22]

- Microsoft Excel 2019: To analyze and export the files of top-cited or productive authors, countries/regions, publications, journals, and institutions. H-index (a hybrid index proposed by Hirsch) was used to evaluate academic achievements.[23]
- CiteSpace: Is an information visualization tool in the domain of knowledge graphs developed at Drexel University (USA)[17] that allows the analysis and visualization of trends and patterns in a research area[24,25] and facilitates the analysis of emerging trends in a knowledge domain. The version used in this research is Version 6.1.R3 (64-bit) (updated on September 22, 2022).
- VOSviewer: Is a scientific knowledge graph application that can be launched directly from the web page, developed by the Centre for Science and Technology Studies (CWTS) at Leiden University (Netherlands). This software can depict structure, coordination, progression, and other features of knowledge fields by constructing linkages, visually analyzing literary knowledge items and visualizing bibliometric networks with individual publications, researchers, or journals and based on co-citation, bibliographic coupling, or co-authorship relations.[26] A text mining

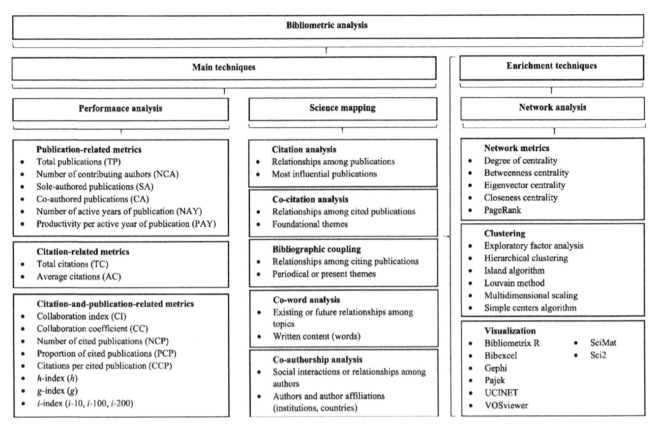

FIG. 2   The bibliometric analysis toolbox.

functionality makes it possible to build co-occurrence networks of important terms extracted from a corpus of scientific literature. Moreover, it is possible to study whether there is a link between two items through the curved lines representing the interlinks: more robust is the link and higher is the positive arithmetic value.

- Biblioshiny: Is the Bibliometrix (R language programmed) web-based graphical interface developed by Massimo Aria and Corrado Cuccurullo from the University of Naples and University of Campania Luigi Vanvitelli (Italy).[27] Biblioshiny's possible analysis is subdivided into seven categories: (1) Overview, (2) Sources, (3) Authors, (4) Documents, (5) Conceptual structures, (6) Intellectual structure, and (7) Social structure. This platform contains the most extensive set of techniques implemented and, with the easiness of its interface, it could be an excellent software for practitioners.[28]
- Altmetrics: Is an additional statistic-free browser plugin (https://www. altmetric.com/), introduced in 2012, even if Jason Priem formally used the term Altmetric two years before, in 2010. It stands for "alternative metrics" and is different from traditional metrics like citation count and h-index. When available and accessible, it provides the popularity of the research articles or items and is used to monitor reader behaviors and interactions with content and social media.[29,30] It includes the social media presence on Facebook, Twitter, LinkedIn, and blogs, as well as views, counts, reads online, and downloads mentioned on different new trends. Altmetrics allows the performing of various functions:
  - I. Provide an early indicator of the newly published article.
  - II. How a publication performs after publishing. In contrast to the traditional metric, it provides the instant performance of an article and research items after publishing.
  - III. Social Media popularity (Online News media, Blogs, Tweets, etc.).
  - IV. Online reference manager: chase and follow up the citation counts of the articles and discussions.
  - V. Measurement of traditional metric.

In this research, it is used to calculate the Altmetrics as "Almetric Attention Scores," an important score that could be applied to research promotion and tenure extension, funding/grant applications, and for ranking newly published articles. This score is essential for researchers because it provides the statistical data of published articles and allows them to understand how many times they have been downloaded; who is reading the work (on ResearchGate,

Mendeley and other bookmarking sites, etc.); if there are other researchers of the same discipline or in other disciplines commenting on it; how many times were they shared (on a blog post or websites); and which countries are looking at the research.

3. Results

The analysis covers 10 years of scientific production (2012–22). We gathered 2834 documents from the Web of Science Core Collection (WoSCC) database, comprising 2128 articles and 706 reviews, published in 518 sources consisting mainly of scientific journals. The number of keywords Plus (ID) used was 4754, and the number of Author's keywords (DE) was 6343, almost twice and half times the number of articles.

3.1 Global trends of publication and citation

As of the search date (October 15, 2022), all papers have been cited 33,738 times, with an h-index of 91 and an average citation count per item of 15.7. The most significant increase in published articles has occurred in the last 3 years, with a peak in 2021. On average, each article was written by five authors (5.2), and the Collaboration Index (CI), which is designed as total authors of multi-author articles/total multi-author articles,[31] is 5.36. During the earlier years analyzed, the number of published papers was small (only 224/2834, equal to only 8% until 2017). Fig. 3 shows that since 2017, Artificial Intelligence research in Medicine has continuously expanded, year after year, and the number of publications has steeply increased between 2020 and 2022, accounting for almost 77% (2090/2720) of all included papers and reaching the peak in 2021 with 820 papers. From 2012 to 2022, the average annual growth rate of scientific research papers on medicine and healthcare-related AI research was 53.15%, decreasing by 4.76% between 2021 and 2022. The phenomena demonstrate that the application of Artificial Intelligence and Machine Learning in medical research is gaining traction, and the quality of papers in the field has been improved (Fig. 4).

3.2 Sources impact and dynamics

All the papers were published in 518 journals with a not significantly concentrated distribution. Table 1 shows TP=total publication in the AI field; TC=total citations in the AI field; CPP=citation per AI publications; SNIP=source normalized impact per paper (2021); and SJR=Scimago journal ranking (2021) of the first 10 sources for the number of total publications. The mean number of publications is distributed in three sources: "Medical Physics," with 121 articles, is at the top of the three most productive journals, followed by "Diagnostics," with 91 articles and "Journal of healthcare engineering," with 90 articles. Also, "Cancer," with 78 articles and "Npj digital medicine," with 75, are important sources. The indicator citation per publication (CPP) was presented in this study to assess the impact of article output per year for different countries, institutes, and authors worldwide. The journal's impact factor is checked in the 2022 edition of the *Journal Citation Reports*. Furthermore, the total number of citations

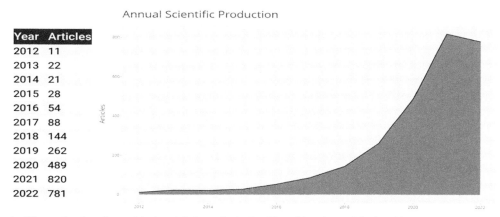

Year	Articles
2012	11
2013	22
2014	21
2015	28
2016	54
2017	88
2018	144
2019	262
2020	489
2021	820
2022	781

FIG. 3 Annual scientific production chart with the global trend of scientific publications of the last 10 years.

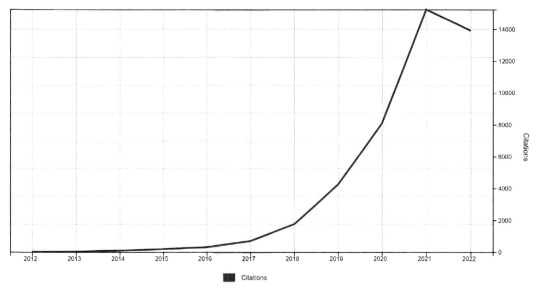

FIG. 4   Bar chart showing the growing number of citations about Artificial Intelligence and Machine Learning in Medicine in the last 10 publication years.

TABLE 1   Source impact information.

Rank	Journal Title	Country	TP (AI)	TC (AI)	CPP (AI)	IF (2021)	CiteScore	SNIP	SJR	PY start	JCI category	H-index
1	Medical Physics	USA	121	4020	33	4506	6.7	1.523	1.174	2012	Radiology and medical imaging	31
2	Diagnostics	Switzerland	91	590	6.5	3992	2.4	11	0.658	2020	General and Internal medicine	13
3	Journal of Healthcare Engineering	England	90	549	6	3822	2.9	1.449	0.684	2014	Healthcare sciences and services	12
4	Cancers	Switzerland	78	392	5	6575	5.8	1.265	1.349	2019	Oncology	10
5	Npj Digital Medicine	England	75	3745	50	15,357	11.8	3.717	3.326	2018	Medical informatics -Healthcare sciences & services	28
6	Journal of personalized medicine	Switzerland	66	197	3	3508	1.8	0.887	0.757	2018	Healthcare sciences & services – General & Internal medicine	7
7	BMC Medical Informatics and decision-making	England	64	503	8	3298	4.6	1.387	0.833	2012	Medical informatics	12
8	Artificial Intelligence in medicine	Netherlands	59	708	12	7011	10.4	224	1.497	2013	Biomedical Engineering-Medical informatic-Computer science, Artificial Intelligence	15
9	Neural computing and applications	England	59	585	10	5102	8.7	1.653	1.072	2018	Computer science, Artificial Intelligence	13
10	Frontiers in Oncology	Switzerland	56	756	13.5	5738	4.5	1.191	1.291	2016	Oncology	15

in "Medical Physics" was 4020, much higher than in other publications. On the other hand, the most locally cited sources were "PLoS ONE," "Scientific Reports," "Radiology," and "The New England Journal of Medicine."

3.3 Document's citation analysis

Citation analysis is a scientific mapping method based on the fact that citations reflect intellectual linkages between publications, formed when one publication cites the other.[32] Therefore, the number of citations is the most objective and straightforward means to measure the impact of a publication.[33] The ranks of research impact of the different countries and journals were also given based on the citation rates. Table 2 lists the 20 most cited articles in the field of AI in medicine and healthcare. All the papers were published before the SARS-CoV-2 pandemic, and most of them

TABLE 2 Most 20 global cited documents.

Document	Title	Year	Local citations	Global citations
Deo, 2015, Circulation[34]	Machine Learning in Medicine	2015	70	981
Jiang, 2017. Stroke Vasc Neurol[9]	Artificial Intelligence in healthcare: past, present and future	2017	63	815
Rajkomar A, 2018, Npj Digit Med[35]	Scalable and accurate deep learning with electronic health records	2018	46	782
Johnson, 2018, J Am Coll Cardiol[36]	Artificial Intelligence in Cardiology	2018	44	336
Krittanawong C, 2017, J Am Coll Cardiol[37]	Artificial Intelligence in Precision Cardiovascular Medicine	2017	40	334
Motwani M, 2017, Eur Heart J[38]	Machine learning for prediction of all-cause mortality in patients with suspected coronary artery disease: a 5-year multicentre prospective registry analysis	2017	36	334
Zhang J, 2018, Circulation[39]	Fully Automated Echocardiogram Interpretation in Clinical Practice	2018	35	288
Madani A, 2018, Npj Digit Med[40]	Fast and accurate view classification of echocardiograms using deep learning	2018	29	219
Lee Jg, 2017, Korean J Radiol[41]	Deep Learning in Medical Imaging: General Overview	2017	27	460
Bi Wl 2019, Ca-Cancer J Clin[42]	Artificial Intelligence in cancer imaging: Clinical challenges and applications	2019	26	479
Abramoff Md, 2018, Npj Digit Med[43]	Pivotal trial of an autonomous AI-based diagnostic system for detection of diabetic retinopathy in primary care offices	2018	24	422
Shameer K, 2018, Heart[44]	Machine learning in cardiovascular medicine: are we there yet?	2018	24	183
Lundervold, 2019. Z Med Phys[45]	An overview of deep learning in medical imaging focusing on MRI	2019	23	616
Antropova N, 2017, Med Phys[46]	A deep feature fusion methodology for breast cancer diagnosis demonstrated on three imaging modality datasets	2017	19	184
Park Sh, 2018, Radiology[47]	Methodologic Guide for Evaluating Clinical Performance and Effect of Artificial Intelligence Technology for Medical Diagnosis and Prediction	2018	19	309
Miller Dd, 2018, Am J Med[48]	Artificial Intelligence in Medical Practice: The Question to the Answer?	2018	18	226
Sidey-Gibbons Jam, 2019, Bmc Med Res Methodol[49]	Machine learning in medicine: a practical introduction	2019	18	250
Cikes M, 2019, Eur J Heart Fail[50]	Machine learning-based phenogrouping in heart failure to identify responders to cardiac resynchronization therapy	2019	18	91
Han X, 2017, Med Phys[51]	MR-based synthetic CT generation using a deep convolutional neural network method	2017	16	360
Ibragimov B, 2017, Med Phys[52]	Segmentation of organs-at-risks in head and neck CT images using convolutional neural networks	2017	16	279

mainly focused on cardiovascular medicine (6/20) and Medical Imaging (6/20). The mean citation count of the 20 most globally cited articles was 397.4 (range, 91–981).

The first in the list[34] was written by Rahul C. Deo, belonging to the Cardiovascular Research Institute, Department of Medicine and Institute for Human Genetics, University of California, San Francisco.

3.4 Contributions of top productive countries/regions

The first country in the ranking is the USA, with major studies and projects related to Artificial Intelligence and Machine Learning in medicine and healthcare. Following for dissemination of articles, there are China, England, Germany, and Italy (Fig. 5).

It is evident how the theme is developed in countries located on different continents, from the West to the East, with little evidence of African nations and developing countries. The most cited countries, as shown in the following figure, are the United States and China, with Korea in the third position (Figs. 6 and 7).

Table 3 shows that the United States ranked top in overall citations (18,927 times), outnumbering China, which ranks second (4716 times). Norway has, instead, the highest average citations.

3.5 Cooperation and networking between countries

The red lines on the map in Fig. 8 represent the existence of cooperation in research with other nations worldwide. All countries with more publications, especially those most frequently mentioned, have cooperated closely with other countries.

The most productive countries for Single Country Publications (SCPs) and Multiple Country Publications (MCPs) are the USA and China, as shown in Fig. 9.

VOSviewer was applied to examine the collaboration, as shown in the following figure. Setting the minimum number of documents of a country at higher than 5, of the 114 nations, 65 met the thresholds and were included. Fig. 10 shows the map of the clustered collaboration network analysis of the most productive countries. Following figure shows 886 links with different collaboration clusters:

- Purple: the USA, Germany, Switzerland, Israel, South Africa.
- Red: China, India, South Korea, Saudi Arabia, Japan, Singapore, and other eastern and African countries.
- Green: England, Italy, Netherlands, Spain, Belgium, Greece, Hungary, and some Balkan countries.
- Yellow: Canada, Australia, northern European countries (Sweden, Norway, Denmark, Poland, and Finland), Ireland, and Scotland.

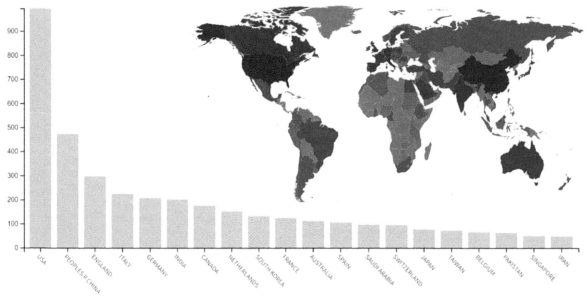

FIG. 5   Most 20 countries for scientific production over the last 10 years.

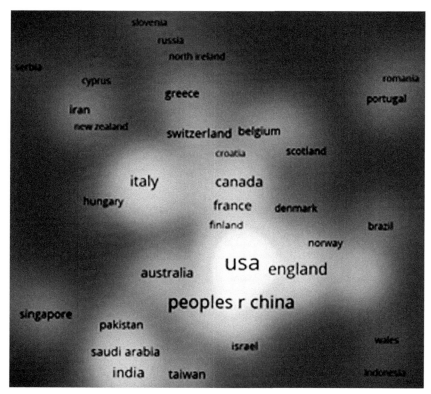

FIG. 6 Countries' density visualization with VOSviewer.

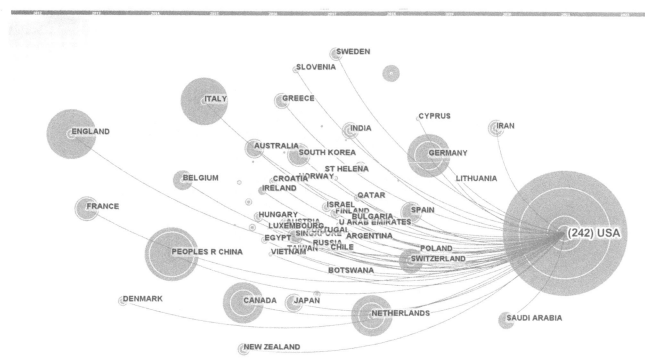

FIG. 7 Countries' citation burst with CiteSpace.

TABLE 3   Average article citations.

Country	Total citations	Average article citations
USA	18,927	26.397
China	4716	12.378
Korea	2110	21.313
United Kingdom	2041	14.076
Germany	1823	16.133
Italy	1578	10.450
Canada	1186	12.227
Netherlands	905	15.339
India	877	7.189
France	762	11.373
Spain	686	12.035
Norway	638	127.600
Australia	634	10.567
Austria	634	45.286
Switzerland	615	16.184
Japan	599	11.302
Hungary	439	48.778
Malaysia	397	18.905
Singapore	352	12.571
Saudi Arabia	321	8.447

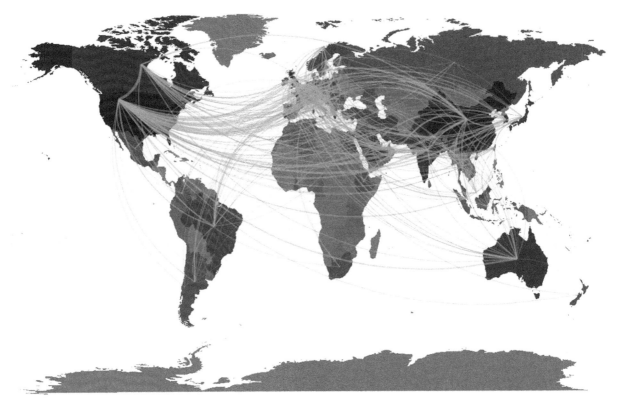

FIG. 8   Countries' collaboration map.

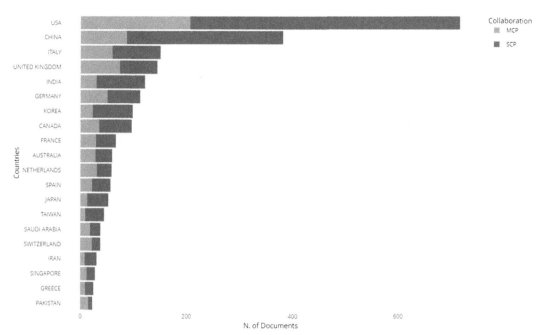

FIG. 9 Most productive countries' chart, divided by Single Country Publications (SCPs) and Multiple Country Publications (MCPs).

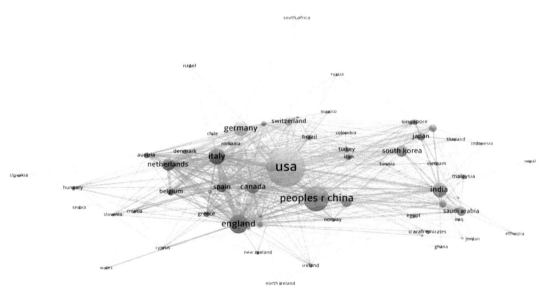

FIG. 10 Bibliometric map of co-authorship from VOSviewer using countries.

– Blue: France, Switzerland, Portugal, Turkey, Iran, Tunisia, and South American countries (Brazil, Colombia, Mexico, and Argentina).

The strength of collaboration and co-authorship between countries is given by the thickness of the lines that connect the nodes. The thicker the lines are, and more robust the collaboration between nations. Closer the two countries are located in VOSviewer and stronger is their relatedness (Fig. 11).

The top six TLS (total link strength) countries were the United States, England, Germany, Italy, Netherlands, and China. The United States had the closest collaboration with England (link strength: 96) and China (link strength: 75). Other countries' cooperation was not so strong.

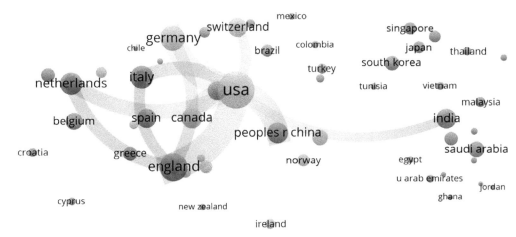

FIG. 11 The countries/regions' citation network visualization map was generated by using VOSviewer. The thickness of the lines reflected the citation strength.

3.6 Analysis of institution and co-institution

Of the 4629 organizations, we can see in the figure later the first 50 that played an active role in AI applied research, with more than 17 publications, classified for the number of citations. Although the Harvard Medical School (HMS), in close collaboration with the Massachusetts General Hospital, is the Institution with more publications, the University of California, San Francisco (UCSF), is that with more citations (Figs. 12 and 13).

3.7 Bibliometric analysis of authorship and co-authorship

3.7.1 Most relevant authors

Analyzing the data in Table 4, Zhang Yi is the author with more publications in the AIM field (36 articles). Li Juan and Li Xiaogang are the following authors with significant publications, 29 each one, followed by a long list of Chinese authors with 20–30 publications for each.

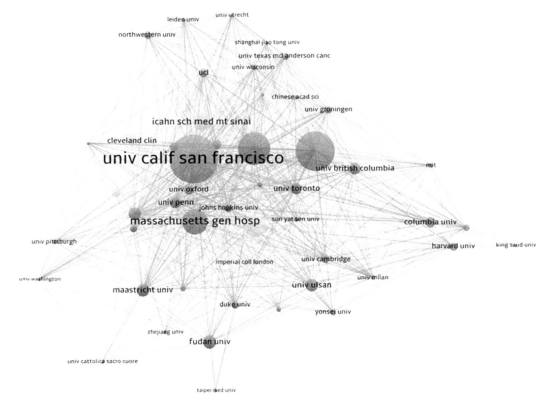

FIG. 12 First 50 institutions for the weight of citations using VOSviewer.

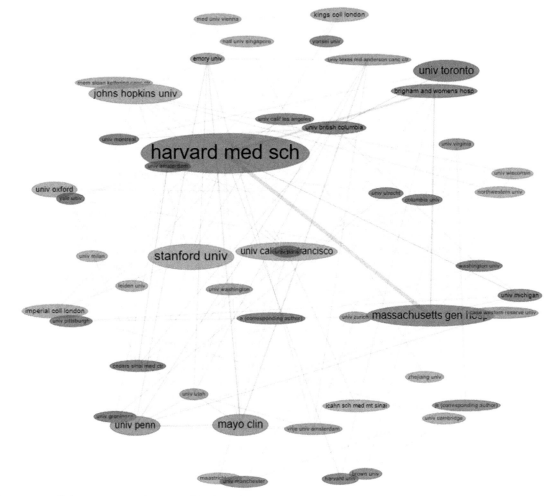

FIG. 13 Institution collaboration network using Biblioshiny for Bibliometrix.

TABLE 4 Top 20 authors by the number of articles.

Authors	Publications
Zhang Y	36
Li J	29
Li X	29
Wang Y	28
Li Y	27
Wang J	26
Chen Y	25
Zhang X	24
Zhang J	23
Liu X	22
Liu Y	22
Wang Z	22
Liu Z	21
Zhang Z	21
Wang X	20
Zhang H	19
Zhang L	19
Wang L	18
Chen J	17
Liu H	17

TABLE 5 Top 20 authors' impact.

Author	h_index	g_index	m_index	TC	NP	PY_start
Zhang Y	11	34	1222	1197	35	2014
Li J	10	22	1429	499	29	2016
Li X	9	19	1.5	386	27	2017
Wang Y	7	27	1167	960	27	2017
Li Y	9	24	1.5	591	27	2017
Wang J	10	21	1429	453	26	2016
Chen Y	7	17	0.875	315	25	2015
Zhang X	8	12	0,889	154	24	2014
Zhang J	8	20	1	429	22	2015
Liu X	8	22	0.889	1052	22	2014
Liu Y	8	19	1333	390	21	2017
Wang Z	8	22	0.889	695	22	2014
Liu Z	8	18	1333	329	21	2017
Zhang Z	8	15	1143	250	20	2016
Wang X	8	13	1143	183	20	2016
Zhang H	6	18	1.2	328	19	2018
Zhang L	9	13	1.8	174	19	2018
Wang L	8	17	1333	332	17	2017
Chen J	6	17	1	356	17	2017
Liu H	7	16	1.75	256	17	2019

Some authors have been primary authors, while most have been co-authors.

In Table 5, we can study the impact of each author through the total number of publications, the total number of citations, and three different indexes: H-index,[53] g-index,[54] and m-index.[55]

The author with the most significant impact is Zhang Yi, a senior lecturer at the UTS Australian Artificial Intelligence Institute as an expert in bibliometrics, intelligent bibliometrics, technology management, and tech mining.

The authors with more citations are as follows: Yann LeCun, Silver Professor of the Courant Institute of Mathematical Sciences at New York University; Leo Breiman, a distinguished statistician at the University of California, Berkeley; Andre Esteva, CEO of Artera and previously Head of Medical AI of Salesforce Research; Philippe Lambin, Professor at the Universities of Maastricht and Eindhoven.

Empirical data suggest that influential authors, as measured by the total number of citations and the number of citations per paper, are often those who either lead a field and stay productive throughout their careers or invent a method applicable in various research areas. This pattern has been observed in other studies, such that senior and productive authors will drive the productivity of their collaborators.[56]

3.7.2 Analysis of the co-authorship

To create the map in VOSviewer, we chose 2 as value, both for the minimum number of documents and for the minimum number of citations of an author. Of the 15854 authors, 1326 met the thresholds (Fig. 14).

The most extensive set of related items consisted of 552 because some of these still needed to connect in the network. Gichoya and Judy Wawira, from Emory University, a private research University in Atlanta in Georgia, had nine papers and the most links (27 for accuracy). The total link strength was 85 (Fig. 15).

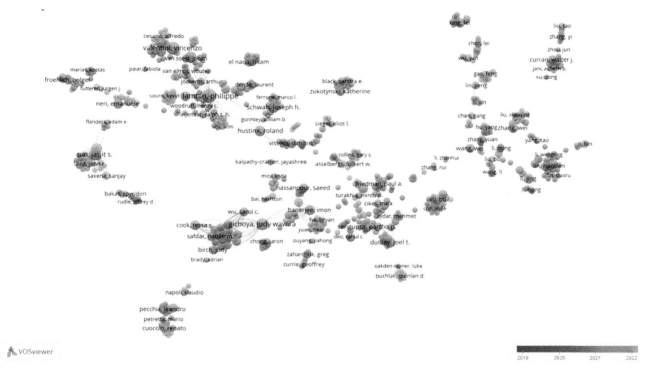

FIG. 14 Bibliometric map of co-authorship from VOSviewer using author names with two as the minimum number of documents and citations of an author.

FIG. 15 Author collaboration network using Biblioshiny for Bibliometrix.

3.8 Analysis of the bibliographic coupling and co-citation

This analysis can provide a representation of the state-of-the-art of research field. It focuses on dividing publications into thematic clusters, based on shared references,[57] formed based on the citing publications and therefore updated.

We did the analysis using VOSviewer, where different colors indicate different research areas. The size of the circles represented the counts of co-citations. The distance between the two circles showed their correlation.

Putting 5 in VOSviewer as the minimum number document citations, eleven clusters were obtained. Among them, the three most significant were as follows:

- Cluster 1 (shown in red) with 446 items and "Machine learning in Medicine" by Deo, Rahul C. (2015),[34] the item with more citations (978);
- Cluster 2 (shown in green) with 182 items and "An overview of deep learning in medical imaging focus on MRI" by Lunrvold et al. (2019),[45] the article with more citations (616);
- Cluster 3 (shown in blue) with 152 items and "Artificial Intelligence in cardiology," by Johson, Kipp W. Et al. (2018),[36] the publication with more citations (335) (Fig. 16).

Proceeding with the bibliographic coupling of source analysis, choosing 5 as the minimum number of documents of a source, among the 518 sources, 123 met the thresholds. The analysis highlighted four clusters with 42, 33, 29, and 19 items from the largest to the smallest, as shown in Fig. 17.

Putting 20 as the minimum number of citations of a cited reference, among the 120216 cited references, 183 met the threshold. Five clusters of the cited references were obtained by bibliometric analysis. The top three clusters are shown in red, green, and blue. Between the network, the publication with more citations and the strongest total link was that published in Nature in 2017 about deep neural networks for the classification of skin cancer.[58]

Looking the Attention Score, that is a weighted count that represents a weighted count of the amount of attention for the research output, with an Altmetric Attention score of 2930, the article "Dermatologist-level classification of skin cancer with deep neural networks"[58] by Andre Esteva of the Department of Electrical Engineering, Stanford

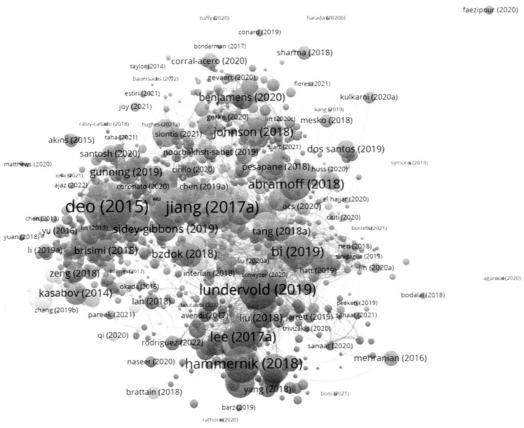

FIG. 16   Bibliometric analysis of the bibliographic coupling of documents.

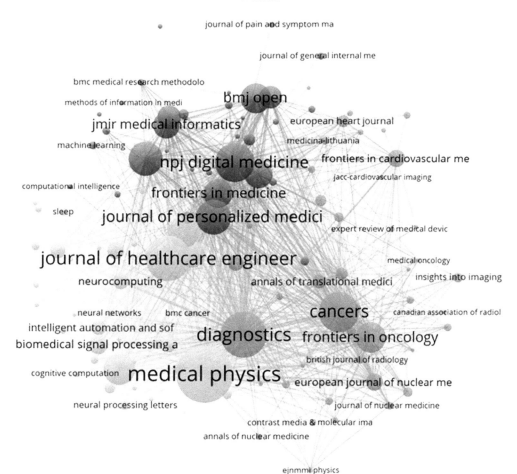

FIG. 17   Bibliometric analysis of the bibliographic coupling of sources.

University, California, USA, is the most influential in social media and other networks, having been referenced by 6182 Mendeley, 2284 tweeters, and 44 Facebook pages.

As regards the analysis of co-citation of cited sources, putting 20 as the limit of citations of a source, 1088 met the threshold among 25,701 total sources. The most significant clusters of cited sources included 316 and 251 items, respectively. The representative journals were the International Journal of Scientific Reports and PLoS One, as shown in Fig. 18.

3.9 Clustering analysis using CiteSpace

According to the CiteSpace v. 6.1.R3 analysis results, the network consists of eleven clusters that help to study the hotspots and cutting-edge content of the applications of Artificial Intelligence in medicine and healthcare in recent years. The Modularity Q of 0.6975 and the mean Silhouette S of 0.8656 indicated a quite good clustering effect and strong network homogeneity. The clusters were labeled using subject categories and fields of study. The major citing article in the first cluster follows: An overview of deep learning in medical imaging focusing on MRI[45]; Radiomics: data are also images[59] in #1; Standardized data collection to build prediction models in oncology: a prototype for rectal cancer[60] in #2; e-Doctor: machine learning and the future of medicine[61] in #3; Deep learning for cardiovascular medicine: a practical primer[62] in #4; Artificial Intelligence in cardiovascular imaging: state-of-the-art and implications for the imaging cardiologist[63] in #5; Artificial Intelligence: reshaping the practice of radiological sciences in the 21st century[64] in #6; Artificial Intelligence-enhanced electrocardiography in cardiovascular disease management[65] in #7; Canadian association of radiologists white paper on Artificial Intelligence in radiology[66] in #8; Deep pain: exploiting long short-term memory networks for facial expression classification[67] in #9; and An efficient sleep scoring system based on EEG (electroencephalography) signal using complex-valued machine learning algorithms[68] in #10.

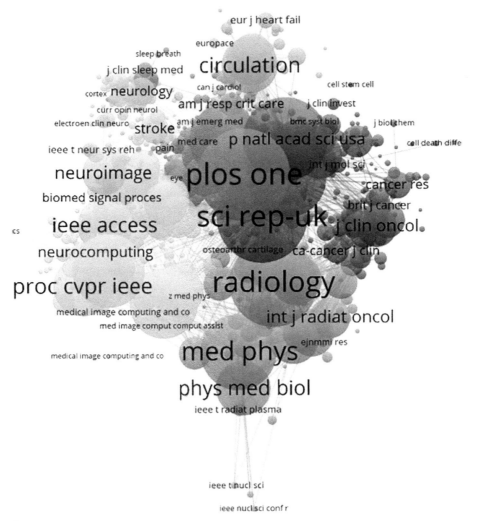

FIG. 18   Co-citation of sources.

3.10 Analysis of keywords and co-occurrence

A bibliometric analysis of the keywords in publications on Artificial Intelligence and Machine Learning in medicine and healthcare was done using the software VOSviewer. This analysis is essential to determine research trends and identify any gaps and fields of interest as research areas. Keywords provided by the paper's authors and occurred more than five times in the WoS core database were enrolled in the final analysis. Of the 6391 keywords, 348 met the threshold. The following figure shows the keywords in the top 50 positions. It is noteworthy to mention that this study considered author keywords, not index keywords (Figs. 19 and 20).

Fig. 21 is an example of co-word (keyword co-occurrence) network visualization in VOSviewer. Each node in the network represents a keyword. The colors represent a thematic cluster, wherein links and nodes can be utilized to interpret the theme's (cluster's) coverage of topics (nodes) and relationships between the topic (nodes) manifesting under that theme (cluster). In particular:

- node's size indicates the occurrence of the keyword (i.e., the number of times that the keyword occurs);
- the link between the nodes stands for the co-occurrence between keywords (i.e., keywords that co-occur or occur together);
- link's thickness represents the occurrence of co-occurrence between keywords (i.e., the number of times that the keywords co-occur or occur together); the occurrence more significant of the keyword increases with the increasing node's size and thicker is the link between nodes, more significant is the occurrence of co-occurrences between keywords. The keywords that appeared most were "Machine Learning" (total link strength 2106) with 319 links, "Artificial Intelligence" (total link strength 1532) with 272 links and "Deep Learning" (total link strength 1164) with

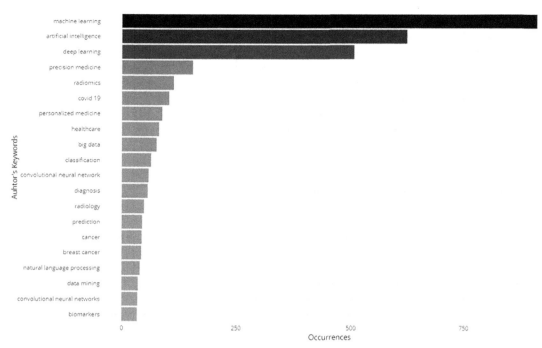

FIG. 19   The 20 most relevant words.

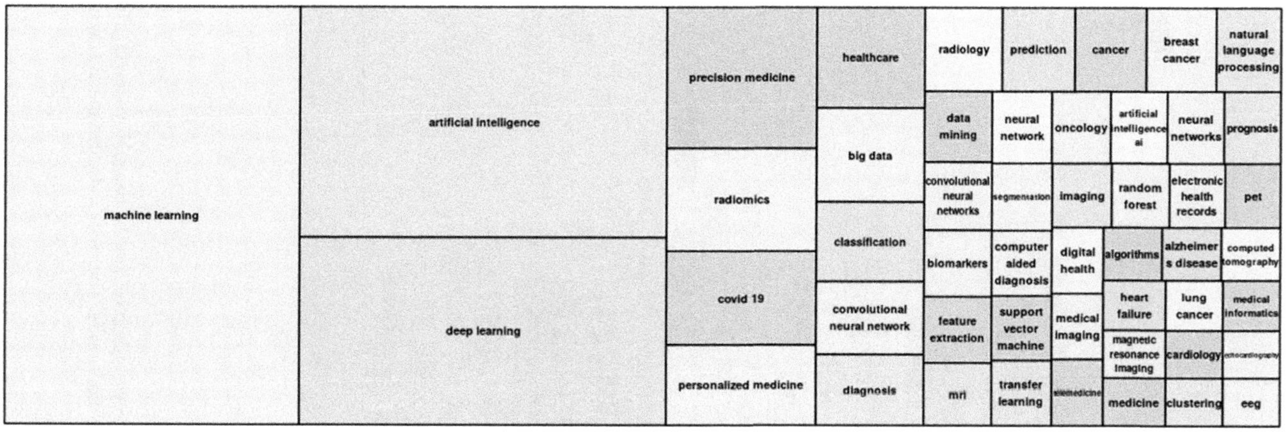

FIG. 20   TreeMap of the 50 most frequent author keywords and their relationship. The TreeMap highlights, also the combination of possible keywords.

252 links. The keyword "Machine Learning" is generally more connected with the other main keywords than "Artificial Intelligence," with stronger links. This applies to the following keywords: "Precision medicine" (81 VS 51), "Personalized medicine" (46 VS 27), "Radiomics" (49 VS 31), and "COVID-19" (23 VS 21). Only one of the most common keywords, "Radiology," has stronger links with "Artificial Intelligence" than "Machine Learning" (21 VS 36). "Machine Learning," "Artificial Intelligence," "Deep Learning," "Precision medicine," and "Radiomics" had frequencies of more than 100 times, and "COVID-19," "Personalized medicine," "Healthcare," "Big Data," "Classification," "convolutional neural network," and "Diagnosis" were reasonably high with frequencies of over 50 times.

The frequency of occurrence is connected to the size of the nodes. The curves between the nodes represent their co-occurrence in the same publication. The distance between the nodes gives the number of co-occurrence of keywords. Shorter is the distance between two nodes, and more significant is the number of co-occurrences of the two keywords. Link strength in co-occurrence analysis stands for the number of journals in which two keywords appear together.[69]

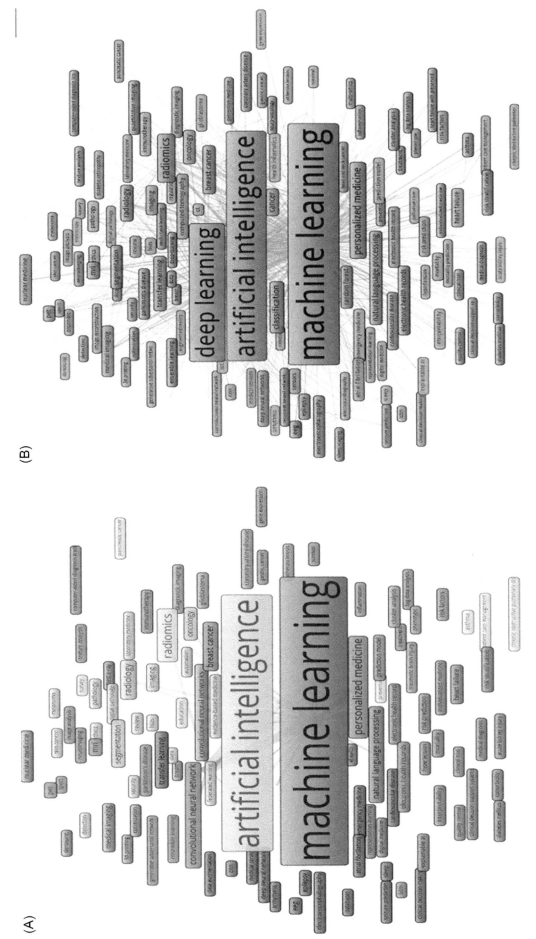

FIG. 21 (A) The network visualization map of the 348 author keywords generated by using VOSviewer. Minimum occurrences of a keyword are set to five. (B) A screenshot of the bibliometric map created based on author keywords co-occurrence with overlay visualization mode. The color indicates the average publication year of the documents in which a keyword occurs.

(Continued)

(C)

Keyword	Occurrences	Total link strength ∨
machine learning	898	2106
artificial intelligence	617	1532
deep learning	496	1164
precision medicine	155	419
radiomics	111	320
big data	76	258
covid-19	99	255
personalized medicine	88	252
healthcare	81	217
diagnosis	56	177
radiology	49	162
classification	64	159
convolutional neural network	59	146
breast cancer	43	122
prediction	45	119
oncology	30	115
cancer	44	110
data mining	36	107
feature extraction	31	98

FIG. 21, CONT'D (C) First 20 keywords for occurrences.

A word cloud was also created to show the frequency of the keywords, where the font size represents the frequency of occurrence (Fig. 22). For example, "Artificial Intelligence" was the most frequent keyword, followed by "Deep learning" and "Precision Medicine."

3.11 Bibliometric analysis of themes and trend topics

Radiomics and precision medicine have remained research hotspots through 2022 and might be research hotspots in the near future.

Radiomics, presented for the first time by Lambin et al.,[70] aims to capture additional information via advanced feature analysis from medical imaging and involves the high-throughput extraction of image features from large numbers of medical images. Its workflow comprises different steps: imaging data collection and preprocessing, identification and segmentation of the region/volume of interest, feature extraction and selection, model establishment, and validation.[71,72] Generally, radiomics extracts large volumes of quantitative data from digital images and amalgamates these with patient and clinical data into shared databases that combinate genetic and radiomic data. An example of this application is in oncology, where radiogenomics integrates, into mathematical modelling, large volumes of quantitative significant imaging phenotypes, extracted from medical digital images, and tumour genetic profiles, derived from sequencing, together with clinical–epidemiological data. This methodology shows excellent prospects in precision medicine.[73]

The term "precision medicine" identifies an approach that uses a person's genetics, environment, and lifestyle to help determine the best approach to prevent or treat a disease.[74] It has become very popular recently, fueled by scientific and political perspectives.[62,74–78] It has superseded the term "personalized medicine,"[75] developing a customized medicine or treatment for providing better treatment to patients,[79] incorporating a wide array of individual data, including clinical, lifestyle, genetic, and further biomarker information.[80]

(A)

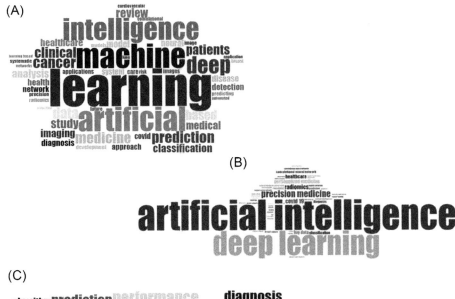

(B)

(C)

FIG. 22   (A) Word Cloud of the most frequent 50 author's keywords. (B) Word Cloud for the most frequent 50 words in the titles. (C) Word Cloud for the most frequent 50 words in the abstracts.

Precision medicine requires AI to provide personalized healthcare[81] in a continuous process of feedback loops that newly gained knowledge improving accuracy.[80]

Rapid advances in computational power; massive, linked databases; plummeting costs of genetic testing; and new targeted therapies are making it increasingly possible to prevent or treat illnesses based on an individual patient's characteristics.[82]

In Fig. 23, we see a dendrogram representing the hierarchical order and the relationship between keywords generated by hierarchical clustering. The representation denotes the weights for each object according to the clusters and measures the links. Each object refers to a set of keywords associated with Artificial Intelligence and Machine Learning in medicine and healthcare.

4. Discussion

To the best of our knowledge, this study cannot be considered the first intensive global mapping and analysis of scientific research on AI in health and medicine because other studies before analyzed this topic.[83–85] In the past 10 years, the exponential growth of computing power and data storage capacity[86–88] rapidly grew scientific literature on AI. The United States and China are the most significant contributors to overall AI research worldwide.[87] The top 20 authors by the number of articles have all Chinese origins. However, the same thing cannot be said regarding the top 20 authors by citations. China came late in the field of Artificial Intelligence in medicine, and this can be the reason why the number of citations per paper by Asian researchers is significantly lower than that of their Western peers. Future research should focus on the factors that explain the differences in research output and the impact of citations between China and the USA.

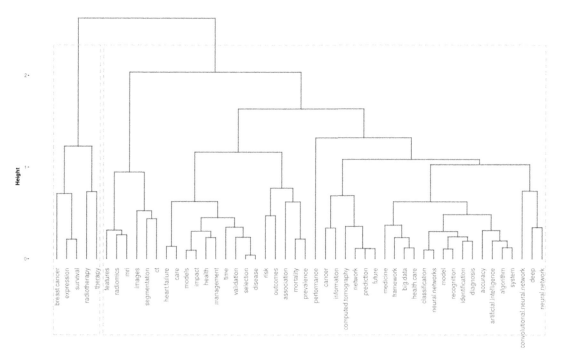

FIG. 23 Dendrogram of the topics addressed.

The top research domains were General & Internal Medicine (543 papers); Computer Science (500 papers); Radiology, Nuclear Medicine & Medical Imaging (499 papers); Health Care Sciences & Services (417 papers); Oncology (351 papers); Neurosciences & Neurology (8255 papers); Cardiovascular System & Cardiology (203 papers); and Engineering (66 papers).

Although a higher number of publications in the radiomic field, the volume of publications on AI applications in cancer was the highest. It should be noted that the scientific community focuses differently on different types of cancer. The most studied is breast cancer, followed by colon-rectal, lung, prostate, skin, and ovarian cancer.

In this research, we find a plethora of AI applications in healthcare: for assisting experts (e.g., pathologists) for more accurate diagnoses (e.g., cancer); for better and targeted treatment/healthcare (patient journey); for patient-flow optimization (real-time); for increasing access to healthcare, for personalized healthcare plans and automation of healthcare's most repeated processes; for risk prediction – predictive modeling; for symptoms and cure checker; for revolutionized endoscopy and precision treatment/surgery; for learning and treating rare diseases; and for medical imaging – looking behind the data. Even if in a minor way, we can find some studies concerning other uses of AI in healthcare, such as AI for clinical trials, for developing new medicines, and for cloud-based digital drug discovery.

Furthermore, radiomics and precision medicine have remained research hotspots through 2022 and might be research hotspots in the near future.

Finally, an aspect that must be stressed is that the word "ethics" is almost absent in the research subjects, keywords, and abstracts. This is an essential point because the application of AI in healthcare has colossal potential to transmute it for the better. Still, it also enhances ethical challenges,[89] and ethical issues must be addressed. Primary ethical concerns are safety and transparency, those more involved in developing trust among patients and healthcare specialists. Also, the field of trust toward these AI-based technologies, which is vital for the success of the theme in healthcare, is rarely faced.

4.1 Implications for policy, practice, and research

Our findings revealed that, removing China and India, which are emerging as top players in the field, most of the countries involved are Western countries, and only some research comes from African ones. Therefore, one of the essential points to stress is that developing countries should look for investment in research in medical AI as soon as possible to avoid being marginalized by new developments in the field. The research confirmed the difficulty of having large clinical datasets, especially those with labels requiring medical expert annotation, high costs, and much time to collect.[58,90,91] For this reason, sophisticated data augmentation techniques have recently been proposed to enrich the training datasets to better characterize the data distribution. Convolutional neural networks (CNN), Artificial neural networks (ANN). and support vector machines (SVM) have the highest impact on healthcare, but, in the next future, the use of other techniques, including feature space data augmentation[92,93] and data synthesis using complex, deep neural network models, notably generative adversarial networks (GAN),[94–97] will be increasingly widespread. It is difficult to predict if one specific technique will prevail, but the surging trend is inexorable, to the extent that entrepreneurial attempts and policymaking changes will have to adapt.[84]

Future AI development trends will focus on Machine Learning based on data obtained from state-of-the-art imaging methods to predict treatment responses,[98,99] especially in areas where there is a lack of objective diagnostic methods, e.g., psychiatric disorders[100] and, above all, from the latest diagnostic modalities, including multi-omics (e.g., genomics, metabolomics).[101] Study findings are consistent with prior evidence, suggesting that, given the large amount of health data collected in support of treating cancer, future applications of AI in medicine will be increasingly helpful in aiding diagnosis and clinical treatment.

However, to accelerate the application and expansion of AI in medicine, it is critical to develop global and national protocols and regulations to frequently review and justify the validity of AIM products in clinical and practical environments.[84] Furthermore, though AI algorithms are utilized to deliver automatic decision-making, it is advisable that healthcare experts and practitioners need poise in AI-driven technologies' efficacy and observance of current legislation. Furthermore, a key challenge for governments is that AI development should be conducted in a way that is easy to approach and aligned with the public interest.

The achievement of AIM progress awareness might entail several future interventions for reducing societal concerns to minimize possible risks of critical barriers and nonacceptance. The policies and subsequent intervention strategies for digital healthcare should comprehend the investment in AIM workshops able to provide closer and better access, first to health professionals and then to the general population, for training them on AIM mechanisms and possible benefits.

4.2 Limitations

The study is based on bibliometrics, a method not free from shortcomings that include bibliometric inability to predict the long-term impact of research, the validity of qualitative pronouncements made, based on quantitative tools and problems arising from data sources.

Our major limitation is that we only included English articles and reviews and we excluded the non-English ones. That made the number of English-speaking countries' publications, but in general Western countries' publications, more than that of other continents like Asia or Africa. Secondly, we might have missed many studies related to AI and medicine; the restriction on searchable research publications on Artificial Intelligence's practical applications and the exclusion of other documents focused only on theoretical studies may impact the thoroughness of the results.

Nonetheless, a useful proxy for the overall content of these papers is the bibliometric analysis of a large volume of publications and the summary of keywords. Furthermore, we had not considered multiple data sources and only extracted and analyzed data from the Web of Science; that is, however, an extensive database that offers a wide variety of research and includes all SCI and SSCI-listed journals. Future studies to compare the outputs from multiple databases, such as Scopus and PubMed, are recommended for a more comprehensive analysis.

Despite its weaknesses and limitations, this study provides detailed and complete state-of-the-art research concerning Artificial Intelligence's applications in medicine and healthcare and might become a helpful starting point for creating a more enabling environment in which AI developers and health researchers will work.

5. Conclusion

AI has been applied for various purposes, especially in healthcare. This study analyzes the development of AI-related research conducted in this field and provides relevant information on trends and future implications. AIM is a topic in continuous evolution and, although the current applications focus on radiomics and cancer medicine, the research in other medical fields is very productive and constantly evolving. In addition, there is a plethora of activities that still need to be reported in scientific journals.

Although AI technologies are attracting significant consideration in medical research, real-life implementation still needs to be improved. The main hurdles are two: regulations and data exchanges.[9] It should be noted that, seemingly large enough medical data sets and good learning algorithms have been available and although the existence of thousands of papers applying Machine Learning algorithms to medical data, very few of them have contributed meaningfully to clinical care.[34]

In the near future, it will be fundamental to strengthen cooperation between countries and institutions to fill the gap between theoretical AI research and clinical applications and study physicians' trust and attitude toward AI. In fact, although AI models have achieved humanlike performance, physicians' use is still limited because they are often seen as a black box.[10] This lack of trust is undoubtedly an important reason for their everyday use in practice, especially in healthcare, and represents a field that must be investigated. Necessary is also further research to explore ethical and social issues.

Ethical statement

The authors ensure that questions related to the integrity or accuracy of any part of the work are appropriately examined and resolved.

Conflict of interest

The authors declare no conflict of interest.

References

1. Evans R, Kurantowicz E, Lucio-Villegas E. Introduction. In: *Researching and Transforming Adult Learning and Communities: The Local/Global Context.* Brill; 2016:1–12.
2. Ramesh AN, Kambhampati C, Monson JR, Drew PJ. Artificial intelligence in medicine. *Annals of the Royal College of Surgeons of England.* 2004;86:334.
3. Gunn AA. The diagnosis of acute abdominal pain with computer analysis. *Journal of the Royal College of Surgeons of Edinburgh.* 1976;21:170–172.
4. Ridharan N. *Artificial Intelligence.* 1978;11:1–4.
5. Shortliffe EH. The adolescence of AI in medicine: Will the field come of age in the '90s? *Artificial Intelligence in Medicine.* 1993;5:93–106.
6. Yu K-H, Beam AL, Kohane IS. Artificial intelligence in healthcare. *Nature Biomedical Engineering.* 2018;2:719–731.
7. Niu J, Tang W, Xu F, Zhou X, Song Y. Global research on artificial intelligence from 1990–2014: spatially-explicit bibliometric analysis. *ISPRS International Journal of Geo-Information.* 2016;5:66.
8. Patel VL, Shortliffe EH, Stefanelli M, et al. The coming of age of artificial intelligence in medicine. *Artificial Intelligence in Medicine.* 2009;46:5–17.
9. Jiang F, Jiang Y, Zhi H, et al. Artificial intelligence in healthcare: past, present and future. *Stroke Vasc Neurol.* 2017;2:230–243.
10. Loh HW, Ooi CP, Seoni S, Barua PD, Molinari F, Acharya UR. Application of explainable artificial intelligence for healthcare: a systematic review of the last decade (2011–2022). *Computer Methods and Programs in Biomedicine.* 2022;226, 107161.
11. Yakimenko Y., Stirenko S., Koroliouk D., Gordienko Y., Zanzotto F.M. Implementation of personalized medicine by artificial intelligence platform [internet]. In: Ranganathan G., Fernando X., Piramuthu S., editors. Soft Computing for Security Applications. Singapore: Springer Nature Singapore; 2023 [cited 2022 Nov 4]. page 597–611. Available from: https://doi.org/10.1007/978-981-19-3590-9_46.
12. Ramos-Rodríguez A-R, Ruíz-Navarro J. Changes in the intellectual structure of strategic management research: a bibliometric study of the strategic management journal, 1980–2000. *Strat Mgmt J.* 2004;25:981–1004.
13. Makarius EE, Mukherjee D, Fox JD, Fox AK. Rising with the machines: a sociotechnical framework for bringing artificial intelligence into the organisation. *Journal of Business Research.* 2020;120:262–273.
14. Ellegaard O, Wallin JA. The bibliometric analysis of scholarly production: how great is the impact? *Scientometrics.* 2015;105:1809–1831.
15. Cobo MJ, López-Herrera AG, Herrera-Viedma E, Herrera F. An approach for detecting, quantifying, and visualizing the evolution of a research field: a practical application to the fuzzy sets theory field. *Journal of Informetrics.* 2011;5:146–166.
16. Donthu N, Kumar S, Mukherjee D, Pandey N, Lim WM. How to conduct a bibliometric analysis: an overview and guidelines. *Journal of Business Research.* 2021;133:285–296.
17. Chen C, Hu Z, Liu S, Tseng H. Emerging trends in regenerative medicine: a scientometric analysis in *CiteSpace. Expert Opinion on Biological Therapy.* 2012;12:593–608.
18. Yu Y, Li Y, Zhang Z, et al. A bibliometric analysis using VOSviewer of publications on COVID-19. *Ann Transl Med.* 2020;8:816.
19. Ma D, Yang B, Guan B, et al. A bibliometric analysis of Pyroptosis from 2001 to 2021. *Frontiers in Immunology.* 2021;12, 731933.
20. Yin M, Xu C, Ma J, Ye J, Mo W. A bibliometric analysis and visualization of current research trends in the treatment of cervical Spondylotic myelopathy. *Global Spine J.* 2021;11:988–998.
21. Fu R, Xu H, Lai Y, et al. A VOSviewer-based bibliometric analysis of prescription refills. *Frontiers in Medicine.* 2022;9, 856420.
22. Musa IH, Afolabi LO, Zamit I, et al. Artificial intelligence and machine learning in Cancer research: a systematic and thematic analysis of the top 100 cited articles indexed in Scopus database. *Cancer Control.* 2022;29. 107327482210959.
23. Ioannidis JPA, Baas J, Klavans R, Boyack KW. A standardized citation metrics author database annotated for scientific field. *PLoS Biology.* 2019;17, e3000384.

24. Chen C. CiteSpace II: detecting and visualizing emerging trends and transient patterns in scientific literature. *Journal of the American Society for Information Science*. 2006;57:359–377.

25. Chen C, Song M. Visualizing a field of research: a methodology of systematic scientometric reviews. *PLoS One*. 2019;14, e0223994.

26. van Eck NJ, Waltman L. Citation-based clustering of publications using CitNetExplorer and VOSviewer. *Scientometrics*. 2017;111:1053–1070.

27. Aria M, Cuccurullo C. Bibliometrix : an R-tool for comprehensive science mapping analysis. *Journal of Informetrics*. 2017;11:959–975.

28. Moral-Muñoz J.A., Herrera-Viedma E., Santisteban-Espejo A., Cobo M.J. Software tools for conducting bibliometric analysis in science: An up-to-date review. *EPI* [Internet] 2020 [cited 2022 Nov 1]; 29. Available from: https://revista.profesionaldelainformacion.com/index.php/EPI/article/view/epi.2020.ene.03.

29. James A, Raux M. Altmetrics scores: what are they? *Anaesthesia Crit Care Pain Med*. 2020;39:443–445.

30. Saud S, Traboco L, Gupta L. Harnessing the true power of Altmetrics to track engagement. *Journal of Korean Medical Science*. 2021;36, e330.

31. Elango B, Rajendran P. Authorship trends and collaboration pattern in the marine sciences literature : a Scientometric study. *International Journal of Information Dissemination and Technology*. 2012;2:166–169.

32. Appio FP, Cesaroni F, Di Minin A. Visualizing the structure and bridges of the intellectual property management and strategy literature: a document co-citation analysis. *Scientometrics*. 2014;101:623–661.

33. Pieters R, Baumgartner H. Who talks to whom? Intra- and interdisciplinary communication of economics journals. *Journal of Economic Literature*. 2002;40:483–509.

34. Deo RC. Machine learning in medicine. *Circulation*. 2015;132:1920–1930.

35. Rajkomar A, Oren E, Chen K, et al. Scalable and accurate deep learning with electronic health records. *NPJ Digital Medicine*. 2018;1(18). https://doi.org/10.1038/s41746-018-0029-1.

36. Johnson KW, Torres Soto J, Glicksberg BS, et al. Artificial Intelligence in Cardiology. *Journal of the American College of Cardiology*. 2018;71:2668–2679.

37. Krittanawong C, Zhang H, Wang Z, Aydar M, Kitai T, et al. Artificial intelligence in precision cardiovascular medicine. *Journal of the American College of Cardiology*. 2017;69(21):2657–2664. https://doi.org/10.1016/j.jacc.2017.03.571.

38. Motwani M, Dey D, Berman DS, et al. Machine learning for prediction of all-cause mortality in patients with suspected coronary artery disease: a 5-year multicentre prospective registry analysis. *European Heart Journal*. 2017;38(7):500–507. https://doi.org/10.1093/eurheartj/ehw188.

39. Zhang J, Gajjala S, Agrawal P, et al. Fully automated echocardiogram interpretation in clinical practice. *Circulation*. 2018;138(16):1623–1635. https://doi.org/10.1161/CIRCULATIONAHA.118.034338.

40. Madani A, Arnaout R, Mofrad M, Arnaout R, et al. Fast and accurate view classification of echocardiograms using deep learning. *NPJ Digital Medicine*. 2018;1(6). https://doi.org/10.1038/s41746-017-0013-1.

41. Lee JG, Jun S, Cho YW, et al. Deep learning in medical imaging: general overview. *Korean Journal of Radiology*. 2017;18(4):570–584. https://doi.org/10.3348/kjr.2017.18.4.570.

42. Bi WL, Hosny A, Schabath MB, et al. Artificial intelligence in cancer imaging: clinical challenges and applications. *CA: A Cancer Journal for Clinicians*. 2019;69(2):127–157. https://doi.org/10.3322/caac.21552.

43. Abràmoff MD, Lavin PT, Birch M, Shah N, Folk JC, et al. Pivotal trial of an autonomous AI-based diagnostic system for detection of diabetic retinopathy in primary care offices. *NPJ Digital Medicine*. 2018;1(39). https://doi.org/10.1038/s41746-018-0040-6.

44. Shameer K, Johnson KW, Glicksberg BS, Dudley JT, Sengupta PP, et al. Machine learning in cardiovascular medicine: are we there yet? *Heart*. 2018;104(14):1156–1164. https://doi.org/10.1136/heartjnl-2017-311198.

45. Lundervold AS, Lundervold A. An overview of deep learning in medical imaging focusing on MRI. *Zeitschrift für Medizinische Physik*. 2019;29:102–127.

46. Antropova N, Huynh BQ, Giger ML, et al. A deep feature fusion methodology for breast cancer diagnosis demonstrated on three imaging modality datasets. *Medical Physics*. 2017;44(10):5162–5171. https://doi.org/10.1002/mp.12453.

47. Park SH, Han K, et al. Methodologic guide for evaluating clinical performance and effect of artificial intelligence technology for medical diagnosis and prediction. *Radiology*. 2018;286(3):800–809. https://doi.org/10.1148/radiol.2017171920.

48. Miller DD, Brown EW, et al. Artificial intelligence in medical practice: the question to the answer? *American Journal of Medicine*. 2018;131(2):129–133. https://doi.org/10.1016/j.amjmed.2017.10.035.

49. Sidey-Gibbons JAM, Sidey-Gibbons CJ, et al. Machine learning in medicine: a practical introduction. *BMC Medical Research Methodology*. 2019;19(1). https://doi.org/10.1186/s12874-019-0681-4.

50. Cikes M, Sanchez-Martinez S, Claggett B, et al. Machine learning-based phenogrouping in heart failure to identify responders to cardiac resynchronization therapy. *European Journal of Heart Failure*. 2019;21(1):74–85. https://doi.org/10.1002/ejhf.1333.

51. Han X. MR-based synthetic CT generation using a deep convolutional neural network method. *Medical Physics*. 2017;44(4):1408–1419. https://doi.org/10.1002/mp.12155.

52. Ibragimov B, Xing L, et al. Segmentation of organs-at-risks in head and neck CT images using convolutional neural networks. *Medical Physics*. 2017;44(2):547–557. https://doi.org/10.1002/mp.12045.

53. Koltun V, Hafner D. The h-index is no longer an effective correlate of scientific reputation. *PLoS One*. 2021;16, e0253397.

54. Abbas AM. Bounds and inequalities relating h-index, g-index, e-index and generalized impact factor: an improvement over existing models. *PLoS One*. 2012;7, e33699.

55. Thompson DF, Callen EC, Nahata MC. New indices in scholarship assessment. *American Journal of Pharmaceutical Education*. 2009;73:111.

56. Probst L., Pedersen B., Lefebvre V., Dakkak L. USA-China-EU plans for AI: where do we stand. Digital Transformation Monitor of the European Commission 2018.

57. Zupic I, Čater T. Bibliometric methods in management and organization. *Organizational Research Methods*. 2015;18:429–472.

58. Esteva A, Kuprel B, Novoa RA, et al. Dermatologist-level classification of skin cancer with deep neural networks. *Nature*. 2017;542:115–118.

59. Hatt M, Le Rest CC, Tixier F, Badic B, Schick U, Visvikis D. Radiomics: data are also images. *Journal of Nuclear Medicine*. 2019;60:38S–44S.

60. Meldolesi E, van Soest J, Damiani A, et al. Standardized data collection to build prediction models in oncology: a prototype for rectal cancer. *Future Oncology*. 2016;12:119–136.

61. Handelman GS, Kok HK, Chandra RV, Razavi AH, Lee MJ, Asadi H. eDoctor: machine learning and the future of medicine. *Journal of Internal Medicine*. 2018;284:603–619.

62. Krittanawong C, Johnson KW, Rosenson RS, et al. Deep learning for cardiovascular medicine: a practical primer. *European Heart Journal*. 2019;40:2058–2073.

63. Siegersma KR, Leiner T, Chew DP, Appelman Y, Hofstra L, Verjans JW. Artificial intelligence in cardiovascular imaging: state of the art and implications for the imaging cardiologist. *Netherlands Heart Journal*. 2019;27:403–413.

64. El Naqa I, Haider MA, Giger ML, Ten Haken RK. Artificial intelligence: reshaping the practice of radiological sciences in the 21st century. *BJR*. 2020;93:20190855.

65. Siontis KC, Noseworthy PA, Attia ZI, Friedman PA. Artificial intelligence-enhanced electrocardiography in cardiovascular disease management. *Nature Reviews Cardiology*. 2021;18:465–478.

66. Tang A, Tam R, Cadrin-Chênevert A, et al. Canadian Association of Radiologists White Paper on artificial intelligence in radiology. *Canadian Association of Radiologists Journal*. 2018;69:120–135.

67. Rodriguez P, Cucurull G, Gonzalez J, et al. Deep pain: exploiting long short-term memory networks for facial expression classification. *IEEE Transactions on Cybernetics*. 2022;52:3314–3324.

68. Peker M. An efficient sleep scoring system based on EEG signal using complex-valued machine learning algorithms. *Neurocomputing*. 2016;207:165–177.

69. Md Khudzari J, Kurian J, Tartakovsky B, Raghavan GSV. Bibliometric analysis of global research trends on microbial fuel cells using Scopus database. *Biochemical Engineering Journal*. 2018;136:51–60.

70. Lambin P, Rios-Velazquez E, Leijenaar R, et al. Radiomics: extracting more information from medical images using advanced feature analysis. *European Journal of Cancer*. 2012;48:441–446.

71. Pinker K, Chin J, Melsaether AN, Morris EA, Moy L. Precision medicine and Radiogenomics in breast Cancer: new approaches toward diagnosis and treatment. *Radiology*. 2018;287:732–747.

72. Lambin P, Leijenaar RTH, Deist TM, et al. Radiomics: the bridge between medical imaging and personalized medicine. *Nature Reviews Clinical Oncology*. 2017;14:749–762.

73. Li S, Zhou B. A review of radiomics and genomics applications in cancers: the way towards precision medicine. *Radiation Oncology*. 2022;17:217.

74. Council NR. Toward Precision Medicine: Building a Knowledge Network for Biomedical Research and a New Taxonomy of Disease; 2011.

75. Behrens MK. Priorities for Personalized Medicine; 2008.

76. Rubin MA. Health: make precision medicine work for cancer care. *Nature*. 2015;520:290–291.

77. Robinson PN. Deep phenotyping for precision medicine. *Human Mutation*. 2012;33:777–780.

78. Hamburg MA, Collins FS. The path to personalized medicine. *The New England Journal of Medicine*. 2010;363:301–304.

79. Nayak S, Patgiri R. A study on big cancer data. In: *International Conference on Intelligent Systems Design and Applications*; 2018.

80. König IR, Fuchs O, Hansen G, von Mutius E, Kopp MV. What is precision medicine? *The European Respiratory Journal*. 2017;50:1700391.

81. Reddy B, Hassan U, Seymour C, et al. Point-of-care sensors for the management of sepsis. *Nature Biomedical Engineering*. 2018;2:640–648.

82. Weil AR. Precision medicine. *Health Affairs*. 2018;37:687.

83. Guo Y, Hao Z, Zhao S, Gong J, Yang F. Artificial intelligence in health care: bibliometric analysis. *Journal of Medical Internet Research*. 2020;22, e18228.

84. Tran B, Vu G, Ha G, et al. Global evolution of research in artificial intelligence in health and medicine: a bibliometric study. *JCM*. 2019;8:360.

85. Yoon HY, Lee H, Yee J, Gwak HS. Global research trends of gender-related artificial intelligence in medicine between 2001–2020: a bibliometric study. *Frontiers in Medicine*. 2022;9, 868040.

86. de Kleijn M, Siebert M, Huggett S. Artificial Intelligence: How knowledge is created, transferred and used; 2017.

87. Fleming N. How artificial intelligence is changing drug discovery. *Nature*. 2018;557:S55.

88. Mayer-Schönberger V, Cukier K. Big Data: A Revolution that Will Transform how we Live, Work, and Think. Houghton Mifflin Harcourt; 2013.

89. Santosh K., Gaur L. Artificial Intelligence and Machine Learning in Public Healthcare: Opportunities and Societal Impact [Internet]. Singapore: Springer Singapore; 2021 [cited 2023 Jan 27]. Available from: https://doi.org/10.1007/978-981-16-6768-8.

90. Do T-T, Hoang T, Pomponiu V, et al. Accessible melanoma detection using smartphones and Mobile image analysis. *IEEE Transactions on Multimedia*. 2018;20:2849–2864.

91. Nejati H, Ghazijahani HA, Abdollahzadeh M, et al. Fine-grained wound tissue analysis using deep neural network. In: *2018 IEEE International Conference on Acoustics, Speech and Signal Processing (ICASSP)*. IEEE; 2018:1010–1014.

92. Dixit M, Kwitt R, Niethammer M, Vasconcelos N. Aga: Attribute-guided augmentation. In: *Proceedings of the IEEE conference on computer vision and pattern recognition*; 2017:7455–7463.

93. Liu B, Wang X, Dixit M, Kwitt R, Vasconcelos N. Feature space transfer for data augmentation. In: *Proceedings of the IEEE conference on computer vision and pattern recognition*; 2018:9090–9098.

94. Goodfellow I.J., Pouget-Abadie J., Mirza M., Xu B., Warde-Farley D., Ozair S., Courville A., Bengio Y. In: Proceedings of the 27th International Conference on Neural Information Processing Systems. 2014. page 2672–80.

95. Lim SK, Loo Y, Tran N-T, Cheung N-M, Roig G, Elovici Y. Doping: Generative data augmentation for unsupervised anomaly detection with GAN. In: *2018 IEEE International Conference on Data Mining (ICDM)*. IEEE; 2018:1122–1127.

96. Frid-Adar M, Diamant I, Klang E, Amitai M, Goldberger J, Greenspan H. GAN-based synthetic medical image augmentation for increased CNN performance in liver lesion classification. *Neurocomputing*. 2018;321:321–331.

97. Tran N-T, Bui T-A, Cheung N-M. Improving GAN with neighbour embedding and gradient matching. In: *Proceedings of the AAAI conference on artificial intelligence*; 2019:5191–5198.

98. Ho C.S.H., Zhang M.W.B., H. RCM. Optical topography in psychiatry: a chip off the old block or a new look beyond the mind–brain frontiers? Frontiers in Psychiatry [Internet] 2016; 7 [cited 2023 Jan 27]. Available from: https://doi.org/10.3389/fpsyt.2016.00074.

99. Lai CYY, Ho CSH, Lim CR, Ho RCM. Functional near-infrared spectroscopy in psychiatry. *BJPsych Adv*. 2017;23:324–330.

100. Athreya A, Iyer R, Neavin D, et al. Augmentation of physician assessments with multi-omics enhances predictability of drug response: a case study of major depressive disorder. *IEEE Computational Intelligence Magazine*. 2018;13:20–31.

101. Liu D, Ray B, Neavin DR, et al. Beta-defensin 1, aryl hydrocarbon receptor and plasma kynurenine in major depressive disorder: metabolomics-informed genomics. *Translational Psychiatry*. 2018;8:10.

CHAPTER

12

Ethics and regulations for AI in radiology

Filippo Pesapane[a] and Paul Summers[b]

[a]Breast Imaging Division, Radiology Department, European Institute of Oncology (IEO), IRCCS, Milan, Italy
[b]Radiology Division, Radiology Department, European Institute of Oncology (IEO), IRCCS, Milan, Italy

1. Introduction

The transformation of medical data from sets of records considered in isolation during the care of individual patients into big data on which machine learning, and in particular artificial intelligence (AI) models can be trained and operate to generate insights for both the individual and the many represents a new frontier in healthcare research. The COVID-19 pandemic triggered an unprecedented upsurge in the development of, and demand for medical AI technologies; the use of which demonstrated its potential to drive beneficial outcomes when given access to suitable and sufficient medical information,[1–3] but also gave some warning signs of the risks of these developments in health care[4] as the embryonic legal framework and emerging ethical issues seek to respond to this new development.

Implementing AI in radiology raises many regulatory issues and ethical dilemmas due to their potential impacts on patient care, clinical working practices, and the roles of regulators and healthcare policy. This is particularly important since the new AI systems may not be limited to processing information to assist humans in making decisions of consequence, but could directly provide sensitive services that when performed by humans would require training and certification.[5–9] These issues need to be carefully and continually addressed as AI research requires robust and ethical guidelines, demanding an update of the legal and regulatory framework.

It is a widely shared opinion that radiologists, and physicians in general, will remain essential to medical practice, because medicine requires unique human characteristics[10,11]: if AI is based on a huge increase in data and information, the hallmark of intelligence will be in reducing such information to what is really relevant.[12,13] The gain in efficiency provided by AI will hopefully allow physicians to perform more value-adding tasks, such as integrating patients' clinical and imaging information, having more professional interactions, becoming more visible to patients, and playing a vital role in integrated clinical teams.[13–15] AI in health care encourages the creation of organizations specifically oriented toward This novelty and potential change of roles has led many professional organizations to actively observe and respond to developments through training, delineation of positions,[16–18] and the creation of new bodies, such as the Data Science Institute, which the American College of Radiology has dedicated to the field.[19,20]

Ethics and regulation exhibit diverse forms and originate from distinct institutions, yet they exert mutual influence and support each other. The incorporation of ethical considerations within regulatory processes and the presence of guidelines and regulations are essential to enforce ethical standards and commitments.

Regulation is deemed crucial to both foster AI development and effectively handle associated risks. This entails striking a balance between the need for well-defined rules and guidelines to ensure a proper and established implementation of AI in health care and the requirement for regulatory oversight that remains flexible and proactive enough to facilitate the progress of AI as a beneficial tool for patients.

As technology advances, new situations will arise that necessitate the creation of new regulations and ethical standards by policymakers. Nonetheless, physicians and healthcare workers must never lose sight of their duty to serve and, therefore, strictly adhere to the principle of "primum non nocere" (do no harm). Consequently, a thorough evaluation of regulatory and ethical issues, policy initiatives, data protection, data ownership, and the associated accountability is imperative to realize the potential of AI in healthcare systems while upholding respect and ethical practices.

2. Ethics, transparency, and patients' trust

While medical ethics has traditionally focused on interactions between humans as involving the human body and psyche, the ethics of AI focus on interactions with "data," which is of a clearly different nature. Firstly, data do not have clear borders and boundaries, but they may represent a specific person, are often distributed across many data repositories, and can be accessed by many people at the same time. Secondly, interacting with a person's data is not comparable to having the person undergo a radiological exam, but may similarly have implications for the person's health. Thirdly, there is often no clear beginning and no clear end to an "operation" on a dataset—data can be interrogated continuously and for different endpoints.

Although talk of ethics and ethical regulation may suggest prohibiting or mandating specific forms of innovation, ethics can promote or even enhance a complex system such AI because by helping to gain patient trust.[21] Some ethical challenges are straightforward and need to be guarded against, like the concern that AI algorithms may mirror human biases in decision-making. In many applications such as assessing image quality, predicting equipment failure, or optimizing patient throughput, ethical considerations might not play a significant role in the problem to be solved. This creates a misunderstanding that the problem of AI bias is irrelevant in such cases leaving many to believe wrongly that the algorithms are not biased.[15] In general, however, bias in clinically oriented AIs is likely to occur as the algorithms are trained on data of patients from a small number of centers and thus reflect the characteristics and drivers that are specific to the patient base of those center due to their location, referral profile, technology in use, and local practices, with the consequence that the algorithm performs suboptimally for patients in other centers. A particular risk of this type is that ethnic biases could be inadvertently built into medical algorithms since current healthcare delivery often varies by ethnicity.

A distinct perspective arises when we take into account that the data utilized to train AI at present are derived from the existing rules that guide clinicians' thinking and approach to specific medical conditions. These data determine the behavior of each algorithm but may lack significant information due to current limitations in data acquisition. As a result, there is a potential bias toward reproducing current performance levels rather than pushing forward clinical practice.

As the accuracy of algorithms relies heavily on the accuracy of the underlying annotations of the training data, poorly labeled data will yield poor results.[22] Transparency of labeling allows others to critically evaluate the training process for potential biases. AI might even help resolve healthcare disparities if designed to compensate for known biases.[19,23]

Transparency regarding model form and weights is similarly important if model interpretability is to permit humans to understand how a given technology reached a certain result.[19] Especially in the context of unsupervised AI it is often difficult, if not impossible, to know how the software arrived at a specific outcome because the path to achieving the outcome was not designed into the system. This lack of transparency regarding the bases for their operation often leads AIs to be referred to as "black box" models and has led some authors to argue that the use of unsupervised AI in health care is ethically more problematic than supervised AI.[24] The black box nature of AI represents a main challenge for researchers who want to understand how the AI algorithm comes to its conclusion, which features have been selected, how to detect possible failure, and most importantly, communicate to patients, the rationale behind their diagnosis or treatment planning.[25,26] Enforcing transparency in AI is necessary to justify a particular diagnosis, treatment recommendation, or outcome prediction when using such technology for patients.[13]

The intent behind, or target of an AI also needs to be considered because they could be trained to perform in ways that do not reflect the patients' best interests. This could occur if the AI guides users toward clinical that increase profits for their providers but do not impart better care, for instance by recommending exams, drugs, or referrals in which they hold a stake.[5]

Some initiatives are underway concerning the ethical, social, and legal aspects of AI. OpenAI, for example, is a research laboratory based in San Francisco (California, US) that aims to produce open source AI code as part of their mission to ensure that artificial general intelligence benefits all of humanity.[27] Similarly, the Machine Intelligence Research Institute is a research non-profit studying the mathematical underpinnings of intelligent behavior with a mission to develop formal tools for the clean design and analysis of general-purpose AI systems, with the intent of making such systems safer and more reliable when they are developed.[28]

While the above-mentioned initiatives have a broad scope in the field of AI, their efforts toward transparency and openness of AI are hoped in part to foster a patient willingness to share personal data if they believe there will be downstream benefits, but they want to be confident it will not be shared in ways they do not understand.[29,30] This latter point touches on two of the cardinal points of most existing ethical frameworks. First, the individual should be informed about the nature of data being collected and intended use of that data. Second they provide explicit consent to said collection and use of their data; without which the collection and use do not proceed. As will be discussed in more detail below, one of the regulatory responses to abuses of data usage within and beyond the healthcare sector, in some jurisdictions (most notably perhaps, Europe and California), has been to effectively enshrine informed consent for data usage as a right of the person or obligation of the potential data user[31,32]; the ability to replicate, and share data easily remains.

3. Regulatory issues and policy initiatives for AI in health care

Health care is highly regulated, with national and international governing bodies seeking to promote quality and ensure patient safety.[15] The contrast between the two guiding principles[33] is useful to illustrate how the spectrum of ethical and societal mores under which legislators operate impacts the thinking that goes into such policy-making. The "precautionary principle" approach imposes limits or even outright bans on certain applications due to their potential risks: this means that these systems are never tested because of what could happen in the worst-case scenarios. Conversely, the "permissionless-innovation" approach allows experimentation to proceed freely: addressing the issues that arise as they emerge.

One of the first issues to be faced with medical AI applications is where they fit in the current legal framework and how this may vary between jurisdictions. In European Union (EU), the term "medical device" is applied to any instrument or other tool intended by the manufacturer to be used for human beings for the purpose, among others, of diagnosis, prevention, monitoring, treatment, or alleviation of disease, according to the definition of medical device provided by Article 1(2) of Directive 93/42/EEC.[34] This definition has been endorsed by the Medical Device Academy, a nonlegally binding guideline drafted by the European Commission to guide stakeholders in complying with legislation related to medical devices,[35] but has propagated into the current Medical Devices Regulations (MDR) and In Vitro Diagnostic Medical Device Regulation (IVDR).[33,34] Notably, in the United States (US) the 21st-Century Cures Act[36] of 2016 defines the medical device as a tool "intended for use in the diagnosis of disease or other conditions, or in the cure, mitigation, treatment, or prevention of disease, in man or other animals, or intended to affect the structure or any function of the body of man or other animals".[37]

Despite the differences in definition, it is generally the case that where an AI is to be used in the care of patients, it is to be considered a medical device, but that is not to say all AI technologies used in the healthcare space will be considered medical devices. Systems that analyze large amounts of data to develop knowledge about a disease, rather than to decide on treatment options for an individual patient, may not necessarily be considered as having a medical purpose, and hence as a medical device.[38]

A second issue relates to the potential of the AI application to integrate and adapt to new information even after they have been put into use. This represents an important distinction from traditional medical devices where a user becomes more familiar and practiced with the device and can adapt their patient management considering this experience. Instead, the adaptation lies within the AI itself and may over time lead to patients in objectively identical conditions receiving different outputs or recommendations from the AI without the clinician understanding the basis for the difference. Historically, changes to the means of operation of a medical device would require revision of their approval by regulatory bodies. The US Food and Drug Administration (FDA) and the International Medical Device Regulators Forum (IMDRF) have recognized the uniqueness of AI technologies in comparison with traditional medical devices. The IMDRF is a voluntary group of medical device regulators including EU, the United States, Canada, Australia, Brazil, China, Japan, Russia, Singapore, and South Korea, working toward harmonizing international medical device regulation. The collaboration between IMDRF and FDA had defined a new category called Software as Medical Device (SaMD) pointing out for the need for an updated regulatory framework[19,30] that takes into account the safety challenges AI systems have to face in the forms of complex environments, periods of learning which may result in significant variation in the system's performance.[30] Their guidance recommends a continuous iterative process based on real-world performance data and states that low-risk SaMD may not require independent review.[19]

It is important to acknowledge that AI is entering the healthcare field within the broader context of a digital revolution, where data play a crucial role, and there is an increasing recognition and concern regarding the possibilities and risks associated with data usage.

These circumstances elucidate the reasons why the regulation of medical devices remains a contentious issue, influenced by guidelines and subjective interpretations by authorities. In general, the AI sector in the United States has thrived in an environment that promotes innovation without explicit permission, while decision-makers in the EU have implemented more stringent policies for this transformative technology sector.[15,33,39] These variations are evident

TABLE 1   Key-requirements considered by the EU Commission for high-risk AI applications like medical-devices.

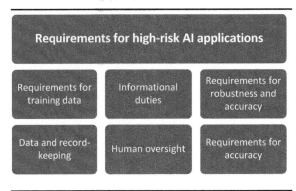

in the regulations and laws that have emerged in recent years, aiming to uphold societal oversight over AI technology in the healthcare sector. In this section of the chapter, we provide an overview of the existing regulatory landscape for AI in health care in both the United States and the EU.

3.1 Regulatory framework in the EU

Although each EU country has its own national strategies toward regulating AI, these are largely convergent,[15,19] guided by the "European Strategy on Artificial Intelligence," supported by the "High-Level Expert Group on Artificial Intelligence",[40] and the EU Commission's "White Paper on Artificial Intelligence - A European approach to excellence and trust",[41] the latter of which outlines the EU's approach for a regulatory framework for AI (Table 1).

The current regulatory framework for medical devices in the EU is composed of the Medical Devices Regulation (MDR)[42] (that replaced the EU Medical Device Directive in 2021) and the In Vitro Diagnostic Medical Device Regulation (IVDR)[43] (Table 2). Their main characteristics are the following:

– extended scope to include a wider range of products;
– extended liability in relation to defective products;
– strengthening of requirements for clinical data and traceability of the devices;
– more rigorous monitoring of notified bodies;
– and improved transparency through making information relating to personal data used for developing and training AI algorithms public.[44]

The MDR[33] applies to software (ranging from full executable programs down to macros embedded in general purpose programs and extending to responsive websites, and models that adapt based on patient-specific inputs) that is intended to provide information concerning diagnosis, prevention, monitoring, treatment, or alleviation of disease.[42]

TABLE 2   Regulatory framework in the European Union on medical devices.

MEDDEVS

• Non-binding guidelines on legislation related to medical devices

MDR

• Regulation on medical devices
• Applies from 26 May 2020
• Repeals Directive 93/42/EEC

IVDR

• Regulation on in vitro diagnostic medical devices
• Applies from 26 May 2022

MDR = Medical Device Regulation; IVDR = In Vitro Diagnostic Medical Device Regulation; EEC = European Economic Community.

Notably, qualifying as a medical device is independent of the software's complexity, intended user, or risk to the patient or user. Moreover, the software may be stand-alone (a device in its own right) or a component in a hardware medical device. Software that qualifies as a medical device must comply with a set of "General Safety and Performance Requirements." This compliance is formally verified before the CE marking (a manufacturer's declaration that a product complies with the EU's New Approach Directives) can be affixed and the product placed on the European market.[16]

The purposes of the MDR and IVDR do not substantially deviate from those of the previous Directives, with the new Regulations aiming to:

— harmonize the single market by granting uniform standards for the quality and safety of medical devices;
— classify medical devices and in vitro diagnostics based on the relevant risk profile, and require specific assessment procedures that depend on said classification;
— Highlight responsibilities of notified bodies and competent authorities

In August 2021,[45] the European Medicines Agency (EMA) published a report together with the International Coalition of Medicines Regulatory Authorities (ICMRA) identifying key issues linked to the regulation of future therapies using AI and making recommendations to foster the uptake of AI in medicine development. Some of their main findings and recommendations include

— Regulators may need to apply a risk-based approach to assessing and regulating AI, which could be informed through exchange and collaboration in the International Coalition of Medicines Regulatory Authorities;
— Sponsors, developers, and pharmaceutical companies should establish strengthened governance structures to oversee algorithms and AI deployments that are closely linked to the benefit/risk of a medicinal product;
— Regulatory guidelines for AI development, validation and use with medicinal products should be developed in areas such as data provenance, reliability, transparency and understandability, and real-world monitoring of patient functioning.[45]

The main reasons behind these regulatory changes are divergent interpretations of the previous Directives, incidents concerning product performance, and lack of control of notified bodies. Such weaknesses of the legal system created in the 1990s rendered it unfit to deal with new technologies like AI. The new Regulations aim to ensure a consistently high level of health and safety protection for EU patients, as well as the free and fair trade of the products throughout the EU.

The MDR also introduces requirements applicable to the clinical use of software (including AI models) developed "in-house" by healthcare providers, creating a degree of consistency across commercial and own-use applications.[33,46] Notably the CE marking is not necessary for "in-house" software provided the hosting institution justifies the use of the software as satisfying a patient need that cannot be appropriately met by a device already on the market, and the software is not transferred to another institution (considered putting on the market and thus necessitating CE marking).

The value of developing in-house software solutions may be questioned in situations where market-available solutions with adequate performance already exist. Unless there is an intention to proceed with commercialization, such in-house reinventions would likely have limited prospects for clinical utilization beyond their potential use in research endeavors.

The lack of a CE marking requirement, however, does not exonerate the hosting institution from obligations under MDR tied to General Safety and Performance Requirements:

— Document the software design and development
  ○ intended use
  ○ risk classification and management
  ○ GSPRs and other applicable standards
  ○ technical documentation
— Document the performance of the software
  ○ verification and validation
  ○ clinical evidence and monitoring
  ○ change management
— Declaration of conformity

For software that is intended to become commercial products, the process further includes

– defining the commercialization strategy
– full CE marking conformity assessment
– registration of the product
– postmarket clinical follow-up

Given that many software implementations in healthcare institutions emerge out of research activities, the above requirements argue for imposing robust and rigorous software development practices in the research phase so that extension to clinical use is not hampered. For an excellent review of the implications of the MDR for healthcare institutions, see Ref. 46.

3.2 Regulatory framework in the United States

Discussions on regulation of AI in the United States have included topics such as the timeliness of regulating AI, the nature of the federal regulatory framework to govern and promote AI, including what agency should lead, the regulatory and governing powers of that agency, and how to update regulations in the face of rapidly changing technology, as well as the roles of state governments and courts.

In January 2019, the "White House's Office of Science and Technology Policy" released a draft entitled "Guidance for Regulation of Artificial Intelligence Applications," which included ten principles for United States agencies when deciding whether and how to regulate AI[47] (Table 3). Subsequently, the US Federal Trade Commission published further guidance regarding the ethical and commercial use of AI technology, acknowledging that while AI has significant positive potential, it also presents the risk of arriving at unfair or discriminatory outcomes or entrenching existing disparities. This guidance suggests that companies:

– be transparent with consumers;
– explain how AI algorithms make decisions;
– ensure that decisions are fair, robust, and empirically sound;
– hold themselves accountable for compliance, ethics, fairness, and nondiscrimination.

However, no institutional body is still designated for enforcing AI-related policies in the United States so far.

The rapid growth in the number of AI learning applications being developed has been recognized as creating a challenge for the FDA to carry out its approval process in a timely fashion, given the volume and the complex nature of testing and verification involved. There is of course pressure not to repeat the drawn-out approval seen at the introduction of computer-assisted detection (CAD) software for mammography in 1998,[48] which took many years to obtain clearance from the FDA to be used as a second screening reader. Yet, AI systems that do not need radiologist supervision and cannot be compared to predicated medical devices warrant a more exhaustive FDA clearance process compared to CAD systems. Companies and developers therefore usually present AI systems as aid tools for radiologists rather than as a tool that substitutes them.[14]

As yet, the FDA has only cleared or approved AI-based medical devices that include algorithms that are locked prior to marketing. Algorithm changes will likely require FDA premarket review for changes beyond the original market authorization. This complicates the situation for AI algorithms that can adapt over time, continuously learning from real-world experience and this may provide a different output in comparison to the output initially cleared for a given set of inputs. To face this new highly autonomous and adaptive nature of AI tools, the FDA is working on an innovative regulatory approach that facilitates a rapid cycle of product improvement and allows these devices to continually improve while providing effective safeguards.[49]

TABLE 3   Regulatory framework in the European Union on data protection.

Directive 95/46/EC	Directive on data protection Has been be replaced by the GDPR
GDPR	Regulation on data protection Applies from 24 May 2018 Replaces Directive 95/46/EC
Directive (EU) 2016/1148	Directive on cybersecurity Applies from 10 May 2018

GDPR, General Data Protection Regulation; EU, European Union.

4. Data protection issues

With data being essential for the development of healthcare AI, it is important to address a number of questions that relate to the responsible use of data:

- Who owns and who can use medical data?
- What are the conditions for the use of medical data?
- How can the individuals to whom the data pertains be protected?

The data required for the training of healthcare AIs naturally relate to medical aspects of individuals, and this gives it particular valence. Personal data are defined in the EU[31] as information about an identified or identifiable living person, thus medical data about individual persons is personal data. The data may come from a variety of sources (from wearable devices to diagnostic and interventional procedures) and covers a wide spectrum of data items, some of which the person may want to keep confidential or private, and some may expose the person to harm if it were to be known or used by others. Moreover, the information may relate to others as well, as in the case of a family history or a genetic profile.

The generation and sharing of information in the course of a patient–clinician interaction, however, usually forms part of the care of the patient directly. Historically there has not had much scope for secondary use beyond possible analyses for scientific advancement and process audit (likely to be seen favorably by the patient), or for altering risk ratings for insurance purposes (likely to be seen unfavorably). For healthcare AI development, access to medical data is so critical, which commercial developers of healthcare AIs actively seek and are generally willing to pay for relevant medical data so that preparation of their product can move forward. The emergence of such overt interest in healthcare data for purposes other than the patient's care is similar to what has been seen regarding one's internet browsing or streaming activities, where third parties have an interest in personal data for targeting of advertisements, but potentially also for more sinister applications.

The storage of medical data on the part of those who produced it (e.g., an imaging center) or used it (e.g., the hospital where treatment occurred) serves to render subsequent patient-clinician interactions more efficient and is also typically required by law as part of medico-legal obligations. This preservation of the data tends to be seen as ownership by healthcare organizations, and sometimes even by clinicians. Others have argued that the patients themselves should be the owners of their health data, with those who use and store the data being guardians and processors of said data. In fact, patients typically only have a fraction of the medical data about themselves in their own possession. For the developers of healthcare AIso, it is therefore far more efficient to deal with healthcare organizations when seeking data for training and analysis, and such organizations see a potential financial benefit from making the data available. The patient, however, may be rightfully concerned that such an exchange of data between a healthcare organization and AI developer puts their privacy at risk, oversteps the boundaries regarding the use of the data they agreed to when making it available to their clinicians, and fails to recognize their contribution in the generation of the data.

Reflecting this growing interest in, and by the same token growing concern for the use of personal data, the EU has enacted the General Data Protection Regulations (GDPR) to provide a common basis for data protection laws that have subsequently been passed in the member states.[31] The legal aspects of dealing with related personal data form a special, somewhat more restrictive case under GDPR. California's Consumer Privacy Rights Act (CPRA)[32] is, for its part, primarily interested in the data exchanged in the course of business dealings but includes consideration of sensitive information and specific exemptions in relation to clinical trials.

It is important to note that the GDPR avoids the use of the term "ownership", but rather expresses the roles and obligations of individuals and entities dealing with personal data to ensure the protection of the natural person (data subject) to whom the data pertains and their enjoyment of rights in relation to that data.[31] In accordance with this, healthcare organizations occupy the roles of controllers and processors of patient data generated in the healthcare system, with the responsibility to serve as guardians of the data and the rights of the associated data subjects. The specific obligations and rights designed to protect the data subjects under GDPR[31] in the EU and CPRA[32] are outlined in Table 4.

Both the GDPR and CPRA legitimately try to regulate the use of health data.[8] Patient confidentiality is fundamental to the patient–clinician relationship, and to be used by healthcare AIs, medical data must be shared with other parties. The legal obligation to protect the privacy of personal health data is a critical priority as the unregulated circulation of confidential information would expose the data subjects to a variety of risks. Through such regulations, the states seek to ensure that health operators take appropriate measures to minimize the impact of incidents and to preserve service continuity (Table 5).[50]

TABLE 4   Summary of obligations and rights designed to protect data subjects under the General Data Protection Regulations (GDPR) and California Privacy Rights Act (CPRA).

GDPR	CPRA
– Obligation (of data controller) to inform data subject of collection and processing	– Right to know what personal information is being collected.
– Right to access	– Right to access personal information
– Right to rectification	– Right to correct inaccurate personal information
– Right to be forgotten	– Right to delete personal information
– Right to restrict processing	
– Right to data portability	
– Right to object to processing	– Right to limit use and disclosure of sensitive personal information
– Rights not to be subject to automated decision-making and profiling	– Right to opt-out of sale or sharing of personal information
– Obligation (of data controller) to inform data subject of personal data breach	– Right of no retaliation following opt-out or exercise of other right

TABLE 5   10 Principles of White House Office of Science and Technology Policy (OSTP).

Public trust in AI

• "It is … important that the government's regulatory and non-regulatory approaches to AI promote reliable, robust and trustworthy AI applications."

Public participation

• Agencies should provide "opportunities for the public to provide information and participate in all stages of the rulemaking process" and should promulgate and "promote awareness and widespread availability of standards and… other informative documents."

Scientific integrity and information quality

• "It is … important that the government's regulatory and non-regulatory approaches to AI promote reliable, robust and trustworthy AI applications."

Risk assessment and management

• "It is not necessary to mitigate every foreseeable risk… Instead, a risk-based approach should be used to determine which risks are acceptable and which risks present the possibility of unacceptable harm, or harm that has expected costs greater than expected benefits. Agencies should be transparent about their evaluations of risk and re-evaluate their assumptions and conclusions at appropriate intervals so as to foster accountability."

Benefits and costs

• Where agency action is required, agencies should "carefully consider the full societal costs, benefits, and distributional effects before considering regulations," including "the potential benefits and costs of employing AI, when compared to the systems AI has been designed to complement or replace, whether implementing AI will change the type of errors created by the system, as well as comparison to the degree of risk tolerated in other existing ones. Agencies should also consider critical dependencies when evaluating AI costs and benefits." The guidance specifically notes that bringing clarity to "questions of responsibility and liability for decisions made by AI" is an area that may require agency action.

Flexibility

• "Rigid, design-based regulations that attempt to prescribe the technical specifications of AI applications will in most cases be impractical and ineffective… To advance American innovation, agencies should keep in mind international uses of AI, ensuring that American companies are not disadvantaged by the United States' regulatory regime."

Fairness and non-discrimination

• — Agencies should consider "issues of fairness and non-discrimination with respect to outcomes and decisions produced by the AI application at issue, as well as whether the AI application at issue may reduce levels of unlawful, unfair, or otherwise unintended discrimination as compared to existing processes."

Disclosure and transparency

• "In addition to improving the rulemaking process, transparency and disclosure can increase public trust and confidence in AI applications. At times, such disclosures may include identifying when AI is in use, for instance, if appropriate for addressing questions about how the application impacts human end users."

TABLE 5 10 Principles of White House Office of Science and Technology Policy (OSTP)—cont'd

Safety and security

- Agencies should consider "issues of fairness and non-discrimination with respect to outcomes and decisions produced by the AI application at issue, as well as whether the AI application at issue may reduce levels of unlawful, unfair, or otherwise unintended discrimination as compared to existing processes."

Interagency coordination

- Agencies should coordinate with each other to share experiences and to ensure consistency and predictability of AI-related policies." The Office of Management and Budget's Office of Information and Regulatory Affairs will require that stakeholder agencies have an opportunity to provide input on any AI-related draft regulatory action it designates "significant."

In place of the ownership of data, these regulations build around the acceptance on the part of the data subject of use of their data for specific purposes and by specific users (called data controllers and data processors under GDPR). Consequently, informed consent from patients is mandatory for use of their data not only in the course of their direct medical care,[15] but beyond that, including its use to develop AI solutions.[51]

In the last decade, two issues have arisen that complicate the management and use of health data. First, the healthcare system, in the midst of a slow transition from a hospital-centric data model to a more patient-centric data model[52] has seen a substantial acceleration in point of use and health wearable data generation, namely, devices that consumers can wear to collect the data of their personal health and exercise. This expansion of data sources, often involving providers outside the conventional healthcare system complicates the unification of data, while also requiring expanding circles of trust. Second, open data policies are increasingly advocated by governments, and those who fund research, resulting in growing collections of data available in the cloud. As access to huge amounts of medical data is needed to train healthcare AI algorithms,[53] policies should prevent the collection of illicit or unverified sensitive data[54] and, although privacy concerns are growing, there is still a lack of clear regulations in data protection and cybersecurity regulations.[55] Soon the AI Act (currently in initial stages of approval) may fill this gap in Europe.

Healthcare operators and regulatory bodies are called to closely protect patients' health data. This extends beyond potential misuse by those to whom a data subject grants consent for a given data use, to avoid unintended access or outright theft of data. As with all digital data, healthcare data is threatened by cyberattacks. With its Cybersecurity Directive,[50] the EU has set out requirements for its member states that aim to prevent cyberattacks and limit their consequences. Among other things, European countries are required to ensure that operators of essential services take appropriate measures to prevent and minimize the impact of incidents and to preserve service continuity (Articles 14(2) and 16(2)), and to ensure that supervisory authorities are notified of incidents without undue delay (Articles 14(3) and 16(3)).[50]

In the United States, the Health Insurance Portability and Accountability Act (HIPAA) focuses on health information, defining standards and safeguards that protect patients' health records as well as personal health information that apply to all healthcare providers, insurers, and other healthcare entities.[56] This Act includes requirements for the formulation of policies and training systems for those who have access to sensitive data. HIPAA does not hinder the action of individual states to further protect the individuals' right to privacy but rather establishes national standards to protect individuals' electronic personal health information that is created, received, used, or maintained by an approved entity.[56] Cybersecurity, as dealt with by the FDA, requires providers to report only a limited number of risks their devices present and the actions are taken to minimize vulnerability.[39]

Finally, the development of large patient datasets incorporating wide ranges of clinical, and imaging data and pathologic information across multiple institutions for the development of AI algorithms will necessitate a thorough re-examination of issues surrounding patient privacy and informed consent.[15] Only the collaboration between patients, healthcare operators, and policymakers will be able to prevent the risks of inappropriate use of sensitive datasets and inaccurate or inappropriate disclosures. The concept of doctor–patient confidentiality requires that a physician withholds information from the medical record in line with the patient's wishes, as long as this poses no risk to the patient or others: once a clinical decision based on AI algorithms is integrated into clinical care, withholding information from electronic records will impair the validity of algorithm-driven medical practice.[23]

4.1 The problem of anonymization

The correct balance between privacy and achieving the goals of AI algorithms via personal data usage should be reached by anonymization, allowing data about patients to be used without the risk of revealing their identity.[57] Notably, rendering data anonymous also removes the data from the domain covered by GDPR insomuch as it would no longer relate to an identified or identifiable data subject. Unfortunately, the requisites for determining whether a data subject is identifiable are somewhat open-ended and subject to interpretation, stating that re-identification should not be reasonably likely for anyone – including the data controller, using the data directly or in combination with other data sources and techniques available at the time of processing or technological developments. Due to the level of detail in many medical datasets (be it unimodal—e.g., genetic or imaging, or multifaceted—e.g., combinations of many data elements that render the data effectively unique), it is often extremely difficult to achieve anonymization in a strict sense without greatly reducing the data content that serves for AI training.

Current methodologies for anonymization are often suboptimal[58] and there are no currently available certifications for tools and methods for anonymization. Nonetheless, steps need to be taken to reduce the risk of data anonymization, and they should be applied as early as possible in any data processing pipeline as possible, and as completely as possible while permitting the data processing goal to be completed. This typically includes the substitution of the name with an unrelated placeholder value (pseudonymization), elimination or substitution of directly identifying attributes such as address, birthdate, and national or institutional identifiers (de-identification), and removal of data that is superfluous in the required processing (minimization). Steps should also be taken to avoid indirect identification through combination with outside data sources. This may include masking or eliminating data such as the site, time and date of healthcare procedures, and the pooling of values (e.g., age into bands rather than the precise values) to avoid unique combinations of attributes being present. Lastly, data exchange should be avoided, if possible, thus limiting the number of copies of the data in circulation. This last is of particular relevance for AI training, because it is quite common for data from multiple centers to be required.

New solutions are demanded to conceal identities effectively both protecting individual privacy and still maintaining the full value of the same data for AI algorithms. These include distributing the learning to the sites of origin, thus restricting the pool of data processors and controllers for the data, while still permitting multicentric data to be used in the model creation.[32] Other approaches that have been proposed include homomorphic encryption—encrypting the data in ways that permit the data to be processed without requiring decryption,[59] and the use of an AI system to generate realistic, but artificial information that can be used in place of the personal information.[46] In light of the emerging legal requirements to restrict and control use of the data, data-centric security which includes not only s.

The wide acceptance of the DICOM format for the storage and exchange of medical images is an advantage for the radiology community as it means that Current repositories of research data such as The Cancer Imaging Archive (TCIA)[60] still have a workflow in place where curators visually check and when needed correct every DICOM file (image and header) entered into their database to ensure data privacy and correct handling of the data. The challenge here is the fact that DICOM headers may contain proprietary information that is not part of the standard DICOM but could include information on the acquisition or nature of the imaging data enclosed which is vital for adequate postprocessing of the data.[29]

A further issue specific to the field of radiology is that facial features can easily be obtained from imaging datasets of the head by performing surface or volume rendering reconstruction of those datasets. With the face of the subject thus rendered their appearance becomes visible. Studies have shown that facial recognition technology is able to match the data to actual photographs (for example, from social media) of individuals in research studies to such rendered images,[61,62] and could be more generally applicable. This issue has been recognized since before the growth of social media, though this has made the likelihood of recognition far greater, and several software packages for analysis of neuroimaging studies (see Ref. 31 for a recent comparison) contain de-facing algorithms. It is also common for de-facing to be performed as part of de-identification of data in clinical studies but has not been so widely adopted for data exchange in clinical practice. With face recognition providing a possible means of reidentifying research participants from their imaging examinations the current standard in many centers of removing only metadata in medical images may be insufficient to prevent the reidentification of participants in research.[62] In some cases, however, de-facing may not be desirable for AI purposes as doing so may affect the results of training or render it impossible (say for facial tumor radiomics). A recent study also suggests that even de-facing may not be sufficient as the shape of the cranium is relatively predictive of facial shape.

In the current scenario, privacy protection and data value tend to be in conflict due to opposing requirements. Moreover, variability in data content between sources and lack of standardization hamper the automation of this process.[29] These are major issues in the development of research collaboration between institutions for sharing data to perform AI studies. In the last few years, both EU and US authorities have started to promote data sharing.[63] This was part of the motivation for the HIPAA legislation in the clinical domain and is further pressed in the research domain by nongovernmental funding agencies in order to improve the efficiency of research funding. One manifestation of this change in policy is the emergence of anonymized benchmarking datasets with known diagnoses, that are updated and calibrated at regular intervals using local data from the contributing institutions to provide reference standards.[64]

Of radiological relevance beyond the above-mentioned TCIA,[60] are imaging and tissue biobanks and international consortia for medical imaging databases and other clinical data, such as the Cardiac Atlas Project,[65] the Kaggle Data Science Bowl,[19] and the Visual Concept Extraction Challenge in Radiology Project.[66]

Despite these promising starts, the extent of data sharing required for the widespread adoption of AI technologies across health systems will require more expansive efforts and it will probably depend more on the policy context of the health system in question rather than on the technology itself, which has already been showed to be available and ready.

5. Accountability of AI in health care

Because AI algorithms are capable of analyzing a much more exhaustive configuration space than conventional statistical analyses, their decisions do not always share a common basis with those we may have used in the past. In consequence, their conclusions may be both unpredictable and difficult to understand for humans.[67] Moreover, because AI algorithm decisions are based on the collected data on which the algorithm is trained, they are prone to suffer from biases and possible errors in the training data, and such training must be bound by core ethical principles, such as beneficence and respect for patients.[23]

When AIs make decisions that influence the diagnosis or management of patients, legal questions arise about accountability. A complicating factor is to determine the legal status of an AI system. Personhood in a legal sense is not carved in stone; there is the elasticity of the concept due to the evolution of societal needs, dependent on what is deemed acceptable within certain social, cultural, and geographical parameters.[29]

According to a Canadian Association of Radiologists white paper,[30] as an intended use statement must be submitted by the manufacturer to receive approval for an AI by the FDA and other institutional bodies, liability may rest with the health care practitioner using that device. Other authors have argued that ethical and legal responsibility for decision-making, even with AI, will remain with the natural intelligence of physicians.[7]

Modern medicine is shaped around a multidisciplinary approach, which involves not only medical professionals with different fields of expertise and levels of experience but also professionals from different backgrounds, such as biomedical engineers and medical physicists. Multidisciplinary teamwork has greatly enhanced the level of health care provided to patients. From this viewpoint, it is probable that multidisciplinary boards will take responsibility in difficult cases, considering relevant but not always conclusive what the AI provided. On the other hand, such an approach also comes with its unique shortcomings, which include uncoordinated administrative support, insufficient circulation of relevant information, and an excessive focus on one's own specific point of view, to the detriment of a holistic, comprehensive evaluation of the patient's case. This is a significant challenge not only from a clinical perspective but also from a juridical one, as they alter the ordinary criteria that regulate the assessment of medical accountability that are traditionally shaped with reference to the individual, rather than to a team of different professionals.

In the EU, the principles that govern the assessment of professional accountability within a medical team consider each member of the team as having a specific duty to challenge the decisions made by his colleagues anytime he has reasons to believe that those decisions could be detrimental to the patient's well-being. If the same criterion is applied to a potential collaboration between an AI and a radiologist, it would be crucial to establish what is the inherent value to be attributed to the opinion expressed by the AI, also considering that, in most cases, the reasoning behind the AI's opinion is not evident to the radiologist, as AI devices cannot explain nor elaborate on the outcome of their analysis. As long as the opinions expressed by AI align with the opinion of the radiologist, there is no particular issue[39] but if the opinions differ the radiologist will need to choose whether to trust the AI device over his own judgment. Accordingly, the radiologist may be exposed to liability arising from the (potential) mistake committed by AI as well as that from his own mistakes. This is not an easy choice and radiologists, as other medical professionals, should not be left alone. It is essential that both hospitals and professional associations take an active step toward their employees and members by offering specific instruments (such as guidelines, protocols, and training programs) that can help medical professionals understand the functioning of the AI devices they are using and, therefore, to better assess the reliability of the opinions offered by those same devices, also to the aim of solving possible discrepancies.

To understand accountability in AI, the uncontrolled reliance on automatic medical decisions may be distinguished from technical malpractice, in which AI achieves clinical certification despite undocumented, untested, or overlooked erratic behavior that can lead to wrong decisions.[68] While it seems that physicians tend to blame responsibility for wrong decisions on system providers, the same system provides tend to contractually exclude such liabilities, probably generating future law controversies.[69] The EU has recently faced this delicate issue and published a report that looks at whether the existing liability regimes are sufficient for the purposes of attributing liability in relation to highly complex tools such as AI.[41] Their report suggests that a clinician using a technology that has a certain degree of autonomy should not be less accountable for harm caused than if said harm had been caused by a human aide. However, as AI technology will continue to evolve, the current legislative framework for tort and product liability will need to be adapted accordingly.

Finally, as medical liability cases essentially revolve around the patient or the patient's family, educating patients about the potential benefits and limits coming from the use AI devices is just as important, from a legal perspective, as increasing the sensitivity of policymakers toward such subject.[23,39]

6. Conclusions

The development of AI has been considerable over the past several decades, and it could potentially be widely applied in the medical field. However, it is essential to assess the issues to ensure innovation, regulations, and ethics continue together. That triple goal is not impossible but responsible innovation requires great effort.

Although data privacy concerns have been growing in the last decade, we still face a lack of unique and clear regulations in data protection and cybersecurity regulations.[55] The ownership of health data is also part of the discussion on the application of different ownership rules to original, de-identified, anonymized, and processed data.[17]

In daily practice, radiologists will ultimately decide based upon two elements: regulatory approval and the standards of care. This means that AI algorithms also need to be accepted and approved by the latest consensus of the professional societies including their subspecialty sections and, responsible for issuing international guidelines on the practice of medicine.[5,6,18,22]

This book highlights the extensive potential of AI, but healthcare systems are confronted with a critical decision: whether to dampen the enthusiasm surrounding AI's potential in day-to-day clinical practice or to address the ethical and regulatory challenges. Without resolving these issues, the opportunities presented by AI to the healthcare system will remain unrealized possibilities. It is imperative to foster a global collaborative effort that engages in an open and mature dialogue about the most effective regulatory and ethical requirements, ensuring the safe realization of AI's potential across health systems. This conversation must involve policymakers at national and international levels, physicians, radiologists, lawyers, patients, data scientists, as well as representatives from industry and academia. By undertaking this endeavor appropriately and promptly, the value of AI in health care can be immeasurable.

References

1. Barbieri D, Giuliani E, Del Prete A, Losi A, Villani M, Barbieri A. How artificial intelligence and new technologies can help the management of the COVID-19 pandemic. *Int J Environ Res Public Health*. 2021;18(14):7648.
2. Schiaffino S, Codari M, Cozzi A, et al. Machine learning to predict in-hospital mortality in COVID-19 patients using computed tomography-derived pulmonary and vascular features. *J Pers Med*. 2021;11(6):501.
3. Pesapane F, Penco S, Rotili A, et al. How we provided appropriate breast imaging practices in the epicentre of the COVID-19 outbreak in Italy. *Br J Radiol*. 2020;93(1114):20200679.
4. Clift AK, Coupland CAC, Keogh RH, et al. Living risk prediction algorithm (QCOVID) for risk of hospital admission and mortality from coronavirus 19 in adults: national derivation and validation cohort study. *BMJ*. 2020;371, m3731.
5. Thrall JH, Li X, Li Q, et al. Artificial intelligence and machine learning in radiology: opportunities, challenges, pitfalls, and criteria for success. *J Am Coll Radiol*. 2018;15(3 Pt B):504–508.
6. Yi PH, Hui FK, Ting DSW. Artificial intelligence and radiology: collaboration is key. *J Am Coll Radiol*. 2018;15:781–783.
7. King Jr BF. Artificial intelligence and radiology: what will the future hold? *J Am Coll Radiol*. 2018;15(3 Pt B):501–503.
8. Ravi D, Wong C, Deligianni F, et al. Deep learning for health informatics. *IEEE J Biomed Health Inform*. 2017;21(1):4–21.
9. Calo R. Artificial Intelligence Policy: A Primer and Roadmap: Social Science Research Network; 2017. Available from: https://lawreview.law.ucdavis.edu/issues/51/2/Symposium/51-2_Calo.pdf.
10. Verghese A, Shah NH, Harrington RA. What this computer needs is a physician: humanism and artificial intelligence. *JAMA*. 2018;319(1):19–20.
11. Miller DD, Brown EW. Artificial intelligence in medical practice: the question to the answer? *Am J Med*. 2018;131(2):129–133.
12. Jha S. Will Computers Replace Radiologists?; 2016. Available from: https://www.medscape.com/viewarticle/863127.
13. Pesapane F, Codari M, Sardanelli F. Artificial intelligence in medical imaging: threat or opportunity? Radiologists again at the forefront of innovation in medicine. *Eur Radio Exp*. 2018;2(1):35.
14. Recht M, Bryan RN. Artificial intelligence: threat or boon to radiologists? *J Am Coll Radiol*. 2017;14(11):1476–1480.
15. Pesapane F, Volonte C, Codari M, Sardanelli F. Artificial intelligence as a medical device in radiology: ethical and regulatory issues in Europe and the United States. *Insights Imaging*. 2018;9:745–753.
16. Beckers R, Kwade Z, Zanca F. The EU medical device regulation: implications for artificial intelligence-based medical device software in medical physics. *Phys Med*. 2021;83:1–8.
17. Rosenstein BS, Capala J, Efstathiou JA, et al. How will big data improve clinical and basic research in radiation therapy? *Int J Radiat Oncol Biol Phys*. 2016;95(3):895–904.

18. Mohan CS. Artificial intelligence in radiology—are we treating the image or the patient? *Indian J Radiol Imaging*. 2018;28(2):137–139.

19. He J, Baxter SL, Xu J, Xu J, Zhou X, Zhang K. The practical implementation of artificial intelligence technologies in medicine. *Nat Med*. 2019;25 (1):30–36.

20. Langlotz CP, Allen B, Erickson BJ, et al. A roadmap for foundational research on artificial intelligence in medical imaging: from the 2018 NIH/ RSNA/ACR/the academy workshop. *Radiology*. 2019;291(3):781–791.

21. Pesapane F, Rotili A, Valconi E, et al. Women's perceptions and attitudes to the use of AI in breast cancer screening: a survey in a cancer referral centre. *Br J Radiol*. 2023;96(1141):20220569.

22. Hashimoto DA, Rosman G, Rus D, Meireles OR. Artificial intelligence in surgery: promises and perils. *Ann Surg*. 2018;268(1):70–76.

23. Char DS, Shah NH, Magnus D. Implementing machine learning in health care—addressing ethical challenges. *N Engl J Med*. 2018;378 (11):981–983.

24. Boddington P. Towards a Code of Ethics for Artificial Intelligence. 1st ed. Springer International Publishing; 2017.

25. Hosny A, Parmar C, Quackenbush J, Schwartz LH, Aerts H. Artificial intelligence in radiology. *Nat Rev Cancer*. 2018;18(8):500–510.

26. Derevianko A, Pizzoli SFM, Pesapane F, et al. The use of artificial intelligence (AI) in the radiology field: what is the state of doctor-patient communication in cancer diagnosis? *Cancers (Basel)*. 2023;15(2):470.

27. Open AI. 2020 [Available from: http://open.ai/.

28. MIRI. The Machine Intelligence Research Institute; 2020. Available from: https://intelligence.org/about/.

29. Ranschaert ER, Sergey M, Algra PR. Artificial Intelligence in Medical Imaging. Springer; 2019.

30. Jaremko JL, Azar M, Bromwich R, et al. Canadian association of radiologists white paper on ethical and legal issues related to artificial intelligence in radiology. *Can Assoc Radiol J*. 2019;70(2):107–118.

31. Theyers AE, Zamyadi M, O'Reilly M, et al. Multisite comparison of MRI defacing software across multiple cohorts. *Front Psych*. 2021;12.

32. Konečný J, McMahan B, Ramage D. Federated optimization: distributed optimization beyond the datacenter. *ArXiv*. 2015. 1511.03575.

33. Thierer AD, O'Sullivan A, Russel R. Artificial Intelligence and Public Policy Mercatus Research Paper; 2017. Available from: https://www.mercatus.org/system/files/thierer-artificial-intelligence-policy-mr-mercatus-v1.pdf.

34. European Economic Community. 93/42/EEC—Council Directive concerning Medical Devices Official Journal of the European Communities; 1993. [Available from: http://ec.europa.eu/growth/single-market/european-standards/harmonised-standards/medical-devices_en.

35. European Commission. MDCG 2018–2 Future EU Medical Device Nomenclature—Description of requirements; 2018. Available from: https:// ec.europa.eu/docsroom/documents/28668.

36. 114th Congress (2015–2016). H.R.34—21st Century Cures Act 2016, updated December 13, 2016. Available from: https://www.congress.gov/ bill/114th-congress/house-bill/34.

37. U.S. Food & Drug Administration. Is The Product A Medical Device? U.S. Department of Health and Human Services; 2018. updated 22/03/ 2018. Available from: https://www.fda.gov/MedicalDevices/DeviceRegulationandGuidance/Overview/ClassifyYourDevice/ucm051512. htm.

38. Tsang L.K.D., Mulryne J., Strom L., Perkins N., Dickinson R., Wallace V.M., Jones B. The Impact of Artificial Intelligence on Medical Innovation in the European Union and United States 2017. Available from: https://www.arnoldporter.com/~/media/files/perspectives/publications/ 2017/08/the-impact-of-artificial-inteelligence-on-medical-innovation.pdf.

39. Pesapane FBD, Mulligan J, Lanzavecchia MB, et al. Legal and regulatory framework for AI solutions in healthcare in EU, US, China, and Russia: new scenarios after a pandemic. *Radiation*. 2021;1(4):261–276.

40. Communication Artificial Intelligence for Europe, (2021).

41. European Commission. White Paper on Artificial Intelligence: A European Approach to Excellence and Trust; 2020.

42. The European Parliament and the Council of The European Union. Regulation (EU) 2017/745 of the European Parliament and of the Council on medical devices, amending Directive 2001/83/EC, Regulation (EC) No 178/2002 and Regulation (EC) No 1223/2009 and repealing Council Directives 90/385/EEC and 93/42/EEC Official Journal of the European Communities2017. Available from: https://eur-lex.europa.eu/ legal-content/EN/TXT/?uri=CELEX%3A32017R0745.

43. The European Parliament and the Council of the European Union. Regulation (EU) 2017/746 of the European Parliament and of the council on in vitro diagnostic medical devices and repealing directive 98/79/EC and commission decision 2010/227/EU official journal of the European Communities; 2017. Available from: https://eur-lex.europa.eu/legal-content/EN/TXT/?uri=CELEX%3A32017R0746.

44. Crossley S, LLP E. EU Regulation of Health Information Technology, Software and Mobile Apps. Global Guide; 2016.

45. Informal Innovation Network—Horizon Scanning Assessment Report—Artificial Intelligence, (2021).

46. Lu Y, Shen M, Wang H, Wei W. Machine learning for synthetic data generation: a review. *ArXiv*. 2023. 2302.04062.

47. Inside Tech Media. AI Update: White House Issues 10 Principles for Artificial Intelligence Regulation; 2020. Available from: https://www. insidetechmedia.com/2020/01/14/ai-update-white-house-issues-10-principles-for-artificial-intelligence-regulation/.

48. Mendez AJ, Tahoces PG, Lado MJ, Souto M, Vidal JJ. Computer-aided diagnosis: automatic detection of malignant masses in digitized mammograms. *Med Phys*. 1998;25(6):957–964.

49. FDA. Proposed Regulatory Framework for Modifications to Artificial Intelligence/Machine Learning (AI/ML)-Based Software as a Medical Device (SaMD) - Discussion Paper and Request for Feedback; 2021. Available from: https://www.fda.gov/files/medical%20devices/ published/US-FDA-Artificial-Intelligence-and-Machine-Learning-Discussion-Paper.pdf.

50. The European Parliament and the Council of The European Union. Directive (EU) 2016/1148 of the European Parliament and of the Council concerning measures for a high common level of security of network and information systems across the Union Official Journal of the European Communities; 2016. Updated 19/07/2016. Available from: https://eur-lex.europa.eu/legal-content/EN/TXT/?toc=OJ:L:2016:194:TOC&uri= uriserv:OJ.L_.2016.194.01.0001.01.ENG.

51. Mandl KD, Szolovits P, Kohane IS. Public standards and patients' control: how to keep electronic medical records accessible but private. *BMJ*. 2001;322(7281):283–287.

52. Rajkomar A, Dean J, Kohane I. Machine learning in medicine. *N Engl J Med*. 2019;380(14):1347–1358.

53. Kruskal JB, Berkowitz S, Geis JR, Kim W, Nagy P, Dreyer K. Big data and machine learning-strategies for driving this bus: a summary of the 2016 intersociety summer conference. *J Am Coll Radiol*. 2017;14(6):811–817.

54. Castelvecchi D. Can we open the black box of AI? *Nature.* 2016;538(7623):20–23.
55. Dilsizian SE, Siegel EL. Artificial intelligence in medicine and cardiac imaging: harnessing big data and advanced computing to provide personalized medical diagnosis and treatment. *Curr Cardiol Rep.* 2014;16(1):441.
56. Tsang L, Mulryne J, Strom L. The Impact of Artificial Intelligence on Medical Innovation in the European Union and United States; 2017.
57. Moore SM, Maffitt DR, Smith KE, et al. De-identification of medical images with retention of scientific research value. *Radiographics.* 2015;35(3):727–735.
58. Aryanto KY, Oudkerk M, van Ooijen PM. Free DICOM de-identification tools in clinical research: functioning and safety of patient privacy. *Eur Radiol.* 2015;25(12):3685–3695.
59. Munjal K, Bhatia R. A systematic review of homomorphic encryption and its contributions in healthcare industry. *Complex Intell Syst.* 2022. https://doi.org/10.1007/s40747-022-00756-z.
60. The Cancer Imaging Archive. TCIA. Available from: http://www.cancerimagingarchive.net.
61. Mazura JC, Juluru K, Chen JJ, Morgan TA, John M, Siegel EL. Facial recognition software success rates for the identification of 3D surface reconstructed facial images: implications for patient privacy and security. *J Digit Imaging.* 2012;25(3):347–351.
62. Schwarz CG, Kremers WK, Therneau TM, et al. Identification of anonymous MRI research participants with face-recognition software. *N Engl J Med.* 2019;381(17):1684–1686.
63. Jiang F, Jiang Y, Zhi H, et al. Artificial intelligence in healthcare: past, present and future. *Stroke Vasc Neurol.* 2017;2(4):230–243.
64. Wu H, Chan NK, Zhang CJP, Ming WK. The role of the sharing economy and artificial intelligence in health care: opportunities and challenges. *J Med Internet Res.* 2019;21(10), e13469.
65. Fonseca CG, Backhaus M, Bluemke DA, et al. The Cardiac Atlas Project—an imaging database for computational modeling and statistical atlases of the heart. *Bioinformatics.* 2011;27(16):2288–2295.
66. Jimenez-Del-Toro O, Muller H, Krenn M, et al. Cloud-based evaluation of anatomical structure segmentation and landmark detection algorithms: VISCERAL anatomy benchmarks. *IEEE Trans Med Imaging.* 2016;35(11):2459–2475.
67. Scherer MU. Regulating artificial intelligence systems: risks, challenges, competencies, and strategies. *Harv J Law Tech.* 2016;29(2):354–400.
68. Bal BS. An introduction to medical malpractice in the United States. *Clin Orthop Relat Res.* 2009;467(2):339–347.
69. Braun M, Hummel P, Beck S, Dabrock P. Primer on an ethics of AI-based decision support systems in the clinic. *J Med Ethics.* 2020;47:e3.

13

The role of artificial intelligence in radiology and interventional oncology

Carolina Lanza[a],*, Serena Carriero[a],*, Pierpaolo Biondetti[b], Salvatore Alessio Angileri[b], Anna Maria Ierardi[b], and Gianpaolo Carrafiello[b,c]

[a]Postgraduate School in Radiodiagnostics, Università degli Studi di Milano, Milan, Italy [b]Diagnostic and Interventional Radiology Department, Fundation IRCCS Cà Granda-Ospedale Maggiore Policlinico, Milan, Italy [c]Department of Health Science, Università degli Studi di Milano, Milan, Italy

1. Artificial intelligence

The term "artificial intelligence"(AI) includes computational algorithms that can perform tasks considered typical of human intelligence, with partial to complete autonomy, to produce new beneficial outputs from specific inputs.[1,2]

AI is an umbrella category that includes machine learning (ML) and deep learning (DL). Machine learning (ML) is based upon the so-called "reverse training" method, in which computer systems focus on specific pathological features identified during a training period, and once trained, the computer can apply this information even to new cases never seen before. A common machine learning approach involves the use of artificial neural networks (ANNs).[3,4]

A convolutional neural network (CNN) is a type of deep artificial neural network that is well suited for imaging. Convolutional neural networks are inspired from the connectivity pattern of visual cortex neurons, scanning an image with receptive fields and serving as an input to a deep neural network. Similar to artificial neural networks, convolutional neural networks include input, output, and multiple hidden layers. However, the hidden layers are specialized, consisting of convolutional, pooling, and fully connected layers.[5,6]

2. Radiomics

AI finds its field of application in radiomics. Radiomics, an expansion of computer-aided diagnosis, provides computer-extracted characteristics related to tumor biology and other clinical, pathologic, and genomic data.[7]

Radiomics has recently gained traction as a popular tool because of its applications to image analysis, precision medicine, and oncology. Radiomics uses computer methods to extract features of medical images that go beyond the visible features.[6]

These features include both semantic and agnostic data. Semantics are typically used by radiologists to describe tumors and include size, shape, location, vascularity, necrosis, etc. However, agnostics are more specific to higher dimensional analysis in radiomics and include histograms, Haralick textures, laws textures, wavelets, Laplacian transforms, and several others. This provides a lot of data that can be analyzed and combined with clinical information to optimize ML models.[6,7]

Interventional oncology can benefit greatly using AI through enhanced image analysis and intraprocedural guidance. For example, the identification of an accurate method to predict the success rate of a specific treatment in a

---

* Both authors contributed equally to the drafting of the chapter.

specific patient could reduce unnecessary and useless procedures and interventions, reducing healthcare costs and the risk for the patient.[8]

Classification of patients as a responder (complete or partial) or nonresponder could potentially be used in daily clinical practice as an indicator to decide whether or not a specific intervention should be performed. For instance, the performance of preablation CT texture features may predict posttreatment local progression and survival in patients who undergo tumor ablation, using ML to identifying specific CT texture patterns, as demonstrated by Daye et al. for adrenal metastases.[8]

3. Virtual reality

Among the field of application of AI, Augmented Reality (AR) or Virtual Reality (VR) can be supportive during the preprocedural and intraprocedural assessment. Through advanced 3D rendering and manipulation of imaging in space, AR and VR allow operators to conceptualize difficult anatomy, to increase realism in procedural planning (when compared with standard 2D images), and to improve procedural skills in a previous simulated environment.[9]

Both VR and AR, although distinct from each other, refer to simulations in which virtual elements are used to replace or supplement native sensory input. VR is a fully immersive simulation that generates the perception of being present in a nonphysical virtual world; AR differs from VR because virtual objects are superimposed on the real world and the user is able to interact with the real world and virtual objects simultaneously.[9]

4. Fusion imaging

Fusion imaging is a technique that fuses more different imaging modalities to better exploit the characteristics of each, eliminating or reducing to a minimum the weaknesses of each individual mode. The process consists of the overlapping imaging dataset, obtained from different imaging modalities, into a single composite imaging dataset.[10]

There are many applications of fusion imaging, and the current application is in the setting of the oncologic percutaneous procedures, such as biopsies and thermal ablations.

In this field of application, fusion imaging allows to precisely localize the target tumor and to guide the antenna placement.[11]

The first step of imaging fusion is the importation of data from a previous CT/MR/PET exam.

The second step is the spatial alignment of the imaging dataset, and both anatomical landmarks and external markers can be used. Imaging registration can be carried manually by the operator, automatically based on matching common anatomical landmarks, or semi-automatically using a combination of both techniques. Appropriate alignment of anatomical landmarks is fundamental to ensure the proper targeting.[12]

When an appropriate alignment is complete, real-time US and CT/MR/PET images are overlaid on the US monitor, displaying the same plane and moving synchronously together.[11,12]

US guidance provides a real-time visualization of needle placement, does not use ionizing radiation, and is easily accessible. However, the limitations of US are represented by the deep lesions and/or large patients with a no-complete visualization of target lesion.

CT and MRI are not a real-time imaging techniques guidance but offer superior three-dimensional visualization of the needle and electrode and target.[12]

FDG-PET/CT fusion is a tool used to characterize malignancy based on tumor metabolic activity.[13]

The association of the advantages of different imaging techniques by fusion imaging improves the performance during the interventional radiology procedures.

Currently, the use intraprocedural CBCT has been increased for the percutaneous oncologic procedures. CBCT allows volumetric data acquisition with a single rotation of an X-ray source and a flat-panel detector, mounted at the ends of the C-arm of the angio-suite.[14]

CBCT-derived volumetric data can be merged with preprocedural cross-sectional images and/or combined with dedicated software for needle trajectory planning and ablation volume prediction.

Navigation software such as XperGuide (Philips Allura Xper FD20; Philips Healthcare, Best, The Netherlands) is used for the planning of needle trajectory, monitoring needle progression by merging fluoroscopic images with the preliminary CBCT dataset.

XperCT software (Philips Allura Xper FD20; Philips Healthcare, Best, The Netherlands), on the other hand, is used to predict ablation volume. Merging the intraprocedural CBCT images and the preprocedural CT/MR/PET images, a "virtual antenna" can be located exactly over the real one and after choosing the preferred power and ablation time. Then, an ablation volume is automatically produced, based on the MWA manufacturer's data (Figs. 1 and 2).

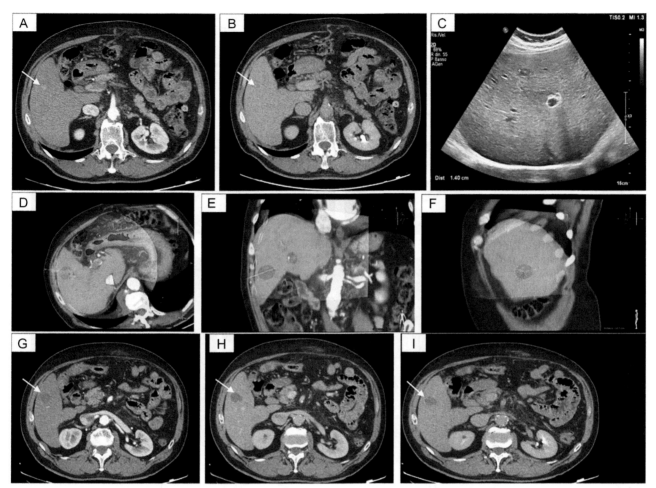

FIG. 1 Preprocedural CECT shows the presence of HCC nodule in S5 with wash-in in the arterial phase (A) and wash-out in the delayed phase (B) (white arrows). (C) Preprocedural US demonstrates the visibility of lesion by a subcostal approach. (D, E, F) Axial, sagittal, and coronal sections of fusion imaging between preprocedural CECT in the arterial phase and intraprocedural CBCT and prediction of ablated volume using XperCT software (Philips). MWA with a power of 100 W for 3.30 min. One-month follow-up CECT shows in arterial (G), venous (H), and (I) delayed phase the presence of hypodense area without signs of residual disease. (white arrows). Abbreviations: CECT: contrast-enhanced computed tomography; CBCT: cone-beam CT; HCC: hepatocellular carcinoma; US: ultrasound.

5. Robotics

The use of robotics in IR is applied in both percutaneous interventions as well as in endovascular procedures. One of the main potential advantages of robotics is the reduction of radiation for the operator while working from a remote console, as well as on the patients' side in the case of reduced procedure and radiation times.[15]

To improve ablative radio-oncologic procedures in IR, there have been recent developments in assistance in trajectory planning and placement of the instruments with the use of navigational devices and image registration. Navigational systems can be distinguished from tracking systems and robotic systems, in which robot-assisted systems do not trace the instrument, but rather deliver active guidance for the placement of the probe or electrode. These robotic systems are calibrated to a CT scanner and deliver active guidance probe placement, where the robotic arm moves toward the targeted position. The target is defined prior to the intervention using data on the access point, angle, and depth of the probe. After the probe is placed, the correct position is then confirmed by control imaging.[16]

IR robotic systems can be used for both percutaneous and endovascular procedures. Different kinds of imaging modality guidance can be used integrated with IR robotic systems, such as CT, MRI, US, and fluoroscopy. IR robots in addition to receiving guidance input by single modality imaging can receive the guidance by fused multimodality imaging. Some devices are completely integrated into the machine and are able to perform all steps of image capture, registration, fusion, and to adequately insert a needle with an imaging guidance with semiautonomous autonomous operations.[16,17]

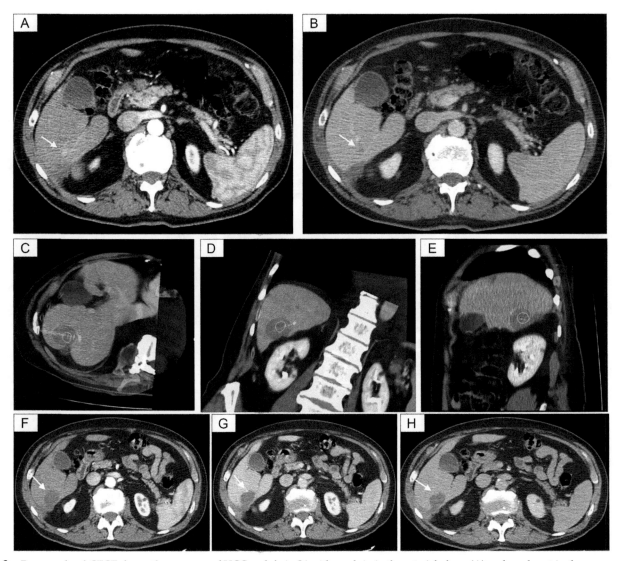

FIG. 2   Preprocedural CECT shows the presence of HCC nodule in S6 with wash-in in the arterial phase (A) and wash-out in the venous phase (B) (white arrows). (C, D, E) Axial, coronal, and sagittal sections of fusion imaging between preprocedural CECT and intraprocedural CBCT and prediction of ablated volume using XperCT software (Philips). MWA with a power of 100 W for 4 min. One-month follow-up CECT shows in arterial (G), venous (H), and (I) delayed phase the presence of hypodense area without signs of residual disease. (white arrows). Abbreviations: CECT: contrast-enhanced computed tomography; CBCT: cone-beam CT; HCC: hepatocellular carcinoma.

Other prototypes of robot are patient-mounted and may be either CT- US-, or MR-compatible with multiple degrees of freedom during device actuation.

The endovascular robotic systems represent another type of IR robotic system, capable of ensuring precise and stable catheter navigation and, above all, reducing radiation exposure during the procedures. Endovascular robotic systems can be used both for small caliber arteries and large caliber arteries. Current endovascular robotic systems consist of two components: the patient-side mechanical robot and the operator control station.[18]

6. Immunotherapy and the interventional oncology

6.1 What is interventional oncology?

Interventional oncology (IO) is a subspecialty field of interventional radiology focused on the diagnosis and treatment of cancer by using minimally invasive procedures performed under image guidance. Interventional oncologists actively participate in the diagnosis and treatment of cancer patients by observing patients in the clinic, admitting patients to hospitals, serving on tumor review committees, and multidisciplinary treatment teams. The combination of radiological knowledge and interventional procedure expertise enables interventional radiologists to perform minimally invasive procedures in the most challenging areas of the body with a low-risk complications. The interventional oncologist has a pivotal role in for the patient with cancer. IO, the youngest and most rapidly growing offshoot of interventional radiology, plays a central role in integrated cancer care and is part of the four pillars of cancer care with medical, surgical, and radiation oncology.[19] IO is focused on three main areas in cancer management: diagnosis, therapy, and symptom palliation. The top cause of death worldwide is currently cancer, surpassing cardiovascular disorders. In modern medicine, there is a growing demand for faster, increasingly individualized, and more affordable healthcare solutions. IO is a technology-driven specialty, minimally invasive that is able to perform personalized procedure. A highly qualified interventional oncologist must be fluent in oncological medicine; knowing the fundamentals of the other oncologic disciplines must become a prerequisite for every interventional oncologist. A lot of progress has been made over the past decade; interventional radiologist had influenced the clinical guidelines in primary hepatocellular carcinoma (HCC) with ablation and trans arterial chemoembolization (TACE).[20]

6.2 The connection between immune system and cancer

The hypothesis that immune system can control cancer has been the subject of debate for over a century. Nowadays, it is established that cancer-associated inflammation, which is present at different stages of tumorigenesis, contributes to epigenetic modification, genomic instability, induction of cancer cell proliferation, enhancement of cancer antiapoptotic pathways, stimulation of angiogenesis, and cancer dissemination. Studies during the past two decades have demonstrated that inflammatory immune cells are essential players of cancer-related inflammation.[21] Nowadays, it is known that chronic inflammation is a critical hallmark of cancer, with at least 25% of cancers associated with it,[22] and possible underlying causes include microbial infections, autoimmunity, and immune deregulation.

The immune system keeps an appropriate balance between identifying and eliminating foreign antigens and suppressing an uncontrolled immune response.[23] Antigen-presenting cells (APCs) and CD8 effector T cells, often known as cytotoxic T cells, are the main players in the immune system. Cytotoxic T cells recognize "self" and "nonself" antigens tied up to major histocompatibility class I complexes that are expressed on APCs. Due to genetic mutations or errors, cancer cells have undergone major modifications that have led to the development of neo-antigens expression of proteins that are not normally expressed. Neo-antigen-presenting cells can be recognized as "nonself" and destroyed by cytotoxic T cells. Lewis Thomas and Frank Macfarlane Burnet described for the first time this this concept of the "immunological surveillance" of cancer.[24] On the other hand, cancer cells can escape from immune surveillance by with several mechanisms as secretion of immunosuppressive cytokines (trans- forming growth factor b (TGF-b) and interleukin 10 (IL-10), downregulation of surface major histocompatibility complex (MHC) class I molecules, loss or alteration of specific antigens or antigenic machinery, promotion of an immune-tolerant microenvironment, and upregulation of the expression of immune checkpoint molecules.

In 2001, it was discovered that the immune system controls both tumor quantity and tumor quality (immunogenicity concept)[25]; this concept induced to a major revision of the cancer immunosurveillance hypothesis. Cancer immunoediting is based on both function of immune system: the protection of the host against tumor formation and the modeling of tumor immunogenicity.[26]

Cancer immunoediting consists of three sequential phases: elimination, equilibrium, and escape.

1. *Elimination phase*: Innate and adaptive immunity work together to destroy developing tumors before they become clinically apparent. If this phase goes to completion, the host remains free of cancer. However, if a rare tumor cell variant is undestroyed in this phase, it may then enter the equilibrium phase.
2. *Equilibrium phase*: In this phase, tumor outgrowth is prevented by immunologic mechanisms. T lymphocytes, IL-12, and IFN-g are essential to keep tumor cells functionally dormant. Editing of tumor immunogenicity occurs in the equilibrium phase. Equilibrium may also indicate the end step of the cancer immunoediting process, preventing the spread of occult tumors throughout the duration of the host's life.

   However, in this phase may emerge tumor cell variants because of constant immune selection pressure placed on genetically unstable tumor cells. Tumor cell variants no longer detected by adaptive immunity as antigen loss variants or tumor cells that have deficiencies in antigen processing or presentation become insensitive to immune effector mechanisms and generate an immunosuppressive state within the tumor microenvironment. These tumor cells may then undergo the phase of escape.
3. *Escape phase*: Immunity no longer inhibits tumor growth at this stage. These tumor cells proliferate and generate clinically visible disease.

On the other hand, tumor has the ability to evade immune system with a lot of different strategy:

1. *Loss of antigenicity*: Tumors can express a variety of nonmutated and mutated antigens that have the potential to elicit tumor-specific immune responses. However, to avoid immune-mediated elimination, cancer cells may lose their antigenicity. Loss of antigenicity can arise due to the immune selection of cancer cells that lack or mutate immunogenic tumor antigens as well as through the acquisition of defects or deficiencies in antigen presentation (e.g., loss of major histocompatibility (MHC) expression or dysregulation of antigen processing machinery).[26]
2. *Loss of immunogenicity*: Tumors can escape elimination by decreasing their immunogenicity. IFN-γ produced by tumor infiltrating lymphocytes can induce the upregulation of the immunoinhibitory molecule PD-L1 on malignant cells.[24] Membranous PD-L1 expression by tumor cells has been shown to strongly correlate with lymphocyte-rich regions of a tumor and with objective responses to anti-PD-1 antibody therapy.[27]
3. *Immunosuppressive microenvironment*: Tumors may also escape immune elimination by promoting an immunosuppressive microenvironment. For successful immune mediated elimination, leukocyte infiltration into tumor tissue and recognition of malignant cells is necessary. Studies had shown that reverse immune suppression through elimination of immunosuppressive cell populations have been found to restore T cell infiltration into tumor tissue and the capacity of T cells to mediate antitumor activity.[28] These findings suggest that some tumors may retain sufficient antigenicity and immunogenicity for recognition by tumor-specific T cells but evade immune elimination by orchestrating a suppressive microenvironment.[28]

A new era in cancer therapy began with the blockage of the inhibitory signaling pathways called "checkpoint inhibitors" (CPIs) that has shown to provide a significant benefit against different solid tumors.[29]

6.3 The checkpoint inhibitors CPIs

CPIs are a type of immunotherapy drugs that can be used to treat cancer. CPIs inhibit the regulatory steps of activation and proliferation of T cells. CPIs targets are specific proteins on immune cells, known as checkpoints, that are involved in regulating the immune response. The fundamental action of CPI is blocking these checkpoints to obtain the inhibition of the negative regulation of T cells. T-cells mediated immune response is fundamental in control of intensity and duration of the immune response.[30] CPIs activate the immune system against cancer to obtain a more effective activation of it. There are three main types of checkpoint inhibitors with Food and Drug Administration approval (FDA): Cytotoxic T lymphocyte antigen-4 (CTLA-4) antibodies, programmed cell death (PD-1), and programmed cell death ligand (PD-L1 and PD-L2) antibodies.

PD-1 inhibitors, such as pembrolizumab and nivolumab, target the PD-1 receptor found on T cells, B cells and dendritic cells (DC), macrophages, and natural killer (NK), promoting self-tolerance by suppressing T-cell activation and promoting self-tolerance. When activated, PD-1 suppresses immune cells activity, and some cancer cells can exploit this mechanism to evade the immune system. PD-1 inhibitors block the PD-1 receptor, allowing T cells to attack cancer cells more effectively.[31]

CTLA-4 inhibitors, such as ipilimumab, target the CTLA-4 receptor found on T cells. CTLA-4 is another checkpoint protein important in regulating immune response. This drug, by blocking CTLA-4, can activate T cells and enhance the immune response against cancer cells.

Checkpoint inhibitors have shown promise in the treatment of several types of cancer as metastatic melanoma, advanced non–small cell lung cancer (NSCLC), Hodgkin's disease, and bladder cancer. Nivolumab (Opdivo) and pembrolizumab (Keytruda) (drugs that block PD-1 antibodies) have received FDA approval in metastatic melanoma, advanced non–small cell lung cancer (NSCLC), RCC, and Hodgkin's disease.[32] Atezolizumab (Tecentriq) is the first FDA-approved antibody that blocks the PD-1 ligand.[33] This treatment has been approved for locally advanced or metastatic urothelial carcinoma and metastatic NSCLC patients who have progressed with frontline chemotherapy. However, these drugs can have side effects, such as autoimmune reactions, that need to be carefully managed. Ongoing research is focused on identifying new targets for checkpoint inhibition and developing combination therapies that can enhance the effectiveness of these drugs.

6.4 The connection between immune system and interventional radiology

Ablation caused necrotic cell death dropping numerous tumor antigens and inducing a noninfectious inflammatory response, which conducts to the proliferation of tumor-specific T cells and APC infiltration into tumors.[34]

Ablation can have different effects depending on the specific circumstances. For example, HCC ablation causes an increase in T cells specific against HCC antigens; the number of specific against HCC T cells correlates with a low recurrence of HCC.[35]

Ablation reduces the tumor burden after surgical excision and may also stimulate the immune system to mount a stronger defense against any cancer cells that may still be present. For example, in colorectal liver metastases, ablation before surgery of the primary tumor has been shown to affect lymphocyte tumor infiltration of primary tumor.[36]

Given the things mentioned earlier, in some cases, ablation can be used in conjunction with immunotherapy. Animal and human studies indicate that the combination of ablation and CPIs do indeed provide synergistic responses.

Ablation techniques could induce local and systemic antitumor immune responses, but these responses are relatively weak, and cannot completely control the tumor. This reason explains the high local recurrence rates after treatment. We can obtain the enhancement of the immune response with check point inhibitors with a lot of interventional radiology procedures as TACE, ablation with radiofrequency (RFA), microwave (MWA), and irreversible electroporation (IRE).

Ablative therapies induce a peripheral immune response that may enhance the effect of anti-CTLA4 treatment in patients with advanced hepatocellular carcinoma (HCC). As an example, tremelimumab in combination with MWA is a potential new treatment for patients with advanced HCC and leads to the accumulation of intratumoral CD8+ T cells. Positive clinical activity was seen, with a possible surrogate reduction in HCV viral load.[37]

Nivolumab is used in treatment of HCC and is well tolerated; combination of TACE and nivolumab, in the treatment of HCC resulted in improved overall survival compared to TACE alone.[38] Huang et al. in their study affirm that combination of MWA and anti-PD-1 therapy resulted in the inhibition of distant tumor growth and the construction of a systemic antitumor immune environment that can reduce recurrence.[38]

Some clinical studies have shown that IRE combined with immunotherapy is effective in prolonging OS in cancer patients.[39]

Alnaggar et al. show in their study that IRE combined with allogeneic NK cell immunotherapy significantly increases the median OS of patients with stage IV HCC.[39]

Moreover, we can use also other immunotherapies as allogeneic γδ T-cell infusion in combination with ablation techniques. Lin et al. showed that IRE combined with allogeneic γδ T-cell infusion is a promising strategy to enhance the antitumor efficacy in LAPC patients, yielding extended survival benefits.[40]

Nowadays, there are a lot of studies about the combination of ablation and immunotherapy, and this field has a great potential and may become a promising choice for patients with unresectable tumors.

References

1. Roberto I., S.N. Goldberg, B. Merlino, A. Posa, V. Valentini, R. Manfredi, Artificial intelligence in interventional radiology: a literature review and future perspectives, J Oncol, vol. 2019, Article ID 6153041, 5 pages, 2019.
2. Waller J, O'Connor A, Rafaat E, et al. Applications and challenges of artificial intelligence in diagnostic and interventional radiology. *Pol J Radiol.* 2022;87:e113–e117. https://doi.org/10.5114/pjr.2022.113531. 35280945. PMCID: PMC8906183.
3. D'Amore B, Smolinski-Zhao S, Daye D, et al. Role of machine learning and artificial intelligence in interventional oncology. *Curr Oncol Rep.* 2021;23:70. https://doi.org/10.1007/s11912-021-01054-6.
4. B. Letzen, et al., The Role of Artificial Intelligence in Interventional Oncology: A Primer, J Vasc Interv Radiol, Volume 30, Issue 1, 38–41.e1.
5. Bishop C. Pattern Recognition and Machine Learning. New York: Springer-Verlag; 2006.
6. Chartrand G, Cheng PM, Vorontsov E, et al. Deep learning: a primer for radiologists. *Radiographics.* 2017;37:2113–2131.
7. Gillies RJ, Kinahan PE, Hricak H. Radiomics: images are more than pictures, they are data. *Radiology.* 2015;278:563–577.
8. Daye D, et al. CT texture analysis and machine learning improve post-ablation prognostication in patients with adrenal metastases: a proof of concept. *Cardiovasc Intervent Radiol.* 2019;42(12):1771–1776. https://doi.org/10.1007/s00270-019-02336-0.
9. Elsayed M, Kadom N, Ghobadi C, et al. Virtual and augmented reality: potential applications in radiology. *Acta Radiol.* 2020;61(9):1258–1265. https://doi.org/10.1177/0284185119897362.
10. Chehab MA, Brinjikji W, Copelan A, Venkatesan AM. Navigational tools for interventional radiology and interventional oncology applications. *Semin Intervent Radiol.* 2015;32(4):416–427. https://doi.org/10.1055/s-0035-1564705.
11. European Society of Radiology (ESR). Abdominal applications of ultrasound fusion imaging technique: Liver, kidney, and pancreas. *Insights Imaging.* 2019;10(1):6. https://doi.org/10.1186/s13244-019-0692-z.
12. Krücker J, Xu S, Venkatesan A, et al. Clinical utility of real-time fusion guidance for biopsy and ablation. *J Vasc Interv Radiol.* 2011;22(4):515–524. https://doi.org/10.1016/j.jvir.2010.10.033.
13. Fontana F, Piacentino F, Ierardi AM, et al. Comparison between CBCT and fusion PET/CT-CBCT guidance for lung biopsies. *Cardiovasc Intervent Radiol.* 2021;44(1):73–79. https://doi.org/10.1007/s00270-020-02613-3.
14. Monfardini L, Gennaro N, Orsi F, et al. Real-time US/cone-beam CT fusion imaging for percutaneous ablation of small renal tumours: a technical note. *Eur Radiol.* 2021;31(10):7523–7528. https://doi.org/10.1007/s00330-021-07930-w.
15. Solomon SB, Patriciu A, Bohlman ME, Kavoussi LR, Stoianovici D. Robotically driven interventions: a method of using CT fluoroscopy without radiation exposure to the physician. *Radiology.* 2002;225(1):277–282. https://doi.org/10.1148/radiol.2251011133.

16. Yanof J, Haaga J, Klahr P, et al. CT-integrated robot for interventional procedures: preliminary experiment and computer-human interfaces. *Comput Aided Surg.* 2001;6(6):352–359. https://doi.org/10.1002/igs.10022.

17. Cleary K, Melzer A, Watson V, Kronreif G, Stoianovici D. Interventional robotic systems: applications and technology state-of-the-art. *Minim Invasive Ther Allied Technol.* 2006;15(2):101–113. https://doi.org/10.1080/13645700600674179.

18. Beaman CB, Kaneko N, Meyers PM, Tateshima S. A review of robotic interventional neuroradiology. *Am J Neuroradiol.* 2021;42(5):808–814. https://doi.org/10.3174/ajnr.A6976.

19. Kim HS, Chapiro J, Geschwind JH, Imaging B. *HHS Public Access.* 2017;22:363–364. https://doi.org/10.1097/PPO.0000000000000235. Interventional.

20. Galle PR, Forner A, Llovet JM, et al. Clinical practice guidelines OF HEPATOLOGY EASL clinical practice guidelines: management of hepatocellular carcinoma q. *J Hepatol.* 2018;69:182–236. https://doi.org/10.1016/j.jhep.2018.03.019.

21. Hanahan D, Weinberg RA. Review hallmarks of cancer: the next generation. *Cell.* 2011;144:646–674. https://doi.org/10.1016/j.cell.2011.02.013.

22. Coussens LM, Werb Z. Inflammation and cancer. *Nature.* 2010;420:860–867. https://doi.org/10.1038/nature01322.

23. Ribatti D. The concept of immune surveillance against tumors: the first theories. *Oncotarget.* 2017;8:7175–7180.

24. Dunn GP, Bruce AT, Ikeda H, et al. Cancer immunoediting: from immunosurveillance to tumor escape. *Nat Immunol.* 2002;3:991–998. https://doi.org/10.1038/ni1102-991.

25. Schreiber RD, Old LJ, Smyth MJ. Cancer immunoediting: integrating suppression and promotion. *Science.* 2011;331:1565–1570.

26. Taube JM, Klein A, Brahmer JR, et al. Association of PD-1, PD-1 ligands, and other features of the tumor immune microenvironment with response to anti-PD-1 therapy. *Clin Cancer Res.* 2014;20:5064–5074. https://doi.org/10.1158/1078-0432.CCR-13-3271.

27. Lesokhin AM, Hohl TM, Kitano S, et al. Monocytic CCR2(+) myeloid-derived suppressor cells promote immune escape by limiting activated CD8 T-cell infiltration into the tumor microenvironment. *Cancer Res.* 2012;72:876–886. https://doi.org/10.1158/0008-5472.CAN-11-1792.

28. Kyi C, Postow MA. Immune checkpoint inhibitor combinations in solid tumors: opportunities and challenges. *Immunotherapy.* 2016;8:821–837. https://doi.org/10.2217/imt-2016-0002.

29. Duran ADR, Hocquelet KHLEKA, T-cell CAR. Cancer immunotherapy: a simple guide for interventional radiologists of new therapeutic approaches. *Cardiovasc Intervent Radiol.* 2019;42:1221–1229. https://doi.org/10.1007/s00270-018-2074-1.

30. Zou W, Wolchok JD, Chen L. PD-L1 (B7-H1) and PD-1 pathway blockade for cancer therapy: mechanisms, response biomarkers, and combinations. *Sci Transl Med.* 2016;8:328rv4. https://doi.org/10.1126/scitranslmed.aad7118.

31. Reck M, Rodríguez-Abreu D, Robinson AG, et al. Pembrolizumab versus chemotherapy for PD-L1-positive non-small-cell lung Cancer. *N Engl J Med.* 2016;375:1823–1833. https://doi.org/10.1056/NEJMoa1606774.

32. Fehrenbacher L, Spira A, Ballinger M, et al. Atezolizumab versus docetaxel for patients with previously treated non-small-cell lung cancer (POPLAR): a multicentre, open-label, phase 2 randomised controlled trial. *Lancet (London, England).* 2016;387:1837–1846. https://doi.org/10.1016/S0140-6736(16)00587-0.

33. Wissniowski TT, Hänsler J, Neureiter D, et al. Activation of tumor-specific T lymphocytes by radio-frequency ablation of the VX2 hepatoma in rabbits. *Cancer Res.* 2003;63:6496–6500.

34. Mizukoshi E, Yamashita T, Arai K, et al. Enhancement of tumor-associated antigen-specific T cell responses by radiofrequency ablation of hepatocellular carcinoma. *Hepatology.* 2013;57:1448–1457. https://doi.org/10.1002/hep.26153.

35. Ahmed M, Kumar G, Moussa M, et al. Hepatic radiofrequency ablation-induced stimulation of distant tumor growth is suppressed by c-met inhibition. *Radiology.* 2016;279:103–117. https://doi.org/10.1148/radiol.2015150080.

36. Duffy AG, Ulahannan SV, Makorova-Rusher O, et al. Tremelimumab in combination with ablation in patients with advanced hepatocellular carcinoma. *J Hepatol.* 2017;66:545–551. https://doi.org/10.1016/j.jhep.2016.10.029.

37. Pinter M, Ulbrich G, Sieghart W, et al. Hepatocellular carcinoma: a phase II randomized controlled double-blind trial of Transarterial chemoembolization in combination with biweekly intravenous Administration of Bevacizumab or a placebo. *Radiology.* 2015;277:903–912. https://doi.org/10.1148/radiol.2015142140.

38. Huang S, Li T, Chen Y, et al. Microwave ablation combined with anti-PD-1 therapy enhances systemic antitumor immunity in a multitumor murine model of Hepa1-6. *Int J Hyperthermia.* 2022;39:278–286. https://doi.org/10.1080/02656736.2022.2032406.

39. Alnaggar M, Lin M, Mesmar A, et al. Allogenic natural killer cell immunotherapy combined with irreversible electroporation for stage IV hepatocellular carcinoma: survival outcome. *Cell Physiol Biochem.* 2018;48:1882–1893. https://doi.org/10.1159/000492509.

40. Lin M, Zhang X, Liang S, et al. Irreversible electroporation plus allogenic Vγ9Vδ2 T cells enhances antitumor effect for locally advanced pancreatic cancer patients. *Signal Transduct Target Ther.* 2020;5:215. https://doi.org/10.1038/s41392-020-00260-1.

14

The multiomics revolution in the era of deep learning: Allies or enemies?

Justine Labory[a,b,c] and Silvia Bottini[a,c]

[a]Université Côte d'Azur, Center of Modeling, Simulation and Interactions, Nice, France [b]Université Côte d'Azur, Inserm U1081, CNRS UMR 7284, Institute for Research on Cancer and Aging, Nice (IRCAN), Centre hospitalier universitaire (CHU) de Nice, Nice, France [c]INRAE, Université Cote d'Azur, Institut Sophia Agrobiotech, Sophia-Antipolis, France

1. Introduction

In the past decade, a large number of different data types has been generated thanks to the development of high-throughput technologies giving rise to "omics" studies.[1] Each omic represents different levels of information ranging from DNA level to metabolite level, including data such as genome, transcriptome, proteome, and metabolome.[2,3] All these omics data attempt to capture the essence of the biological machinery occurring in a living being, providing a high level of information. However, each omic layer individually cannot depict the entire biological complexity of most human diseases. Therefore, the combination of several of these omics data generates a more complete molecular profile of the disease in order to offer patients a personalized medicine approach called precision medicine. Here, multiomics integration is considered a process of combining different single-omics data.

Lately, the development of precision medicine has seen unprecedented growth, supported by machine learning approaches,[4–6] and data mining tools[7–9] applied to multiomics integration. In the first instance, machine learning has enabled the development of diagnostic, prognostic, and predictive tools based on simple omics data.[10–12] However, statistical machine learning models can have large variations in high-dimensional contexts such as analysis of gene expression data for example.[13] Thus, these models are now being applied to multiomics data to study and interpret inter- and intrarelationships between omics layers. Both supervised and unsupervised methods can be employed to solve multiomics integration. Supervised methods can be applied to predict how to classify subject samples after the exposure to a specific factor, the application of a certain treatment, the disease status (normal/disease), the disease progression (early/late-stage), or the survival time. Unsupervised methods are used to classify samples or patients and discover new biomarkers for the disease by making inferences and finding patterns in input multiomics datasets.

In this book chapter, we investigate different strategies in both supervised and unsupervised models, which are commonly used within the context of multiomics integration. Various learning models are described for different purposes such as patient stratification or identification of molecular signatures. This paper is organized as follows. Section 2 provides a short background related to simple omics technologies. Section 3 describes the different challenges encountered in multiomics integration analyses. In Section 4, main objectives of multiomics data integration studies are presented. Section 5 lists multiomics methods for patient stratification, while Section 6 provides multiomics methods for molecular signatures and disease pathway identification. Finally, conclusions and perspectives are presented in Section 7.

2. Simple omics

Omics technologies provide a global view of the molecules that compose a cell, tissue, or organism. They are mainly aimed at the universal detection of genes (genomics), mRNAs (transcriptomics), proteins (proteomics), and metabolites (metabolomics) in a specific biological sample. The fundamental aspect of these approaches is that a complex system can be understood more thoroughly if it is considered a whole. Each omics represents a layer of information of this complex system, and the objective is to study the biological mechanisms in their entirety and the complexity of their interactions.

The areas of application of omics technologies may concern normal physiological processes in order to better understand them, but they may also play a role in pathological processes, notably in screening, diagnosis, and prognosis.

These omics approaches are already widely used in complex pathologies such as cancer or rare diseases, or in better-known pathologies such as obesity or cardiovascular diseases. They have made it possible to discover new targets to adapt treatments to patients and to develop new drugs.

In the near future, through the use of omics technologies, the objective is to be able to develop new approaches to predictive and preventive personalized medicine.

2.1 Genomics

Genomics is the oldest omics technology. It is the systematic study of the genome, which is the entire DNA of a cell or organism. The human genome contains approximately 30,000–40,000 protein-coding genes.[14] The next generation sequencing (NGS) has revolutionized genomics, generating massive amounts of DNA sequence data that require large computing capacity to store and analyze. NGS has enabled whole exome sequencing (WES), which consists of sequencing the coding parts of the genome representing 2% of the genome, and whole genome sequencing (WGS), which is the sequencing of the entire genome.[15] The identification of anomalies such as insertions and deletions of nucleotides (indels), nucleotide changes (single nucleotide variations, SNVs), or abnormal chromosome numbers is then possible. SNVs and indels, also called genetic variants, are the most common variants. They can be found at different places in the gene, and the consequences can be multiple and more or less serious, up to the alteration of the gene. These genetic variants are the cause of many Mendelian diseases, which is why genomics is widely used in diagnosis.[16]

2.2 Transcriptomics

Transcriptomics is the study of RNA transcripts that are produced by the genome and the changes in transcripts in response to regulatory processes. The development of NGS allows high-throughput RNA sequencing (RNA-seq), which enables the entire transcriptome to be sequenced. This makes it possible to reflect the level of gene expression and thus to identify deregulated transcripts, to discover new transcripts (de novo transcripts), and to identify long noncoding RNAs. Transcriptomics has led to a better understanding of the regulatory mechanisms that may explain certain complex diseases such as cancer.[17] Transcriptomics also serves as a model for protein synthesis.

2.3 Proteomics

Proteomics is the large-scale study of the proteins produced in an organism, system, or biological context, which is called the proteome. The proteome is dynamic, changing over time and differing from cell to cell. The proteome can be said to reflect the underlying transcriptome, but the expression of proteins depends on many other factors in addition to the level of expression of the gene concerned.[18]

Proteomics allows the determination of protein expression and protein modifications, including posttranslational modifications, such as phosphorylation, interaction between two proteins, and the involvement of proteins in biological and metabolic pathways.

The technique used in proteomics is mass spectrometry (MS). MS is a primary protein characterization technique that can be used to determine the amino acid sequence of a protein and PTM sites. MS measures charged molecules based on their mass-to-charge ratios, where the mass analyzer characterizes molecules by their mass-to-charge ratios, and the signal intensities of charged peptides reflect the quantity.[19]

2.4 Metabolomics

Metabolomics is the most recent omics and its development has seen a leap in the last few decades thanks to the improvement of MS, which has become more sensitive, allowing better coverage of metabolites.[20] Metabolomics simultaneously quantifies metabolites that are multiple small-molecule types, such as amino acids, fatty acids, carbohydrates, or other products of cellular metabolic functions. Tens of thousands of metabolites are found in plasma. Since the circulating blood collects metabolites from all organs, metabolomic profiling provides very integral data of human physiology.[21] The metabolome changes constantly over time and in response to myriad factors, complicating the interpretation of results, but at the same time opening a unique opportunity for comprehensive analysis. Metabolite levels and relative ratios reflect metabolic function, and out-of-normal range perturbations are often indicative of disease. Quantitative measures of metabolite levels have made possible the discovery of novel genetic loci regulating small molecules, or their relative ratios, in plasma and other tissues. Additionally, metabolomics in combination with modeling has been used extensively to study metabolite flux. Associated technologies include MS-based approaches to quantify both relative and targeted small-molecule abundances.

3. Challenges in multiomics integration analysis

The use of learning algorithms to perform integrated analysis of high-throughput generated multiomics data poses key unique challenges that are summarized as follows.

3.1 Heterogeneity, sparsity, and uneven datasets

This refers to the disparate nature of high-throughput sources used to generate different omics data are usually heterogeneous.[22] For example, when the genome is queried, usually the outcome is a list of variants (i.e., genomic positions in which a mutation has been found in the sample under investigation compared to the reference genome). Mutation profiles are extremely sparse and take binary values.[23] On the other hand, transcriptomics and proteomics are continuous values, but they follow different distributions, thus using different normalization and scaling techniques before omics analysis. This leads to different dynamic ranges and data distribution. Furthermore, some omics are more prone to generating sparse data than others. For instance, transcriptomic data usually contain several very low values and very few transcripts with high values. Also, omics datasets can differ vastly in size. For example, proteomics and metabolomics technologies produce more sparse and smaller datasets than RNA-seq. In addition, there are omics-specific noise, sources of variation, and confounding effects in each omics measurement.

3.2 More features than data ($p \gg n$)

One of the main issues with multiomics data is the classical "curse of dimensionality" problem, i.e., having much fewer observation samples (n) than multiomics features (p).[24] Data collection is financially costly, and the number of clinical research participants is usually limited. Depending on the omics, the number of measurable molecules largely exceeds the thousands making very difficult to have a balanced number of patients. On top of that, most of the features are highly correlated and some features are not always directly connected with disease explanation, thus resulting high-dimensional space composed of many redundant and noninformative features that can mislead the algorithm training.[25] When these irrelevant and redundant features in each omics data type are integrated into the multiomics analysis, it would produce a model with unlimited generalizability to unseen samples. Usually, feature selection or feature extraction techniques can be applied on each omics data separately as a preprocessing step before integration. Feature extraction refers here to techniques computing a subset of representative features, which summarize the original dataset and its dimensions. On the other hand, feature selection finds a subset of the *original* features that maximize the accuracy of a predictive model.[26] It can be based on prior knowledge, i.e., evident from known literature or based on a database such as a biofilter.[27] Formally, feature selection methods can be classed as *filter* (Information gain,[28] ReliefF,[29] Chi-square statistics,[30] *wrapper* (Recursive feature elimination,[31] Sequential feature selection[32]), and *embedded* (such as LASSO (Least Absolute Shrinkage and Selection Operator)[33]) techniques. Xu et al.[34] and Stańczyk[35] provide an excellent resource for understanding and exploring the use of different dimensionality reduction techniques in the generic ML domain. Meng et al.[36] offer a review of these methods from the perspective of multiomics data analysis. When feature selection is applied at the single-omic level, the redundancy among features across omics datasets can be missed, resulting in low-performance multiomics analysis. A very unpopular strategy is to perform feature selection after multiomics dataset merging. The drawback of these methods is the tremendously high computational cost. A widely used strategy to reduce the dimensions of the input data is feature extraction, in which a new representation is constructed by projecting the initial feature set into a new space with lower dimensions. Techniques often used include PCA (principal component analysis),[37] LDA (linear discriminant analysis),[38] and MDS (multidimensional scaling).[39]

Missing data. Datasets can contain also missing values. For instance, in the case of metabolomics, there can be missing values because of detection limits and hence assigned null values.[40] In this case, imputation[41] and outlier detection[42] can be employed for each omic separately, before planning their integration. During the process of integration, especially when integrating datasets from different experiments, random features or even whole omics measurements or some samples can be missing. This can hinder the learning process.[43] In the case of subtype identification, the grouping obtained might be driven predominantly by variation in transcriptomics.

3.3 Class imbalance and overfitting

A major problem with multiomics data is the imbalance either at the class or feature level. Regarding class imbalance, usually the class of healthy samples is less represented that the unhealthy. Furthermore, certain disease classes are rarer than others, which can cause a class imbalance in the multiomics dataset.[44] This can lead to overfitted model, i.e., high accuracy for training data but underperformance for unseen test data. Some approaches can be used to deal with class imbalance. The best option would be to collect more data, but usually very hardly possible. Over or under-sampling the under or over-represented class respectively is another valuable possibility, including synthetic sample generation (such as SMOTE[45] or ADASYN[46]) for the under-represented class. Lately, a lot of effort has been done to produce multiomics simulation tools such as InterSIM,[47] MOSim,[48] and OmicsSIMLA.[49] Despite the good performances achieved by these tools, they are usually employed more for tool benchmarking rather than to increment the cohort sizes. Another option is to adopt techniques such as regularization, bagging, hyper-parameter tuning, and cross-validation to balance the bias–variance trade-off.[50] Finally, another suggestion can be considered using weighted or normalized metrics to measure the classifier performance (such as F1-Score or Kappa[51]). On the other hand, feature imbalance refers to the different distribution of feature dimensionality within each omics data. One omics may have only hundreds of features, while another may contain thousands. As a result, the learning model is more likely to pay more attention to omics with a larger number of features, leading to a learning imbalance. To deal with this problem, various strategies have been introduced, ranging from dimensionality reduction to late fusion.

3.4 Computation and storage cost

The use of learning models for multiomics integration comes with computational and data storage costs.[52] High computation power and large volumes of storage capacity to save the logs, results, and analysis are needed. Recently,[53] cloud computing platforms are the more and more accessible,[54] such as Amazon EC2,[55] Microsoft Azure,[56] and Google Cloud Platform,[57] with the drawback of a related cost to be considered before planning to include learning models in the multiomics analysis pipeline. In order to define the most adapted computation infrastructure to perform multiomics integration, it is crucial to define in advance which learning model is more suitable to address the tasks of the study. Some computational performance criteria include whether the algorithm can scale to large number of samples, if it is easy and efficient to run, if it is robust, and whether it can converge to an optimal solution in a set number of runs. Therefore, it is crucial to define criteria that should be objective-specific, to help assess their strengths.

3.5 How to choose a good model to perform the integration?

Based on the considerations in the previous paragraphs, each multiomics dataset is unique, thus finding the appropriate method to perform a successful integration is crucial. Recently, various artificial platforms and tools, including learning models for multiomics integration,[58–60] have also emerged; however, they are computationally expensive, and mainly they are not easily adaptable to different number and type of omics. Depending on the omics data that the user disposes of and the biomedical question to answer, diverse methodologies should be employed. In the next paragraphs, we will discuss the main objectives that multiomics integration can address.

4. Main objectives of multiomics data integration studies

We have identified two main biomedical questions that can be addressed by multiomics integration studies, and each of them can be articulated in different subquestions.

- Patients' grouping/stratification

  Subtype identification: The discovery of disease subtypes can improve the definition of personalized and thus more effective treatments, including biological drugs, hormonal therapy, and immunotherapy. Also, subtype identification can identify heterogeneous groups within cancer cohorts with differences in disease progression or response to treatment. Usually, histopathology features, patient clinical profiles, and symptoms are used by physicians to stratify patients accordingly. Currently, research studies are investigating new methodologies to assess disease subtype classifications by finding signatures at the molecular level. At first, these signatures were investigated at the single-omics level, for example, by finding common genes with perturbed expression. Recently, multiomics study signatures are used to determine disease subtypes.

  Drug response prediction: Patients affected by the same disease can respond to drug treatment differently. One of the central questions nowadays to achieve successful personalized medicine approaches is to be able to predict whether a drug will work on a group of patients with a similar molecular profile. Multiomics integration analysis can be useful to study drug effects on specific cell lines or patient cells tailoring the way toward personalized medicine.

- Molecular signatures and salient disease pathway identification

  Detect disease-associated molecular patterns: Similar to the previous objective and more generally, the identification of molecular markers associated with clinical markers or measurable characteristics is valuable in clinical practice. These molecular markers can be used as disease stage indicators or to identify disease-specific pathways and mechanisms. Multiomics integration methods can reveal disease-associated molecules leading to the identification of salient pattern signature as relationships or patterns.

  Understand regulatory processes. The previous objective can lead to the inference of disease-specific gene regulatory networks (GRNs) by combining measurements from multiomics studies.[61]

  Diagnosis/prognosis: The diagnosis of multifactorial diseases can be difficult to assess due to their complex genotype and phenotype. Thus, diagnosis can be tedious and very long, resulting in patients in diagnostic stalemate. By using integrated multiomics analysis, complex molecular signatures can be identified by employing approaches that are able to catch complex relationships among different molecular layers. By identifying the relationship between these indicators at the molecular level, a better explanation of the complex phenotype can be achieved and allowed the prediction of disease progression and severity and course.

5. Multiomics methods for patient grouping/stratification

5.1 Concatenation-first approaches

The concatenation-first approach consists to create a unique dataset by joining all omics containing all features. These methods take advantage of all the concatenated features to select the most discriminating features for a given phenotype.[62–68] This is the easiest strategy for analyzing continuous or categorical data, and the final comprehensive dataset can be used as the input for numerous classical machine learning algorithms such as artificial neural networks,[69] support vector machines (SVM)[70], decision trees,[66] random forests (RF),[71] and k-nearest neighbors.[67] Similarly, multivariate LASSO models have been investigated in Refs. 33, 72, 73. A joint matrix of multiomics features (including gene expression, copy number variation, and mutation) was used with classical RF and SVM to predict anticancer drug response.[74] Furthermore, boosted trees[75] and SVR (support vector regression)[76] have been employed to identify predictors of glycemic health.[77] Other than classical learning algorithms, such as deep neural networks,[78] have also been widely used, or instance to identify robust survival subgroups of liver cancer using RNA, miRNA, and methylation data.[79]

The drawback of these methodologies consists of training difficulties due to the high dimensionality of features of the joint dataset compared to the relatively small number of patients/samples, which decreases the performance and increases the computational time. Because of the striking difference in the feature dimensionality in multiomics data, another pitfall of this technique is the model's tendency to learn more from the omics with the larger number of features.

5.2 Dimensionality reduction approaches

To minimize the number of features and avoid the problems of using a learning algorithm on the concatenated multiomics dataset, one can select a subset of more relevant features (feature selection) or apply a dimensionality reduction technique in the preprocessing by keeping a small number of discriminating features (feature extraction).[80–84] This approach is based on the selection of the most salient features independently on each omic, either by selecting a subset of features based on some knowledge-based criteria or by using a feature extraction algorithm.[85] Sometimes a combination of the two techniques is used, because even after feature selection, most multiomics datasets might still have too many features and high ratio of features/samples. Overall, the pitfall of these methods consists of a possible loss of relationship inter-omics due to the feature selection performed before integration.

5.3 Feature selection

In computational modeling, it is common practice to use any prior knowledge of the system to include into the model to achieve better performances. Therefore, biological expertise can offer allow to select the features to include in the model with the highest probability to be relevant. Athreya et al. reduced over 7 million features consisting of SNPs and metabolites, to 65 predictor variables by using several biological-driven criteria.[86] Usually, regarding transcriptome, only the genes showing the highest variability among samples showing different phenotypes are retained, whereas genes with consistently low activity levels are usually discarded. Similarly, relevant features from epigenomic data can be selected by only keeping the loci near relevant genes or regions encompassing multiple methylation sites.

5.3.1 Feature extraction

Feature extraction is the process of condensing features into a lower number of new features (decided by the user). Despite the efficacy of these algorithms, the degree of explainability is sometimes lost since it is not always easy to explain what the new features are and how they are connected to the original ones. This is by far the widest application of learning algorithms to multiomics integration studies. Several methods have been proposed, listed hereafter.

5.4 Factorization

Factorization-based techniques take all omics as input matrices and decompose them into two parts: (i) factors that are common to all omics and (ii) weights for each omic. Common factors can be utilized for patient clustering/stratification, and weights help identify disease-causing molecules and/or biomarkers. The assumption behind these models is that the biological mechanisms under investigation can be revealed by biological factors shared among multiple omics. This type of approach allows to identify complex inter-omics structures and can be accomplished in two ways: tensor-based and matrix-based. Factorization-based approaches have been extensively investigated in the literature for multiomics integration; however, the assumption is to consider a global shared space among omics while neglecting partial common structures prevents the identification of indirect mechanisms.

5.4.1 Matrix-based factorization

The main idea is to factorize multiomics data matrices into the product of several matrices, including omics-specific weight matrices and a factor matrix. The most popular matrix factorization method is the principal component analysis (PCA), which decomposes the covariance matrix of data to extract hidden biological factors. A downside of PCA is that data are linearly transformed to generate the new features, whereas in real life, the relationship is rarely linear.[87] Multiomics factor analysis (MOFA) is a generalization of principal component analysis (PCA) to multiomics data. It aims to capture maximum variance of the data in the generated subspace, while eliminating unwanted variance. MOFA is an unsupervised method for integrating multiomics data types on the same or partially overlapped samples. It infers a low-dimensional representation of the data in terms of a small number of (latent) factors that capture the global sources of variability. It uses a probabilistic Bayesian framework for model formulation that can support combination of different noise models to integrate multiple data types such as numerical (continuous and count) and categorical (binary) data. MOFA uses linear models to represent relationships between omics data, so the drawback is that it is impossible to capture strong nonlinear relationships between and within omics data.[88] Like MOFA, joint and individual variation (JIVE) is an extension of the PCA to multiomics data. JIVE is an integrative method that decomposes a dataset into a sum of three terms: two low-rank approximation terms, one for capturing joint variation between datasets and another for capturing individual variations to each data, and a term for residual noise.[89] The nonnegative matrix factorization (NMF) method is widely used in analyzing high-dimensional data sets, and various extensions of this method are developed for better interpretation of multiomics data. It factorizes a matrix into two non-negative matrices, one containing the basis vectors and the other containing the coefficient vectors. jNMF, iNMF, and jNMFMA are all extensions of NMF. Joint NMF (jNMF) integrates multiple datasets with common observations.[90] The problem is that jNMF does not distinguish between different variable sources when integrating, which is problematic for heterogeneous data. Integrative NMF (iNMF) was developed to overcome limitations of jNMF, and it takes into account heterogeneous effects when integrating multiple data sources.[91] jNMFMA (joint NMF transcriptomics data meta-analysis method) is a new meta-analysis method for DEG identification based on joint NMF that decomposes multiple transcriptome data matrices into one common submatrix and multiple individual submatrices simultaneously as a joint version.[92] ICluster uses similar principles to NMF but allows integration of datasets that have negative values.[93] It is a clustering method that uses use a Gaussian latent variable model where the latent variables form a set of principle coordinates collectively capturing the correlative structure of multiomics data. The goal is to obtain joint clustering of samples and identify cluster-relevant features across datasets. The major drawback is that it cannot handle both categorical and continuous variables together. To overcome limits of iCluster, the iCluster+ tool has been proposed.[94] It is able to incorporate various omics data modalities, including binary, categorical, and continuous values, allowing the data to have different distributions other than Gaussian. ICluster+ decomposes each omics data type into a component factor and loading factors based on assumptions for different omics data types. In this way, iCluster+ allows us to explicitly model the assumptions about the distributions of different omics data types and leverage the strengths of Bayesian inference. However, a limitation of this method is that statistical inference (statistical selection of the final model) is not straightforward owing to its computationally intensive approach. A more recent version of the iCluster+, iClusterBayes, uses a Bayesian integrative clustering approach and overcomes the limitations of the iCluster+.[95] The MoCluster proposed by Meng,[96] defines a set of latent variables representing joint patterns across multiple omics datasets by employing a multiblock multivariate analysis. Then, the latent variables are clustered using classic methods such as hierarchical or K-means to discover joint patterns. MoCluster was validated by integrating proteomic and transcriptomic data and shows a noticeably higher clustering accuracy and lower computation cost in comparison with both iCluster and iCluster+. LRAcluster (low-rank approximation-based multiomics data clustering)[97] was developed to integrate high-dimensional multiomics data and find low-dimensional manifolds to identify molecular subtypes of cancer. Each input omics data are conditional on a size-matched parameter matrix, and this matrix can be decomposed into a low-dimensional representation of the original data. Then, clustering is done on the reduced subspace.

5.4.2 Tensor-based factorization

Matrix factorization can be applied only to two omics data; however, it can be convenient to integrate more than two entities. Tensor factorization is a generalization of matrix factorization. Typically, it identifies higher-order relationships among biological variables by extracting factors that play essential roles in describing these relationships.[98]

5.4.3 Kernel-based approach

Kernel-based approach is a form of transformation that uses kernel functions to map original features onto a new space with higher dimensions. Kernels allow such methods to work in high-dimensional space to explore similarities and relationships between samples. Support Vector Machine and multiple kernel learning (MKL) are common machine learning algorithms for working with kernels. Despite the attractive performances, this approach is computationally expensive compared to other transformation-based techniques. The kernel-based integration approaches include the following methods. In the SDP-SVM method, semidefinite programming (SDP)[99–101] is used to select the best parameters to optimize SVM kernel function and to simplify SVM operation.[102] The SDP method is a convex optimization problem that maximizes or minimizes a linear function, but the constraint is that the affine combination of a symmetric matrix is positive and semidefinite. SDP-SVM algorithm is an improvement of SVM algorithm. Through appropriate selection of the SVM classifier parameters, the classification accuracy can be maximized while maintaining good generalization capability. Another method is FSMKL (Multiple Kernel Learning with Feature Selection). This is a supervised classification method that uses multiple kernels to capture the similarity between datasets, each encoded in a basic kernel. A feature selection algorithm then finds the most relevant kernel and its importance within the multiple datasets. Prior knowledge in the form of pathways can be incorporated into computing base kernels.[103] The Relevance Vector Machine (RVM) is a probabilistic sparse kernel model that adopts a Bayesian approach to learning to infer the model weights connecting feature space to output.[104,105] Adaboost is a machine learning algorithm that can combine different types of learners to improve the final performance. It requires no prior knowledge or learning process, and this signifies that boosting is achievable without a trade-off between classification accuracy and training time. As RVM is computationally intensive, using AdaBoost for RVM could address the problem of large-scale learning and lower the computational cost.[106] fMKL-DR is a method that generates kernel matrices from each input omics data, then combines them and finally uses SVM to stratify the data.[107]

5.5 Neural network-based

This is a new and fast-growing area of research in multiomics integration due to its superior performance in numerous domains of multimodal learning. Usually, a network is trained for each omic to learn a joint representation of the inputs. The hidden layers of the built networks are then passed into another neural network. They are particularly suitable for multiomics integration because their particular structure allows for learning complex nonlinear relationships of features. Furthermore, they can deal with both structured data, like gene or protein expressions[108] and unstructured data, such as medical images.[109,110] Several neural network-based approaches for feature extraction use autoencoders and variants. Autoencoders compress the original input data (i.e., multiomics dataset) into a lower dimensional representation ("bottleneck" layer) and reconstruct them by minimizing the difference between original and reconstructed inputs (i.e., "reconstruction loss").[111] An advantage of autoencoders is that by adding several layers of a neural network with nonlinear activation functions, the technique can model complex nonlinear functions. Some examples of this methodology are implemented in the following methods. In Split-AutoEncoders (Split-AEs),[112] an AE is created for each view with each encoder projecting the input domain to a common latent space and each decoder projecting the data back to the starting input space. The field of multiview feature learning and dimensionality reduction[113,114] has made extensive use of canonical correlation analysis (CCA) and kernel variants.[115,116] CCA is used to learn an integration with as few correlations between features as possible. By considering the features discovered from one or more views, the correlation of features can be determined. It is possible to learn complementary features from each view by imposing a noncorrelation between them. A full extension of deep neural networks (DNNs) called Deep CCA (DCCA) was only presented in the paper,[117] despite many attempts to learn a CCA-like neural network model.[116] In DCCA, a single nonlinear representation is extracted from each input view by the learning of two DNNs. Deep canonically correlated autoencoders (DCCAE)[118] add an autoencoder regularization term to DCCA. They use two autoencoders that optimize the combination of canonical correlation between the learned bottleneck representations and the autoencoder reconstruction errors. The aim of the DCCAE is to strike a balance between, on the one hand, information about the input data and features captured in the mapping of each view and, on the other hand, information about the relationships between features across views. Recently, MOSAE (multiomics supervised autoencoder)[119] was developed for pan-cancer analysis and compared with conventional ML methods such as SVM, DT, Naïve Bayes, KNN, RF, and AdaBoost. MOSAE uses a specific AE for each omics, according to their size of dimensions to generate omics-specific representations. Then, a supervised autoencoder is constructed based on specific autoencoder by using labels to enforce each specific autoencoder to learn both omics-specific and task-specific representations. Finally, MOSAE fuses all different omics-specific representations generated from supervised AEs and the fused representation is used for predictive tasks. HI-DFNForest (hierarchical integration deep flexible neural forest) framework[120] was developed, which uses a stacked autoencoder[121] to learn high-level representations from three omics datasets. Later, these representations are integrated and final learned representations from the SAE are used to predict cancer subtype classification using deep flexible neural forest (DFNForest) model. MAUI (multiomics autoencoder integration) is a nonlinear dimension reduction method for multiomics integration based on the use of variational AE to produce latent features that can be used for either clustering or classification.[122] DeepProg is a semisupervised machine learning framework that takes multiple omics data matrices and survival information as the input. This method is divided into two parts: one unsupervised and the other supervised. In the first part, an AE for each omics data type is used to transform them and survival-associated latent-space features are selected from the bottleneck layer of autoencoders. The selected survival-associated latent-space features from all the omics are then combined for clustering analysis. The second part is the prediction of new samples.[123]

Beyond AEs, other neural network algorithms have been investigated for feature extraction from multiomics data. The Neural Graph Learning for Data Fusion (NGL—F) is a gradient-based neural network, which uncovers topological sample-to-sample relationships using multiple data sources. The output of NGL-F is a set of graphs. For each input dataset, NGL-F aims at finding a graph where nodes represent cluster centroids, while edges represent cluster topological properties. Then, the learned topology described by such graphs is used to create the sample adjacency matrix. The information contained in the matrix represents all datasets, and it can be used to uncover latent patterns among samples. The sample adjacency matrix is used to build a unique graph (sample graph) in which nodes represent samples and the edges are derived from the sample adjacency matrix. NGL-F is composed of a set of dual multilayer perceptrons (MLPs), one foreach dataset and weights are estimated by backpropagation.[54] The input of each network is a dataset represented as a matrix, and each MLP provides as output a set of vectors representing cluster centroids for the input data. For each data source taken into consideration, a multilayer neural network is instantiated. Once all networks terminate the training procedure, the resulting clusters are analyzed. For each dataset, two samples are considered near to each other in case they belong to the same cluster; far from each other in case, they belong to different clusters. Finally, MOLI (multiomics late integration)[124] is a deep-learning model that uses distinct encoding subnetworks to learn features of each omics data type. Then, the final network uses the concatenated features to classify the response of cancer cells to a given drug.

Despite their incredible success in several tasks, their performances are strongly dependent on training sample size, unfortunately usually limited in the multiomics field. Moreover, the lack of interpretability, which is fundamental to identify biological functions, prevents their large employment in this field.

6. Multiomics methods for molecular signatures and salient disease pathway identification

Another goal of multiomics integration is to connect phenotypes to biological mechanisms and their regulators. High-throughput data from large-scale experiments are often analyzed via different pathway and functional enrichment analyses, by filtering and combining with relevant clinical data (if available) to comprehend the physiological relevance. Some methods include the use of multiple models, one for each omic as an intermediary step before creating an integrated model from these intermediate models.[125,126] The advantage of these techniques is that they can be used on different omic types and allow a more straightforward understanding of the observed phenotypes.

6.1 Regression models

The earliest methods, including learning models for multiomics integration, were mainly based on regression techniques. Usually, in these models, the expression of each gene is represented by a regression model that includes measurements from other omic datasets and their parameters. Thus, inferring the relationship between a set of N genes and their regulators is decomposed into a set of N regression problems. iGRN[127] was used to infer a gene regulatory network from human brain data of patients with three psychiatric disorders: schizophrenia, bipolar disorder, and major depression. The samples have 25 k gene expression (GE), 1028 copy number variations (CNVs), and 24 k sites for DNA methylation. The method produces a gene-to-gene adjacency matrix and two bi-adjacency matrices for the interactions of CNV and DNA methylation with genes. The expression of each gene is then modeled by a sparse linear model incorporating other genes and also interaction effects of its nearby CNVs and DNA methylations. Another example is BMNPGRN.[128] It uses nonconvex penalty-based regression methods as an alternative to LASSO when dealing with sparse problems such as estimating interactions from multiomics datasets. They studied the mechanisms of breast cancer, using to a multiomics dataset of 760 cases and 80 control samples, and identified potential regulators for key driver genes in the context of breast cancer.

6.2 Network-based approach

Network-based approach is one of the most used techniques for multiomics integration in biomedical and healthcare studies. These techniques are capable to capture molecular interactions, thus allowing to perform sample classifications and disease subtyping. Two network-based techniques are employed. The first one models each omic as a network and combines them to make a unified network for carrying out further analysis and is usually combined with clustering methods. A network is created for each omic, the nodes represent samples, and the edges represent relationships between pairs of samples. Then, networks are converted to similarity matrices in an iterative optimization process or single iteration algorithm. Similarity network fusion (SNF)[129] and neighborhood-based multiomics (NEMO)[130] clustering are two examples belonging to this category. They perform a three-stage conversion. In the first stage, each omic is converted into a similarity matrix based on patient relationships. Then, matrices were fused to generate a relative similarity matrix in a single iteration. Finally, samples are clustered with the spectral clustering algorithm. The resulting network of clusters of similar patients can then be used to derive information about the very basic molecules that caused these patient clusters to form. If these molecules are consistently present in more than one patient, the SNF can be inferred to be highlighting pertinent disease-related molecules.[129] The second strategy network integrates latent representation spaces of networks into a joint representation (also known as network embedding) and feeds into machine learning models for classification purposes. In other words, each omic represented as a network is encoded into a low-dimensional space to reflect the network topology. Then, latent representations are combined to perform the downstream task.

The advantage of these techniques is that since networks are formed based on samples rather than features, the complexity of the whole pipeline does not significantly increase by adding new omics.

6.3 Multilayer network and network propagation

Another way to use networks for multiomics integration is to build molecular networks. In these networks, nodes represent molecules (genes, proteins, and metabolites), connected by edges that represent the pairwise relationships and interactions between two molecules. Networks are used to represent all relevant interactions taking place in biological systems,[131] for example, transcriptional regulation mechanisms, physical protein–protein interactions,[132,133] and correlation between RNA networks and protein structure or metabolic reactions.[134] Then, topological features are evaluated, including degree distribution to identify highly connected nodes (hubs) or shortest paths that determine the proximity between two nodes. Networks can also be divided into modules, namely, subnetwork with highly connected nodes concerning the rest of the network. The nodes in these modules often share a similar function. Thus, by applying the "guilt by association" property, unknown entities in modules highly connected with known molecules are assumed to be functionally related.[135] Inference methods to apply this principle are often applied to a single-omic layer to identify interactions between molecules. However, to elucidate interaction across multiple omics, the different layers should be connected. To connect these layers, one approach uses correlations-based methods between molecules based on multiomics data to infer the interactions. Another method is to use prior knowledge across omic molecular networks such as publicly available databases to create inter-omics edges.[136] This latter is known as network propagation, based on the work of Page et al.,[137] and lately, they have become the state-of-the-art to investigate gene–disease associations and also gene function prediction.[138,139] Network propagation involves mapping the omics data onto predefined molecular or genetic networks that can be obtained from public databases. The most exploited are BioGRID,[140] IntAct,[141] String,[132] and UniProtKB.[142] A large set of databases is referenced in startbioinfo.org and pathguide.org.[143] Several mathematical formulations of network propagation exist, such as Random Walk, Random Walk with Restart (RWR),[144] and Heat Diffusion (HD).[145] Briefly, the basic concept is that the signal is iteratively propagated through the network from previous knowledge. The scores attributed to each node are "spread" to neighboring nodes through the edges of the network. The node scores are updated using the weighted average of the neighboring nodes. This averaging or smoothing of node scores will emphasize regions in the network that are particularly associated with the phenotype, whereas regions with small changes around zero will be dampened.

6.4 Graph convolutional network

Graph deep learning has recently emerged to incorporate graph structures into a deep learning framework. In particular, graph convolutional networks (GCNs) are able to classify unlabeled nodes in a network on the basis of both their associated feature vectors, as well as the network's topology, making it possible to integrate graph-based data with feature vectors in a natural way. Advances in feature interpretation strategies for DNNs make it also possible to investigate the decision of such methods, leveraging a deep understanding of the underlying data.[146] MoGCN[147] is an example of a tool for multiomics integration based on a GCN. It first uses an autoencoder (AE) to reduce the dimensionality of multiomics patient data and SNF method to build a patient similarity network (PSN). Then, new features found by the AE and PSN are the input to GCN for training and testing and to allow the classification of patients. Another method is MOGONET (MultiOmics Graph cOnvolutional NETworks), a supervised multiomics data classification model that uses GCN incorporating patient associations.[67] First, from each omics data, a PSN is generated. Then, GCN is used for multiomics-specific learning taking advantage of both the omics features and the correlations among patients described by the PSN. From initial predictions from each omics-specific GCN, the cross-omics discovery tensor is calculated and forwarded to View Correlation Discovery Network (VCDN) for multiomics integration. Finally, the explainable multiomics graph integration (EMOGI) method[148] combines multidimensional multiomics data as gene features with protein–protein interaction (PPI) networks to learn more abstract gene features by using GCN.

6.5 Pathways as networks

These methods first construct networks by using pathways as sources of information to infer links among entities. Then, each pathway network is independently analyzed to obtain the summary statistics for each element. Finally, graph-based analyses are performed to calculate each pathway's P-value and network score. Methods in this category include PARADIGM,[149] Subpathway-GM,[150] microGraphite,[151] mirIntegrator,[152] MOSClip,[153] IMPRes-Pro,[154] ATHENA,[69] and rPAC.[155] For a complete overview, we refer to Maghsoudi et al.[156] Pathway Recognition Algorithm using Data Integration on Genomic Model (PARADIGM) is one of the earliest tools.[149] Lemon-Tree[157] has recently been expanded to allow the integration of multiomics data for module network inference.

PAMOGK[158] is a pathway-based multiomic graph kernel clustering method that integrates multiomics patient data with existing biological knowledge on pathways. Patient similarities are evaluated based on a single molecular alteration type in the context of a pathway by graph kernel. Multiview kernel clustering is used to support multiviews of patient and molecular alteration combinations.[158] It used somatic mutations, transcriptomics, and proteomics data to find subgroups of kidney cancer.

6.6 Omics as an image

Although these works have been devised to use embedding and conventional machine learning approaches, the use of deep learning on multiomic data integration is still in its infancy. Deep artificial neural networks are widely acknowledged for their ability to perform automatic feature extraction from raw data. Hence, a deep learning-based model has the capacity to develop a single-step phenotype prediction procedure where omics data would be directly used to classify the outcome without prior feature selection. The absolute superiority of convolutional neural networks (CNNs) in image classification has been widely acknowledged but not yet sufficiently leveraged for analyzing multiomics data. Intuitively, CNN's convolution operators extract local spatial features from an input image. The local information is then combined, via pooling aggregations, to higher-order special information from a large image region, which would eventually be used to distinguish among different image types. Therefore, the utility of CNN is in the automated extraction of local and global special features from input images where adjacent pixels are interrelated and share similar information. To convert omics data represented as numerical matrices to an image requires the definition of spatially coherent pixels in local regions to incorporate interrelationships and local/global patterns in molecular profiles into phenotype prediction. While converting omics data to images is a relatively new concept in the field of bioinformatics, former studies have used different CNN architectures to classify biological or clinical samples based on omics measurements, mainly gene expression data, converted into two-dimensional images. Lyu and Haque[159] converted RNA-seq data into 2-D images and used a CNN to classify 33 tumor types obtained from The Cancer Genome Atlas, TCGA (www.cancer.gov/tcga). Lopez et al.[160] used the molecular function of the genes as a methodology to transform gene expression vectors into images. Sharma and Kumar[161] proposed three methods to transform a 1-D vector into a 2-D image, which were used to predict breast cancer using numerical vectors of patients' clinical information obtained from Wisconsin Original and Diagnostic Breast Cancer datasets from UCI library.[162] Sharma et al.[163] developed DeepInsight, which is the most acknowledged algorithm for transforming nonimage data into images. The advantage of this method is that it can be applied to different data types, including RNA-seq, vowels, text, and synthetic data. Finally, Zandavi et al.[164] proposed to convert nonimage omics data into images using Fast Fourier Transform (FFT) to map features onto a complex Cartesian plane.

7. Conclusions and perspectives

This work reviews various multiomics integration methods using machine learning. First, we focused on the challenges encountered in multiomics integration analyses. Multiomics datasets come from different sources, are obtained with different techniques, and are therefore very heterogeneous. After preprocessing, some omics are expressed as binary values, while others are represented by continuous measurements. They have different data distribution; therefore, they undergo different normalization strategies before integration leading different dynamic ranges. Depending on the number of molecules measured in each layer, different dataset sizes are expected for each omic. Since the number of molecules in each layer will always be larger than the number of samples collected, multiomics dataset will always be affected by "the curses of dimensionality." This explains why feature selection and/or extraction methods are the most explored approaches to perform multiomics integration. Another major challenge is imbalance at the class or feature level. Regarding class imbalance, usually the class of healthy samples is less represented than the unhealthy samples, which may lead to an overfitted model.

Concerning feature imbalance, the distribution of feature dimensionality is different in each omics data. The use of learning models for the integration of multiomics data can also be problematic due to computational and data storage costs. It is very important to define in advance the tasks to be performed and the algorithm that will constitute the optimal solution. Finally, the most difficult part is to choose the best model to perform the multiomics integration. This depends on many criteria such as the biological context or the question to be answered.

Several multiomics integration methods are available for patient stratification. The main objective is to find disease subtypes and predict drug response. The discovery of disease subtypes allows treatments to be tailored to patients and to be more effective. In patients with the same disease, the drug response may be different due to interindividual variability. Multiomics integration analysis can therefore be used to study the effects of drugs on specific cell lines or on patient cells. These methods can be classified in three groups: concatenation-first approaches, dimensionality reduction methods, and factorization approaches. Concatenation-first approaches are simple and straightforward, but they are difficult to train because of the high dimensionality of features in the join dataset compared to the very small number of samples, which increases computational time and decreases performance. For dimensionality reduction methods, two approaches are possible on simple omics before the integration. To reduce the number of features, feature selection can be used to select the more relevant features or feature extraction applies a dimensionality reduction technique to keep a smaller number of more discriminating features. The use of these methods reduces computational costs, but inter-omics relationships are lost due to the selection or extraction of features prior to integration. The last group of methods is factorization methods. They take all omics as input matrices and decompose them into two parts: the factors common to all omics and weights for each omic. They can be divided into four categories: matrix-based, tensor-based, kernel-based, and neural network-based. In matrix-based approaches, the multiomics data matrices are factorized into the product of several matrices, including omics-specific weight matrices and a factor matrix. Tensor-based approaches are a generalization of matrix factorization, while kernel-based approaches use kernel functions to map original features into a new higher dimensional space. Neural network-based approaches allow the learning of complex nonlinear relationships of features. The performance of factorization methods is highly dependent on training sample size, which is limited in multiomics analyses. With all these machine learning methods, patient stratification opens the way to personalized medicine.

Other multiomics integration methods are designed to identify important molecular signatures and pathways. The idea is to detect molecular patterns associated with disease, to understand regulatory processes, and to establish a diagnosis and prognosis. They can be divided into six categories: regression models, network-based, multilayer network, graph convolutional network, pathway as networks, and omics as an image. In regression models, gene expression is represented by a regression model that includes measurements from other omics data sets. In network-based methods, the idea is to create a network for each omic dataset where nodes represent samples and edges represent relationships between pairs of samples, whereas in neural network-based methods, molecular networks are constructed where nodes represent molecules (genes, proteins, and metabolites), connected by edges that represent pairwise relationships and interactions between two molecules. GCNs are able to classify unlabeled nodes in a network based on their associated feature vectors and the network topology. In pathways as networks models, known pathways are used to construct networks and infer links between entities. In omics as image models, deep learning-based model develops a single-step phenotype prediction procedure where omics data are directly used to classify the outcome without prior feature selection.

As future directions, we envisage three main roads: (1) to integrate a priori biological knowledge in the model, (2) to integrate omics data with other types of data (clinical measurements and environmental data), and (3) to develop a universal model to answer different biomedical questions. We extensively discussed about the small sample size issue of biomedical datasets that yields several challenges in the application of learning models to multiomics integration. A possibility could be to add a priori biological knowledge into the model to balance the small sample size. Deep learning methods offer a good opportunity to combine omics measurements with biological structure to leverage this extra biological a priori information. Nowadays, most of the available multiomics methods are conceived to integrate two or three specific omics; thus, more effort should be done to produce flexible tools and models able to integrate any omic type and more than three omics. To conclude, multiomics integration methods are designed to answer one specific task each, while usually multiple outcomes are needed; thus, it would be advantageous to have combined multivariate models to provide such multiple answers yielding a more powerful significance.

References

1. Lightbody G, Haberland V, Browne F, et al. Review of applications of high-throughput sequencing in personalized medicine: barriers and facilitators of future progress in research and clinical application. *Brief Bioinform*. 2019;20(5):1795–1811.
2. Beale DJ, Karpe AV, Ahmed W. Beyond metabolomics: A review of multi-omics-based approaches. In: Beale DJ, Kouremenos KA, Palombo EA, eds. *Microbial Metabolomics: Applications in Clinical, Environmental, and Industrial Microbiology*. Springer International Publishing; 2016:289–312. https://doi.org/10.1007/978-3-319-46326-1_10.
3. Hasin Y, Seldin M, Lusis A. Multi-omics approaches to disease. *Genome Biol*. 2017;18(1):1–15.
4. Delavan B, Roberts R, Huang R, Bao W, Tong W, Liu Z. Computational drug repositioning for rare diseases in the era of precision medicine. *Drug Discov Today*. 2018;23(2):382–394.
5. Peterson TA, Doughty E, Kann MG. Towards precision medicine: advances in computational approaches for the analysis of human variants. *J Mol Biol*. 2013;425(21):4047–4063.

6. Zou Q, Chen L, Huang T, Zhang Z, Xu Y. Machine learning and graph analytics in computational biomedicine. *Artif Intell Med*. 2017;83:1.
7. Chawla NV, Davis DA. Bringing big data to personalized healthcare: a patient-centered framework. *J Gen Intern Med*. 2013;28:660–665.
8. Cheng PF, Dummer R, Levesque MP. Data mining the Cancer genome atlas in the era of precision cancer medicine. *Swiss Med Wkly*. 2015;145 (3738):w14183.
9. Margolies LR, Pandey G, Horowitz ER, Mendelson DS. Breast imaging in the era of big data: structured reporting and data mining. *AJR Am J Roentgenol*. 2016;206(2):259.
10. Dias-Audibert FL, Navarro LC, de Oliveira DN, et al. Combining machine learning and metabolomics to identify weight gain biomarkers. *Front Bioeng Biotechnol*. 2020;8:6.
11. Mamoshina P, Volosnikova M, Ozerov IV, et al. Machine learning on human muscle transcriptomic data for biomarker discovery and tissue-specific drug target identification. *Front Genet*. 2018;9:242.
12. Sonsare PM, Gunavathi C. Investigation of machine learning techniques on proteomics: a comprehensive survey. *Prog Biophys Mol Biol*. 2019;149:54–69.
13. Kim AA, Zaim SR, Subbian V. Assessing reproducibility and veracity across machine learning techniques in biomedicine: a case study using TCGA data. *Int J Med Inform*. 2020;141, 104148.
14. Lander ES, Linton LM, Birren B, et al. Initial sequencing and analysis of the human genome. *Nature*. 2001;409(6822):860–921. https://doi.org/10.1038/35057062.
15. Koboldt DC, Steinberg KM, Larson DE, Wilson RK, Mardis ER. The next-generation sequencing revolution and its impact on genomics. *Cell*. 2013;155(1):27–38.
16. Eichler EE. Genetic variation, comparative genomics, and the diagnosis of disease. *N Engl J Med*. 2019;381(1):64–74.
17. Wang Z, Gerstein M, Snyder M. RNA-Seq: a revolutionary tool for transcriptomics. *Nat Rev Genet*. 2009;10(1):57–63. https://doi.org/10.1038/nrg2484.
18. Aslam B, Basit M, Nisar MA, Khurshid M, Rasool MH. Proteomics: technologies and their applications. *J Chromatogr Sci*. 2016;1–15.
19. Wilhelm M, Schlegl J, Hahne H, et al. Mass-spectrometry-based draft of the human proteome. *Nature*. 2014;509(7502):582–587.
20. Zampieri M, Sekar K, Zamboni N, Sauer U. Frontiers of high-throughput metabolomics. *Omics*. 2017;36:15–23. https://doi.org/10.1016/j.cbpa.2016.12.006.
21. Guo L, Milburn MV, Ryals JA, et al. Plasma metabolomic profiles enhance precision medicine for volunteers of normal health. *Proc Natl Acad Sci*. 2015;112(35):E4901–E4910.
22. Bersanelli M, Mosca E, Remondini D, et al. Methods for the integration of multi-omics data: mathematical aspects. *BMC Bioinform*. 2016;17 (2):167–177.
23. Hofree M, Shen JP, Carter H, Gross A, Ideker T. Network-based stratification of tumor mutations. *Nat Methods*. 2013;10(11):1108–1115. https://doi.org/10.1038/nmeth.2651.
24. Misra B, Langefeld C, Olivier M, Cox L. Integrated Omics: Tools, Advances and Future Approaches; 2019. https://doi.org/10.1530/JME-18-0055.
25. Gareth J, Daniela W, Trevor H, Robert T. An Introduction to Statistical Learning: With Applications in R. Springer; 2013.
26. Guyon I, Elisseeff A. An introduction to variable and feature selection. *J Mach Learn Res*. 2003;3(Mar):1157–1182.
27. Bush WS, Dudek SM, Ritchie MD. Biofilter: A knowledge-integration system for the multi-locus analysis of genome-wide association studies. In: *Biocomputing 2009*. World Scientific; 2009:368–379.
28. Roobaert D, Karakoulas G, Chawla NV. Information gain, correlation and support vector machines. In: *Feature Extraction: Foundations and Applications*; 2006:463–470.
29. Beretta L, Santaniello A. Implementing ReliefF filters to extract meaningful features from genetic lifetime datasets. *J Biomed Inform*. 2011;44 (2):361–369.
30. Lee I-H, Lushington GH, Visvanathan M. A filter-based feature selection approach for identifying potential biomarkers for lung cancer. *J Clin Bioinform*. 2011;1:1–8.
31. Guyon I, Weston J, Barnhill S, Vapnik V. Gene selection for cancer classification using support vector machines. *Mach Learn*. 2002;46:389–422.
32. Pudil P, Novovičová J, Kittler J. Floating search methods in feature selection. *Pattern Recogn Lett*. 1994;15(11):1119–1125.
33. Zou H. The adaptive lasso and its oracle properties. *J Am Stat Assoc*. 2006;101(476):1418–1429.
34. Xu X, Liang T, Zhu J, Zheng D, Sun T. Review of classical dimensionality reduction and sample selection methods for large-scale data processing. *Neurocomputing*. 2019;328:5–15.
35. Stańczyk U, Jain LC. Feature Selection for Data and Pattern Recognition: An Introduction. Springer; 2015.
36. Meng C, Zeleznik OA, Thallinger GG, Kuster B, Gholami AM, Culhane AC. Dimension reduction techniques for the integrative analysis of multi-omics data. *Brief Bioinform*. 2016;17(4):628–641.
37. Jolliffe IT. Principal Component Analysis for Special Types of Data. Springer; 2002.
38. Martinez AM, Kak AC. Pca versus lda. *IEEE Trans Pattern Anal Mach Intell*. 2001;23(2):228–233.
39. Hamer RM, Young FW. Multidimensional Scaling: History, Theory, and Applications. Psychology Press; 2013.
40. Antonelli J, Claggett BL, Henglin M, et al. Statistical workflow for feature selection in human metabolomics data. *Metabolites*. 2019;9(7):143.
41. Liew AW-C, Law N-F, Yan H. Missing value imputation for gene expression data: computational techniques to recover missing data from available information. *Brief Bioinform*. 2011;12(5):498–513.
42. Vivian J, Eizenga JM, Beale HC, Vaske OM, Paten B. Bayesian framework for detecting gene expression outliers in individual samples. *JCO Clin Cancer Inform*. 2020;4:160–170.
43. Picard M, Scott-Boyer M-P, Bodein A, Périn O, Droit A. Integration strategies of multi-omics data for machine learning analysis. *Comput Struct Biotechnol J*. 2021;19:3735–3746. https://doi.org/10.1016/j.csbj.2021.06.030.
44. Haas R, Zelezniak A, Iacovacci J, Kamrad S, Townsend S, Ralser M. Designing and interpreting 'multi-omic' experiments that may change our understanding of biology. *Curr Opin Syst Biol*. 2017;6:37–45.
45. Chawla NV, Bowyer KW, Hall LO, Kegelmeyer WP. SMOTE: synthetic minority over-sampling technique. *J Artif Intell Res*. 2002;16:321–357.
46. He H, Bai Y, Garcia EA, Li S. ADASYN: adaptive synthetic sampling approach for imbalanced learning; 2008:1322–1328.

47. Chalise P, Raghavan R, Fridley BL. InterSIM: Simulation tool for multiple integrative 'omic datasets'. *Comput Methods Programs Biomed.* 2016;128:69–74. https://doi.org/10.1016/j.cmpb.2016.02.011.
48. Martínez-Mira C, Conesa A, Tarazona S. MOSim: multi-omics simulation in R. *BioRxiv.* 2018;421834. https://doi.org/10.1101/421834.
49. Chung R-H, Kang C-Y. A multi-omics data simulator for complex disease studies and its application to evaluate multi-omics data analysis methods for disease classification. *GigaScience.* 2019;8(5):giz045. https://doi.org/10.1093/gigascience/giz045.
50. Lee JK. Statistical Bioinformatics: For Biomedical and Life Science Researchers. John Wiley & Sons; 2011.
51. Jeni LA, Cohn JF, De La Torre F. Facing imbalanced data recommendations for the use of performance metrics. In: *Proceedings of the International Conference on Affective Computing and Intelligent Interaction Workshops*; 2013:245–251.
52. Herrmann M, Probst P, Hornung R, Jurinovic V, Boulesteix A-L. Large-scale benchmark study of survival prediction methods using multi-omics data. *Brief Bioinform.* 2021;22(3):bbaa167.
53. Schmidhuber J. Deep learning in neural networks: An overview. *Neural Netw.* 2015;61:85–117.
54. Armbrust M, Fox A, Griffith R, et al. A view of cloud computing. *Commun ACM.* 2010;53(4):50–58.
55. AWS | Amazon EC2—Service d'hébergement cloud évolutif. (n.d.). Amazon Web Services, Inc. Retrieved March 15, 2023, from https://aws.amazon.com/fr/ec2/.
56. Cloud Computing Services | Microsoft Azure. (n.d.). Retrieved March 15, 2023, from https://azure.microsoft.com/en-gb/.
57. Services de cloud computing | Google Cloud. (n.d.). Retrieved March 15, 2023, from https://cloud.google.com/?hl=fr.
58. Feurer M, Klein A, Eggensperger K, Springenberg J, Blum M, Hutter F. Efficient and robust automated machine learning. *Adv Neural Inform Process Syst.* 2015;28.
59. Olson RS, Sipper M, Cava WL, et al. A system for accessible artificial intelligence; 2018:121–134.
60. Waring J, Lindvall C, Umeton R. Automated machine learning: review of the state-of-the-art and opportunities for healthcare. *Artif Intell Med.* 2020;104, 101822.
61. Liu E, Li L, Cheng L. Gene Regulatory Network Review. In: Ranganathan S, Gribskov M, Nakai K, Schönbach C, eds. *Encyclopedia of Bioinformatics and Computational Biology.* Academic Press; 2019:155–164. ISBN:9780128114322.
62. Acharjee A, Kloosterman B, Visser RG, Maliepaard C. Integration of multi-omics data for prediction of phenotypic traits using random forest. *BMC Bioinform.* 2016;17(5):363–373.
63. Auslander N, Yizhak K, Weinstock A, et al. A joint analysis of transcriptomic and metabolomic data uncovers enhanced enzyme-metabolite coupling in breast cancer. *Sci Rep.* 2016;6(1):1–10.
64. Ding MQ, Chen L, Cooper GF, Young JD, Lu X. Precision oncology beyond targeted therapy: combining omics data with machine learning matches the majority of Cancer cells to effective therapeutics assigning cancers to effective drugs with big data. *Mol Cancer Res.* 2018;16(2):269–278.
65. Kim M, Tagkopoulos I. Data integration and predictive modeling methods for multi-omics datasets. *Mol Omics.* 2018;14(1):8–25.
66. Lin E, Lane H-Y. Machine learning and systems genomics approaches for multi-omics data. *Biomarker Res.* 2017;5(1):1–6.
67. Wang T, Shao W, Huang Z, et al. MOGONET integrates multi-omics data using graph convolutional networks allowing patient classification and biomarker identification. *Nat Commun.* 2021;12(1):1–13.
68. Zhang L, Lv C, Jin Y, et al. Deep learning-based multi-omics data integration reveals two prognostic subtypes in high-risk neuroblastoma. *Front Genet.* 2018;9:477.
69. Kim D, Li R, Dudek SM, Ritchie MD. ATHENA: identifying interactions between different levels of genomic data associated with cancer clinical outcomes using grammatical evolution neural network. *BioData Mining.* 2013;6(1):1–14.
70. Ma S, Ren J, Fenyö D. Breast cancer prognostics using multi-omics data. *AMIA Summits Transl Sci Proc.* 2016;2016:52.
71. Ma B, Meng F, Yan G, Yan H, Chai B, Song F. Diagnostic classification of cancers using extreme gradient boosting algorithm and multi-omics data. *Comput Biol Med.* 2020;121, 103761.
72. Mankoo PK, Shen R, Schultz N, Levine DA, Sander C. Time to recurrence and survival in serous ovarian tumors predicted from integrated genomic profiles. *PloS One.* 2011;6(11), e24709.
73. Nicolai M, Peter B. Stability selection. *J R Stat Soc Series B Stat Methodology.* 2010;72(4):417–473.
74. Stetson LC, Pearl T, Chen Y, Barnholtz-Sloan JS. Computational identification of multi-omic correlates of anticancer therapeutic response. *BMC Genomics.* 2014;15:1–8.
75. Elith J, Leathwick JR, Hastie T. A working guide to boosted regression trees. *J Anim Ecol.* 2008;77(4):802–813.
76. Awad M, Khanna R, Awad M, Khanna R. Support vector regression. In: *Efficient Learning Machines: Theories, Concepts, and Applications for Engineers and System Designers*; 2015:67–80.
77. Prélot L, Draisma H, Anasanti MD, et al. Machine learning in multi-omics data to assess longitudinal predictors of Glycaemic health. *BioRxiv.* 2018;358390.
78. Tang B, Pan Z, Yin K, Khateeb A. Recent advances of deep learning in bioinformatics and computational biology. *Front Genet.* 2019;10:214.
79. Chaudhary K, Poirion OB, Lu L, Garmire LX. Deep learning-based multi-omics integration robustly predicts survival in liver cancer using deep learning to predict liver cancer prognosis. *Clin Cancer Res.* 2018;24(6):1248–1259.
80. Cantini L, Zakeri P, Hernandez C, et al. Benchmarking joint multi-omics dimensionality reduction approaches for the study of cancer. *Nat Commun.* 2021;12(1):1–12.
81. Mirza B, Wang W, Wang J, Choi H, Chung NC, Ping P. Machine learning and integrative analysis of biomedical big data. *Genes.* 2019;10(2):87.
82. Spicker JS, Brunak S, Frederiksen KS, Toft H. Integration of clinical chemistry, expression, and metabolite data leads to better toxicological class separation. *Toxicol Sci.* 2008;102(2):444–454.
83. Wang D, Gu J. Integrative clustering methods of multi-omics data for molecule-based cancer classifications. *Quant Biol.* 2016;4(1):58–67.
84. Wörheide MA, Krumsiek J, Kastenmüller G, Arnold M. Multi-omics integration in biomedical research—a metabolomics-centric review. *Anal Chim Acta.* 2021;1141:144–162.
85. Wu C, Zhou F, Ren J, Li X, Jiang Y, Ma S. A selective review of multi-level omics data integration using variable selection. *High-Throughput.* 2019;8(1):4.
86. Athreya A, Iyer R, Neavin D, et al. Augmentation of physician assessments with multi-omics enhances predictability of drug response: a case study of major depressive disorder. *IEEE Comput Intell Mag.* 2018;13(3):20–31.

87. Zuin J, Roth G, Zhan Y, et al. Nonlinear control of transcription through enhancer–promoter interactions. *Nature*. 2022;604(7906):571–577.

88. Argelaguet R, Velten B, Arnol D, et al. Multi-omics factor analysis—a framework for unsupervised integration of multi-omics data sets. *Mol Syst Biol*. 2018;14(6), e8124.

89. Lock EF, Hoadley KA, Marron JS, Nobel AB. Joint and Individual Variation Explained (JIVE) for Integrated Analysis of Multiple Data Types; 2013. https://doi.org/10.1214/12-AOAS597.

90. Zhang S, Liu C-C, Li W, Shen H, Laird PW, Zhou XJ. Discovery of multi-dimensional modules by integrative analysis of cancer genomic data. *Nucleic Acids Res*. 2012;40(19):9379–9391. https://doi.org/10.1093/nar/gks725.

91. Yang Z, Michailidis G. A non-negative matrix factorization method for detecting modules in heterogeneous omics multi-modal data. *Bioinformatics*. 2016;32(1):1–8.

92. Wang H-Q, Zheng C-H, Zhao X-M. JNMFMA: a joint non-negative matrix factorization meta-analysis of transcriptomics data. *Bioinformatics*. 2015;31(4):572–580.

93. Shen R, Olshen AB, Ladanyi M. Integrative clustering of multiple genomic data types using a joint latent variable model with application to breast and lung cancer subtype analysis. *Bioinformatics*. 2009;25(22):2906–2912. https://doi.org/10.1093/bioinformatics/btp543.

94. Mo Q, Wang S, Seshan VE, et al. Pattern discovery and cancer gene identification in integrated cancer genomic data; 2013. https://doi.org/10.1073/pnas.1208949110.

95. Mo Q, Shen R, Guo C, Vannucci M, Chan KS, Hilsenbeck SG. A fully Bayesian latent variable model for integrative clustering analysis of multi-type omics data. *Biostatistics*. 2018;19(1):71–86.

96. Meng C, Helm D, Frejno M, Kuster B. moCluster: identifying joint patterns across multiple omics data sets. *J Proteome Res*. 2016;15(3):755–765.

97. Wu D, Wang D, Zhang MQ, Gu J. Fast dimension reduction and integrative clustering of multi-omics data using low-rank approximation: application to cancer molecular classification. *BMC Genomics*. 2015;16(1):1–10.

98. Jung I, Kim M, Rhee S, Lim S, Kim S. MONTI: a multi-omics non-negative tensor decomposition framework for gene-level integrative analysis. *Front Genet*. 2021;1635.

99. Boyd S, Boyd SP, Vandenberghe L. Convex Optimization. Cambridge University Press; 2004.

100. Nesterov Y, Nemirovskii A. Interior-Point Polynomial Algorithms in Convex Programming. SIAM; 1994.

101. Vandenberghe L, Boyd S. Semidefinite programming. *SIAM Rev*. 1996;38(1):49–95.

102. Lanckriet GR, Cristianini N, Bartlett P, Ghaoui LE, Jordan MI. Learning the kernel matrix with semidefinite programming. *J Mach Learn Res*. 2004;5(Jan):27–72.

103. Seoane JA, Day IN, Gaunt TR, Campbell C. A pathway-based data integration framework for prediction of disease progression. *Bioinformatics*. 2014;30(6):838–845.

104. Bowd C, Medeiros FA, Zhang Z, et al. Relevance vector machine and support vector machine classifier analysis of scanning laser polarimetry retinal nerve fiber layer measurements. *Invest Ophthalmol Vis Sci*. 2005;46(4):1322–1329.

105. Tipping ME. Sparse Bayesian learning and the relevance vector machine. *J Mach Learn Res*. 2001;1(Jun):211–244.

106. Wu C-C, Asgharzadeh S, Triche TJ, D'Argenio DZ. Prediction of human functional genetic networks from heterogeneous data using RVM-based ensemble learning. *Bioinformatics*. 2010;26(6):807–813.

107. Giang T-T, Nguyen T-P, Tran D-H. Stratifying patients using fast multiple kernel learning framework: case studies of Alzheimer's disease and cancers. *BMC Med Inform Decis Mak*. 2020;20(1):1–15.

108. Chen Y, Li Y, Narayan R, Subramanian A, Xie X. Gene expression inference with deep learning. *Bioinformatics*. 2016;32(12):1832–1839.

109. Liu X, Song L, Liu S, Zhang Y. A review of deep-learning-based medical image segmentation methods. *Sustainability*. 2021;13(3):1224.

110. McBee MP, Awan OA, Colucci AT, et al. Deep learning in radiology. *Acad Radiol*. 2018;25(11):1472–1480.

111. Kramer MA. Nonlinear principal component analysis using autoassociative neural networks. *AIChE J*. 1991;37(2):233–243.

112. Ngiam J, Khosla A, Kim M, Nam J, Lee H, Ng AY. Multimodal Deep Learning. ICML; 2011.

113. Dhillon P, Foster DP, Ungar L. Multi-view learning of word embeddings via cca. *Adv Neural Inform Process Syst*. 2011;24.

114. Vinokourov A, Cristianini N, Shawe-Taylor J. Inferring a semantic representation of text via cross-language correlation analysis. *Adv Neural Inform Process Syst*. 2002;15:1–8.

115. Akaho S. A kernel method for canonical correlation analysis; 2006. ArXiv Preprint Cs/0609071.

116. Lai PL, Fyfe C. Kernel and nonlinear canonical correlation analysis. *Int J Neural Syst*. 2000;10(05):365–377.

117. Andrew G, Arora R, Bilmes J, Livescu K. Deep canonical correlation analysis. In: *Proceedings of Machine Learning Research*; 2013:1247–1255.

118. Wang W, Arora R, Livescu K, Bilmes J. On deep multi-view representation learning; 2015:1083–1092.

119. Tan K, Huang W, Hu J, Dong S. A multi-omics supervised autoencoder for pan-cancer clinical outcome endpoints prediction. *BMC Med Inform Decis Mak*. 2020;20(3):129. https://doi.org/10.1186/s12911-020-1114-3.

120. Xu J, Wu P, Chen Y, Meng Q, Dawood H, Dawood H. A hierarchical integration deep flexible neural forest framework for cancer subtype classification by integrating multi-omics data. *BMC Bioinform*. 2019;20(1):527. https://doi.org/10.1186/s12859-019-3116-7.

121. Vincent P, Larochelle H, Lajoie I, Bengio Y, Manzagol P-A, Bottou L. Stacked denoising autoencoders: learning useful representations in a deep network with a local denoising criterion. *J Mach Learn Res*. 2010;11(12):3371–3408.

122. Ronen J, Hayat S, Akalin A. Evaluation of colorectal cancer subtypes and cell lines using deep learning. *Life Sci Alliance*. 2019;2(6):e201900517.

123. Poirion OB, Jing Z, Chaudhary K, Huang S, Garmire LX. DeepProg: an ensemble of deep-learning and machine-learning models for prognosis prediction using multi-omics data. *Genome Med*. 2021;13(1):112. https://doi.org/10.1186/s13073-021-00930-x.

124. Sharifi-Noghabi H, Zolotareva O, Collins CC, Ester M. MOLI: multi-omics late integration with deep neural networks for drug response prediction. *Bioinformatics*. 2019;35(14):i501–i509.

125. He H, Lin D, Zhang J, Wang Y, Deng H-W. Biostatistics, data mining and computational modeling. *Appl Clin Bioinform*. 2016;23–57.

126. Ritchie MD, Holzinger ER, Li R, Pendergrass SA, Kim D. Methods of integrating data to uncover genotype–phenotype interactions. *Nat Rev Genet*. 2015;16(2):85–97. https://doi.org/10.1038/nrg3868.

127. Zarayeneh N, Ko E, Oh JH, et al. Integration of multi-omics data for integrative gene regulatory network inference. *Int J Data Min Bioinform*. 2017;18(3):223–239.

128. Yuan L, Guo L-H, Yuan C-A, et al. Integration of multi-omics data for gene regulatory network inference and application to breast cancer. *IEEE/ACM Trans Comput Biol Bioinform*. 2018;16(3):782–791.

129. Wang B, Mezlini A, Demir F, et al. Similarity network fusion for aggregating data types on a genomic scale; 2014. https://doi.org/10.1038/nmeth.2810.

130. Rappoport N, Shamir R. NEMO: cancer subtyping by integration of partial multi-omic data. *Bioinformatics*. 2019;35(18):3348–3356.

131. Newman MEJ. 78Biological networks: a discussion of various networks of interest in biology, including biochemical networks, neural networks, and ecological networks. In: Newman M, ed. *Networks: An Introduction*. Oxford University Press; 2010. https://doi.org/10.1093/acprof:oso/9780199206650.003.0005.

132. Szklarczyk D, Gable AL, Lyon D, et al. STRING v11: protein–protein association networks with increased coverage, supporting functional discovery in genome-wide experimental datasets. *Nucleic Acids Res*. 2019;47(D1):D607–D613.

133. Warde-Farley D, Donaldson SL, Comes O, et al. The GeneMANIA prediction server: biological network integration for gene prioritization and predicting gene function. *Nucleic Acids Res*. 2010;38(suppl_2):W214–W220.

134. Montenegro JD. Gene co-expression network analysis. In: *Plant Bioinformatics*. Springer; 2022:387–404.

135. van Dam S, Võsa U, van der Graaf A, Franke L, de Magalhães JP. Gene co-expression analysis for functional classification and gene–disease predictions. *Brief Bioinform*. 2018;19(4):575–592. https://doi.org/10.1093/bib/bbw139.

136. Glass K, Huttenhower C, Quackenbush J, Yuan G-C. Passing messages between biological networks to refine predicted interactions. *PloS One*. 2013;8(5), e64832.

137. Page L, Brin S, Motwani R, Winograd T. The PageRank Citation Ranking: Bringing Order to the Web. Stanford InfoLab; 1999.

138. Biran H, Kupiec M, Sharan R. Comparative analysis of normalization methods for network propagation. *Front Genet*. 2019;10:4.

139. Cowen L, Ideker T, Raphael BJ, Sharan R. Network propagation: a universal amplifier of genetic associations. *Nat Rev Genet*. 2017;18(9):551–562.

140. Oughtred R, Rust J, Chang C, et al. The BioGRID database: a comprehensive biomedical resource of curated protein, genetic, and chemical interactions. *Protein Sci*. 2021;30(1):187–200.

141. Hermjakob H, Montecchi-Palazzi L, Lewington C, et al. IntAct: an open source molecular interaction database. *Nucleic Acids Res*. 2004;32(suppl_1):D452–D455.

142. UniProt Consortium. UniProt: a worldwide hub of protein knowledge. *Nucleic Acids Res*. 2019;47(D1):D506–D515.

143. Bader GD, Cary MP, Sander C. Pathguide: a pathway resource list. *Nucleic Acids Res*. 2006;34(Suppl. 1):D504–D506.

144. Köhler S, Bauer S, Horn D, Robinson PN. Walking the interactome for prioritization of candidate disease genes. *Am J Human Genet*. 2008;82(4):949–958.

145. Carlin DE, Demchak B, Pratt D, Sage E, Ideker T. Network propagation in the cytoscape cyberinfrastructure. *PLoS Comput Biol*. 2017;13(10), e1005598.

146. Wang D, Gu J. VASC: dimension reduction and visualization of single-cell RNA-seq data by deep Variational autoencoder. *Bioinform Commons (II)*. 2018;16(5):320–331. https://doi.org/10.1016/j.gpb.2018.08.003.

147. Li Y, Qian B, Zhang X, Liu H. Graph neural network-based diagnosis prediction. *Big Data*. 2020;8(5):379–390.

148. Schulte-Sasse R, Budach S, Hnisz D, Marsico A. Integration of multiomics data with graph convolutional networks to identify new cancer genes and their associated molecular mechanisms. *Nature Mach Intell*. 2021;3(6):513–526. https://doi.org/10.1038/s42256-021-00325-y.

149. Vaske CJ, Benz SC, Sanborn JZ, et al. Inference of patient-specific pathway activities from multi-dimensional cancer genomics data using PARADIGM; 2010. https://doi.org/10.1093/bioinformatics/btq182.

150. Li C, Han J, Yao Q, et al. Subpathway-GM: identification of metabolic subpathways via joint power of interesting genes and metabolites and their topologies within pathways. *Nucleic Acids Res*. 2013;41(9):e101.

151. Calura E, Martini P, Sales G, et al. Wiring miRNAs to pathways: a topological approach to integrate miRNA and mRNA expression profiles. *Nucleic Acids Res*. 2014;42(11):e96.

152. Diaz D, Draghici S. mirIntegrator: Integrating miRNAs into Signaling Pathways. In: R, ed. *R Package*. Bioconductor; 2015.

153. Martini P, Chiogna M, Calura E, Romualdi C. MOSClip: multi-omic and survival pathway analysis for the identification of survival associated gene and modules. *Nucleic Acids Res*. 2019;47(14):e80.

154. Jiang Y, Wang D, Xu D, Joshi T. IMPRes-pro: a high dimensional multiomics integration method for in silico hypothesis generation. *Methods*. 2020;173:16–23.

155. Joshi P, Basso B, Wang H, Hong S-H, Giardina C, Shin D-G. RPAC: route based pathway analysis for cohorts of gene expression data sets. *Methods*. 2022;198:76–87.

156. Maghsoudi Z, Nguyen H, Tavakkoli A, Nguyen T. A comprehensive survey of the approaches for pathway analysis using multi-omics data integration. *Brief Bioinform*. 2022;23(6):bbac435.

157. Bonnet E, Calzone L, Michoel T. Integrative multi-omics module network inference with lemon-tree. *PLoS Comput Biol*. 2015;11(2), e1003983.

158. Tepeli YI, Ünal AB, Akdemir FM, Tastan O. PAMOGK: a pathway graph kernel-based multiomics approach for patient clustering. *Bioinformatics*. 2020;36(21):5237–5246.

159. Lyu B, Haque A. Deep learning based tumor type classification using gene expression data; 2018:89–96.

160. Lopez-Garcia G, Jerez JM, Franco L, Veredas FJ. Transfer learning with convolutional neural networks for cancer survival prediction using gene-expression data. *PloS One*. 2020;15(3), e0230536.

161. Sharma A, Kumar D. Classification with 2-D convolutional neural networks for breast cancer diagnosis. *Sci Rep*. 2022;12(1):21857.

162. Asuncion A, Newman D. UCI machine learning repository; 2007.

163. Sharma A, Vans E, Shigemizu D, Boroevich KA, Tsunoda T. DeepInsight: a methodology to transform a non-image data to an image for convolution neural network architecture. *Sci Rep*. 2019;9(1):11399.

164. Zandavi SM, Liu D, Chung V, Anaissi A, Vafaee F. Fotomics: Fourier transform-based omics imagification for deep learning-based cell-identity mapping using single-cell omics profiles. *Artif Intell Rev*. 2022;1–16.

15

Artificial intelligence in behavioral health economics: Considerations for designing behavioral studies

Nadja Kairies-Schwarz[a] and Andrea Icks[a,b]

[a]Institute for Health Services Research and Health Economics, Centre for Health and Society, Medical Faculty and University Hospital Düsseldorf, Heinrich-Heine-University Düsseldorf, Düsseldorf, Germany [b]Institute for Health Services Research and Health Economics, German Diabetes Center, Leibniz Center for Diabetes Research at Heinrich-Heine-University Düsseldorf, Düsseldorf, Germany

1. Introduction: Why is artificial intelligence relevant to behavioral health economists?

1.1 What is behavioral economics?

The traditional "homo oeconomicus" model that is widely used in economics assumes that individuals are perfectly rational in their decision-making. In the last decades, this assumption has been vividly tested and various empirical studies suggest individuals often systematically deviate from this assumption in a variety of situations. Individuals, for example, show inconsistent behavior in relation to the individual's own preferences (e.g., risk and time), use of heuristics, or nonselfish (e.g., altruistic) behavior. These systematic observations have then been integrated into mathematically formal models, and behavioral economics has evolved as a new branch of economics. Behavioral economics studies how people make decisions and combines insights from other disciplines psychology, medicine (especially neuroscience), environmental research, sociology, anthropology, but also technical sciences (e.g., environmental research) to understand why people behave in certain ways and how these behaviors affect economic behavior.

1.2 What is behavioral health economics?

Since the importance of testing model assumptions against actual individual behavior has become more important in the last decades, behavioral economics in general has de facto found its way into all applied areas of economics, including health economics. In health care the outcome of medical treatment is highly influenced by the decisions of healthcare providers (e.g., physicians) and the individual's health behavior. While there are many aspects that are not easy to control within the process of treating a patient, e.g., a patient's age, gender or genetic disposition, or a physician's medical equipment, numerous aspects rely on individual preferences and behavior. The contribution of behavioral health economics is that it provides new explanations for modeling agents' preferences and behaviors when they either receive or provide health-related services.

1.3 What are the applications of behavioral economics in health care?

For physicians, behavioral economics has a long legacy and dates back to the Hippocratic Oath. The latter formulates altruistic preferences (so-called "other regarding altruistic preferences") as a fundamental ethical norm for physicians.[1,2] In general, the concept of altruism entered the field of health economics with Arrow[3] and has since then been taken into account as an assumption in many formal models (see, e.g., Ref. 4). Experimental evidence shows that individuals in the healthcare sector, such as physicians, are best characterized by (semi-)altruistic preferences and thus deviate in their behavior from the neoclassical model of "pure" profit-maximizing agents (see e.g., Refs. 5–8). Furthermore, medical decisions in clinics are often made under high pressure and great uncertainty. Under such conditions, healthcare providers are especially prone to behavioral biases or heuristics in decision making often leading to suboptimal decisions. Singh,[9] for instance, show that physicians' treatment decisions in the delivery room (i.e., vaginal versus a cesarean delivery mode) are influenced by the availability heuristic: In case of previous complications with one of the two modes of delivery, a physician will be more likely to switch to the respective other mode irrespective of a patient's indications. They also show that this behavior has small negative effects on patient health (e.g., an increase in maternal and neonatal mortality). Typical policy interventions on the supply side include, for example, the optimal design of reimbursement systems (see, e.g., Ref. 10), organizational structures, or decision support systems to ensure the highest possible quality and efficiency in healthcare.

On the patient side, chronic diseases such as type 2 diabetes mellitus or cardiovascular diseases are to some degree influenced by individual behavior that is reflected in western lifestyles such as tobacco consumption, excessive alcohol consumption, lack of exercise, and stress. These behaviors can be explained by models from behavioral economics such as inconsistent time preferences with hyperbolic discounting.[11,12] While a rational individual has a constant discount rate and would always make the same decision regarding healthy behaviors irrespective of the point of time, the empirical evidence shows that due to time-inconsistent preferences individuals might make plans to engage in healthy behaviors such as exercising or eating well in the future, but in the respective moment of the actual decision they do not stick to their previous plan anymore and decide for the unhealthy alternative.[13–15] Mørkbak et al.[16] also show that a strong preference for the present can even lead to an early start of type 2 diabetes mellitus. In order to induce behavioral changes in the field of health, e.g., in patients through new and sustainable prevention or therapy approaches (see, e.g., Ref. 17), an in-depth understanding of the behavioral economic aspects in modeling interventions is therefore of high importance.

An improved or refined understanding of the actual preferences and behaviors of agents better then also allows to design policy interventions (e.g., payment reforms), decision support systems, or prevention and treatment strategies more efficiently and more tailored to the individual. Both can in turn lead to improved health outcomes.

1.4 What are the opportunities of AI in behavioral health economics?

Similar to the application of AI in all areas of health from primary health care to rare disease care, emergency medicine, basic biomedical research, as well as healthcare management (cf. Ref. 18; or 19), the evolution of artificial intelligence (AI) has raised new opportunities for studying topics in behavioral health care.

According to Luxton,[20] there are four main benefits of AI for behavioral health care. The first one is that AI-based intelligent machines or decision support systems are less prone to behavioral biases such as the availability heuristic or stereotyping than a human decision maker. Evidence also shows that patients were actually more willing to disclose information to digital humans for clinical interviews than to actual humans.[21]

The second one includes that AI can improve self-care and access to care. Concerning access, AI methods can increase the potential of telemedicine, e.g., by giving access to virtual human healthcare providers who are continuously available from anywhere via mobile devices.[22] Self-care can, for instance, be improved by new wearables such as smart watches or biosensors, which increase the number of individual data points. Based on the latter, individuals can receive more information on medical markers such as the heart rate as well as progress toward health targets such as the number of steps.

The third benefit of AI in health care is its potential to optimize care, i.e., make health care more patient-centered. For a patient with a diagnosed type 2 diabetes mellitus who is wearing a smartwatch or biosensor, these data could be integrated into physician decision support systems using AI methods to optimize individual treatment strategies. This is possible since AI methods are able to model high-dimensional, complex, and nonlinear relationships very accurately and quickly for instance through the use of machine learning. In case of nonadherence to a physical activity target of increasing the number of steps, the intelligent system could, for instance, identify a certain measure such as sending daily reminders to increase adherence. Based on the additional info such as gender, age, family situation, or socioeconomic status in the intelligent system, the timing, form of message, or frequency of the message sent to the respective patient could also be automatically customized to an individual's needs and preferences.

Finally, as a consequence of these advances, AI also has the potential to increase economic benefits. The central aspect is that processes of healthcare delivery can become more efficient for both providers and consumers. For instance, a first-time patient could go through a virtual anamnesis upon arrival. The information can then be automatically integrated into intelligent AI-based decision support systems facilitating diagnosis and enabling a physician to use the time spent with the patient more effectively (e.g., with a greater focus on interpersonal aspects rather than purely informational aspects). The further treatment of a patient who is, for instance, diagnosed with type 2 diabetes mellitus can then be optimized by wearables or biosensors, which track individual behavior that is fed directly into the system. This facilitates self-care, e.g., via self-assessment of medical markers and/or health targets such as daily number of steps, as well as the continuous optimization of treatment strategies, and may ultimately lead to better health outcomes increasing in turn patient benefits while simultaneously further decreasing healthcare costs. This individually customized or patient-centered care is particularly relevant in the field of chronic diseases such as type 2 diabetes mellitus or cardiovascular diseases where individual health behaviors play a substantial role in prevention and/or progress.

In this context, behavioral health economics can particularly contribute to the aspects of increasing self-care and making health care more patient-centered by identifying behavioral features, which for instance inform how healthcare consumers respond to different incentives to increase healthy behaviors (e.g., how patients with chronic diseases such as type 2 diabetes mellitus respond to different forms of financial rewards to increase physical activity). The behavioral variables can be integrated into intelligent machines using AI methods, which can translate the information to customized treatment strategies for an individual or in the sense of public policy into more effective policy interventions.

Behavioral research using AI methods can be conducted using observational as well as interventional studies. For the identification of new behavior with AI variables especially interventional studies are of interest, e.g., studies in which participants in the treatment group continuously wear smartwatches and are given financial rewards for achieving a certain health goal. The more forms and variations of treatments, e.g., height or frequency of the financial reward, are tested in such behavioral studies, the more potential behavioral health care has to become more efficient in the light of AI. Behavioral studies using interventions should therefore be designed in a way that recognizes the technological advancements of AI in healthcare. The aim of this chapter is to give an introduction to the fundamentals in the research field of behavioral health economics and give a guide to designing interventional behavioral studies in the light of AI.

The remaining chapters are structured as follows. Chapter 2 gives an introduction to the fundamentals in the research field of behavioral health economics in the light of AI. It elaborates on its theory-based nature and how AI can help to improve the interplay between theory and empirical observations. Thereby, it also introduces the reader to the basic classifications of the different types of experimental approaches for behavioral studies. In Chapter 3, we will then describe the traditional approach of designing behavioral studies and give a guide on important aspects to be considered for the design of behavioral studies, as well as opportunities and limitations in the light of using AI methods.

2. The fundamentals of behavioral health economics and AI

2.1 The interplay between theory and empirical evidence in behavioral health economics

As with other disciplines, (behavioral health) economics is a theory-based research field in which often a formal model serves as the basis for research questions. The evolution of this research field crucially depends on the interplay between theory and empirical evidence: empirical observations inform theory, which in turn can be adjusted and empirically tested again (see, e.g., Robert Wilson, Paul Milgrom, and Al Roth in[23] for market design). The idea behind this continuous adjustment of the underlying model parameters is summarized by Duflo[24] with the term *"tinkering"*:

> *"Plumbers try to predict as well as possible what may work in the real world, mindful that tinkering and adjusting will be necessary since our models gives us very little theoretical guidance on what (and how) details will matter."*

Such tinkering can be found in all areas of behavioral health economics. Consider, for example, healthy behaviors and the underlying theories of inconsistent time preferences, which are modeled via an individual's utility function, aim to explain why individuals plan to behave in a healthy way, yet do not stick to it. Interventions with different incentives, such as financial incentives or social incentives to increase healthy behaviors, might affect an individual's utility within the model context. Behavioral studies can then test how the different types of incentives affect patients' behavior, e.g., adherence. The empirical observations can then feed back into the formal models.

2.2 How can AI enhance the interplay between theory and empirical evidence in behavioral health economics?

Similar to other disciplines, behavioral health economic models can greatly benefit from AI techniques in various dimensions. Particularly, AI methods may enable a more accurate and *dynamic adjustment of parameters* within such behavior-based models. Athey,[25] among various others, predicts that this so-called *"economist as plumber"* approach will be generally reinforced by AI in the future and that this will be even more relevant. In the case of the previous example, health behaviors in the form of physical exercise might be tracked by wearables allowing for a large number of data points per individual. AI-driven methods can be used to find and analyze new relationships between individuals' health behaviors and outcomes, providing further insight into the role that various factors may play in influencing health outcomes.

In general, new approaches to model policy interventions or prevention strategies (e.g., the introduction of new explanatory approaches) in behavioral health economics are often motivated by findings from psychology, medicine (especially neuroscience), environmental research, sociology, anthropology, but also technical sciences (e.g., environmental research). Therefore, behavioral health economics is at most interdisciplinary. Methodologically, this interdisciplinary approach also includes the application of "new" statistical methods such as the application of AI methods *for feature exploration (variable identification), model specification, and prediction of actual behavior*. Using new methodological approaches of AI can hence enrich the interplay between theory and empirics.

2.3 Types of experimental studies in behavioral economics and external vs. internal validity

The research design of a behavioral interventional study is of special interest. It is, hence, central to consider which type of *experimental study* is suitable for answering the research question. According to the classification of Harrison and List,[26] there are four distinguished types of experimental studies in behavioral economics:

(1) A *"conventional lab experiment"* is carried out often with students, has an abstract "framing," takes place in the laboratory, and has fixed rules.
(2) An *"artefactual field experiment"* differs from a "conventional lab experiment" in that real decision-makers such as patients or physicians are also involved.
(3) A *"framed field experiment"* has a field context in terms of the subject, the stakes, the task, and the information.[a]
(4) In a *"natural field experiment,"* the subjects act in their natural environment and are not aware of the fact that they are taking part in an experiment.

A new form of field experiments is "massive filed experiments" or so-called *"mega studies"* (see, e.g., Ref. 27 or 28). While traditional field studies usually test only one or two treatments (e.g., a financial reward for a certain number of steps per week or a larger one per month) compared to a control group (e.g., without a financial reward) in these studies the effects of many different treatments on the same quantitatively measurable outcome are tested simultaneously within one large sample.

The experimental designs differ

- in their relative degree of control and the possibility of establishing causalities (*internal validity*), as well as
- in their relative degree of realism of the decision scenario (*external validity*).

Framed field experiments, mega studies, and *natural experiments* are characterized by their comparatively high external validity. Realistic decision scenarios enable the collection of many different variables in interdisciplinary settings. They are therefore in particular suitable to allow AI techniques to identify new explanatory variables (features) that improve behavior-based intelligent machines or policy interventions. *Mega studies* come with the additional advantage that the relative efficacy of different treatments to change behavior can be directly tested within one study. They are therefore a particularly promising means to identify new explanatory behavioral variables with AI methods.

Conventional lab experiments and *artefactual field experiments* are carried out under controlled laboratory conditions. This high *internal validity* makes it possible to identify causalities. In case, for example, either the amount or the form of remuneration for physicians is changed and everything else, such as the patient pool, is kept constant, a change in the

---

[a] A framed field experiment is comparable to a so-called Randomized Controlled Trial (RCT) in clinical research or, often more pragmatic, in health services research (evaluation of complex interventions). In clinical research, a "traditional" RCT (e.g., to evaluate the efficacy of a pharmaceutical agent under strict experimental conditions), is assumed to have a high internal validity. Pragmatic RCTs (pRCTs), which are conducted under more real-world conditions, increase the external validity.

provision of medical services can be traced back solely to the respective change in remuneration. This form of behavioral economics experiments is an established and complementary approach to field data or framed fields and natural experiments. If, for example, associations between behavioral variables and other variables are found on the basis of field data, causalities can be better researched. These identified causalities can then provide new insights for behavioral economic models. This shows that, in addition to the interdisciplinary nature of the data, the complementarity of the study design also plays an important role.

In addition to the form of the study design, other aspects should also be considered. According to Galizzi and Wiesen,[29] the subjects' decisions should have actual consequences, i.e., there is a suitable incentive structure. In conventional lab and artefactual experiments, a suitable incentive structure can be easily implemented through monetary payments. Such a monetary incentive structure has some advantages. Thus, money is an easily interpreted metric that is relatively unaffected by nonrandom measurement errors. It also allows easy comparison between individuals and avoids hypothetical response bias. The latter may occur when participants' hypothetical responses in surveys or experimental studies do not collide with their real behaviors. However, a functional monetary incentive structure (e.g., monetary rewards conditional on achieving a certain health goal) may be difficult to implement in large-scale studies based on, e.g., framed field experiments, mega studies, or natural experiments. The latter may, for instance, have very large differences in income and hence respond differently to the same-sized monetary reward. To achieve statistical power, one will need a very large number of participants, which in turn increases the costs of such studies. This must either be taken into account at an early stage in the planning or other questionnaire instruments that have already been experimentally validated in the field must be used instead. An often-used alternative to financial incentives in behavioral studies is nudges, which gently nudge or steer individuals to their desired choices.[30,31] Nudges may include reminders (e.g., to exercise), or giving information (e.g., about potential benefits of exercising or potential losses of not exercising). Behavioral nudges in the form of reminders as well as digital public health interventions in the form of social media advertisement have for instance been shown to be effective at increasing the uptake of COVID-19 vaccinations (see, e.g., Ref. 32 or 33).

3. What has to be considered in designing experimental studies in the field of behavioral health economics?

3.1 "Traditional" approach

In this section, we will discuss considerations for the experimental design of behavioral studies using AI methods. While many aspects also apply to observational studies, our example focuses on behavioral interventions.

Designing an experimental study can be structured in a variety of ways. However, like in other research disciplines, a typical experimental study in behavioral health economics starts with the *research question*. The research question is then broken down into (various) hypotheses that can be empirically tested. Follow-up questions include which subjects (e.g., patients, physicians) are relevant for answering the research question (*study group*) as well as which is the best *study design* (e.g., conventional lab experiment or framed field experiment). The study design also defines the *outcome measure(s)*. In order to apply statistical hypothesis testing and achieve a certain desired level of statistical significance, a *minimum sample size* needs to be determined and subjects need to be randomly assigned to the intervention and the control group(s). Data collection and hypothesis testing are typically restricted to the research question (and the related hypothesis).

This "traditional" approach has its merits but the application of AI in the field of behavioral health economics commonly involves:

- a more *interdisciplinary* approach that in particular also includes data scientists that help with their specific expertise (e.g., with respect to data collection, storage, model selection and tuning, and deployment) but often do not have specific domain knowledge in behavioral health economics, and
- a more rigorous *process model* that ensures that all parties involved in the study design establish a joint understanding of what the research question is, what data are needed to investigate the research question, and apply AI methods within the study design.

As such, "standard" methods that are commonly applied in data analytics projects can help behavioral health economists to better design (not only from a methodological point of view but also in terms of costs and time efficiency) and carry out data-driven experimental studies.

3.2 CRISP–DM process model

As a common widely used methodology for data analytics projects, the CRoss Industry Standard Process for Data Mining (acronym "CRISP–DM") is a very popular process model[b] that serves as the base for data analytics projects. The CRISP–DM approach can be easily adapted for the design of experimental studies in behavioral health economics. The following six phases describe—along the lines of the traditional CRISP–DM process—the different steps:

1. **Understanding the health context:** Similar to the traditional approach, researchers first define the research question and develop the hypotheses, which can then be empirically tested. In this phase, a joint understanding of the behavioral study's objective from a behavioral health perspective is secured by involving all nondomain experts such as data scientists.
2. **Understanding the data:** The necessary data sources are defined and a joint understanding of the content and caveats is established in the second phase. This includes the identification of missing data sources, estimating data quality, and calculation of the necessary sample size for the study (and control) groups.
3. **Data collection:** In this phase, the data are collected, quality is assessed, the data are transformed (e.g., merged), as well as it is dealt with missing and outlier data in the data preparation.
4. **Modeling::** The modeling phase involves model selection and model optimization based on predefined performance measures.
5. **Evaluation:** The evaluation phase assesses the performance of the applied model and the validity of the findings. Also, any errors or biases in the data that could impact the results are evaluated.
6. **Deployment:** In this phase, the insights of the behavioral study can be implemented (e.g., insights on patient behavior can be transferred to the design of new patient-centered prevention or treatment strategies).

Fig. 1 illustrates the process phases: The CRISP–DM process model is a well-established methodology that ensures a high degree of transparency across all phases in conducting an experimental behavioral study. This is of great importance in an interdisciplinary team and also allows to communicate very easily to the public.

In the following, the different phases and particularities to be considered in designing experiments in behavioral health economics when using AI methods are explained in more detail.

3.3 Understanding the health context

3.3.1 Research question, hypothesis, and study design

Similar to the traditional approach, researchers first define the (theory-based) research question and develop the testable hypotheses. To do so, knowledge in the domain of behavioral health economics is the prerequisite. In order to apply AI methods, experts with presumably little or no domain knowledge in behavioral health economics such as data scientists need to be involved. They also need to develop a clear understanding of the motivation and relevance of the research question and the related hypotheses. Assume for instance, the aim of the behavioral study is to increase physical activity among patients with an established type 2 diabetes mellitus via a certain form of intervention using financial and/or social incentives. The choice for the respective incentive to be implemented in an intervention should be clearly communicated based on the previous empirical evidence and theoretical behavioral model(s). This may

FIG. 1   CRISP–DM process model in behavioral health economics. *Adapted from Chapman P, Clinton J, Kerber R, Khabaza T, Reinartz T, Shearer C, Wirth R. (1999, March). The CRISP-DM user guide. In 4th CRISP-DM SIG Workshop in Brussels in March (Vol. 1999).*

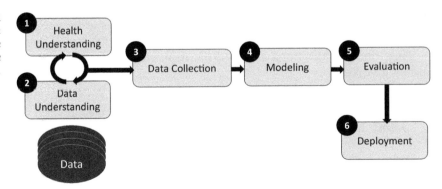

include the behavioral economics knowledge on the impact of, for instance, the height, frequency, framing, or timing of financial incentives to increase physical activity (see, e.g., Refs. 34–39) as well as the medical knowledge on which type of medical markers (e.g., blood glucose levels for type 2 diabetes mellitus patients) might be affected by a change in physical activity. Communicating this expertise with respect to the outcome measures to data scientists is of particular relevance since their expertise is needed in the second phase with respect to the necessary data. Finally, the research question must be embedded in a suitable study design that allows for rigorous hypothesis testing with the application of AI methods (cf. Section 2.3). This may also include a combination of different types of experimental studies. A controlled laboratory or artefactual experiment may, for instance, inform a framed field experiment on the effects of different forms of (financial) incentives on (work) motivation prior to its implementation in the field.

3.3.2 Enhanced interplay between theory and empirics

As such, the two first phases of the CRISP–DM approach (understanding the health context and data understanding) simultaneously secure a common understanding of all experts involved in the experimental behavioral study. If the joint understanding is secured, AI methods can help to identify new explanatory influencing factors independently of a theoretical foundation, which has not been considered to date or has not been fully considered. Also, AI methods are able to model high-dimensional, complex, and nonlinear relationships very accurately and quickly, e.g., through the use of machine learning. Both approaches allow to enhance the interplay between the theoretical basis of experimental design and the actual behavior of individuals. A prerequisite for this is the identification of a broad set of data points in an interdisciplinary and broad manner. Given our previous example, in addition to variables such as counted steps, heart rate, or blood glucose levels of a participant, data points may include the room temperature during sleep, the weather conditions, the mental fitness, or the socioeconomic status before and/or during the intervention, etc. In this respect, as many predictive explanatory variables (features) as possible shall be considered and an interdisciplinary approach is the necessary prerequisite for those parties involved in data collection.

3.3.3 Increasing complexity

As such, in the future experimental studies in behavioral health will become even more fundamentally interdisciplinary *complex*, for example, by linking economic, health-related, environmental, technical, psychological, sociological, anthropological, and neuroscientific data points in an interdisciplinary linked database. However, interdisciplinarity is challenging to implement in the concrete research project work, since this requires the same understanding of the features and variables of interest to be collected and the exact content of the data variables collected. Therefore, a joint understanding of both, the health context and the data analytics requirements, is of the highest importance. Albeit this seems trivial with respect to "traditional" experimental behavioral studies, more complex experimental designs such as mega studies require particular emphasis on a joint understanding of experts involved.

Key Aspects: In the "understanding the health content" phase, it is crucial to develop a joint understanding of all experts involved with respect to

- what is the research question and why is it relevant,
- what are related hypotheses,
- what the variable(s) of interest are from a health point of view,
- what is the most suitable study design and
- what interdisciplinary explanatory variables can be considered in the hypothesis testing.

3.4 Data understanding

3.4.1 Necessary data variables

A prerequisite for the successful application of AI techniques is data.[c] Therefore, in the "data understanding" phase, the necessary data variables that shall be analyzed in the study are defined from a data science point of view and a joint understanding of the content of those from a health perspective is established. This includes interalia the identification of interdisciplinary data sources, the calculation of the necessary sample size for the study (and control) groups, as well as estimating the expected data quality. Given our previous example, this includes practical aspects of how the data points of interest such as counted steps, heart rate, blood glucose levels of a participant, as well as the room temperature during sleep, the weather conditions, the mental fitness, or the socioeconomic status are measured and coded.

---

[c] This if often referred under the slogan "Data is food for AI" according to Ng.[54]

The first CRISP–DM phase and this second phase typically involve iterative steps to establish a joint understanding from a health, behavioral health economic, as well as technical data analytics perspective.

3.4.2 New interdisciplinary data sources

Future experimental behavioral studies will likely follow a more interdisciplinary approach and combine different data sources such as environmental data to identify new patterns, e.g., the link between air pollution or temperature and the level of physical activity (e.g., number of steps) and the medical outcome (e.g., blood glucose levels). Apart from an interdisciplinary data matching, behavioral studies using AI methods, can also greatly benefit from combining different data sources available within a research area.[40] Behavioral interventions in the healthcare context usually affect both the demand and supply side (patients and providers of health services), as well as the medical "setting" (e.g., hospitals, pharmacies, etc.) even if they are targeted at one side only. Hence, given our example of an intervention to increase physical activity on the patient side, one may, for example, also match electronic patient records, which give more information on the treating physician such as gender, age, experience, different types of medical prescriptions, or healthcare costs.

3.4.3 Amount of data

Related to this, an important aspect that should be considered in the data collection process is the *necessary amount of data points*. In terms of AI methods, new results can be expected, especially if a large number of individual data points are collected. This may be done by continuous data collection within a given period. Given our example this may include the number of steps or heart rate collected with smartwatches or biosensors. This continuous aspect should also be considered in the study design (cf. Section 2.3). While laboratory experiments are typically rather short compared to field experiments, such continuous tracking of the heart rate may even yield a sufficient amount of data points in relatively short laboratory experiments. Additionally, the number of data points can be increased by the period of time individuals participate. In laboratory experiments, this is typically only a relatively short period of time. In contrast, framed field experiments or mega studies offer the opportunity to collect behavioral data from participants over longer periods of time. However, dropouts are to be expected over longer periods of time. This should be taken into account from the start when calculating the required number of participants. Multicenter designs may be used to enable the recruitment of a large number of participants and also the external validity of the results. Natural field experiments are also suitable for collecting data over longer periods of time. Apart from the continuous collection of data points, the amount of data can also be achieved via the interdisciplinary approach of collecting many different variables an individual, ideally from different disciplines originates, raises, and connects in a structured way. These data may be merged with the data from the behavioral study irrespective of the study design.

3.4.4 Identifying confounding variables

Another key aspect of the experimental design is controlling for confounding variables that could affect the outcome of an experiment.[d] Confounding variables are factors that are associated with both the exposure (i.e., the intervention being tested) and the outcome (i.e., the behavioral health outcome being measured). While a laboratory experiment can minimize confounding variables, AI methods can be used to identify potential confounding variables and to control for them in field studies or natural experiments. For example, machine learning algorithms can be used to identify confounding variables with the goal to increase the number of steps. Such confounding variables that are associated with both the exposure and the outcome may include an individual's physical state of health and personal motivation for the intervention, as well as the weather conditions, access to public or private transportation, or access to (safe) walking spaces. AI methods can then also be used to adjust for these factors in the analysis of the data.

3.4.5 Intervention/treatment groups

Since AI methods benefit greatly from larger data sets, the traditional approach that aims for a "minimum" of data points per study group is not suitable anymore. AI methods are able to explore fine differences between intervention and control groups. In the case of our example, this may include clear criteria for the treatment or intervention group. Furthermore, for each study group, sample sizes need to be large enough to provide a sufficient basis for hypothesis testing and statistical significance (see, e.g., Ref. 41). This aspect should also be considered in the study design (cf. Section 2.3).

---

[d] In theory, there should not be confounding variables in studies using an experimental design: using randomization, intervention and control group should be equal, the only difference should be the intervention. However, in reality, a perfect equality with respect to all characteristics will not be achieved, so that a number of imbalances will remain.

3.4.6 Data quality and missing data

When combining various and "new" data sources, the data quality to be expected is also a crucial point. In a perfect world, AI requires completeness, correctness, and relevance of the variables. The completeness and correctness of the collected data can be improved with automated screening approaches. However, data collection is still comparatively complex (the 80/20 rule between data collection and modeling or evaluation often applies) and the data quality is still not perfect (completeness, correctness, relevance). Data protection requirements must be observed, which makes it difficult to link person-specific data points in a database. New methods of anonymizing data ("privacy-preserving methods", cf. Ref. 25; or 42) could establish standards here. Particularly, behavioral studies, which collect many personal variables such as a number of steps, heart rate, and medical markers as in our example can greatly benefit from such techniques, which protect the privacy of individuals while still making the analyses on an individual level possible.

Key Aspects: In the "data understanding" phase, it is crucial to develop a joint understanding of all experts involved with respect to

- what data sources are needed and available,
- what is the health and/or economic content behind each variable,
- what new interdisciplinary data sources can be used,
- what the expected data quality is and
- what the necessary sample size per study group is.

3.5 Data collection

3.5.1 Collection strategy

New AI methods require large and high-quality data sets. Although the special requirements for the collection, preparation, and storage of data are an important aspect of every empirical research, they are particularly important in the field of AI. Complementary to the methodological development of AI, further developments in computer science have significantly improved data collection strategies. This includes, among other things technological advances in the field of data storage, which make it possible to store more data ("big data"), and collect it continuously (e.g., with smart watches or biosensors, which continuously track the number of steps, heart rate, or oven blood glucose levels), and access larger data sets via cloud services.

A further aspect to be considered is that data collection in behavioral studies is currently often rather event-driven (e.g., before and after a surgery or diagnosis) than continuous. This type of data collection can lead to systematically distorted data sets, in which weak characteristics are rarely or systematically not recorded (e.g., no data collection a few weeks after a surgery or diagnosis). An example of for systematically not recorded data is a too narrow time frame for two few points of observation within the intervention. Patients with a newly diagnosed type 2 diabetes mellitus might increase their steps within an intervention period of four weeks after the diagnosis, yet then decrease the level again after the four weeks of the intervention. In case, the individual is only tracked for 4 weeks, relevant behavioral information is missing. The observational period should therefore be sufficiently long.

There is a fundamental risk here that AI methods of machine learning based on distorted data sets will lead to poor models or that the importance of explanatory variables will not be recognized (cf. Ref. 43,44). Comparable to the problem of discrimination, this can also be recognized by the fact that the performance of the algorithm is comparatively poor when validating the data set on new data (mitigation of underfitting). Here, too, rebalancing methods can be used to at least mitigate distorted data collection (cf. Ref. 25,45,46). Therefore, it is to be expected that improved data literacy will identify distorted data sets and avoid possible false conclusions, such as the intervention lead to an increase in physical activity ex-post diagnosis, using the methods mentioned.

In the design of an experimental behavioral study, particular emphasis should therefore be put on continuous and sufficiently long-term data collection procedures, e.g., through biosensors or wearables for patients.

3.5.2 Communication strategy

Furthermore, the communication of the data collection strategy is a sensitive matter in the data collection process of individual health-related data points. In conventional, artefactual, and field experiments, participants know that they are participating in a study. However, if studies become more subtle for participants, e.g., if a wearable smartwatch or biosensor continuously monitors a patient, the awareness of participation in a study vanishes. This aspect can be enhanced if the data collection is embedded in health platforms or decision support systems that are easily accessible to participants (patients, physicians). Then, the communication strategy becomes even more important (cf. EU Proposal 2022).[47] It should ideally be clear and patient/person-centered.

3.5.3 Ethics and discrimination

Health is a public good from which no one may be excluded. AI methods such as machine learning (e.g., neural networks) optimize the models on the basis of preselected data (training data sets). If these data sets are unbalanced (e.g., mainly men with a diagnosed type 2 diabetes mellitus are prevalent in the training data set), a machine learning algorithm will—a priori—be able to "describe" other groups of people (e.g., women) less accurately if they systematically differ from the male individuals contained in the training data set. Possible interventions to change behavior could therefore lead to misguided conclusions or are inaccurate for individual groups (e.g., women with a diagnosed type 2 diabetes mellitus). This problem can, for example, be "detected" by the fact that the performance of the algorithm is comparatively "poor" in the validation of the data set on new data (e.g., with balanced proportions between men and women).

As this is a "standard" problem with the application of AI, as well as with other statistical models, solution strategies are available. The problem can at least be mitigated using re-balancing methods (cf. Refs. [25,45,46]). It should also be noted that machine learning algorithms can typically respond much better to any systematic differences between groups using the flexibility in the estimation function compared to more traditional approaches such as linear regression models.

However, if predictions or the identification of new essential discriminatory influencing factors are only possible to a limited extent, e.g., are forbidden from a legal perspective (e.g., in relation to age, gender, religion, sexual orientation, etc.), it is a simple solution not to include these explanatory variables in the optimization of the algorithm to be included (cf. Ref. 25). Given our example, one might find that interventions to increase physical activity are not cost-effective for certain types of patients for which discrimination in treatment strategies or insurance coverage is legally not allowed.

Taken together, problems of possible discrimination and the consideration of ethical manners are not new (also present in classic linear regression models), but may become more visible or amplified when using applications of AI. Better data literacy on the part of the user could make such discrimination effects directly recognizable even with classic methods.

Key Aspects: In the "data collection" phase, the

- collection strategy,
- amount of data,
- communication strategy

needs to be defined. Furthermore,

- discrimination and
- distortion

must be avoided.

3.6 Modeling

3.6.1 Traditional econometrics vs. AI methods

AI methods such as machine learning have great strengths in flexibly selecting the functional forms of the estimator (e.g., nonlinear, combination of different functional forms). What many AI methods have in common is that they use data-driven automated (rather than manual) model selection (e.g., in relation to the functional form, choice of hyperparameters). For example, the functional form is a function of the available data or the data determines it (grid search approaches in the hyperparameter optimization of the models). A countable number of alternative model specifications are estimated and then the "best" model (automated) is selected from among them, which maximizes a certain criterion (e.g., accuracy, precision). In classical econometrics, on the other hand, only individual estimates (model specifications) are usually carried out manually. However, the automated model specifications of the AI tend to lead to better model specifications and may also have greater transparency compared to an untransparent manual selection of an estimate. This transparency about the selection mechanism for the "best" model specification is important in order to increase the overall acceptance of statistical methods. In this respect, the automated model specifications of the AI have an advantage over the manual and selective selection methods of classical econometrics.

3.6.2 Model optimization

After the selection of the modeling technique, the initial parameter settings are chosen and based on the model performance optimized ("hyper parameter tuning"). This is done based on the initial step of the CRISP-DM approach

("Understanding the health context") that has defined the relevant performance metrics such as the number of steps, heart rate, mental fitness, or blood glucose of a participant, the room temperature during sleep, or the weather conditions before and/or during the intervention. Analogously to the model specification in traditional econometrics, new AI methods are commonly optimized automatically (e.g., with the help of grid search approaches) and not manually. Therefore, in this step, a transparent communication strategy for all parties involved in the experimental design is of great importance.

3.6.3 Transparency

A major driver of the application of AI, in particular in the acceptance of more advanced AI modeling approaches, is increasing data literacy. The increasing data literacy in the field of behavioral health economics not only refers to the improvement of existing models through more explanatory variables and automated and continuous model optimization, but also regarding transparency of the model selection process and communicating this to all not-so-AI-affine users (such as some physicians or patients).

Key Aspects: The "model" phase involves

- the model selection,
- the model optimization and
- transparency regarding the model selection process.

3.7 Evaluation

3.7.1 Model performance

The model results based on the model performance metrics as defined in the initial step of the CRISP–DM approach ("understanding the health context") are evaluated with respect to the initial research question (derived hypothesis). As such, the evaluation phase ideally shows the "success" (benefit) of the AI application compared to more traditional econometric methods on the basis of the applied experimental design. Given our example, this may, for instance, imply that our model can predict the success of a behavioral intervention to increase physical activity for a certain patient type with a (much) higher accuracy than a logistic regression.

3.7.2 Identification of new and relevant variables (features)

Typical examples of new insights from the application of AI methods are the identification of new and relevant explanatory variables (features) that increase the predictive power of the estimated models. If this is the case, behavioral health economics can be better applied, e.g., to develop new effective policy designs or patient-centered treatment or prevention strategies that allow individuals to make healthier decisions or avoid unhealthy decisions. Such new variables may be that higher air pollution or high room temperature decreases the likelihood of a successful behavioral intervention with financial rewards to increase physical activity, which is measured by the number of steps per day.

The basis for the identification of new behavioral variables is usually interdisciplinary model approaches that can more accurately depict the actual human behavior of consumers and providers of healthcare services. An increasing wealth of experience in the concrete application of these new methods of AI, as well as better data literacy on the application side, means that considerable progress can be expected (cf. Ref. 25).

3.7.3 Interplay between theory and empirics

Therefore, the identification of new relevant variables and the consideration of these can not only increase the explanatory content of a statistical model per se but also improve the quality of the estimated influence of all previously considered explanatory variables. In addition to this statistical effect, the identification of "subtle" and comparatively small effects (effect sizes) also allows more advanced theoretical behavioral health economics models. For example, differences between groups of individuals (e.g., with certain response patterns to different forms of financial incentives to increase physical activity) can be recognized automatically and more precisely. Those patterns can then be integrated into existing theoretical models.

3.7.4 Black–box problem

Some AI techniques show superior predictive power but on the other hand "*suffer*" from algorithms that are too complicated for humans to comprehend (e.g., since they are highly recursive like deep learning). This complexity paired with the lack of interpretability and transparency (e.g., it is unclear how the variables relate to each other) is typically referred to as "the" Black–Box problem. Compared to other interpretable model approaches, the accessibility for users (e.g., physicians and patients without a data science background) is then limited. Related to this, some authors argue that the Black–Box problem can be avoided by using interpretable approaches and that better predictive power is either comparable or not necessary for the problem at hand (cf. Ref. 48). However, if the accessibility in terms of interpretability and transparency is not of the highest importance, the Black–Box problem as such is also less relevant.

Key Aspects: In the evaluation phase

- the model performance based on predefined performance metrics is assessed,
- new and relevant explanatory variables are identified and
- existing theoretical models are tested against new empirical insights based on AI methods.

3.8 Deployment

3.8.1 Stability

The idea behind the AI approach of machine learning is to use a training data set to develop model predictions for validation of the effects of behavioral interventions (e.g., financial rewards on healthy behaviors or different payment schemes for physicians treatment quality). As with other statistical methods (e.g., classic regression analysis), it is important to note that systematic changes in the data basis are not "automatically" reflected in the model prediction. If, for example, the height of conditional payments to exercise within the intervention is changed from 100€ for 70,000 steps per week to 500€ for the same number of steps, machine learning algorithms that have been trained on the previous (systematically different) intervention with the much lower financial incentive are not necessarily suitable for making a meaningful prognosis or the algorithm adapts incompletely.[49] This aspect has been recognized as part of the "prediction policy" problem,[50] and various approaches to solving this problem have also been discussed (e.g., comparison of the validation data set, cf. Ref. 25). Ideally, the data collection is therefore dynamic (cf. EC Proposal, 2021) and the algorithm is also regularly "adjusted." Good data literacy is even more important so that this possible problem is addressed and taken into account in the context of conception, modeling. and implementation.

3.8.2 Manipulation

As with other statistical methods, knowledge of the data collection can lead to data sets being collected selectively and manipulatively. In the context of our example, this may be the systematic selection (or de-selection) of certain medically related variables (e.g., comorbidities or prescribed medication) or patient groups. Since the collection of data sets is a particularly controversial topic when using machine learning, methods of data set evaluation (forensic approaches) can lead to uncovering systematic manipulation. Complete documentation of the data collection, data processing (data preparation), modeling approach. and model evaluation is necessary so that systematic manipulation can also be effectively uncovered. This is also ensured by the iterative application of the CRISP–DM approach. AI algorithms can also be used to automate the steps from data collection to modeling.

3.8.3 Transparency

Transparency of the data collection process, data processing (data preparation), modeling approach, and model evaluation is an important prerequisite for the acceptance of AI methods. As part of greater data literacy, users will increasingly question these aspects and, for example, the documentation of the model selection including hyperparameter selection, training, and validation dataset and monitoring (e.g., with regard to optimized performance indicators, evaluation, robustness, cf. EU regulation, 2017[51]). In the positive case, the results of the applied method should not only be accepted by users but also be reproducible and evaluable.

3.8.4 Usage of AI tools

A central prerequisite of the deployment phase is that the tools envisaged (e.g., physical activity apps connected to smartwatches or physician decision support systems which are based on patients' behavioral data) have practicable interfaces and offer meaningful services/support features. Their usage should always be easy and hence transform into a natural habit of their users. Illiteracy of the tool can lead to incorrect or irregular usage resulting in the data collection phase being prone to user-related errors. Hence, ideally, the tools are developed in a user-centered way, e.g., by Discrete Choice Experiments, which test users' preferences for certain tool features,[52] and are then tested rigorously with potential users. Moreover, education on AI-related topics and tools (data literacy) increases the initial uptake and adherence of usage. This may include education on AI-based decision support systems in medical schools as well as patient education.

Key Aspects: In the "deployment" phase, the

- stability of the experimental insights,
- potential manipulation,
- transparency and
- practical usage of AI tools

must be considered.

4. Outlook

The previous chapter has highlighted important aspects to be considered when applying AI methods in designing experimental studies in behavioral health economics. These experimental studies are important in improving the efficiency of health care via interventions that target the behavior of agents on the supply and demand side (e.g., physicians or patients). Typical interventions may include increasing the quality or efficiency of care by designing payment incentives or decision support systems for physicians, or financial incentives or nudges such as reminders to uptake healthy behaviors such as exercising for patients.

The aim was to give a guide to designing interventional studies in a behavioral health economics context aiming to implement such behavioral interventions when applying AI methods. In contrast to the "traditional" approach, the application of AI in behavioral studies commonly involves a more *interdisciplinary* approach and a more rigorous *process model* that ensures that all parties involved in the study design establish a joint understanding of what the research question is and what data are needed to apply AI methods within the study design.

A challenge of behavioral research within the context of AI is that human behavior is difficult to change and realistic estimates of treatment effects call for statistical power and hence very large number of observations in the respective treatments (see, e.g.,[41]). While this may be achieved by fostering interdisciplinary (e.g., medicine, economics, ethics, psychology, social sciences, or law) and multicenter research clusters, the high costs of a large number of participants need to be considered. From a technical perspective, the advancement of the application of AI methods in the field of behavioral health economics calls for relevant, representative, and interdisciplinary mass databases.

Furthermore, it is necessary to increase the acceptance of the methodology. This can be achieved by comprehensible documentation and transparency of the algorithms on the part of the users (e.g., clinics) and the data suppliers (e.g., patients), for instance by a well-established and systematic process as the CRISP–DM approach.

In addition to the purely technical optimization of the algorithms, the human assessment of the algorithms should be guaranteed in order to gain robust and accurate insights from the application of the method. AI methods are hence supposed to support decision-making rather than be used autonomously as a decision-making tool.

Finally, it is crucial to increase the uptake of behavioral study participation by improving and communicating data security, particularly with regard to cyberattacks on medical AI technologies such as wearables (e.g., smart watches or biosensors), the practicability of the intervention (e.g., interface of the decision support system for physicians), as well as clarification of ethical concerns.

References

1. Beauchamp TL, Childress JF. Principles of Biomedical Ethics. 5th ed. Oxford University Press; 2001.
2. Pellegrino ED. Altruism, self-interest, and medical ethics. *JAMA.* 1987;258:1939–1940. https://doi.org/10.1001/jama.1987.03400140101036.
3. Arrow KJ. Uncertainty and the welfare economics of medical care. *Am Econ Rev.* 1963;53:941–973.
4. Ellis RP, McGuire TG. Provider behavior under prospective reimbursement: cost sharing and supply. *J Health Econ.* 1986;5:129–151.
5. Attema AE, Galizzi MM, Groß M, Hennig-Schmidt H, Karay Y, Wiesen D. The Formation of Physician Altruism; 2021. Working Paper.
6. Brosig-Koch J, Hennig-Schmidt H, Kairies-Schwarz N, Wiesen D. Using artefactual field and lab experiments to investigate how fee-for-service and capitation affect medical service provision. *J Econ Behavior Organiz.* 2016;131(Part B):17–23.
7. Brosig-Koch J, Hennig-Schmidt H, Kairies-Schwarz N, Kokot J, Wiesen D. Physician performance pay: Experimental evidence. In: *HERO Working Paper Series 2020:3.* University of Oslo; 2020.
8. Godager G, Wiesen D. Profit or patients' health benefit? Exploring the heterogeneity in physician altruism. *J Health Econ.* 2013;32(6):1105–1116.
9. Singh M. Heuristics in the delivery room. *Science.* 2021;374(6565):324–329.
10. Kairies N. Pay-for-performance, reputation, and the reduction of costly overprovision. *Econ Bull.* 2013;33(3):A211.
11. Laibson D. Why don't present-biased agents make commitments? *Am Econ Rev.* 2015;105(5):267–272.
12. O'Donoghue T, Rabin M. Doing it now or later. *Am Econ Rev.* 1999;89(1):103–124.
13. Barlow P, McKee M, Reeves A, Galea G, Stuckler D. Time-discounting and tobacco smoking: a systematic review and network analysis. *Int J Epidemiol.* 2016;46(3):860–869.

14. Barlow P, Reeves A, McKee M, Galea G, Stuckler D. Unhealthy diets, obesity and time discounting: a systematic literature review and network analysis. *Obes Rev.* 2016;17(9):810–819.

15. Story G, Vlaev I, Seymour B, Darzi A, Dolan R. Does temporal discounting explain unhealthy behavior? A systematic review and reinforcement learning perspective. *Front Behav Neurosci.* 2014;8:76.

16. Mørkbak MR, Gyrd-Hansen D, Kjær T. Can present biasedness explain early onset of diabetes and subsequent disease progression? Exploring causal inference by linking survey and register data. *Soc Sci Med.* 2017;186:34–42.

17. Lamiraud K, Geoffard PY. Therapeutic non-adherence: a rational behavior revealing patient preferences? *Health Econ.* 2007;16(11):1185–1204.

18. Roski, J., Chapman, W., Heffner, J., Trivedi, R., Del Fiol, G., Estiri, H. & Pierce, J. (2019). How artificial intelligence is changing health and health care. In Artificial Intelligence in Health Care: The Hope, the Hype, the Promise, the Peril, 58.

19. Fihn SD, Saria S, Mendonça E, et al. Deploying AI in clinical settings. In: Matheny M, Israni ST, Ahmed M, Whicher D, eds. *Artificial Intelligence in Health Care: The Hope, the Hype, the Promise, the peril'.* Washington, DC: National Academy of Medicine; 2019.

20. Luxton DD. An introduction to artificial intelligence in behavioral and mental health care. In: *Artificial intelligence in behavioral and mental health care.* Academic Press; 2016:1–26.

21. Lucas GM, Gratch J, King A, Morency LP. It's only a computer: virtual humans increase willingness to disclose. *Comput Hum Behav.* 2014;37:94–100.

22. Rizzo A, Shilling R, Forbell E, Scherer S, Gratch J, Morency LP. Autonomous virtual human agents for healthcare information support and clinical interviewing. In: *Artificial Intelligence in Behavioral and Mental Health Care.* Academic Press; 2016:53–79.

23. Roth AE. The economist as engineer: Game theory, experimentation, and computation as tools for design economics. *Econometrica.* 2002;70(4):1341–1378.

24. Duflo E. The economist as plumber. *Am Econ Rev.* 2017;107(5):1–26.

25. Athey S. The impact of machine learning on economics. In: Agrawal A, Gans J, Goldfarb A, eds. *The Economics of Artificial Intelligence: An Agenda*; 2019.

26. Harrison GW, List JA. Field experiments. *J Econ Literat.* 2004;42(4):1009–1055.

27. Milkman KL, Gromet D, Ho H, et al. Megastudies improve the impact of applied behavioral science. *Nature.* 2021;600(7889):478–483.

28. Duckworth AL, Milkman KL. A guide to megastudies. *PNAS Nexus.* 2022;1(5):214.

29. Galizzi MM, Wiesen D. Behavioral Experiments in Health. Oxford Encyclopedia in Economics and Finance; 2018.

30. Thaler RH, Sunstein CR. Libertarian paternalism. *Am Econ Rev.* 2003;93(2):175–179.

31. Thaler RH, Sunstein CR. Nudge: Improving Decisions About Health, Wealth, and Happiness. Yale University Press; 2008.

32. Dai H, Saccardo S, Han MA, et al. Behavioural nudges increase COVID-19 vaccinations. *Nature.* 2021;597(7876):404–409.

33. Athey S, Grabarz K, Luca M, Wernerfelt N. Digital public health interventions at scale: the impact of social media advertising on beliefs and outcomes related to COVID vaccines. *Proc Natl Acad Sci.* 2023;120(5), e2208110120.

34. Carrera M, Royer H, Stehr M, Sydnor J. Can financial incentives help people trying to establish new habits? Experimental evidence with new gym members. *J Health Econ.* 2018;58:202–214.

35. Charness G, Gneezy U. Incentives to exercise. *Econometrica.* 2009;77(3):909–931.

36. Homonoff T, Willage B, Willén A. Rebates as incentives: the effects of a gym membership reimbursement program. *J Health Econ.* 2020;70, 102285.

37. Hunter RF, Tully MA, Davis M, Stevenson M, Kee F. Physical activity loyalty cards for behavior change: A quasi-experimental study. *Am J Prev Med.* 2013;45(1):56–63. https://doi.org/10.1016/j.amepre.2013.02.022.

38. Pope L, Harvey-Berino J. Burn and earn: A randomized controlled trial incentivizing exercise during fall semester for college first-year students. *Prev Med.* 2013;56(3–4):197–201. https://doi.org/10.1016/j.ypmed.2012.12.020.

39. Royer H, Stehr M, Sydnor J. Incentives, commitments, and habit formation in exercise: evidence from a field experiment with workers at a fortune-500 company. *Am Econ J Appl Econ.* 2015;7(3):51–84. https://doi.org/10.1257/app.20130327.

40. Gómez-González, E. & Gómez Gutiérrez, E. (2020). Artificial Intelligence in Medicine and Healthcare: applications, availability and societal impact. *EUR 30197 EN. Publications Office of the European Union,* Luxembourg, 2020.

41. DellaVigna S, Linos E. RCTs to scale: comprehensive evidence from two nudge units. *Econometrica.* 2022;90(1):81–116.

42. Komarova T, Nekipelov D, Yakovlev E. Estimation of treatment effects from combined data: Identification versus data security. In: *Economic Analysis of the Digital Economy.* University of Chicago Press; 2015:279–308.

43. Campello VM, Gkontra P, Izquierdo C, et al. Multi-centre, multi-vendor and multi-disease cardiac segmentation: the M&Ms challenge. *IEEE Trans Med Imaging.* 2021;40(12):3543–3554.

44. Subbaswamy A, Saria S. From development to deployment: dataset shift, causality, and shift-stable models in health AI. *Biostatistics.* 2020;21(2):345–352.

45. Cabitza F, Rasoini R, Gensini GF. Unintended consequences of machine learning in medicine. *JAMA.* 2017;318(6):517–518.

46. Ghassemi M. Exploring healthy models in ML for health. In: *AI for Healthcare Equity Conference.* AI & Health at MIT; 2021.

47. Lekadir K, Quaglio G, Garmendia AT, Gallin C. Artificial Intelligence in Healthcare—Applications, Risks, and Ethical and Societal Impacts. European Parliament; 2022.

48. Rudin C. Stop explaining black box machine learning models for high stakes decisions and use interpretable models instead. *Nat Mach Intell.* 2019;1:206–215. https://doi.org/10.1038/s42256-019-0048-x.

49. Yu KH, Kohane IS. Framing the challenges of artificial intelligence in medicine. *BMJ Qual Saf.* 2019;28(3):238–241.

50. Kleinberg J, Ludwig J, Mullainathan S, Obermeyer Z. Prediction policy problems. *Am Econ Rev.* 2015;105(5):491–495.

51. EU. EU are the 2017/745 Medical Devices Regulation (MDR) and the 2017/746; 2017.

52. Landsat E, Louviere J. Conducting discrete choice experiments to inform healthcare decision making: a user's guide. *Pharmacoeconomics.* 2008;26:661–677.

53. Chapman P, Clinton J, Kerber R, et al. The CRISP–DM user guide. In: *4th CRISP–DM SIG Workshop in Brussels in March (Vol. 1999);* 1999, March.

54. Ng A. Fortune; 2021. November 8th, 2021.

16

Artificial intelligence and medicine: A psychological perspective on AI implementation in healthcare context

Ilaria Durosini[a], Silvia Francesca Maria Pizzoli[a], Milija Strika[a,b], and Gabriella Pravettoni[a,b]

[a]Department of Oncology and Hematology-Oncology (DIPO), University of Milan, Milan, Italy [b]Applied Research Division for Cognitive and Psychological Science, European Institute of Oncology (IEO), IRCCS, Milan, Italy

1. Introduction

In recent years, the advances of new technologies allowed the collection of a large amount of data through devices, tools, and sensors installed in the spaces (*big data*). A large amount of data is challenging to analyze by the human mind but could be easily managed by technological entities, such as artificial intelligence (AI). AI uses machine learning and algorithms to manage *big data* in a relatively short time. Algorithms allow the detection of similarities and associations to predict specific outcomes. Machines can learn from experience and, simulating human intelligence, adapt their actions and output to new scenarios.[1] Even if AI could find solutions to specific problems, there are some relevant human characteristics that machines can not completely reproduce. This represents a fundamental difference between human cognition and artificial computation.

In any case, machine learning is present in technologies that people use daily, such as social media, email, and software (e.g., Refs. 2,3). AI helps humans in some business, workplace, and industrial areas (e.g., economic and scientific areas) and is preparing to improve more and more labor productivity (e.g., Ref. 4), making the delivery and the production of services and goods much faster and easier. Thus, artificial entities promise to act as active collaborators of humans to define activities and tasks.

More recently, AI has been used in the context of health, allowing the identification of medical treatments and diagnosis in a relatively short time.[5] Therefore, the study of AI implementation within real-world fields becomes an important aspect of the promotion of better applications of these techniques in human activities.

In this contribution, we focused our attention on the implementation of AI in the healthcare context, highlighting the possible benefits and dysfunctional effects. We discussed the use of AI in health care and the possible challenges of implementing artificial entities in the medical field. Then, the possible impact of the presence of AI in a doctor–patient relationship will be explained, focusing on the differences between humans and artificial technologies. The important role of emotional intelligence in clinical consultations will also be discussed.

2. Artificial intelligence in healthcare context

Up to now, *evidence-based medicine* has been considered one of the most valuable innovations in medicine and health. Evidence-based medicine is *"the conscientious, explicit and judicious use of current best evidence in making decisions about the care of individual patients"* (Ref. 6, p. 71) and has its roots in the mid-19th century Paris.[7] Thanks to this approach, the healthcare system began to stand or support prescriptions and decisions based on evidence-proven scientific data.

Evidence-based medicine is currently the mainstream approach to deciding treatments and interpreting data, relying on the systematic synthesis of data (meta-analysis, systematic reviews) or controlled studies (randomized controlled trials) as a primary source of treatment decisions. However, the importance of real-world data or real-word evidence[8] posed challenges in integrating evidence-based medicine principles with this new kind of data. Real-world evidence relies on data continuously monitored through different sources of information (for example, clinical recordings, databases from hospitals, and recordings on effective treatments delivered) and not from controlled studies.[9] While evidence-based medicine relies mainly on the quality and solidity of the evidence retrieved by studies summarizing evidence from specific populations, real-world evidence uses data related to patients' health status or healthcare procedures, which are consistently recorded and collected from a variety of sources.[9] Currently, real-world data are used by the Federal Drug Administration to monitor postmarket safety and side effects of drugs and treatments and by the healthcare community to develop guidelines and decision aids.[8] Partnerships between pharmaceutical and technology companies intend to analyze big data in less time through the use of AI. For example, AI was used during the COVID-19 pandemic to accelerate the development process of vaccines or drugs against the virus. As we know, the COVID-19 quarantine represented a unique phenomenon that affected people's lives in several ways and led to several psychological consequences (e.g., Ref. 10). Microsoft created *COVID Moonshot*, a collaborative open-science project started in March 2020 intending to develop an un-patented oral antiviral drug to treat SARS-CoV-2 that exploits *PostEra's machine learning* to design the synthesis of all 2000 compounds. This is a brief example of the application of artificial entities in health care, and its potential is rapidly expanding.

More specifically, literature recognized the employment of AI in the context of care in four areas (Fig. 1):

(a) AI can be used as a diagnosis support tool: Healthcare professionals could use artificial entities to identify patients' diseases as a diagnostic support tool.[11] AI may use machine learning and algorithms to assess the presence or absence of certain symptoms and compare this information with available literature from clinical results, genetic testing, diagnostic imaging, and other available data. For example, some Google AI researchers have fed a huge amount of CT images of lung lesions into a computer to create an algorithm capable of assessing by itself the presence or absence of lung cancer in a group of patients.[12]

(b) AI can be used to identify personalized therapies: Artificial entities can be used to detect individualized treatments based on patient's symptomatology. This will allow clinicians to administer more precise therapies following the concept of precision medicine. The use of AI for this scope could be interesting for the identification of the best treatment for patients and for the provision of early intervention for chronic disease. For example, AI could be used to identify adequate treatment for dementia.[13] The effects of drugs recommended for dementia were analyzed using a large observational dataset of real patients. The differential effects of drugs were assessed by combining demographic data, longitudinal cognitive measures, and creating a cognitive score prediction model based on deep neural networks to find the most optimal medication for treating cognitive decline in dementia for each patient. According to some studies, the application of AI in this area was very promising, allowing the identification at the level of the individual patient of the most effective drug to reduce cognitive impairment within two years.[13] Additionally, some types of AI can help clinicians improve palliative care decisions.

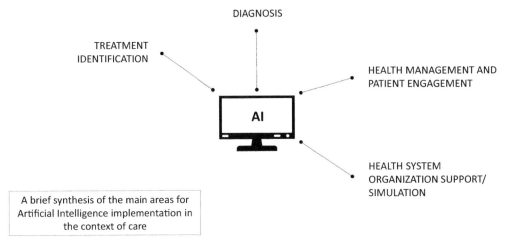

FIG. 1   A synthesis of the main areas for artificial intelligence implementation in medicine and health care.

These technologies can help doctors identify high-mortality risk patients or unsuccessful/inappropriate treatments, helping promptly decisions based on patients' needs.[14]

(c) **AI can be used to promote patient engagement**: AI can be used as a tool to promote patient engagement. Involving patients in the process of care is a key element in achieving good health outcomes.[15] Some existing digital devices can collect patients' data, monitor their health status, and support them in managing their symptoms, such as Digital Therapeutics and eHealth. An example is the interactive platform *Patients Like Me*. This platform allows patients to communicate about their illnesses with others and simultaneously allows doctors to collect important data about their patients' physical and psychological needs.[16] This allows clinicians to stay in contact and treat patients outside of the health consultation, promoting the management of patients' symptoms in their homes. Through AI for this scope, patients can receive assistance at any moment, becoming more responsible for their symptoms and the cure of their clinical conditions.

(d) **AI can be used to empower medical institution organizations**: AI can be used to improve medical institutions' organizational infrastructures by optimizing the flow of care and improving doctors' productivity.[5,17] Additionally, thanks to AI, patients can be monitored remotely and the costs of using emergency rooms and hospitalizations can be reduced.[18] For example, AI allowed the management of the scheduling of operating rooms, obtaining data on the estimated duration of the surgical case and leading to more precise planning and a reduction in the waste of resources. In addition, AI could also predict the risk of cancellation of surgeries, allowing the planning of preventive measures to reduce the cancellation rate and save economic resources.[19]

To summarize, AI could use real-world data to promote more advanced suggestions and outcomes in the healthcare context.[20] However, this context of application is not free of challenges.[1,21] Challenges related to the use of AI in the context of care still exist, and it is essential to underline the obstacles to its implementation. In the following section, we will underline some of the main challenges that organizations, practitioners, users, and researchers face regarding implementing AI.

3. The challenges of AI

The introduction of AI within the context of care is raising some crucial challenges linked to technical, social, and psychological aspects:

(a) **AI-Explanation**: The first challenge is related to the AI explanation and the difficulty of using data provided by artificial entities to communicate and make decisions in the context of care. The outputs of complex AI systems are often perceived as a black box by users without expertise in the field.[22] One of the possible ways to address this challenge relies on the concept of *eXplainable Artificial Intelligence* (XAI),[23] which suggests the need to make transparent and understandable computer outputs that can shape people's decisions.

Acceptance of technological devices is a complex process that is not related only to technological aspects of the functionality of the machine but also to psycho-social and sociodemographic aspects. For example, women eligible for breast cancer screening with a higher education level showed better opinions on the application of AI in medicine and in helping radiologists with the diagnosis than others.[24]

Physicians make diagnoses and prescribe therapies, but they have also to relate to patients and their needs, goals, and emotions and make decisions that can have a major impact on quality of life and survivorship. In addition to the ethical and deontological delicacy that this entails, physicians deal with the risk of incurring litigation and disciplinary action regarding their actions and decisions. One consequence of this phenomenon, independent of the implementation of technologies, is so-called defensive medicine, conduct whereby physicians prescribe additional tests and therapies that they would not consider it necessary in order to defend themselves in case of controversies.[25,26] The overuse of medical prescriptions and exams, even if they are not necessary, causes a significant increase in costs across the healthcare system.[27]

(b) **AI Acceptance**: The acceptance of technologies is a process that involves many factors and does not depend only on the functionality of the technology. For example, an aspect contributing to the acceptance of technology is related to how it is perceived by the users. A well-known model that assesses the acceptance of artificial entities is the technology acceptance model (TAM):[28] according to the TAM, the effective predictors of the acceptance of technology are the perceived utility and ease of use. These opinions are strongly influenced by other factors, including preexisting beliefs and experiences, social influences, persuasion, or the perceived correspondence between technology and personal intentions.[29] In the context of care, doctors can show doubts and mistrust about introducing technologies for patient care. As suggested by the literature, most of the doubts may be related to doctors' difficulty in understanding the machine learning process and, therefore, the inability to understand their outcomes and effective use in clinical practice. This can also be linked to the difficulty of being able to justify one's choices in case of disputes or legal controversies.

But also the promotion of a culture in which new technologies can be used in the clinical context can lead to aspects that need attention: *overconfidence and deskilling*.[18,30,31] Overconfidence is the tendency to rely on technology for tasks other than those it was originally designed to perform. The risk related to overconfidence is the development of improper ways of using technology that can have consequences for the psychological and physical safety of users.[32] An example of overconfidence can emerge in the context of health, especially when professionals delegate tasks and activities to AIs even if they cannot complete them.

Another risk is related to Deskilling, considered as the tendency to reduce personal abilities because some tasks can be performed by technologies.[30] When we get used to technology that automates a task or activity we previously carried out in person, we can gradually lose that ability. Therefore, the health professional must be adequately trained in using technologies to avoid incurring the risks of overconfidence or deskilling and be adequately aware of human and machine potential.

(c) *AI in the doctor–patient relationship*: From a psychological point of view, it is important to understand the impact of new technologies on doctor–patient relationships and guarantee a collaborative and individualized assessment procedure.[33] In the near future, technologies that include machine learning have the potential to become more than simple "tools" that clinicians may use for diagnosis, treatment identification, health management, and health systems organization support, but may become real interlocutors of healthcare professionals that help in decision-making processes and medical tasks. The presence of these technologies in clinical practice could influence doctor–patients communication and their relationships.[34]

Even if the literature lacks scientific research that comprehensively assesses the impact of AI in healthcare practice, it is possible to prefigure some psychological and social reactions that people may have before using artificial entities. In 2020, Triberti, Durosini, and Pravettoni described the *"third wheel effect"* as a phenomenon related to the effect of AI implementation in the healthcare context. This phenomenon tries to depict the impact of artificial entities on patients' perceptions and on doctor–patient relationship. The "third wheel" effect will be discussed in the next paragraph.

4. When AI comes into the medical consultation with patients: The "Third Wheel Effect"

Generally, the expression "third wheel" refers to a person who feels himself/herself out of place in the company of a romantic couple. This person goes somewhere with a couple of lovers, and the couple may feel uneasy due to this third presence, negatively influencing the general mood and experience. In this line, as stated by Triberti, Durosini, and Pravettoni,[34] we can use this expression to refer to the third presence of AI in a doctor–patient relationship, generating three possible effects of artificial entities in a medical consultation with patients: *decision paralysis*, *"confusion of the tongues"*, or *role ambiguity*. These three facets of the "third wheel" effect are explained below:

- *Decision paralysis*: As we stated previously, using AI in the context of care could lead to numerous advantages in terms of diagnosis and treatment identification. However, the AI process that generates specific outcomes needs to be more transparent for users. This could lead professionals who use AI for their clinical practice to be doubtful about the generated outcomes due to the absence of a clear representation of the inner process behind the AI process. On these bases, implementing AI in the consultation plan could introduce new time-consuming tasks clinicians need to manage to promote better patient assistance. In the context of care, doctors need to review and use AI's recommendations, explain these aspects to patients, and answer their questions. In other words, the doctor needs to use their human abilities to stay in contact with the patients, introduce technologies in the clinical scenarios, and translate the AI report into a comprehensible language. This "mediation" role may generate delays, uncertainties, or decision paralysis in the traditional procedure. Therefore, clinicians must act as a mediator in the relationship with their patients and explain the role of IA in clinical planning.[34]
- *Role ambiguity*: Sometimes, the presence of artificial entities in the healthcare scenario creates role ambiguity from the side of patients. A survey conducted by PwC that involved 11.000 patients residents in twelve countries highlighted that 54% of participants were amenable to the idea of receiving assistance and cure from artificial innovations. However, 38% of participants were against these entities, and the remaining 8% were uncertain about them. The results of this survey pointed out the need to introduce and explain the role of AI entities to patients. Communicate to patients the value of AI in the clinical context, allowing them to recognize the possible role of this

technology in the healthcare journey, avoiding the risk that patients perceive that technologies take the place of humans. People who receive clinical care may need more certainty about the role of human doctors and AI in the medical context. This may create a sense of general confusion about clinicians' authority and competence.

If the diagnosis provided by artificial entities is not in line with the clinical evaluation of human counterparts, which information is considered? The incongruence in the clinical opinion provided by human healthcare professionals and AI may generate ambiguity in patients regarding who provides the correct information and who is doing the doctor's work. In this scenario, patients may ask: "Who really works to help me to identify the right diagnosis and treatment?".[34]

- **"Confusion of the Tongues"**: According to Triberti et al.,[34] this expression—originally used by psychologist Frernczi to describe the obstacles in adult—child communication—could be useful for considering the possible obstacles to utilizing AI in clinical consultation. In doctor–patient consultation, the active role of healthcare professionals is crucial. The active role of doctors during the process allows the translation of information from patients to AI according to specific formats, categories, and languages that the artificial entities can understand and analyze (e.g., data). This is useful, especially in the case of symptoms that are hard to describe and categorize into specific categories. In addition, human doctors may use their emotional abilities (such as emotional intelligence) to understand patients' needs, symptoms, and requests and adapt them to the language of AI.[34]

These three possible effects of AI in clinical consultation with patients help shed light on the importance of considering not only technical aspects related to the implementation of technologies but also the possible psychological and social implications of their use.

5. Artificial intelligence and humans: The role of emotional intelligence

In the previous sections, we described the roles of artificial entities in the context of care, helping professionals and healthcare organizations in the definition of complex diagnoses, identification of individualized treatments, promotion of patients' engagement, and empowerment of medical institutions. However, despite the role of machines in health care, their introduction is exposed to challenges and risks (e.g., Refs. 35,36). Paying attention to these aspects is essential for the promotion of the correct use of technologies and for enhancing the relationship between doctor and patient.

Published evidence clearly states the uniqueness of the "human doctor" figure in the process of care, and, despite the recent advantages of technologies, humans cannot be replaced by machines.[34] Certainly, AIs can find solutions to specific problems, but there are some relevant human characteristics that machines cannot completely reproduce. The aspects that make human doctors unique in the context of care are the psychological characteristics that are used in the relationship with patients, such as emotional intelligence. Emotional intelligence emerged as a psychological construct in the 1990s. In 1990, Salovey and Mayer defined emotional intelligence as a type of intelligence that involves the humans' ability to monitor, perceive, and express one's and others' emotions, discriminate among them, and use that information to manage one's actions.[37] Subsequently, in 1995, Goleman[38] conceptualized emotional intelligence as the ability to regulate, recognize, and manage one's and other's emotions. Literature underlines the importance of emotions and emotional intelligence for humans.[39–41]

We can easily understand how emotional intelligence and emotion-related abilities are relevant within a healthcare context, in which contact with fear, pain, and suffering can negatively impact the patient's psychological well-being, motivation, and participation and commitment to care.[39,41–43] For healthcare professionals, developing and increasing one's emotional intelligence is a fundamental aspect that needs to be used in the context of the clinical relationship (e.g., Refs. 44,45). With emotional intelligence, doctors can emerge as irreplaceable figures and develop positive relationships with patients. Conversely, the absence of empathy can generate dissatisfaction and misunderstandings in the context of care (e.g., Ref. 46). An example of dissatisfaction emerged in the case of Ernest Quintana, a man admitted to the Kaiser Permanente Medical Centre in Fermont, California. The case is discussed worldwide and reported in some of the most relevant newspapers.[47] Quintana and his family received a bad diagnosis through a robot with a video screen. The doctor appeared on the video screen and communicated the unfortunate diagnosis. The family was shocked by this experience and considered the use of this robot a disservice to the hospital.[47]

This episode underlines the relevance of human relationships and how much the human being is unique in the clinical context and cannot be replaced by machines, especially in front of negative symptoms, grief, or traumatic diagnoses.[48] In the context of treatment, it is essential to consider the psychological and emotional impact of the disease and the relevance of doctor–patient relationships.

6. Conclusion

Implementing AI in care could lead to different advantages for doctors, patients, and medical institutions. However, it is essential to manage some challenges related to using AI in clinical practice.[35] The management of these aspects helps promote better use of technologies and implementation in the doctor–patient relationships. As described, it is important to consider the possible effects of artificial entities in a medical consultation with patients, avoiding the negative impact of technologies in the consultations (e.g., *"third wheel" effect*).[34] AI could be employed in the care context for treatment identification, diagnosis detection, health management, and patient engagement and to support health system organization. Despite the use of AI in these areas, professionals must consider the possible challenges related to AI implementation.[1] According to Topol,[49] using AI in medicine could positively affect healthcare practice, but it is essential to consider doctors' attitudes toward these technologies. Scientific research needs to understand this aspect to implement AI in the care context better. Topol suggested that if AI were to take on technical and administrative tasks, the time saved could be used by doctors to stay in contact with their patients, recovering the "lost time" for consultation. An empathic relationship with patients and positive listening can be promoted using the new technologies, also improving shared decision-making. In this scenario, AI would become the go-between patients and healthcare professionals, helping people understand humans' vital role in real care and supporting the use of technologies to promote emotional-related abilities in clinical consultation.

Acknowledgments

I.D. and S.F.M.P. were supported by Fondazione Umberto Veronesi. M.S. is a Ph.D. student within the European School of Molecular Medicine (SEMM).

References

1. Triberti S, Durosini I, La Torre D, Sebri V, Savioni L, Pravettoni G. Artificial intelligence in healthcare practice: How to tackle the "human" challenge. In: *Handbook of Artificial Intelligence in Healthcare*. Cham: Springer; 2022:43–60.
2. Karim A, Azam S, Shanmugam B, Kannoorpatti K, Alazab M. A comprehensive survey for intelligent spam email detection. *IEEE Access*. 2019;7:168261–168295.
3. Ozbay FA, Alatas B. Fake news detection within online social media using supervised artificial intelligence algorithms. *Physica A: Stat Mech Appl*. 2020;540, 123174.
4. La Torre D, Colapinto C, Durosini I, Triberti S. Team formation for human- artificial intelligence collaboration in the workplace: a goal programming model to foster organizational change. *IEEE Trans Eng Manage*. 2021.
5. Yu KH, Beam AL, Kohane IS. Artificial intelligence in healthcare. *Nature Biomed Eng*. 2018;2(10):719–731.
6. Sackett DL, Rosenberg WM, Gray JM, Haynes RB, Richardson WS. Evidence based medicine: what it is and what it isn't. *BMJ*. 1996;312(7023):71–72.
7. Sackett DL. Evidence-based medicine. *Semin Perinatol*. 1997;21(1):3–5.
8. Jarow JP, LaVange L, Woodcock J. Multidimensional evidence generation and FDA regulatory decision making: defining and using "real-world" data. *JAMA*. 2017;318(8):703–704.
9. Hampton JR. Evidence-based medicine, opinion-based medicine, and real-world medicine. *Perspect Biol Med*. 2002;45(4):549–568.
10. Durosini I, Triberti S, Savioni L, Pravettoni G. In the eye of a quiet storm: a critical incident study on the quarantine experience during the coronavirus pandemic. *PloS One*. 2021;16(2), e0247121.
11. Sarwar S, Dent A, Faust K, et al. Physician perspectives on integration of artificial intelligence into diagnostic pathology. *NPJ Dig Med*. 2019;2(1):28.
12. Ardila D, Kiraly AP, Bharadwaj S, et al. End-to-end lung cancer screening with three-dimensional deep learning on low-dose chest computed tomography. *Nat Med*. 2019;25:954–961.
13. Liu Q, Vaci N, Koychev I, et al. Personalised treatment for cognitive impairment in dementia: development and validation of an artificial intelligence model. *BMC Med*. 2022;20:45.
14. Peruselli C, De Panfilis L, Gobber G, Melo M, Tanzi S. Intelligenza artificiale e cure palliative: opportunità e limiti [Artificial intelligence and palliative care: opportunities and limitations]. *Recenti Prog Med*. 2020;111(11):639–645.
15. Davenport T, Kalakota R. The potential for artificial intelligence in healthcare. *Future Healthcare J*. 2019;6(2):94–98.
16. Hendler J, Mulvehill AM, Hendler J, Mulvehill AM. Who will be your next doctor? In: *Social Machines: The Coming Collision of Artificial Intelligence, Social Networking, and Humanity*; 2016:14–28.
17. Weng SF, Vaz L, Qureshi N, Kai J. Prediction of premature all-cause mortality: a prospective general population cohort study comparing machine-learning and standard epidemiological approaches. *PloS One*. 2019;14(3), e0214365.
18. Triberti S, Durosini I, Curigliano G, Pravettoni G. Is explanation a marketing problem? The quest for trust in artificial intelligence and two conflicting solutions. *Public Health Genomics*. 2020;23(1–2):2–5.
19. Bellini V, Guzzon M, Bigliardi B, Mordonini M, Filippelli S, Bignami E. Artificial intelligence: a new tool in operating room management. Role of machine learning models in operating room optimization. *J Med Syst*. 2020;44(1):20.
20. Triberti S, Durosini I, Lin J, La Torre D, Ruiz Galán M. On the "human" in human-artificial intelligence interaction. *Front Psychol*. 2021;12, 808995.
21. Yu KH, Kohane IS. Framing the challenges of artificial intelligence in medicine. *BMJ Qual Saf*. 2019;28(3):238–241.

22. Wadden JJ. Defining the undefinable: the black box problem in healthcare artificial intelligence. *J Med Ethics*. 2022;48(10):764–768.

23. Arrieta AB, Díaz-Rodríguez N, Del Ser J, et al. Explainable artificial intelligence (XAI): concepts, taxonomies, opportunities and challenges toward responsible AI. *Inform Fusion*. 2020;58:82–115.

24. Pesapane F, Rotili A, Valconi E, et al. Women's perceptions and attitudes to the use of AI in breast cancer screening: a survey in a cancer referral Centre. *Br J Radiol*. 2023;95(1141):20220569.

25. Sekhar MS, Vyas N. Defensive medicine: a bane to healthcare. *Ann Med Health Sci Res*. 2013;3(2):295–296.

26. Young PL, Olsen L. The Healthcare Imperative: Lowering Costs and Improving Outcomes: Workshop Series Summary. The National Academies Press; 2010.

27. Rothberg MB, Class J, Bishop TF, Friderici J, Kleppel R, Lindenauer PK. The cost of defensive medicine on 3 hospital medicine services. *JAMA Intern Med*. 2014;174(11):1867–1868.

28. Venkatesh V, Davis FD. A theoretical extension of the technology acceptance model: four longitudinal field studies. *Manage Sci*. 2000;46(2):186–204.

29. Triberti S, Villani D, Riva G. Unconscious goal pursuit primes attitudes towards technology usage: a virtual reality experiment. *Comput Hum Behav*. 2016;64:163–172.

30. Lu J. Will Medical Technology Deskill Doctors? International Education Studies; 2016.

31. Triki A, Weisner MM. Lessons from the literature on the theory of technology dominance: possibilities for an extended research framework. *J Emerging Technol Account*. 2014;11(1):41–69.

32. Lewis DR. The perils of overconfidence: why many consumers fail to seek advice when they really should. *J Finan Services Market*. 2018;23:104–111.

33. Durosini I, Aschieri F. Therapeutic assessment efficacy: a meta-analysis. *Psychol Assess*. 2021;33(10):962.

34. Triberti S, Durosini I, Pravettoni G. A "third wheel" effect in health decision making involving artificial entities: a psychological perspective. *Front Public Health*. 2020;8:117.

35. Goodman K, Zandi D, Reis A, Vayena E. Balancing risks and benefits of artificial intelligence in the health sector. *Bull World Health Organ*. 2020;98(4):230.

36. Wang F, Preininger A. AI in health: state of the art, challenges, and future directions. *Yearb Med Inform*. 2019;28(01):016–026.

37. Salovey P, Mayer JD. Emotional intelligence and its relationship to other intelligences. *Imagin Cogn Pers*. 1990;9(3):185–211.

38. Goleman DD. Emotional Intelligence: Why it Can Matter More than IQ for Character, Health and Lifelong Achievement. Bantam Books; 1995.

39. Durosini I, Masiero M, Casini C, Pravettoni G. Tobacco smoking behaviors in Cancer survivors: the mediation effect of personality and emotional intelligence. *Curr Oncol*. 2022;29(12):9437–9451.

40. Durosini I, Triberti S, Ongaro G, Pravettoni G. Validation of the Italian version of the brief emotional intelligence scale (BEIS-10). *Psychol Rep*. 2021;124(5):2356–2376.

41. Durosini I, Triberti S, Savioni L, Sebri V, Pravettoni G. The role of emotion-related abilities in the quality of life of breast Cancer survivors: a systematic review. *Int J Environ Res Public Health*. 2022;19(19):12704.

42. Durosini I, Savioni L, Triberti S, Guiddi P, Pravettoni G. The motivation journey: a grounded theory study on female cancer survivors' experience of a psychological intervention for quality of life. *Int J Environ Res Public Health*. 2021;18(3):950.

43. Savioni L, Triberti S, Durosini I, Sebri V, Pravettoni G. Cancer patients' participation and commitment to psychological interventions: a scoping review. *Psychol Health*. 2022;37(8):1022–1055.

44. Filipponi C, Pizzoli SF, Masiero M, Cutica I, Pravettoni G. The partial mediator role of satisficing decision-making style between trait emotional intelligence and compassion fatigue in healthcare professionals. *Psychol Rep*. 2022. 00332941221129127.

45. Johnson DR. Emotional intelligence as a crucial component to medical education. *Int J Med Educ*. 2015;6:179.

46. Strzelecka A, Stachura M, Wójcik T, et al. Determinants of primary healthcare patients' dissatisfaction with the quality of provided medical services. *Ann Agric Environ Med*. 2021;28(1):142.

47. Nichols G. Terminal Patient Learns he's Going to Die from a Robot Doctor; 2019. Retrieved at: https://www.zdnet.com/article/terminal-patient-learns-hes-going-to-die-from-a-robot-doctor/. Accessed 26 March 2019.

48. Durosini I, Tarocchi A, Aschieri F. Therapeutic assessment with a client with persistent complex bereavement disorder: a single-case time-series design. *Clin Case Stud*. 2017;16(4):295–312.

49. Topol E. Deep Medicine. New York, NY: Basic Books; 2019.

17

AI for outcome prediction in Radiation Oncology: The present and the future

Stefania Volpe[a,b], Lars Johannes Isaksson[a,b], and Barbara Alicja Jereczek-Fossa[a,b]

[a]Department of Radiation Oncology, European Institute of Oncology (IEO), IRCCS, Milan, Italy
[b]Department of Oncology and Hematology-Oncology (DIPO), University of Milan, Milan, Italy

1. Fundamentals of radiation oncology

Cancer is a leading cause of death worldwide, accounting for approximately 10.0 million deaths, and an estimated 19.3 million new diagnoses in 2020.[1] In the last decades, the capability of diagnosing and treating cancer has evolved deeply, as novel tools have progressively become available to physicians. These include, but are not limited to, more accurate diagnostic systems (e.g., computed tomography, magnetic resonance, positron emission tomography) and more effective drugs, which can either replace or be added to the administration of classical chemotherapy (e.g., immunotherapy, targeted therapies). Another shift in the paradigm of cancer treatment is the integration of multiple modalities: surgery, radiation therapy, and systemic therapies may all be indicated, with a complementary role in disease control.

Radiation therapy is a treatment modality consisting of the delivery of ionizing radiation (mainly, high-energy X-rays, but also electrons or charged particles such as protons and carbon ions, based on the clinical indication). To do so, different forms of linear accelerators can be used depending on the anatomical site to be irradiated, and on other factors such as the way the dose is being delivered (e.g., high or conventional doses per fraction, which is generically defined as "fractionation"). Radiotherapy can be indicated in different scenarios. It can be curative when the intent is disease eradication, postoperative when delivered after surgery, and palliative/symptomatic when it is delivered to alleviate cancer-related symptoms (e.g. bone-metastasis-related pain, or bleeding). Overall, radiotherapy is a part of radiation oncology, a clinical specialty that involves not only treatment delivery but also patient consultations, management of cancer symptoms, treatment-related side effects, and follow-up.

The rationale behind the use of ionizing radiation lies in its ability to induce either lethal or sublethal damage to the DNA of proliferating cancer cells, preventing them from reproducing and causing disease progression. To date, ultimate generation linear accelerators allow for the delivery of highly conformed doses to the target volume(s), thus reducing the dose to the surrounding healthy tissues (e.g., the highly conformed irradiation of a peripherical lung carcinoma allows for the reduction of unintended dose to the healthy lung parenchyma, the ribs, and the spinal cord). This is achieved, thanks to high-precision techniques, such as intensity-modulated radiotherapy and stereotactic body radiotherapy. Additionally, the use of image-guided radiotherapy allows radiation therapists and radiation oncologists to verify the exact position of the target volume before radiation is delivered. This limits the risk of the so-called "geographical misses" (i.e., when parts of the target are not adequately irradiated) and reduces the risk of irradiating nearby healthy tissues. This significantly limits the risk of developing radiation-related side effects deriving from the tissue response to ionizing radiation—what is commonly referred to as toxicities.

Given that radiotherapy is a local treatment, its side effects are generally limited to the area close to the irradiated site(s). Based on tissue response to ionizing radiation, toxicities can be classified into "acute" and "late." The former is mostly due to acute inflammatory reactions of the irradiated tissues. The most common acute side effects are dermatitis (skin irritation including erythematous, itchy, and/or dry skin) and fatigue, a systemic symptom causing a feeling of exhaustion affecting psychological function and everyday life activities.[2] Other acute toxicities are more specific to the irradiated site. For example, patients treated for head and neck cancers may experience side effects such as dysphagia (difficulty swallowing), dysgeusia (altered taste), and xerostomia (reduction of the salivary flow). Conversely, common acute toxicities of pelvic irradiation (e.g., curative-intent RT for prostate cancer) include proctitis and cystitis (inflammation of the rectum and of the bladder, respectively). Late toxicities occur after a minimum time of three months since treatment completion and are mostly due to fibrosis (i.e., an altered process of wound repair causing the replacement of normal tissue with connective tissue, also called "scar"). As fibrosis is a nonreversible process, it usually persists over time, with a potentially relevant impact on patients' well-being and quality of life. Fibrosis can not only manifest on the skin (e.g., following breast irradiation), but it can involve any healthy tissue following exposure to radiation, including the bladder, the lungs, and the esophagus, with varying degrees of functional impairing (from subclinical modifications that can be assessed by imaging only to moderate–severe dysfunctions altering patients' quality of life). Importantly, acute inflammation leading to acute toxicities can persist into chronic inflammation. Therefore, the same symptoms described above can be persistent (e.g., dysphagia, dysgeusia, and xerostomia following treatment for head and neck cancer, or proctitis and cystitis following pelvic irradiation for either gynecological malignancies or prostate cancer).

Despite the fact that high-precision techniques are both common and recommended these days, the risk of clinically relevant toxicities still exists. The primary countermeasure for preventing treatment-related side effects is accurate segmentation. Segmentation consists of the delineation of the target volume(s) (e.g., the cancer nodule), and the surrounding tissues, defined as "organs at risk" (OARs). Segmentation can be performed manually or through semiautomated or fully automated tools, which are especially useful for segmenting OARs in anatomically complex body regions (e.g., the head and neck, and the pelvis). As a reference, it has been estimated that the segmentation of a head and neck cancer case candidate to curative radiotherapy requires approximately 3.0 h due to both the complexity and the large number of OARs involved. Regardless of the segmentation method (i.e., manual, semi-automated, or fully automated), accurate segmentation is paramount to optimize treatment planning, which can be defined as the calculation of the dose delivered to the target volume(s) and to the OARs.

Fig. 1 provides an example of a real-life treatment plan. Specifically, Fig. 1A shows a primary lung cancer tumor of nonsmall cell histology and its associated dose distribution: it can be noted that the prescription dose falls only in close proximity to the treated areas (i.e., ipsilateral lung and the mediastinal vessels), thus minimizing the risk of toxicity. On the other hand, Fig. 1B shows the dose-volume graph: this is a type of representation used in radiation oncology to quantify the dose received by the volumes of interest, which include both the target and surrounding healthy structures. In the right portion of the graph are the curves for the lung tumor, meaning that this volume is adequately reached by the prescription dose. In contrast, the left portion shows curves for the neighboring healthy organs (in this case, the lungs, the mediastinum, the esophagus, the trachea, and the spinal cord), indicating that all of these structures receive a minimal dose. In essence, the more separate the dose-volume curves of target volumes and volumes to be spared, the better, as adequate irradiation of the disease and preservation of healthy organs are ensured at the same time.

However, given the same conditions (e.g., patients' demographics, cancer diagnosis and stage, and treatment planning), outcomes may differ in terms of both disease control and treatment-related outcomes. This derives from the fact that multiple individual factors are involved in determining response to radiation. Therefore, there is a large unmet need to fully understand the mechanisms underlying treatment response, and the onset of toxicity in each patient, to combine the achievement of maximal oncological outcomes and null to minimal side effects. Recently, radiation oncology is benefiting from advances in the fields of quantitative imaging and radiogenomics.[3,4] Such "big data" approaches are gradually being integrated into a more traditional body of knowledge on tumor biology and interpatient variability and may represent a meaningful step toward a personalized medicine approach. Nonetheless, this growing amount of information is difficult for single practitioners to manage, and there is an increasing demand for novel, informatics-based tools to structure and solve complex clinical questions. Machine learning (ML), a branch of artificial intelligence (AI) that relies on patterns and inference to perform a specific task, could provide accurate models to Radiation Oncologists to optimize patients' care paths.

The following section will provide an overview of the most common ML algorithms that are being developed and/or validated in radiation oncology, with a dedicated focus on the prediction of oncological and toxicity outcomes. Further ML applications (e.g., automated segmentation, treatment planning) are beyond the scope of this chapter and can be found elsewhere.

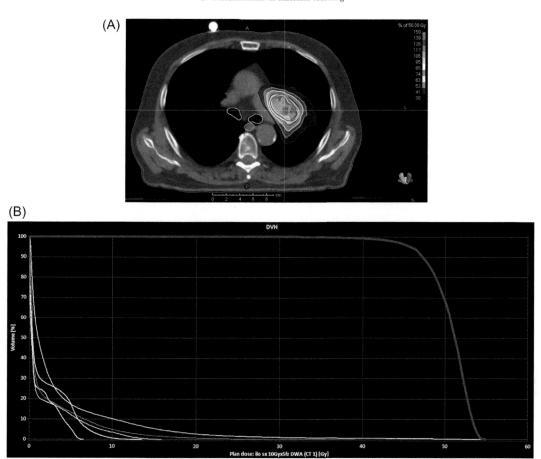

FIG. 1 A treatment plan for a lung cancer patient. (A) Dose distribution overlaid on a CT scan of the patient and (B) corresponding dose-volume graph.

2. Fundamentals of machine learning

Albeit the term "machine learning" was first introduced in 1959 by Arthur Samuel,[5] it was not until recently that advances in technology and computational abilities favored the integration of these tools into the experimental and clinical practice of health sciences. In its broadest sense, ML is a subset of AI relying on inference and patterns to execute a specific task (e.g., making a prediction). More specifically, ML encompasses a set of algorithms capable of building a model from sample data (namely, the training set), without an explicit implementation of the solution. ML, as opposed to statistical methods, focuses on identifying predictive patterns rather than drawing conclusions from a sample. Statistical models aim to assess whether a relationship between two or more variables describes a true effect and to interpret the extent of the above-mentioned relationship, beginning with sampling and power calculations. As a result, a quantitative measure of confidence can be provided to test hypotheses and/or verify assumptions.[6] On the other hand, ML employs general-purpose algorithms with no or minimal assumptions. While this may lead to results that are difficult to interpret and generalize, ML can be useful in cases of poorly understood and complex phenomena, such as when the number of input variables exceeds the number of subjects and complicated nonlinear interactions are present.[7] Remarkably, statistics- and ML-based models, should not be considered either antagonistic or mutually exclusive. For example, some methods (such as bootstrapping) can be used for both statistical inference and the development of ML models, and the distinction between the two is not always clear.

The selection of the best ML algorithm to solve a given problem begins with the characterization of available data, which can be labeled (e.g., implemented with additional information, such as: "this computed tomography (CT) slice contains the contour of the tumor") or unlabeled (e.g., data do not contain any supplementary tag, such as a collection of CT slices). In the first case, the learning problem is supervised, which means that the algorithm learns patterns that are characteristic of all samples with a given label. The model then assigns class labels to previously unseen, unlabeled instances using the same labels it saw from the training set. Unsupervised learning, on the other hand, uses unlabeled data to identify previously undetected patterns and to react to the presence or absence of such patterns in new

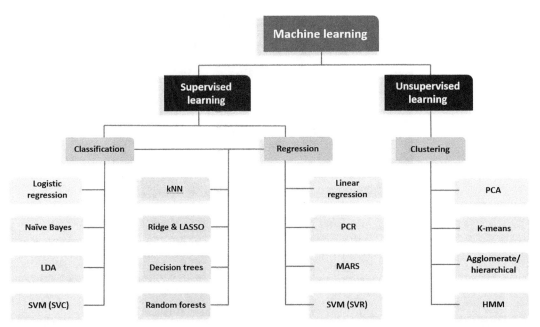

FIG. 2   Taxonomic overview of some of the most popular machine learning algorithms in healthcare. Note that most regression algorithms can be made to perform classification given a suitable mapping from numbers to classes (the converse is also often true since many classification algorithms implicitly convert their output to classes). What is pictured is more or less their most common application. Artificial neural network approaches are not pictured; they can be made to perform all of the above approaches depending on how they are constructed. LDA: linear discriminant analysis, SVM: support vector machine, SVC: support vector classifier, SVR: support vector regressor, kNN: k nearest neighbors, PCR: principal component regression, PCA: principal component analysis, HMM: hidden Markov models.

instances without requiring human intervention. Fig. 2 provides an overview of the most common algorithms, tested for both medical and nonmedical purposes, but a detailed description of individual classification, regression, and clustering algorithms is beyond the scope of this chapter.

Other than by input data type, models can be categorized according to the type of output the algorithm aims to predict. Generally, predictive modeling can be defined as the mathematical problem of approximating a mapping function (f) from input variables (x) to output variables (y). This is called the problem of function approximation. Therefore, the task of the modeling algorithm is to find the best mapping function given the data, time, and computational resources available. Broadly, function approximation tasks can be categorized into classification tasks and regression tasks[8]:

- *Classification tasks*: In classification, the predictive function maps the input variables to discrete output variables (y), which are often referred to as "labels" or "categories." In other words, the prediction task is to predict the class or category for a new observation (e.g., spam filters act as classifiers, by assigning new emails to either the "spam" or "not spam" class). Classification problems can be either binary, as in the example above, or multiclass in case the algorithm is required to assign the observation to one among three or more possible classes (e.g., identify car types in images from a booklet). While there are multiple methods to assess the performance of a classification predictive model, perhaps the most common is to calculate the classification accuracy (i.e., the percentage of observation being correctly classified out of all predictions).
- *Regression tasks*. Unlike classification tasks that focus on assigning data points to predefined categories, regression tasks involve predicting continuous numerical values based on input features. As such, regression targets tend to be quantities/amounts/sizes/etc., e.g., the temperature on a coming day given input variables like atmospheric pressure, wind speed, humidity, and previous records. The goal of a regression task is to build a model that can accurately estimate or forecast a target variable based on the relationships and patterns observed in the training data. One thing to keep in mind, however, is that classification accuracy is not generally appropriate for continuous output variables. Instead, a common measure of the error in these predictions is the root mean squared error (RMSE), which is defined as the square root of the mean value of the squared error terms, i.e. $\text{RMSE} = \sqrt{\frac{1}{N}\sum_i^N c_i^2}$. Another way to look at the RMSE is in terms of the standard deviation of the residuals, where the residuals measure how far the predictions are from the regression line (see Fig. 3).

FIG. 3 Illustration of the RMSE loss function. A target function (depicted in orange (gray in print version)) on an input variable X is estimated by a model producing discrete predictions (depicted as crosses). The error of the predictions (epsilon) is the distance from the predicted y-values ($\hat{y}$) to the real y-values (y) on the orange function, i.e., $equation$ (depicted with a blue curly bracket). The RMSE is the square root of the mean value of the squared error terms: $\sqrt{\frac{1}{N}\sum_i^N \epsilon_i^2}$.

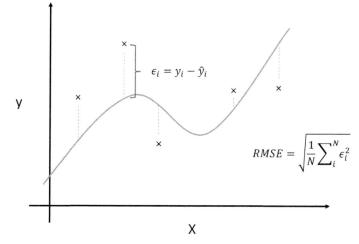

$$\epsilon_i = y_i - \hat{y}_i$$

$$RMSE = \sqrt{\frac{1}{N}\sum_i^N \epsilon_i^2}$$

One of the most widespread applications of unsupervised learning is data clustering, which is a procedure where the input data are grouped into clusters of internally coherent samples. Hence, after clustering, the data samples in cluster A will all be somewhat similar, and collectively different from the samples in cluster B. Generally speaking, the clustering procedure recognizes patterns inside the data, computes their similarity, and identifies the most efficient way to group them into clusters given some measure of similarity and some constraints. Different approaches to clustering can be suitable in different contexts, and the best algorithm depends on the user's preferences and the algorithm's ability to fit the specific data distribution.[9]

3. Data quality and preprocessing

As ML models "learn" from the data in the training set, it stands to reason that the characteristics and quality of the collected data are paramount; "garbage in, garbage out," as the saying goes. This is a phrase used to describe the fact that if the input data fed into an ML model is of poor quality, the model will produce poor-quality output. If the input data contains errors, biases, or irrelevant information, the model will be unable to learn the correct relationships and will produce inaccurate predictions. Thus, it's important to ensure the input data is high-quality and properly preprocessed before training an ML model. As such, exploring, understanding, and assessing the quality of the available data is an essential prerequisite of data processing and data modeling. The overall process of exploring and dissecting data through the use of statistical, summarization, and plotting techniques is called exploratory data analysis (EDA, for short). Regardless of the composition of the data and the analyses to be performed later, EDA allows for identifying and uncovering possible errors (incorrectly labeled data, missing values, poor encoding of variables, etc.), outliers, relationships between variables (correlations), redundancies, and more. Until recently, both academia and industry have focused almost exclusively on introducing and improving ML models rather than addressing data challenges like cleaning, preparing, and collecting data in effective ways. Recently, however, the quality of training data has been shown to limit the performance of AI-enhanced systems in practice, which has prompted a small shift from model-centric to data-centric approaches to building AI systems.[10]

Errors in data collection may derive from different sources, including erroneous user input (e.g., typos), measurement error, sampling bias, aggregation errors (errors resulting from formatting data from different sources into a common standard), and noise. One way to measure this error is called data accuracy, which is defined as the extent to which collected data agree with the real ground truth (i.e., the higher the deviation from the real value, the lower the accuracy within the dataset). Data balance is another common issue; if, e.g., one class is overrepresented in the training dataset, the ML model may learn a skewed relationship. Additional indexes of data quality include but are not limited to, completeness (i.e., the ratio between nonmissing values and the total number of samples in the dataset), uniqueness (i.e., the quantity of duplicate, nonunique values), and consistency (i.e., if all records use the same units of measurement or if the data follows a logical structure).

The recognition and management of missing values, outliers, duplicates, and other inconsistencies (e.g., mislabels) before analyses are performed, is called data cleaning and has been recognized as a significant problem in ML.[11] Specifically, it has been demonstrated that missing values and outliers can significantly impact the performance of downstream ML algorithms,[12] and that data-cleaning pipelines can be automatized through dedicated tools and algorithms.[13,14] To date, the main issues preventing a consistent implementation of such tools stem from the difficulty in generalizing data-cleaning pipelines into a one-size-fits-all fashion that can be used off the shelf for most real-world datasets. A prevalent example of efforts to overcome this include the AutoML framework.[15] For such systems to be effective in practice, they must automatically choose an appropriate algorithm and preprocessing steps, as well as their hyperparameters. Some errors within data may be better identified following multiple iterations and/or transformation procedures (e.g., imputation of missing values may facilitate the discovery of outliers), which warrants multiple rounds of cleaning and wrangling of the initial dataset.[16]

4. Machine learning and personalized medicine in radiation oncology

Given the growing availability of big data in cancer care, there has been increasing interest in the use of ML algorithms to solve clinically relevant problems. These may range from predicting patients' response to a certain drug to stratifying patients into prognostic groups based on medical history and estimated side effects. In radiation oncology, it is easy to envision algorithms being helpful in solving issues related to virtually every step of the clinical workflow, from patient admission to release/follow-up. From a clinical point of view, generating personalized outcome predictions tailor-made for individual people is widely considered to be the next big leap in medicine, and has come to be known simply as Personalized Medicine. This concept embodies the fundamental objective of current Medicine, aiming to overcome the old paradigm of "one size fits all"-type approaches, where decisions are made based on patient labels instead of individual needs. Indeed, the outlook for personalized medicine looks promising given the large influx of new knowledge, novel techniques, and more data. To promote a personalized framework, the integration of data from multiple sources becomes necessary, and ML appears to become an indispensable tool given the potential complexity of all the interacting parts. Considering outcome prediction, the main points of interest for radiation oncologists involve oncological and toxicological outcomes.

Oncological prediction relates to the capability of predicting disease control in terms of recurrence within the site of origin of the tumor (referred to as local recurrence, or loco-regional recurrence if recurrence within nearby nodal regions is considered), and survival outcomes. Survival is most commonly analyzed in terms of overall survival or cancer-specific survival. Overall survival considers the time from the date of diagnosis (or the start of treatment) to the date of death. Note that this also includes noncancer-related deaths such as cardiovascular diseases or traffic accidents. By contrast, cancer-specific survival only considers deaths from strictly cancer-related complications.

As mentioned earlier, a wide range of acute and late radiation-related toxicities may occur, mainly depending on the irradiated site, the surrounding healthy tissue, and the total delivered dose. However, different patients irradiated at the exact same site with the exact same dose can still exhibit vastly different toxicity profiles. Hence, there is a strong need for a better understanding of the mechanisms and interactions involved in toxicity development. One such approach is radiogenomics; the study of the relationship between image characteristics and gene expression. In radiogenomics, the genetic profile of the target site is sampled and analyzed together with the radiological images (and their features) that are acquired as part of the treatment process.[17]

In more recent years, radiogenomics has been frequently associated with radiomics, which is the extraction of descriptive quantitative features from routinely acquired images without explicitly incorporating genetic information. These radiomic features are extracted using data-mining algorithms and typically describe things related to the image intensities within a region (e.g., their kurtosis), its shape (e.g., the maximum diameter), or texture. As suggested by an increasing albeit preliminary amount of evidence, these radiomic features can be associated with previously known biological features, such as necrosis, cell cycle phase, or white blood cell activation.[18]

Overall, the goal of radiotherapy—like that of any medical intervention—is to achieve maximal efficacy at the lowest rate of complications/toxicities. Therefore, the ideal radiation treatment is the one that can effectively control the disease (or the symptom), without inducing either acute or late adverse events. In practice, one method to quantify the probability of achieving tumor control, or to determine the onset of toxicity, is provided by the TCP (tumor control probability) and NTCP models (normal tissue complication probability), respectively. Specifically, the latter can be classified as mechanistic (or analytical) and data-driven (or semi-empirical)[19]:

– Mechanistic or analytical models rely on explicitly defining algorithms that describe a simplified characterization of the interaction between radiation and tissue. Among the analytical models, the most common is the Lyman–Kutcher–Burman model, which can be used to predict the risk of normal tissue complication probability in patients receiving irradiation treatment. The model has been implemented into several commercial treatment planning systems to allow for a biological optimization of the delivered dose.[20,21]

– Data-driven or semi-empirical models assume that interactions between radiation and healthy tissue cannot be represented explicitly (in so far as to still be useful and intelligible for medical practitioners). Instead, these models aim to adequately fit the input data to predict the outcome of interest. The input data can be of different origins: clinical (e.g., a patient's gender and age), dosimetric (e.g., data derived from the quantitative estimation of the dose distribution, such as DVH points), and image-based (e.g., information derived from functional imaging, such as the magnetic resonance imaging).

In general, these approaches can be further distinguished into well-established statistical techniques (e.g. regression), and more novel approaches based on AI and ML. Since ML models learn from available data, it follows that the availability of well-structured datasets is crucial. Specifically, if the training dataset is sparse and/or of low quality, models typically fail to learn a representative set of parameters that can be generalized to instances not included in the dataset. This issue, generally defined as overfitting or overtraining, arises when a model is trained on limited datasets, or when the model encompasses the characteristics of a dataset too closely. When the number of features/measures greatly exceeds the number of samples they are made on, the risk of overfitting is high, and a compromise needs to be found to identify a model that performs acceptably both on the training and on the test sets. Overfitting can occur for a variety of reasons and should always be a major concern when constructing an ML model, particularly in medical scenarios.

5. Toxicity prediction in radiation oncology

Toxicity prediction is an extremely relevant endpoint in radiation oncology because it relates directly to the resulting quality of life of the patient and affects the choice of treatment. With the plethora of possible variables that can lead to toxicity, ML approaches are particularly well suited to model the relationship between treatment-induced side effects and related covariates. As an example, the use of spatial dose metrics, such as the gradient and direction of the irradiating beam, may complement the information provided by absolute mean and maximum doses. Additionally, genetic determinants of toxicity are thought to impact individual radiosensitivity/resistance of healthy tissues. ML has the potential to combine these emerging factors with more established toxicity aspects such as patient data, systemic therapy administration, and absolute dosimetric parameters. For example, adequate consideration of these covariates in dedicated algorithms could discern the probability for a given patient to experience a specific type of toxicity. Thus, ML and computer-aided decision tools could contribute to refining clinical decisions for the better (e.g., by assisting with the feeding tube placement in patients diagnosed with head and neck cancer at high risk for severe weight loss).[22,23]

An increasing number of works and literature reviews have been published in the last few years to investigate the potential of ML-based approaches in the field of radiation oncology. A recent narrative review[24] has summarized current data, identifying a total of 53 publications, mainly focused on prostate, lung, and head & neck cancers (16, 15, and 13 published papers, respectively). As far as mathematical modeling is concerned, the vast majority of prediction models are built upon structured data in the form of tables and spreadsheets with traditional ML models, with a small minority focusing on the application of neural networks directly on the images. In particular, 29 and 15 studies used logistic regression (LR), and support vector machines, respectively. These are linear models that can be easily implemented and interpreted. Moreover, LR naturally integrates with statistical inference techniques such as the likelihood ratio test, which simplifies the statistical analysis and interpretation. However, one could argue that their performance may be insufficient for reliable clinical integration since they are often outclassed by nonlinear models in terms of pure performance (at least in complex nonlinear scenarios; see e.g., Ref. 25. Nonlinear models like RF and neural networks therefore often achieve better performance in scientific studies, particularly with larger sample sizes and high-dimensional input, but this comes at the price of being more easily overfit. Regardless of whether these models are suitable for clinical integration, they can still uncover important details about the relationships between data and clinical observations. Therefore, it is paramount to balance the pros and cons of various models when designing studies in the clinical setting.

Considering ML application for toxicity prediction in head and neck cancers, the most common clinical endpoint is the prediction of xerostomia, which can be defined as the reduction (from mild to severe) of the salivary flow. It is a complex phenomenon with a potentially relevant impact on patients' quality of life since it may induce complications like difficulty swallowing and dental problems. Xerostomia (also referred to as "dry mouth") can develop during the course of treatment as a consequence of acute inflammation, and persist over time due to the onset and maintenance of fibrotic reactions compromising the function of the salivary glands (namely, the parotids, the submandibular glands, and the sublingual glands). As an example, a 2018 study by Gabrys et al. looked at different models for the prediction of early (defined as xerostomia diagnosed during treatment and within 6 months after its completion), late (defined as xerostomia diagnosed between 6 and 15 months after treatment completion), long-term (defined as xerostomia diagnosed between 15 and 24 months after treatment completion), and any-time xerostomia.[26] Interestingly, ML classifiers outperformed NTCP models based on the sole mean dose to the parotid glands. This underlines the need for complex models incorporating multiple parameters for accurate outcome prediction (i.e., gland volume and dose gradients in the right–left and anterior–posterior direction for long-term xerostomia).

Overall, the prevalence of models operating on structured data has been one of the driving factors behind efforts to represent nonstructured data such as images in terms of tables and spreadsheets. The current prime example of such efforts is the emergence of radiomics, where quantitative features are extracted from medical images. This enables researchers to incorporate information from the images while employing the same techniques and may be easier and more transparent than modes operating directly on the images. Also, alternative techniques such as variations of artificial neural networks, have also demonstrated great success in various image analysis domains, not the least medical image analysis. An example of successful implementation of radiomic features for the prediction of toxicity outcomes has been provided, among others, by Bourbonne et al., who applied radiomic analysis of 3D dose distribution to predict lung and esophageal toxicity in 167 patients with lung cancer treated with radiotherapy.[27] Specifically, the authors applied a supervised NN approach to build a clinical model, a clinico-dosimetic model, and a clinico-radiomic-dosimetric model considering all available parameters (namely, clinical characteristics, DVH, and dose map radiomic features). These results (albeit preliminary and not externally validated) showed that this method is applicable and has the potential to improve the prediction of acute and late pulmonary toxicities in real-world patients.

6. Oncological outcome prediction and decision support tools in radiation oncology

Outcome prediction is crucial in the field of radiation oncology, especially in the era of personalized treatments. In radiation oncology, various de-intensification strategies are being tested in clinical trials for several disease types, and as biological and quantitative imaging parameters are gaining the spotlight as promising prognosticators, there is an increasing need for effective models integrating this growing body of information.[28] Many different approaches have been tested for modeling oncological outcomes, including SVM, Bayesian networks, ANNs, decision trees, and ensemble methods.[29]

A typical issue in outcomes prediction is the management of time-dependent endpoints, e.g., overall survival, local control, and progression-free survival. When these outcomes have not occurred for all patients at the time of the last follow-up, but may occur at a later time, they are said to be "right censored" since it is unknown how far to the "right" (on a horizontal time axis) the event (e.g., death) will occur. Inappropriate recognition and management of right-censored events may lead to poor model calibration, regardless of the specific algorithm of choice.[30]

In general, the most common oncological outcomes of interest are

- Overall survival is defined as the time from either the date of diagnosis or the start of treatment for a disease, such as cancer, up to the time of death, for any cause.
- Cancer-specific survival is defined as the time from either the date of diagnosis or the start of treatment for a disease, such as cancer, up to the time of disease-related death.
- Progression-free survival is defined as the time from the start of treatment for a disease, such as cancer, up to the time the disease progresses, or death occurs.

A recent systematic review of ML application for head and neck cancers has shown that oncological outcome prediction was a frequent endpoint, being the target of prediction in one-fourth of the scientific papers published between 1998 and 2021.[31] The review highlighted the use of both supervised and unsupervised models, with overall satisfactory performance in small-to-medium-sized datasets. Neural networks were implemented in only two of the identified studies, both of which demonstrated the superiority of DL compared to competing algorithms in predicting recurrence in nasopharyngeal carcinoma (in the first case),[32] and overall survival of mixed locally advanced head and neck cancers patients (in the second case).[33] Another relevant finding was that radiomics is gaining progressive interest in the field, with six works implementing texture analysis, mainly derived from CT images. However, the use of feature selection methods was quite uncommon, as it was implemented in only two of the radiomic-based works.[24,30]

Oncological outcome modeling is closely intertwined with decision-making tools. Traditionally, decision-making has been managed by physicians, either alone or in multidisciplinary team discussions with other clinical practitioners. However, the increasing availability of complex, high-throughput data has made the process more complex and has spurred a need for tools that support decisions and are capable of synthesizing the myriad of clinical, pathological, and omics-derived information. To this aim, clinical decision support tools aim to provide evidence-based personalized information to better orient clinicians' decisions. Several such tools have already been validated in the field of Radiation Oncology, and include applications for prostate, breast, and metastatic colorectal cancer.[34–36] Remarkably, cost-effectiveness considerations can be implemented into the systems such that the estimation of the likely benefit of one treatment over another can be considered both in terms of cost and availability. In particular, proton therapy and photon therapy are two competing treatments of peculiar interest, as the number of proton facilities has increased worldwide in recent years, thus making this alternative form of radiation therapy applicable to a wider number of potential candidates. The advantages of proton therapies rely on their capability of delivering beams with ballistic precision, thus sparing the surrounding normal tissues, which could translate into a clinically relevant benefit in patients with higher sensitivity to radiation, or to those who have received prior radiation courses. In addition, due to their biological properties, protons can be used for the treatment of hypoxic and radioresistant tumors, which usually do not benefit from classical photon-based irradiation. An example of such a decision support tool has been provided by Cheng et al., who developed an online platform for proton decision support using dose metrics, toxicity, and cost-effectiveness parameters.[37]

7. Most common machine learning algorithms in radiation oncology

In medical research, simple linear algorithms such as logistic regression (which is overwhelmingly used as a classifier) or LASSO regression are often preferred when building prediction models, in large part because they are easily interpretable. Linear models produce scalar coefficients for each input variable, which are then linearly combined, meaning that one can simply inspect the variable coefficients to get an idea of how impactful each variable is. This can be particularly important in medical scenarios where users (e.g., doctors and other medical practitioners) need to be aware of how the model works so they can communicate the details to their patients if needed. This is also a good way to explore relationships and interactions between variables and conditions, even if linear models tend to be less successful in terms of pure performance compared to their nonlinear counterparts. An additional benefit of many linear models is that they naturally integrate with statistical inference such as the likelihood ratio test, which is useful for hypothesis testing.

Logistic Regression is a widely used statistical approach to binary classification problems, where the goal is to model the relationship between a set of predictor variables and the target variable, which is binary in nature (0 or 1). The algorithm models this relationship by transforming the input features into a probability score that indicates the likelihood of a given data point belonging to a certain class. The core of the model relies on the logistic function, which maps the input features to a value between 0 and 1. This value, referred to as the predicted probability, is then thresholded to generate binary predictions. The coefficients of the model are determined through the optimization of the maximum likelihood estimation, which adjusts the model to minimize the difference between the predicted probabilities and the actual class labels. What makes the model linear is that the input to the logistic function is a linear combination of the variables; the model is linear in its argument. As such, the core difference between linear and logistic regression is that the latter is transformed with the logistic function (which makes it suitable for classification purposes). These two models have traditionally been the most prevalent in medical research by far, but more advanced and higher-performing (nonlinear) models have started to become more common in recent years.

Other common classification algorithms include the naïve Bayes classifier, discriminant analysis (most commonly linear, but quadratic models also exist), and support vector machines (e.g., support vector classifiers). The Naive Bayes classifier is a probabilistic machine learning model that utilizes Bayes' theorem for binary and multiclass classification problems. It uses Bayes' theorem and assumes independence between predictor variables to calculate the probability of each class given the input features and make predictions based on the class with the highest probability. It can be well suited for medical applications since it is robust to irrelevant features and can be good at handling small datasets. Like linear models, it is also easily interpreted since the probabilities calculated can provide insight into the contributions of each feature, which can be useful in medical applications where understanding the decision-making process is important. Discriminant analysis (DA) is a family of statistical approaches to supervised classification problems in which the primary objective is to find a linear combination of the predictor variables that maximizes the separation between the classes, referred to as discriminant functions. The DA classifier generates a prediction for a new data point based on the class with the highest discriminant score. It is simple, interpretable, and efficient, making it a suitable alternative to the other classification models. Support vector machines (SVMs) are a type of supervised machine learning algorithm used for both classification and regression problems. SVMs find the optimal boundary, referred to as the maximum margin hyperplane, that separates the classes by maximizing the margin between the closest data points of each class, known as support vectors. The optimal boundary is chosen such that it has the largest margin between the two classes, which makes the model robust to outliers and reduces the generalization error. An interesting property of SVMs is that they can be extended to nonlinearly separable data using the kernel trick, which maps the data into a higher-dimensional space where a linear boundary can be found. This makes SVMs suitable for a wide range of classification problems, including those with complex decision boundaries.

Apart from linear regression (which is a special case of polynomial regression in which the relationship between the independent variable x and the dependent variable y is modeled as a first-degree polynomial in x) and support vector regressors, two less common regression models that are principal component regression (PCR) and multivariate adaptive regression splines (MARS). PCR is a regression method that utilizes principal component analysis (PCA) to reduce the dimensionality of the predictors (the independent variables). The idea is to capture the maximum amount of variance in the predictors while retaining only a small number of the most important components. In PCR, the original set of predictor variables is transformed into a smaller set of principal components through PCA. These principal components are then used as predictors in a standard linear regression model. The primary goal of PCR is to reduce the complexity of the model while retaining its predictive power, thereby avoiding overfitting and improving the interpretability of the model. Due to its dimensionality reduction properties, PCA is more commonly used as a feature selection or dimensionality reduction technique and is especially well suited for data sets where there is a large number of predictor variables. This can help to avoid the curse of dimensionality, where the number of predictors becomes too large relative to the number of observations. MARS, on the other hand, is a flexible, nonparametric regression technique that is well-suited for complex and nonlinear relationships between predictor variables and the target variable. MARS uses piecewise linear regression models, which are defined by knots, to model the relationship between the predictors and the target variable. MARS starts by considering a single predictor and constructing a simple linear regression model. Then, it adds additional predictors to the model and fits nonlinear functions of these predictors, where the nonlinearities are defined by knots. The model continues to grow, adding additional knots and predictor variables, until a stopping criterion is reached, such as a minimum improvement in the fit of the model. One advantage of MARS is that it is able to capture complex relationships between predictors and the target variable, as well as interactions between predictors, without the need for prior knowledge of the relationships. Additionally, MARS is highly interpretable, as it can be visualized as a collection of piecewise linear models.

Some of the most common and powerful models are those that are able to perform both classification and regression tasks, perhaps most notably decision trees and random forests. A decision tree is a tree-based model where the relationships between the predictor variables and the target variable are represented by a series of splits. At each node in the tree, a split is made on one of the predictors, and the tree branches in two directions. The process continues until a stopping criterion is met, such as a minimum number of observations in a terminal node or a maximum tree depth. Random forests, on the other hand, are an ensemble of decision trees. In a random forest, multiple decision trees are grown using bootstrapped samples of the data, and the final prediction is made by combining the predictions from all the trees. Random forests can improve the performance and stability of decision trees by reducing overfitting, which is a common problem with decision trees. Both decision trees and random forests are highly interpretable and easy to use, which makes them particularly suitable for medical applications. Random forest-derived approaches have gained particular interest lately due to their easy integration with gradient boosting techniques, which have largely been popularized with the help of packages such as XGBoost, LightGBM, and CatBoost. Boosting is a simple concept wherein an ensemble model is trained by iteratively training weak learners. The key insight is that every added weak learner can be trained to predict the error of the previous ones, which allows one to iteratively reduce the error by adding more and more learners. This works well with decision trees because they are extremely fast to train, but the catch is that one loses most of the interpretation abilities of decision trees. kNN (k-nearest neighbors) models are based on the idea of making predictions based on the closest examples in the training data. kNN assigns a new observation to the class with the majority of the k nearest training examples. The distance between the new observation and the training examples can be calculated using various metrics, such as Euclidean distance or Manhattan distance. The standout element of kNN is the fact that it is a nonparametric and instance-based method, which means that it does not make any assumptions about the distribution of the data and it does not fit a model to the training data. Instead, kNN stores the training data and makes predictions based on the nearest neighbors. This makes it simple, easy to implement and interpret, and capable of handling both categorical and continuous predictor variables, which is a major benefit in medical applications. Ridge and LASSO models are an interesting class of models that implicitly make a type of variable selection during their training. Though they can be used for classification in some contexts, they are overwhelmingly used for regression. They are designed to reduce the complexity of the model and promote sparsity by adding a penalty term to the objective function. This results in a sparse solution where only a subset of the predictors is selected. LASSO is useful for selecting relevant predictors and reducing variance but has limitations such as dependence on the penalty parameter, sensitivity to the scale of the predictors, and potential loss of information.

Apart from the above-mentioned classification and regression models, there are also numerous clustering algorithms, which are unsupervised learning techniques used to group similar observations or features into clusters based on their similarities. The goal of clustering is to identify patterns and relationships within the data. Common clustering algorithms include k-means, hierarchical clustering, and density-based clustering. In health care, clustering is useful for identifying subgroups within a population, understanding patient similarities and differences, reducing data dimensions, and supporting personalized medicine. For instance, clustering algorithms can be used to identify subgroups of patients with similar disease progression, which can aid in developing targeted treatment plans.

Survival models are another class of statistical models that are used to analyze time-to-event data in healthcare and radiology. The goal of these models is to estimate the probability of an event occurring as a function of time, given the covariates. The event of interest can be death, failure, hospitalization, or any other outcome that occurs over a period of time. The overwhelmingly most common survival model is the Cox proportional hazards model, but other forms also exist such as accelerated failure time models, and Aalen's additive hazard models. These models are useful in healthcare for predicting the risk of events, analyzing the effect of different treatments or interventions on survival outcomes, and making personalized recommendations for diagnosis and treatment.

The final class of models we will mention are of course artificial neural networks and deep learning approaches. Crucially, they are flexible enough that they can be applied to virtually any task and use any data modality depending on how they are constructed, but we will not describe them in detail here. Surprisingly, they are not used as much in health care and radiology applications as one might suspect, primarily due to their relative propensity to overfit in combination with the prevailing small dataset sizes.

A quick search on Google Scholar for *"[model name]" + radiology* gives 470 k hits for logistic regression, 286 k for linear regression, 116 k for neural networks (91.7 k for deep learning), 92.8 k for Cox proportional hazards, 32.2 k for decision trees, 29.9 k for kNN, 27.1 k for random forests, 23.4 k for LDA, and 20.2 k for naïve Bayes, which should give a rough estimate of their relative usage.

8. Limitations and open questions

One of the main criticisms raised toward ML applications in medicine is the prevailing small sample sizes. In a recent review covering 53 studies of ML for toxicity prediction, the median sample size was just 173 patients (with an average of 357), and ten studies had even fewer than 50 patients. Similarly, according to a recent review of 54 prostate cancer radiomics studies,[38] the largest sample was just 489 patients. This is not surprising given that collecting large samples of high-quality data from patients is time-consuming, expensive, and requires legal and ethical systems in place. There are public datasets available but compared to other areas in ML they are few and far between. More importantly, public datasets are seldom representative of the particular distribution the researchers try to model. For example, the data generated by imaging machines such as MRI scanners vary drastically depending on manufacturer and settings, which means that a model developed for one setting typically performs very poorly on a different setting, potentially even with the exact same scanner model. Moreover, geographical differences in populations can be deceptively adverse, as was the case when AI-powered automatic soap dispensers failed to recognize the hands of black people during the COVID-19 pandemic. Some recent efforts have tried to remedy this, for instance by generating artificial data (perhaps most notably with diffusion models), but such models are least effective in the areas where they are needed the most. This is because they need large amounts of data to be trained, but with such an amount of data available, the need for generating new data is not as great in the first place. At the end of the day, it is important to remember that products need to be developed in the setting they are intended for, which means that it may be more worthwhile to collect and acquire high-quality data than to circumvent the problem with shortcuts.

On a note related to the sample size issue is the problem of comparing models developed by different research groups or organizations. In contrast to many other ML domains, healthcare applications typically lack widespread benchmark datasets (in many ways due to the issues mentioned above) which makes direct comparisons of different studies hopeless. Not only are the testing data from different sets of patients, but they can also be of vastly different sizes and have drastically different class distributions. Moreover, different studies do not necessarily report the same performance metrics, and there are active debates about which metrics are most suitable for clinical applications. As is well known, most classification metrics are not invariant to differences in class distributions, so the performance reported in a particular data set can be misleading if one does not pay attention to the details. As an example, consider a simple classifier that classifies all samples into the majority class: in an even split of 50 patients in class A and

50 patients in class B, the classifier will have an accuracy of 50%, but in a split of 98/2, the classifier will have an accuracy of 98% even though the classifier is worthless in practice. In other words, the performance alone is not enough to accurately determine the quality of a classifier. As a consequence, medical researchers are often forced to implement all the different models should they wish to properly compare them, which is neither easy nor effective.

The lack of standardization for reporting results in healthcare research adds a level of ambiguity when evaluating studies, but an even more dominant problem is the lack of methodological standardization. This issue comes into play at both a clinical level and a study design level. At a clinical level, different institutions may have different procedures for collecting information and treating patients, which results in different data distributions and different effects on the patients. An example of this is the different scanner settings. In fact, various settings might even change within a single institution since doctors may need to change the parameters, for example, specific acquisition parameters may be required to emphasize some features of the lesion of interest (e.g., vascular pattern). Arguably, there is no tractable solution to this, but it nevertheless adds a dimension of variability that needs to be accounted for in studies and products. At the study design level, multiple facets have the potential to be standardized, perhaps most notably the training and validation procedures of the ML models. As in other areas of ML, it is critical to employ a rigorous validation procedure that does not leak information from the target variable into the training process, such as proper cross-validation (or nested cross-validation if model parameters are tuned) withheld-out test sets. However, one problem is that different dataset sizes may call for different procedures, and there is no silver bullet that works for all scenarios when it comes to validation. Other study design aspects that could benefit from standardization are things like data collection and consent.

As with other areas of ML and data science, there is also an ever-present worry about overfitting the models. While this can be ameliorated by proper validation on larger datasets, the issue is poignant enough to warrant a separate discussion. If a model is overfit, it may provide misleading results, leading to incorrect diagnoses, treatments, and patient care, and it is therefore critical that the issue is taken seriously. A strongly related problem is the curse of dimensionality, which refers to the phenomenon in which the number of features or dimensions in a dataset increases, causing the amount of data required to accurately model the data to increase exponentially. This presents a challenge in healthcare research where high-dimensional data is commonly generated, such as genomics or imaging data. This curse results in models that are highly complex and very likely to overfit the data, leading to poor generalization and inaccurate predictions when applied to new data.

The small datasets in healthcare research exacerbate the problems associated with the curse of dimensionality and overfitting since there is limited information available to model the underlying relationships in the data, making it more challenging to develop accurate and generalizable models. At the same time, small datasets are more prone to overfitting, as even small variations in the data can have a significant impact on the model's predictions. This can result in models that perform well on the training data but poorly on independent validation data. To mitigate these issues, healthcare models can benefit from ensemble methods, transfer learning, or augmentation of the data through synthetic data generation to increase the size of the dataset and improve model performance. As always, it is also essential to use appropriate validation techniques, such as cross-validation, to evaluate the performance of a model on independent data. To overcome the curse of dimensionality, feature selection, and dimensionality reduction techniques can be applied, such as principal component analysis or feature importance ranking, which can select the most relevant and informative features and reduce the number of dimensions in the data.

References

1. Sung H, Ferlay J, Siegel RL, et al. Global cancer statistics 2020: GLOBOCAN estimates of incidence and mortality worldwide for 36 cancers in 185 countries. *CA Cancer J Clin.* 2021;71:209–249.
2. Bower JE. Cancer-related fatigue—mechanisms, risk factors, and treatments. *Nat Rev Clin Oncol.* 2014;11:597–609.
3. Jethanandani A, Lin TA, Volpe S, et al. Exploring applications of radiomics in magnetic resonance imaging of head and neck cancer: a systematic review. *Front Oncol.* 2018;8:131.
4. Wong W, Sundar G, Chee C, et al. Clinical spectrum, treatment and outcomes of uveal melanoma in a tertiary centre. *Singapore Med J.* 2019;60:474–478.
5. Samuel AL. Some studies in machine learning using the game of checkers. *IBM J Res Dev.* 1959;3:210–229.
6. Bzdok D, Altman N, Krzywinski M. Statistics versus machine learning. *Nat Methods.* 2018;15:233–234.
7. Bzdok D, Krzywinski M, Altman N. Machine learning: a primer. *Nat Methods.* 2017;14:1119–1120.
8. Pugliese R, Regondi S, Marini R. Machine learning-based approach: global trends, research directions, and regulatory standpoints. *Data Sci Manage.* 2021;4:19–29.
9. Xu D, Tian Y. A comprehensive survey of clustering algorithms. *Ann Data Sci.* 2015;2:165–193.
10. Jarrahi MH, Memariani A, Guha S. The Principles of Data-Centric. AI (DCAI); 2022.
11. Feurer M, Klein A, Eggensperger K, et al. Auto-sklearn: efficient and robust automated machine learning. In: Hutter F, Kotthoff L, Vanschoren J, eds. *Automated Machine Learning.* Cham: Springer International Publishing; 2022:113–134.

12. Li P, Rao X, Blase J, et al. CleanML: a study for evaluating the impact of data cleaning on ML classification tasks. In: *IEEE 37th International Conference on Data Engineering (ICDE), Chania, Greece*. IEEE; 2021:13–24.

13. Krishnan S, Haas D, Franklin MJ, et al. Towards reliable interactive data cleaning: a user survey and recommendations. In: *Proceedings of the Workshop on Human-In-the-Loop Data Analytics, San Francisco, California*, ACM; 2016:1–5.

14. Mathew C, Güntsch A, Obst M, et al. A semi-automated workflow for biodiversity data retrieval, cleaning, and quality control. *Biodiversity Data Journal*. 2014;2:e4221.

15. He X., Zhao K., Chu X. AutoML: a survey of the state-of-the-art. Epub ahead of print 2019. doi:10.48550/ARXIV.1908.00709.

16. Stonebraker M, Ilyas IF. Data integration: the current status and the way forward. *IEEE Data Eng Bull*. 2018;41:3–9.

17. Mazurowski MA. Radiogenomics: what it is and why it is important. *J Am Coll Radiol*. 2015;12:862–866.

18. Aerts HJWL, Velazquez ER, Leijenaar RTH, et al. Decoding tumour phenotype by noninvasive imaging using a quantitative radiomics approach. *Nat Commun*. 2014;5:4006.

19. Nuraini R, Widita R. Tumor control probability (TCP) and normal tissue complication probability (NTCP) with consideration of cell biological effect. *J Phys Conf Ser*. 2019;1245:012092.

20. Allen Li X, Alber M, Deasy JO, et al. The use and QA of biologically related models for treatment planning: short report of the TG-166 of the therapy physics committee of the AAPM: TG-166 report. *Med Phys*. 2012;39:1386–1409.

21. Van Den Bosch L, Van Der Schaaf A, Van Der Laan HP, et al. Comprehensive toxicity risk profiling in radiation therapy for head and neck cancer: a new concept for individually optimised treatment. *Radiother Oncol*. 2021;157:147–154.

22. Scaife JE, Barnett GC, Noble DJ, et al. Exploiting biological and physical determinants of radiotherapy toxicity to individualize treatment. *The British Journal of Radiology*. 2015;88:20150172.

23. Yang D-W, Wang T-M, Zhang J-B, et al. Genome-wide association study identifies genetic susceptibility loci and pathways of radiation-induced acute oral mucositis. *J Transl Med*. 2020;18:224.

24. Isaksson LJ, Pepa M, Zaffaroni M, et al. Machine learning-based models for prediction of toxicity outcomes in radiotherapy. *Front Oncol*. 2020;10:790.

25. Isaksson LJ, Repetto M, Summers PE, et al. High-performance prediction models for prostate cancer radiomics. *Inf Med Unlocked*. 2023;37:101161.

26. Gabryś HS, Buettner F, Sterzing F, et al. Design and selection of machine learning methods using radiomics and dosiomics for normal tissue complication probability modeling of xerostomia. *Front Oncol*. 2018;8:35.

27. Bourbonne V, Da-ano R, Jaouen V, et al. Radiomics analysis of 3D dose distributions to predict toxicity of radiotherapy for lung cancer. *Radiother Oncol*. 2021;155:144–150.

28. Wong AJ, Kanwar A, Mohamed AS, et al. Radiomics in head and neck cancer: from exploration to application. *Transl Cancer Res*. 2016;5:371–382.

29. Field M, Hardcastle N, Jameson M, et al. Machine learning applications in radiation oncology. *Phys Imaging Radiat Oncol*. 2021;19:13–24.

30. Parmar C, Grossmann P, Rietveld D, et al. Radiomic machine-learning classifiers for prognostic biomarkers of head and neck cancer. *Front Oncol*. 2015;5. https://doi.org/10.3389/fonc.2015.00272. Epub ahead of print 3 December.

31. Volpe S, Pepa M, Zaffaroni M, et al. Machine learning for head and neck cancer: a safe bet?—a clinically oriented systematic review for the radiation oncologist. *Front Oncol*. 2021;11:772663.

32. Bryce TJ, Dewhirst MW, Floyd CE, et al. Artificial neural network model of survival in patients treated with irradiation with and without concurrent chemotherapy for advanced carcinoma of the head and neck. *Int J Radiat Oncol Biol Phys*. 1998;41:339–345.

33. Li S, Wang K, Hou Z, et al. Use of radiomics combined with machine learning method in the recurrence patterns after intensity-modulated radiotherapy for nasopharyngeal carcinoma: a preliminary study. *Front Oncol*. 2018;8:648.

34. Shariat SF, Kattan MW, Vickers AJ, et al. Critical review of prostate cancer predictive tools. *Future Oncol*. 2009;5:1555–1584.

35. Olivotto IA, Bajdik CD, Ravdin PM, et al. Population-based validation of the prognostic model ADJUVANT! For early breast cancer. *Journal of Clinical Oncology*. 2005;23:2716–2725.

36. Engelhardt EG, Révész D, Tamminga HJ, et al. Clinical usefulness of tools to support decision-making for palliative treatment of metastatic colorectal cancer: a systematic review. *Clin Colorectal Cancer*. 2018;17:e1–e12.

37. Cheng Q, Roelofs E, Ramaekers BLT, et al. Development and evaluation of an online three-level proton vs photon decision support prototype for head and neck cancer—comparison of dose, toxicity and cost-effectiveness. *Radiother Oncol*. 2016;118:281–285.

38. Ferro M, De Cobelli O, Musi G, et al. Radiomics in prostate cancer: an up-to-date review. *Ther Adv Urol*. 2022;14:175628722211090.

18

Artificial intelligence in neurologic disease

David McEvoy[a], Katherine Zukotynski[b], Sandra E. Black[c],
Vincent Gaudet[d], and David Koff[b]

^aMichael G. DeGroote School of Medicine, McMaster University, Hamilton, ON, Canada ^bDepartment of Radiology, McMaster University, Hamilton, ON, Canada ^cSunnybrook Research Institute and the University of Toronto, Toronto, ON, Canada ^dDepartment of Electrical and Computer Engineering, University of Waterloo, Waterloo, ON, Canada

1. Introduction

Over the past century, medical science has significantly advanced. In addition to a revolution in available pharmaceuticals and medical equipment, recent software developments have led to a proliferation of clinical applications for artificial intelligence (AI). In particular, the application of AI in neurologic disease may enable physicians to solve problems that have long seemed elusive. We start this chapter with a brief background on AI followed by a short overview illustrating the spectrum of AI applications in neurological disease.

2. Artificial intelligence

AI can be divided into two main categories: virtual and physical.[1] Physical AI refers to what we colloquially call robots: tangible, mechanical constructions that perform physical tasks in the real world. We can find physical AI throughout our environment, from assembly lines in the manufacturing industry, to aiding in education for children with special needs, and in some cases assisting in complex medical surgeries. Virtual AI refers primarily to software implementations of machine learning: algorithms capable of processing and analyzing large or complex datasets and making inferences on new data.[1] These algorithms are able to learn from the data they process and update themselves to incorporate newly discovered patterns therein. Machine learning is particularly well-suited to analyzing large and complex data sets.[2] Training of machine learning models includes supervised learning (SL), unsupervised learning (UL), or a combination of these.

SL requires data to be input that has been previously labeled. These data are then used to train an algorithm to recognize those features in the labeled data that are predictive of a known outcome, enabling future analysis of unlabeled input data. For example, we might want to classify patients into one of two categories: normal cognition versus Alzheimer's disease (AD). Input data such as clinical tests or imaging may have features labeled by a physician that could be used to train an algorithm to detect features predictive of normal cognition versus AD. Subsequently, the algorithm could categorize unlabeled patient data into one of these two categories. While these algorithms might not extrapolate pertinent features on their own, they can suggest features that are most predictive of a given outcome. Importantly, SL learns from input data, in other words, requires "supervision."[2] This means mistakes made by the teacher can seriously impact the efficacy of the algorithm. Common SL algorithms include support vector machines (SVM), random forests, a variety of neural network models, and regression.

UL uses unlabeled or raw data as the input. The algorithm then, on its own, analyzes and sorts that data based on shared characteristics. In this model, the same clinical data as above could be used, but the algorithm does not know which data belong to the normal cognition group, and which belong to the AD group. The algorithm attempts to categorize the data according to commonalities, finding unique features and relationships, perhaps previously unknown to a clinician. Ultimately, an expert is needed to make clinical sense of the findings as the machine is only able to find commonalities, not make determinations about what those commonalities mean.[2] Common UL algorithms include K-means clustering or principal component analysis.

Deep learning (DL) refers to a multilayered machine learning approach that may use SL, UL, or a combination of algorithms and typically requires lots of input data (big data). These algorithms can extract features from data that might not have been apparent based on human review of the raw, unlabeled data.[2] DL, including deep neural networks, is modeled on the human brain. These algorithms are well-suited to analyzing complex input data like images, or speech, using a combination of raw and prelabeled data as input. For example, a DL algorithm might compare previously identified imaging features with corresponding clinical features to extrapolate new features. DL requires a high baseline resource investment but may necessitate little human input and provide complex data analysis exceeding human ability.

The performance of a machine learning algorithm can be evaluated using several metrics, where each one is related to the problem at hand: classification accuracy or receiver operating characteristic (ROC) area under the curve (AUC) can be used in classification problems, whereas mean square error can be used for regression problems.[2] Classification accuracy is the proportion of correct predictions given as a percentage: (true positives + true negatives)/all predictions. The AUC considers the ability of the algorithm to predict a true positive versus a true negative, providing information about sensitivity and specificity at various threshold settings. The AUC approach is useful because it is more resistant to errors introduced by skewed data sets. For example, if the data set used to test an algorithm has more patients with a disease than healthy controls, the algorithm might return a falsely high accuracy percentage, and the AUC might be a better measure of algorithm performance.

In the subsequent sections, we provide a brief overview of AI applications in neurological disease. We begin by examining dementia. This will be followed by sections exploring other areas including Parkinson's Disease, epilepsy, multiple sclerosis (MS), and stroke.

3. Dementia

Dementia is characterized by a decline in more than one domain of cognitive function resulting in impairment in the individual's ability to work or perform the so-called instrumental (high-level) activities of daily life (ADLs), such as managing finances, workplace demands, or physical self-care ADLs such as bathing and dressing. With an estimated global prevalence of 7% among individuals over the age of 65,[3] dementia is one of the most common neurological conditions seen in medicine today.

3.1 AI software and data mining

Currently, the diagnosis of dementia is made clinically, based on neurologic assessment, including family history, imaging, and laboratory analysis, although this is now changing and plasma biomarkers are becoming increasingly available as a detection tool. Still today, often, people with suspected dementia are only brought to medical attention late in the course of the disease. AI models can process massive quantities of data routinely obtained by public registries quickly, potentially identifying people at risk despite limited symptoms. High-risk individuals could then be referred for cognitive testing or advanced laboratory analysis/imaging.[2] For example, a UL model developed in 2018 analyzing social data and physical comorbidities—such as hypertension, diabetes, and body mass index, among others—identified individuals at high-risk for dementia with an accuracy of 93.1% and an AUC of 0.91.[4] By comparison, an algorithm that included Mini-Mental Status Examination (MMSE) scores and a clinical assessment of cognitive function had AUC of 0.92.[5] Another algorithm including MMSE scores, Verbal Fluency Test scores, the Clinical Dementia Rating (CDR), and the Ascertaining Dementia tool (AD8) as well as gender, age, and level of education to classify patients as cognitively normal, mild cognitive impairment (MCI), or AD had accuracy of 96.8%, sensitivity of 0.98 and specificity of 0.96.[6] Of note, the MMSE is a 30-item questionnaire which assesses complex attention, learning, memory, language, and orientation to person, place, and time. The verbal fluency test asks patients to generate as many words as possible according to a specific parameter in a period of time, usually a minute. This might include using a starting letter (i.e., list as many words as you can which begin with the letter S) or a semantic category (i.e., list as many animals as you can). The CDR is a 90-min clinical interview. The AD8 is a tool that utilizes data obtained from a family member or caregiver regarding cognition and activities of daily living. These tests can help assess cognition;

however, no one test alone provides the diagnosis and each test has limitations. For example, cultural bias and level of education can distort MMSE and verbal fluency test scores, the CDR relies on the subjective opinion of a patient and care partner and includes some specifically probing a patient's recollection of recent events to test episodic memory of the patient based on prior information obtained from the care partner, and the accuracy of the AD8 relies on a caregiver's testimony.[6] Ultimately, AI algorithms that incorporate multiple sources of data often have slightly improved performance compared with those that use limited data as input.

The digitization of a patient's health history with the electronic medical record (EMR) has created a wealth of data for machine learning. Currently, there are electronic profiles for millions of people. The International Classification of Diseases (ICD) system assigns a numerical code to a specific disease state. Developed by the World Health Organization, the idea was to aid in information sharing and disease categorization. Digital tags, embedded into EMRs, can help to assess health trends across global populations that may have disparate diagnostic or categorization practices. In 2023, Gao et al. used over 11,000 ICD codes in combination with demographic data and polygenic risk scores (PRS) from the AD genetic consortium with an AI algorithm to detect features predictive of AD.[7] Patients were divided for algorithm training into one of two categories based on age, 40+ and 65+, and labeled as healthy control versus AD. The most predictive features for the 40+ group were age, PRS, household income, and primary hypertension. Top features for the 65+ group were age, PRS, household income, and body mass index. ICD codes ranked among the most predictive included N390: urinary tract infection, E119: type-2 diabetes without complications, F32: depressive episode, R55: syncope and collapse, and R074: chest pain unspecified. While AI may be helpful to identify features predictive of dementia, underlying disease pathology is often multifactorial.

A paper by Alexander et al. studied a clustering algorithm to identify shared characteristics in AD patients.[8] The study utilized anonymized data from the Clinical Practice Research Datalink, a database containing clinical data collected from general practices in the UK and 3 categories of variables by which to cluster patients: symptoms of AD, comorbid conditions, and social demographic features. To determine symptoms and comorbid conditions, the researchers conducted a systematic literature review. Length of time on cholinesterase inhibitors, time from diagnosis to assisted living, annual MMSE scores, degree of healthcare utilization, and mortality provided information on disease severity, rate of progression, and mortality for each patient. Four AI algorithms were used: K-means, Kernel K-means, affinity propagation, and latent class analysis. The results for each method were evaluated to determine how distinct were clusters, how often clusters recurred, the concordance of results, and potential clinical utility. Among other results, the researchers found a hypertension cluster across all clustering methods, cerebrovascular disease implicated by 3 of 4 methods, and mental health/smoking implicated in early-onset disease by 3 of 4 methods. Outcome analysis suggested rate of disease progression was faster among certain clusters, such as those with early-onset disease. Similar findings have been identified by other machine learning models such as the one studied by Xu et al.[9] and Landi et al.[10] While more research is needed, it seems possible AI can identify and expand our understanding of at-risk patients.

3.2 Robotic AI

The use of robots to aid in dementia care is also an area of active research. Social robots are in essence machines designed to interact with humans in a meaningful way. They may be broadly placed into one of three categories: socially assistive robots, pet robots, or telepresence robots.[11] Socially assistive robots can perform a variety of functions to assist users in completing their activities of daily living.[12] Pet robots may physically resemble animals and are designed to mimic their emotional responses. These devices can serve as a nonliving pet replacement providing the user with emotional and psychological comfort.[11] Telepresence robots are intended to facilitate connections between two humans and usually feature a social networking video interface mounted on a robotic base.[11] These machines can enhance a feeling of connection for individuals with mobility issues.

The robotic seal PARO is one of the most ubiquitous and well-studied social robots.[13] Approved by the FDA and utilized internationally in healthcare facilities since 2003, PARO is designed to look like a baby harp seal. As this is an animal unfamiliar to most individuals, PARO has the advantage of being approached by individuals free of preconceptions or expectations. It contains software for behavior and voice recognition and is able to respond to light, touch, temperature, and posture. Programmed to emulate animal behavior, PARO's AI allows it to develop a unique "character" over time-based on its experiences. The device is intended to lower stress, reduce anxiety, and improve depression. A study by Peterson et al. investigated PARO's effectiveness in dementia care.[13] Assessment metrics included the Rating for Anxiety in Dementia (RAID), the Cornell Scale for Depression in Dementia (CSDD), pulse rate, pulse oximetry, galvanic skin response (GSR), and medication utilization. The treatment group received three 20-min interactive sessions with PARO per week while the control group received the standard of care: 20-min sessions which included music, physical activity, and mental stimulation. Study participants were volunteers aged 65 years or older with a previous physician diagnosis of mild to moderate dementia. After 3 months, treatment subjects relative to control subjects showed increases in pulse oximetry and GSR as well as decreases in pulse rate, pain, and behavior medication utilization, and improved scores on the RAID and CCSD assessments. These results suggest robots may help reduce anxiety, depression, and pain in patients with dementia. Several similar studies in the literature suggest social robotics are promising; the true efficacy of current technologies in dementia care requires further study.

3.3 Additional AI applications

Machine learning has the potential to detect patients with AD and commonly uses input data such as amyloid-beta42 or tau levels in cerebral spinal fluid, MRI, and amyloid brain PET.[14] SL classification algorithms are among the most ubiquitous including input image processing, feature detection, and classification.[15] SL approaches based on random forests have been used to classify amyloid brain PET as positive or negative for amyloid deposition,[16] or to identify brain regions associated with MoCA scores.[17] Similarly, UL approaches based on K-means clustering have been used to classify amyloid brain PET.[18] Transfer learning is a concept whereby algorithms trained on one dataset can be adapted to another and has shown promising results in AD.[15,19–21] While imaging datasets typically include MRI and PET, retinal imaging has also shown good results and may, one day, provide an inexpensive tool for detecting patients with AD.[22,23]

A study by Kim et al. highlights the utility of the FreeSurfer software in classifying different subtypes of dementia based on MRI data.[24] Utilizing T1-weighted MR brain imaging, researchers trained a classifier with a supervised approach to differentiate cognitively normal subjects from those with either Alzheimer's dementia or one of three clinical subtypes of frontotemporal dementia (FTD). The FreeSurfer software performed automated modeling and measuring of each subject's cortical thickness from the MR images. Following analysis of this data, the ML classifier was able to distinguish between cognitively normal subjects and those with either AD or FTD with an accuracy of 86.1%, AD vs. FTD with an accuracy of 90.8%, behavioral variant FTD vs. nonfluent variant primary progressive aphasia (nfvPPA) with an accuracy of 86.9%, and nfvPPA vs. semantic variant PPA with an accuracy of 92.1%. In Zhao et al., volumetric measurement of cognitively relevant areas and patterns of atrophy served as the input for a SVM model.[25] This model was able to achieve a high accuracy of greater than 90% in classifying MCI/subjective cognitive decline (SCD) vs normal control. The model was, however, limited in its ability to distinguish between MCI and SCD, achieving an accuracy of less than 63% for this task.

Wang et al. utilized T1-weighted structural and diffusion MR brain images combined with morphometry and connectomics to create an ML model capable of classifying AD vs. cognitively normal subjects with an accuracy of 97%.[26] The work of Nguyen et al. demonstrates that rs-fMRI may also play a significant role in the future of dementia diagnosis.[27] Their study utilizes a SVM to analyze data extracted from rs-fMRI related to voxel changes in regional coherence and functional connectivity during the resting state. Maximum classification accuracy achieved by their model was 98.86% in the differentiation of AD/MCI from cognitively normal subjects. Finally, a novel approach from Yamashita et al. introduced a new image descriptor, the Residual Centre of Mass (RCM), and compared its utility to other imaging hallmarks typically used in ML dementia research.[28] The RCM uses image moments to highlight brain boundaries. In the classification of normal subjects vs. those with AD, the SVM using RCM achieved an accuracy of 95.1% when using FDG-PET scans and 90.3% when using MRI. Other types of input data can potentially be derived from smartphones or watches. Currently, smartphone ownership is at 85% in the United States[29] and 67% globally.[30] The Apple Watch has health monitoring capabilities which can be set up to record ECGs and detect the presence of arrhythmia such as atrial fibrillation. While this feature only has a sensitivity of 43% (Series 4), it has a specificity of 100%.[31] Research by Akl et al.[32] suggested movement patterns of older individuals in their homes could be helpful to assess cognitive status. Building upon research suggesting walking speed and variability could distinguish patients with MCI from those with normal cognition,[33–35] this study used motion sensors in the home.[32] Choosing subjects who lived alone, the sensors recorded the subjects' walking speeds in their home over 3 years. Measures associated with weekly walking speed and level of activity were used and participants were assessed annually for cognitive impairment. The researchers found the trajectory of walking was the most effective tool for distinguishing cognitively normal from MCI patients. Including parameters such as the coefficient of the variation of walking speed, the coefficient of the variation of morning and evening walking speeds, participant age, and gender, their AI algorithm could classify participants as cognitively normal or MCI with AUC of 0.97. This was nice because individuals were assessed in their own homes, going about daily routines. Gwak et al.[36] also used walking speed to distinguish MCI from cognitively normal patients.

However, rather than using motion sensors planted around the homes of study participants, this study used a smartwatch (the Samsung Gear Live), a pulse oximeter, and a smartphone to record data ultimately yielding a classification accuracy of 86%. While further research is needed, these results provide a glimpse of our potential future regarding dementia assessment.

The process of handwriting is complex, requiring both cognitive and motor skills to be executed correctly.[37] It is perhaps because of this that changes in handwriting may serve as an indication of cognitive decline. Building on research that established certain handwriting features as biomarkers for cognitive dysfunction,[38,39] Angelillo et al.[37] developed an algorithm to detect cognitive impairment. Their algorithm used an adapted digital version of the Attentional Matrices Test (AMT). Features determined to have the most relevance to cognitive status classification included the total time to complete the test, among others. The accuracy of the algorithms was 84%. Ashraf et al.[40] analyzed subjects' handwashing behavior using an overhead video camera. Recruiting seniors from a long-term care facility, participants in the study were instructed to wash their hands by a researcher who was present in the room. Data were recorded over a period of three months, resulting in 1309 complete video recordings. Using various algorithms, the accuracy for cognitive classification was approximately 70%. The ability to speak is also linked with cognitive status. Studies suggest the neuropathology of AD begins decades prior to the onset of clinical symptoms.[41] Language deficits such as word retrieval difficulty may be associated with dementia.[42] A study by Toth et al. tasked patients with MCI and healthy controls to recall the content of 2 short black-and-white films. Their spontaneous speech was recorded, and acoustic parameters such as speech tempo, length, and number of pauses, among others were extracted using both manual and automated software. Their classification model for distinguishing MCI from healthy cognition had accuracy of 75%.[43] Another study, Balagopalan et al.[44] focused on transcribed speech with 83% classification accuracy. Of course, features related to speech such as syntax, semantics, and cadence, among others vary from one language to another and results from one study may not generalize well when applied to another language. Also, speech is often analyzed in the context of a clinical test and not in the context of everyday conversation, this can be problematic in cases of more advanced cognitive decline. Ultimately, there are a host of different types of data input and algorithms that can be used to detect, diagnose, and assist in the care of dementia patients.

4. Parkinson's disease

It has been estimated that Parkinson's disease (PD) is among the fastest-growing neurological diseases in the world.[45] Affecting 4 million individuals worldwide, PD has an estimated prevalence of 0.3% in industrialized nations.[45] In addition to motor symptoms which include resting tremor, bradykinesia, postural instability, and rigidity, PD is characterized by non-motor symptoms such as cognitive decline, depression, anxiety, and sleep disturbances.[45] Studies have shown that comorbid dementia and PD has a prevalence as high as 30–40%.[45] There is no known pharmacological intervention that can stop the progression of the disease.[45] Diagnosis is clinical and is assessed primarily through the evaluation of motor dysfunction. Because motor symptoms tend to appear years after disease onset, diagnosis is often delayed.[45] Lack of an early diagnostic method leads to limit in eligible patients for clinical trials, potentially delaying drug discovery and advances in treatment. Identification of biomarkers that precede the onset of motor symptoms could significantly help PD research.

Research by Yang et al.[46] developed an AI model to detect the presence of PD by utilizing data on subjects' nocturnal breathing patterns. The relationship between disordered breathing and PD is a long-established one, with several studies showing that PD leads to degeneration of areas in the brainstem that regulate breathing.[47] Weakness in respiratory muscle function and sleep breathing disorders are symptoms that often precede motor dysfunction by several years.[48,49] Working with the hypothesis that nocturnal dyspnea may be an early diagnostic biomarker, researchers set out to create an AI model that could interpret and classify subjects according to observed trends.

A large and diverse dataset was utilized by combining data from several sources including the Mayo clinic, Massachusetts General Hospital sleep lab, clinical trials sponsored by the Michael J. Fox Foundation, the National Institutes of Health Udall Centre, and an observational study conducted by the Massachusetts Institute of Technology. The combined dataset includes 11,964 nights with over 120,000 h of nocturnal breathing signals from 757 Parkinson's disease subjects and 6914 control subjects.[46] Included data were obtained via two methods and separated into two datasets accordingly. The first dataset consists of subjects whose nocturnal breathing was analyzed via polysomnography. This technique requires the subject to wear a breathing belt around their abdomen or chest to physically measure nocturnal breathing patterns. The second dataset made use of a completely noninvasive radio device that utilizes a sensor deployed in the subject's bedroom to analyze radio reflections from the environment and thereby extract the subject's breathing signal.

Having a diverse and large dataset comprised of information from multiple institutions allowed researchers to uniquely assess their model's generalizability. They systematically examined cross-institution prediction performance by training the model on data from every institution except one and then using the excluded data for classification testing. This process was repeated for each institution and the best results were achieved using the data acquired by the radio device. In the classification task of identifying PD vs non-PD, the model achieved an AUC of 0.892 for the Michael J. Fox Foundation data, 0.884 for the NIH set, 0.974 for the MGH set, and 0.916 for the MIT set. These results show that the model can accurately identify the presence of PD for types of data it never encountered during training. This is significant because it reveals that performance was not due to leveraging institution-related information or due to misattribution of institution-related information to the disease.[46]

The Movement Disorder Society's Unified Parkinson's Disease Rating Scale, or the MDS-UPDRS, is the most used method for evaluating disease severity in PD. It requires patients to present in the clinic to be assessed by trained clinicians who perform an evaluation using quasi-subjective criteria. As such, this represents a fairly high-effort, resource-intensive assessment. Researchers attempted to determine if their sleep analysis AI model could provide an alternative autonomous assessment of disease severity. Using the radio device dataset for patients with available MDS-UPDRS scores, the model was trained on 25 PD subjects with 1263 nights' worth of data and 28 control subjects with 1338 nights' worth of data. The model achieved a strong correlation with the subjects' MDS-UPDRS scores, yielding an r-value of 0.94. These promising results reveal that such a model may be useful as a less burdensome, resource-intensive means of assessing disease severity in PD.

Finally, researchers tested whether their model could identify the presence of PD before it had been formally diagnosed by a clinician. To this end, the MrOS dataset was utilized which contains breathing data obtained from subjects on two separate visits occurring 6 years apart. A prodromal Parkinson's group was established by selecting subjects who did not have a diagnosis on their first visit but did have a diagnosis by the time of their second visit ($n = 12$). A control group was constructed using subjects who did not have a PD diagnosis, matching for gender and age nearly 40 subjects for everyone subject in the prodromal group ($n = 476$). Testing the model on data from the first visit, when neither group had a diagnosis of PD, the model identified 75% of the members of the prodromal group as having PD.

The use of nocturnal breathing patterns as a biomarker of PD has the potential to change diagnostics, the assessment of disease severity, and may contribute to the development of an effective early screening tool. The model is notable not only for its identification of a new potential biomarker, but also for its ability to diagnose, stage, and predict PD in an autonomous, non-invasive manner. With further refinement, it may be able to reduce diagnostic costs, eliminate clinical subjectivity, provide inexpensive and noninvasive home monitoring for high-risk or already diagnosed patients, and reduce the length and cost of clinical trials. Because PD progresses slowly, and clinical assessments of disease progression are imprecise, trials often take many years to effectively assess the progression of PD.[45] The model developed by Yang et al. may be able to significantly reduce the time required to observe disease progression in clinical trials. This would result in the rapid advancement of drug development and treatment efficacy, improving the lives of millions of patients currently suffering from PD. Also, interesting REM sleep disorder may precede the onset of PD and combining detection of this as well as nocturnal breathing patterns may prove to be an interesting area of future research.

5. Epilepsy

Affecting 70 million people worldwide, epilepsy represents a symptom complex with multiple risk factors, rather than a disease with a singular expression and etiology.[50] Its hallmark feature is a predisposition to unprovoked seizures. A precise diagnosis requires a thorough investigation of the nature of the seizures, level of consciousness during seizure activity, and assessment for the underlying causes and comorbidities that may be contributing to the condition.[50] ECGs are used to rule out cardiogenic causes and imaging, principally MRI, is used to assess for underlying structural abnormalities. The diagnosis of epilepsy, however, relies primarily on clinical findings and electroencephalography, or EEG.[50] A non-invasive means to measure the electrical activity of the brain, EEG is able to detect interictal epileptiform discharges (EDs). These "spikes" in electrical activity represent important biomarkers of epilepsy and can be detected on EEG in-between seizure events. Technological advancements and improvements in patient care have led to increased use of EEG, and while this has resulted in improved diagnostics and monitoring of the condition, it has also substantially increased the demand placed on clinicians to provide accurate and timely interpretation.[51] Additionally, research has shown that interrater agreement among experts on the identification of epileptiform discharges is low.[51] These observations make it clear that a reliable, standardized, automated means of interpreting EEGs could substantially improve the diagnostics of epilepsy and aid clinicians in handling the increasing burden of interpretation.

Furbass et al.[51] developed a machine learning algorithm to automatically detect epileptiform discharges on EEG. Using a semi-supervised approach, researchers used both labeled EEGs, for which experts had identified the presence of EDs, and unlabelled EEGs to train their model. A preliminary model named DeepSpike was trained on labeled data alone. It was then exposed to unlabelled long-term EEGs—greater than 36 h—taken from patients without epilepsy. Synthetic EEG samples were also used for training which included digitized drawings of artificial spike waveforms taken from EEG handbooks. The inclusion of synthetic EEG data allowed researchers to train their model with not just one particular spike variant of dipole and spatial orientation, as would be seen on an authentic EEG, but with every conceivable variant. This diversity of spike orientation greatly increases the model's generalizability.

Validation was performed using a testing set consisting of 100 EEG samples taken from 100 patients. Accuracy was assessed by examining the model's ability to detect which EEGs had at least one ED as well as its ability to detect each individual ED. The sensitivity of the algorithm in detecting which EEGs had an ED event was 88.89%, with a specificity of 69.57% and an overall accuracy of 80.00%. At the level of individual EDs, the algorithm achieved a sensitivity of 81.63%, a specificity of 46.38%, and an overall accuracy of 67.07%. The high sensitivities achieved by the model reveal that machine-learning approaches can aid clinicians in expediting the evaluation of studies. However, at this point in the technology's development, expert supervision is still required for confirming clusters of measured EDs and for describing clinical correlates. With some refinement, machine learning approaches have the potential to automate EEG interpretation, which would drastically alter the landscape of epilepsy screening and diagnosis.

6. Multiple sclerosis

MS is a degenerative autoimmune disease of the central nervous system that affects 140 people for every 100,000 in North America.[52] The prevalence of MS is 2–3 times higher in women than in men.[52] Onset typically occurs in younger adults, between the ages of 20 and 40, with clinical features including optic neuritis, neuropathic pain, and cerebellar dysfunction characterized by gait abnormalities, scanning speech, nystagmus, and intention tremor.[52] Demyelination and axonal loss occur even in the early stages of the disease and despite advancements in treatment, MS patients have a shorter expected lifespan by 10 years compared to the average individual.[52]

MRI has become an indispensable tool in the diagnosis and monitoring of MS. The administration of gadolinium contrast allows for improved visualization of acute lesions that appear hyper-attenuated on post-gadolinium T1-weighted images. These acute lesions represent areas of blood–brain barrier disruption and are useful indicators of acute disease activity. As such, T1wGd images are highly useful in monitoring the progression and activity of MS and in guiding therapeutic intervention.[53]

Recent studies have shown that gadolinium deposits remain in brain tissue long after Gd-enhanced imaging is performed.[54] A heavy metal, gadolinium is toxic to humans but is administered in chelated form for imaging procedures to prevent toxicity. Despite a lack of evidence that the presence of gadolinium deposits secondary to contrast injection is harmful to humans, there has been a push to reassess the need for contrast-indicated studies due to the uncertainty surrounding their long-term effects. Zhang et al.[53] studied an imaging technique that utilizes an ML algorithm to semi-autonomously identify acute MS lesions without using Gd contrast. Their approach makes use of quantitative susceptibility mapping (QSM), an advanced MRI technique that allows for the visualization of the magnetic susceptibility of certain substances, such as iron and myelin.[53] Histological studies have shown that myelin is broken down and digested by macrophages in active MS lesions with iron increasing in concentration due to persistent microglial activation. Gd-enhancing MS lesions therefore tend to initially appear isointense or slightly hyperintense on QSM, and as they transition from Gd-enhancing to non-enhancing over time their susceptibility values increase, leading to a more hyperintense appearance on QSM.[53] The basis of the study by Zhang et al. is that QSM lesion values can predict lesion enhancement status, thereby eliminating the need for visual inspection and subsequently Gd use.

Thirty-three patients were included in this retrospective analysis study.[53] All had a diagnosis of MS, at least 2 MRI scans performed within a 3-year period, and at least one Gd-enhancing lesion present on their second scan which was not present on their first. T2-weighted FLAIR images for each subject were first normalized for intensity, and subtraction was then applied. An in-house statistical detection of changes (SDC) algorithm was applied to each patient's T2w images to autonomously detect any differences present between the first and the second scan. This algorithm can identify new lesions on the second scan that were not present on the first by analyzing changes in voxel signal intensity according to the currently accepted minimum MS lesion size requirement of 3 mm. The algorithm placed a color-coded box around each of the new lesions to aid in visual recognition by the radiologists who would participate in the next phase of the study.

After T2w normalization and analysis by the SDC algorithm, two experienced radiologists reviewed T1w and T1wGd images using standard side-by-side comparison in order to identify all new enhancing lesions present on the second scan of each patient. T2w images were not used during this first phase of evaluation but once all discrepancies had been resolved, the SDC analyzed T2w images with color-coded boxes included. Both radiologists repeated their evaluation using T2w SDC, T1w, and T1wGd images to attempt to identify both the presence of any new lesions and their enhancement status. Following a 4-week washout period instituted to eliminate recall bias, radiologists repeated their assessment using only T2w SDC images and QSM analysis to predict the presence and enhancement status of new lesions, this time blinded to the gadolinium-enhanced T1w scans.

Initially using only the T1w and T1wGd scans, radiologists identified 49 new enhancing lesions among the 33 patients included in the study. The addition of the T2w SDC scans led to the identification of 54 new enhancing lesions: this included five enhancing lesions that were initially missed by radiologists using only the standard side-by-side comparison of T1w and T1wGd images. This first phase assessment was used as the standard against which the accuracy of the QSM analysis was measured. T2w SDC and QSM analysis yielded an overall sensitivity of 90.7% and specificity of 85.6% in the prediction of new enhancing lesions and an AUC of 0.93 in the discrimination between enhancing and non-enhancing lesions when lesions were $15\,mm^3$ or larger. These results demonstrate that machine learning analysis of T2w subtraction images is a highly sensitive technique for the detection of new enhancing MS lesions and outperforms conventional analysis using T1w and T1wGd side-by-side comparison. Additionally, these results show that the T2w SDC and QSM analysis represents an accurate and reliable method for assessing the presence of new MS lesions without the need for Gd-enhanced imaging. This potential means of monitoring disease progression in MS patients would eliminate the need for frequent and repeated contrast injection and this new contrast-free monitoring technique would reduce imaging costs, mitigate possible risk by reducing the accumulation of gadolinium deposits in the brain, and provide effective monitoring for patients with an allergic or nephrotic contraindication to contrast administration. The limitations of small sample size, only two diagnosing radiologists, and a brief 4-week period to prevent recall bias notwithstanding, further research into QSM may enable future effective monitoring of MS using semi-autonomous, contrast-free imaging.

7. Stroke

Stroke is the leading cause of hospitalization in neurologic disease, a significant contributor to the development of disability, and the fifth leading cause of death in the United States.[55] Incidence has declined in recent years due primarily to improvements in treatments for hypertension, diabetes mellitus, hyperlipidemia, and cardiac arrhythmias, as well as a reduction in cigarette use. As age is the most significant demographic risk factor, the lifetime risk of stroke continues to increase due to the extension of the average expected lifespan.

In ischemic stroke, vessel occlusion leads to inadequate blood supply of cerebral tissue. This results initially in a reversible loss of tissue function but if occlusion persists long enough can progress to infarction and deterioration of neurons and supportive structures. Cerebral tissue ischemia results in a loss of electrical function, which triggers a chain reaction characterized by membrane dysfunction, calcium influx, generation of reactive oxygen species, and finally destruction of cell membranes and cell lysis. Because of the acute nature of stroke and the time-dependent progression from reversible to irreversible loss of tissue function, the time taken to diagnose and intervene largely determines the resultant extent of damage. As such, clinicians and researchers are continually looking for new methods to expedite these processes and the autonomous nature of AI makes it well-suited to these purposes.

Treatment of acute ischemic stroke focuses on achieving timely reperfusion of tissue at risk for infarction. The elapsed time from symptom onset or from the time the patient was last observed at baseline is the primary factor used to guide decisions around which reperfusion therapy is most appropriate. IV-administered tissue-plasminogen activator (tPA) is indicated in patients who present within 3h of symptom onset or in select patients who present within 4.5h.[55] All patients presenting within 6h and select patients presenting within 24h are candidates for endovascular thrombectomy.[55] Selecting which patients qualify for endovascular thrombectomy beyond the typical 6-h window relies on either computed tomography perfusion (CTP) imaging or dynamic susceptibility contrast (DSC) perfusion MRI. While CTP is widely available and relatively quick to perform, it subjects patients to a high dose of ionizing radiation as it requires continuous exposure during the passage of iodinated contrast medium.[56] DSC perfusion MRI is the preferred imaging method used to make determinations for thrombectomy beyond the 6-h window, but it requires the administration of gadolinium contrast. Because gadolinium is contraindicated in patients with renal impairment, and most patients presenting with ischemic stroke have vascular risk factors, extra steps and time are needed to ensure this modality can be performed safely.

In a study from 2019, Wang et al.[56] analyzed the effectiveness of a DL algorithm in selecting patients for thrombectomy using 3-dimensional pseudo-continuous arterial spin labeling (pCASL). Arterial spin labeling can provide information about cerebral blood flow without requiring contrast administration. This comes with the obvious advantage of expediting and broadening the inclusion process, allowing patients with renal impairment and other at-risk populations like children and pregnant women to be assessed for reperfusion thrombectomy. Determining the precise delineation of ischemic tissue using arterial spin labeling is challenging however due to the low signal-to-noise ratio of this modality.

A DL model was trained using a supervised approach. DSC perfusion MRI data was utilized along with pCASL to teach the neural network to recognize ischemic tissue in the pCASL scans. 167 image sets from 137 patients were used for training and 10-fold cross-validation was employed. The Highres3Dnet network, a form of convolutional neural network that deals with 3D inputs, was then tested on a cohort of 12 pCASL images from 12 patients. The algorithm was able to identify DSC-defined hypoperfusion regions with a voxel-wise AUC of 0.958. Retrospective eligibility for thrombectomy treatment was determined using the criteria of perfusion/diffusion mismatch as defined by the DEFUSE 3 trial. The algorithm achieved an accuracy of 92% with a sensitivity of 0.89 and a specificity of 0.95 in its assessment of which patients were eligible for endovascular thrombectomy. These results demonstrate that pCASL may have the potential to serve as a diagnostic tool in assessing which patients qualify for endovascular thrombectomy beyond the standard 6-h window, thereby eliminating the need for gadolinium contrast administration. Due to the high risks associated with intracranial hemorrhage and tPA administration, however, higher accuracies than 92% will need to be achieved before such a model will have clinical utility. In this time-sensitive diagnostic domain, the potential of AI to expedite clinical procedures continues to be explored from multiple angles.

The Alberta Stroke Program Early CT Score (ASPECTS) is a qualitative method used to evaluate focal hypoattenuation in early acute stroke. It assesses 10 middle cerebral artery vascular territories looking for hypoattenuation in the cortex and basal ganglia, a reduction in gray and white matter differentiation, and the loss of the "insular ribbon sign," which is loss of the gray-white matter interface in the insular cortex secondary to edema due to ischemic injury. A maximum score of 10 is calculated with one point being subtracted for each region displaying signs of early infarction.[57] Many of the randomized controlled clinical trials that helped to establish endovascular thrombectomy as a standard intervention used an ASPECT score of 6 or greater as an inclusion criterion for patients. This has led to the incorporation of the ASPECT evaluation into most international guidelines surrounding reperfusion thrombectomy. As such, accurate and timely ASPECTS calculation is necessary to facilitate effective reperfusion therapy in the context of acute ischemic stroke.

Two software programs are currently available that are capable of clinically acceptable autonomous calculation of ASPECTS. Maegerlein et al.[57] compared the accuracy of the RAPID ASPECTS software in calculating an ASPECT score using noncontrast CT imaging with that of two experienced neuroradiologists. In the first stage of this study, neuroradiologists conducted a reading of all available imaging on two cohorts of patients ($n = 100$ and $n = 52$) to obtain a baseline consensus. Imaging assessed at this stage included noncontrast CT obtained at initial presentation, perfusion CT, digital subtraction angiography imaging, and follow-up MRI. Discrepancies in ASPECT scores at this stage were resolved through joint review and unanimous decision. In the second stage, following a six-week washout period to eliminate recall bias, the same neuroradiologists independently assessed only the noncontrast CTs obtained at the time of the patient's initial presentation. All information regarding vessel occlusion, time metrics, and other imaging was withheld for this review; the readers were only informed about which hemisphere was affected. In the final stage, the RAPID ASPECTS software generated an automated score using the initial presentation noncontrast CT imaging. Its automated score is generated via a series of operations which include applying a standardized atlas to create an individualized grid corresponding to the 10 ASPECTS regions in each hemisphere, calculating the Hounsfield unit values and other relevant parameters for each region, and classifying each region as either normal or abnormal. A square-rated κ, a statistical measure of interrater reliability, was calculated to quantify the level of agreement between scores from the second and third stages of the study and the consensus scores from stage 1. A predefined table of weights was utilized for this quantification method meaning more significant disagreements are weighed more heavily than minor disagreements.

Neuroradiologists showed mild agreement with the consensus scores, with one achieving a κ of 0.57 and the other a κ of 0.56. The RAPID ASPECTS software achieved substantial agreement with the consensus score attaining an overall κ of 0.9. When taking into consideration the time lapse between when imaging was obtained and symptom onset, the software attained a κ of 0.78 when imaging was obtained 1h or more after symptom onset, and a κ of 0.92 when imaging was obtained 4h or more after symptom onset; the neuroradiologists achieved comparable results only in the four hour or more period (κ = 0.83 and κ = 0.76).

With automated software outperforming experienced radiologists, particularly in the window wherein imaging was obtained 1–4h following symptom onset, the future of acute stroke diagnosis and treatment may look quite different. An automated means of triaging patients for reperfusion therapy would save precious time and might allow patients on the cusp of qualifying for treatment the chance to receive life-changing intervention. Automated software used to assess medical imaging continues to struggle with flexibility, however, and the software studied here is no exception: 32 CT datasets were excluded because they could not be analyzed by the RAPID ASPECTS software. This stands in stark contrast to the three datasets that the human readers deemed to be of unacceptable quality. The software excluded many scans because the field of view was too small and others seemingly due to the presence of artifacts. While these results are extremely impressive, human readers continue to demonstrate more flexibility in their ability to interpret imaging of varying quality, and for AI to attain genuine clinical utility, more technical refinement of this technology is needed.

8. Conclusion

Our discussion has explored some of the most exciting research to emerge in recent years pertaining to the intersection of neurologic disease and AI. We have seen that AI in neurologic disease is not merely conceptual, but in many cases represents a highly effective diagnostic, screening, or treatment tool with practical, working models that in many cases outperform current clinical gold standards. The methods we have explored seem poised to initiate mass automated screening programs, provide personalized diagnoses, ease follow-up burden, and conserve healthcare resources by reducing clinical workload. We have observed throughout that despite the extraordinary promise of machine learning, many of the studies we have reviewed are limited by small sample sizes and poor generalizability. Many of the techniques we have explored seem hindered by expensive or cumbersome technology. AI is often also held back by its lack of transparency—the rationale for decisions made by some AI models is not always clear, sometimes making it difficult to use without further human involvement. The years to come will surely reveal whether the promising models we have discussed can be refined to attain genuine clinical utility. The future of neurologic disease will undoubtedly be shaped by AI to some degree; the precise extent of its influence will be determined by the next generation of researchers and clinicians devoted to advancing the research we have detailed here.

References

1. Hamet P, Tremblay J. Artificial intelligence in medicine. *Metabolism.* 2017;69(S):S36–S40.
2. Graham S, Lee E, Jeste D, et al. Artificial intelligence approaches to predicting and detecting cognitive decline in older adults: a conceptual review. *Psych Res.* 2020;284, 112732.
3. Gale S, Acar D, Daffner K. Dementia. *Am J Med.* 2018;131(10):1161–1169.
4. Langavant L, Bayen E, Bachoud-Levi AC, Yaffe K. Approximating dementia prevalence in population-based surveys of aging worldwide: an unsupervised machine learning approach. *Alzheimers Dement (NY).* 2020;6(1), e12074.
5. Na KS. Prediction of future cognitive impairment among the community elderly: a machine-learning based approach. *Sci Rep.* 2019;9:3335.
6. Lins AJCC, Muniz MTC, Garcia ANM, Gomes AV, Cabral RM, Bastos-Filho CJA. Using artificial neural networks to select the parameters for the prognostic of mild cognitive impairment and dementia in elderly individuals. *Comput Methods Programs Biomed.* 2017;152:93–104.
7. Gao XR, Chiariglione M, Qin K, et al. Explainable machine learning aggregates polygenic risk scores and electronic health records for Alzheimer's disease prediction. *Sci Rep.* 2023;13(1):450.
8. Alexander N, Alexander DC, Barkhof F, Denaxas S. Identifying and evaluating clinical subtypes of Alzheimer's disease in care electronic health records using unsupervised machine learning. *BMC Med Inform Decis Mak.* 2021;21(1):343.
9. Xu J, Wang F, Xu Z, et al. Data-driven discovery of probable Alzheimer's disease and related dementia subphenotypes using electronic health records. *Learn Health Syst.* 2020;4(4), e10246.
10. Landi I, Glicksberg BS, Lee H-C, et al. Deep representation learning of electronic health records to unlock patient stratification at scale. *NPJ Digit Med.* 2020;17(3):96.
11. Koh WQ, Felding SA, Budak KB, et al. Barriers and facilitators to the implementation of social robots for older adults and people with dementia: a scoping review. *BMC Geriatr.* 2021;21:351.
12. Yu C, Sommerlad A, Sakure L, Livingston G. Socially assistive robots for people with dementia: systematic review and meta-analysis of feasibility, acceptability and the effect on cognition, neuropsychiatric symptoms and quality of life. *Ageing Res Rev.* 2022;78, 101633.
13. Petersen S, Houston S, Qin H, Tague C, Studley J. The utilization of robotic pets in dementia care. *J Alzheimers Dis.* 2017;55(2):569–574.
14. Atri A. The Alzheimer's disease clinical Spectrum: diagnosis and management. *Med Clin North Am.* 2019;103(2):263–293.
15. Richardson A, Robbins C, Wisely C, Henao R, Grewal D, Fekrat S. Artificial intelligence in dementia. *Curr Opin Ophthalmol.* 2022;33(5):425–431.
16. Zukotynski K, Gaudet V, Kuo P, et al. The use of random forests to classify amyloid brain PET. *Clin Nucl Med.* 2019;44(10):784–788.
17. Zukotynski K, Gaudet V, Kuo P, et al. The use of random forests to identify brain regions on amyloid and FDG PET associated with MoCA score. *Clin Nucl Med.* 2020;45(6):427–433.

18. Zukotynski K, Black SE, Kuo P, et al. Exploratory assessment of K-means clustering to classify [18F]Flutemetamol brain PET as positive or negative. *Clin Nucl Med*. 2021;46(8):616–620.

19. Helaly HA, Badawy M, Haikal AY. Deep learning approach for early detection of Alzheimer's disease. *Cogn Comput*. 2022;14:1711–1727.

20. Agarwal D, Marques G, de la Torre-Díez I, Franco Martin MA, García Zapiraín B, Martín RF. Transfer learning for Alzheimer's disease through neuroimaging biomarkers: a systematic review. *Sensors (Basel)*. 2021;21(21):7259.

21. Koga S, Ikeda A, Dickson DW. Deep learning-based model for diagnosing Alzheimer's disease and tauopathies. *Neuropathol Appl Neurobiol*. 2022;48(1), e12759.

22. Wisely CE, Wang D, Henao R, et al. Convolutional neural network to identify symptomatic Alzheimer's disease using multimodal retinal imaging. *Br J Ophthalmol*. 2022;106(3):388–395.

23. Zhang Q, Li J, Bian M, et al. Retinal imaging techniques based on machine learning models in recognition and prediction of mild cognitive impairment. *Neuropsychiatr Dis Treat*. 2021;17:3267–3281.

24. Kim JP, Kim J, Park YH, et al. Machine learning based hierarchical classification of frontotemporal dementia and Alzheimer's disease. *Neuroimage Clin*. 2019;23, 101811.

25. Zhao W, Luo Y, Zhao L, et al. Automated brain MRI volumetry differentiates early stages of Alzheimer's disease from normal aging. *J Geriatr Psychiatry Neurol*. 2019;32(6):354–364.

26. Wang Y, Xu C, Park JH, et al. Alzheimer's disease neuroimaging initiative. Diagnosis and prognosis of Alzheimer's disease using brain morphometry and white matter connectomes. *Neuroimage Clin*. 2019;23, 101859.

27. Nguyen DT, Ryu S, Qureshi MNI, Choi M, Lee KH, Lee B. Hybrid multivariate pattern analysis combined with extreme learning machine for Alzheimer's dementia diagnosis using multi-measure rs-fMRI spatial patterns. *PloS One*. 2019;14(2), e0212582.

28. Yamashita AY, Falcão AX, Leite NJ. Alzheimer's disease neuroimaging initiative. The residual Center of Mass: an image descriptor for the diagnosis of Alzheimer disease. *Neuroinformatics*. 2019;17(2):307–321.

29. Mobile Fact Sheet. (2023, March 2). Pew Research Center: Internet, Science & Tech. https://www.pewresearch.org/internet/fact-sheet/mobile/.

30. Global Smartphone Penetration 2016–2021. Statista; 2023. January 17 https://www.statista.com/statistics/203734/global-smartphone-penetration-per-capita-since-2005/#:~:text=The%20global%20smartphone%20penetration%20rate,population%20of%20around%207.4%20billion.

31. Seshadri DR, Bittel B, Browsky D, et al. Accuracy of apple watch for detection of atrial fibrillation. *Circulation*. 2020;141(8):702–703.

32. Akl A, Taati B, Mihailidis A. Autonomous unobtrusive detection of mild cognitive impairment in older adults. *IEEE Trans Biomed Eng*. 2015;62(5):1383–1394.

33. Aggarwal NT, Wilson RS, Beck TL, Bienias JL, Bennett DA. Motor dysfunction in mild cognitive impairment and the risk of incident Alzheimer disease. *Arch Neurol*. 2006;63(12):1763–1769.

34. Verghese J, Robbins M, Holtzer R, et al. Gait dysfunction in mild cognitive impairment syndromes. *J Am Geriatr Soc*. 2008;56(7):1244–1251.

35. Camicioli R, Howieson D, Oken B, Sexton G, Kaye J. Motor slowing precedes cognitive impairment in the oldest old. *Neurology*. 1998;50(5):1496–1498.

36. Gwak M, Sarrafzadeh M, Woo E. Support for a clinical diagnosis of mild cognitive impairment using photoplethysmography and gait sensors. In: *Proceedings, APSIPA Annual Summit and Conference*; 2018. 12–15 November2018, Hawaii http://www.apsipa.org/proceedings/2018/pdfs/0000671.pdf.

37. Angelillo MT, Balducci F, Impedovo D, Pirlo G, Vessio G. Attentional pattern classification for automatic dementia detection. *IEEE Access*. 2019;7:57706–57716.

38. De Stefano C, Fontanella F, Impedovo D, Pirlo G, Scotto di Freca A. Handwriting analysis to support neurodegenerative diseases diagnosis: a review. *Pattern Recogn Lett*. 2019;121:37–45.

39. Impedovo D, Pirlo G. Dynamic handwriting analysis for the assessment of neurodegenerative diseases: a pattern recognition perspective. *IEEE Rev Biomed Eng*. 2019;12:209–220.

40. Ashraf A, Taati B. Automated video analysis of handwashing behavior as a potential marker of cognitive health in older adults. *IEEE J Biomed Health Inform*. 2016;20(2):682–690.

41. Albert MS, DeKosky ST, Dickson D, et al. The diagnosis of mild cognitive impairment due to Alzheimer's disease: recommendations from the National Institute on Aging-Alzheimer's Association workgroups on diagnostic guidelines for Alzheimer's disease. *Alzheimers Dement*. 2011;7(3):270–279.

42. Mueller KD, Hermann B, Mecollari J, Turkstra LS. Connected speech and language in mild cognitive impairment and Alzheimer's disease: a review of picture description tasks. *J Clin Exp Neuropsychol*. 2018;40(9):917–939.

43. Toth L, Hoffmann I, Gosztolya G, et al. A speech recognition-based solution for the automatic detection of mild cognitive impairment from spontaneous speech. *Curr Alzheimer Res*. 2018;15(2):130–138.

44. Balagopalan A, Eyre B, Robin J, Rudzicz F, Novikova J. Comparing pre-trained and feature-based models for prediction of Alzheimer's disease based on speech. *Front Aging Neurosci*. 2021;13, 635945.

45. Hayes MT. Parkinson's disease and parkinsonism. *Am J Med*. 2019;132(7):802–807.

46. Yang Y, Yuan Y, Zhang G, et al. Artificial intelligence-enabled detection and assessment of Parkinson's disease using nocturnal breathing signals. *Nat Med*. 2022;28(10):2207–2215.

47. Benarroch EE, Schmeichel AM, Low PA, Parisi JE. Depletion of ventromedullary NK-1 receptor-immunoreactive neurons in multiple system atrophy. *Brain*. 2003;126:2183–2190.

48. Baille G, Perez T, Devos D, Deken V, Defebvre L, Moreau C. Early occurrence of inspiratory muscle weakness in Parkinson's disease. *PloS One*. 2018;13(1), e0190400.

49. Pokusa M, Hajduchova D, Buday T, Kralova TA. Respiratory function and dysfunction in Parkinson-type neurodegeneration. *Physiol Res*. 2020;69(Suppl 1):S69–S79.

50. Thijs RD, Surges R, O'Brien TJ, Sander JW. Epilepsy in adults. *Lancet*. 2019;393(10172):689–701.

51. Fürbass F, Kural MA, Gritsch G, Hartmann M, Kluge T, Beniczky S. An artificial intelligence-based EEG algorithm for detection of epileptiform EEG discharges: validation against the diagnostic gold standard. *Clin Neurophysiol*. 2020;131(6):1174–1179.
52. Oh J, Vidal-Jordana A, Montalban X. Multiple sclerosis: clinical aspects. *Curr Opin Neurol*. 2018;31(6):752–759.
53. Zhang S, Nguyen TD, Zhao Y, Gauthier SA, Wang Y, Gupta A. Diagnostic accuracy of semiautomatic lesion detection plus quantitative susceptibility mapping in the identification of new and enhancing multiple sclerosis lesions. *Neuroimage Clin*. 2018;18:143–148.
54. Kanda T, Nakai Y, Hagiwara A, Oba H, Toyoda K, Furui S. Distribution and chemical forms of gadolinium in the brain: a review. *Br J Radiol*. 2017;90(1079):20170115.
55. Feske SK. Ischemic stroke. *Am J Med*. 2021;134(12):1457–1464.
56. Wang K, Shou Q, Ma SJ, et al. Deep learning detection of penumbral tissue on arterial spin labeling in stroke. *Stroke*. 2020;51(2):489–497.
57. Maegerlein C, Fischer J, Mönch S, et al. Automated calculation of the Alberta stroke program early CT score: feasibility and reliability. *Radiology*. 2019;291(1):141–148.

19

Should I trust this model? Explainability and the black box of artificial intelligence in medicine

Jeremy Petch[a], Juan Pablo Tabja Bortesi[b], Walter Nelson[b,c], Shuang Di[a,d],
and Muhammad Hasnain Mamdani[e]

[a]Centre for Data Science and Digital Health, Hamilton Health Sciences, Hamilton, ON, Canada [b]CREATE, Hamilton Health Sciences, Hamilton, ON, Canada [c]Department of Statistical Sciences, University of Toronto, Toronto, ON, Canada [d]Dalla Lana School of Public Health, University of Toronto, Toronto, ON, Canada [e]Department of Medicine, Faculty of Medicine, University of Toronto, Toronto, ON, Canada

We are surrounded by AI in our daily lives, from virtual assistants that use AI voice recognition technology to streaming video and music services that use AI to recommend new content based on our personal tastes. Few would question that artificial intelligence (AI) holds enormous promise for medicine. From assisting with early diagnoses, to providing clinical decision support, to automating time-consuming tasks, AI could one day help us simultaneously improve both the quality and efficiency of health care.

Yet, adoption of AI into health care has seemed to lag behind other industries, including other high-stakes industries like aviation and automotive, where (like health care) mistakes can be fatal. This apparent lag is due in large part to the fact that medical AI simply has not performed particularly well in the real world, underscored by high-profile failures like Watson Health.[1] Poorer performance compared to some other industries has been driven to a large degree by the relatively low volume of healthcare data available to develop data-hungry machine learning models. Unlike the aviation and automotive industries, healthcare data are closely regulated to protect patient privacy. As a result, the kind of granular clinical data that would be useful to train AI systems is typically siloed across hundreds of individual healthcare organizations, and thus not easily available to the technology companies developing these commercial AI systems.

1. The problem of the "black box"

However, even as better-performing medical AI systems become available, barriers to adoption remain. Chief among these are concerns among the medical community about the "black box" nature of medical AI. In engineering and computer science, a black box is any system that can be viewed entirely in terms of inputs and outputs, without any knowledge of the system's internal workings. In a medical context, a classic example of a black box AI system is an early warning system that can be understood by its users in terms of inputs like vital signs and lab values, as well as its output, typically an alarm that triggers if a patient is in danger. Clinicians can make use of such a system without any knowledge about how the warning system works internally (i.e., what precise combination of vital signs measurements result in an alarm), so long as they are aware of which inputs to provide it and what to do with the output.

Most of the time, black box systems are not a problem. Indeed, in our day-to-day lives, we treat nearly all the technology we rely on as black boxes (e.g., few nonradiologists could provide more than a rudimentary explanation of how an MRI actually works). But concerns with the black box system arise when the reliability of those systems is in question and the stakes are high. No diagnostic test or risk prediction model is perfect, and AI is no exception: any black box AI will get it wrong some of the time. But most of the time, imperfect performance is not a deal-breaker. Many will continue to use speech-to-text apps on their phone to send messages even when those apps garble the occasional text message. But few would rely on those same apps to enter complicated medication orders for a patient, because the stakes are just too high to take the chance. It is the combination of unreliability (real or perceived) of medical AI combined with the high-stakes nature of medical decision-making that makes black box AI so concerning in the medical industry.

In contrast to black box AI methods, interpretable mathematic models are ubiquitous in medicine. Among the most common of these are risk scores for managing the health of populations, such as the Framingham Risk Score[2] for cardiovascular disease and the FINDRISC[3] score for diabetes. While both are based on sophisticated statistical modeling of population-level data, their implementation involves simple addition of risk factors based on preestablished thresholds. Similarly, commonly used early warning systems like the Modified Early Warning Score,[4] the Hamilton Early Warning Score,[5] and the National Early Warning Score[6] were developed through large-scale data analysis, but are implemented through established physiological thresholds that are easy for a clinician to interpret. Even risk scores that implement mathematical models like logistic regression directly are inherently interpretable since the models' odds ratios can be used to discern how they function.

But with black box models, the scale and the structure of their computations render them uninterpretable, even when they are based on familiar mathematical operations like linear algebra. Deep learning, for example, employs matrix multiplication as a core computational function, but while the individual operations may be interpretable, the resulting models become so complex through their implementation that they are rendered uninterpretable to humans. Similarly, ensemble machine learning methods take decision tress, which on their own are entirely interpretable, then iterate them hundreds or thousands of times, sacrificing interpretability through sheer scale.

In practical terms, black box models in medicine become a challenge when their output conflicts with a clinician's judgment. For example, when a black box warning system indicates that a patient is at high risk, but a clinician believes the patient is fine. The stakes in this case are high: missing deterioration could harm the patient, but so could unnecessary medical intervention. What is the clinician to do? Ideally, they would be able to interrogate *why* the model is indicating a high level of risk. Has the model picked up a subtle trend in the patient's vital signs that the clinician missed? Or is the model responding to faulty data, like a falsely elevated blood pressure reading caused by a too-tight cuff? Or perhaps the AI model was developed on a predominantly white patient population, but the current patient is from an ethnic group that was not represented in the data set and the model does not know what to do with them. Without being able to interrogate *why* a black box AI is making a particular decision, a clinician who disagrees with the AI is put in a tenuous position.

In addition to clinical acceptability, interpretability of predictive models is increasingly recognized as essential for establishing fairness in AI. The danger of AI encoding racial and other types of bias into predictive models is now well established.[7,8] This can occur when AI is trained on data that reflect larger social patterns of injustice, as well as cases where a class of persons is underrepresented in a training data set. One of the most dramatic examples of this phenomenon was observed in an algorithm used for population health management, where the algorithm was shown to be more likely to provide preventive health services to white patients, even when black patients were objectively in greater need of those services.[9] Many healthcare data sets have significant imbalances, such as clinical trials, which have historically underrepresented women and nonwhite populations.[10] Interpretability provides an approach by which such biases in a model can be straightforwardly investigated during model development, versus black box models where such biases are often discovered only after being deployed in the real world (potentially after much damage has already been done).

Interpretability may also become part of the regulatory framework for AI as lawmakers become increasingly concerned about transparency and privacy. Europe's General Data Protection Regulation (GDPR) introduced language around the need for technology companies to provide explanations of fully automated decisions made by AI systems, but it is unclear whether the European courts would interpret that language to imply that GDPR provides an individual "right to explanation" for AI decision-making.[11] Similarly, the California Consumer Privacy Act (CCPA) stops short of explicitly requiring AI models to be interpretable, but does require companies to disclose (and be able to destroy upon request) all consumer data that were used by a black box model to make its predictions.[12] Interpretability is also on the radar of healthcare regulatory agencies like the FDA and Health Canada. While the FDA does not yet require medical AI systems to be interpretable, it has suggested that black box AI products could require a higher standard of evidence than interpretable ones.[13]

Yet, despite the challenges associated with black box models, they are increasingly dominating the commercial AI field. This is due in large part to the perceived performance improvements that can be achieved by black box models compared to previous (more interpretable) approaches to AI. But while the performance of black box AI on unstructured data like images and text is undeniable, black box techniques rarely achieve superior performance on well-structured tabular data. Yet, technology companies continue to favor black box models even when interpretable methods may achieve comparable performance. In such cases, the lack of transparency provided by black box models may be more of a feature than a bug, in that the uninteroperability of their inner workings provides an extra layer of protection to technology companies' intellectual property.[14]

2. From interpretability to explainability

The challenges with black box models have given rise to a relatively new field of machine learning research, which aims to generate *explanations* of black box models. While the models themselves remain uninterpretable, these explainability methods seek to reveal how black box models are really working "under the hood." Ultimately, the promise of these methods is to let us bake our cake and eat it too: to achieve the state-of-the-art performance of modern neural network-based AI, without all the drawbacks associated with black box models.

What exactly are explainability methods explaining? There are broadly two types of methods. The first provide *global* explanations. Global explanations account for how a model works in general, rather than trying to explain why a model made a specific recommendation for a specific patient. In contrast, *local* model explanations provide information about why a model made a single specific prediction, but do not provide insight into how a model works as a whole. Global explainability techniques are most often used during model development, while local techniques are most often used during clinical deployment to provide some measure of transparency to end users.[15]

What all explainability methods have in common is that they are not direct accountings of how a model functions or why it makes the predictions it does. Rather, all explainability methods approximate the workings of black box models, with varying degrees of resolution. In other words, the goal of explainable AI is not to account for all the intricacies of an AI's computations, but rather to provide users with a high-level understanding of how the model works and why it makes specific decisions. The upside of this approach is that these explanations are intelligible to humans. The downside is that some fidelity is inevitably lost in translation.

While the promise of explainability methods is significant, they have come under criticism. Because these methods provide only intelligible approximations (rather than direct accountings) of black box models' structures and behavior, Babic et al. worry that these explanations will provide clinicians only an "ersatz understanding" of black box models.[16] In a similar vein, Ghassemi et al. argue that explainability methods present a "false hope" for medical AI, because they leave an interpretation gap for human intuition to fill, which introduces a risk of bias.[17] Similar concerns over the limitations of these methods led Rudin to argue that we should avoid the use of black box models altogether for high-stakes decisions in favor of interpretable models.[14]

These critiques of explainable AI should not be dismissed out of hand, but they may be tempered in part by considering an analogy to how clinicians communicate with patients. By law, patients must be able to provide informed consent to medical treatment, but a few patients have sufficient medical background to understand all the intricacies of a clinician's reasoning for offering a particular treatment. Thus, clinicians must routinely explain their reasoning to patients in a fashion that is intelligible to those who do not have advanced training in medicine. The act of distilling learning from medical school, residency, medical literature, and decades of clinical experience into a short and accessible explanation inevitably involves significant abstraction and loss of fidelity. Yet, while a clinician's explanation is likely just an intelligible approximation that may not reflect the intricacies of their real reasoning, we nonetheless believe these explanations, assuming they accurately describe the potential benefits and risks of treatment, are sufficient for patients to be able to provide informed consent. By analogy then, it may be appropriate to acknowledge the limitations of explainability methods, while simultaneously believing they are sufficiently informative to make use of.

3. Explainability methods

There are currently three major approaches to explaining black box AI models. The first of these are visualization methods, which seek to illustrate the operations of a model by graphing some of its key statistical functions in two- or three-dimensional plots. The second family of methods are variable importance techniques (or "feature importance" among AI researchers), which aim to create transparency by identifying the relative contribution each of an AI's input variables make to the AI's outputs. Finally, the third major group is surrogate methods, which train new interpretable models that are intended to faithfully represent the predictions of black box AI models.

3.1 Visualization methods

Visualization methods all aim to visually illustrate the relationships between the inputs and outputs of an AI system. They typically work by creating two- or three-dimensional plots that graph how an output variable changes in relationship to changes in input variables. Visualization methods provide global explanations, in that they provide explanations of an AI's function as a whole, rather than explaining why an AI provided a specific output. The most common visualization methods are centered individual conditional expectation (ICES) plots,[18] accumulated local effects (ALE) plots,[19] and partial dependence plots (PDPs).

Visualization methods have been used to examine the nature of the relationships between EHR variables and in-hospital acute kidney injury,[20] between factors related to in vitro fertilization and clinical pregnancy,[21] and between longitudinal exposures and poor self-perceived health.[22]

Fig. 1 illustrates how visualization methods can work in practice. In this figure, a PDP is used to model how an AI system's prediction of a patient's risk of heart disease relates to changes in age and cholesterol level. From this illustration, several of the advantages of visualization methods are apparent. First, the visual nature of the explanation provides a relatively simple and intuitive illustration of how an AI's output will change in response to changes in inputs. Second, visualization allows for a direct illustration of the nonlinear relationship between age and risk of heart disease (modeling of nonlinear relationships being one of the major advantages of AI over linear statistical models). Finally, these methods allow us to visualize the interaction between these two inputs to illustrate how they combine to influence risk of heart disease.

While they offer several advantages over other explainability techniques, visualization methods have limitations. Key among these is that because humans' visual perception is limited to three dimensions, visualization methods can illustrate a maximum of two inputs at a time, when an AI model may use dozens or even hundreds of input variables. Visualization methods may therefore be unable to capture particularly complex interactions between large sets of variables. PDPs like the one illustrated in Fig. 1 also assume that the variables illustrated in the figure are not correlated with other variables used by an AI, which can produce misleading explanations if that is not in fact the case. Visualization methods are also not suited to providing explanations for specific (local) AI decisions, which may limit their value in a clinical setting.

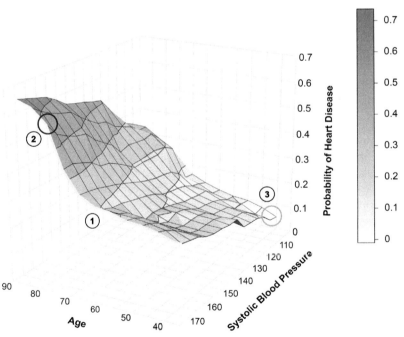

FIG. 1 Visualized global explanation of a black box AI for predicting risk of heart disease. This figure illustrates the relationship between age and systolic blood pressure with respect to how an AI model predicts the probability of having heart disease. Annotations have been added to acclimatize readers to this type of plot. The *yellow line (light gray in print version)* (1) shows the nonlinear effect of age on risk of heart disease, in the subgroup of patients with high blood pressure (>170). The *red circle (dark gray in print version)* (2) indicates that patients over 75 with high blood pressure levels have a relatively higher risk of heart disease. The *green circle (gray in print version)* (3) illustrates that relatively younger patients with lower blood pressure levels are at much lower risk of heart disease.

3.2 Variable importance methods

Variable importance methods all aim to quantify the relative contribution each input variable makes to an AI model's output. Thus, they explain how a model functions insofar as they can document which factors are the most predictive of a particular outcome. Variable importance methods provide global explanations and are used extensively during AI development, where they provide an indication of whether a model is learning correctly and whether the variables it is relying on are clinically appropriate. For example, if developing an AI for mortality risk prediction in an ICU, variable importance methods can help identify when an AI may be learning to "cheat" to get very high accuracy, such as predicting mortality based off the variable *consult to spiritual care*. Variable importance methods include Mean Decrease in Impurity,[23] Permutation Importance,[24] and Conditional Variable Importance.[25]

Variable importance methods have been used to assess the contribution of model features in the prediction of 5-year overall survival in oral squamous cell carcinoma patients,[26] in the prediction of hepatitis B surface antigen seroclearance from laboratory and clinical data,[27] and in the differentiation of benign and malignant breast lesions.[28]

Fig. 2 illustrates how variable importance methods are typically reported. This example uses permutation importance, which works by continually retraining an AI model, but each time with one variable's values shuffled randomly. By doing this over and over and measuring the degree of performance degradation when each variable has its values shuffled, permutation importance generates an estimate of each variable's relative contribution to an AI model's predictions (the thinking being that if a variable's values are shuffled and it makes no difference to a model's accuracy, then the AI model is not making much use of that variable). This provides a clinician with some ability to validate that the AI model in Fig. 2 is relying on clinically appropriate variables, since stress tests are generally accepted to be more important to establishing the risk of heart disease than fasting blood sugar.

The chief advantage of variable importance methods is that they are intuitive and thus easy to interpret. However, variable importance methods are not always entirely accurate. For example, permutation importance is known to produce unreliable results when an AI model is making use of highly correlated variables.[25] These methods also provide a limited amount of information. For example, Fig. 2 illustrates which variables the AI model is using, but it is not able to illustrate *how* the model is making use of those variables. For example, how chest pain type and ST depression may be interacting to affect risk, or whether the effect of age on risk is linear. Thus, while variable importance may provide some useful information to establish face validity for an AI model, it arguably stops well short of an explanation of how that model really works.

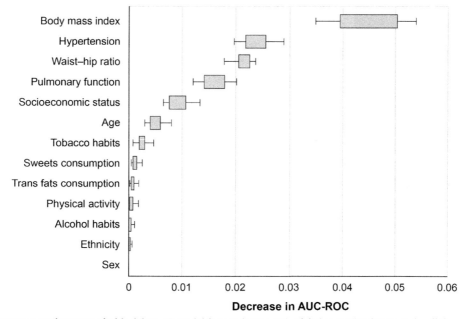

FIG. 2 Variable importance explanation of a black box AI model for predicting risk of diabetes. This figure ranks all the variables used by a black box AI based on their relative importance in predicting risk of heart disease. It illustrates the decrease in the AI's performance when each variable's values are randomly shuffled.

3.3 Surrogate methods

Surrogate methods aim to provide explanations of black box AI by training a second, interpretable model that faithfully reproduces the predictions of a black box model. Since this second model will be inherently interpretable, an end user can interpret the workings of the second model as a surrogate for the black box model. The surrogate model is trained to reproduce the predictions of the black box model, rather than independently predicting the outcome variable, in order to ensure the surrogate model is as faithful a recreation of the black box model as possible. In practice, surrogate methods are most often used to provide local explanations (to explain specific decisions made by a black box AI), though they can also be used to provide global explanations. The most common surrogate methods are Local Interpretable Model-agnostic Explanations (LIME)[29] and Shapley Values (SHAP).[30] Local surrogate methods tailored for image classification tasks include integrated gradients,[31] guided backpropagation,[32] and Gradient-Weighted Class Activation Mapping (Grad-CAM).[33]

Surrogate methods have been employed to explain models that predict mortality in COVID-19 patients in the ICU,[34] models that perform glioma grading,[35] and models that predict postoperative delayed remission in patients with Cushing's disease.[36]

Imaging-specific surrogate methods have been used to identify regions of pelvic radiographs contributing to detection of hip fractures,[37] to visualize the fundus autofluorescence image pixels being used for etiology-based classification of retinal atrophy,[38] and to highlight MRI regions that are important in distinguishing between Alzheimer's disease and frontotemporal dementia.[39]

Fig. 3 illustrates how explanations from a surrogate method like LIME can be directly integrated into an electronic health record in order to provide clinical decision support at the point of care. In this case, the variables (and their values) contributing most to the black box AI's prediction are displayed next to each patient's risk score, which is intended to both enhance transparency and actionability of the AI's output.

Fig. 4 illustrates how image classification explanations (Grad-CAM, in this case) systems operate. Like the previous example, the data elements (pixels) contributing most to the black box AI's prediction are highlighted in warmer colors, while those not as important to the prediction are highlighted in cooler colors. Thus, a clinician seeking to validate a black box AI's outputs can refer to the image to verify whether it is using the clinically relevant areas to make its determination, such as the neovascularization of the disc highlighted in Fig. 4, which is indicative of retinopathy.

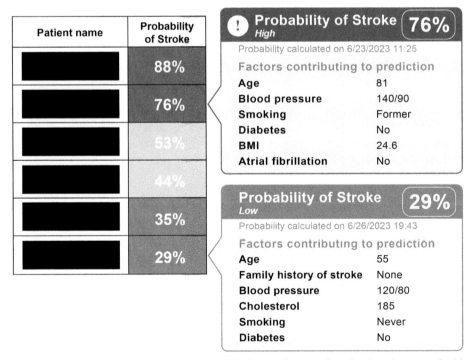

FIG. 3 Black box AI-generated risk scores with local explanations. This figure illustrates how local explanations for black box AI are typically integrated into electronic medical records. AI-generated risk scores are color-coded to draw clinicians' attention to patients at highest risk. Clinical characteristics most contributing to each risk score are provided as explanations of the AI's reasoning.

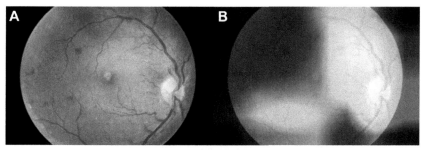

FIG. 4 Black box AI classification of diabetic retinopathy from retinal fundus photograph with local explanation. The photo on the left (A) was classified as having proliferative diabetic retinopathy. The photo on the right (B) is a local explanation generated by Grad-CAM, with the pixels most contributing to the prediction *shaded yellow (light gray in print version)*, and those contributing least *shaded blue (dark gray in print version)*. The area most contributing to the prediction is consistent with neovascularization of the disc, which is characteristic of retinopathy.

The chief advantage of surrogate methods is that they can produce local explanations and are thus suitable for providing explanations at the point of care, potentially addressing one of the chief barriers to the adoption of AI in health care. Moreover, their output appears intuitive, particularly in the case of medical images. However, surrogate methods have significant limitations. Chief among these is that their "explanations" may bear little resemblance to how a black box AI actually operates. This is because while the machine learning algorithms behind black box AIs can model nonlinear relationships, most surrogate methods rely on interpretable methods that are linear in nature. Similarly, since no well-fit model has perfect accuracy, no surrogate model will be entirely faithful in its reproduction of a black box AI, which further erodes the fidelity of surrogate explanations. Moreover, like variable importance methods, surrogate methods only indicate which data elements were important to a particular prediction, not how or why those data elements were used. This creates an interpretation gap for an end user to fill, which introduces a risk of cognitive bias.[17]

3.4 Should I trust this model?

Many hope that explainable AI methods will reduce barriers to AI adoption in health care. Frequently, this is framed in terms of explainability enhancing clinician trust or confidence in AI models.[40,41] Yet is it not obvious that we should want clinicians to trust AI systems. Automation bias—the tendency to overrely on automation—has been studied across fields, including health care.[42] While clinical decision support systems can improve care delivery, there is a well-documented tendency to overlook new errors they can introduce.[43] When users come to rely too heavily on automation, they become less vigilant in using their own clinical judgment, which can result in both following incorrect advice, as well as failing to act because of not being prompted to do so.[44]

Concern with the framing of trust or confidence is not a mere semantic quibble, in that this framing shapes the design of explainable AI deployment. Fig. 3 is designed to mirror the explainability features of a number of algorithms that are deployed in a market-leading electronic medical record. It is arguably designed to enhance clinician trust, in that it confidently displays the clinical factors believed to contribute to the model's predictions. But this deployment is arguably designed to promote automation bias. For example, there is no transparency with respect to the underlying AI model's accuracy or degree of calibration in the local population, both of which might be quite poor given the limited generalizability of most AI models. Nor is there any indication with respect to the nature of the AI model or how well the explanation represents the model itself. While not being transparent about the potential weaknesses of the model might enhance the confidence of the end user, this confidence might not be well placed and, more importantly, does not equip the end user to critically appraise the AI model's outputs to come to their own clinical determination of how to act. Thus, if explainability methods are to improve outcomes, and not just increase AI adoption, they should be designed not simply to increase trust, but to be genuinely transparent to reduce the risk of automation bias and enhance (not undermine) clinician vigilance.

3.5 Guidelines for when to use black box AI with explanations

Given the limitations of explainability methods, those developing AI systems for health care should not default to black box models. Rather, they should decide between using interpretable models and black boxes with explanations based on two factors: (1) the magnitude of the trade-off between performance and interpretability, and (2) the stakes of the recommendation being made by an AI.[45]

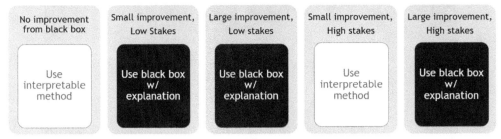

FIG. 5   Guidelines for when to use interpretable versus black box AI models with explanations.

When developing a new AI system, data scientists should train AI models using both interpretable and black box methods to assess whether there is in fact a performance vs interpretability trade-off in the specific case on which they are working. If there no meaningful difference in performance between an interpretable model and a black box, then an interpretable method is more appropriate. However, if a black box model does provide greater performance, then the stakes of the decision should be considered. If the decision that will be informed by the model is relatively low stakes (such as substituting a generic medication for a brand name drug), then a small improvement in accuracy may justify the use of a black box. However, if the stakes are high (such as whether to intubate a patient), it is reasonable to require a greater improvement in accuracy before sacrificing interpretability. Importantly, gains in performance from black box methods for high-stakes decisions must be sufficient to translate into meaningful improvements in clinical outcomes, such as reduced morbidity or mortality. Only if the use of a black box model can be justified should explainability techniques be employed to make the model and its predictions as transparent as possible, but clinicians should be aware of their limitations and be cautious of overinterpreting, which can lead to narrative fallacies (Fig. 5).[16]

4. Conclusions

Explainability techniques for AI hold considerable promise: to provide all the advantages of state-of-the-art machine learning without the drawbacks of black box models. Yet, these methods have important limitations that undermine their reliability. While it is justifiable to use black box models with explanations in some circumstances, developers should only adopt black box AI after evaluating the degree of performance improvement over interpretable methods and confirming that the stakes are appropriate.

References

1. O'Leary L. How IBM's Watson Went From the Future of Health Care to Sold Off for Parts. Slate; 2022, January 31. https://slate.com/technology/2022/01/ibm-watson-health-failure-artificial-intelligence.html.
2. D'Agostino RB, Vasan RS, Pencina MJ, et al. General cardiovascular risk profile for use in primary care: the Framingham heart study. *Circulation.* 2008;117(6):743–753. https://doi.org/10.1161/CIRCULATIONAHA.107.699579.
3. Lindström J, Tuomilehto J. The Diabetes Risk Score: a practical tool to predict type 2 diabetes risk. *Diabetes Care.* 2003;26(3):725–731. https://doi.org/10.2337/DIACARE.26.3.725.
4. Suppiah A, Malde D, Arab T, et al. The modified early warning score (MEWS): an instant physiological prognostic Indicator of poor outcome in acute pancreatitis. *J Pancreas.* 2014;15(6):569–576. https://doi.org/10.6092/1590-8577/2829.
5. Skitch S, Tam B, Xu M, McInnis L, Vu A, Fox-Robichaud A. Examining the utility of the Hamilton early warning scores (HEWS) at triage: retrospective pilot study in a Canadian emergency department. *Can J Emerg Med.* 2018;20(2):266–274. https://doi.org/10.1017/CEM.2017.21.
6. Kostakis I, Smith GB, Prytherch D, et al. The performance of the National Early Warning Score and National Early Warning Score 2 in hospitalised patients infected by the severe acute respiratory syndrome coronavirus 2 (SARS-CoV-2). *Resuscitation.* 2021;159:150–157. https://doi.org/10.1016/j.resuscitation.2020.10.039.
7. Benjamin R. Assessing risk, automating racism. *Science.* 2019;366(6464):421–422. https://doi.org/10.1126/science.aaz3873.
8. Buolamwin J, Gebru T. Gender shades: intersectional accuracy disparities in commercial gender classification. In: *Proceedings of Machine Learning Research;* 2018. https://proceedings.mlr.press/v81/buolamwini18a/buolamwini18a.pdf.
9. Obermeyer Z, Powers B, Vogeli C, Mullainathan S. Dissecting racial bias in an algorithm used to manage the health of populations. *Science.* 2019;366(6464):447–453. https://doi.org/10.1126/SCIENCE.AAX2342/SUPPL_FILE/AAX2342_OBERMEYER_SM.PDF.
10. Ma MA, Gutiérrez DE, Frausto JM, Al-Delaimy WK. Minority representation in clinical trials in the United States: trends over the past 25 years. *Mayo Clin Proc.* 2021;96(1):264–266. https://doi.org/10.1016/j.mayocp.2020.10.027.
11. General Data Protection Regulation; 2016.
12. California Consumer Privacy Act; 2018. https://leginfo.legislature.ca.gov/faces/codes.xhtml.
13. FDA. Proposed Regulatory Framework for Modifications to Artificial Intelligence/Machine Learning (AI/ML)-Based Software as a Medical Device (SaMD)-Discussion Paper and Request for Feedback; 2019. https://www.fda.gov/downloads/medicaldevices/deviceregulationandguidance/guidancedocuments/ucm514737.pdf.

14. Rudin C. Stop explaining black box machine learning models for high stakes decisions and use interpretable models instead. *Nat Mach Intell.* 2019;1(5):206–215. https://doi.org/10.1038/s42256-019-0048-x.

15. Molnar C. Interpretable Machine Learning. A Guide for Making Black Box Models Explainable; 2023. https://christophm.github.io/interpretable-ml-book.

16. Babic B, Gerke S, Evgeniou T, Cohen IG. Beware explanations from AI in health care. *Science.* 2021;373(6552):284–286. https://doi.org/10.1126/science.abg1834.

17. Ghassemi M, Oakden-Rayner L, Beam AL. The false hope of current approaches to explainable artificial intelligence in health care. *Lancet Digit Health.* 2021;3(11):e745–e750. https://doi.org/10.1016/S2589-7500(21)00208-9.

18. Goldstein A, Kapelner A, Bleich J, Pitkin E. Peeking inside the black box: visualizing statistical learning with plots of individual conditional expectation. *J Comput Graph Stat.* 2015;24(1):44–65. https://doi.org/10.1080/10618600.2014.907095.

19. Apley DW, Zhu J. Visualizing the effects of predictor variables in black box supervised learning models. *J R Stat Soc Ser B Stat Methodol.* 2020;82(4):1059–1086. https://doi.org/10.1111/rssb.12377.

20. Kim K, Yang H, Yi J, et al. Real-time clinical decision support based on recurrent neural networks for in-hospital acute kidney injury: external validation and model interpretation. *J Med Internet Res.* 2021;23(4), e24120. https://doi.org/10.2196/24120. https://www.jmir.org/2021/4/e24120.

21. Wang CW, Kuo CY, Chen CH, Hsieh YH, Su ECY. Predicting clinical pregnancy using clinical features and machine learning algorithms in in vitro fertilization. *PloS One.* 2022;17(6), e0267554. https://doi.org/10.1371/JOURNAL.PONE.0267554.

22. Loef B, Wong A, Janssen NAH, et al. Using random forest to identify longitudinal predictors of health in a 30-year cohort study. *Sci Rep.* 2022;12(1):1–13. https://doi.org/10.1038/s41598-022-14632-w.

23. Breiman L, Friedman JH, Olshen RA, Stone CJ. Classification and regression trees. In: *Classification and Regression Trees.* Routledge; 1984. https://doi.org/10.1201/9781315139470.

24. Altmann A, Toloşi L, Sander O, Lengauer T. Permutation importance: a corrected feature importance measure. *Bioinformatics.* 2010;26(10):1340–1347. https://doi.org/10.1093/bioinformatics/btq134.

25. Strobl C, Boulesteix AL, Kneib T, Augustin T, Zeileis A. Conditional variable importance for random forests. *BMC Bioinform.* 2008;9(1):307. https://doi.org/10.1186/1471-2105-9-307.

26. Karadaghy OA, Shew M, New J, Bur AM. Development and assessment of a machine learning model to help predict survival among patients with oral squamous cell carcinoma. *JAMA Otolaryngol Head Neck Surg.* 2019;145(12):1115–1120. https://doi.org/10.1001/JAMAOTO.2019.0981.

27. Tian X, Chong Y, Huang Y, et al. Using machine learning algorithms to predict hepatitis B surface antigen seroclearance. *Comput Math Methods Med.* 2019;2019. https://doi.org/10.1155/2019/6915850.

28. Sun K, Jiao Z, Zhu H, et al. Radiomics-based machine learning analysis and characterization of breast lesions with multiparametric diffusion-weighted MR. *J Transl Med.* 2021;19(1):1–10. https://doi.org/10.1186/S12967-021-03117-5/FIGURES/3.

29. Ribeiro MT, Singh S, Guestrin C. Model-agnostic interpretability of machine learning. In: *WHI*; 2016. http://arxiv.org/abs/1606.05386.

30. Lundberg SM, Lee SI. A unified approach to interpreting model predictions. In: *Advances in Neural Information Processing Systems, 2017-Decem*; 2017:4766–4775.

31. Sundararajan M, Taly A, Yan Q. Axiomatic attribution for deep networks. In: *34th International Conference on Machine Learning, ICML 2017. vol. 7*; 2017:5109–5118.

32. Springenberg JT, Dosovitskiy A, Brox T, Riedmiller M. Striving for simplicity: the all convolutional net. In: *3rd International Conference on Learning Representations, ICLR 2015—Workshop Track Proceedings*; 2015:1–14.

33. Selvaraju RR, Cogswell M, Das A, Vedantam R, Parikh D, Batra D. Grad-CAM: visual explanations from deep networks via gradient-based localization. *Int J Comput Vis.* 2020;128(2):336–359. https://doi.org/10.1007/s11263-019-01228-7.

34. Pan P, Li Y, Xiao Y, et al. Prognostic assessment of COVID-19 in the intensive care unit by machine learning methods: model development and validation. *J Med Internet Res.* 2020;22(11), e23128. https://doi.org/10.2196/23128. https://www.jmir.org/2020/11/e23128.

35. Wang X, Wang D, Yao Z, et al. Machine learning models for multiparametric glioma grading with quantitative result interpretations. *Front Neurosci.* 2019;13(JAN):1046. https://doi.org/10.3389/FNINS.2018.01046/BIBTEX.

36. Fan Y, Li Y, Bao X, et al. Development of machine learning models for predicting postoperative delayed remission in patients with Cushing's disease. *J Clin Endocrinol Metabol.* 2021;106(1):e217–e231. https://doi.org/10.1210/CLINEM/DGAA698.

37. Cheng CT, Ho TY, Lee TY, et al. Application of a deep learning algorithm for detection and visualization of hip fractures on plain pelvic radiographs. *Eur Radiol.* 2019;29(10):5469–5477. https://doi.org/10.1007/S00330-019-06167-Y/FIGURES/4.

38. Miere A, Capuano V, Kessler A, et al. Deep learning-based classification of retinal atrophy using fundus autofluorescence imaging. *Comput Biol Med.* 2021;130:104198. https://doi.org/10.1016/J.COMPBIOMED.2020.104198.

39. Hu J, Qing Z, Liu R, et al. Deep learning-based classification and voxel-based visualization of frontotemporal dementia and Alzheimer's disease. *Front Neurosci.* 2020;14. https://doi.org/10.3389/FNINS.2020.626154.

40. Lahav O, Mastronarde N, van der Schaar M. What is Interpretable? Using Machine Learning to Design Interpretable Decision-Support Systems; 2018. http://arxiv.org/abs/1811.10799.

41. Tonekaboni S, Joshi S, McCradden MD, Goldenberg A. What clinicians want: contextualizing explainable machine learning for clinical end use. In: Doshi-Velez F, Fackler J, Jung K, Kale D, Ranganath R, Wallace B, Wiens J, eds. *Proceedings of the 4th Machine Learning for Healthcare Conference.* vol. 106. PMLR; 2019:359–380. https://proceedings.mlr.press/v106/tonekaboni19a.html.

42. Skitka LJ, Mosier KL, Burdick M. Does automation bias decision-making? *Int J Hum-Comput Stud.* 1999;51(5):991–1006. https://doi.org/10.1006/IJHC.1999.0252.

43. Goddard K, Roudsari A, Wyatt JC. Automation bias: a systematic review of frequency, effect mediators, and mitigators. *J Am Med Inform Assoc.* 2012;19(1):121–127. https://doi.org/10.1136/AMIAJNL-2011-000089/3/AMIAJNL-2011-000089FIG2.JPEG.

44. Koppel R, Metlay JP, Cohen A, et al. Role of computerized physician order entry systems in facilitating medication errors. *JAMA.* 2005;293(10):1197–1203. https://doi.org/10.1001/JAMA.293.10.1197.

45. Petch J, Di S, Nelson W. Opening the black box: the promise and limitations of explainable machine learning in cardiology. *Can J Cardiol.* 2022;38(2):204–213. https://doi.org/10.1016/j.cjca.2021.09.004.

Index

Note: Page numbers followed by *f* indicate figures and *t* indicate tables.